CORE TAX ANNU

Corporation

CORE TAX ANNUALS
Corporation Tax 2009/10

Juliana Watterston MSc FCA CTA (Fellow)

Series General Editor: Mark McLaughlin CTA (Fellow) ATT TEP

Bloomsbury Professional

Bloomsbury Professional Ltd, Maxwelton House, 41–43 Boltro Road, Haywards Heath, West Sussex, RH16 1BJ

© Bloomsbury Professional Ltd 2009

Cover illustration © Marcus Duck 2009

Marcus Duck is a Brighton-based graphic designer and photographer.

Contact:marcus@marcusduckdesign.com

Previously published by Tottel Publishing Ltd

A CIP Catalogue record for this book is available from the British Library.

ISBN: 978 1 84766 327 6

Typeset by Phoenix Photosetting, Chatham, Kent
Printed and bound in the UK by CPI William Clowes Beccles NR34 7TL

Preface

Welcome to Corporation Tax 2009/10, now published by Bloomsbury Professional, and one of their six Core Tax Annuals. This book aims to provide an up-to-date guide to the principles and practice of corporation tax and is specific to the needs of businesses and their advisers.

Corporation tax is a cost to business. Responsible directors will monitor this cost and minimise the risks associated with poor compliance. HMRC's new compliance assurance powers and procedures and responsibilities of the Senior Accounting Officer, which have a direct bearing on company behaviour were introduced in 2009 and are covered in Chapter 18. Changes to the self-assessment procedures and the new Tribunal procedures to settle disputes between HMRC and company taxpayers are covered in Chapter 2.

Companies exist in order to carry on a business. All businesses receive relief for their business expenditure against their profits chargeable to corporation tax, but businesses that make use of new technologies, engage in research projects and carry out regeneration works receive the tax breaks. The energy savings reliefs, the business renovation allowance and the flat conversion allowance are covered in Chapter 6. Research and development reliefs and reliefs for the remediation of contaminated land are covered in Chapter 8. The special reliefs for the corporate venturing scheme and the community investment scheme are addressed in Chapter 12.

Legislative changes have been made during 2009 to simplify the taxation of controlled foreign companies and foreign dividends and these are discussed in Chapter 13.

Although, many companies are finding it difficult to survive in the current economic climate, this is an opportunity to maximise a company's available loss relief. Loss relief and group planning matters are discussed in Chapters 9 and 10. General tax planning matters are discussed in Chapter 22. In addition, the Corporation Tax Act 2009 was introduced in 2009 to which reference is made in this book throughout.

Corporation tax is very much a boardroom topic, and one on which directors should ensure they are adequately informed to enable them to provide shareholder value. The commentary is supported by over 100 worked examples and is cross-referenced to case law, statute law and HMRC practice. The law is stated, as at 1 August 2009. Tax planning and cost cutting ideas are detailed alphabetically in Chapter 22. The retail price indices used in capital gains calculations are given in appendix 1. Reference copies of forms CT600 are included in appendix 2.

Preface

We trust that you find this book useful and we always welcome feedback from our readers.

Needless to say, it has not been possible to cover all areas, and readers will need to turn to additional texts for in-depth coverage of certain areas such as leasing and specialised businesses.

Once again many thanks to the Bloomsbury Professional staff, especially Sarah Blair and Heather Saward for their assistance in producing this book.

Juliana Watterston
watterston@mac.com
August 2009

Contents

Contents

Contents

Table of statutes

Table of statutes

Table of statutory instruments

[All references are to paragraph numbers]

Table of european legislation

Table of cases

S

Table of cases

List of abbreviations

ACT	advance corporation tax
ADP	acceptable dividend policy
AIM	alternative investment market
APA	advance pricing agreement
APR	agricultural property relief
ARC	Accounting Regulatory Committee
ASB	Accounting Standards Board
BA	balancing allowance
BMT	bereaved minor trust
BPR	business property relief
CA	Companies Act
CAA 2001	Capital Allowances Act 2001
CFC	controlled foreign company
CIHC	close investment holding company
CTA 2009	Corporation Tax Act 2009
CTF	child trust fund
CTO	Capital Taxes Office
CTT	capital transfer tax
EEA	European Economic Area
EIS	enterprise investment scheme
ESC	Extra-statutory Concession
EUFT	eligible unrelieved foreign tax
FA	Finance Act
FSMA 2000	Financial Services and Markets Act 2000
FRS	Financial Reporting Standard
FRSSE	Financial Reporting Standard for Smaller Entities
FYA	first year allowance
GWR	gift with reservation
HMRC	HM Revenue and Customs
IA	initial allowance
IA 1986	Insolvency Act 1986
IAS	International Accounting Standards
IASB	International Accounting Standards Board
IBA	industrial building allowance
ICTA 1988	Income and Corporation Taxes Act 1988
IFRS	International Financial Reporting Standards
IHT	inheritance tax
IHTA 1984	Inheritance Tax Act 1984

IHTM	Inheritance Tax Manual
ITEPA 2003	Income Tax (Earnings and Pensions) Act 2003
ITTOIA 2005	Income Tax (Trading and Other Income) Act 2005
LLP	limited liability partnership
OECD	Organisation for European Cooperation and Development
OEIC	open ended investment company
PCTCT	profits chargeable to corporation tax
PET	potentially exempt transfer
POA	pre-owned asset
R&D	research and development
SDLT	stamp duty land tax
SE	small enterprise
SI	Statutory Instrument
SME	small and medium-sized enterprise
SSAP	Statement of Standard Accounting Practice
SSCBA 1992	Social Security Contributions and Benefits Act 1992
TAAR	target anti-avoidance rule
TCGA 1992	Taxation of Chargeable Gains Act 1992
TMA 1970	Taxes Management Act 1970
TSI	transitional serial interests
UITF	Urgent Issue Task Force
UK GAAP	UK Generally Accepted Accounting Principles
UTR	Unique Taxpayer Reference
VCT	venture capital trust
VOA	Valuation Office Agency
WDA	writing down allowance
WDV	written down value

Chapter 1

Introduction to corporation tax

CORPORATION TAX LEGISLATION

1.1 First introduced in 1965, the UK corporation tax legislation is currently being re-drafted and re-enacted in the government's tax law rewrite project. The corporation tax provisions contained in the first new Act, the *Corporation Tax Act 2009* (*CTA 2009*), come into force for accounting periods ending on or after 1 April 2009; the income tax and capital gains tax provisions come into force for the tax year 2009/10 and subsequent tax years. It was announced on 13 July 2009 that the rewrite project would be complete in 2010. The second Corporation Tax Bill and the Taxation (International and Other Provisions) Bill have been drafted but have yet to be enacted. The former deals mainly with provisions that affect investment institutions and charities, and the latter deals with international and miscellaneous regulations. Until the corporation tax law rewrite project is complete, we are working with the new *CTA 2009* and the remaining legislation that is to be found in the *Income and Corporation Taxes Act 1988* and subsequent Acts. The government's intention in drafting *CTA 2009* was not to change the existing legislation, but to make it clearer. *CTA 2009* references are used in this book where applicable. For details of prior legislation, please refer to *Corporation Tax 2008/09* (Tottel Publishing).

FORMATION OF A UK COMPANY

1.2 Corporation tax is charged on the profits of UK resident companies (*CTA 2009, s 2(1)*); the vast majority of which are formed in the UK.

A UK company is formed by providing Companies House with details of its Memorandum and Articles of Association, directors, company secretary and members and registered office. The registrar of companies checks the documents and if approved retains them for public inspection. The new company may be a private company that is limited by shares, or by guarantee or it may be unlimited. Alternatively, the company may be a public company that is also limited by shares. If limited by shares, the members will subscribe to the company's share capital, which in turn forms their initial investment in the company. The liability of each member is restricted to the amount of his or her investment. A public company can offer its shares to the public, whereas a private company cannot. If a company is to be limited by guarantee, the members make no contribution upon formation or during the company's lifetime, but agree instead to contribute an amount to the company's assets upon winding-up. Members of a private unlimited company have unlimited liability, and the company need not necessarily have a share capital. A company limited by shares is by far the most common structure, and is the arrangement on which the commentary in this book is based. From 8 October 2004, it has been possible to establish a European company or Societas Europaea ('SE') in Great Britain (England, Scotland and Wales) (*SI 2004/ 2326*), and an SE is treated much like a PLC.

The company has a separate legal personality to its members. A company is required to maintain statutory books to record its constitution and structure and books of account to record its transactions. Documents notifying changes in structure must be filed at Companies House. Statutory accounts must be prepared annually and filed at Companies House. A company is also required to file an annual return with the Registrar of Companies every year.

COMPANIES ACT 2006

1.3   UK companies are regulated by the companies' legislation that emanates from the nineteenth century. As a result of the Company Law Review 1998, various Law Commission recommendations and EU Directives, this legislation was completely recast and redrafted, and the *Companies Act 2006* received Royal Assent on 8 November 2006; its commencement was effectively complete with effect from October 2009 (*SI 2008/2860*). References, where appropriate, are made in this book to the *Companies Act 2006*. For previous legislation, see *Corporation Tax 2008/09* (Tottel Publishing). Under the new Act, public companies have more regulation, whilst deregulation is the order of the day for private companies. This may encourage more companies to remain or convert to being private; which may bring even more UK companies within the close company status (see **Chapter 4**).

Changes have been made to the format of the Memorandum of Association, with additional information to be supplied to the Registrar in the form of a series of statements made in the application for registration or in the articles. Other changes include the requirement that a company must have at least one director who is a natural person (*CA 2006, s 155*) and a private company is no longer required to appoint a company secretary, although in practice they may choose otherwise (*CA 2006, s 270*). The requirement is maintained for public companies (*CA 2006, s 271*). See www.companieshouse.gov.uk for subsequent changes.

THE BASIS OF CORPORATION TAX

1.4   The UK operates a free enterprise economy and any person or persons can subscribe to a company. The shareholder reward for his, her or their investment in the company is a distribution of profits, commonly known as a dividend.

The profits of a company are brought to charge to tax under the corporation tax régime. Corporation tax is directly levied on the profits of companies and is payable by the company. Profits are the company's income less expenses, together with its chargeable gains. A dividend payment is not an expense of the company; it is a distribution payment. There is no relief for corporation tax. Instead, each qualifying distribution to a shareholder who is an individual carries a tax credit of 1/9 of the distribution; which effectively satisfies the liability of a basic rate taxpayer, but not a higher rate taxpayer. Company shareholders are not chargeable to corporation tax on distributions from other UK companies.

Corporation tax rates have varied over the years but, generally speaking, current UK corporation tax rates are at their lowest (see **Chapter 3**). The main rate of corporation tax was set to decrease even further, whilst the small company rate was set to increase, but rates have now been held in view of the current financial crises. The tax base is also subject to characteristic annual *Finance Act* changes, to target avoidance or to provide incentives, and corporation tax is part of the government's tax rewrite project (see **1.1** above).

LIABILITY TO CORPORATION TAX

Definition of a company

1.5   A company is not the only 'person' that is liable to corporation tax. This is because a company is defined as 'any body corporate or unincorporated association' (*ICTA 1988, s 832(1)*). Therefore members' clubs, societies and trade and voluntary associations will find themselves within the ambit of corporation tax (see **5.76–5.79**). The *s 832* definition of a company excludes a partnership, a local authority or a local authority association. Therefore partnerships, trustees, local authorities and local authority associations are not chargeable to corporation tax. Please see *Income Tax 2009/10* (Bloomsbury Publishing) for partnerships, and *Trusts and Estates 2009/10* (Bloomsbury Publishing) for trustees. Local authorities and local authority associations are exempt from corporation tax, income tax and capital gains tax (*ICTA 1988, s 519(2) and TCGA 1992, s 271(3)*).

The extent of the corporation tax charge

1.6   It is immaterial where and how a UK company earns its profits because all UK resident companies are liable to corporation tax on their profits wherever they arise and whether or not they are received or transmitted to the UK (*CTA 2009, s 5(1)*). The UK (United Kingdom) for these purposes includes Great Britain and Northern Ireland but not the Irish Republic, the Isle of Man or the Channel Islands.

A company is UK resident if it is incorporated in the UK, ie registered at Companies House. If it is not incorporated in the UK but is managed and controlled from the UK, it will most likely be resident in the UK for corporation tax purposes. These concepts are discussed in **Chapter 13**.

If a non-UK resident company carries on a trade in the UK through a permanent establishment, it will be liable to corporation tax on the profits directly attributable to the permanent establishment. A permanent establishment could amount to an overseas company's UK branch, UK office or UK agency. Such profits may emanate directly or indirectly from the permanent establishment and will include income from trades, property, intangibles and gains (*CTA 2009, s 19(2), (3)*).

Taxation of company profits

1.7   *Section 2(2) of the Corporation Tax Act 2009* brings a company's profits into charge to corporation tax by stating that the profits that are chargeable to corporation tax consist of income and chargeable gains. Dividends and distributions received from UK resident companies are excluded (*CTA 2009, s 1285*). With effect from 1 July 2009, dividends received from foreign companies are also excluded. See **Chapter 13**. The profits for each accounting period are then chargeable to corporation tax at the appropriate rate (*CTA 2009, s 8(3)*). Corporation tax rates are fixed for financial years. The financial year (for corporation tax) commences on 1 April in one year and ends on 31 March in the next year and is known as the calendar year on which it commences, eg the financial year 2009 commences on 1 April 2009 and ends on 31 March 2010.

Like its income tax counterpart – *Income Tax (Trading and Other Income) Act 2005 (ITTOIA 2005)* – *CTA 2009* refers to an income source by its name, rather than a case or schedule category. In addition, it removes the distinction between UK and foreign source income, when taxing that income, but retains the distinction when granting loss relief.

Computation of income and gains

1.8   Corporation tax is charged on income and chargeable gains, but is not charged on dividends and distributions.

Each source of income and each chargeable gain are computed separately, in accordance with corporation tax law and practice.

Thus, the corporation tax computation and the corporation tax return bring together the company's total assessable income from trading and other sources, and chargeable gains. Deductions such as allowable losses and charges on income are taken into account in arriving at the company's profit chargeable to corporation tax (PCTCT).

The various sources of income and reliefs are discussed as follows:

Source	Type of income	Chapter
Property income	Profits from rents and other income from property in the UK and overseas	12
Trading income	Profits from a trade	5
Loan relationships	Interest and other income arising from money debts	11
Miscellaneous income	Sundry income	5
Chargeable gains	Profits and losses arising from the disposal of capital assets	20
	Type of relief	
Management expenses	Expenses relating to investment business	12
Charges on income	Expenditure deducted from total income	9
Loss relief	Relief for excess of expenditure over income against other sources of income	9, 10

COMPANY ACCOUNTS AND DIRECTORS' DUTIES

Duty to prepare accounts

1.9   The company's financial results are presented in a company's accounts. Preparation of accounts is a duty of the directors. *Section 394* of the *Companies Act 2006* states that the directors of every company shall prepare accounts for the company for each of its financial years. The accounts may be prepared either under the 'Companies Act individual accounts' accounting framework or under the 'IAS individual accounts' framework (*CA 2006, s 395*). Directors of a company must not approve accounts unless they are satisfied that those accounts give a true and fair view of the assets, liabilities, financial position and profit or loss of a company (*CA 2006, s 393(1)*). *Companies Act 2006, s 386* states that every company shall keep adequate accounting records for the company for each of its financial years. Under the *Companies Act 2006* with effect from 6 April 2008, the auditor will also report on whether the company has maintained 'adequate records' (*CA 2006, s 498*). Prior to this, the auditor had to report on whether proper accounting records were kept (*CA 2006, s 237*).

Companies Act accounts

1.10 *Companies Act* individual accounts comprise a balance sheet as at the last day of the financial year, and a profit and loss account for each financial year, which are known as individual accounts (*CA 2006, s 396(1)*). The balance sheet must give a true and fair view of the state of the company's affairs as at the end of the financial year, and the profit and loss must give a true and fair view of the profit or loss of the company for the financial year. The individual accounts may be prepared in accordance either with *Companies Act* or IAS frameworks (*CA 2006, s 395*).

IAS individual accounts are accounts that comply with international accounting standards. If IAS are used, the notes to the accounts must state that the accounts have been prepared in accordance with international standards (*CA 2006, s 397*).

Group accounts may be prepared on a similar basis, either *Companies Act* group accounts or 'IAS group accounts', which are in accordance with international accounting standards. Listed companies, as required by European law, must use IAS when preparing their consolidated accounts. If IAS group accounts are prepared, the directors must state in the notes to those accounts that they have been prepared in accordance with international accounting standards (*CA 2006, s 406*).

Accounting standards

1.11 The Accounting Standards Board (ASB), an independent body, sets the accounting standards that apply to all UK and Republic of Ireland entities that have not chosen to use International Financial Reporting Standards (IFRS). The Board has adopted a strategy of convergence with international standards.

The International Accounting Standards Board (IASB) sets the accounting standards to be used, with effect from 1 January 2005, by all listed groups. The standards are referred to as International Accounting Standards (IAS) or International Financial Reporting Standards (IFRS). UK companies may not use a standard as written by the IASB unless it has been adopted by the

European Union. The European Commission set up the Accounting Regulatory Committee (ARC), which is chaired by the Commission and composed of representatives from member states. The ARC provides an opinion on Commission proposals of whether or not to endorse an international accounting standard (see **17.5–17.6**).

UK GAAP

1.12   The vast majority of UK companies apply UK GAAP. Over the past few years there have been many changes to UK GAAP. This is largely due to the ASB's focus to bring the UK's accounting standards in line with the international standards.

UK GAAP includes accounting standards, Urgent Issues Task Force (UITF) abstracts, the Companies Act and Stock Exchange requirements and other accepted industry practices. Until 1970 the *Companies Act* was the only regulatory force that governed the preparation of companies' financial statements. Since then accounting standards have developed commencing with statements of standard accounting practice (SSAPs), Financial Reporting Standards (FRSs) and latterly International Accounting Standards and International Financial Reporting Standards. The purpose of the accounting standards is to give an authority as to how a certain type of transaction should be recorded in the accounts to reflect a 'true and fair view'.

Smaller companies may adopt the Financial Reporting Standard for Smaller Entities (FRSSE), which is within UK GAAP. The FRSSE may be applied to small companies and groups as defined in the *Companies Act* (see **1.13** and **1.14** below). Large or medium-sized groups cannot use the FRSSE. The FRSSE exempts the small company from complying with other accounting standards and UITF abstracts unless the company is preparing consolidated accounts. FRSSE embodies FRS 5 *Reporting the Substance of Transactions* and FRS 18 *Accounting Policies* (see **17.12** and **17.18**) principles amongst others. An International Accounting Standard for smaller entities IFRS for SMEs was published on 9 July 2009.

SMEs (small and medium-sized enterprises) and SEs (small enterprises)

1.13   *Companies Act 2006, ss 382, 383, 465* and *466* define small and medium-sized enterprises by a limiting criteria of turnover, assets and the number of employees. The criteria are as follows:

	Small company	Medium-sized company
	Not more than	Not more than
Turnover	£5.6 million	£22.8 million
Balance sheet total	£2.8 million	£11.4 million
Number of employees	50	250

The balance sheet total is the aggregate of the company's assets, as shown on the balance sheet, before both current and long-term liabilities. The amounts are reduced proportionately for accounting periods of less than 12 months.

For the first year that a company satisfies two or more of the above-mentioned requirements, it qualifies as an SME for that financial year. Once a company has qualified as an SME, it will continue to be treated as such unless it fails to meet the requirements for two consecutive years. If a large company reduces in size to become an SME, it will not be treated as such unless it has met the requirements for two successive years.

Groups

1.14   The definitions of a small and a medium-sized group are as follows:

	Small group		Medium-sized group	
	Not more than	Not more than	Not more than	Not more than
	Net	Gross	Net	Gross
Turnover	£5.6 million	£6.72 million	£22.8 million	£27.36 million
Balance sheet total	£2.8 million	£3.36 million	£11.4 million	£13.68 million
Number of employees	50		250	

The balance sheet total 'net' is the aggregate of the company's assets, as shown on the balance sheet, before both current and long-term liabilities, with inter-company balances 'netted' off.

The balance sheet total 'gross' is the aggregate of the company's assets, as shown on the balance sheet, before both current and long-term liabilities. Inter-company group balances are included.

Companies Act directors' duties

1.15   It is important to be aware of a director's duty under the *Companies Act* because, with effect from accounting periods beginning on or after 21 July

2009, the senior accounting officer of a qualifying company is mandated under the *Corporation Tax Act 2009* to ensure that the company's accounting systems are sufficiently robust in order to supply HMRC with accurate information (see **18.37**). A director who lapses in his duties may fall foul of more than one statute.

Companies Act 2006 sets out seven statutory duties of directors (*CA 2006, ss 170–181*):

- a duty to act within powers,

- a duty to promote the success of the company,

- a duty to exercise independent judgment,

- a duty to exercise reasonable care, skill and diligence,

- a duty to avoid conflicts of interest,

- a duty not to accept benefits from third parties, and

- a duty to declare interest in proposed transaction or arrangement.

(*CA 2006, ss 171–177*)

Pre-existing case law on any issue still stands (*CA 2006, s 170(4)*).

In promoting the success of the company, it is stated that the director should consider:

- the likely consequences of any decision in the long term,

- the interests of the company's employees,

- the need to foster the company's business relationships with suppliers, customers and others,

- the impact of the company's operations on the community and the environment,

- the desirability of the company maintaining a reputation for high standards of business conduct, and

- the need to act fairly as between members of the company.

(*CA 2006, s 172(1)*)

Directors are required to act responsibly in relation to all company dealings; this will include corporation tax compliance and corporation tax planning. In fulfilling their duties, it is hoped that directors will not become too involved in the minutiae of making and recording decisions. Overall it is hoped that directors will be able to follow the spirit of the law by ensuring the 'long-term best interests of the company'. Therefore, it seems that strategic decisions, based on and around a business culture with clear policies supported by robust budgeting and forecasting, may be more appropriate.

TAXATION AND ACCOUNTS

Legislation

1.16 A company may have many sources of income but the vast majority of UK companies carry on a trade of some sort. Over the years, the courts have applied GAAP as the rationale for determining the profits of a trade for taxation purposes. Accounts are treated as prepared according to GAAP for tax purposes even if they have not been so prepared: see *Threlfall v Jones (HM Inspector of Taxes); Gallagher v Jones (HM Inspector of Taxes)* (1993) 66 TC 77, [1993] STC 537, [1994] 2 WLR 160, [1994] Ch 107 and *Tapemaze Ltd v Melluish (HM Inspector of Taxes)* (2000) 73 TC 167, [2000] STC 189. HMRC acknowledge that profits computed in accordance with UK generally accepted accounting practice, subject to adjustments, form the starting point for the computation of taxable profits (HMRC Business Income Manual BIM 31019). The accounts could be prepared under international GAAP but the occurrence is not as common as UK GAAP. Also, small companies are within the realms of UK GAAP if they choose to adopt the FRSSE.

The accounting basis is embodied in statute by *Corporation Tax Act 2009, s 46* that states that the profits of a trade must be computed in accordance with GAAP. The inference is, of course, that by using GAAP the accounts will show a true and fair view. UK GAAP or international GAAP may be used, and the legal override for accounting adjustments remains.

HMRC practice

1.17 HMRC discuss FRS 18 *Accounting Policies* in HMRC Business Income Manual BIM 31032.

FRS 18 sets the framework for GAAP; IAS 8 being the international equivalent. The standard provides definitions of accounting policies, estimation techniques and measurement bases: accounting policies are the manner in which certain types of transaction should be presented; estimation techniques are the methods used to arrive at an estimated monetary amount; and measurement bases are the monetary attributes that are reflected in the accounts.

For example, if a company changed its method of stock valuation from average cost to FIFO, this would be a change of accounting policy. If, on the other hand, the company changed its method of ascertaining the cost of stock from a percentage of selling price to actual invoiced cost, this would only be a change in estimation techniques.

FRS 18, para 14 states that 'an entity should adopt accounting policies that enable its financial statements to give a true and fair view. Those accounting policies should be consistent with the requirements of accounting standards, Urgent Issues Task Force (UITF) Abstracts and companies legislation'.

The standard also states that a business must select those policies that 'are judged by the entity to be most appropriate to its particular circumstances for the purpose of giving a true and fair view'. What is 'appropriate' is left to each business to determine and is not defined in the standard. Instead the standard provides guidance on how the appropriateness of the accounting policies is to be judged. There are four objectives:

- relevance,

- reliability,

- comparability, and

- understandability (FRS 18, para 30).

Balancing the four objectives and the cost/benefit balance of providing the information constrains the four objectives. There are two bases of accounting in the preparation of financial statements and these are going concern and accruals. A going concern basis is always used unless the entity concerned has ceased trading or is to be liquidated. The accruals concept determines that transactions should be reflected in the accounts in the period they are incurred as opposed to the period in which they are received or paid. However, a deferral of costs under FRS 18 is not permitted unless the corresponding debit on the balance sheet meets the definition criteria of an asset under FRS 5 *Reporting the Substance of Transactions* (FRS 18, para 27).

HMRC particularly note that FRS 18 states that that prudence requires accounting policies to take account of uncertainty about the existence of assets, liabilities, gains, losses and changes to shareholders' funds or the amount at which they should be measured. FRS 18 also states that there is no need to exercise prudence where there is no uncertainty, nor should prudence be used as a reason to create, for example, hidden reserves or excessive provisions, deliberately understating assets or gains, or deliberately overstating liabilities or losses. To do that would mean that the financial statements are not neutral and therefore not reliable.

In Business Income Manual BIM 31040, HMRC acknowledge the importance of SSAP 17 *Accounting for post balance sheet events*, by referring to comments in *Symons v Weeks (as personal representative of Lord Llewelyn-*

Davies) (1982) 56 TC 630, [1983] STC 195. In this case it was commented that 'where facts are available they are preferable to speculative estimates'. For tax purposes it is not acceptable to ignore facts if by so doing an unreal loss is provided for. SSAP 17 has now been replaced by FRS 21 Events after the Balance Sheet Date (see **17.11**).

Although HMRC recognise that accounts are to be drawn up in accordance with GAAP, they seem uneasy with the notion of materiality, presumably because *CTA 2009, s 8(3)* states that tax is to be charged on the full amount of profits arising in the accounting period.

Materiality is closely related to the relevance objective. Accounting practice considers that an item would be material to the financial statements if its misstatement or omission might reasonably be expected to influence the economic decisions of the users of the statements. As such it acknowledges materiality as an accountancy concept and not as a taxation concept (HMRC Business Income Manual BIM 31047). Materiality is a judgment to be made in the light of the circumstances and the event. They suggest that the factual accuracy of any item in the accounts is not for the company, nor its accountants, nor indeed HMRC, but for the tribunal to decide. Appeals before the tribunal are discussed in **Chapter 2** (see **2.23–2.32**).

The objective of FRS 5 *Reporting the substance of transactions* is to ensure that the substance of any transaction is reported in the financial statements. The commercial effect of all transactions is therefore recorded in the financial statements. The standard predisposes that economic substance takes precedence over legal form. HMRC consider that, by and large, FRS 5 is a sound basis for the preparation of accounts for taxation purposes (HMRC Business Income Manual BIM 31055).

1.18   The basic premise is that the accounting profits form the taxable profits, unless overridden by taxation law (*CTA 2009, s 46(1)*). It is the overriding taxation law that we seek to examine in the following chapters. A further discussion of accounting and taxation is given in **Chapter 17**, together with a list of the UK and International Reporting Standards.

Chapter 2

Self-assessment

INTRODUCTION

2.1   Self-assessment for companies was introduced in 1999, effectively for accounting periods ended after 30 June 1999. Companies are empowered to determine their own corporation tax liability and pay corporation tax based on this self-assessment to Her Majesty's Revenue and Customs (HMRC). HMRC are an integrated revenue department that was formed on 18 April 2005 by the merger of the Inland Revenue (IR), the government department responsible for direct tax, and Customs and Excise (CE), the government department responsible for indirect taxes. HMRC have organised themselves into customer units – large business and employers; small and medium-sized enterprises (SMEs); individuals; and frontiers – whose focus is on compliance assurance in order to minimise the risk of loss of tax to the government through taxpayer error, non-payment, evasion and fraud. This chapter comments on the self-assessment regulations, and **Chapter 18** comments on compliance assurance.

COMPANY TAX RETURN

2.2   Companies report their liability to corporation tax to HMRC through the self-assessment procedures. Any notice served by HMRC on the company should be served on the 'proper officer' that is the company secretary or the person acting as the company secretary (*TMA 1970, s 108(3)*). In cases of liquidation, the liquidator is responsible or any other person with implied or apparent authority. The treasurer or person acting as treasurer is responsible in the case of unincorporated associations. A company tax return includes a declaration by the person making the return that to the best of his knowledge and belief the return is correct and complete (*FA 1998, Sch 18, para 3(3)*).

Companies are also required to deliver a copy of their statutory accounts to HMRC (*FA 1998, Sch 18, para 11*). The company must calculate its own 'self-assessment' (*FA 1998, Sch 18, para 7*). Companies will prepare a corporation tax computation to calculate the corporation-tax due and submit this together with the corporation tax return including the supplementary pages and the statutory accounts to HMRC. A return is strictly not 'delivered' to HMRC unless it is accompanied by 'all the information, accounts, statements and reports' *(FA 1998, Sch 18, para 4)*. The CT600 asks the company to confirm that the accounts and computations are included. HMRC reject returns where delivery is incomplete.

A complete company tax return should include:

- a completed form CT600;

- any appropriate supplementary pages;

- a set of accounts, appropriate to the type of company (if registered at Companies House the statutory accounts required under the *Companies Acts*); and

- a tax computation showing how the figures on the CT600 have been derived from the accounts (detailed trading and profit and loss accounts are usually included).

If a company or a company's agent sends a CT600 without supporting accounts and tax computations, HMRC will return the CT600 to the company or the agent because it does not meet the legal return requirement (Working Together, Issue 18, November 2004).

HMRC may by notice require a company to deliver a corporation tax return to the issuing officer, together with any information and reports relevant to the tax liability *(FA 1998, Sch 18, para 3(1))*. If a company is chargeable to corporation tax for an accounting period, it is required to give notice to HMRC within 12 months of the end of the accounting period concerned that it is so liable. If the company fails to do so, it will incur a penalty *(FA 1998, Sch 18, para 2)*.

The accuracy of the preparation of the corporation tax return and the completion of the Company Tax return is a prime management responsibility. Company Tax Return CT600 (2008) Version 2 and CT600 (Short) Version 2 are reproduced by kind permission of HMRC as Appendices. An outline corporation tax computation is included in **22.2**.

CONTACTING HMRC

2.3   A company or an organisation must inform HMRC within three months in writing when it comes within the charge to corporation tax *(FA 2004, s 55)*. The information required is as follows:

- the company's name and registered number;

- the address of the company's registered office;

- the address of the company's principal place of business;

- the nature of the business being carried on by the company;

- the date to which the company intends to prepare accounts;

- the full name and home address of each of the directors of the company;

- if the company has taken over any business, including any trade, profession or vocation formerly carried out by another;

- the name and address of that former business;

- the name and address of the person from whom that business was acquired;

- the name and registered office of the parent company (if any); and

- the date that the company is required to register for PAYE.

(*Corporation Tax (Notice of Coming within Charge–Information) Regulations 2004, SI 2004/2502.*)

In practice, Companies House will inform HMRC of the formation of a new company and, as a result, HMRC will contact the company requesting information shown on form CT41G, which requests identical information as shown above. However, if HMRC do not contact the company for this information, it is still the company's responsibility to supply the information and CT41G may be completed and submitted independently. Failure to notify will result in a penalty. Penalties cannot be imposed after the failure is rectified (*TMA 1970, s 98(3)*). See **18.21** for details of provisions applying for accounting periods commencing on or after 1 April 2008. For details of the penalty provisions applying for accounting periods commencing before 1 April 2008, see *Corporation Tax 2008/09* (Tottel Publishing).

If a company fails to inform HMRC, HMRC will assume that the first accounting period runs for 12 months from the date of incorporation.

HMRC will maintain the company's details on their database. HMRC use the database to issue returns and other communications to corporate taxpayers, and it is important to keep HMRC informed of any changes in the company's accounting period or address.

COMPANY RECORDS

2.4   A company has a requirement to keep and preserve records together with supporting documents to enable it to deliver a complete and correct corporation tax return for each relevant accounting period.

2.4 *Self-assessment*

If a company complies with *Companies Act 2006, ss 386* and *387* it will maintain sufficient records to prepare its statutory accounts. Good accounting records should in most cases form good records for corporation tax purposes. Under self-assessment a company is specifically required to keep records of:

'(a) all receipts and expenses in the course of a company's activities and the matters in respect of which they arise and

(b) in the case of a trade involving dealing in goods, all sales and purchases made in the course of the trade.'

(FA 1998, Sch 18, para 21(5))

The type of records retained will vary with the industry, but it is important to bear in mind that information must be available on how a matter arises. Current legislation and HMRC often look behind a transaction and it can be important to demonstrate how a business decision or transaction was actioned at the time. When self-assessment was first introduced, HMRC commented that if a company satisfied what is now *CA 2006, ss 386* and *387* it will have satisfied the requirements to keep and preserve records for corporation tax self-assessment (*Revenue Tax Bulletin 37*, October 1998, p 587). Although that was some time ago, the article is still current.

In recent years, examinations of supporting vouchers by professionals acting for the company may have reduced due to the relaxation in the criteria for a statutory audit and also where the statutory audit concentrates on a risk-based approach. The onus for maintaining the supporting vouchers rests with the company and the supporting documents required are identified as 'accounts, books, deeds, contracts, vouchers and receipts' (*FA 1998, Sch 18, para 21(6)*). HMRC will accept alternative forms of records such as optical imaging systems. This is admissible evidence in Commissioner hearings (*FA 1998, Sch 18, para 22(2)*). As part of new HMRC powers (see **18.2** et seq), *FA 2008, Sch 37, para 9* states that the records may be kept in any form and by any means subject to any exceptions made by HMRC in writing. Companies are not required to keep records relating to distributions and tax credits and details of gross and net interest payments (*FA 1998, Sch 18, para 22(3)*). The records must be kept for six years from the end of the relevant accounting period (*FA 1998, Sch 18, para 21(3)*). With effect from 1 April 2009, as part of the new powers, HMRC may reduce this period below the six-year time limit (*FA 2008, Sch 37, para 8(3)*). Records should be kept longer if:

● a return is under enquiry more than six years after the end of the accounting period;

● the company makes its return late; or

● the records relate to a continuing transaction that may affect current years.

Penalties for failing to provide information to support the company tax return will be invoked under the new penalty régime, effective for tax periods commencing on or after 1 April 2008 that are due to be filed on or after 1 April 2009, see **18.21**. There is no penalty for failing to keep or preserve records, which might have been needed, only for the purposes of claims, elections or notices not included in the return (*FA 1998, Sch 18, para 23(3)*).

Additional documentary evidence may be required to support arm's-length dealings under transfer pricing legislation. The records required to enable a company to deliver a correct and complete return in this instance go beyond the Companies Act requirements. This is discussed in **14.23** and **14.25**.

COMPANY TAX RETURN

Corporation tax accounting periods

2.5   Under the Companies Act 2006, directors of UK companies are required to prepare and file statutory accounts for every 12-month accounting period. Usually, from three to seven weeks after the end of the accounting period from information held in its database, HMRC will send the company a 'Form CT603 Notice to deliver its company tax return by the due date'. The notice will specify a 12-month period for which HMRC consider that a return is due (*FA 1998, Sch 18, para 5(1)*). In general, the corporation tax accounting period follows the statutory accounting period but for corporation tax purposes there are specific points at which an accounting period will begin or end.

A corporation tax accounting period first begins when a company comes within the scope of corporation tax by acquiring a source of income or becoming UK resident.

An accounting period ends on the earliest of the following events:

- 12 months from the beginning of the accounting period;

- the date on which the company draws up its accounts;

- the company begins or ceases to trade or ceases to be within the charge to corporation tax in respect of its trade or trades if more than one;

- the company begins or ceases to be UK resident;

- the company begins or ceases to be in administration; or

- the company goes into liquidation or winds up.

(*ICTA 1988, s 12.*)

Therefore, an accounting period will generally last for 12 months and will usually coincide with the period for which the company draws up accounts. If the statutory period of account exceeds 12 months, it is divided for corporation tax purposes into one or more accounting periods of 12 months, with a further accounting period covering the remainder of the period of account.

Each event will require the preparation of a separate company tax return.

Example 2.1—Commencement to trade

A Ltd incorporated on 1 January 2009. It completes form CT41G and commences trading on 1 April 2009. Form CT603 is issued on 1 April 2010. The company prepares accounts for the three months to 31 March 2009 and for the 12 months to 31 March 2010 and then to 31 March each year.

A Ltd is required to prepare company tax returns from 1 January 2009 to 31 March 2009 and from 1 April 2009 to 31 March 2010. The latest filing date for the 31 March 2009 return will be 30 June 2010 being three months after receipt of the Form CT603. The latest filing date for the 31 March 2010 return will be 31 March 2011 being 12 months after the year end (see **2.15**).

Example 2.2—Change in accounting date

B Ltd has always prepared accounts to 30 September each year. In January 2009 it changes its accounting date to 31 December and prepares accounts for the 15 months to 31 December 2009.

B Ltd is required to prepare company tax returns from 1 October 2008 to 30 September 2009 and from 1 October 2009 to 31 December 2009. The filing date for both returns is 31 December 2010 being 12 months after the end of the period of accounts.

2.6   An accounting period of more or less than 12 months may result in profits being apportioned. As a general rule these should be apportioned on a time basis, according to the number of days in the accounting period (*ICTA 1988, s 834(4)*). Chargeable gains are apportioned to the period in which they occur (*TCGA 1992, s 8(3)*).

Example 2.3

	Days
A company prepares statutory accounts for the period 1 January 2009 to 31 March 2010. The company is trading throughout the whole period. Its total profits chargeable to corporation tax amount to £500,000	456

Its corporation tax accounting periods are:

	Days
First accounting period (12 months) from 1 January 2009 to 31 December 2009	365
Second accounting period (balance) from 1 January 2010 to 31 March 2010	91

The total profit is apportioned to accounting periods as follows:

	£
First accounting period profit is (£500,000 ÷ 456) × 365	400,219
Second accounting period profit is (£500,000 ÷ 456) × 91	99,781

(Working Together, Issue 18, August 2004—Company Tax Return Helpful Hints Example adapted).

2.7 Profits may be apportioned on a time basis if this gives more of an accurate result. This occurred in the case of *Marshall Hus & Partners Ltd v Bolton* (1980) 55 TC 539, [1981] STC 18. Marshall Hus & Partners Ltd was a property company that had not prepared accounts for six years. The time came for the company to fulfil its corporation tax requirements. In order to allocate its profits to the corporation tax accounting periods it averaged the profits over the entire period. The Inland Revenue objected because they had discovered that the first five accounting periods resulted in profits and the last in a substantial loss. The taxation legislation restricts the carry back of loss relief against profits of earlier periods: see **9.11**. The judges upheld the Inland Revenue's contention commenting that it was not obligatory for the Inland Revenue to divide and apportion profits where a 'more accurate and a fairer estimate of profit or loss' of the chargeable periods was available.

HMRC consider that transactions can only be matched with accounting periods where there are a few easily identifiable transactions (HMRC Company Taxation Manual CTM 01405).

CT600

2.8   In practice, shortly after the commencement of the accounting period, HMRC will issue the company with a form CT 603 'Notice to deliver a corporation tax form'. HMRC will then issue the company with a company tax return CT600 (2008) Version 2.

Companies may also use the shorter version of the form CT600 (Short) (2008) Version 2 if this is sufficient to cover their activities (both forms are reproduced in the appendices). The shorter version omits overseas income, tonnage tax profits, intra-group activities and management expenses for companies with investment business. Additional or replacement copies may be obtained from the HMRC Orderline (telephone: 0845 300 6555 or fax: 0845 300 6777) or from the HMRC website (www.hmrc.gov.uk). HMRC also accept an HMRC-approved substitute version.

If relevant to the company's activities, the following supplementary pages must also be submitted together with the main return:

Supplementary pages

2.9

CT600A	Loans to participators by close companies	See **Chapter 4**
CT600B	Controlled foreign companies	See **Chapter 13**
CT600C	Group and Consortium	See **Chapter 10**
CT600D	Insurance	
CT600E	Charities and Community Amateur Sports Clubs (CASCs)	See **Chapter 5**
CT600F	Tonnage Tax	
CT600G	Corporate Venturing Scheme	See **Chapter 12**
CT600H	Cross-border royalties	See **Chapter 3**
CT600I	Supplementary charge in respect of ring fence trade	
CT600J	Disclosure of tax avoidance schemes	See **Chapter 18**

FILING DATE

2.10   The company tax return must be filed on the last day of whichever of the following periods is last to end:

- within 12 months of the end of the accounting period for which it is made;

- if the company's statutory accounting period is longer than 12 months but no longer than 18 months, 12 months from the beginning of the accounting period;

- if the company's statutory accounts are for a period longer than 18 months then 30 months from the beginning of that period;

- alternatively if the notice to deliver a return is given late then three months after the notice was served (*FA 1998, Sch 18, para 14*).

A company may amend its company tax return within 12 months of the filing date. Therefore if a company's accounting period is 31 December 2008, its filing date is 31 December 2009 and it is able to file an amendment to the return anytime up to 31 December 2010. If a company makes a return for a wrong period it can correct the position any time up to 12 months after the filing date on the assumption that the return had been made for the correct period (*FA 1998, Sch 18, para 15*).

HMRC also have the power to amend returns for errors and omissions but can only do so for up to nine months after the return was filed, or nine months after an amendment was made if the correction follows an amendment. The company can in turn reject the correction within its amendment period or within three months of receipt of HMRC's amendment if later (*FA 1998, Sch 18, para 16*). With effect from 1 April 2009, an HMRC officer may also amend a return for anything else that he or she has reason to believe is incorrect, in the light of information available to him or her (*FA 2008, s 119(2)(b)*).

ERROR OR MISTAKE CLAIM

2.11   A company that considers that it has paid too much tax because of an error in a return may submit an error or mistake claim to HMRC within six years after the end of the year to which the claim relates, Upon receipt, HMRC will enquire into the claim and give what relief they consider to be reasonable and just in respect of that relief. No relief is available for the basis on which the return was submitted or in respect of a mistake in a claim or election which is included in the return (*FA 1998, Sch 18, para 51*). These rules are to change with effect from 1 April 2010 (see **3.30**).

ONLINE FILING

2.12   Corporation tax returns can be filed online with HMRC by using the online facility at www.hmrc.gov.uk/businesses. The company tax return

2.12 *Self-assessment*

(CT600), supplementary pages A to J, the statutory accounts and computations can be filed with HMRC over the internet. Attachments should be sent in PDF format.

Taxpayers registering for the first time will be asked to enter their name and to select a password. After successful registration a username will be displayed on screen. The company will then receive confirmation by post of the company's User ID and Activation PIN(s) to the address that HMRC have on their database within seven days of registering. The User ID is required together with the password every time the company logs in. The service must be activated within 28 days of the Activation PIN letter date.

HMRC have given the following information on their frequently asked questions on their website. It is advisable to check this information for technological changes.

To use our Online Services, you will require access to a computer with an Internet connection

Operating system and browser requirements

Windows users:

- *Internet browsers: Internet Explorer 5.0 or above or Opera 7.0.*

Mac users:

- *Safari 2.0.4 or above and Opera 7.0.*

Please also note that your Internet browser must have JavaScript and cookies enabled and be capable of supporting 128-bit SSL.

Other operating systems and browsers

Browsers and versions, other than those listed above, such as Mozilla Firefox, may allow you to access the site and use the pages but might not display the site as designed or allow you to access all the functionality. To check for the latest version of your browser, please visit the supplier's website and follow any instructions provided.

(Frequently asked questions HMRC Website.)

Any company with a CT Unique Taxpayer Reference can register and use corporation tax online filing. The Unique Taxpayer Reference (UTR) is made up of ten numbers and is shown on the company tax return, a notice to complete a company tax return or on the statement of account. It may also be on other documents from HMRC. Depending on the document or piece of correspondence, it may be printed next to the heading 'Tax Reference', 'UTR', or 'Official Use'.

Taxpayers may use HMRC's free online tax return—CT or any of the available third party products, which have successfully passed HMRC testing procedures.

Only the full company tax return may be filed online. The short return is a paper only option. The corporation tax software guides the user to the relevant sections of the full return. Questions are posed relating to the circumstances. It is important to understand the meaning of these questions and the consequences of the response. The software will perform the calculation. After successful submission the software will display an online message indicating that the return has been received and accepted. HMRC will also send an email confirming that the return has been received and accepted, if an email address has been given. Taxpayers have the facility to print out a copy of the return from the online return software.

An agent may submit an online return on behalf of a client and complete the declaration if the following are met:

- Authorisation is in place with a form 64-8 signed by a proper officer of the company.

- The agent must make a copy of the relevant information before it is sent.

- A proper officer of the company, (or other person authorised to make the return on behalf of the company) must confirm that the information is correct to the best of his knowledge and belief before the information is sent by the agent. The officer must approve and sign the copy approved as such.

This does not apply where the agent is a person authorised by the company to make the return on its behalf (*Income and Corporation Tax (Electronic Communications) Regulations 2003, SI 2003/282*).

It is envisaged that all company tax returns will be delivered online from 31 March 2011 for accounting periods ending after 31 March 2010 (HMRC Press Release 19 June 2009).

PAYMENT

2.13   Electronically coded payslips are included within form CT603 notice to deliver a company tax return. Payment can be made electronically by BACS (Bankers Automated Clearing Services) or CHAPS (Clearing House

Automated Payments System) or by cheque to HMRC accounts office. It is important to use the payslip that corresponds to the relevant accounting period, otherwise the company's cheque may be misallocated.

A payment by cheque is deemed to be made on the day that the cheque is received by HMRC (*TMA 1970, s 70A*). *Finance Act 2007* includes provisions to enable HMRC to make regulations to treat the payment as being made when the cheque clears (*FA 2007, s 95(1)*).

Interest is charged on any corporation tax paid late. Interest is earned on any overpaid corporation tax. The interest receivable calculations are based on the premise that the tax paid last is repaid first: see **3.18**. Interest on tax debts and repayment amounts is brought into account as a loan relationship debit or credit (*CTA 2009, s 482(1)*; *TMA 1970, s 90(2)*).

It is envisaged that all corporation tax payments will be made electronically after 31 March 2011 (HMRC Press Release 19 June 2009).

FAILURE TO DELIVER A RETURN BY THE FILING DATE

Rules – prior to Finance Act 2009, Sch 55

2.14   *Finance Act 2009, Sch 55* has introduced new penalty rules regarding the late submission of a company tax return. These rules have yet to take effect, but it is anticipated that they will be introduced for returns for tax periods ended after 1 April 2008 that are due to be filed before 1 April 2009. See **18.21** for details of the new provisions. Under the existing rules, failure to deliver a return on time incurs a flat rate penalty of £100 if the return is up to three months late and £200 in any other case. These penalties are increased to £500 and £1,000 where failure occurs for a third successive time (*FA 1998, Sch 18, para 17*). These penalties are not tax-related and will not reduce if the tax liability reduces. If an accounting period is longer than 12 months and HMRC has not been advised of the change, an automatic late filing penalty will be issued to meet the 12-month deadline. Companies should inform HMRC of any changes in accounting periods without delay.

If a company fails to deliver a return within 18 months of the end of an accounting period or by the later filing date then, in addition to the flat rate penalty, it will be liable to a tax-related penalty. The penalty is 10% of the unpaid tax if the return is delivered within two years after the end of the period for which the return is required or 20% of the unpaid tax in any other case (*FA 1998, Sch 18, para 18*).

There is no flat rate penalty where accounts are required under the *Companies Act* and the return is delivered no later than those accounts are required at Companies House (*FA 1998, Sch 18, para 19*). This would happen where a company extends its accounting period beyond 12 months.

Example 2.4

Renaldo Ltd, a small private company, prepares accounts to 31 March each year. However, the 2008 accounting period is extended to 30 September 2008. Renaldo Ltd prepared two corporation tax returns; the first to 31 March 2008 and the second to 30 September 2008. The two returns were submitted to HMRC on 30 April 2009. Provided Renaldo Ltd submitted the accounts to 30 September 2008 to Companies House by 30 June 2009 no penalty will ensue. If HMRC raise a penalty notice, the company should appeal under *FA 1998, Sch 18, para 19*.

HMRC's computer system (COTAX) automatically issues flat rate and tax-related penalty notices shortly after the date the penalty is incurred. Additionally, tax-related penalty determinations are automatically amended when the amount of tax payable recorded on COTAX is revised. A further flat rate penalty notice will be issued automatically when incurred after three months unless the initial flat rate penalty is under appeal (Working Together, Issue 13, June 2003).

A company is liable to a tax-related penalty if it makes a fraudulent or negligent return, which is incorrect. It is also liable to a tax-related penalty if it discovers that it has made an incorrect return, which was not made fraudulently or negligently, but which it does not correct without unreasonable delay (*FA 1988, Sch 18, para 20*). Such penalties are normally negotiated with HMRC. These rules are replaced under the new penalty regime, see **18.21.** All tax-related penalties carry interest. The rates are the same as for interest on unpaid tax: see **3.15** (*TMA 1970, s 103A*).

ENQUIRY

Time

Accounting periods ending prior to 31 March 2008

2.15   HMRC may by notice enquire into a company tax return any time within 12 months of the filing date, if the return was filed on or before the filing date. If the return was delivered late the enquiry time is extended to 12 months after the next 31 January, 30 April, 31 July or 31 October following the date the return was delivered. Similarly, if the company has made any amendments to the return, the enquiry time is extended to 12 months after the next 31 January, 30 April, 31 July or 31 October following the date the amendment was made (*FA 1998, Sch 18, para 24*). If the time limit has expired for enquiry into the main return but not the company amendments, then HMRC may only enquire into those amendments (*FA 1998, Sch 18, para 25*). If the time limit for a self-assessment enquiry has expired, HMRC may make a discovery assessment (*FA 1998, Sch 18, para 41(1)*). See **2.22**

The enquiry notice must be received by the company before the time limit. It is assumed that second-class post takes four working days to be delivered and first-class post takes two working days to be delivered. Working days do not include Saturdays, Sundays or Bank Holidays (HMRC Enquiry Manual EM 1506). It would seem that notices or assessments received outside the statutory time limit may only be disputed by noting the post-mark on the envelope in which the notice was sent. Electronic filing is more efficient in this respect.

Small companies

2.16   For accounting periods ended after 31 March 2008, the time span for which HMRC may give notice of an enquiry into a single company, or a company that is a member of a small group, is shortened to 12 months from the date when the return was delivered to HMRC (*FA 2007, s 96(3), (4)*). A small group takes the *Companies Act* definition: see **1.13** and **1.14**. A company is required to indicate on the front of form CT600 if it is part of a group that is not small.

Large and medium-sized companies

2.17   As regards large and medium-sized companies, HMRC have assured that they will endeavour only to raise an enquiry within 12 months of the filing date on which the last company tax return for the group was filed. Companies are requested to agree a time-table with HMRC and to notify HMRC in writing of when the last return is filed. This is a non-statutory arrangement and HMRC are able to revert to the statutory time period if need be.

Procedure

2.18   Where fraud is not suspected, HMRC conduct their enquiries according to set practices, which are set out in its Codes of Practice ('COP'). COP14 'Corporation tax self-assessment enquiries' details the procedures regarding a corporation tax enquiry.

To begin an enquiry, HMRC will issue a notice, copied to an appointed agent, in the form of a letter that they intend to enquire into the company tax return (*FA 1998, Sch 18, para, 24(1)*). Copies of these letters are reproduced in Working Together, Issue 12, February 2003.

The scope of the enquiry can extend to any item included in the return, any amount that affects the tax payable by the company for another accounting period and the tax liability of another company for any accounting period together with all claims and elections. The enquiry may also extend to the transfer pricing information. See **Chapter 14** for a discussion on transfer pricing. If a return is made for the wrong period, HMRC may enquire into the period for which it should have been made (*FA 1998, Sch 18, para 26*).

Overall, the company is responsible for its affairs, even if it has appointed a professional adviser, who should be fully informed of the facts of the case. HMRC will deal with a professional adviser if one has been appointed. If matters are not progressing with the adviser with sufficient speed, HMRC will advise the company and may then deal with the company direct.

In most cases, enquiries take the form of an aspect enquiry; in other words, just dealing with one or two issues on a claim or return. In-depth enquiries do occur, with HMRC conducting a wide-ranging examination into some companies' tax affairs. In such an event, HMRC will undoubtedly require to see and have the power to obtain the records from which the return was prepared. Thus the importance of keeping good accounting records manifests itself. Good accounting records are the company's only real defence in disputing HMRC claims. HMRC may ask to examine the records at the business premises or they may ask for them to be sent. With the withdrawal of the company statutory audit requirement and the influx of effective electronic systems into business life, the supporting evidence and vouchers are often ignored. The astute director/shareholder will ensure that he maintains good systems and company records. See **18.2** for HMRC powers.

In *Ferribly Construction (UK) Ltd v Revenue & Customs Commissioners* (2007) SpC 635, a construction company declared a profit on its self-assessment corporation tax return, which it later claimed should have been a loss. The company was unable to produce proper books and records to HMRC in support of the loss claim. The assessment therefore remained unchanged.

Whether or not a professional adviser can be sued by a client in the wake of a full-scale HMRC enquiry, for not warning him to keep better records, is a moot point. Companies must realise that maintaining good records is not just an administration function but also a statutory function.

Course of enquiry

2.19 Normally the course of enquiry involves the company and/or the professional agent supplying information and documents to HMRC in response to their queries. There is a period of time over which this happens, and replies to the Revenue officer conducting the enquiry should be given accurately and in good time. In any event, if any enquiry is in progress it should not hold up the submission of the next year's tax return, even if best estimated entries are included when preparing the return.

In addition, HMRC may call a meeting with the directors, company secretary or even the employees to discuss the company's business affairs. Many, indeed, will feel nervous and intimidated in such a situation. HMRC cannot compel those involved to attend a meeting. A professional adviser may attend as well as or instead of the company attendees. In all circumstances, whether or not a meeting takes place, HMRC must be provided with all the information necessary to answer their enquiries. HMRC have powers to call for information (see **18.2**).

If a meeting takes place, HMRC have formal procedures which they must follow.

They require the company representatives to bring the necessary records, either to answer HMRC's questions or to support their own queries. HMRC will make a written record of what is said at the meeting. The company may ask to see the notes.

HMRC may even go as far as requesting the company to sign a copy of their notes to signify agreement. HMRC cannot compel the company to do so. The company, of course, may comment on the notes if it wishes. The worth of attendance at a meeting from the taxpayer's perspective must be judged on its own merits in each and every case.

Corporation tax return amendment

2.20 HMRC may, by notice, amend the self-assessment calculation during the course of the enquiry if they consider it insufficient. The company has a 30-day time limit to lodge an appeal against the amendment (*FA 1998, Sch 18, para 30*). Similarly, the company may amend its return during the course of the enquiry. This will not restrict the scope of the enquiry, but it may be taken into account. The amendment will not take effect until the enquiry is finished (*FA 1998, Sch 18, para 31*). During the course of the enquiry, if the company considers that it may have additional tax to pay it can make an additional payment to reduce any interest charges that might arise. Overpayments are always repaid if incorrect. If, during the course of the enquiry, it is discovered that there is a period for which a return is required but for which none has been submitted, then such a return is required to be submitted within 30 days of the final determination (*FA 1998, Sch 18, para 35*).

COMPLETION OF ENQUIRY

2.21   The enquiry is complete when HMRC issue their closure notice to the company stating their conclusions (*FA 1998, Sch 18, para 32*). The closure notice must either state that, in the officer's opinion, no amendments are required as a result of the enquiry, or if amendments are required to amend the corporation tax return accordingly (*FA 1998, Sch 18, para 34* as amended by *FA 2008, s 119(6)*). The additional corporation tax payments will most likely include interest on overdue tax and may include a penalty.

DETERMINATIONS AND DISCOVERY ASSESSMENTS

2.22   If a company fails to submit a corporation tax return by the filing date, in response to a notice to deliver a corporation tax return, HMRC may at any time during the next five years estimate the amount of corporation tax due in a determination assessment (*FA 1998, Sch 18, para 36*). *FA 2008, Sch 39, para 38* has reduced this period to three years, for periods commencing after 1 April 2010 (*SI 2009/403*). Alternatively, if a return is filed for that period that is the subject of the notice to deliver, but there is another accounting period ending during that return period, HMRC may issue a determination for that period within any time during the next five years (*FA 1998, Sch 18, para 37*). *FA 2008, Sch 39, para 39* has reduced this period to three years, for periods commencing after 1 April 2010. These determinations are treated as the company's self-assessment (*FA 1998, Sch 18, para 39*). If a self-assessment return is subsequently filed, it will replace the determination, but the return must be filed no later than five years after HMRC were able to issue the determination assessment, or one year after the date of the determination assessment (*FA 1998, Sch 18, para 40*). *FA 2008, Sch 39, para 40* has reduced the five years to three years, for periods commencing after 1 April 2010. If a company has delivered a return, HMRC may make a discovery assessment or determination in cases where there is a loss of tax that was brought about 'carelessly or deliberately' by the company or by a person acting on its behalf (*FA 1998, Sch 18, paras 42* and *43*). *FA 2008, Sch 39, para 41* has specified 'carelessly' and 'deliberately', for periods commencing after 1 April 2010. Prior to this, the words 'fraud or negligent conduct' are applied.

The time limit for cases of fraud and negligence are 21 years from the end of the accounting period to which it relates (*FA 1998, Sch 18, para 46(2)*). With effect from 1 April 2010, an assessment for a loss of tax brought about carelessly by the company or a related person may be made at any time not more than six years after the end of the accounting period to which it relates. In cases of loss of tax brought about deliberately by the company or a related person, a failure to comply with an assessment raised because it acted carelessly, or a failure to comply with a tax avoidance scheme obligation (see **Chapter 18**), the period is 20 years from the end of the accounting period, subject to any condition existing at the time which allows a longer period (*FA 1998, Sch 18, para 46; FA 2008, Sch 39, para 42*).

If HMRC discover that the amount assessed on a company tax return is insufficient, or the relief has become excessive, they may make a discovery assessment. They may also make a discovery assessment if there has been fraudulent or negligent conduct. A discovery assessment may be made at any time, even if the enquiry time had elapsed or they had completed their enquiries into the return, if they could not be reasonably expected, on the basis of the information made available to them, to be aware of the errors in the return. In *Revenue and Customs Commrs v Household Estate Agents Ltd* (2007) All ER(D) 175 (Jul), a company submitted a corporation tax return in accordance with prevailing practice. An employee benefit trust deduction was treated as an allowable deduction from profits, but following a later ruling was no longer held to be allowable. The company made no adjustment to its corporation tax computation. HMRC had opened enquiries into the following two returns and, in the course of those enquiries, enquired about payments into the trust. HMRC made a discovery assessment, which the company claimed was precluded by *FA 1998, Sch 18, para 45*. It was held that HMRC were not prevented from making a discovery assessment, because it would have been reasonable for the inspector, if he had thought about it, to initiate an enquiry, which could have been expected to reveal the full facts. It was further decided that the burden of proof as to whether a taxpayer had not made a return in accordance with generally prevailing practice lay on the taxpayer and not the Revenue.

Information is regarded as being made available to HMRC if:

(i)   it is included in a company tax return or in the documents accompanying the return;

(ii)   it is contained in a relevant claim made by the company or in any accounts, statements or documents accompanying any such claim;

(iii)   it is contained in any documents, accounts or information produced or provided by the company to HMRC for the purposes of an enquiry into a return or claim; or

(iv)   it is information, the existence and relevance of which could reasonably be expected to be inferred by HMRC from the information supplied in circumstance (i), (ii) or (iii) above or is notified to HMRC (*FA 1998, Sch 18, para 44*).

It is therefore important to supply clear information to HMRC to support the return or the queries raised in order to avoid a discovery assessment.

Similar powers are afforded to HMRC in respect of a recovery of an excessive repayment (*FA 1998, Sch 18, para 53*). The normal time limit was six years, but this has been reduced to four years for periods commencing after 1 April 2010 (*FA 2008, Sch 39, para 44*).

APPEALS PROCEDURES

Tribunal reform

2.23   The *Tribunals, Courts and Enforcement Act 2007*, which received Royal Assent in July 2007, reforms all central government administrative tribunals including the tax appeal tribunals. The new rules take effect from 1 April 2009. For details of the previous rules, see *Corporation Tax 2008/09* (Tottel Publishing).

The *Tribunals, Courts and Enforcement Act 2007* introduced a two-tier tribunal system, the First-tier Tribunal and the Upper Tribunal. The two tribunals are organised into Chambers, which have specific functions, to which existing tribunal jurisdictions have been transferred (*SI 2008/2684*). The new system is administered centrally by the Tribunals Service.

The First-tier Tribunal is the first instance tribunal for most jurisdictions. There is a right of appeal on points of law, except in the case of excluded decisions, to the Upper Tribunal. The Upper Tribunal acts in the main (but not exclusively) as an appellate tribunal from the First-tier Tribunal, but it also has power to deal with judicial review work delegated from the High Court and Court of Session. A decision of the Upper Tribunal may be appealed to the Court of Appeal. The grounds of appeal must always relate to a point of law (*SI 2008/2707*). The Senior President of Tribunals maintains judicial oversight of the whole system.

Tax tribunals

2.24   With effect from 1 April 2009, the existing tax tribunals were abolished and all functions of the Special Commissioners, the VAT and duties tribunals, the tribunal established under *ICTA 1988, s 706* (regarding a tax advantage in dealing in securities) and under *ITA 2007, s 704* (transactions in securities) were transferred to the new tribunal. The General Commissioners are retained to deal with existing cases (*Transfer of Tribunal Functions and Revenue and Customs Appeal Order 2009, SI 2009/56*). The new provisions, *TMA 1970, ss 49A to 49I*, apply to corporation tax appeals (*TMA 1970,* *s 48(2))*. The First-tier tax chamber has an appointed President, and the Upper Tribunal has an appointed President and Vice-President.

COMPANY APPEAL

Introduction

2.25   Under the new appeal procedures, a company can appeal an HMRC decision directly to the First-tier Tribunal. Previously, HMRC controlled the cases that were listed before the Commissioners. Alternatively, the company can ask HMRC to carry out an internal review of the decision. There is a 30-day time limit. HMRC will accept late appeals if there is a reasonable excuse; if not, the company has the option to ask the tribunal for permission to make a late appeal.

Company disagrees with an HMRC decision

2.26   If a company disagrees with an HMRC decision, it may appeal direct to HMRC *(TMA 1970, s 49A)*, in which case there are three possible outcomes:

- the company may ask HMRC to carry out an independent review of the matter in question (see **2.27**);

- HMRC may offer to review the matter in question (see **2.28**), or

- the company may appeal directly to the tribunal (see **2.29**).

Alternatively, the parties may agree to settle by mutual agreement *(TMA 1970, s 54)*.

HMRC have confirmed that 'all reviews will be done by a trained review officer, who has not previously been involved with that decision, who will be able to offer a balanced and objective view. In the vast majority of cases the review officer will be outside the immediate line management chain of the decision maker' (HMRC Brief 10/2009 16 March 2009).

Company requests HMRC to carry out an independent review

2.27   The company may request an HMRC review, and HMRC must give their response within 30 days of receipt of that request *(TMA 1970, s 49B)*.

HMRC must carry out the review that they consider to be appropriate in the circumstances. They must take account of all steps taken before the beginning of the review, both by HMRC and other parties, in resolving the matter in question. They must take all company representations into account. HMRC may conclude that the decision is to be upheld, varied or cancelled, and must notify the company of their decision. Notification must be given within 45 days from the day when HMRC notified the company of their view of the matter in question.

If HMRC do not give notice of their conclusions within the 45-day time period, the review is to be treated as having concluded that HMRC's view of the matter in question is upheld. Notification in any case should be given to the company (*TMA 1970, s 49E*).

HMRC offers to carry out an independent review

2.28   HMRC's review offer must include their view of the matter in question. The company has an acceptance period of 30 days, beginning with the date of the notification document of the offer, to review the matter in question and to accept the offer. If the company does not give notice of its acceptance within the acceptance period, HMRC's view of the matter in question is final. The company can appeal direct to the tribunal (*TMA 1970, s 49C*).

HMRC must carry out the review that they consider to be appropriate in the circumstances. They must take account of all steps taken before the beginning of the review, both by HMRC and other parties, in resolving the matter in question. They must also take all company representations into account. HMRC may conclude that the decision is to be upheld, varied or cancelled, and must notify the company of their decision within 45 days of HMRC's receipt of the company's acceptance of a review offer.

If HMRC do not give notice of their conclusions within the 45-day time period, the review is to be treated as having concluded that HMRC's view of the matter in question is upheld. Notification in any case should be given to the company (*TMA 1970, s 49E*).

HMRC cannot offer the company a review if:

- a review offer has already been made;
- the company has requested a review; or
- the company has appealed direct to the First-tier Tribunal.

(*TMA 1970, s 49C*)

Company appeal to the tribunal following HMRC review

2.29   If the company has appealed a decision to HMRC, it may also notify the appeal to the tribunal for it to decide the matter in question. There is no such appeal if HMRC have given notice of their view of the matter following a review at the instigation of either the company or HMRC, unless the following circumstances are met (*TMA 1970, s 49D*).

If HMRC have carried out a review, and whether or not the 45-day time limit has been adhered to for giving notice of its conclusions, the company may still appeal to the tribunal within the post-review period.

The post-review period is:

- *where HMRC give notification of its conclusions within the 45-day time limit*

  the period of 30 days beginning with the date of the review conclusion notification document; or

- *where HMRC fails to give notification of its conclusions within the 45-day time limit*

  the period that begins with the day following the last day of the HMRC 45-day notification period (or other period as agreed) and ends 30 days after the date of the document in which HMRC give notice of their conclusions of the review.

Appeals to the tribunal outside the post-review period are subject to the tribunal's permission (*TMA 1970, s 49G*).

Company appeal to the tribunal having declined an HMRC review

2.30   If a company declines the offer of an HMRC review, it may notify its appeal to the tribunal within the acceptance period. Appeals to the tribunal outside the acceptance period are subject to the tribunal's permission (*TMA 1970, s 49H*).

HMRC have issued guidance material on the new tribunal system – in particular, see HMRC Brief 10/2009 16 March 2009 and the Appeal, reviews and tribunals guidance Manual (www.hmrc.gov.uk).

Reviews in the transitional period

2.31   The new review provisions also apply where a company sent its appeal to HMRC before 1 April 2009, provided neither HMRC nor the taxpayer have taken any steps before that date to secure a hearing of the appeal by the General or Special Commissioners or the new tribunal.

Where a corporation tax appeal was sent to HMRC before 1 April 2009, and the option to have a review is exercised before 1 April 2010, the period within which HMRC must notify the review conclusions (subject to any other period being agreed) is 90 days, rather than the usual period of 45 days (HMRC Guidance 10 March 2009).

Excluded decisions

2.32   A company has no right of appeal against the following decisions:

- *ICTA 1988, s 215(7)* – advance clearance of distributions and payments; see **16.18**;

- *FA 2000, Sch 15, para 91(b)* – corporate venturing scheme: advance clearance; see **12.48**;

- *CTA 2009, s 833(2), (3)* – gains and losses from intangible fixed assets: transfer of business or trade; see **7.26** (*SI 2009/275*).

Chapter 3

Rates and payment of corporation tax

RATES OF CORPORATION TAX

Full rate

3.1   The corporation tax chargeable is calculated by applying the applicable corporation tax rate to the company's profits chargeable to corporation tax (PCTCT). The main rate of corporation tax for the financial year 2009 is 28% (*FA 2008, s 6*). The main rate of corporation tax for the financial year 2010 will remain at 28% (*FA 2009, s 7*). A 30% rate applies to 'ring fence profits'. Ring fence profits are a company's profits or gains from oil extraction and oil rights in the UK and the UK Continental shelf (*FA 2009, s 7*).

Small companies rate

3.2   The small companies rate of corporation tax is 21% for the financial years 2008 and 2009 (*FA 2009, s 8*). It has been announced that the small companies rate will increase to 22% for the financial year 2010 (Pre-Budget Report 2008 PRRN 02). The fraction for calculating marginal relief is 7/400ths.The 19% small companies rate and the 11/400ths small companies fraction (see **3.4** below) apply to small companies with ring fence profits.

Starting rate and non-corporation distribution rate

3.3   Both the corporation tax starting rate and the non-corporate distribution rate were abolished with effect from 1 April 2006 (*FA 2006, ss 26(1)* and *(2)*). For further discussion of these topics, see *Corporation Tax 2006/07* (Tottel Publishing), Chapter 2.

Table of rates

3.4   The rates of corporation tax for the financial years 2009 and 2008 are:

	Financial Year 2009 Commencing 1 April 2009	Financial Year 2008 Commencing 1 April 2008
Full rate	28%	28%
Small companies' rate	21%	21%
Profit limit for small companies' rate	£300,000	£300,000
Profit limit for small companies' marginal relief	£1,500,000	£1,500,000
Marginal relief fraction for profits between £300,000 and £1,500,000	7/400ths	7/400ths

In addition, loans to participators attract *ICTA 1988, s 419* tax at 25% on the outstanding amount: see **4.14–4.22**.

Marginal rates of corporation tax

3.5   The small companies rate of corporation tax is applied to profits chargeable to corporation tax (PCTCT) if company profits for a financial year are £300,000 or less. Profits above £300,000 are chargeable at the full rate of corporation tax subject to the company's claim for marginal relief. This limit is proportionately reduced where the company has one or more associated companies (by dividing it by one plus the number of associated companies) and for accounting periods of less than 12 months (*ICTA 1988, s 13(3)*). (See **4.27–4.33**). Profits for this purpose are measured as PCTCT plus non-group FII. FII is the net dividend plus the 10/90 tax credit. With effect from 1 July 2009, foreign dividends are included (*FA 2009, Sch 14, para 3*). A group for this purpose is the parent and any of the 51% subsidiaries (*ICTA 1988, s 13*).

A company may claim marginal relief by completing box 64 of the company tax return (*ICTA 1988, s 13(2)*).

Marginal relief is calculated as follows:

Fraction × (Upper relevant amount—profits) × (PCTCT ÷ profits)

Example 3.1

Apple Ltd's profits chargeable to corporation tax for the accounting period ended 31 March 2010 amount to £350,000. The company received a dividend of £9,000 from Pear Ltd a non-group company during the year. No dividends were paid during the year and there are no associated companies.

Corporation tax payable is calculated as follows:

	£
350,000 @ 28%	98,000
Less marginal relief:	
$7/400 \times (1,500,000 - 360,000) \times (350,000 \div 360,000)$	19,396
	78,604

FII = £(9,000 × 100/90)

Effective rates of corporation tax

3.6   For the financial years 2008 and 2009, in cases where no dividends are received corporation tax payable may be more simply calculated where marginal relief is involved by applying the following effective rates of corporation tax.

Corporation tax rates

	Financial year 2009		*Financial year 2008*	
	Rate of corporation tax	*Maximum corporation tax payable*	*Rate of corporation tax*	*Maximum corporation tax payable*
£	%	£	%	£
0–300,000	21	63,000	21	63,000
300,001–1,500,000	29.75	357,000	29.75	357,000
1,500,000+	28	420,000	28	420,000

The eventual corporation tax payable is corporation tax chargeable less: marginal relief (if any) less CVS Investment Relief (see **12.41**), community investment tax relief (see **12.56**), double taxation relief (see **13.22**), ACT (see **16.10**) plus tax payable under *s 419* (see **4.16**), any supplementary charge in respect of ring-fence trades, sums chargeable in respect of controlled foreign companies (see **13.23**) less research and development tax credit (see **8.25**), together with any income tax deducted at source (*FA 1998, Sch 18, para 8*).

PAYMENT OF CORPORATION TAX

Payment

3.7 Electronically coded payslips are included within form CT603 'notice to deliver a company tax return'. If paying by cheque, it is important to use the payslip that corresponds to the relevant accounting period, otherwise the company's cheque may be misallocated. If there is no payslip, the following details should be included with the cheque sent to HMRC:

- company name;

- address;

- telephone number;

- CT reference number;

- accounting period for which payment is being made; and

- amount of the corporation tax payment.

A payment by cheque is deemed to be made on the day that the cheque is received by HMRC (*TMA 1970, s 70A*). *Finance Act 2007* includes provisions to enable HMRC to make regulations to treat the payment as being made when the cheque clears (*FA 2007, s 95(1)*).

Payment can also be made by direct debit, internet telephone banking, by BACS (Bankers Automated Clearing Services), CHAPS (Clearing House Automated Payments System), debit or credit card over the internet, Bank Giro and at the Post Office. For further details, see www.hmrc.gov.uk – Paying Corporation Tax. No payslip is required for an electronic payment.

If a company pays tax by credit card and gives a telephone authorisation, HMRC will charge a fee of 0.91% of the payment (*SI 2008/1948*). If a company pays corporation tax on the internet by credit card, a fee of 1.25% of the payment will be charged (*SI 2008/2991*).

Interest is charged on any corporation tax paid late. Interest is earned on any overpaid corporation tax. The interest receivable calculations are based on the premise that the tax paid last is repaid first: see **3.18**. Interest on tax debts and repayment amounts is brought into account as a loan relationship debit or credit (*CTA 2009, s 482(1)*; *TMA 1970, s 90(2)*).

Electronic payment of all corporation tax liabilities is scheduled after 31 March 2011 (HMRC Press Release 19 June 2009).

PAYMENT DATES

3.8   The corporation tax payment due date is nine months and one day following the end of the accounting period concerned (*TMA 1970, s 59D(1)*).

Small and medium-sized companies

3.9   A small or medium-sized company's corporation tax is due and payable nine months and one day after the end of the accounting period (*TMA 1970, s 59D*). Small and medium-sized companies are not required to pay corporation tax by quarterly instalments (see **3.11**).

Large companies

3.10   Large companies are charged to corporation tax at the 28% full rate. A company is large if its 'profits' plus franked investment income exceed the upper relevant amount, currently £1,500,000 for a year. Franked investment income (FII) is the company's UK dividends that it has received during the accounting period plus the corresponding tax credit. Dividends received from other group members are not included. Groups are discussed in **Chapter 10**. This limit is proportionately reduced where the company has one or more associated companies (by dividing it by one plus the number of associated companies) and for accounting periods of less than 12 months (*ICTA 1988, s 13(3)*). (See **4.27–4.33**). Hence a company with a large number of associates may be a 'large' company even though its profits are relatively small.

Quarterly instalments

3.11   Unlike small and medium-sized companies, 'large' companies are required to pay their corporation tax liabilities in up to four quarterly instalments, based on the company's estimated liability for that accounting period.

A company will not be required to pay by instalments in an accounting period where its PCTCT plus non-group FII (see **3.5**) for that period does not exceed £10m and it was not large for the previous year.

A company is not treated as large for an accounting period if its corporation tax liability does not exceed £10,000.

The £10m and the £10,000 limits mentioned above are reduced proportionately if the accounting period is less than 12 months. The limits are also reduced if the company has associated companies by dividing the limits by one plus the number of associated companies (see **4.27**) (*Corporation Tax (Instalment Payments) Regulations 1998, SI 1998/3175*).

Corporation tax is payable in four quarterly instalments, which are due:

Instalment	Due
First	Six months and 13 days after the start of the accounting period
Second	Three months after the first instalment
Third	Three months after the second instalment
Final	Three months and 14 days after the end of the accounting period.

Example 3.2

Twelve month accounting period ended 31 December 2009.

Instalment	Due
First	14 July 2009
Second	14 October 2009
Third	14 January 2010
Final	14 April 2010

3.12 If the accounting period is less than 12 months, the final instalment is due as normal three months and 14 days after the end of the accounting period. The earlier instalments only fall due if the payment date falls before the due date for the final instalment.

Example 3.3

Six month accounting period ended 30 June 2010.

Instalment	Due
First	14 July 2010
Final	14 October 2010

Calculation of tax due

3.13 A company, which considers that it is large, should calculate its quarterly payment at each due date. If it considers that it has paid too much tax for a quarter, it may deduct the overpayment from the next quarter's liability.

The liability is calculated as follows:

3 × (Company's total liability ÷ Number of months in the accounting period)

Example 3.4

Wood Ltd's corporation tax liability for the year ended 31 December 2010 is £1,000,000.

Instalments are 3 × (1,000,000 ÷ 12) = £250,000

The liability for the year is payable as follows:

Instalment	Due	Amount
First	14 July 2010	£250,000
Second	14 October 2010	£250,000
Third	14 January 2011	£250,000
Final	14 April 2011	£250,000

3.14   Interest is charged on instalments paid late at the late instalment rate (see **3.15**).

If a company should have made quarterly instalment payments, regardless of whether or not it made such payments a cross should be placed in box 95. HMRC regard electronic payments as more efficient than payments by post. The HMRC website (www.hmrc.gov.uk/howtopay) gives more information on how to make electronic payments (Working Together, Issue 18, August 2004—Company Tax Return—Helpful Hints). See HMRC Company Taxation Manual CTM 92500 onwards for more information on quarterly instalments.

INTEREST

Late payment interest

3.15   If a company pays its corporation tax beyond the due date (nine months and one day after the end of the accounting period) it will be charged late payment interest under *TMA 1970, s 87A* on the corporation tax that it pays late. HMRC will not charge the company interest on interest paid late.

Late payment interest is calculated from the day after the normal due date until the effective date of payment. HMRC's computer system is programmed to calculate the interest due. Situations not covered by the programmes are calculated manually by HMRC clerical staff.

The most current rates are:

Corporation tax interest on unpaid tax

From	*%*
24 March 2009	2.5
27 January 2009	3.5
6 January 2009	4.5
6 December 2008	5,5
6 November 2008	6.5
6 January 2008	7.5
6 August 2007	8.5
6 September 2006	7.5
6 September 2005	6.5
6 September 2004	7.5
6 December 2003	6.5

REPAYMENTS

3.16   If a company has overpaid tax it may make a repayment claim. Normally a company is only able to ascertain whether it has made an overpayment when it prepares its corporation tax computation and company tax return. The repayment claim is made by placing a cross in the appropriate repayment claim box on the front of form CT600 and by completing the relevant repayment claim sections of CT600 or CT600 (Short). HMRC advise that a company will receive its repayment faster if it files online. The fastest and most secure repayment method is direct credit to the company bank account (by BACS). For this to take place the company must ensure that the 'Bank Details' section of the return is fully completed (page 12 of the main return and page 4 of the short return) (Working Together, Issue 18, August 2004—Company Tax Return—Helpful Hints).

If a company does not consider the overpayment to be worth claiming, it may indicate on the return by completing the CT600 boxes 139 or 140 that small overpayments are to be set against future liabilities instead of being repaid.

Income tax

3.17   A company may claim an income tax repayment. This can arise if the company has received income from which tax has been deducted at source. The claim must be made on the company tax return or on an amended return (*FA 1998, Sch 18, para 9*). Box 142 is the requisite box for completion (see **3.24** and Example 3.6 for an income tax calculation). Tax deduction vouchers are not required in support of the claim and will only be requested if the return is under enquiry.

Repayment interest

3.18   If a company overpays corporation tax it will be entitled to repayment interest. Repayment interest is calculated from the later of the day after the normal due date or the date the payment was made to the material date (*ICTA 1988, s 826(1)*).

The material date is either the date when the repayment was issued or the HMRC allocation. HMRC assume that the tax paid last is repaid first. If there are no loss carry-backs for an accounting period the material date is the date the corporation tax was paid or, if later, the normal corporation tax due date (*ICTA 1988, s 826(2)*). For R&D and land remediation tax credits, the material date is the later of the filing date for the company's tax return and the date on which an amended tax return including the claim is delivered to HMRC (*ICTA 1988, s 826(3A)*). If losses are carried back to an accounting period wholly within the previous 12 months, the material date is the due date for the accounting period in which the tax was overpaid (*ICTA 1988, s 826(7A)*).

If the accounting period against which the losses are set does not fall wholly within the previous 12 months, the material date becomes the due date of the accounting period in which the losses arise (*ICTA 1988, s 826(7A)*).

When a non-trading loan relationship deficit or double tax relief is carried back to an earlier period, the material date is the due date for the accounting period in which the deficit or the double tax arose (*ICTA 1988, s 826(7C), (7BB)*).

The most current rates are:

Corporation tax repayment interest

From	%
24 March 2009	0
27 January 2009	0
6 January 2009	1
6 December 2008	2
6 November 2008	3
6 January 2008	4
6 August 2007	5
6 September 2006	4
6 September 2005	3
6 September 2004	4
6 December 2003	3

Interest rate formulae

3.19 The interest rates charged are calculated using the formula given in *Taxes (Interest Rate) Regulations 1989, SI 1989/1297, regs 3ZA* and *3ZB* (inserted by *Taxes (Interest Rate) (Amendment No. 2) Regulations 1998, SI 1998/3176, reg 6)*. This results in late payment interest being charged at approximately 2.5% above base rate, and overpayment interest being credited at 1% less than base rate.

Late payment interest where there is a carry-back of losses or a non-trading deficit

3.20 Companies that have incurred a trading loss or a non-trading deficit may elect to carry that loss back to be set against the total profits of the previous accounting period under *ICTA 1988, s 393A* and *FA 1996, s 83(2)(c)* respectively: see **Chapter 9**, in particular the temporary extension of trading loss carry-back. In anticipation of so doing they may not pay the corporation tax due for the previous period. The company must be aware that the late payment interest will run from the normal due date to the due date of the later accounting period (*TMA 1970, s 87A(4A)*).

Example 3.5

Roquet Ltd anticipates a trading loss for the year ended 31 December 2009 of £200,000. For the accounting period ended 31 December 2008 it had a trading profit of £100,000. The company has no other source of income. On 1 October 2009 the directors consider that it is not worth paying the corporation tax due for the year ended 31 December 2008 because of the forthcoming loss.

Roquet Ltd will be charged interest on the corporation tax due on £100,000 for the period from 1 October 2009 until 1 October 2010.

QUARTERLY INSTALMENTS

Debit and credit interest

3.21   A large company that pays corporation tax by instalments will be charged interest on late quarterly instalment payments and will receive interest on quarterly instalment payments paid in advance (*Corporation Tax (Instalment Payments) Regulations 1998, SI 1998/3175, regs 7* and *8*). Interest paid is known as debit interest and interest received is known as credit interest. The interest rate formulae are similar to late payment interest but result in lower rates. Debit interest is approximately 1% above base rate and credit interest is approximately 0.25% below base rate.

Debit interest is charged from the quarterly instalment due date until the earlier of the date of payment of the tax and the normal due date, being nine months and one day after the end of the accounting period (see **3.7**).

The most current rates are:

Debit interest charged on underpaid quarterly instalment payment

From	To	%
16 March 2009		1.50
16 February 2009	15 March 2009	2.00
19 January 2009	15 February 2009	2.50
15 December 2008	18 January 2009	3.00
17 November 2008	14 December 2008	4.00
20 October 2008	16 November 2008	5.50
21 April 2008	19 October 2008	6.00
18 February 2008	20 April 2008	6.25
17 December 2007	17 February 2008	6.50
16 July 2007	16 December 2007	6.75
21 May 2007	15 July 2007	6.50

22 January 2007	20 May 2007	6.25
20 November 2006	21 January 2007	6.00
14 August 2006	19 November 2006	5.75
15 August 2005	13 August 2006	5.5
16 August 2004	14 August 2005	5.75
21 June 2004	15 August 2004	5.5

Credit interest will accrue from the date on which the overpayment arises or from the due date for the first instalment payment, if later to the earlier of:

● the date the overpayment is removed by being utilised as payment for another quarter; and

● the normal due date, being nine months and one day after the end of the accounting period.

The most recent rates are:

Credit interest paid on overpaid quarterly instalment payments and on early payments of corporation tax not due by instalments

From	*To*	*%*
16 March 2009		0.25
16 February 2009	15 March 2009	0.75
19 January 2009	15 February 2009	1.25
15 December 2008	18 January 2009	1.75
17 November 2008	14 December 2008	2.75
20 October 2008	16 November 2008	4.25
21 April 2008	19 October 2008	4.75
18 February 2008	20 April 2008	5.00
17 December 2007	17 February 2008	5.25
16 July 2007	16 December 2007	5.50
21 May 2007	15 July 2007	5.25
22 January 2007	20 May 2007	5.00
20 November 2006	21 January 2007	4.75
14 August 2006	19 November 2006	4.5
15 August 2005	13 August 2006	4.25
16 August 2004	14 August 2005	4.5
21 June 2004	15 August 2004	4.25

GROUP PAYMENT ARRANGEMENTS

3.22 *FA 1998, s 36* allows one company in a group to attend to the administration of the corporation tax payments on behalf of the other group members if it enters into a group payment arrangement 'GPA' contract with HMRC. Details of the contract can be downloaded from HMRC's website: 'The Group Payment Arrangement Document and Schedule'.

In order to be eligible, group members must have a 51% group relationship and be up-to-date with their filing and payment obligations. A company can only be a member of one GPA. If any group member is liable to make quarterly instalment payments, the paying company should enter into the standard contract at least two months prior to the due date for the first payment. Payment of tax must be by electronic funds transfer.

A GPA also covers interest and penalties, and each individual company remains liable for its own corporation tax (see Application for a Group Payment Arrangement—Notes for Guidance and Working Together, Issue 20, February 2005).

QUARTERLY ACCOUNTING

CT61 procedures

3.23 Companies are required to make a return to the Collector of Taxes of income tax deducted and claimed in respect of certain interest and charges on income, through the completion of form CT61, obtainable from HMRC.

There are normally four quarterly CT61 return periods, plus a fifth where the company's accounting period does not coincide with one of the quarter ends (*ICTA 1988, Sch 16, para 2*). The return periods are to 30 March, 30 June, 30 September and 31 December. The company's first return will run from the start of its accounting period to the end of the relevant quarter. Subsequent returns will follow a quarterly cycle, and a fifth return (where appropriate) will cover the period from the end of the previous quarter to the end of the company's accounting period, if it does not coincide with the end of a normal return period. The completed CT61 return and any tax liability is due 14 days after the end of the return period.

Deduction of tax

3.24 Annual interest and other annual payments (eg copyright royalties) are generally paid under deduction of income tax (*ITA 2007, ss 874 and 914*).

Companies are not required to deduct tax from interest, royalties, annuities and annual payments where the recipient is a company, which is chargeable to corporation tax in respect of that income (*ITA 2007, s 914*). See HMRC Double Taxation Guidance Note 11: Cross Border interest and Royalty payments.

Companies also have the option to pay royalties overseas without deduction of tax at source (or at a reduced rate) without the approval of HMRC in advance, provided that there is a reasonable belief that the non-resident is entitled to relief from UK tax on those royalties under a double tax treaty (*ITTOIA 2005, s 758*).

Interest and royalty payments between associated companies in the UK and other EU states are not subject to deduction of income tax at source if the companies are at least 25% associates. HMRC must have issued an exemption notice in relation to interest payments, and a company making royalty payments must have a reasonable belief that the recipient company is entitled to the exemption (*ITTOIA 2005, ss 761, 762*).

The CT61 return allows for the offset of income tax due on relevant payments against tax deducted from the company's income. Where such payments exceed income, income tax is due only on the excess. Where income exceeds payments for a return period, income tax paid in an earlier return period may be repaid. At the end of an accounting period, if total income exceeds total interest and/or annual payments, the balance of tax suffered is offset against the company's corporation tax liability; any excess tax suffered is repaid (*ICTA 1988, Sch 16*). No repayment interest will be paid.

Example 3.6

S Ltd prepares accounts each year to 31 October. During the year ending 31 October 2010, it pays the following interest:

		£
21 December 2009	(net of tax @ 20%)	8,000
4 January 2010	(net of tax @ 20%)	5,600
9 August 2010	(net of tax @ 20%)	8,000
21 October 2010	(net of tax @ 20%)	12,000

All the interest is paid to individuals.

S Ltd will enter the following figures into its CT61 returns and account for tax as follows:

49

3.25 *Rates and payment of corporation tax*

Return periods	Payments	Income tax paid
	£	£
1 November 2009 to 31 December 2009	8,000	2,000
1 January 2010 to 31 March 2010	5,600	1,400
1 April 2010 to 30 June 2010	(no return)	
1 July 2010 to 30 September 2010	8,000	2,000
1 October 2010 to 31 October 2010	12,000	3,000
Total income tax paid		£8,400

Penalties for failing to pay tax on time

3.25   A penalty can arise if a company fails to pay its corporation tax in time. A new penalty regime will be introduced by Treasury Order. *Finance Act 2009, Sch 56* gives details of the relevant taxes and the dates from which the penalty arises.

The penalty date for an outstanding corporation tax liability or quarterly instalment payments is the filing date for the company tax return for the period in which the tax is due (*FA 1998, Sch 18, para 14*). If the tax liability is still outstanding in whole or in part after the end of three months beginning with the penalty date, a penalty of 5% of the outstanding amount is charged. If the tax liability is still outstanding in whole or in part after the end of nine months beginning with the penalty date, a penalty of another 5% of the outstanding amount is charged (*FA 2009, Sch 56, para 4*).

If HMRC raise a determination under *FA 1998, Sch 18, para 36* or *37*, the penalty date is also the filing date for the company tax return for which the tax is due. If the tax liability is still outstanding in whole or in part after the end of five months beginning with the penalty date, a penalty of 5% of the outstanding amount is charged. If the tax liability is still outstanding in whole or in part after the end of 11 months beginning with the penalty date, a penalty of 5% of the outstanding amount is charged (*FA 2009, Sch 56, para 3*).

If an amount charged by correction to the corporation tax liability, a quarterly instalment or a determination assessment is paid late, it will attract a penalty from the later of 30 days after the payment date or 30 days after the amendment or correction was made.

Special reduction

3.26   If HMRC consider that special circumstances apply, they may reduce any penalty arising. Special circumstances do not include the company's inability to pay, or the fact that a potential loss of revenue from one taxpayer is balanced by a potential over-payment by another (*FA 2009, Sch 56, para 9*).

Suspension of penalty during currency of agreement for deferred payment

3.27 If HMRC agree to a company's request for deferral of a tax liability before a penalty becomes due, the company will not become liable to a penalty unless it breaks the terms of the agreement (*FA 2009, Sch 56, para 10*).

Assessment

3.28 In order to collect the penalty, HMRC must raise an assessment, notify the company and give details in the notice of the period in respect of which the penalty is assessed. The company has 30 days, beginning with the day on which notice of the assessment of the penalty is issued, to pay the penalty. For procedural purposes, the penalty is treated in the same way as tax (*FA 2009, Sch 56, para 11*).

HMRC have a time limit for raising the penalty assessment. This is on or before the later of:

● the last day of the period of two years beginning with the tax due date (this is, in effect, the last date on which tax can be paid without incurring a penalty); and

● the last day of the period of 12 months beginning with:

– the end of the appeal period for the assessment of the amount of tax in respect of which the penalty is assessed, or

– if there is no such assessment, the date on which that amount of tax is ascertained.

(*FA 2009, Sch 56, para 12*)

3.29 A company may appeal against an HMRC decision that a penalty is payable; the tribunal may then affirm or cancel HMRC's decision. A company may appeal against the amount of the penalty, in which case, the tribunal will substitute another decision within HMRC's powers. In this case, they may apply HMRC's rules in reducing the penalty (*FA 2009, Sch 56, para 13*). Appeals against a penalty are treated in the same way as an appeal against a tax liability – see **2.25**. The penalty is not due for payment before the appeal is determined (*FA 2009, Sch 56, paras 14* and *15*). If the company can satisfy the tribunal that there is a reasonable excuse, no penalty will arise. An insufficiency of funds is not a reasonable excuse, unless the insufficiency is attributable to events outside the company's control. Reliance on a third party is not a reasonable excuse, unless the company took reasonable care to avoid the failure. If the company had a reasonable excuse for the failure but the excuse has ceased, the company is to be treated as having continued to have the excuse if the failure is remedied without unreasonable delay after the excuse ceased (*FA 2009, Sch 56, para 16*).

CLAIMS FOR OVERPAID CORPORATION TAX

3.30   If a company has overpaid its corporation tax, or has been assessed to corporation tax that it considers is not due, it may make a claim for recovery or discharge of that tax as appropriate (*FA 2009, Sch 52, para 13*; *FA 1998, Sch 18, para 51*).

The new legislation introduced with effect from 1 April 2010 identifies seven cases A to G where HMRC are not liable to give relief:

Case A

Where the amount paid, or liable to be paid, is excessive because of:

- a mistake in a claim, election or a notice;
- a mistake consisting of making or giving, or failing to make or give, a claim, election or notice;
- a mistake in allocating expenditure to a capital allowance pool or a mistake consisting of making, or failing to make, such an allocation, or
- a mistake in bringing a capital allowance disposal value into account or a mistake consisting of bringing, or failing to bring, such a value into account. (See **Chapter 6** for capital allowances).

Case B

Where the company is or will be able to seek relief by taking other steps under the *Corporation Tax Acts*.

Case C

Where the company:

- could have sought relief by taking such steps within a period that has now expired, and
- knew, or ought reasonably to have known, before the end of that period that such relief was available.

Case D

Where the claim is made on grounds that:

- have been put to a court or tribunal in the course of an appeal by the company relating to the amount paid or liable to be paid, or

- have been put to HMRC in the course of an appeal that is settled by agreement under *section 54* of the *Taxes Management Act 1970.*

Case E

Where the company knew, or ought reasonably to have known, of the grounds for the claim before the latest of the following:

- the date on which an appeal by the company relating to the amount paid, or liable to be paid, in the course of which the ground could have been put forward (a 'relevant appeal') was determined by a court or tribunal (or is treated as having been so determined);

- the date on which the company withdrew a relevant appeal to a court or tribunal; and

- the end of the period in which the company was entitled to make a relevant appeal to a court or tribunal.

Case F

Where the amount in question was paid or is liable to be paid:

- in consequence of proceedings enforcing the payment of that amount brought against the company by HMRC; or

- in accordance with an agreement between the company and HMRC in settling such proceedings.

Case G

Where:

- the amount paid, or liable to be paid, is excessive by reason of a mistake in calculating the company's corporation tax liability; and

- the liability was calculated in accordance with the practice generally prevailing at the time.

(FA 2009, Sch 52, para 13; FA 1998, Sch 18, para 51A)

Making a claim

3.31   A claim for overpaid or over-assessed corporation tax is not to be included in a company tax return and may not be made more than four years after the end of the relevant accounting period.

If the company has overpaid corporation tax, the relevant accounting period is:

- the accounting period to which the company tax return relates (or first return relates if more than one) if the corporation tax paid, or liable to be paid, is excessive by reason of a mistake in that return or those returns, and

- in all other cases, the accounting period in which the corporation tax was paid.

If the company considers that it has been over-assessed to corporation tax, the relevant accounting period is the accounting period to which that corporation tax assessment, determination or direction relates.

Where a right of corporation tax set-off exists between two parties, only the company against whose corporation tax liability the set-off is made can make the claim *(FA 2009, Sch 52, para 13)*; *FA 1998, Sch 18, para 51C)*. If the company is a partner in a partnership carrying on a trade or business, only the nominated partner may make the claim *(FA 2009, Sch 52, para 13)* ; *FA 1989, Sch 18, para 51D)*.

If the grounds for the claim bring about a discovery assessment or discovery determination on the company in respect of any accounting period, the assessment or determination may still be made even if the statutory time limit has expired. If the assessment or determination depends on these provisions, it must be made before the claim is finally determined *(FA 2009, Sch 52, para 13; FA 1998, Sch 18, para 51E)*. The same criteria apply to the amendment of a partnership assessment *(FA 2009, Sch 52, para 13; FA 1998, Sch 18, para 51F)*.

Contract settlements

3.32 A contract settlement can result from an enquiry, and normally takes the form of a letter of offer from the company in respect of unpaid tax and interest. Overpaid tax includes amounts paid by contract settlement. If the company that paid the amount under the contract settlement ('the payer') and the company from which the tax was due ('the taxpayer') are not the same, and if the grounds for the claim bring about a discovery assessment or discovery determination on the company in respect of any accounting period, HMRC may set any amount repayable to the payer against the amount payable by the taxpayer *(FA 2009, Sch 52, para 13; FA 1998, Sch 18, para 51G)*.

Equitable liability

3.33 In the past, HMRC adopted a concessional practice to excessive assessments. Information received after the statutory deadlines had passed might be accepted as evidence that the finalised liabilities were too high, and could lead to a decision not to pursue recovery of the full amount of tax. This treatment is to be withdrawn with effect from 1 April 2010. HMRC may accept late returns or information affecting liability where the request for the relief under the concession is made before 1 April 2010 and in accordance with Tax Bulletin 18 (HMRC Statement 22 May 2009).

Business Payment Support Service

3.34   A company in financial difficulty can agree to vary the timing of its payments through the Business Payment Support Service. HMRC provide this service for companies that are in genuine difficulty, unable to pay their tax on time but are likely to be able to pay if allowed more time to do so. Payment arrangements are agreed on a case-by-case basis. Details are available on www.hmrc.gov.uk or by calling the Business Payment Support Line (Tel 0845 302 1435, Monday–Friday 8.00am to 8.00pm, Saturday and Sunday 8.00am–4.00pm).

Managed payment schemes

3.35   A company may prefer to spread its corporation tax payments rather than pay on the normal due date (see **3.7**); if so, it may find that a managed payment scheme is appropriate. The managed payment plan is an agreement between the company and HMRC for the company to pay its main corporation tax liability by instalments. The plan is so structured that the instalments paid before the due date are balanced by those paid after it. Group companies within a group payment arrangement (see **3.22**) cannot make use of the managed payment plan *(FA 2009, s 111(3))*.

The general rule is that all instalments paid on time and in accordance with the plan satisfy the corporation tax liability as if paid on the normal due date *(FA 2009, s 111(4))*. Payments made late or not in accordance with the plan attract late payment interest or penalties, which run from the normal due date *(FA 2009, s 111(5))*. If a company were to be charged late payment interest, any payments that it made before the normal due date will attract credit interest *(FA 2009, s 111(6))*.

POWER TO OBTAIN CONTACT DETAILS OF DEBTORS

Debtor contact details

3.36   A company may receive a written notice from HMRC to supply them with contact details of a debtor. HMRC can only make this request if amounts are owed by the debtor, and HMRC reasonably believe that the company obtained these details when carrying out its business (*FA 2009, Sch 49 para 1*). The company is required to comply with the request within the time limit prescribed in the request. The company has a right of appeal on the ground that it would be unduly onerous to comply with the notice or requirement (*FA 2009, Sch 49, para 4*).

See **2.25** onwards for the appeal procedure. Failure to comply with the notice brings about a £300 penalty on the company.

Chapter 4

Close companies and connected issues

INTRODUCTION

4.1   Ownership of a company is vested in its shareholders. A share is a bundle of rights; namely voting rights, dividend rights and a right to assets in a winding-up. Companies owned by a small number of individuals are in a position to control a company to their advantage. The corporation tax legislation looks through these relationships and modifies the corporation tax rules in particular in relation to:

- close companies;

- close investment holding companies; and

- associated companies.

CLOSE COMPANIES

Consequences

4.2   The close company provisions were included within corporation tax provisions when they were first introduced in 1965 and similar legislation was in existence before then.

The effect of the provisions (and if all the related conditions apply) is to widen the scope of a distribution to include shareholder and shareholder family member benefits (see **Chapter 16** for distributions). The provisions regard some loans to shareholders as an extraction of profits and seek to tax the loan. Close investment holding companies are prevented from applying the lower rate of corporation tax on their profits.

Status

4.3   A close company is defined as:

'a "close company" is one which is under the control of five or fewer participators, or of participators who are directors ...' *(ICTA 1988, s 414(1))*.

Control

4.4 Control is the ability to exercise, or entitlement to acquire, direct or indirect control over the company's affairs, including the ownership of, or entitlement to acquire the greater part (over 50%) of the company's share capital; voting rights, distributable income or distributable assets *(ICTA 1988, s 416(2))*. If the rights and powers of two or more persons taken together amount to the greater part of the company's share capital etc, these two or more persons will control the company.

Rights and powers of a nominee, an associate and any company of which the person has control or he or she and or her associates (including nominees of associates but not associates of associates) have control are attributable to the person *(ICTA 1988, s 416(5), (6))*.

Exceptions

4.5 As with all definitions there are exceptions and a company with the following criteria is not close (or is open):

- a company not resident in the UK;

- a registered industrial and provident society or building society;

- a company controlled by or on behalf of the Crown;

- a UK resident company controlled by a non-resident company (unless the non-resident company would itself be close if resident in the UK);

- a company controlled by a non-close company or companies, where it cannot be treated as a close company except by including a non-close company as one of its five or fewer participators;

- a quoted company:

  — where 35% or more of the company's voting power is held by the 'public' (excluding shares entitled to a fixed rate of dividend); and

  — within the preceding 12 months those voting shares have been the subject of dealings on a recognised stock exchange unless the total voting power of the company's 'principal members' exceeds 85% (including shares entitled to a fixed rate of dividend) *(ICTA 1988, s 414(1))*.

A recognised stock exchange is any HMRC designated market of a UK or overseas recognised investment exchange *(FA 2007, s 109, Sch 26, para 1)*.

Public

4.6   In this sense, the public excludes directors and their associates, any company controlled by them, any associated company, any fund for the benefit of past or present employees, directors or dependants of the company or associated companies, and the principal members *(ICTA 1988, s 415(5))*.

Principal member

4.7   A principal member is a person holding more than 5% of the company's voting power or where there are more than five such persons, one of the five possessing the greatest percentages. Where two or more persons hold equal percentages, so that the greatest percentages are held by more than five persons, a principal member is any one of that number *(ICTA 1988, s 415(6))*.

Director

4.8   A director includes any person who acts in that capacity whatever name is given to him. A director is also someone who gives directions upon which directors are accustomed to act or who is concerned in the management of the company's business and controls. A director is also someone who is able, either directly or indirectly, to control 20% or more of the company's ordinary share capital *(ICTA 1988, s 417(5))*.

Close company tests

4.9   In order to determine whether a company is close, HMRC apply five tests (HMRC Company Taxation Manual CTM 60102):

Test	Answer	Result
1. Is the company within one of the specific exceptions that exclude it from being a close company?	Yes	The company is not close.
	No	Consider further tests.
2. Who are the participators in the company and what powers or rights do they possess or are they entitled to acquire?		

Test	Answer	Result
3. What rights and powers of other persons are attributable to the participators?		
4. Having regard to the rights, etc, of each participator, and other persons' rights, etc, which are attributed to the participator, do:		
(i) five or fewer participators control the company, or	Yes	The company is close.
	No	Consider further tests.
(ii) participators who are directors control the company?	Yes	The company is close.
	No	Consider further tests
5. Would more than half the assets of the company be ultimately distributed to five or fewer participators, or to participators who are directors, in the event of the company being wound up?	Yes	The company is close
	No	The company is not close

The result as to which participators control the company should always be inferred from the minimum controlling holding. X, Y and Z may each own 33.33% of the company. Therefore control in applying the tests is given to X and Y or Y and Z or X and Z but never X, Y and Z (*ICTA 1988, s 416(3)*).

Participator

4.10   Test 2 requires the identity of the participator to be determined. The full definition of a participator is given as:

'A participator is any person having a share or interest in the capital or income of the company ... and includes:

(a)   any person who possesses or is entitled to acquire share capital or voting rights in the company;

(b)   any loan creditor of the company;

(c)   any person who possesses or is entitled to acquire a right to receive or participate in distributions of the company ... or in any amounts payable by the company (in cash or kind) to loan creditors by way of premium or redemption;

(d)   any person who is entitled to secure that income or assets (whether present or future) of the company will be applied directly or indirectly for his benefit.' (*ICTA 1988, s 417(1)*.)

Generally speaking a participator is anyone who has a financial interest in a close company, ie who has invested into share capital or who has provided loan finance. A participator is 'entitled to acquire' or 'entitled to secure' if he has a contractual right to do so (see *R (on the application of Newfields Developments Ltd) v IRC* (2001) 73 TC 532, [2001] STC 901, [2001] 1 WLR 1111, [2001] 4 All ER 400 on this point).

The definition of a participator can be extended through a company structure (*ICTA 1988, s 419(7)*).

Example 4.1

In the following circumstances all companies are close:

Fact	Result
A is a shareholder of A Ltd.	A is a participator of A Ltd
A Ltd owns all the shares in B Ltd.	A is also a participator in B Ltd
If B Ltd makes a loan to A.	The loan is within ICTA 1988, s 419

Loan creditor

4.11   A loan creditor is also a participator and is defined as:

' "loan creditor" means a creditor in respect of any debt incurred by the company:

(a)   for any money borrowed or capital assets acquired by the company, or

(b)   for any right to receive income created in favour of the company, or

(c)   for consideration the value of which to the company was (at the time when the debt was incurred) substantially less than the amount of the debt (including any premium thereon),

or in respect of any redeemable loan capital issued by the company.' (*ICTA 1988, s 417(7)*)

Normal company trade creditors are not included in the definition. Any holder of redeemable capital is a loan creditor. Hire purchase arrangements are not regarded as part of loan capital. Arrangements where a person makes annual payments to a company in exchange for a capital sum at some future date treats the person as a participator.

Loans in the normal course of banking business do not bring about a loan creditor relationship (HMRC Company Taxation Manual CTM 60130).

Associate

4.12   An associate of a participator includes the following:

- any 'relative': spouses or civil partners, parents or remoter forebear, children or remoter issue, brothers or sisters (but not aunts, uncles, nephews and nieces). Separated spouses and half-brothers or sisters are associated, but divorced spouses and step-brothers or sisters are not;

- any business partner;

- the trustee(s) of any settlement in which the participator (or any living or dead 'relatives') is or was the settlor; and

- the trustee(s) of a settlement or personal representatives of an estate holding company shares in which the participator has an interest (where the participator is a company, any other company interested in those shares is also an associate) (*ICTA 1988, s 417(3), (4)*).

Benefits to participators

4.13   Benefits or services provided to close company participators, who are also directors or other employees, will be treated as remuneration and will be assessed to income tax, as calculated under the taxable benefit rules for employments (*ICTA 1988, s 418(3), (4)*). Payments to a non-working participator or the non-working associate of a participator cannot be classed as employment income and will be treated as a distribution to the participator. Hence the 'distributions' will not be an allowable expense of the company (*ICTA 1988, s 418(2)*).

Loans to participators

4.14   The company must self-assess tax liabilities in respect of any loans not in the ordinary course of business to participators or associates, which can result in the requirement to make tax payments to HMRC equal to 25% of the outstanding loan or advance made during the accounting period. The tax need not be paid if the loan has been repaid, released or written off within nine months and one day following the end of the accounting period. Where the loan or advance is repaid, released or written off more than nine months after the end of an accounting period, the tax paid can be repaid nine months after the end of the accounting period in which the repayment, release, etc takes place.

Self-assessment disclosure

4.15   Loans to participators or their associates made during the accounting period must be disclosed on the corporation tax return. Supplementary page

CT600A (2006) Version 2 (loans to participators by close companies) is used for this purpose and is reproduced in the Appendices. Details of the name of the participator or associate to whom the loan was made and the amount of the loan outstanding at the end of the accounting period for which the return has been made must be disclosed in Part 1.

If the loan has been repaid, released or written off within nine months and one day after the end of the accounting period, details of the name of the participator or associate whose loan has been repaid, released or written off, together with the amount and date repaid, released or written off, must be disclosed in Part 2.

The effect of completion of both Parts 1 and 2 will result in no liability to *s 419* tax at 25%. The practical implication is that HMRC will now have been informed of the amounts loaned to the participators and the associates and will be able to follow through the beneficial loan declarations on form P11D for directors, other employed participators and their associates. A benefit in kind may arise on a participator who is an employee or director in respect of direct loans. A benefit in kind may also arise on a participator who is an employee or a director in respect of direct loans made to their associates.

Relief is given if the loan is repaid, released or written off (*ICTA 1988, s 419(4)*). If the loan has been repaid, released or written off later than nine months and one day after the end of the accounting period, details of the name of the participator or associate whose loan has been repaid, released or written off, together with the amount and date repaid, released or written off must be disclosed in Part 3. It follows that if the loan has not been repaid, released or written off at all then neither Part 2 nor Part 3 can be completed. The effect of completion of Part 3 or non-completion of Parts 2 and 3 is that the *s 419* liability will be shown in box A13. This amount should be shown in box 79 on CT600 (the corporation tax self-assessment return for the year). Corporation tax software and online filing will automatically make these calculations but manual completion following the step-by-step instructions on form CT600A should arrive at this result. The tax at 25% of the outstanding loan then becomes payable with the main corporation tax. Any late payment falls within the normal interest provisions. Interest is charged on any outstanding liability from the due date until the earlier of the payment of the *s 419* tax and the date that the loan or part is repaid, released or written off (*TMA 1970, ss 87A(1), 109(3A)*). If the repayment, release or write-off of a loan takes place earlier then nine months and one day after the end of the accounting period in which the loan was made repayment interest will accrue from the later off nine months after the end of that accounting period and the date the tax was paid. If the loan is repaid, release or written-off more than nine months after the end of the accounting period in which the loan was made interest will accrue from the later of nine months after the end of the accounting period in which the loan was cleared and the date the tax was paid (*ICTA 1988, s 826(4)*). HMRC may make enquiries into the loan accounts as part of their corporation tax self-assessment enquiries.

Loans within s 419(1)

4.16 To be within *s 419(1)* the loan must have been made 'otherwise than in the ordinary course of a business carried on by it which includes the lending of money'. The principle of the lending of money was tested in *Brennan v Denby Investment Co Ltd* (2001) 73 TC 455, [2001] STC 536 and resulted in the comment that 'business requires some regularity of occurrence'. It would seem that without doubt a commercial lending bank's business includes lending money. HMRC state that they will look at the following characteristics to determine whether there is a money lending trade:

- Money lending advertisements aimed at the general public.

- Interest rate publication.

- Receipt of loan applications from the public.

- Commercial interest rate charge.

- *In situ* debt collection personnel and procedures.

- Legally enforceable written repayment term contracts.

- A reasonable number of existing loans (usually 200+) enabling inter alia loan set-off.

- Matched time period borrowing and lending.

If indeed there is a money lending business the loan to the participator must be made to the participator on the same commercial lending terms (HMRC Company Taxation Manual CTM 61520).

Loans to employee share schemes and employee benefit trusts are within *s 419*. *Section 419(1)* is applied at the time of the loan, if the trust is a shareholder or individual trustees are participators in the company. HMRC state that *ICTA 1988, s 419(5)* may apply when the trustees make payments to existing shareholders for their shares (HMRC Company Taxation Manual CTM 61525).

Loans to a tax transparent partnership, where a participator is a member are within *s 419*.

HMRC state that they will not apply *s 419* where money is lent to a partnership of which the company is a member where there is a genuine partnership with bona fide arrangements. However, HMRC may invoke *s 419(5)*. This section enables HMRC to assess a loan not made by the close company but by arrangements not in the ordinary course of business to *s 419(1)* (HMRC Company Taxation Manual CTM 61515). Payments by a company to a director in respect of the directors private business were held to be within *s 419* in *Grant (Andrew) Services Ltd v Watton (Inspector of Taxes) (aka HCB Ltd v HM Inspector of Taxes)* (1999) 71 TC 333, [1999] STC 330.

Loans not within s 419(1)

4.17   Not only are loans and advances that a company makes to its participators and/or their associates, other than in the ordinary course of business, within *s 419(1)*, but also:

- any debt due by the participator or associate to the company (*ICTA 1988, s 419(2)(a)*);

- any debt due to a third party, which has been assigned by the third party to the company (*ICTA 1988, s 419(2)(b)*); or

- the provision of goods or services in the ordinary course of trade or business to a participator on credit terms that exceed six months or are longer than normally given to the company's customers (*ICTA 1988, s 420(1)*).

As regards debts due to a third party, HMRC acknowledge that a debt can only be assigned by the third party. If the debtor (the person to whom the money is lent) and the close company of which he is a participator agree that the close company will pay the debt on his behalf, *ICTA 1988, s 419(2)(b)* cannot apply. However, a debt due from the participator to the close company may arise when the close company pays the debt to the third party on the participator's behalf, which will fall under *ICTA 1988, s 419(2)(a)*. Indeed, depending on the facts of the case, HMRC may treat the amount as remuneration or a distribution (HMRC Company Taxation Manual CTM 61535).

As regards the provision of goods or services, HMRC acknowledge that a credit period runs from the time that goods are delivered or services are performed until time of payment (*Grant (Andrew) Services Ltd v Watton* (1999) 71 TC 333, [1999] STC 330; HMRC Company Taxation Manual CTM 61535).

Section 419 does not apply to loans less than £15,000, where the borrower is a full-time working director or employee of the close company or of an associated company with no material interest in the company (*ICTA 1988, s 420(2)*). No material interest means 5% or less direct or indirect control (associates included) of the ordinary share capital or the assets in winding-up (*ITEPA 2003, s 68*). HMRC interpret full-time as not less than three-quarters of the normal working hours of the close company (HMRC Company Taxation

Manual CTM 61540). As soon as the conditions of *s 420(2)* are no longer met, for example, by the borrower acquiring an interest of more than 5% then *s 419* will apply from that time. Spouses and civil partners, if employees of the company, have their own £15,000 limit.

Loan accounts

4.18   For accounts purposes if a loan is made to a participator the company will record the loan in its nominal ledger as a 'loan account'. Director loan accounts are a common feature of owner-managed companies, which are invariably close companies. HMRC will not concur to the netting off of one loan account against another unless there is a genuine joint loan, for example, as between spouses, where a joint nominal ledger loan account would be operated. A participator or director may have more than one nominal ledger loan account with the company, where loans carrying different terms are recorded. The fact that one loan account may be in debit and another in credit has no avail with HMRC. This is because HMRC treat all loan accounts as separate loans. If a genuine posting is made to clear the two loan accounts then this is treated as though the loan had been repaid under *ICTA 1988, s 419(4)*. The posting date is the repayment date (HMRC Company Taxation Manual CTM 61550).

Actual repayment by the participator or a third party takes place on the date that payment is made. A director's loan account may be cleared by a bonus payment. *ITEPA 2003, s18* onwards determines the date that the bonus is received by the director for income tax purposes. For *s 419* purposes the date of repayment is the date that the bonuses are voted or the date on which PAYE was operated if earlier (HMRC Company Taxation Manual CTM 61605).

The director/participator may wish to use a dividend payment to clear the loan account. In practice, the company's constitution should be examined for any matters that may affect dividend payments. A dividend may only be declared if there are sufficient net realised profits.

A dividend is paid when it is due and payable (*ICTA 1988, s 834(3)*) but for *s 419(4)* purposes *s 834(3)* does not apply and until the dividend is paid the debt remains outstanding to the company (HMRC Company Taxation Manual CTM 61605). 'A dividend is not paid and there is no distribution, unless and until the shareholder receives money or the distribution is otherwise unreservedly put at their disposal, perhaps by being credited to a loan account on which the shareholder has the power to draw' (HMRC Company Taxation Manual CTM 20095). Evidence of the payment or credit should be shown in the company's books of account. If a dividend is paid unlawfully and the shareholder knew or was in a position to know of this fact, he or she is liable to return the distribution to the company *(CA 2006, s 847; It's a Wrap (UK) Ltd (in liquidation) v Gula* [2006] EWCA Civ 544).

HMRC acknowledge that, in many small private companies, the directors and shareholders are one and the same. A dividend is only paid when the money is placed unreservedly at the disposal of the directors/shareholders as part of their current accounts with the company. So, payment is not made until such a right to draw on the dividend exists (presumably) when the appropriate entries are made in the company's books.

If, as may happen with a small company, such entries are not made until the annual audit, and this takes place after the end of the accounting period in which the directors resolved that an interim dividend be paid, then the 'due and payable' date is in the later rather than the earlier accounting period.

A director may clear the account shortly before the year end by borrowing from an external third party shortly before the year end only to reinstate the loan at the beginning of the accounting period. HMRC will regard the company as supplying a false document under the *Finance Act 2007* penalty regime, see **18.21–18.30** (HMRC Enquiry Manual EM 8565).

Section 419 tax repayment

4.19   When the loan is actually repaid the company will be due the *s 419* tax that it has already paid, but this is not due for repayment until nine months after the accounting period in which the loan is repaid *(ICTA 1988, s 419(4A))*. There is no facility for setting the repayable overpaid *s 419* tax against the corporation tax liability for the year in which the repayment is made. The company will need to complete an amended Part 3 CT600A for the accounting period in which the loan was made. If the loan is repaid in time to enable the amended CT600A to be completed and submitted within the 12-month enquiry period, this will act as an amended return and repayment will be issued. Alternatively, if submission is outside the enquiry period, the revised form will act as a separate claim under *TMA 1970, Sch 1A*.

Section 419 loan released

4.20   If the loan is released or written off, the same procedures apply to the company as for repayment but the individual participator will be treated as receiving a distribution net of the 10% tax credit *(ICTA 1988, s 421)*. The *s 421* charge takes precedence over the employment income charge (HMRC Company Taxation Manual CTM 61630).

Circuitous and indirect loans

4.21   Circuitous and indirect loans are also caught by *s 419*. In particular, HMRC quote the situation whereby, for example, a close company makes a loan to an employee who is not a participator and that employee applies the loan in purchase of the shares from an existing shareholder. The existing shareholder is a 'deemed borrower' under *ICTA 1988, s 419(5)* and *s 419(1)* can apply (HMRC Company Taxation Manual CTM 61540).

This is because *s 419(5)* catches the situation where a close company makes a loan but no *s 419(1)* liability arises. A third party then makes a payment or transfers property to a participator or releases a participator's debt. HMRC give the following examples:

Example 4.2

Company D is a close company. Instead of making a loan directly to D, an individual participator, it makes it to an associated company, Company E. Company E then passes the loan to D. The loan by one company to the other is treated as if it had been made direct to D.

Example 4.3

Company T, a close company, makes a loan to A. A is an individual participator in Company W but not in Company T. Company W, acting in concert with Company T, then makes a loan to D, an individual participator in Company T. Company T and Company W have swapped loans to participators and are treated as if they had made loans to their own participators.

Such loans should be assessed to *s 419(1)* in the normal way except where the amounts form assessable income receipts for the individual concerned (HMRC Company Taxation Manual 61670 and 61680).

Anti-avoidance

4.22   *ICTA 1988, s 422* (extension of *s 419* to loans by companies controlled by close companies) is an anti-avoidance clause. A loan to a participator by a third party, directly or indirectly financed by the participator's close company, is within *s 419(1)* by virtue of *TA 1988, s 422*. In addition, a loan to a participator by a company controlled by a close company is within *s 419(1)*. A loan to a company that is acting in a fiduciary or representative capacity of a participator is also within *s 419 (ICTA 1988, s 419(6))*.

CLOSE INVESTMENT HOLDING COMPANIES

Consequences

4.23   Trading uncommercially or letting property to connected parties may mean that a close company becomes a close investment holding company.

The small company corporation tax rate can be utilised by a close company, but not by a 'close investment holding company', which will pay corporation tax at the full rate, regardless of profit levels (*ICTA 1988, s 13(1)(b)*).

Status

4.24   A close company will *not* be a close investment holding company if throughout the period it exists wholly or mainly for one or more of the following purposes:

- carrying on a trade on a commercial basis;
- making investments in land or estates or interests in land and in cases where the land is or is intended to be let to persons other than:
    - any person connected with the close company, or
    - any person who is the wife or husband of an individual connected with the relevant company, or is a relative, or the wife or husband of a relative, of such an individual or of the husband or wife of such an individual,
- the purpose of holding shares in and securities of, or making loans to, one or more companies each of which is a qualifying company or a company which:
    - is under the control of the relevant company or of a company that has control of the relevant company, and
    - itself exists wholly or mainly for the purpose of holding shares in or securities of, or making loans to, one or more qualifying companies;
- the purpose of co-ordinating the administration of two or more qualifying companies;
- the purpose of a trade or trades carried on on a commercial basis by one or more qualifying companies or by a company that has control of the relevant company; and

- the purpose of the making, by one or more qualifying companies or by a company, which has control of the relevant company, of investments as mentioned in lands or estates as set out above *(ICTA 1988, s 13A(1), (2))*.

In general terms a 'qualifying company' is a trading company or a property investment company *(ICTA 1988, s 13A(3))*.

Letting of land to a connected person

4.25   Letting of land to a connected person may bring the company into the close investment holding company regime. Connection is defined here in *ICTA 1988, s 839(5), (6)*.

Connection to another company

'A company is connected with another company

(a)   if the same person has control of both, or a person has control of one and persons connected with him, or he and persons connected with him, have control of the other, or

(b)   if a group of two or more persons has control of each company, and the groups either consist of the same persons or could be regarded as consisting of the same persons by treating (in one or more cases) a member of either group as replaced by a person with whom he is connected.' *(ICTA 1988, s 839(5))*

Connection with another person

'A company is connected with another person if that person has control of it, or if that person and persons connected with him together have control of it.' *(ICTA 1988, s 839(6).)*

Control is given the same meaning as at **4.4** *(ICTA 1988, s 416(2))*.

Letting of land

4.26   Land let to a relative may also bring the company within the close investment holding company regime.

A relative includes a brother, sister, ancestor or lineal descendant *(ICTA 1988, s 839(8))*. Lettings to a relative of the individual's spouse, or the spouse of a relative of the individual will affect the close investment holding company status.

Example 4.4

Facts

Joe is married to Mary. Joe owns 100% of Joe Ltd, a building and construction company in the South of England. Joe would like to provide Mary's mother Mrs K with a home where she could reside independently of Joe and Mary.

On 1 January 2008, Joe forms Mrs K Ltd, a 100% subsidiary of Joe Ltd. The subsidiary buys a plot of land with development value on which stands Plum Cottage, a Victorian property. Mrs K moves into the cottage and pays her landlord Mrs K Ltd a full market rent for the property. Mrs K maintains her independence and pays for the upkeep of Plum Cottage herself.

Comments

The facts appear to fall under *ICTA 1988, s 13A(2)(b)(ii)*.

This would bring the company within the close investment holding company regime. Corporation tax will be payable on profits at the full 30% rate.

Joe formed the company in order to buy a property suitable for his mother-in-law's occupation. The land on which the property stood had development value.

If the situation were reversed such that Joe bought land with development value (albeit through Mrs K Ltd) for use in his trade on which stood a vacant cottage, there may be an argument that the company had a trading 'purpose'. This would mean that the company might fall out of the close investment holding company regime. There is also the possibility that the company would pay corporation tax at the full rates because of the associated company rules.

ASSOCIATED COMPANIES

Consequences

4.27   Associated companies share the small companies rate band by dividing the lower relevant amount and the higher relevant amount equally between them. (See **3.5** and Example 4.7.)

A company is to be treated as an associated company of another at a given time if at that time one of the two has control of the other, or both are under the control of the same person or persons (*ICTA 1988, s 13(4)*).

Status

4.28   The same definition of control is used as for close companies (see **4.3** and **4.4**).

For these purposes, not only are the rights of the person concerned taken into account, but also the rights and powers of associates that can be attributed to that person (*ICTA 1988, s 416(6)*). Associates are as defined in **4.12**. HMRC expressly state that rights and powers of associates must not be attributed to the person concerned (HMRC Company Taxation Manual CTM 03750). However, rights and powers of the person's nominees must be attributed to the person (*ICTA 1988, s 416(5)*).

Associated companies share the £300,000 lower and £1,500,000 higher corporation tax profit limit bands between them, with the result that, if there are two associated companies, the small company rate band for each will only reach £150,000 and the full rate band will commence at £750,000.

STATUTORY EXCEPTIONS

Partners

4.29   Partners within the meaning of *ICTA 1988, ss 416(6)* and *417(3)(a)* (see **4.12**), with whom the company's shareholders or participators are within a business partnership, are only associated persons for small company rate purposes, if there are or have been tax planning arrangements in relation to the company, which will include its formation (*ICTA 1988, s 13(4A)–(4C)* inserted by *FA 2008, s 35*). Arrangements include any agreement, understanding, scheme, transaction or series of transactions (whether or not legally enforceable) other than any guarantee, security or change given to or taken by a bank. This will be particularly relevant where a shareholder or participator is a member of a partnership, whose number of partners is unrestricted. The rights will only be attributed to other shareholders and participators in circumstances where tax planning arrangements exist and the small companies' rate reduces the corporation tax payable. These rules are effective from 1 April 2008; prior to that it was possible for a participator's business partners' interests to be attributed to him. The Chartered Institute of Taxation (CIOT) have raised this point with HMRC. HMRC responded on 24 July 2008 and confirmed the following:

- Unless the case is selected for full enquiry, the existence of associated companies is relevant only in cases where the amount of tax at risk is significant;

- There is a clear recognition that, in many cases, individuals will have no information whatsoever about the business affairs of other individuals who are partners in the same partnership, and certainly will have no right to request such information, and Local Compliance have been asked to take a practical approach; and

- Enquiries should only be pursued in cases where it is possible to establish evidence of associated companies.

The CIOT have been advised that, whilst the legislation was not backdated, HMRC's practice regarding earlier years will, in most cases, be influenced by the new rules. HMRC also confirmed that they do not expect an agent to embark on fact-finding exercises in cases where an individual is a partner in a substantial partnership, or has invested in a film partnership, where it would not be reasonable for him to know of the business affairs of his fellow partners (*CIOT – Associated Companies – Claims to the small company rate of corporation tax*, 20 February 2009: www.tax.org.uk).

Non-trading companies

4.30   An associated company that has not carried on any trade or business during the accounting period in question is excluded from the count of associated companies (*ICTA 1988, s 13(4)*).

A trading company that ceased to trade and placed its surplus funds on a non-actively managed bank deposit account was regarded as dormant (*Jowett (Inspector of Taxes) v O'Neill and Brennan Construction Ltd* (1998) 70 TC 566, [1998] STC 482). A company that ceased trading but continued to receive rent from an established source that required little administration was also excluded from the count of associated companies (*Salaried Persons Postal Loans Ltd v HMRC* [2006] EWHC 763 (Ch), [2006] STC 1315).

A close company, which merely holds a bank deposit account, will fall into the definition of a close investment holding company and will be liable to corporation tax at the full rate, but can still be included in the count of associated companies.

A non-trading holding company is excluded from the count of associated companies provided that throughout the accounting period all the following conditions apply:

- Its only assets are its shares in its 51% subsidiaries.

- There is no deduction entitlement for charges or management expenses.

- It has no income of gains other than dividends, which it has distributed to its shareholders and which amount to franked investment income if distributed to a company (SP 5/94).

Rights of attribution

4.31   In practice the rights of attribution are an important consideration for close companies. By concession HMRC, in cases where there is no substantial commercial interdependence between companies, will only treat spouses, civil partners and minor children as relatives. HMRC interpret companies' interdependence in the commercial sense as reliance upon one another for trade or services etc. HMRC amongst other things will look at common administration or joint directorships, use of staff and facilities, purchasing and selling arrangements, co-operation on joint projects and inter-company loans and guarantees. HMRC interpret substantial in relative terms as not being insubstantial and as a guide anything more than 10% will be substantial (HMRC Company Taxation Manual CTM 03770).

Neither will HMRC attribute shares held by a trustee company to the party concerned if there is no other past or present connection with the trustee company (ESC C9).

In *R (on the application of Newfields Developments Ltdv IRC* (2001) 73 TC 532, [2001] STC 901, [2001] 1 WLR 1111, [2001] 4 All ER 400 the Revenue's power to exercise attribution under *ICTA 1988, s 416(6)* was taken to the House of Lords.

The facts of this case are briefly as follows. Before his death, Mr W created a will trust in favour of his wife, Mrs W. The trustees of W's trust (Trustees A) owned shares in N Ltd for which the small companies rate of corporation tax was claimed. In his lifetime Mr W had also created a discretionary trust and had appointed separate trustees (Trustees B). Trustees B controlled a separate company L Ltd. The point of issue was whether N Ltd was associated with L Ltd.

The result of the House of Lords decision was as follows:

Mrs W was a participator. Her husband (a relative of hers) was the settlor of both the will trust and the discretionary trust. Therefore, by reason of *ICTA 1988, s 417(3)(b)*, Mrs W was an associate of Trustees A and Trustees B. The rights and powers of both Trustees A and Trustees B could be attributed to her, even though she personally, owned no shares in the companies concerned. Therefore, indirectly, N Ltd and L Ltd were controlled by the same 'person' simply because of the rules of attribution and hence were associated companies.

In addition, it was further decided that HMRC have neither discretion as to whether or not they should operate the rules of attribution, nor indeed in deciding whether companies are associated.

In *Gascoignes Group Ltd v Inspector of Taxes* [2004] EWHC 640 (Ch), [2004] STC 844 the Revenue exercised the powers of attribution. In this case Mr D held 71% of the shares in G Ltd. Mr & Mrs G had created a settlement in favour of their three children. The settlement owned 99% of the shares in S Ltd. Mr D was a participator and therefore associated by reason of *ICTA 1988, s 417(3)(b)* with the trustees of the settlement. The rights and powers of the trustees must be attributed to him and hence he controls G Ltd and S Ltd and therefore these companies are associated companies for small companies rate purposes.

In HMRC Company Taxation Manual CTM 03750, HMRC acknowledge that attribution rights in some cases are limited by ESC C9. However, even if ESC C9 applies, rights will always be attributed to:

• spouse (civil partner) and minor children;

• business partners (but see **4.29**);

• trustee or trustees of a settlement where that person is the settlor, or the settlor's spouse or minor child.

The following examples are given:

Example 4.5

F Ltd and C Ltd have the following shareholders. Mr F and Mrs F are married to each other. Mr B and Mr C have no connection at all.

F Ltd	Shares	C Ltd	Shares
Mr F	60	Mrs F	75
Mr B	40	Mr C	25
Total issued shares	100	Total issued shares	100

Neither B nor C is an associate of Mr F or Mrs F. Mr F controls Company F. Mr F is a participator and under *ICTA 1988, s 416(6)* Mrs F's rights may be attributed to him. He therefore controls C Ltd. The two companies are associated whether or not there is substantial commercial interdependence between them because ESC C9 does not ignore the inter-spousal relationship.

Example 4.6

The situation is the same as **Example 4.5** except that Mrs C is Mr F's sister.

F Ltd	Shares	C Ltd	Shares
Mr F	60	Mrs C	75
Mr B	40	Mr C	25
Total issued shares	100	Total issued shares	100

Neither Mr B nor Mr C is an associate of Mr F. Mrs C is an associate of Mr F. Mrs C's rights may be attributed to Mr F. However, this will only occur if there is substantial commercial interdependence between F Ltd and C Ltd.

4.32 By concession, HMRC do not consider a company to be controlled by another (non-close) company if that control derives solely from preference shares or loans and that is the only connection (ESC C9). The loan in question must be a commercial loan. HMRC disregard fixed rate preference shares where the company takes no part in the management of the company and they have been subscribed for in the ordinary course of its business (HMRC Company Taxation Manual CTM 03810). In addition, the fixed rate preference shares must be issued for new consideration, carry no conversion rights and have no rights to dividend other than the fixed dividend together with redemption rights at a reasonable commercial rate of return.

Company tax return

4.33 The corporation tax return form CT600 requires the number of associated companies to be entered in boxes 39, 40 and 41. This is necessary in order to determine the company's entitlement to small or marginal relief as appropriate, which must be the subject of a claim.

Example 4.7

Facts

The following companies are all wholly owned by Bill. They each make up accounts to 31 March each year.

A Ltd	B Ltd	C Ltd	D Ltd
£100,000	(£220,000)	£390,000	£20,000

Assessable profits and allowable losses for the year ended 31 March 2010 are shown.

Comments

The lower and upper relevant amounts of £300,000 and £1,500,000 are divided by 4, resulting respectively in bands of £75,000 and £375,000.

The effective corporation tax paid by each company is as follows:

	A Ltd £	*Tax*	B Ltd £	*Tax*	C Ltd £	*Tax*	D Ltd £	*Tax*
Profits	100,000		Nil		390,000		20,000	
21%	75,000	15,750			75,000	15,750	20,000	4,200
29.75%	25,000	7,438			300,000	89,250		
28%					15,000	4,200		
Total corporation tax		23,188		Nil		109,200		4,200

Although B Ltd has made a trading loss it must still be included in the count of associated companies.

The company's total results are below £300,000, being £290,000, but it is not possible to make full use of the small companies rate. Bill may wish to consider restructuring the group to either put all activities into one company or to form a group. (See **Chapter 9** regarding losses and **Chapter 10** regarding group relief). Bill may also wish to consider reducing A Ltd's profits that fall within the marginal rate band.

CORPORATION TAX ACT 2009

4.34   *Corporation Tax Act 2009* has adopted in general the *ICTA 1988, s 839* meaning to define connection and the *ICTA 1988, s 840* meaning to define control (*CTA 2009, s 1316*).

Companies are connected with each other if one controls the other, or both are under the same control. A company is connected with a person that is not a company if that person or his or her connected parties have control of it. For *s 839*, control is defined in accordance with *ICTA 1988, s 416* (see **4.4**).

ICTA 1988, s 840 defines control as being able to determine the affairs of the company in accordance with a person's wishes by means of a shareholding or the possession of voting power in or in relation to the company; or by any powers conferred by the articles of association or other document regulating the company's affairs.

HUSBAND AND WIFE COMPANIES

4.35   Spouses or civil partners, who jointly own and manage a private company, each have a personal allowance and the various tax brackets to apply to any income withdrawn from the company. In some circumstances, HMRC regard all the income as falling to the income-producing spouse by means of a settlement where the other spouse is seen as taking no part in the function of the business and possessing a holding that only reflects an income right. This situation was tested in *Jones v Garnett (Inspector of Taxes)* [2005] UKHL 35, [2005] EWCA Civ 1553 and a settlement was found not to exist. However, each case must be reviewed on its merits. See *Income Tax 2009/10* (Bloomsbury Professional).

Income shifting

4.36   The government proposed to introduce 'income shifting' legislation in the *Finance Act 2009* to counter situations where an individual is able to move taxable income to someone else with a lower rate of tax than him or herself. However, given the current economic conditions, the government is deferring this action and keeping the issue under review instead (Pre-Budget Report 2008 – PN1).

Chapter 5

Trading income

INTRODUCTION

5.1   The *Corporation Tax Act 2009 (CTA)* has come into force for accounting periods ending on or after 1 April 2009. The new Act updates part of the original legislation. This chapter deals with the new and the remaining trading income provisions. For details of the previous provisions, please see *Corporation Tax 2008/09* (Tottel Publishing).

Corporation tax is charged on a company's profits for each financial year, in accordance with the corporation tax statutes *(CTA 2009, s 2(1))*. A company's profits are its income and its chargeable gains, subject to any specific exemptions *(CTA 2009, s 2(2))*

TRADE PROFITS

5.2   The profits of a trade are chargeable to corporation tax *(CTA 2009, s 35)*. Normally it is a question of fact as to whether a trade is being carried on, but certain activities are statutorily deemed to be trades or non-trades, as the case may be.

For corporation tax purposes, the profits of a trade must be calculated in accordance with generally accepted accounting practice (GAAP), subject to any overriding statutory adjustment. Accruals accounting is required, and cash accounting is not allowed. The *Corporation Tax Act 2009* imposes no requirement to comply with the *Companies Act 2006* or its related subordinate legislation, except as to the basis of calculation; neither does it impose any requirements as to audit or disclosure *(CTA 2009, s 46)*.

Accounting principles do not apply where they conflict with the tax legislation and case law. As a result, a company's PCTCT will usually differ from the profit shown in the company's profit and loss account or income statement. See **Chapter 17** on accounting and taxation for the interaction of accounting standards and taxation law.

The same calculation rules apply regardless of whether the result is a profit or a loss (*CTA 2009, s 47*).

TRADE

Meaning of a trade

5.3   A trade is defined as 'every trade, manufacture, adventure or concern in the nature of trade' (*ICTA 1988, s 83(1)*). As to whether a trade is being carried on is a question of fact. The badges of trade established by the Royal Commission on the Taxation of Profits and Income in 1955 look to the subject matter of the transaction, the period of ownership, the frequency of the transactions, the supplementary work, the circumstances or method of realisation and the motive. In other words, has the company acquired products or services over a short space of time that had no use to the company, which it enhanced in some way or to which it added its own identity, which it has then sold in a strategic manner in order to make a profit

Case law

5.4   There is a substantial body of case law relating to trading activities, which confirms the 'badges of trade', of which the following are a selection:

Subject matter of transaction. In *Rutledge v CIR* (1929) 14 TC 490 the taxpayer bought and sold a large quantity of toilet rolls in an isolated transaction. The subject matter of the transaction determined that this was a trading transaction.

Period of ownership. In *Martin v Lowry* (1926) 11 TC 297, [1927] AC 312 an agricultural machinery merchant with no previous connection with the linen trade bought a surplus of government stock of 44,000,000 yards of linen. Negotiations for sale to the linen manufacturers fell through. The taxpayer advertised the linen and eventually all was sold within a year to numerous purchasers. The goods were sold swiftly at a profit. It was held that this was an adventure in the nature of trade.

Frequency of transactions. In *Pickford v Quirke* (1927) 13 TC 251 the taxpayer was a member of four different syndicates involved in buying and selling cotton spinning mills. It was held that the repetition of this transaction implied a trading intention. In *Leach v Pogson* (1962) 40 TC 585, [1962] TR 289 the taxpayer founded a driving school which he later sold at a profit. He then founded 30 more driving schools. Once the schools were operational he transferred them to companies, partly for shares and partly for cash. Because of the frequency of the transactions, the taxpayer was found to be trading.

Supplementary work. In *Cape Brandy Syndicate v CIR* (1921) 12 TC 358, [1921] 2 KB 403 three wine merchants all from different firms bought a quantity of South African brandy. Most of the brandy was shipped to the UK where it was blended with French brandy, re-casked and sold in numerous lots. It was held that the transactions amounted to a trade.

Circumstances or method of realisation. In *West v Phillips* (1958) 38 TC 203, [1958] TR 267 a retired builder owned 2,495 houses, of which 2,208 had been built as investments and 287 for eventual sale. After a period of time, the taxpayer began to sell the houses. It was held that 287 houses were sold as trading stock, but the sale of the remainder held for investment purposes was not a trade.

Motive. In *Wisdom v Chamberlain* (1968) 45 TC 92, [1969] 1 WLR 275, [1969] 1 All ER 332 the taxpayer made a profit on the purchase and sale of silver bullion. The bullion was bought to protect his wealth against the devaluation of sterling. It was held that this was a trading activity because the silver had been purchased for the specific purpose of realising a profit.

Of more recent importance is the decision in *Marson v Morton* (1986) 59 TC 381, [1986] STC 463, [1986] 1 WLR 1343. In this case, factors that should be considered as to whether a particular transaction was a trading transaction were summarised as follows:

Factor to consider	*Comment*
Was the transaction a one-off transaction?	Frequency of transactions indicate a trade, but a one-off transaction may still constitute a trade, depending on intention and other factors.
Was the transaction in some way related to a trade carried on by the taxpayer?	If related to the trade, this will point to a trading transaction.
Was the transaction in a commodity of a kind which is normally the subject matter of trade?	If yes, this will point to a trading transaction.
Was the transaction carried out in a manner typical of a trade in a commodity of that nature?	If yes, this will point to a trading transaction.
How was the transaction financed?	If financed by borrowings, this often indicates that a trade is being carried on.

Factor to consider	Comment
Was work done on the item before resale?	If yes, it is more likely to be a trading transaction.
Was the item purchased broken down into several lots?	If so, there is an indication that a trading transaction has taken place.
What were the purchaser's intentions at the time of purchase? Was it intended to hold the asset as an investment?	If held as an investment, its resale is unlikely to be a trading transaction.
Did the asset purchased either provide enjoyment for the purchaser, or produce income?	The production of income points to a trading transaction.

The issues can be transferred to professional income but here, more than likely, the central issue is whether professional skills are sold and marketed for remunerative gain.

The Act makes no reference to the carrying on of a profession or a vocation, for which there is no statutory definition. A profession is normally understood to mean a high degree of skill or competence attributed to an individual, for which he or she has undergone specialised training.

Commentary on the Act has suggested that a corporate body cannot carry on a profession that depends on the knowledge and skill of the individual. If a corporate body carries on a business consisting of the provision of professional services, the practice is to treat it as a trade. A vocation is a specific career that can only be undertaken by an individual and requires a personal commitment to a particular activity (*Corporation Tax Act 2009*, Explanatory Notes, Annex 1).

All these indications point to whether a trade is being carried on. Overall, the company's activities must be looked at as a whole. A company may carry on a trade and an investment business. Transactions for each must be kept separate, as the rules for each are different. See **Chapter 11** for investment business.

On the premise that a trade is being carried on, the company must establish whether its receipt is from the trade and whether it is a capital or a revenue item. It is an established principle that trading income is received when it is recognised in the trader's accounts (HMRC Business Income Manual BIM 40070). See **Chapter 17** on accounting and taxation.

Commencement of a trade

5.5   A company is treated as starting or ceasing to carry on a trade when it becomes chargeable or ceases to be within the charge to corporation tax in respect of that trade. Therefore, if a proprietorship business were to incorporate, the trade then carried on by the company would be treated as a new commencement (*CTA 2009, s 41*).

Commencing or ceasing to trade, or the receipt of income from any source, is a question of fact. However, whether or not a company is within the charge to corporation tax can often, in practice, be more difficult to ascertain where the company is not in receipt of any income, *ICTA 1988, s 832(1)* states that a source of income is 'within the charge to corporation tax' if corporation tax would be chargeable on that income were there to be any from that source. The company in *Centaur Clothes Group Ltd v Walker* (2000) 72 TC 379, [2000] STC 324, [2000] 1 WLR 799, [2000] 2 All ER 589 was not carrying on a trade but had potential sources of income from an inter-company debt and an agency agreement. The company was held to be within the charge to corporation tax. The case overturned the established principle in *National Provident Institution v Brown* (1921) 8 TC 57, [1921] 2 AC 222 whereby a company had to be in receipt of a source of income to be within the charge to corporation tax. If a company is not carrying on any activity whatsoever, it is a dormant company. See **4.30** for further commentary.

SELF-ASSESSMENT OF TRADING INCOME

Company tax return

5.6   On the assumption that a company is carrying on a trade or profession, the company is required to declare its turnover in box 1 of the company tax return. This information should be available from the company's accounts. Box 2 is for use by financial concerns such as banks, building societies and insurance companies. On the assumption that all information is to hand, the company can now calculate its trading profits. If the result is positive, this amount should be shown in box 3 of the company tax return. If the result is negative, box 3 should be left blank.

Adjusted trade profits

5.7   The company must then compute its adjusted trade profit, to enable it to complete box 3 of the company tax return. The profit for each trade must be computed on separate computations, and a calculation of the capital allowances claimed should also be provided.

5.8 *Trading income*

The accounting profits form the basis of the taxable profits, and so the starting point for computing the assessable trade profit is the reported profits.

In computing the assessable trade profits, it is first necessary to eliminate the non-trade source income from those profits, eg capital items, property income and non-trade loan relationship income that is assessed to corporation tax under its own rules. Special rules also apply to intangible assets (**Chapter 7**), research and development (**Chapter 8**) and investment business (**Chapter 12**). A transfer pricing adjustment increases taxable profits but never decreases them (**Chapter 14**).

Receipts and expenses

5.8   The new Act uses the terms 'receipts' and 'expenses' for the accounting credits and debits that are brought into account in calculating trade profits. The use of the words 'receipts' or 'expenses' does not mean that an amount has actually been received or paid (*CTA 2009, s 48*). Capital allowances are treated as an expense, and balancing charges are treated as receipt of the trade, as are debits and credits arising from the company's trading loan relationships, derivative contracts debits and intangible assets (*CTA 2009, s 49*).

Calculation of adjusted trade profits

5.9   If a company is operating GAAP correctly, there are unlikely to be too many adjustments to trade profits, but tax law takes precedence over accounting practice.

In order to calculate the adjusted trade profits, the profit as shown in the company's accounts is taken. That accounts profit is then reduced by any non-trading income and increased by any non-deductible expenses included in the accounts. It is then increased by any trading income and decreased by any deductible expenses not included in the accounts. Appropriations of profits, such as depreciation and dividend payments, are not an allowable deduction for corporation tax.

Trade profits are adjusted as follows:

Net profit per accounts	+
Less:	
• Non-trade income	−
Trade income per the accounts	

Adjustment for amounts included in the accounts:

• Expenses with a restricted deduction;	+
• Expenses of a specific trade	+
• Receipts not taxable as trading income	−
• Appropriations of profit	+

Adjustment for amounts not included in the accounts:

• Expenses with a permitted deduction;	−
• Expenses of a specific trade	−
• Receipts taxable as trading income.	+
Adjusted profits	=

NON-TRADE INCOME

5.10   Non-trade source income will include capital items and income assessed according to its own rules, such as property income and non-trade loan relationship income. Special rules also apply to intangible assets (**Chapter 7**), research and development (**Chapter 8**) and investment business (**Chapter 12**).

Capital v revenue

5.11   There is a body of case law which established the revenue versus capital principles. A capital receipt is not to be included in taxable trading profits (*CTA 2009, s 93*), and a deduction for capital expenditure in calculating profits of a trade is prohibited (*CTA 2009, s 53*). In general, asset repair carried out during the course of trading activities is a revenue expense. Expenditure in order to put an asset into working order, or the replacement of an entirety, is not a revenue expense. In *Law Shipping Co Ltd v CIR* (1923) 12 TC 621, expenditure on repairs to a ship in order to make it seaworthy shortly after purchase was held to be capital expenditure. In contrast, in *Odeon Associated Theatres Ltd v Jones* (1971) 48 TC 257, [1973] Ch 288, [1971] 1 WLR 442, [1972] 1 All ER 681, expenditure carried out on repairs to a useable cinema over a period of years was held to be revenue expenditure.

In *O'Grady v Bullcroft Main Collieries Ltd* (1932) 17 TC 93 a colliery company built a factory chimney at a cost of £3,067. After several years it became unsafe and was demolished. The company built another improved chimney near the site of the old one and claimed £287 of the cost as repairs. The whole of the cost was found to be capital expenditure because the new chimney was the replacement of an 'entirety'.

5.11 *Trading income*

In *Samuel Jones & Co (Devondale) Ltd v CIR* (1951) 32 TC 513, [1951] TR 411 the company replaced a factory chimney and also incurred costs in respect of the removal of the old chimney. The expenditure was found to be an allowable revenue deduction because it was an integral part of the factory. The chimney was not an entirety as in the case of *O'Grady v Bullcroft Main Collieries Ltd*.

In *Brown v Burnley Football & Athletic Co Ltd* (1980) 53 TC 357, [1980] STC 424, [1980] 3 All ER 244 a stand at the football ground was found to be unsafe. It had been built in 1912 of wood and steel with a brick wall at the back. It was demolished and replaced with a new modern concrete stand. The new stand, with approximately the same capacity, was nearer the pitch but included office and other accommodation not provided by the old stand. The expenditure was held to be capital expenditure because the new stand was a replacement in its entirety.

Expenditure in connection with enduring benefits to a trade is considered to be capital. In *Atherton v British Insulated & Helsby Cables Ltd* (1925) 10 TC 155, [1926] AC 205 a company set up a pension fund and made an initial lump sum contribution to enable the past service of existing staff to rank for pension. The expenditure was held to be capital. The principle was established that expenditure was normally capital if it was made not only once and for all but also with a view to bringing into existence an asset or advantage for the enduring benefit of the trade.

In *Tucker v Granada Motorway Services Ltd* (1979) 53 TC 92, [1979] STC 393, [1979] 1 WLR 683, [1979] 2 All ER 801 the rent, which a company paid to the Ministry of Transport for a motorway service area, was calculated in part by reference to its gross takings. The gross takings included the duty on sales of tobacco. The lease was not assignable. In order to have the duty on sales of tobacco excluded from the gross takings, the company made a once and for all payment of £122,220 to the Ministry of Transport. The expenditure was held to be capital and therefore not deductible from profits. The expenditure related to an identifiable capital asset.

In *Beauchamp v F W Woolworth plc* (1989) 61 TC 542, [1989] STC 510, [1989] 3 WLR 1 a company entered into two loans, each for 50 million Swiss Francs, for five years but repayable earlier at the option of the company, subject to a payment of a graduated premium. The first loan was repaid six months early and the second on the due date, giving rise to losses of £11.4 million, due to currency exchange transactions.

It was held that the loss was incurred in relation to a capital transaction and was therefore not allowable as a revenue deduction. The company had increased its capital employed and thereby obtained an asset or advantage, which endured for five years and, as such, was a capital asset. A loan is only a revenue transaction if it is part of the day-to-day incidence of carrying on the business, which was not the case in this situation. The loss was not deductible.

Often, there is doubt as to whether an item of expenditure is capital or revenue. In *Heather v P-E Consulting Group Ltd* (1972) 48 TC 293, [1973] Ch 189, [1973] 1 All ER 8 it was established that this is the court's decision. In this case a company undertook to pay 10% of its annual profits, subject to a minimum of £5,000, to a trust set up to enable its staff to acquire shares in the company and to prevent the company from coming under the control of outside shareholders. Accountancy evidence given at the time, which was accepted by the Commissioners, confirmed that the expenses were of a revenue nature. Although the Court of Appeal upheld the Commissioners' decision, it was made clear that whether the expenditure was capital or revenue was a matter of law for the court to decide and that accountancy evidence is not conclusive.

It was necessary to turn to the courts to establish whether the cost of airspace was capital or revenue. In *Rolfe v Wimpey Waste Management Ltd* (1989) 62 TC 399, [1989] STC 454 the company purchased several sites on which to tip waste under a contract with its customers. The company claimed that the purchases were revenue expenditure, on the grounds that it had acquired the land in order to use the airspace above it. The expenditure was held to relate to the land and was therefore capital.

Professional and other associated costs in connection with capital expenditure are also disallowed. See HMRC Business Income Manual BIM 35000 onwards for a discussion on the capital/revenue divide.

EXPENSES WITH A RESTRICTED DEDUCTION

5.12   The rules that restrict or allow deductions from trading income are to be found in *CTA 2009, ss 53–92*, and the general restriction on deductions is to be found in *CTA 2009, ss 1288–1309*. It follows that, where any amount that has been allowed as a deduction is subsequently reversed in the accounts, that reversal will be taxable.

These statutorily provided rules are supported by a body of case law and practice that has been established over a number of years.

Wholly and exclusively

5.13   By far the most important rule restricting deductions is the 'wholly and exclusively' rule. Expenditure is only allowed as a deduction if it has been in-curred 'wholly and exclusively' for the purposes of the trade or profession, and losses that are not connected with the trade cannot be deducted in calculating the profits of the trade (*CTA 2009, s 54(1)*). Company expenditure must be reviewed from this perspective. Expenditure on preserving a trade from destruction was treated as incurred wholly and exclusively for the purposes of the trade (*McKnight v Sheppard* (1999) 71 TC 410, [1999] STC 669, [1999] 1 WLR 1133, [1999] 3 All ER 491). If part of an expense is incurred wholly and exclusively for the purposes of the trade, that portion will be an allowable deduction from profits. In practice, this means that the allowable portion of the expenditure must be readily identifiable (*CTA 2009, s 54(2)*).

Trade debts written off

5.14   Trade debts and any other non-monetary debts that are irrecoverable are only deductible against trade profits if an impairment loss (see **17.17**) has been accounted for, or the debt has been released wholly and exclusively for the purposes of the trade, as part of a statutory insolvency arrangement. An asset is impaired when its carrying amount exceeds its recoverable amount, and the loss thereon is to be recognised in the income statement (IAS 39). Therefore, by applying GAAP, the company will obtain immediate bad debt relief.

Car hire charges

5.15   Part of the cost of leasing expensive cars and motor cycles is not allowed as a deduction. A car or motor cycle is any mechanically propelled road primarily suited for the conveyance of goods or burden of any description, or is a type of vehicle not commonly used as a private vehicle and unsuitable for such use (*CTA 2009, s 57*). The restriction on motor cycles only applies to leases entered into before 1 April 2009.

Existing leases that commenced before 1 April 2009

5.16   Where the retail price of a new vehicle (except an electric car with low CO_2 emissions) or a motor cycle exceed £12,000 and is hired for the purposes of the trade, the hire charge is reduced for tax purposes by using the formula $(12,000 + P) \div 2P$, where P is the retail price of the vehicle when new.

Existing leases that commenced on or after 1 April 2009

5.17   Rules introduced by the *Finance Act 2009* reduce the allowable hire charge by a flat 15%, but only for cars with CO_2 emissions exceeding 160g/km and where they are leased for a continuous period of 45 days or more. The new rule applies to leases entered into on or after 1 April 2009 and will no longer affect motor cycles (*CTA 2009, ss 56* and *57*). If the lease includes maintenance, then costs should be excluded if separately identified in the lease agreement. The lease costs will include the 50% VAT charge if the company is VAT registered. The restriction does not apply to the hire of low CO_2 emission cars or electric cars if the hire period commenced before 1 April 2013 (*CTA 2009, s 58*).

Patent royalties

5.18   Patent royalties are not deductible against trading profits. They form part of the intangible assets régime (see **Chapter 7**).

Integral features

5.19   Expenditure on integral fixtures is not deductible instead it is available for capital allowances (see **Chapter 6**).

Business entertainment and gifts

5.20   A company's expenditure on entertainment or gifts is disallowed as a deduction in computing profits, even though it is incurred in connection with a business that the company carries on. This provision overrides the decision in *Bentleys, Stokes and Lowless v Beeson* (1952) 33 TC 491, [1952] WN 280, [1952] 2 All ER 82, where a firm of solicitors discussed business affairs with clients at lunch. In this case, it was decided that there was a business purpose and the provision of lunch was incidental thereto.

Based on VAT decisions, the definition of business entertainment includes hospitality both free and subsidised (*Celtic Football and Athletic Club Ltd v Customs & Excise Commrs* [1983] STC 470). However, hospitality is not defined as business entertainment if it was given 'pursuant to a legal obligation in return for which it obtains proper and sufficient quid pro quo. The quid pro quo may be cash or it may be goods or services.' This also extends to a contractual obligation a company may have to provide hospitality (eg as part of a package).

Not only is relief denied for entertaining expenditure as a deduction in calculating trade profits, but also in calculating the profits of a property business and as management expenses. This will include sums put at the disposal of, or reimbursed to, an employee for meeting the expenditure incurred on entertaining or the provision of a gift (*CTA 2009, s 1298*). Assets used for business entertainment do not qualify for capital allowances. Travel costs associated with business entertainment are not allowable expenses but exceptions exist, such as employees travelling to meet a client.

The entertaining expenditure that any firm incurs, regardless of its trade or business, in entertaining its own staff, including directors and employees, is an exception to the rule. It will be an allowable deduction if incurred wholly and exclusively for the purposes of that trade or business. This does not mean to say that a benefit in kind will not arise upon the employee concerned. The cost of third party entertainment is prohibited as a deduction from business profits of any kind, and so is the expenditure in entertaining employees, if that is incidental to the entertainment of third parties (*CTA 2009, s 1299*).

Another exception occurs if the company's trade consists of the provision of entertainment: any expenses incurred wholly and exclusively for the purposes of that trade, even though of an entertainment nature, will be an allowable deduction from the profits of that trade, eg hospitality provided by restaurants and pubs (*Fleming v Associated Newspapers Ltd* (1972) 48 TC 382, [1973] AC 628, [1972] 2 All ER 574). In addition, if a firm were to incur entertainment expenditure in advertising its trade to the public generally, that would be an allowable deduction from trade profits. Advertising and promotion costs will normally be allowed. A company incurring costs on room hire and entertaining potential customers in order to gain firm orders found that the entertaining costs were disallowed, but the room hire cost was allowable (*Netlogic Consulting Ltd v HMRC*).

Similarly, if a company gifts an item that it provides in its normal course of trade or business to advertise the product to the public generally, the expenditure incurred will be an allowable deduction from trade or business profits. The cost of a gift of any sort that incorporates a conspicuous advertisement of the company is deductible. There is no deduction for gifts of food, drink, tobacco or tokens or vouchers exchangeable for goods. The value of any gifts made to the same person in the same accounting period (with the exception of food, drink, tobacco or a token or voucher exchangeable for goods, which is prohibited in any case) is capped at a deductible amount of £50 for each person. The value of gifts made to employees is deductible in full, but this does not mean to say that a taxable benefit will not arise, but gifts made to employees that are incidental to the gifts made to third parties follow the normal rules. Gifts made to a charity, the Historic Buildings and Monuments Commission for England, or the Trustees of the National Heritage Memorial Fund are deductible in calculating profits (*CTA 2009, s 1300*).

Remuneration

Employees

5.21   Provided the remuneration charged is 'wholly and exclusively' for the purposes of the trade, it should be an allowable deduction (*Copeman v Flood*

(William) & Sons Ltd (1940) 24 TC 53, [1941] KB 202; *LG Berry Investments Ltd v Attwooll* (1964) 41 TC 547, [1964] 1 WLR 693, [1964] 2 All ER 126). An employee will normally have an employment contract with the company, which together with *ITEPA 2003* will determine the time that payment is due to the employee. The existence of a contractual obligation for the company will bring about the allowable deduction, normally at the same time that the remuneration is 'earnings' for the employee. In order to qualify as a deduction from profits, remuneration charged must be paid to the employee within nine months of the year-end *(CTA 2009, s 1288(1))*.

Directors

5.22 A director is any person occupying the position of director by whatever name called *(CA 2006, s 250)*. A shadow director is any person in accordance with whose instructions directors are accustomed to act, with the exception of a professional adviser *(CA 2006, s 251)*. A similar definition is used within *ITEPA 2003, s 67*.

The time that remuneration is due and payable to a director is determined by *ITEPA 2003* and the director's contract of employment.

Directors are treated as having received earnings at the time when they become entitled to be paid them. However, an entitlement to payment is not necessarily the same as the date on which the employee acquires a right to be paid (HMRC Employment Income Manual EIM 42290).

The terms of a service agreement may be written, verbal or implied and may give entitlement to a regular salary or a contractual bonus or other sums. The director would then enjoy rights to earnings under the agreement. The time at which entitlement to earnings under a service agreement arises will be governed by the terms of the agreement.

Both employees' and directors' remuneration is normally paid under deduction of PAYE. See *Income Tax 2009/10* (Bloomsbury Professional), Chapter 5. By concession if a professional partnership holds an office, the income from that office may be taxed as fees rather than employment income (ESC A37 HMRC Employment Income Manual EIM 02500). HMRC when notified will issue an NT coding, PAYE will not be due on these payments but the payments will still be liable to Class 1 NIC (HMRC Employment Income Manual EIM 03002). The directorship should be a normal activity of the professional partnership, the fees are only a small part of the profits and under the partnership agreement the fees are pooled for division amongst the partners. The director concerned must review the situation carefully. There is the possibility that the payment may fall within the personal services régime that can apply to a partnership as well as a company (see **5.41**).

A director or employee may, of course, provide services to a company in a separate business capacity as partner in a professional partnership, eg solicitors, accountants or consultants etc. If the services are provided to the company on the same basis as the director's or employee's other customers, the payment to the director or employee would not be employment income and would not be subject to PAYE or NIC (HMRC Employment Status Manual ESM 4040).

Employee benefit trusts

5.23 An employee benefit trust (EBT) is a discretionary trust set up by an employer for the benefit of its employees and directors. EBTs can be resident in the UK or offshore, and can be subject to UK or foreign law. An 'offshore' EBT is only liable to UK income tax on its UK source income and is not liable to UK capital gains tax. Trustees, who are usually appointed by the company, manage an EBT. The trust fund will comprise of: (a) the initial amount settled by the employer to establish the trust, (b) subsequent contributions from the employer, and (c) sums paid to the trustees by third parties. The beneficiaries and the perpetuity period will be defined in the trust deed (HMRC Business Income Manual BIM 44501 onwards). EBTs are used with employee share schemes, retirement benefit schemes, accident benefit schemes and healthcare trusts. EBTs set up with employee benefit schemes are called employee share ownership trusts (ESOTs); they can also be known as employee share ownership plan (ESOP) trusts. ESOTs may be used by unquoted companies to provide a market for employees' shares (acquired through employee share schemes) that might otherwise not exist, maintain shareholder control and help with business planning and management buy-outs. Established case law has determined that, where the trust is set up for the benefit of employees, the contributions meet the 'wholly and exclusively' test (*Heather v P-E Consulting Group Ltd* (1972) 48 TC 293, [1973] Ch 189, [1973] 1 All ER 8; *Rutter v Charles Sharpe & Co Ltd* (1979) 53 TC 163, [1979] STC 711, [1979] 1 WLR 1429; *Jeffs v Ringtons Ltd* (1985) 58 TC 680, [1985] STC 809, [1986] 1 WLR 266, [1986] 1 All ER 144; *E Bott Ltd v Price* (1986) 59 TC 437, [1987] STC 100). In *Mawsley Machinery Ltd v Robinson* [1998] SSCD 236 the 'wholly and exclusively' test was not met because the reason for the contributions was to facilitate a share purchase (HMRC Business Income Manual BIM 44155).

There is no corporation tax deduction for amounts put into an EBT by an employer until the amount becomes taxable earnings of the employee. For this to occur, the contributions must be paid to the employee within nine months of the end of the year in a form on which PAYE and NIC are charged (*CTA 2009, ss 1203 and 1295*). Securities and options are included as benefits (*Finance (No 2) Act 2005, s 12, Sch 2*; *MacDonald v Dextra Accessories Ltd* [2005] UKHL 47, [2005] STC 1111).

Pension contributions

5.24   Payments to a pension scheme are a revenue expense and will be deductible from profits in the year in which the premium is paid (*FA 2004, s 196(2)(b)*) if the payment meets the 'wholly and exclusively for the purposes of the trade' test. Under FRS 17 the amounts included in the profit and loss account will be based on actuarial assumptions and are unlikely to consist of the premiums paid for the year. Thus, an adjustment will be required for corporation tax purposes that may also be reflected in the deferred tax account (see **17.32**).

Staff pension contributions are allowable unless there is an identifiable non-trade purpose. HMRC have highlighted the following circumstances where, depending on the facts or the circumstances at the time, there may be a non-trade purpose:

- contributions paid in respect of a controlling director or an employee who is a relative or close friend of the controlling director or proprietor of the business;

- contributions made as part of the arrangements for going out of business, in particular where there is no pre-existing contractual obligation to make such a contribution;

- contribution is required to be made pursuant to *Pensions Act 1995, s 75*;

- where, following the issue of a notice by the Pensions Regulator, a person is required to pay a pension contribution;

- where a contribution is in respect of orphaned liabilities;

- contributions made as part of the bargain struck for the purposes of facilitating the sale of shares in a subsidiary;

- contributions made in connection with the pension deficit of another company's trade; and

- where the reputation of the payer's trade or the morale of its staff is not the sole purpose behind the contribution.

Contributions in respect of a controlling director or an employee who is a close friend or relative of the controlling director or proprietor of the business may be queried by HMRC. In establishing whether a payment is for the purposes of the trade, they will examine the company's intentions in making the payment. If the level of the remuneration package is excessive for the value of the work undertaken for the employer by that individual, the contribution may be queried. The pension contribution will be viewed in the light of the overall remuneration package. HMRC acknowledge that employers may make increased pension contributions to remedy under-funding, and will look at the full facts of the case. On the practical side, it is well worth ensuring that employment contracts are in place for directors of close companies. Such directors have the ability to withdraw available funds at will from the company, normally under the rationale that funds are available. Unless this can be proven at the outset by inclusion, say, in a contract, any additional payment may be queried as being not wholly and exclusively for the purposes of the trade.

HMRC will accept that contributions in respect of a director of a close company, or an employee who is a close relative or friend of the director, are paid wholly and exclusively for the purposes of the trade where the remuneration package paid is comparable with that paid to unconnected employees performing duties of similar value. The proportion of any amount not so expended will be disallowed (HMRC Business Income Manual BIM 46035).

An undertaking to provide a pension under an employee's contract of employment will be an allowable deduction from profits. HMRC regard a payment made for the purposes of going out of business or other non-business purposes as a non-allowable deduction, but regard contributions made to preserve the reputation and morale of the staff as an allowable deduction (HMRC Business Income Manual BIM 46040).

Pension contributions in respect of other group company employees whose current employer can no longer contribute are generally deductible by the payer company. The matter may require further investigation if the current employer is in a position to contribute and the payer company's contribution has not been recharged to the current employer (HMRC Business Income Manual BIM 46065).

Pension scheme contributions paid in connection with the sale or transfer of the shares of a subsidiary may not necessarily be for the purposes of that company's trade. It is important for the company to be able to demonstrate that the pension contributions are unrelated to the sale of the company. Again, HMRC regard contributions made to preserve the reputation and morale of the staff as an allowable deduction (HMRC Business Income Manual BIM 46060).

Pension contribution spreading rules

5.25   Contributions paid by an employer to a registered pension scheme in respect of an individual are deductible if the company is carrying on a trade or are deductible as management expenses if the company has an investment activity (*FA 2004, s 196*). If the amount of the contribution for the current chargeable period (CCCP) exceeds 210% of the amount of the contributions paid in the previous chargeable period (CPCP), the payments made in the second period may have to be spread forward. In order to ascertain whether or not this is the case, the company must calculate its relevant excess contributions (REC). The REC is calculated by deducting 110% of the CPCP from the CCCP.

Example 5.1

Wishbone Ltd makes pension contributions of £250,000 in the year ended 31 December 2009. In the year ended 31 December 2010, it makes contributions of £775,000.

	£
CCCP	775,000
Less 110% × £250,000	275,000
REC	500,000

If the REC is less than £500,000, there is no spreading. If the REC is £500,000 or more but less than £1,000,000, one half of the REC is spread into the following accounting period, in this case the year ended 31 December 2011. If the REC is £1,000,000 or more but less than £2,000,000, one-third of the REC is spread into each of the next two accounting periods. If the REC is £2,000,000 or more, one-quarter of the REC is spread into each of the next three accounting periods (*FA 2004, s 197*).

Example 5.2

Wishbone Ltd's pension contribution relief of £775,000 for the year ended 31 December 2010 is spread as follows:

	£
Year ending 31 December 2009	500,000
Year ending 31 December 2010	275,000

Pension commencement of trade

5.26 The cost of setting up a registered pension scheme is capital expenditure and is not an allowable deduction (*Atherton v British Insulated and Helsby Cables Ltd* [1925] 10 TC 155; *Rowntree and Co Ltd v Curtis* [1924] 8 TC 678).

Pension contributions arising from pension scheme obligations taken over on the purchase of a trade as part of the acquisition of the trade are treated as revenue expenditure (*FA 2004, s 196(2)*).

Pension cessation of trade

5.27   Payments by an employer, who has ceased trading, into a registered pension scheme to satisfy a liability falling due under *PA 1995, s 75* or *Art 75* of the *Pensions (Northern Ireland) Order 1995 (SI 1995/3213 (NI22))* are deductible against PCTCT for the final period of trading. The payment is treated as being made on the last day of trading (*FA 2004, s 199*). Thus, it is not necessary for this income to be relieved under the provisions of *CTA 2009, s 196(1), (2)*. Under-funding contributions made because of a direction issued by the Pensions Regulator are normally allowable against profits (HMRC Business Income Manual BIM 46050).

EXPENSES WITH A PERMITTED DEDUCTION

Pre-trading expenses

5.28   Expenditure that a company incurs during the seven years before it starts to carry on a trade, which it cannot relieve because it has no trading income for that trade as yet, but would be allowed if the trade had commenced, is treated as being incurred on the start date of that trade. There is also relief for pre-loan relationship expenditure under the loan relationship rules of *CTA 2009, s 330* – see **11.28** (*CTA 2009, s 61*).

Tenants under taxed leases

5.29   The company as tenant may be required to pay its landlord a capital sum, such as a premium, in respect of a property which it occupies for the purposes of its trade. If so, the landlord will be charged to tax on this receipt, known as a 'taxed receipt' (see **12.21**). This is essentially a capital receipt that is partially taxed as income. The company tenant in turn can claim a proportion of the payment it has made as a deduction from trade profits. The relief is dependent on the amount that has been charged on the landlord and is calculated in the same way as property business deduction – see **12.23** (*CTA 2009, s 62*). A daily amount is calculated according to the formula:

$$\frac{A}{TRP}$$

where A is the landlord's taxable receipt and TRP is the number of days in the receipt period of the taxed receipt (*CTA 2009, s 233(6)*).

Example 5.3

Golding Ltd has been informed that its landlord has a taxed receipt from the lease premium payment of £7,300. The lease runs from 1 January 2010 for 10 years. Golding Ltd prepares accounts to 31 December each year.

The daily deduction for the premium payable is	$\dfrac{£7,300}{365 \times 10} =$	£2
The annual deduction for the premium payable is	£2 × 365 =	£730

If the tenant occupies part of the property for which the landlord paid the premium, the deduction is apportioned according to the proportion occupied.

Replacement and alteration of trade tools

5.30   Expenditure incurred on replacing or altering tools used in a trade is capital by nature. However, a specific deduction is granted for replacing or altering small items used in the trade (*CTA 2009, s 68*).

EXPENDITURE IN CONNECTION WITH EMPLOYEES

Payments for restrictive undertakings

5.31   Certain items in relation to employee expenditure are specifically allowable against profits of a trade. Payments to employees in consideration restricting their activities in some way, although treated as employee earnings under *ITEPA 2003, ss 225* and *226* are capital by nature. A deduction is granted against taxable profits in the accounting period in which the payment is made or is treated as being made (*CTA 2009, s 69*).

Employees seconded to charities and educational establishments

5.32   If an employee is seconded to a charity or an educational establishment on a basis that is stated and intended to be temporary, the costs of that person's employment during the time of his or her secondment are an allowable deduction against the employer company's trading profits. The educational establishment must be situated within the UK and must meet the criteria of an educational establishment (*CTA 2009, ss 70* and *71*).

Contributions to agents' expenses

5.33   An employer company may operate a payroll deduction scheme, whereby it deducts charitable donations from its employees' salaries and pays them to an agent. An employer is allowed a deduction for expenses incurred in operating such schemes (*CTA 2009, s 72*).

Counselling and retraining expenses

5.34   Upon cessation of employment, an employer may offer counselling and other outplacement services to its departing employees. If the conditions of *ITEPA 2003, s 310* are met, the costs of providing such services are deductible against the employer's trading profits, but the costs are not a taxable benefit on the employee. The conditions are, in principle, that:

- the services are in connection with a change of employment;

- the services are to assist the person in finding gainful employment or self-employment;

- the services consist of giving advice, improving skills or allowing the use of equipment or facilities;

- the person has been continually employed in the job concerned for a period of two years ending with the earlier of the time when the services began to be provided or the time when the employment ceased;

- these services are available generally to all employees or a particular class of employees; and

- travel expenses are within the bounds of that employment (*CTA 2009, s 73*).

Retraining courses

5.35   The costs of retraining an employee are deductible against trading profits if the following conditions are met:

- the course must last no longer than two years;

- the course is designed to create or enhance employment or self-employment skills;

- the employee commences the course whilst employed by the employer or within one year after the employment ceases;

- the employee ceases to be employed by the employer within a period of two years beginning with the end of the course and is not re-employed by the employer within a period of two years after that employment ceases;

- the employee has been employed by the employer for a period of two years upon commencement of the course or when leaving the employment if earlier;

- the opportunity to undertake the course on similar terms is available to other employees or a certain class of employees; and

- travelling expenses are within the bounds of that employment (*CTA 2009, s 74*).

The employer must give HMRC notice within 60 days if, subsequently, the employee retraining conditions are not met, in that the employee commences the course after one year of leaving the firm or the employee ceases to be employed by the firm within a period of two years after the end of the course. HMRC can raise a discovery assessment under *FA 1998, Sch 18, para 41* if the employer fails to provide this notice (*CTA 2009, s 75*).

Redundancy payments

5.36 A statutory redundancy payment is an allowable deduction in the accounting period in which it is paid. If paid after the trade has ceased, it is treated as being paid on the last day of trading (*CTA 2009, s 77*).

If the payment partly refers to the trade and partly to another activity, it is to be split on a just and reasonable basis between the two, and the portion allocated to the trade will be deductible against trading income (*CTA 2009, s 78*). If the company employer permanently ceases to carry on a trade or part of a trade and makes a payment to the employee in addition, that payment is also treated as an allowable deduction in the same manner (*CTA 2009, s 79*). Where there are changes in a partnership, the employer is treated as permanently ceasing to carry on the trade unless a company carrying on the trade in partnership immediately before the change continues to carry it on in partnership after the change (*CTA 2009, s 80*). Employee redundancy payments that are paid by the government and then reimbursed by the employer company are an allowable deduction for the employer company (*CTA 2009, s 81*).

Contributions to local enterprise organisations or urban regeneration companies

5.37 Contributions to a local enterprise organisation or urban regeneration company are an allowable deduction, provided the company does not receive or is not entitled to receive a disqualifying benefit therefrom. A benefit is disqualifying if the costs of obtaining, were they incurred by the company contributor, would be disallowed in calculating the profits of the trade. In that case, the amount of the deduction is reduced by the amount of the benefit and any excess is treated as a receipt of the trade (*CTA 2009, s 82*). Reference should be made to *CTA 2009, ss 83–86* for full details of the qualifying organisations

Scientific research

5.38   Expenditure of a revenue nature on research and development undertaken by or on behalf of the company that is related to the trade is an allowable deduction (*CTA 2009, s 87*). Expenditure on the acquisition of research and development rights is not included. Research and development is related to the trade if it may lead to or facilitate an extension of the trade. Research and development expenditure of a medical nature, which has a special relation to the welfare of workers employed in the trade, is also related to the trade (*CTA 2009, s 87*).

Such payments to approved research institutions or universities are allowed in the accounting period in which they are paid (*CTA 2009, s 88*).

Expenses connected with patents, designs or trademarks

5.39   A deduction is allowed for expenses incurred on the grant or extension of a patent's term, or in connection with a rejected or abandoned application, provided such expenditure was incurred for the purposes of the trade (*CTA 2009, s 89*). However, see **Chapter 7** in respect of expenditure on intangible fixed assets. A deduction is allowed for expenses incurred in registering a design or trademark, or for extending the term or renewal of registration (*CTA 2009, s 90*).

Export Credits Guarantee Department and FSMA 2000

5.40   Sums paid to the Export Credits Guarantee Department are deductible if incurred for the purposes of the trade (*CTA 2009, s 91*). Levies payable under the *Financial Services and Markets Act 2000* (*FSMA 2000*) are deductible if incurred for the purposes of the trade (*CTA 2009, s 92*). A repayment of a *FSMA 2000* levy is treated as a trading receipt (*CTA 2009, s 104*).

Relief for employee share acquisitions

5.41   Approved share incentive plans are given specific statutory deductions (*CTA 2009, s 985*). The more common schemes are known as SIP (share incentive plans), CSOP (company share option plans), SAYE (savings-related share option schemes) and QUEST (qualifying share ownership trust).

Companies receive support for share incentive plans in three ways: deductions are allowed for the cost of setting up plans and for running expenses, as well as payments for the acquisition of shares for the plans.

Deductions are allowed for the costs involved in setting up a plan approved by HMRC. Normally, approval will be given within nine months of the expenses being incurred but, if later, then the deduction is allowed in the accounting period in which the company receives the approval (*CTA 2009, ss 987, 999* and *1000*).

Deductions for contributions made by a company to trustees of an approved share incentive plan to cover running expenses are allowable. Running expenses do not cover the cost of share purchases by trustees other than commission and stamp duty (*CTA 2009, s 988*).

An allowable deduction occurs where the company makes a payment to the incentive plan's trustees for the purchase of qualifying shares in the company, or a company which controls it. The trustees must use the payment to acquire shares in the company to the amount of at least 10% of the ordinary share capital. These shares cannot be purchased directly from the company and must carry rightsto at least 10% of the profits available for distribution to the shareholders and 10% of the assets, in a winding up. For the deduction to be allowed:

- the trustees must acquire the shareswithin 12 months from the date of the company's payment(*CTA 2009, s 989 (4)* and *(7)*),

- at least30% of the purchased shares must be distributed by the trustees within a period ending five years from the purchase date (*CTA 2009, s 990(2)*), and

- all the acquired shares must be distributed to qualifying employees within 10 years from when they were acquired by the trustees (*CTA 2009, s 990(3)*).

Shares acquired

5.42 The employer company receives corporation tax relief on the purchase or the exercise of options on non-restricted or non-convertible shares on an amount being the difference between the market value of the shares at the time the employee purchases the shares or exercises an option and the price the employee pays (*CTA 2009, ss 1010* and *1018*). The company also receives relief on the purchase or the exercise of restricted or convertible shares on the difference between the amount that counts as employment income of the employee or, in the case of a qualifying option, the amount that would have counted as employment income and the amount that the employee pays (*CTA 2009, ss 1011* and *1019*). The relief is given in the accounting period in which the option is exercised and the shares acquired (*CTA 2009, ss 1013* and *1021*). The relief applies to enterprise management investment (EMI) scheme options, company share option plans (CSOP), unapproved share option plans, and share acquisitions where the employee is subject to tax. The shares must be ordinary shares in a listed company, single company or holding company (*CTA 2009, ss 1008* and *1016*).

Capital allowances

5.43   A company may be able to claim capital allowances on its expenditure on plant and machinery, industrial and related buildings, agricultural land and buildings, mineral extraction and research and development allowances (*CAA 2001, s 1*) or an annual investment allowance (*FA 2008, s 74*) (see **6.47**) for expenditure incurred on or after 1 April 2008.

A company can also claim capital allowances on expenditure incurred prior to 1 April 2002 on patent rights and know-how. Capital allowances are discussed in **Chapter 6**, and the rates of capital allowances are shown in **6.6**.

Capital allowances are given by reference to accounting periods. Where an accounting period is less than 12 months, writing-down allowances are proportionately reduced. Where a trade starts partway through an accounting period, capital allowances for plant and machinery, research and development etc are also proportionately restricted.

EXPENSES OF A SPECIFIC TRADE

Providing services through a company

Personal service company

5.44   Individuals who provide their services through a company may fall foul of the personal service company or managed service company legislation (see *Income Tax 2009/10* (Bloomsbury Professional)). The deemed employment payments and the employer's national insurance contributions incurred by the contractor company are deductible from profits if treated as made during that accounting period (*CTA 2009, s 139*). Deemed payments are calculated for each income tax year ended 5 April.

Example 5.4

Mr Persona is an IT consultant who provides his services through Persona Services Ltd. It is understood that the personal services legislation applies. Persona Services Ltd prepares accounts to 28 February each year. Mr Persona's deemed payment for the year ended 5 April 2010 is £50,000. Relief for the deemed payment is given against profits for the year ended 28 February 2011.

Managed service company

5.45 A managed service company acts as an umbrella company in raising invoices on a personal service individual's behalf, for which it charges a commission. Managed service companies must account for PAYE and NIC on the full amount invoiced to their clients for the individual's services, rather than the post-commission payment made to the individual (PAYE applies to full invoice payments from 6 April 2007, and NIC applies to full invoice payments from 6 August 2007 (*SI 2007/2070*)). The deemed employment payments and the employer's national insurance contributions incurred by the managed service company are deductible from profits (*CTA 2009, s 141*).

Waste disposal and site preparation expenditure

5.46 A deduction for site preparation expenditure is available against profits to a company that carries on a trade that entails the deposit of waste materials. Either the company itself, or the previous owner, known as the company's predecessor, whose trade the company took over, may have incurred the preparation expenditure on the waste site. The expenditure must have been incurred as a condition of a waste disposal licence or in order to grant or comply with planning permission. Expenditure that qualifies for capital allowances is excluded.

Relief is calculated by the following formula:

$$RE \times \frac{WD}{SV + WD}$$

RE = The residual expenditure
WD = The volume of waste materials deposited on the waste disposal site during the period
SV = The volume of the waste disposal site not used for the deposit of waste materials at the end of the period.

The residual expenditure is the total of the site preparation incurred by the company and its predecessor at any time before the end of the accounting period in question less expenditure allowed as a deduction elsewhere, eg capital expenditure for capital allowances, any expenditure allowed as a deduction against trade profits of the current or a prior accounting period, and the excluded amount of any unrelieved old expenditure if the company was trading before 6 April 1989.

The excluded amount of unrelieved old expenditure is calculated by applying the following formula to the unrelieved old expenditure:

$$\frac{WD}{SV + WD}$$

WD = The volume of waste materials deposited on the waste disposal site before 6 April 1989

SV   = The volume of the waste disposal site not used for the deposit of waste materials immediately before that date.

(CTA 2009, ss 142, 143)

In the case of *Dispit Ltd v Revenue and Customs Commissioners* (2007) SpC 579, it was decided that restoration expenditure was only an allowable expense from trading profits in the accounting period concerned up to the amount of the payments actually made.

DEDUCTIBLE AND NON-DEDUCTIBLE EXPENSES

5.47   The following list is a summary of some of the case law and practice that has been established over a number of years.

Item	*Explanation*	*References*
Accounts preparation	Fees in relation to the preparation of business accounts and other recurring accountancy and legal expenses arising from the preparation are normally allowable. Fee protection insurance charges to cover the risk of incurring additional costs are only allowable if the additional costs are of a revenue nature or if the costs covered would be allowable. The costs of an	HMRC Business Income Manual BIM 46450 HMRC Business Income Manual BIM 46452

Item	Explanation	References
	enquiry that reveals discrepancies resulting from fraud and negligence are not allowable.	
Advertising	Ordinary current expenditure on advertising a company's goods or services is normally allowable.	HMRC Business Income Manual BIM 42550
Animals kept for trade purposes	Animals or other living creatures are accounted for at their capital value on the balance sheet if they are kept wholly or mainly for the work they do in connection with the carrying on of the trade. Otherwise, they are treated as trading stock unless they are part of a herd in relation to which a herd basis election has effect. Part-owned shares in animals or other living creatures are given the same treatment.	*CTA 2009, s 50*
Annuities and annual payments	An annuity or an annual payment is disallowed as a business deduction in accounts under *CTA 2009, s 54*. In general terms, an annual payment will be (a) paid under a legal obligation, (b) annually recurring and (c) pure income profit in the hands of the recipient but may be allowed as a charge on income (see **9.8, 9.16**).	HMRC Business Income Manual BIM 42601. *Gresham Life Assurance Society v Styles* (1890) 2 TC 633, (1890) 3 TC 185, [1892] AC 309.
Assets in satisfaction of trading debts	Companies can accept assets in satisfaction of trading debts. Where the market value of the asset at the date of acceptance of the asset is less than the amount of the outstanding debt, the shortfall may be allowable as a deduction. However, the company must agree to account for any excess as a trading receipt as a result of the disposal of the asset. The excess is excluded from CGT (*TCGA 1992, s 251(3)*).	HMRC Business Income Manual BIM 42735

Item	Explanation	References
Business archives	Costs incurred in maintaining historic business archives will generally be allowable expenses. Company expenditure on the provision of access to archives, and on linked educational services, is also usually allowable.	HMRC Business Income Manual BIM 42501
Capital	Capital payments are disallowed. A company's initial contribution to a staff pension fund was a capital payment because it was made not only once and for all, but also with a view to bringing into existence an asset or an advantage for the enduring benefit of trade.	*Atherton v British Insulated and Helsby Cables Ltd* (1925) 10 TC 155, [1926] AC 205; HMRC Business Income Manual BIM 35320
Company administration	Costs incurred by a company as part of its ordinary annual expenditure on such matters as the keeping of the share register, the printing of annual accounts, and the holding of shareholders' AGMs are normally allowed as trading expenses. Also, the annual cost of a Stock Exchange quotation and the fees paid to newspapers for the inclusion of the company's shares in the newspaper's report of Stock Exchange prices, and annual fees paid to trustees for debenture holders or mortgagees, are treated as allowable expenses.	HMRC Business Income Manual BIM 42510
Compensation and damages	Compensation and damages payments depend on the circumstances of the payment. A compensation payment may be reduced by the reimbursement of trading expenses allowable as a deduction.	HMRC Business Income Manual BIM 42950 BIM 42955

Item	*Explanation*	*References*
	Compensation and damages payments require to be 'wholly and exclusively' for trade purposes and on 'revenue account'.	BIM 42960
	Where compensation relates to normal trading activity and not an identifiable capital asset, it will be an allowable deduction. Compensation for termination of an agency was held to be a trading expense.	*Anglo-Persian Oil Co Ltd v Dale* (1931) 16 TC 253, [1932] 1 KB 124
Computer software	Expenditure may either be capital or revenue expenditure. See **6.15**.	*CAA 2001, ss 71–73*
Crime	No deduction is allowed for crime related payments.	*CTA 2009, s 1304* HMRC Business Income Manual BIM 43100, BIM 43101, BIM 43105, BIM 43115 and BIM43160
Defalcations/ embezzlement	Funds misappropriated by a director, then claimed as a remuneration payment on which PAYE was to be paid, were held not to be an allowable deduction for corporation tax purposes. Losses are allowed as deductions but not misappropriations by a director. Defalcations made good are taxable.	*Bamford v ATA Advertising* (1972) 48 TC 359, [1972] 1 WLR 1261, [1972] 3 All ER 535; *Curtis v Oldfield (J & G) Ltd* (1925) 9 TC 319; *Gray v Penrhyn (Lord)* (1937) 21 TC 252, [1937] 3 All ER 468
Dilapidations	Where the costs of repairs at the end of a lease, called dilapidations, would be the same if the repairs had been undertaken during the course of the lease period, and are not of a capital nature, then they should be allowable (*CTA 2009, s 54*). At the expiry of the lease, the lessee may agree to pay a sum, compensation in lieu of accrued repairs, to the lessor. This payment is allowable if it does not reflect capital costs.	HMRC Business Income Manual BIM 43250, BIM 43251, BIM 43255, BIM 43260, BIM 43265 *Hyett v Lennard* (1940) 23 TC 346, [1940] 2 KB 180, [1940] 3 All ER 133

Item	*Explanation*	*References*
Employees' or directors' remuneration	Remuneration wholly and exclusively for the purposes of trade is deductible. See **5.21**, **5.22**. Remuneration paid to connected parties, say to shareholder's family, must be on arm's-length terms.	*Stott and Ingham v Trehearne* (1924) 9 TC 69; *Earlspring Properties Ltd v Guest* (1995) 67 TC 259, [1995] STC 479; *Robinson v Scott Bader & Co Ltd* (1981) 54 TC 757, [1981] STC 436, [1981] 1 WLR 1135, [1981] 2 All ER 1116
Fee Protection Insurance	A premium for insuring against the costs incurred in the case of a tax enquiry are allowable only to the extent that the costs insured against would themselves be allowable. If the premium covers the cost of accountancy fees incurred in negotiating additional liabilities resulting from negligent or fraudulent conduct, it is not deductible. Apportionment is not permitted.	HMRC Business Income Manual BIM 46452, BIM 46450
Fines	Fines are disallowed, as they are not incurred wholly and exclusively for the purpose of trade—as confirmed in case law. Penalties for breaches of trading regulations are disallowed. Legal costs in defending a business were allowable.	HMRC Business Income Manual BIM 42515. *CIR v Alexander von Glehn & Co Ltd* (1920) 12 TC 232, [1920] 2 KB 553; *McKnight v Sheppard* (1999) 71 TC 419, [1999] STC 669, [1999] 1 WLR 1133, [1999] 3 All ER 491.
Fine (parking)	In situations where the employer pays a parking fine that is in fact the liability of the employee, the cost to the employer will be allowable in determining his trading profit, and the employee will be chargeable on the emolument arising. Fines paid by the company on company cars are not a benefit for the employee, but neither are they deductible for corporation tax.	HMRC Business Income Manual BIM 42515

Item	Explanation	References
	Fines resulting from civil actions arising out of trade may be allowed if not punitive.	*Golder v Great Boulder Proprietary Gold Mines Ltd* (1952) 33 TC 75, [1952] 1 All ER 360
Foreign exchange	Foreign exchange gains and losses are dealt with under the loan relationship provisions (see **Chapter 11**).	HMRC Business Income Manual BIM 45875
Franchise payments	An appropriate part of the initial franchise fee will be considered a revenue payment if the items it represents are revenue items and are not separately charged for in the continuing fees. However, franchise fees are more likely to fall within the intangible assets regime (see **Chapter 7**).	HMRC Business Income Manual BIM 57600–57620
Guarantee payments	Guarantee payments fall within loan relationships (see **Chapter 11**). However, a payment under a loan guarantee is deductible only if the 'wholly and exclusively for the purpose of trade' concept is met at the time it was made and a capital advantage is not secured. Guarantees between grouped and/or associated companies may not fulfil these conditions. Payments under guarantee in respect of an associated company were held to be capital expenditure.	HMRC Business Income Manual BIM 45301 *Milnes v J Beam Group Ltd* (1975) 50 TC 675, [1975] STC 487; *Garforth v Tankard Carpets Ltd* (1980) 53 TC 342, [1980] STC 251; *Redkite v Inspector of Taxes* [1996] STC (SCD) 501; BIM 45305
	An exhibition guarantee payment, made in order to secure work, was considered to be an allowable deduction.	*Morley v Lawford & Co* (1928) 14 TC 229
Hire purchase	Revenue payments for the hire of an asset are deductible. But capital payments for the purchase of an asset are not. Payments under a hire purchase agreement are split between amounts for hire (allowable) and payments for	HMRC Business Income Manual BIM 45351 *Darngavil Coal Co Ltd v Francis* (1931) 7 TC 1 BIM 45351 BIM 45355

Item	*Explanation*	*References*
	the eventual purchase (capital). If ownership of the equipment passes to the purchaser at the time of signing the agreement and payment is via an extra charge, then these payments are capital expenditure.	
	Cost of repairs and renewal to hire purchase assets are allowable as a deduction. SSAP 21 governs the accountancy treatment for hire-purchase contracts (see **Chapter 17**).	BIM 45360
Holding company formation expenses	This is treated as capital expenditure and is not deductible.	*Kealy v O'Mara (Limerick) Ltd* [1942] 2 ITC 265; [1942] IR 616
Incentive and reward schemes	Expenditure on performance related awards and incentive schemes, which satisfy all of the following conditions, may be allowable if (a) the award requires to be based on genuine performance achievement, (b) there is an obligation to provide the gift, and (c) a formal scheme based on known rules is in place.	HMRC Business Income Manual BIM 45080.
	Suggestion scheme awards are treated in a similar manner, provided the award is reasonable.	BIM 47010 BIM 47015
In-house professional fees	A company's in-house professional fees in relation to work involved with the company's capital assets are not allowed. Fees for the maintenance of a company's assets, facilities or trading rights are normally revenue expenses and allowable, but fees in relation to rights or facilities of a capital nature are capital expenses.	HMRC Business Income Manual BIM 46410

Item	*Explanation*	*References*
Insurance	Policies which provide indemnity for loss or damage to fixed or intangible assets, current assets (trading stock or trade debts) are allowable if the business purpose requirement is satisfied (*CTA 2009, s 54*), including policies which cover replacement 'new for old'. Insurance proceeds for stock lost are assessable as trading income.	HMRC Business Income Manual BIM 45501, BIM 45505, *Green v Gliksten (J) & Son Ltd* (1929) 14 TC 364, [1929] AC 381; BIM 45510; *Mallandain Investments Ltd v Shadbolt* (1940) 23 TC 367
	Premiums for policies covering (a) fire at company's premises, (b) interruption or loss of use of income-producing assets, (c) interruption or cessation of the supply of raw materials, or (d) events causing loss of profits for a temporary period, are allowable deductions from trading profits.	BIM 45510
	An indemnity policy premium is allowable where it provides cover for professional negligence. However, damages paid as a result of professional negligence are not.	BIM 45515
	Premiums paid to indemnify employees against legal action taken against them personally, for actions in the course of the employment, are allowable as a deduction in computing the employer's trading profits.	BIM 45520
	Insurance receipts in connection with the trade are taxed as trading receipts.	
Interest on director's property loan	Where interest is paid by a company on a loan (not overdraft) taken out by a director to purchase land or buildings occupied rent-free by the company and used for business purposes, it is	*CTA 2009, s 54* HMRC Business Income Manual BIM 45755

Item	Explanation	References
	considered that the company may obtain relief as a trading expense for the interest in the normal way and that the payments would not normally constitute either remuneration or a benefit of the director.	
Key employee insurance	Premiums on policies in favour of the employer insuring against death or critical illness of key employees are generally allowable, and the proceeds of any such policies are treated as trading receipts. Keyman insurance proceeds were taxable as receipts of the trade. Premiums on policies taken out as a condition of loan finance are not deductible. See **11.29**. An insurance premium covering the payment of compensation to employees is deductible. Life assurance receipts paid to a company in respect of insurance taken out at the request of a shareholder to guarantee the company's bank overdraft were held not to be receipts of the trade and were not taxable.	HMRC Business Income Manual BIM 45525, BIM 45530 *Keir & Cawder Ltd v CIR* (1958) 38 TC 23 *Greycon Ltd v Klaentschi* [2003] STC (SCD) 370 *CIR v Williams' Executor* (1944) 26 TC 23
Launch costs	A company may obtain relief for advertising and launch costs under the intangible assets regime (see **Chapter 7**).	HMRC Business Income Manual BIM 42551
Legal expenses	Legal expenses incurred in maintaining existing trading rights and assets are revenue expenses. The legal costs of defending an overseas branch's title to land in the foreign courts, which it used for the purposes of its trade, was deductible from profits.	 *Southern v Borax Consolidated* (1940) 23 TC 598, [1941] 1 KB 111, [1940] 4 All ER 412;

Item	Explanation	References
	Expenditure on defending a company from public ownership, and thereby the prevention of the seizure of its business and assets, was held to be an allowable business expense.	*Morgan v Tate & Lyle Ltd* (1954) 35 TC 367, [1954] AC 21, [1954] 2 All ER 413
Loan finance	See loan relationships (**Chapter 11**).	
Losses	Losses arising in the normal course of trading are allowable. Losses arising from theft or misappropriation by directors are not allowable.	HMRC Business Income Manual BIM 45851, BIM 45855. *Curtis v Oldfield (J & G) Ltd* (1925) 9 TC 319; *Bamford v ATA Advertising Ltd* (1972) 48 TC 359, [1972] 1 WLR 1261, [1972] 3 All ER 535
Management expenses	HMRC will accept reasonable management expenses allocations to group companies of expenses incurred by a group service company on their behalf. HMRC will investigate arrangements where one company incurs expenditure for the purposes of the trade of another that is outside the scope of UK tax (see **12.3**).	HMRC Business Income Manual BIM 42140,
	However, expenses relating to the trade of one group company will not be allowable against the separate trade of another group member.	BIM 38230
National Insurance Contributions	Secondary Class 1 NICs are deductible in computing profits, as are Class 1A NICs and Class 1B NICs.	*CTA 2009, s 1302*
Onerous contract	Payment of a sum of money to remove a company from an onerous trading contract will usually be considered to be a trading expense.	*Vodafone Cellular v Shaw* (1997) 69 TC 376, [1997] STC 734 (see HMRC Business Income Manual BIM 38220 for details)
	A payment by a company to secure release of an option over a trade investment was held to be a trading expense.	*Walker v Cater Securities Ltd* (1974) 49 TC 625, [1974] STC 390, [1974] 1 WLR 1363, [1974] 3 All ER 63

Item	*Explanation*	*References*
Overseas taxes	Tax of an overseas country charged on the profits arising in that country will be available for tax credit relief in most cases. A deduction may in certain circumstances arise for taxes of a capital nature. Interest payable on overseas tax may be admitted as a trading expense, but not if it relates to a capital tax or overseas tax penalty.	HMRC Business Income Manual BIM 45901, BIM 45905; *Harrods (Buenos Aires) Ltd v Taylor-Gooby* (1964) 41 TC 450
Payments in lieu of notice	Payments in lieu of notice on a cessation of trade were held to be an allowable deduction.	*O'Keefe v Southport Printers Ltd* (1984) 58 TC 88, [1984] STC 443
Political expenses	No deductions are allowable for party political expenditure, but propaganda costs to prevent the loss of business and protect assets may be allowable.	*Morgan v Tate and Lyle Ltd* (1954) 35 TC 367, [1955] AC 21, [1954] 2 All ER 413 HMRC Business Income Manual BIM 42528
Procurement fees	Procuring others to enter into a tax avoidance scheme was not considered to be a trade.	*Ransom v Higgs* (1974) 50 TC 1, [1974] STC 539, [1974] 1 WLR 1594, [1974] 3 All ER 949
Professional fees	Professional fees are not allowable if they are of a capital nature or excluded by statute. Costs of an unsuccessful planning application were held to be capital expenditure.	HMRC Business Income Manual BIM 46405 *ECC Quarries Ltd v Watkis* (1975) 51 TC 153, [1975] STC 578, [1975] 3 All ER 843; *Moore (A & G) & Co v Hare* (1941) 6 TC 572
Professional negligence	Insurance policy premiums to cover professional negligence and employee indemnity risks are usually allowable as a deduction.	HMRC Business Income Manual BIM 45515, BIM 45520
Provisions	If a provision in the accounts satisfies the following requirements: (a) it has been estimated with reasonable accuracy, (b) it does not conflict with any statutory rules, (c) it relates to revenue and not capital expenditure, and (d) agrees with UK GAAP	HMRC Business Income Manual BIM 46510, BIM 46555 *RTZ Oil & Gas Ltd v Ellis* (1987) 61 TC 132, [1987] STC 512, [1987] 1 WLR 1442

Item	Explanation	References
	and FRS 12 principles, it may be allowable (see **17.15**). Case law has disallowed provision in accounts held to be capital expenditure. A company's provisions calculation was held to be insufficiently accurate. To comply with FRS 12, it may be necessary to discount the provision to present value if it is material.	*Owen v Southern Railway of Peru Ltd* (1956) 36 TC 602, [1957] AC 334, [1956] 2 All ER 728 BIM 46525
Purchase of own shares	Fees in relation to raising equity finance, including purchase of own shares, are capital expenses and are not deductible.	HMRC Business Income Manual BIM 46425
Removal expenses	Reasonable employee removal costs due to an employee's change of residence at the employer's request are allowable. Usually, where transactions are completed without delay, profits arising from the purchase and sale of the employee's earlier residence are taxed as a trading receipt and losses as an allowable deduction. Expenses incurred by a company moving to new premises are allowed in most cases.	HMRC Business Income Manual BIM 42531 BIM 42530
Renewal of short lease	Costs in relation to renewal of a short lease (less than 50 years to run) are revenue and allowable. Otherwise, the amounts are capital.	HMRC Business Income Manual BIM 46420
Rent and rates	Costs associated with a company's premises, including rent, rates, repairs and insurance, will normally be allowed.	HMRC Business Income Manual BIM 46801, BIM 46810
Repairs and renewals	Repair costs are normally regarded as revenue expenditure. Repair by replacement of	HMRC Business Income Manual BIM 46900, BIM 46903, BIM 46904, BIM 46906

Item	Explanation	References
	the whole asset is capital expenditure. Mere replacement of parts that are defective by the renewal of those parts is considered to be revenue expenditure. Note the concept of 'entirety' used by courts. Any repair expenditure resulting in an improvement or upgrade to an asset is capital expenditure (see **5.11**).	*Brown v Burnley Football & Athletic Co Ltd* (1980) 53 TC 357, [1980] STC 424, [1980] 3 All ER 244; *Transco plc v Dyall* [2002] STC (SCD) 199
Security expenditure	Where a company needs to protect its employee from a special security threat, because of the nature of the company's business, then the revenue expenditure incurred in providing the required security measures are likely to be allowed if all the qualifying conditions are met under *ITTOIA 2005, s 81*.	HMRC Business Income Manual BIM 47301, BIM 47305, BIM 47310 and BIM 47315
Sponsorship costs	Sponsorship costs are allowable in arriving at the profits of a company, unless they are considered to be capital expenditure or the expenditure is not made wholly and exclusively for business purposes, in which case it is specifically disallowed. If sponsorship contains an element of hospitality, this is disallowable under *CTA 2009, ss 1298* and *1299*. Sums paid as sponsorship to support the personal hobbies and pastimes of a shareholder's family were held not to be deductible from trading profits.	HMRC Business Income Manual BIM 42555, BIM 42560, BIM 42565 *Executive Network (Consultants) Ltd v O'Connor* [1996] STC (SCD) 29
Take-over costs	The acquirer's fees in relation to take-overs are normally capital and disallowable. The target's fees are capital if in	HMRC Business Income Manual BIM 46460, BIM 38260

Item	*Explanation*	*References*
	relation to the structure, but revenue if in connection with protecting the trade.	
Tax appeals	The cost of a tax appeal, even if successful, is not deductible. Additional accountancy expenses incurred as a result of 'in-depth' examination by HMRC will be allowed if this results in no discrepancies. If there are discrepancies, the costs are not allowable, even if the investigation reveals no addition to profits. Costs of an appeal before the Special Commissioners were disallowed.	*Allen v Farquharson Bros & Co* (1932) 17 TC 59 HMRC Business Income Manual BIM 37840
Tied petrol stations	Exclusivity payments made to retailers by petroleum companies were allowed in computing the petroleum companies' profits. In the hands of the retailer, they were held to be trading receipts rather than capital receipts.	*Bolam v Regent Oil Co Ltd* (1956) 37 TC 56, [1956] TR 403; *Tanfield Ltd v Carr* [1999] STC (SCD) 213
Training, education and welfare	A company's expenditure on training, education and welfare is normally allowed.	HMRC Business Income Manual BIM 47080; BIM 47610
Travel and subsistence	Reasonable expenses incurred by an employee on an occasional business journey (or overnight subsistence and accommodation when away from home on business) may be allowed.	HMRC Business Income Manual BIM 47705
Unsuccessful applications	The expenses of unsuccessful applications for licences were held to be not allowable—the company accepted that expenses of successful applications are capital. Costs for variation of a licence were not an allowable deduction.	*Southwell v Savill Bros* (1901) 4 TC 430, [1901] 2 KB 349; *Pyrah v Annis & Co Ltd* (1956) 37 TC 163, [1957] 1 WLR 190, [1957] 1 All ER 196

Item	Explanation	References
Valuations	The costs of valuations for accounts purposes, or as required by the *Companies Act*, are allowable. Valuations in connection with a company reconstruction are not allowable.	HMRC Business Income Manual BIM 42540
VAT	VAT penalties and repayment supplements are not deductible.	HMRC Business Income Manual BIM 31610

RECEIPTS NOT TAXABLE AS TRADING INCOME

Commercial occupation of woodlands

5.48   The commercial occupation of woodlands in the UK is not a trade or part of a trade and the profits arising are ignored for corporation tax purposes. Woodlands are occupied on a commercial basis if they are managed on a commercial basis, and with a view to the realisation of profits (*CTA 2009, ss 37, 208* and *980*).

Credit unions

5.49   Credit unions are cooperative financial institutions that are owned and operated by their members. Loans to members and the investment of surplus funds are not regarded as the carrying on of a trade or part of a trade (*CTA 2009, s 40*).

RECEIPTS TAXABLE AS TRADING INCOME

Trade debts released

5.50   If a trade debt that has been written off against trade profits is subsequently released, either in whole or in part, and the release is not part of a statutory insolvency arrangement, the amount released is treated as a receipt in calculating the profits of the trade for the accounting period in which the release is effected (*CTA 2009, s 94*).

Reverse premiums

5.51   If the company tenant receives a payment from its landlord as an inducement from a new landlord in respect of a property transaction that it or a connected party has entered into, it will be taxable on the company as income. This is if the transaction gives the company or a connected party an entitlement to an estate, interest or right in or over the property and the amount is paid by the grantor of the lease himself or his connected party or a nominee acting on his behalf (*CTA 2009, s 96*). Payments in connection with the sale of a person's principal private residence, or from sale and leaseback arrangements, are not considered to be reverse premiums. Neither is a receipt that reduces expenditure for capital allowances (*CTA 2009, s 97*). A reverse premium is a revenue receipt of the trade, if the property transaction was entered into for the purposes of the trade. If no trade is carried on, the premium is taxable as property income – see **12.24** (*CTA 2009, s 98*).

Non-arm's-length transactions between connected parties are always treated as taking place at market value when the property transaction is first entered into (*CTA 2009, s 99*). For this, persons are connected if they are connected at any time during the period in which the property arrangements are entered into (*CTA 2009, s 100*). 'Connection' is defined in accordance with *CTA 2009, s 1316* (see **4.34**)

Property income treated as trading income

5.52   In general, companies are charged to corporation tax on property income arising from the letting of land and property (see **12.19–12.33**). Income from land and buildings is included in box 11 of the company tax return, and losses are recorded in box 26.

However, certain property income is treated as trading income.

Tied premises

5.53   Where a company carries on a trade in tied premises in which it has an interest, receipts and expenses of the premises are brought into account in computing the profits of the trade. Non-trade amounts are apportioned on a just and reasonable basis (*CTA 2009, s 42*).

Caravan sites where trade carried on

5.54   A company that owns a caravan site may carry on activities that amount to a trade, such as a shop or a café; if so, receipts from the letting of caravans are also treated as trading income. In normal circumstances, income from the letting of caravans is not a trade (*CTA 2009, s 43*).

Surplus business accommodation

5.55   If a company lets or grants a licence to occupy part of its premises where it carries on its trade, and the letting income therefrom is relatively small, that letting income can be included in the company's trading income. This is on the understanding that the premises are not part of the company's trading stock and that the premises are temporarily surplus to the company's trading requirements.

A company will meet the 'temporarily surplus to requirements' condition only if:

● the accommodation has been used within the last three years to carry on the trade or acquired within the last three years;

● the trader intends to use it to carry on the trade at a later date, and

● the letting is for a term of not more than three years.

Accommodation that is temporarily surplus to requirements at the beginning of an accounting period remains so until the end of that period, and all income from the relevant letting must be treated in the same way (*CTA 2009, s 44*).

Payments for wayleaves

5.56   If a company carries on a trade on some or all of the land to which a wayleave relates, the rental income and the expenses in respect of that wayleave can be included in calculating the profits of the company's trade, even if it would normally be assessable as property income under *CTA 2009, s 277*. This is on the condition that no income or expenses in respect of the land are included in a property business carried on by the trader.

For this purpose, a wayleave is an easement, servitude or right in or over land in connection with:

● an electric, telegraph or telephone wire or cable (including the supporting pole or pylon and apparatus used);

● a pipe for the conveyance of any thing, or

● any apparatus used in connection with such a pipe.

The company may still treat the income as trading income (*CTA 2009, s 45*).

Qualifying holiday accommodation

5.57   The commercial letting of furnished holiday accommodation is treated as a trade (*CTA 2009, s 265*). For this to occur, certain conditions apply. In a relevant period, the property must be:

- available for holiday letting to the public on a commercial basis for 140 days or more, and

- let commercially for 70 days or more, and

- not occupied for more than 31 days by the same person in any period of seven months (*CTA 2009, s 267*).

The relevant period is normally the accounting period concerned. If the property was not let as furnished accommodation in the prior accounting period, the 12-month relevant period commences with the date in the accounting period in question that it commenced the furnished holiday letting business. If the property was let as furnished accommodation in the 12 months immediately after the end of the accounting period, the relevant period is 12 months ending with the last day in the accounting period on which it is let by the company as furnished accommodation (*CTA 2009, s 266*). As the income is treated as a trade, loss relief is available but group relief is not available (*CA 2009, s 269(2)(b)*).

These rules apply to UK property businesses only. HMRC have decided that, as these rules may not be compliant with European law, they will be withdrawn from 2010/11. In the meantime, HMRC will treat the rules as being available for all property in the EEA area (HMRC Technical Note, 23 April 2009).

ACTIVITIES TREATED AS A TRADE BY STATUTE

Farming and market gardening

5.58   Farming or market gardening carried on in the UK is treated as a trade or part of a trade, regardless of whether or not the land is managed on a commercial basis and with a view to the realisation of profits. Furthermore, all farming that a company carries on in the UK is treated as one trade, unless the farming is part of another, non-farming trade (*CTA 2009, s 36*).

This does not apply to farming or market gardening by an insurance company on land which is an asset of the company's long-term insurance fund. If the company is a partner in a firm, any farming that is carried on by the firm is not included in any farming trade of the company (*CTA 2009, s 1270(1)*).

Commercial occupation of land other than woodlands

5.59   The commercial occupation of land other than woodlands in the UK is treated as the carrying on of a trade or part of a trade. Land other than woodlands is occupied on a commercial basis if it is managed on a commercial basis, and with a view to the realisation of profits.

Land other than woodlands does not consist of:

- land used for farming or market gardening, see **5.58**;

- land that is being prepared for forestry purposes,;

- commercial woodlands, see **5.48** or

- land occupied by an insurance company of land which is an asset of its long-term insurance fund (*CTA 2009, s 38*).

Profits of mines, quarries and other concerns

5.60   Profits from mines, quarries and other concerns are treated as a trade; these activities are detailed as follows:

- mines and quarries (including gravel pits, sand pits and brickfields);

- ironworks, gasworks, salt springs or works, alum mines or works;

- waterworks and streams of water;

- canals, inland navigation, docks and drains or levels;

- rights of fishing;

- rights of markets and fairs, tolls, bridges and ferries; and

- railways and other kinds of way.

However, concerns carried on by an insurance company on land that is an asset of the company's long-term insurance fund are not included, or if the land is deemed to be commercially occupied other than for woodlands – see **5.6** (*CTA 2009, s 39*).

APPROPRIATIONS OF PROFIT

5.61   Appropriations of profits, ie a distribution or dividend payment, are not deductible from profits. UK corporation tax payments themselves are not deductible, and neither are payments from which tax has been deducted at source. Depreciation is disallowed, but capital allowances are deductible as a trading expense (*CAA 2001, s 352*).

Only the depreciation charged in the profit and loss account must be added back in the corporation tax computation, regardless of any other entry (*Revenue and Customs Comrs v William Grant & Sons Distillers Ltd Small (Inspector of Taxes) v Mars UK Ltd* [2007 All ER (D) 459 (Mar). See also HMRC Business Income Manual BIM 33190.

VALUATION OF STOCKS AND WORK IN PROGRESS

Meaning of trading stock

5.62 The valuation of closing stock has a direct impact on final profits. The higher the closing stock valuation, the higher the reported profits.

Trading stock includes finished goods and work in progress. Trading stock is defined as anything which is sold in the ordinary course of the trade, or which would be so sold if it were mature or its manufacture, preparation or construction were complete. Raw materials and services are not included (*CTA 2009, s 156*). If a company follows GAAP, its stock valuation should be acceptable, being generally the lower of cost and net realisable value. See **Chapter 17** for SSAP 9 and IAS 2. For accounting periods ended after 22 June 2005, companies were required to make a corporation tax adjustment in respect of their professional work in progress. See *Corporation Tax 2008/09* (Tottel Publishing) for details.

Valuation of transfers to and from trading stock

5.63 Case law has determined that the market value rule applies where goods are acquired or appropriated into trading stock, other than in the course of a trade (*Sharkey v Wernher* (1955) 36 TC 275; [1956] AC 58; [1955] 3 All ER 493). *CTA 2009, ss 157* and *158* give statutory effect to these rules.

If any stock is used for non-trade purposes, a taxable receipt is deemed to accrue to the company, equal to the market value of that stock at that time. Any actual receipt is then left out of account (*CTA 2009, s 157(2)*).

Similarly, any item which the company already owns, that it transfers as a finished good or work in progress into stock, is to be valued at market value at the date of transfer (*CTA 2009, s 159*). If an item of stock has been acquired by other means than in the normal course of trade and the transfer pricing rules apply, the transfer pricing valuation will take precedence, which will normally agree with the market valuation (*CTA 2009, ss 160* and *161*).

Valuation of trading stock on the cessation of a trade

5.64   Subject to any transfer-pricing override, the valuation of the closing stock upon the permanent cessation of a trade is dependent upon the seller's relationship to the purchaser (*CTA 2009, s 164*). In this connection, trading stock includes finished goods, work in progress and raw materials, together with the value of any services included therein. The sale includes the transfer of any benefits and rights which accrue, or might reasonably be expected to accrue, from the performance of any such services (*CTA 2009, s 163*). Incomplete services upon the cessation of a company's trade are included in its trading stock (*CTA 2009, s 163(2)*).

Upon cessation of the trade, trading stock is generally valued at its open market price, but special rules apply to sales to: an unconnected person; a connected person; and a connected person where an election is made.

Sale to unconnected person:

- If the sale is to a person carrying on or intending to carry on a trade in the UK where the stock can be deducted as an expense in calculating the profit, the stock is valued at selling price, being the amount realised on the sale. If the stock is sold with other assets, the amount realised on the sale is apportioned on a just and reasonable basis (*CTA 2009, s 165*).

Sale to connected person:

- If the sale is to a buyer connected with the seller who carries on or intends to carry on a trade in the UK where the stock can be deducted as an expense in calculating the profit, the stock is valued at open market value, being the value which would have been realised if the sale had been between independent persons dealing at arm's length (*CTA 2009, s 166*).

Election by connected persons:

- If the open market value of the stock sold exceeds the acquisition cost and the realised proceeds, the buyer and the seller may jointly elect, within two years after the end of the accounting period in which the cessation occurred, for the stock to be valued at the greater of the acquisition cost and realised proceeds (*CTA 2009, s 167*).

Persons can be connected in any one of the following circumstances:

- within the meaning of *ICTA 1988, s 839* (see **4.25**);
- where a company has a share or the right to a share of the assets of an unincorporated business;
- where a company is controlled by another party;

- where the income and asset sharing rights of two unincorporated businesses belong to a third person;

- where either two companies or an unincorporated business and a company are controlled by the other party or both are under the control of a third party (*CTA 2009, s 168*).

Whatever basis the seller adopts in valuing the closing stock upon the cessation of its trade, the buyer will adopt for inclusion as opening stock in its respective trade (*CTA 2009, s 169*). If a transfer of stock is made instead of a sale, the transaction is treated as if it were a sale (*CTA 2009, s 170*). Questions arising from a stock valuation are to be determined in the same way as an appeal (*CTA 2009, s 171*).

CHANGE IN BASIS OF ACCOUNTING

5.65 A company may change its accounting basis from UK GAAP to IFRS, or vice versa, or from a realisation basis to a 'mark to market' basis (*CTA 2009, s 180*). If the last period of account before the change is calculated on the old basis, and the first period of account after the change on the new basis, an adjustment will be required to reconcile the two bases.

A positive adjustment is treated as a taxable trade receipt, and a negative adjustment as a deductible expense, both arising on the first day of the accounting period for which the new basis is adopted. The procedure for calculating the adjustment is contained in *CTA 2009, s 182*. Essentially, receipts and expenses before the change are recalculated on the new basis.

Calculation of the adjustment

5.66 The two bases are compared, and amounts that represent profit understatements and loss overstatements are totalled in Step 1, and the amounts that represent profit overstatements and loss understatements are totalled in Step 2.

The amounts are—

Step 1	Step 2
1. Receipts which would have been brought into account in calculating the profits of the earlier period of account, had they been calculated on the new basis, to the extent that they were not brought into account.	Receipts which were brought into account in the earlier period of account before the change, insofar as they have been brought into account again in calculating the profits on the new basis.

Step 1
2. Expenses brought into account in calculating the profits of the later period, insofar as they were brought into account in calculating the profits of the earlier period.

Step 2
Expenses which were not brought into account in calculating the profits of the earlier period, insofar as they would have been brought into account had the old basis been applied to the later period.

3. The amount by which the value of the opening stock and work in progress of the later period exceeds the value of the closing stock and work in progress of the earlier period.

The amount by which the value of the opening stock and work in progress of the later period falls below the value of the closing stock and work in progress of the earlier period.

4. Depreciation charged in the later period not adjusted for corporation tax purposes but would have been required to be adjusted on the new basis.

Subject to the following additional rules regarding expenses previously brought into account, the adjustment is found by deducting the Step 2 total from the Step 1 total (*CTA 2009, s 182*).

Expenses previously brought into account

5.67   No adjustment is made where the old basis of calculation allowed a tax deduction, but the new basis requires the deduction to be spread over several periods (*CTA 2009, s 183*).

Certain tax adjustments are required to be made in certain periods of account. These are:

Adjustment		*Period in which the adjustment is made*
Closing stock	–	the last period of account before the change.
Opening stock	–	the first period of account on the new basis.
Depreciation	–	when the asset to which it relates is realised or written off.

(*CTA 2009, s 184*)

On a change from a realisation basis to a 'mark to market' basis, a company carrying on the trade may elect for any receipt treated as arising to be spread equally over six periods of account. The election must be made within 12 months of the end of the first accounting period to which the new basis applies. If the trade subsequently ceases, any amounts not accounted for are to be brought into account in calculating the profits of the trade immediately before the cessation (*CTA 2009, ss 185* and *186*).

POST-CESSATION RECEIPTS

5.68   A post-cessation receipt is an amount that the company receives in respect of its prior trading activities after it has permanently ceased to carry on a trade (*CTA 2009, s 190*).

The recovery of trade debts is included, and allowance is granted for any release (*CTA 2009, ss 192* and *193*). Corporation tax is charged on post-cessation receipts as profits of a trade if it has not been charged elsewhere (*CTA 2009, s 189*).

If the company permanently ceased to carry on its trade and sold the right to receive sums from the trade to a third party, if that third party does not carry on the trade the company is treated as receiving a post-cessation receipt (*CTA 2009, s 194*).

On an arm's-length sale, the post-cessation receipt is taken to be the sale proceeds and, on a sale not at arm's length, the arm's-length value is substituted (*CTA 2009, s 194*). If the valuation of closing stock is brought into account upon cessation, any receipts therefrom are not post-cessation receipts (*CTA 2009, s 195*).

Allowable deductions

5.69   Deductions which would have been allowed had the company been trading at the time are allowed against post-cessation receipts (*CTA 2009, s 196*). Losses are deducted from post-cessation receipts from an earlier period before a later period (*CTA 2009, s 197*).

If the company receives a post-cessation receipt in an accounting period beginning not later than six years after the company permanently ceased to carry on the trade, it may elect that the tax chargeable in respect of the receipt is to be charged as if the receipt had been received on the date of the cessation. This election must be made within a period of two years beginning immediately after the end of the accounting period in which the receipt is received, provided there is sufficient income to relieve (*CTA 2009, ss 198* and *199*).

If a company makes an election under *s 198*, the additional tax is payable for the accounting period in which the receipt is received, and not for the accounting period in which the cessation occurred (*CTA 2009, s 200*).

Example 5.5

The following example is illustrative of a corporation tax computation.

Sebastian Ltd is a trading company with the following results. There are no associated companies:

Profit and loss account for the year to 31 March 2010:

	£000	£000
Gross profit		900
Interest on bank deposit	70	
Property income	30	
Profit on sale of UK quoted shares	10	
		110
		1,010
Less:		
Directors' remuneration	100	
Salaries	80	
Repairs	40	
Advertising and promotion	20	
Depreciation	100	
Miscellaneous expenses	50	
Goodwill amortisation	2	
		392
Profit before taxation		618

Miscellaneous expenses:	
Customer entertaining	10
Donation to political party	10
Staff entertaining	14
Christmas gifts:	
5,000 key rings with company name	5
Cigars	1
Other expenses (all allowable)	10
	50

The goodwill was acquired on 1 April 2003 (see **Chapter 7**)

Capital allowances for the year, including the annual investment allowance, amount to £60,000. The chargeable gain on the sales of UK quoted shares is £5,000. The company received no franked investment income.

Adjusted profits for the year ended 31 March 2010:

	£000	£000
Trade Profits:		
Net profit per accounts		618
Add:		
Depreciation	100	
Customer entertaining	10	
Political donation	10	
Gifts—cigars	1	
		121
		739
Less:		
Bank interest	70	
Profit on sale of shares	30	
Property income	10	
Capital allowances	60	170
Trade profits		569

Corporation tax computation for the year ended 31 March 2010:

	£000
Trade profits	569
Loan relationship	70
Chargeable gains	5
PCTCT	644

Corporation tax payable:

	£000
£644,000 at 28%	180,320
Less: 7/400 × (1,500,000 − 644,000)	11,270
Corporation tax liability	169,050

BODIES GRANTED EXEMPTION FROM CORPORATION TAX ON TRADING INCOME

Charities

5.70 Various exemptions are available to a company that meets the charitable status criteria provided by the Charities Commission (*ICTA 1988,* *s 505*). Trading income will be exempt from corporation tax in limited circumstances. Exemption applies if the profits from the trade are applied solely for the purposes of the charity. The trade must be exercised in the course of carrying out a primary purpose of a charity and the work in connection with the trade is mainly carried out by the beneficiaries of the charity (*ICTA 1988, s 505(1)*), eg exhibition profits of a local history society. If a charity franchises its trading activities and receives royalty payments, these will be exempt from tax (*ICTA 1988, s 505(1)(c)(ii)*).

Often, a charity will form a trading subsidiary for the purpose of carrying out all its trading activities that do not meet the exceptions tests. Such a company's income will be taxable, but it can arrange to Gift Aid it to the charity and obtain relief as a non-trading charge on income. The payment to the charity can be made up to nine months after the end of the accounting period (*ICTA 1988, s 339(7AA)*).

5.71   If the profits are not applied solely for the purposes of the charity, the profits are taxable. However, in respect of chargeable periods beginning on or after 22 March 2006, apportionment is available. Where a trade is exercised partly in the course of the actual carrying out of a primary purpose of the charity and partly otherwise, each part is treated as a separate trade. Expenses and receipts are to be apportioned on a reasonable basis (*FA 2006, s 56*).

The separate trade basis also applies where work in connection with the trade is carried out partly, but not mainly, by beneficiaries. Expenses and receipts are apportioned on a reasonable basis.

5.72   If a charity has activities unrelated to its primary purpose, it may operate these through a subsidiary company. A subsidiary company with charity parent companies is able to Gift Aid its profits to its parent by making a charge on income under *ICTA 1988, s 339*.

Cash gifts to charities

5.73   There is no requirement for the company to deduct basic rate income tax for the payment (unlike payments by individuals). The charity, in turn, does not recover any tax from the receipt (*ICTA 1988, s 349(1B)*).

Benefits received

5.74   Close company payments will not qualify as Gift Aid payments if they are subject to conditions that the company is to receive a repayment to the company, or a connected party is to receive benefits in excess of £250 in total. The actual benefits receivable are based on the formula:

Total donations in year	De minimis limit of benefits
£0–£100	25% of value of gift
£101–£1,000	£25
£1,001–£10,000	2.5% of value of gift

(ICTA 1988, Sch 20)

Non-cash gift to charities

5.75   Companies may make gifts of trading stock or plant and machinery to a charity. There is no requirement to show the trading stock disposal in the corporation tax computation or the plant and machinery disposal in the capital allowances computation.

MUTUAL COMPANIES

Mutual trading

5.76   As a person cannot trade with himself or herself, a mutual trader is not liable to tax on any profits arising from their 'mutual' trade.

Mutual trading is a situation whereby an organisation is controlled by the people who use its services. Those, in effect, who contribute to an activity are its sole participators. Arrangements must be in place to ensure that any surplus ultimately finds its way back to the contributors, with no arrangements for it to go to anybody else. Rules that include a winding-up surplus to be gifted to charity will not support mutual trading. Donations to charity are permitted, provided the gift is approved by all members.

In normal circumstances, the *Companies Act* states that, in the event of a winding–up, any surplus available to distribute to members will be distributed pro rata to shareholding.

The normal rules also provide that any such distribution will only be to the members on the register at that time.

For mutual trading purposes, it will be necessary to amend the Articles of Association to state that, on a winding–up, any surplus available for distribution will be returned to contributors in a reasonable proportion to their contribution to that surplus; and that any distribution will also need to include contributors who have left in the last five years.

MEMBERS' SPORTS CLUBS

5.77   Members' sports clubs would normally fall outside the scope of Schedule D Case I. This is because they are usually established by the members for their own social or recreational objects, and any surplus is for distribution amongst the members. They are, therefore, not trading. Services provided commercially to non-members may constitute a trading activity. Expenditure should be allocated on a reasonable basis, but costs specifically in relation to members are not deductible against the non-member-related trading income. Other income received, such as interest or rents, will be taxed in the normal way.

COMMUNITY AMATEUR SPORTS CLUBS (CASCS)

CASC conditions

5.78   Reliefs are available to a community amateur sports club that may register as a CASC, provided certain conditions are satisfied: (1) it is open to the whole community, (2) it is organised on an amateur basis, and (3) its main purpose is the provision of facilities for, and the promotion of participation in, one or more eligible sports (*FA 2002, Sch 18, para 1*).

A club is open to the whole community if membership of the club is open to all without discrimination. Club facilities must be available to members without discrimination, and any fees must be set at a level that does not pose a significant obstacle to membership or use of the club's facilities (*FA 2002, Sch 18, para 2(1)*).

A club is organised on an amateur basis if it is non-profit making and it provides, for members and guests only, the ordinary benefits of an amateur sports club. The constitution must provide for any net assets on dissolution to be applied for approved sporting or charitable purposes (*FA 2002, Sch 18, para 3*).

CASC reliefs

5.79   The CASC may apply for exemption from corporation tax on the following income, provided that it is applied for a qualifying purpose – the qualifying purpose being 'providing facilities for and promoting participation in one or more eligible sports' (*FA 2002, Sch 18, para 16(b)*):

- trading income not exceeding £30,000 (*FA 2002, Sch 18, para 4*);
- interest income and Gift Aid income (*FA 2002, Sch 18, para 5*);

- rental income not exceeding £20,000 (*FA 2002, Sch 18, para 6*); and

- chargeable gains (*FA 2002, Sch 18, para 7*).

Where any income or gains are spent for non-qualifying purposes, the tax exemption is reduced proportionately (*FA 2002, Sch 18, para 8*).

Donor reliefs

5.80   Gifts to a CASC will constitute a charity for Gift Aid and inheritance tax purposes.

CORPORATION TAX SELF-ASSESSMENT

5.81   Clubs and mutual companies are required to self-assess for corporation tax, unless they have agreed otherwise with HMRC. HMRC will prevent the issue of notice to file returns to clubs where the annual corporation tax liability is not expected to exceed £100, and the club or unincorporated association is run exclusively for the benefit of its own members.

The club or unincorporated association will be treated as dormant, but will be subject to a review that will take place at least every five years.

This practice does not apply to: privately owned clubs and unincorporated associations run as commercial enterprises; housing associations or registered social landlords, as designated in the *Housing and Planning Act 1986*; trade associations; thrift funds; holiday clubs; friendly societies; and any company which is a subsidiary of, or wholly owned by, a charity.

For each year of dormancy, the body must have no anticipated allowable trading losses or chargeable assets likely to be disposed of or anticipated payments from which tax is deductible and payable to HMRC.

A flat-owning property management company is also able to benefit from this practice if the company is not entitled to receive income from land and makes no distributions.

The company will be liable to income tax on any interest that it earns from holding service charges on trust received from tenants under *Landlord and Tenant Act 1987, s 42*. The company will be within income tax self-assessment and may be required to make a return to the relevant Trust Office. Income is chargeable at the special trust rates (40% for bank interest) except for the first £1,000, which remains chargeable at basic rates (20% for bank interest).

5.81 *Trading income*

Generally, where the income is below £1,000 and taxed at source, a return will not be required every year (Revenue Announcement, 25 August 2006).

A CASC must give details of its income on supplementary pages CT600E (reproduced in the appendices), which also enables it to recover income tax on its Gift Aid receipts.

Chapter 6

Tangible fixed assets

ACCOUNTANCY TREATMENT

6.1   A company's fixed assets are disclosed in the balance sheet according to the *Companies Act 2006* and to Generally Accepted Accounting Principles (GAAP). The GAAP applied will either be FRSSE or FRS 15 (tangible fixed assets) when using UK GAAP or IAS 16 (property, plant & equipment). Investment properties are accounted for under the FRSSE SSAP 19 (accounting for investment properties) or IAS 40 (investment property). *Companies Act 2006* accounting rules are effective from 6 April 2008. See the *Small Companies and Groups (Accounts and Directors Report) Regulations 2008, SI 2008/409* and the *Large and Medium-sized Companies and Groups (Accounts and Reports) Regulations 2008, SI 2008/410.* These regulations replace *Companies Act 1985, Sch 4.*

FRS 15 defines tangible fixed assets as assets with physical substance that are held for use in the production or supply of goods or services for rental to others or for administrative purposes on a continuing basis in the activities of the reporting entity.

Tangible fixed assets are reported at cost less depreciation at a rate that reflects the economic consumption of the asset by the entity.

TAXATION TREATMENT

6.2   The taxation system maintains the capital/revenue divide for capital assets. This principle was established in *In Re Robert Addie & Sons* CE 1875, 1 TC 1, 12 SLR 274; *Coltness Iron Co v Black* HL 1881, 1 TC 287, 6 AC 315 and *Leeming v Jones* HL 1930, 15 TC 333, (1930) AC 415. Depreciation calculated for accounting purposes is not allowable deduction against income for taxation purposes. Instead, the taxation system grants its own form of depreciation on qualifying assets through the capital allowance and annual investment allowance systems. By claiming capital allowances, a company can deduct capital expenditure from its business profits over a period of years. The system has been amended by various governments to help UK industry develop.

Rules based on safeguarding the environment are steadily being introduced into the taxation system. Expenditure on energy saving and environmentally friendly assets receive the maximum relief. Reliefs are also available for innovative technologies (see **Chapter 8**).

When first introduced in 1945, capital allowances were designed to assist with the industrial regeneration of the UK's post-World War II economy.

Relief for expenditure on industrial buildings in the form of industrial buildings allowances (IBAs) and its mirror relief, agricultural buildings allowance (ABA) (ABAs are not covered in this book), is being removed over the period 1 April 2008 to 31 March 2011. Relief for expenditure on general plant and machinery is available to businesses, but the amounts are restricted.

QUALIFYING EXPENDITURE

Capital allowances claim

6.3   A company may claim capital allowances on its qualifying capital expenditure (*CAA 2001, s 1*). For corporation tax purposes, relief is given in an accounting period (*CAA 2001, s 6(1)(b)*).The reliefs given are a first year allowance (FYA), an annual investment allowance (AIA) (from 1 April 2008) a writing down allowance (WDA), an initial allowance (IA) (currently withdrawn) and a balancing allowance (BA). Capital allowance charges are referred to as balancing charges. The relief must be claimed (otherwise no relief is given) (*CAA 2001, s 3(1)*).

The allowances are claimed by including the amount of the claim in the respective boxes of the company tax return or an amended return. The company need not claim the full amount available. A company may choose either to make a reduced claim or not to claim at all if it wished to maximise a loss in a future accounting period (see **Chapter 9**). The claim is within the normal self-assessment corporation tax return time limits, being two years after the end of the accounting period concerned (*FA 1998, Sch 18, para 82*). The normal time limit is extended in such circumstances where there is an enquiry, amendment or appeal to 30 days after the respected closure notice, amendment or determination. HMRC have the power to extend the statutory time limits in exceptional circumstances, but have stated that they will not extend the time limits in respect of the following:

• A change of mind.

- Hindsight showing that a different combination of claims might be advantageous: for example, the group relief available may be lower than the company expected it to be when it claimed capital allowances. The company may then want to claim further capital allowances. But that is not a circumstance beyond the company's control. It could have claimed sooner.

- Oversight or error, whether on the part of the company or its advisers.

- Absence or indisposition of an officer or employee of the company unless:

  — the absence or illness arose at a critical time, which delayed the making of the claim;

  — in the case of absence, there was good reason why the person was unavailable at the critical time; or

  — there was no other person who could have made the claim on behalf of the company within the normal time limit (HMRC Capital Allowances Manual CA 11140).

HMRC have advised that many companies have requested that their industrial buildings allowance claim be withdrawn for past years by making an error or mistake claim (see **2.11**). HMRC have commented that there would have been a deliberate choice at the time to make the claim, in which case there could have been no mistake. Such claims have been refused (HMRC Brief 12/2009 31 March 2009). Capital allowances given in respect of a trade are deducted from trading income as an adjustment (see **5.43**). Balancing charges are added to trading income. Capital allowances in respect of non-trading activities are generally deducted primarily from the source of income to which they relate, eg property income. If the accounting period is less than 12 months, the WDA and the AIA (but not the FYA) are time-apportioned accordingly. If the accounting period is longer than 12 months, the chargeable period for capital allowance purposes is divided into 12-month periods and the remaining balance.

Capital expenditure incurred—timing

6.4   For the purposes of claiming the allowances, capital expenditure is incurred on the date on which the obligation to pay becomes unconditional even if there is a later payment date (*CAA 2001, s 5(1)*). Delivery of the goods is normally the time when the obligation to pay becomes unconditional. If the contractual payment period is longer than four months the expenditure is treated as incurred on the payment due date (*CAA 2001, s 4(5)*).

For works under contract, expenditure is incurred upon the issue of a certificate of work to date. If a certificate is issued within one month of the end of the accounting period but the asset has become the company's property before the end of the accounting period, the expenditure is deemed to have been incurred on the last day of the accounting period concerned (*CAA 2001, s 5(4)*). However, expenditure incurred before a trade begins is treated as incurred on the first day of trading.

Expenditure still to be incurred under a hire purchase etc contract at the time when the asset is brought into use is treated as incurred on the date on which the asset is brought into use. Expenditure incurred on the purchase of an unused building or structure is deemed to be incurred on the date on which the purchase price becomes payable (HMRC Capital Allowances Manual CA 11800). If a company is not registered for VAT, any VAT paid on the cost of the asset is taken into account when calculating the allowances. If an additional VAT liability is incurred or an additional VAT rebate arises this is treated as taking place on the last day of the relevant VAT interval.

Sales between connected parties are deemed to be made at market value (*CAA 2001, s 567*). Parties under common control may elect for the asset to be transferred at the lower of tax written down value or market value (*CAA 2001, s 569*).

Assets on which capital allowances may be claimed

6.5   The types of capital expenditure that attract a capital allowance claim are:

Para		CAA 2001
6.04	Plant and machinery	Part 2
	The construction of industrial buildings, qualifying hotels, commercial buildings in enterprise zones	Part 3
	The construction of agricultural buildings and works	Part 4
	Flat conversion allowances	Part 4A
	Mineral extraction	Part 5
	Research and development	Part 6
	Know-how	Part 7
	Patents	Part 8
	Dredging	Part 9
	Assured tenancies	Part 10

This chapter discusses plant and machinery (**6.6–6.44**), the annual investment allowance (**6.45-6.53**), leasing (**6.54-6.63**), industrial buildings

(**6.64–6.84**), business premises renovation allowances (**6.85–6.100**) and flat conversion allowances (**6.101–6.110**). Research and development is discussed in **Chapter 8**. Agricultural buildings allowance, mineral extraction and dredging are not discussed. Capital allowances are no longer available on know-how and patents. These are dealt with under the intangible assets regime (see **Chapter 7**) with effect from 1 April 2002. Capital allowances on assured tenancies are no longer available. Capital allowances may also be claimed on other types of expenditure such as agricultural buildings, mineral extraction, dredging etc but these types of expenditure are not covered in this text.

PLANT AND MACHINERY

Rates of allowances

6.6   Current capital allowance rates for plant and machinery are:

Incurred by	*Expenditure incurred*	*Allowance*	*Rate*
All companies	Energy saving plant or machinery	FYA	100%
	Energy service providers		
	Low CO_2 emission cars not exceeding 110g/km (120g/km prior to 1 April 2008)		
	Equipment for refuelling vehicles with natural gas or hydrogen fuel		
	North Sea oil ring-fence plant and machinery		
All companies	General plant and machinery		
	Temporary for expenditure incurred in the 12-month period beginning 1 April 2009	FYA	40%
All companies	Plant and machinery	WDA	20%
	Special rate expenditure		10%
All companies	Annual Investment Allowance	Maximum	£50,000

Subject to the necessary conditions, SMEs (Small and Medium-Sized Enterprises) and SEs (Small Enterprises) could claim FYAs on all their plant and machinery purchases, if the expenditure was incurred prior to 1 April 2008. For details, see *Corporation Tax 2008/09* (Tottel Publishing).

139

Qualifying expenditure

6.7 In order to be able to claim capital allowances for plant and machinery the company must incur qualifying expenditure on a qualifying activity (*CAA 2001, s 11(1)*). Qualifying expenditure is capital expenditure incurred on the provision of plant and machinery, wholly or partly for the purposes of the qualifying activity carried on by the company that incurs the expenditure. As a result of incurring the expenditure, the company 'owns' the asset (*CAA 2001, s 11(4)*).

A qualifying activity may consist of a trade, a property business, or a specialised activity such as a mining or quarrying or other activity giving rise to profits from land charged to tax as a trade in accordance with *CTA 2009, s 39(1)–(5)*, management of an investment company and special leasing business (*CAA 2001, s 15*).

Specific provisions relating to property businesses and investment companies are discussed in **Chapter 12**. This chapter deals with trades as well as the general allowance provisions.

6.8 Capital allowances can only be claimed on the cost of the plant and machinery itself, not the additional costs of interest or commitment fees (*Ben-Odeco Ltd v Powlson* (1978) 52 TC 459, [1978] STC 460, [1978] 1 WLR 1093, [1978] 2 All ER 1111). HMRC only allow professional fees and preliminary fees to be included within the cost on an asset for capital allowance purposes if they relate directly to the acquisition, transport and installation of the plant and machinery (HMRC Capital Allowances Manual CA 20070).

Expenditure on buildings and structures

6.9 In general, plant and machinery expenditure does not encompass expenditure on buildings and structures (*CAA 2001, s 21(1)*). Certain assets are not included in this general rule but, in order for a company to claim plant and machinery capital allowances, they still need to qualify as 'plant' in their own right.

A claim for plant and machinery capital allowances may be made for the following assets, which are not regarded as part of the fabric of the building:

- thermal insulation installed in industrial buildings;
- fire safety (until 1 April 2008);
- safety at designated sports grounds;
- safety at regulated stands at sports grounds;

- safety at other sports grounds;

- personal security;

- software and software rights; and

- integral features (see **6.17**), for expenditure incurred on or after 1 April 2008.

(CAA 2001, s 23(2))

The following items in 'List C' are, again, not regarded as part of the fabric of the building:

1   Machinery (including devices for providing motive power) not within any other item in this list.

2   Gas and sewerage systems provided mainly:

    (a)   to meet the particular requirements of the qualifying activity; or

    (b)   to serve particular plant or machinery used for the purposes of the qualifying activity.

    For expenditure incurred prior to 1 April 2008, electrical systems (including lighting systems) and cold water that meet the criteria above in (a) and (b).

3   *For expenditure incurred prior to 1 April 2008, space or water heating systems; powered systems of ventilation, air-cooling or air purification; and any floor or ceiling comprised in such systems.*

4   Manufacturing or processing equipment; storage equipment (including cold rooms); display equipment; and counters, checkouts and similar equipment.

5   Cookers, washing machines, dishwashers, refrigerators and similar equipment; washbasins, sinks, baths, showers, sanitary ware and similar equipment; and furniture and furnishings.

6   Hoists. *For expenditure incurred before 1 April 2008, lifts, hoists, escalators and moving walkways.*

7   Sound insulation provided mainly to meet the particular requirements of the qualifying activity.

8   Computer, telecommunication and surveillance systems (including their wiring or other links).

9   Refrigeration or cooling equipment.

10   Fire alarm systems; sprinkler and other equipment for extinguishing or containing fires.

11   Burglar alarm systems.

12   Strong rooms in bank or building society premises; safes.

13   Partition walls, where moveable and intended to be moved in the course of the qualifying activity.

14   Decorative assets provided for the enjoyment of the public in hotel, restaurant or similar trades.

15   Advertising hoardings; signs, displays and similar assets.

16   Swimming pools (including diving boards, slides and structures on which such boards or slides are mounted).

17   Any glasshouse constructed so that the required environment (namely, air, heat, light, irrigation and temperature) for the growing of plants is provided automatically by means of devices forming an integral part of its structure.

18   Cold stores.

19   Caravans provided mainly for holiday lettings.

20   Buildings provided for testing aircraft engines run within the buildings.

21   Moveable buildings intended to be moved in the course of the qualifying activity.

22   The alteration of land for the purpose only of installing plant or machinery.

23   The provision of dry docks.

24   The provision of any jetty or similar structure provided mainly to carry plant or machinery.

25   The provision of pipelines or underground ducts or tunnels with a primary purpose of carrying utility conduits.

26   The provision of towers to support floodlights.

27   The provision of:

(a)   any reservoir incorporated into a water treatment works; or

(b)   any service reservoir of treated water for supply within any housing estate or other particular locality.

28   The provision of:

(a)   silos provided for temporary storage; or

(b)   storage tanks.

29   The provision of slurry pits or silage clamps.

30   The provision of fish tanks or fish ponds.

31   The provision of rails, sleepers and ballast for a railway or tramway.

32   The provision of structures and other assets for providing the setting for any ride at an amusement park or exhibition.

33   The provision of fixed zoo cages.

Items 1 to 16 do not include any asset whose principal purpose is to insulate or enclose the interior of a building or to provide an interior wall, floor or ceiling which, in each case, is intended to remain permanently in place.

The following assets are treated as part of the structure of the building and not plant and machinery (*CAA 2001, s 21(3)*). It is not possible to make a claim for plant and machinery capital allowances in their respect:

1   Walls, floors, ceilings, doors, gates, shutters, windows and stairs.

2   Mains services and systems, for water, electricity and gas.

3   Waste disposal systems.

4   Sewerage and drainage systems.

5   Shafts or other structures in which lifts, hoists, escalators and moving walkways are installed.

6   Fire safety systems.

The meaning of plant

6.10   Plant owes its meaning to the development of case law. Plant was first defined in the case of *Yarmouth v France* (1887) 19 QBD 647 as 'whatever apparatus is used by a businessman for carrying on his business—not his stock in trade which he buys or makes for sale but all goods and chattels, fixed or moveable, live or dead, which he keeps for permanent employment in his business'. In other words the assets that enable a business to be carried on. This was confirmed as the functional test in the case of *Benson v Yard Arm Club Ltd* (1979) 53 TC 67, [1979] STC 266, [1979] 1 WLR 347, [1979] 2 All ER 336. Capital allowances were refused on the cost of purchasing and adapting a floating restaurant on the grounds that this was the place where the business was carried on rather than the tools that enable it to be carried on. HMRC regard assets with a life of more than two years as falling within the definition of plant: *Hinton v Madden & Ireland Ltd* (1959) 38 TC 391, [1959] 1 WLR 875, [1959] 3 All ER 356 (HMRC Capital Allowances Manual CA 21100). Whether the setting in which the business is carried on is plant is a question of fact. Lighting that was part of the setting but performed no function was not held to be plant: *J Lyons and Co Ltd v Attorney-General* [1944] 1 All ER 477. Moveable office partitions in a shipping agents office, which were often moved to enable the trade to be carried on, were held to be plant; the partitions performed a function (*Jarrold v John Good & Sons Ltd* (1962) 40 TC 681, [1963] 1 WLR 214, [1963] 1 All ER 141). The law has now been changed on this issue: see item 13 List C at **6.9**. HMRC comment that only moveable partitions that possess mobility as a matter of commercial necessity qualify as plant (HMRC Capital Allowances Manual CA 21120). The function test was also met in *Leeds Permanent Building Society v Proctor* (1982) 56 TC 293, [1982] STC 821, [1982] 3 All ER 925 whereby decorative screens in a building society window were held to be plant. *CIR v Scottish & Newcastle Breweries Ltd* (1982) 55 TC 252, [1982] STC 296, [1982] 1 WLR 322, [1982] 2 All ER 230 was a landmark case in its time. Decorative assets in a pub and restaurant were allowed as plant because they provided atmosphere and ambience, within that trade; proving that assets must be judged within the context of the trade. The law has now been changed on this issue: see item 14 List C at **6.9** HMRC comment that decorative items only qualify as plant if:

- the trade involves the creation of atmosphere/ambience and in effect the sale of that ambience to its customers; and

- the items on which plant or machinery allowances are claimed were specially chosen to create the atmosphere that the taxpayer is trying to sell (HMRC Capital Allowances Manual CA 21130).

HMRC particularly give the example of a painting hanging in an accountant's office not qualifying as plant because selling atmosphere is not part of an accountant's business. The point of course is debatable.

Lighting

6.11   Lighting installed in a building in order to make that building useable was not considered to be plant; it is part of the building. Lighting installed into a useable building to enable a trade to be carried on more effectively was considered to be plant (*Cole Bros v Phillips* (1982) 55 TC 188, [1982] STC 307, [1982] 1 WLR 1450, [1982] 2 All ER 247).

Wimpy International Ltd v Warland (1988) 61 TC 51, [1989] STC 273 generally upheld the decision in *CIR v Scottish & Newcastle Breweries Ltd*. In particular the cost of lighting in a restaurant was allowed because it provided atmosphere and ambience. Since then case law has moved to the function test and whether the piece of equipment is used within the trade. The tests applied in this case which HMRC also apply are:

Questions

1   Is the item stock in trade?

2   Is the item the business premises or part of the business premises (the premises test)?

3   Is the item used for carrying on the business (the business use test)?

Response

If the answers to questions 1 and 2 are negative and the answer to question 3 is positive the item is plant (HMRC Capital Allowances Manual CA 21010 and CA 21140).

In this case it was suggested in order to ascertain whether an asset was part of the premises the following four factors can be considered:

●   Does the item appear visually to retain a separate identity?

●   With what degree of permanence has it been attached to the building?

●   To what extent is the structure complete without it?

●   To what extent is it intended to be permanent or alternatively is it likely to be replaced within a short period?

HMRC accept that electrical installation is plant, if the installation is fully integrated, designed and adapted to meet the particular requirements of the trade, functions as apparatus of the trade and is essential for the functioning of the trade. If the installation fails to qualify as plant, HMRC will adopt a piecemeal approach. The same general and then piecemeal approach is applied to cold water, sewerage and gas systems.

In particular, HMRC will accept that the following elements of an electrical installation are plant:

●   the main switchboard, transformer and associated switchgear provided that a substantial part of the electrical installation—both the equipment and the ancillary wiring—qualifies as plant;

●   a standby generator and the emergency lighting and power circuits it services;

●   lighting in sales areas, if it is specifically designed to encourage the sale of goods on display;

●   wiring, control panels and other equipment installed specifically to supply equipment that is plant or machinery.

Lighting in a sales area will qualify even if there is no other lighting. The public areas in banking businesses are treated as sales areas (HMRC Capital Allowances Manual CA 21180). HMRC also accept that central heating systems, hot water systems, air conditioning systems, alarm and sprinkler systems, ventilation systems, baths, wash basins and toilet suites qualify as plant. Flooring and ceilings are generally considered not to be plant (HMRC Capital Allowances Manual CA 22070 and CA 22080).

Buildings alterations connected with installations of plant or machinery

6.12 Incidental capital expenditure on alterations to an existing building for the installation of plant and machinery for the purposes of the qualifying activity qualifies as plant (*CAA 2001, s 25*). A lift and its necessary wiring qualify as plant. Installation of a lift shaft in an existing building qualifies as plant. Installation of a lift shaft in a new building does not qualify as plant. Plant removal and re-erection costs qualify as plant if not allowable as a deduction from trading profits (HMRC Capital Allowances Manual CA 21190).

Demolition costs

6.13 Net demolition costs of plant and machinery that was last used for the purposes of a qualifying activity may either be added to the cost of the new plant if the plant is replaced, or added to other qualifying expenditure of the same chargeable period as the demolition if the plant is not replaced.

The net demolition costs are the costs of demolition less any money received for the remains of the asset or any insurance receipts (*CAA 2001, s 26*).

Expenditure on required fire precautions

6.14 Expenditure incurred on fire safety equipment such as fire alarms and sprinkler systems by law by a person carrying on a qualifying activity will normally qualify as plant or revenue expenditure. Capital expenditure incurred prior to 1 April 2008, by a business on fire safety equipment in order to meet the requirements of a prohibition order, qualified as plant (*CAA 2001, s 29; FA 2008, s 72*).

Computer software

6.15 Computer software is within the intangible assets regime. An election may be made under *CTA 2009, s 815(1)* for it to be treated as plant for capital allowance purposes within *CAA 2001, s 71*. The election must be made within two years from the end of an accounting period in which the expenditure was incurred.

Thermal insulation of buildings

6.16 Thermal installation is qualifying expenditure for capital allowance purposes. Expenditure incurred prior to 1 April 2008 only qualified if it was incurred in connection with an industrial building. Post 1 April 2008 the expenditure will qualify for a 10% special rate allowance (see **6.38**) if it is incurred by a company on a building used in carrying on one of the qualifying activities within *CAA 2001, s 15* (see **6.7**) (*CAA 2001, s 28(1)*), or on a building let by a property business or an overseas property business (*CAA 2001, s 28(2)*). A dwelling house does not qualify for an allowance (*CAA 2001, s 35*). If an energy savings deduction can be made under *CAA 2001, s 31ZA*, by which a landlord may claim a deduction for expenditure on acquiring and installing an energy-saving item in a dwelling-house or in a building containing the dwelling-house let by him in the course of his business (see **12.26**), no special rate allowance can be claimed (*CAA 2001, s 28(2B)(a)*).

Expenditure on integral features

6.17 A company incurring expenditure on or after 1 April 2008, on the provision or replacement of integral features on a building or structure may claim a 10% annual writing down allowance if the company meets the following conditions:

- it carries on a qualifying activity;

- it uses the building for the purposes of the qualifying activity;

- it owns the plant and machinery as a result of incurring the expenditure.

(*CAA 2001, s 33A(1), (2).*)

Integral features consist of:

- an electrical system (including a lighting system);

- a cold water system;

- a space or water heating system, a powered system of ventilation, air cooling or air purification, and any floor or ceiling comprised in such a system;

- a lift, an escalator or a moving walkway;

- external solar shading.

(*CAA 2001, s 33A(5)*)

Insulation expenditure is specifically excluded from the list. This is covered in *CAA 2001, s 28* (see **6.16**). In practice, some of these additions may also qualify as environmentally beneficial plant and machinery (see **6.21**), in which case the option is available to the company to claim one such allowance, but not both.

An integral feature is 'replaced' if, within 12 months from the time that the initial expenditure was incurred, more than 50% of its cost is spent on its replacement. It may be necessary to apportion the replacement expenditure between two accounting periods (*CAA 2001, s 33B(1)–(4)*). For practical purposes, if it is unknown whether a writing down allowance for the replacement of integral features can be made, the return may be filed and the allowance claimed at a later date (*CAA 2001, s 33B(5)*). A separate deduction for expenditure included in a writing down allowance claim cannot be made when computing the amount of profits chargeable to corporation tax under Case I or Case II of Schedule D (*ICTA 1988, s 74(1)(da)*).

Case law

6.18   There are a number of decided capital allowance cases, besides those mentioned above. A summary of which is given below:

Case	Asset	Held
Yarmouth v France (1887) 19 QBD 647	A horse	Plant
Benson v Yard Arm Club Ltd (1979) 53 TC 67, [1979] 1 WLR 347, [1979] 2 All ER 336	A floating restaurant	Not plant
J Lyons and Co Ltd v Attorney-General [1944] 1 All ER 477	Lighting—as part of the setting	Not plant
Jarrold v John Good & Sons Ltd (1962) 40 TC 681, [1963] 1 WLR 214, [1963] 1 All ER 141	Moveable office partitions	Plant
Leeds Permanent Building Society v Proctor (1982) 56 TC 293, [1982] STC 821, [1982] 3 All ER 925	Window screens—particular to the business	Plant
CIR v Scottish & Newcastle Breweries Ltd (1982) 55 TC 252, [1982] STC 296, [1982] 1 WLR 322, [1982] 2 All ER 230	Lighting and decor providing 'an atmosphere' necessary for the trade	Plant
Cole Bros v Phillips (1982) 55 TC 188, [1982] STC 307, [1982] 1 WLR 1450, [1982] 2 All ER 247	Certain electrical installations	Plant
	Others	Not plant

Case	Asset	Held
Wimpy International Ltd v Warland (1988) 61 TC 51, [1989] STC 273	Decorative items and certain specialist lighting	Plant
	Shop fronts	Not plant
Cooke v Beach Station Caravans Ltd (1974) 49 TC 514, [1974] STC 402, [1974] 1 WLR 1398, [1974] 3 All ER 159	Swimming pool used for a holiday caravan park	Plant
Hampton v Fortes Autogrill Ltd (1979) 53 TC 691, [1980] STC 80	False ceilings in a restaurant to conceal pipes and wires etc	Not plant
Grays v Seymours Garden Centre (Horticulture) (1995) 67 TC 401, [1995] STC 706	An unheated glass house— a planteria	Not plant
St John's (Mountford) v Ward (1974) 49 TC 524, [1975] STC 7	A pre-fabricated fixed school building	Not plant
Munby v Furlong (1977) 50 TC 491, [1976] 1 WLR 410, [1976] 1 All ER 753	A barrister's law books	Plant
Schofied v R & H Hall Ltd (1974) 49 TC 538, [1975] STC 353	Grain silos	Plant
Hinton v Maden & Ireland Ltd (1959) 38 TC 391, [1959] 1 WLR 875, [1959] 3 All ER 356	A shoe repairer's loose tools, knives and lasts—with an expected life of more than two years	Plant
Dixon v Fitch's Garages Ltd (1975) 50 TC 509, [1975] STC 480, [1976] 1 WLR 215, [1975] 3 All ER 455	A garage canopy to protect customers whilst vehicle refuelling	Not plant
Rose & Co (Wallpapers & Paints) Ltd v Campbell (1967) 44 TC 500, [1968] 1 WLR 346, [1968] 1 All ER 405	Wallpaper pattern books	Not plant

6.19 The expenditure is deemed to be incurred at cost on the first day of trading (*CAA 2001, s 12*). Expenditure is deemed to be incurred at the lesser of market value or cost at the date of a change of use if a change of use occurs (*CAA 2001, s 13*).

FIRST YEAR ALLOWANCE

6.20   Companies that invest in 'new' technologies, being energy-saving plant and machinery, receive a 100% first year allowance (FYA) on the full cost of their investment, provided all the necessary criteria are met (see **6.21** et seq). First year allowances on all other plant and machinery were withdrawn for all capital expenditure incurred after 31 March 2007, although they applied for another year to SMEs (small and medium-sized enterprises) and SEs (small enterprises), as defined in the *Companies Act* (see **1.13**). There is a temporary 40% FYA for capital expenditure incurred on general plant and machinery during the 12 months commencing 1 April 2009. Expenditure on long life assets (**6.34**) and integral features (**6.17**) is not included (*FA 2009, s 24*).

An FYA can only be claimed during the chargeable period in which the expenditure is incurred (*CAA 2001, s 52*). (See **6.4** above for the date that expenditure is incurred.) If that is also the period in which the qualifying activity is discontinued, no claim is allowed.

Environmentally beneficial plant and machinery

6.21   Particular plant and machinery that meets environment criteria qualifies for 100% FYA, which may be claimed by companies of any size. This machinery can be found by logging on to www.eca.gov.uk. The technologies that are included are:

- boilers (including oil-fired boilers);
- pipe insulation;
- combined heat and power (CHP);
- radiant and warm air heaters;
- compressed air equipment;
- solar thermal systems;
- heat pumps for space heating;
- thermal screens;
- lighting;
- variable speed drives (VSD);
- motors;
- refrigeration equipment (including display cabinets and compressors);
- automatic monitoring and targeting equipment;

- air-to-air energy recovery equipment;

- compact heat exchangers;

- heating, ventilation and air conditioning zone controls;

- vehicle wash waste reclaim units;

- efficient industrial cleaning; and

- waste management for mechanical seals.

It is necessary for the government to certify that the equipment meets the required standards or that the machinery is a product specified on the product list.

6.22   Certain water technologies and products also qualify for 100% FYA. These fall into classes of: efficient taps, efficient toilets, flow controllers, leakage detection, meters and monitoring equipment, water reuse systems, efficient washing machines, small-scale slurry and sludge dewatering equipment, water efficient industrial cleaning equipment, and water management equipment for mechanical seals (*SIs 2003/2076; 2006/2235; 2008/1916*). Information regarding these products can be found on www.water-eca.gov.uk. See also the *Capital Allowances Energy Saving Plant and Machinery (Amendment) (Order) 2008 (SI 2008/1918)*. Component parts of an asset may meet the environmental criteria. If so, an FYA will be available in respect of these parts. A certificate issued to the buyer will indicate the cost of the environmental components, which should be used in calculating the FYA (*CAA 2001, ss 45H, 45J*). If the total expenditure incurred on the asset containing the qualifying component (or components) is less than the amount specified in the order for the component or components incorporated in that asset, the total expenditure qualifies for 100% FYA (HMRC Capital Allowances Manual CA 23135). If qualifying expenditure is incurred on an asset in stage payment, the payment is allocated pro-rata over the various payments.

If an environmental certificate is revoked, the company should withdraw the 100% FYA claim.

Both the expenditure on the energy-saving plant and machinery (above) and the environmentally beneficial plant and machinery (see **6.21**) may qualify for a payable tax credit (see **9.29**).

Expenditure incurred by energy services provider

6.23   If a company energy service provider of any size supplies energy efficient plant and machinery, which is on the technology list of products list to his client he may be able to claim an FYA. The provider must make an election with this client. The plant must not be for use in a dwelling house and the service provider or another organisation with which it is connected must carry out all or substantially all of the operation and maintenance of the plant and machinery (*CAA 2001, s 180A*).

Expenditure on cars with low carbon dioxide emissions

6.24   Expenditure by any size of company on cars with low carbon dioxide emissions qualifies for an FYA if incurred between 17 April 2002 and 31 March 2013. The car must be unused and not second hand. It can either be an electric car or a car with CO_2 emissions of not more than 110 gm (120 gm for expenditure incurred before 1 April 2008) per km driven. Information regarding a car's carbon dioxide emissions figure can be found on the vehicle registration document (the 'V5') or on the Vehicle Certification Agency's website at www.vca.gov.uk. Neither the rules for cars costing more that £12,000 nor the car hire or leasing expenses restriction applies to these vehicles (*CAA 2001, s 45D*).

Expenditure on natural gas and hydrogen refuelling equipment

6.25   Expenditure incurred on natural gas, biogas (for expenditure incurred after 1 April 2008) and hydrogen refuelling equipment between 17 April 2002 and 31 March 2013 and installed in a refuelling station qualifies for FYA. The stations can be private to the company or open to the public. Eligible expenditure includes storage tanks, compressors, controls and meters, gas connections, and filling equipment (*CAA 2001, s 45E*).

Expenditure on North Sea oil ring-fence plant and machinery

6.26   Extraction of gas or oil in the North Sea trades may claim a 100% FYA on equipment purchased for use in the 'ring-fence' trade. (A ring-fence trade is a trade subject to the supplementary charge.) Long life assets qualify for 24% WDA (*CAA 2001, s 45G*).

Persons who are treated as owners of fixtures

6.27   If the plant and machinery purchased for the purposes of the trade becomes a fixture and the company holds a relevant interest in the land, the company will be able to claim the capital allowances. Where more than one party has an interest in the land the party entitled to claim is normally the party with the lowest interest (*CAA 2001, s 176*) (HMRC Capital Allowances Manual CA 26150).

Lessors and lessees of equipment fixtures used for a qualifying activity of the lessee may jointly elect for the fixture to be treated as belonging to the equipment lessor thus enabling the lessor to claim the capital allowances (*CAA 2001, s 177*). The election must be made within two years of the end of the accounting period for which it is to apply.

EXPENDITURE ON WHICH AN FYA MAY NOT BE CLAIMED

6.28   No FYA is available on the purchase of a car unless it is a low-emission car – see **6.24** (*CAA 2001, s 45D*). No FYA is available on a gifted asset. This is because to qualify for FYA the entity must incur the expenditure (*CAA 2001, s 52*). Similarly, an FYA is not available if a company buys an asset for one purpose and then uses the asset for another purpose. An FYA may not be claimed on the provision of plant and machinery for leasing, unless the expenditure is on qualifying energy saving plant and machinery, cars with low CO_2 emissions or natural gas or hydrogen refuelling equipment. HMRC take the view that the hire of machinery with an operative constitutes contract hire as in the non-tax case of *Baldwins Industrial Services plc v Barr Ltd* [2003] BLR 176. The expenditure is not within finance leasing and an FYA will be available (HMRC Capital Allowances Manual CA 23115). No capital allowances whatsoever are given on assets used for business entertainment (*CAA 2001, s 269*).

The general rule is that no FYA may be claimed on assets purchased from connected parties (*CAA 2001, s 217*). This rule does not apply where the asset is produced by the seller, unused and sold in the ordinary course of the seller's business (*CAA 2001, s 230*). Connection for these purposes is determined by *ICTA 1988, s 839* (see **4.25**). See **6.53** for common AIA provisions.

COMPUTATION OF CAPITAL ALLOWANCES

The pool

6.29   All qualifying expenditure is pooled in a multi-asset pool. Special rate pools are maintained for expenditure on 'expensive cars', being non low emission cars costing more than £12,000, incurred before 1 April 2009 (*CAA 2001, s 74*), and short life assets (*CAA 2001, s 86*). The writing down allowance on an expensive car is restricted to £3,000 per annum (it is anticipated that this transitional period will last for about five years – Budget 2009 BN 65). A separate asset class pool was maintained for expenditure incurred on long life assets (*CAA 2001, s 101*) prior to 1 April 2008. See **22.3** for an outline plant and machinery capital allowance computation.

Allowances

6.30   Four types of adjustment are made: first year allowance (FYA), annual investment allowance (AIA) (post 1 April 2008), writing down allowance (WDA) and a balancing adjustment (BA). An FYA or an AIA can only be claimed in year of purchase. There is no WDA in the accounting period in which an FYA is claimed (*CAA 2001, s 58(5)*). If an AIA is claimed, a WDA may also be claimed in that accounting period (*CAA 2001, s 58(4A)*; *FA 2008, Sch 24, para 5*). WDAs are claimed annually on a reducing balance basis. The WDA is applied to the unrelieved pool of qualifying expenditure at the beginning of the year adjusted for disposals and additions, but not additions on which FYA has been claimed. From 1 April 2008 the rate of WDA has been reduced from 25% to 20% (except for ring fence trades; see **3.1**) (*CAA 2001, s 56(1)*).

Disposal proceeds

6.31   When an asset is disposed of the disposal proceeds up to the amount of the original cost are deducted from the asset balance on the expenditure pool. If a positive balance remains after the deduction on a multi asset or long life asset pool the balance continues to be written off on a reducing balance basis, except in the final period of account when it becomes a balancing allowance that may be deducted from chargeable profits. If a negative balance remains on the pool after the deduction this forms a balancing charge, which must be added to the company's assessable profits. In the case of a single asset pool, a positive balance, after the deduction for sale proceeds, is allowed as a deduction from profits as a balance adjustment. A negative balance will become a taxable balancing charge (*CAA 2001, s 55*). If the assets concerned have not been the subject of a capital allowance claim it is not necessary to deduct the disposal proceeds from the pool. This is not the case if the asset was originally acquired from a connected person or by means of a series of transactions between connected persons and any one person has brought the disposal value into account (*CAA 2001, s 64*). The definition of connection follows *ICTA 1988, s 839* (*CAA 2001, s 575*) (see **4.25**). Expenditure on an asset that is partly used for a qualifying activity and partly for other purposes is put into a separate pool. The expenditure is apportioned on a just and reasonable basis and the allowances are reduced accordingly. If the market value of the asset in the pool exceeds that actual pool value by more than £1 million and there is a significant reduction in the value of the asset, the asset is deemed to have been disposed of at market value for the notional trade and reacquired for the purposes of the separate notional trade (*CAA 2001, s 208*).

Example 6.1

The written down value of Sebastian Ltd's plant, after deduction of capital allowances for the year to 31 March 2009, was £6,660.

In July 2009 the company sold an asset for £300 on which capital allowances had been claimed.

The capital allowance claim is as follows:

Capital allowances—plant and machinery:

	Pool	Allowances
	£	£
WDV b/f	6,660	
Sales proceeds—July 2009	−300	
	6,360	
WDA @ 20%	−1,272	1,272
WDV c/f	5,088	
Allowances		1,272

An asset is disposed of if the person who incurred the qualifying expenditure on the plant and machinery:

● ceases to own the plant or machinery; or

● loses possession of the plant or machinery in circumstances where it is reasonable to assume that the loss is permanent.

The asset is also treated as being disposed of if the plant and machinery:

● has been in use for mineral exploration and access and the person abandons it at the site where it was in use for that purpose;

● ceases to exist as such (as a result of destruction, dismantling or otherwise);

● begins to be used wholly or partly for purposes other than those of the qualifying activity;

or if the qualifying activity is permanently discontinued (*CAA 2001, s 61(1)*).

WRITING DOWN ALLOWANCE FROM 1 APRIL 2008

Transitional rate

6.32   For accounting periods which begin before, but end on or after, 1 April 2008 the rate is calculated according to the following formula:

$$x = \frac{(25 \times BRD)}{CP} + \frac{(20 \times ARD)}{CP}$$

x   rate of writing down allowance rounded to two decimal places
BRD number of days in the accounting period prior to 1 April 2008
ARD number of days in the accounting period on and after the 1 April 2008
CP   number of days in the accounting period

(CAA 2001, s 56(9)–(11); FA 2008, s 80)

Example 6.2

The written down value of Transitio Ltd's plant, after deduction of capital allowances for the year to 30 September 2007 , was £9,000.

The rate of writing down allowance for the year ended 30 September 2008, to be applied is:

$$x = \frac{(25 \times 183)}{366} + \frac{(20 \times 183)}{366} = 22.5\%$$

The capital allowance claim is as follows:

Capital allowances—plant and machinery:

	Pool	Allowances
	£	£
WDV b/f	9,000	
WDA @ 22.5%	−2,025	2,025
WDV c/f	6,975	
ALLOWANCES		2,025

There is a capital allowances ready reckoner on the HMRC website (www.hmrc.gov.uk) to assist in calculating hybrid rates.

Short-life assets

6.33   Assets that are continuously renewed, such as technology assets, may be placed in a separate short life pool. The company must make an irrevocable election for the asset to be treated as 'short life' within two years of the end of the chargeable period for which the expenditure was incurred (*CAA 2001, s 83(b)*). The asset then remains in the short life pool until the earlier of disposal or the fourth anniversary of the end of the chargeable period in which the asset was acquired. If the asset is disposed of, a balancing charge or a balancing allowance will arise. Alternatively, if unsold, the asset's net book value is transferred back to the main pool (*CAA 2001, s 86*).

For accounting periods which begin before, but end on or after, 1 April 2008, the balance of qualifying expenditure less any disposal receipts may be taken in full as the writing down allowance if this amount is equal or less than the annual small pool limit, introduced at £1,000 (*CAA 2001, s 56A*; *FA 2008, s 81(3)*).

Long-life assets

6.34   Expenditure on any asset that is plant and machinery, and whose expected life is 25 years or more, is added to a special rate pool and qualifies for a writing down allowance of 10% (*CAA 2001, s 91*). Expenditure incurred before 1 April 2008 was included in a separate pool to which a 6% writing down allowance applied, the balance on which was then transferred on 1 April 2008 to the special rate pool, from which time a 10% rate applies. See **6.38** and **6.44**. All expenditure incurred on long life assets on or after 1 April 2008 is added to the special rate pool and now qualifies for a 10% rate. Expenditure on plant, machinery and fixtures in a house, hotel, shop or showroom will not qualify. Nor will expenditure on cars or where the total expenditure on long-life assets for the year is £100,000 or less (*CAA 2001, ss 93, 96, 98*; *FA 2008, s 83*).

Reduced allowances

6.35   If the chargeable period is less than 12 months (ie if the accounting period is less that 12 months), the writing down allowance and the annual investment allowance are reduced proportionately (but not the first year allowance). A company may reduce or disclaim the allowances for any chargeable period. The tax written down value is carried forward to the next accounting period and will be written down accordingly (*CAA 2001, s 56*).

Assets purchased under hire purchase

6.36   The asset is treated as that of the hirer who may claim capital allowances (*CAA 2001, s 67*). The full contract cost is treated as expenditure incurred. The disposal value is the proceeds received, together with any unpaid capital instalments (*CAA 2001, s 68*).

6.37   A company may only claim capital allowances on plant and machinery if the assets belong to the company at some time (*CAA 2001, s 11(4)(b)*). HMRC consider that, if there is a contractual relationship that states that 'a company may become the owner of the plant or machinery on the performance of the contract' and the purchasing company pays a deposit for plant that is not supplied, thus incurring abortive expenditure, it will be able to claim capital allowances under *CAA 2001, s 67(1)(a)*. When the beneficial period ends the company must bring a disposal value into account (HMRC Capital Allowances Manual CA 23350 and Tax Bulletin, Issue 2, February 1992).

SPECIAL RATE EXPENDITURE AND THE SPECIAL RATE POOL

Special rate allowance

6.38   The special rate allowance is applied to expenditure on the following types of assets:

From 1 April 2008:

- thermal insulation expenditure (see **6.16**);

- integral fixtures (see **6.17**);

- long-life asset (expenditure incurred before 1 April 2008) (see **6.34**);

long-life asset expenditure incurred on or after 1 April 2008.

From 1 April 2009:

- special rate car.

(*CAA 2001, s 104A; FA 2008, Sch 26*)

A special rate car is not a main rate car (see **6.40**).

Where there is combined special rate and other expenditure, the amounts of expenditure are apportioned on a just and reasonable basis and only the special rate portion of that expenditure will qualify (*CAA 2001, s 104B; FA 2008, Sch 26, para (2)*).

The special rate expenditure must be allocated to a special rate pool or a single asset pool if it is expenditure of that type (see **6.29**) (*CAA 2001, s 104C*). A 10% rate of writing down allowance is applied to the balance of qualifying expenditure less disposal receipts. The rate is also applied to special rate expenditure that has been allocated to a single asset pool (*CAA 2001, s 104C*).

Disposal value of special rate assets

6.39   If a disposal results from a scheme or arrangement entered into to avoid tax, and the actual disposal value is less than the notional written down value, the notional written down value is taken as the disposal value. This is the expenditure incurred less the special rate allowances, which the company could have made for this expenditure (*CAA 2001, s 104E*).

MOTOR CARS

Main rate motor car

6.40   Expenditure on a main rate is allocated to the general pool of expenditure and qualifies for an annual writing down allowance of 20%.

A motor car is classified as main rate if:

- it is first registered before 1 March 2001;

- it has low CO_2 emissions – currently less than 160g/km but more than 110g/km; or

- it is electrically-propelled.

(*CAA 2001, s104AA*; *FA2009, Sch 11 para 8*) .

A car has low CO_2 emissions if it was first registered on the basis of a qualifying emissions certificate and its applicable CO_2 emissions does not exceed 160 grams per kilometre driven. Expenditure on cars with an emission factor of less than 110g/km (see **6.24**) qualifies for a 100% first year allowance.

A qualifying emissions certificate is either an EC certificate of conformity or a UK approval certificate that specifies the emissions in terms of grams per kilometre driven for each type of fuel. Bi-fuel vehicles will have separate emission factors for different fuels (these are cars that run on a combination of road gas and either petrol or diesel).

However, for non bi-fuel vehicles, if only one emissions figure is specified on the certificate, that is the figure to be applied; but, if more than one figure is specified, the combined amount is the figure to be applied (*CAA 2001, s 268C*).

A motor car is classified as electrically propelled if it is propelled solely by external electrical power or from a storage battery that is not connected to any source of power when the vehicle is in motion.

Expenditure on a special rate motor car, that is a motorcar with an emissions factor of more than 160g/km, is added to the special rate pool and qualifies for an annual writing down allowance of 10%. Expenditure on 'expensive' cars (costing more than £12,000) incurred after 1 April 2009 can only be added to the general pool, the special rate pool or qualify for a 100% FYA. Expenditure incurred on 'expensive' cars before 1 April 2009 (see **6.29**) is retained in a separate pool, but the writing down allowances are calculated according to that car's emission factors.

Special rate cars – discontinued activities

6.41 If a company discontinues a qualifying activity that consisted wholly or partly of car hire or leasing (other than incidental) in relation to a special rate car and a balancing allowance arises, it is restricted to the remaining balancing charge after granting relief for its other balancing allowances.

This rule also applies if a company to which group relief would be available (whether or not a claim is made) carries on a qualifying activity that consisted wholly or partly of car hire or leasing (other than incidentally) in relation to a special rate car at any time during the six months after the company's qualifying activity is permanently discontinued (*CAA 2001, s 104F*).

The disposal value to include in such situations is the lower of the market value at the time of the disposable event and expenditure incurred.

It is necessary to make the following calculations:

- the balancing allowance on the special rate pool (SBA);
- the total balancing charge (BC) arising on all assets for the period; and
- the total balancing allowance on all other assets (OBA).

The amount of the balancing allowance that the company then becomes entitled to in respect of the special rate pool is reduced to:

$$BC - OBA$$

The company is then treated as having incurred notional expenditure of an amount by which SBA exceeds:

$$(BC - SOBA)$$

In effect, there is no relief for the notional expenditure, because the qualifying activity will already have ceased. If, as a result, expenditure is allocated to the pre-penultimate chargeable period, it is deemed to have been incurred in the final chargeable period.

Example 6.3

Oswald Limited discontinued its hire car activity on 31 December 2009. The capital allowance computation is as follows:

	Special rate car	Short life assets	Plant and Machinery Pool
	£	£	£
WDV	45,000	7,000	18,000
Sale proceeds	30,000	5,000	26,000
Balancing (charge) or allowance	15,000	(2,000)	8,000
	SBA	OBA	BC

The allowable balancing allowance on the special rate car is restricted to:

$$£8,000 - 2,000 = £6,000$$

Oswald Limited is deemed to have incurred expenditure of:

$$£15,000 - 6,000 = £9,000$$

Sale between connected persons

6.42   A special rate allowance cannot be claimed on sales and subsequent re-sales of integral features between connected parties, where the buyer incurred the original expenditure before 1 April 2008 or incurred expenditure after that date that was not qualifying. The expenditure will be qualifying if the original expenditure was qualifying expenditure or the buyer's expenditure would have been qualifying had it been incurred at the time the original expenditure was incurred (*FA 2008, Sch 26, para 15*). The definition of 'connection' follows *ICTA 1988, s 839 (CAA 2001, s 575)*; see **4.25**.

Intra-group transfers

6.43   Group members may elect to transfer integral features, between themselves, at written down value, where the expenditure was incurred before 1 April 2008. If the expenditure is expenditure of a type on which allowances can be claimed, it will be added to the purchasing company's main pool, and not to the special pool (*FA 2008, Sch 26, paras 16* and *17*). The definition of a group is as for capital gains purposes, see **20.14** and **20.15**.

Existing long-life asset expenditure

6.44   Expenditure on long-life assets that was incurred before 1 April 2008 is to be added to the special rate pool and treated as if it were special rate expenditure. The annual writing down allowance increases from 6% to 10%. The rate for the transitional period covering 1 April 2008 is calculated according to the formula:

$$x = \frac{(6 \times BRD)}{CP} + \frac{(10 \times ARD)}{CP}$$

x   Transitional % rate, rounded to two decimal places.

Number of days in the accounting period:

BRD   before the relevant date – 1 April 2008;

ARD   after the relevant date –1 April 2008;

CP   the complete period.

Any unrelieved qualifying expenditure in a single asset pool at 1 April 2008 is to be treated as if it were special rate expenditure carried forward in the single asset pool (*CAA 2001, s 104D*) (*FA 2008, Sch 26, para 2*).

Example 6.4

The written down value of Constance Ltd's long-life assets after deduction of capital allowances for the year to 30 September 2008, was £10,000. The company has no other assets on which allowances are claimed.

The rate of writing down allowance to be applied for the year ended 30 September 2008 is:

$$x = \frac{(6 \times 183)}{366} + \frac{(10 \times 183)}{366} = 8\%$$

The special rate allowance claim is as follows:

	Special rate pool £	Allowances £
Expenditure transferred from long-life pool	10,000	
WDA @ 8%	–800	800
WDV c/f	9,200	
Allowances		800

THE ANNUAL INVESTMENT ALLOWANCE

Introduction

6.45   The annual investment allowance (AIA) replaces the plant and machinery first-year allowance. The maximum annual allowance is £50,000 for expenditure incurred on plant and machinery. Motor cars are not included (*CAA 2001, s 51A(5)*). The £50,000 allowance can be claimed for each 12-month accounting period beginning on or after 1 April 2008 (*FA 2008, Sch 24, para 23(3)*).

Qualifying expenditure retains the meaning adopted for capital allowances, being capital expenditure incurred on the provision of plant and machinery, wholly or partly for the purposes of the qualifying activity carried on by the company that incurs the expenditure. As a result of incurring the expenditure, the company 'owns' the asset (*CAA 2001, s 11(4)* as modified by *s 11(5)*; see **6.4**). AIA is given for a chargeable period, which is the company's accounting period (*CAA 2001, s 6(1)*). If the accounting period is shorter or longer than a year, the maximum AIA is reduced or increased proportionately (*CAA 2001, s 51A(6)*). A company may claim all or part of an AIA (*CAA 2001, s 51A(7)*).

Although the annual investment allowance may be claimed by an individual, a partnership in which all the members are individuals, or a company, a mixed partnership of which the company is a member, such as a limited liability partnership, may not claim the allowance. Neither may the allowance be claimed by a trust (*CAA 2001, s 38A(3)*). A company is given the same meaning as in *ICTA 1988, s 832(1)* (see **1.5**).

Exclusions

6.46   Certain types of expenditure incurred are excluded from an AIA claim (*CAA 2001, s 38B*). The expenditure is excluded if it is incurred:

- in an accounting period in which a qualifying activity is permanently discontinued;

- on the provision of a car (as defined below);

- wholly for the purposes of a ring fence trade (see **3.1**);

- in circumstances which are connected with a change in the nature or conduct of a trade or business carried on by a person other than the company incurring the expenditure, and the obtaining of an AIA is the main benefit, or one of the main benefits, which could reasonably be expected to arise from the making of the change;

- on plant not originally purchased for use in the qualifying activity;

- on plant purchased for long funding leasing and gifts.

A car is any mechanically propelled road vehicle that is not primarily used for the conveyance of goods or of a type that is not commonly used as a road vehicle (*CAA 2001, s 268A*).

AIA CLAIMS

Single companies

6.47   Regardless of the number of activities that a company carries on, it may only claim a single AIA (*CAA 2001, s 51A(1)*).

Example 6.5

Northco Ltd carries on a manufacturing trade and also runs a property rental business. During the 12-month accounting period to 31 March 2010 the company incurred £40,000 on new plant and machinery for the manufacturing trade and £10,000 on plant used in the letting business.

The company decides to allocate its annual investment claim as follows:

Northco Ltd Annual Investment Capital Allowance claim for the year ended 31 March 2010:

AIA	£
Expenditure incurred re	
Manufacturing trade	
	40,000
Rental business	10,000
Total claim	£50,000

Group companies

6.48   A group of companies is entitled to claim one AIA, which it may allocate to AIA expenditure as it thinks fit, between the companies that incurred the qualifying expenditure (*CAA 2001, s 51C(3)*).

In determining the existence of a group, the definition of a parent undertaking is applied according to *Companies Act 2006, s 1162* (see **10.5**). Where the conditions are met, a company is treated as another company's parent undertaking for any financial year in which the other company's accounting period ends (*CAA 2001, s 51C(5)*). A financial year commences on 1 April and ends on 31 March.

Group companies and other companies under common control

6.49   Groups of companies and other companies under common control in any financial year are only entitled to one AIA, which they may allocate between them as they see fit (*CAA 2001, ss 51D(3), 51E(3)*). Two or more groups of companies are under common control if they are controlled by the same person and are related to one another (*CAA 2001, s 51E(1)*).

A company is controlled by the same person if that person controls it at the end of its chargeable period ending in that financial year (*CAA 2001, s 51F(1)*). Control has the meaning that a person has the power to determine that a company's affairs are conducted in accordance with his wishes (*CAA 2001, s 574(2)*).

Groups of companies and other companies are related to one another if, during the financial year, they either share the same premises, or they derive more than 50 per cent of their respective turnovers from qualifying activities, within the same NACE common statistical classification (Nomenclature générale des activités Économiques dans les Communautés européennes). The NACE classification is the first level of the common statistical classification of economic activities in the European Union, established by Regulation (EC) No

1893/2006 of the European Parliament and the Council of 20 December 2006. The meaning of 'premises' is not defined in the Act (*CAA 2001, s 51J*).

Example 6.6

Ashley Ltd has an accounting period ending on 30 April 2010. It had sole occupation of Ashley House, its business premises. On 1 July 2010, Burton Ltd with an accounting period ending on 31 December 2010, moved into Ashley House. Both companies occupied the premises until 31 December 2010. The companies are related during the financial year 2010.

Short chargeable periods

6.50   A company that has been a member of a group for a period of less than one year can only claim a proportionately reduced AIA (*CAA 2001, s 51A(6)*).

Example 6.7

Mr James controls Cuthbert Ltd, Damian Ltd and Eldridge Ltd. All companies have prepared accounts to 31 March 2010. Eldridge Ltd was formed on 1 July 2009. Each company incurs relevant AIA qualifying expenditure of £100,000, but the maximum allowance that could be allocated to Eldridge Ltd is 9/12ths of £50,000 = £37,500.

Multiple accounting periods

6.51   If a company has more than one accounting period ending in a financial year, each accounting period must be examined separately in order to determine whether or not the related activities conditions are met (*CAA 2001, s 51L(2)*).

INTERACTION WITH CAPITAL ALLOWANCES

Allowance claims

6.52   A company may not claim an annual investment allowance and a first year allowance in respect of the same expenditure (*CAA 2001, s 52A*). Thus, a company could not claim a 100% first year allowance on expenditure on which it had made an annual investment allowance claim.

Example 6.8

Roderick Ltd incurs £100,000 on an item of plant or machinery that appears on the energy technology list, which qualifies for a 100% allowance. Roderick Ltd may either claim energy-saving plant and machinery allowance on the full amount of expenditure incurred, or an AIA of up to £50,000, subject to the company's other expenditure on plant and machinery.

The qualifying expenditure is to be added to and the AIA is deducted from the pool of plant and machinery pool (*CAA 2001, s 58(4A)*; *FA 2008, Sch 24, para 5*).

Example 6.9

Holbein Ltd is a single company. It incurs £20,000 on general plant and machinery during the accounting period ended 31 March 2010. The value of its pool of qualifying capital expenditure brought forward at 1 April 2009 is £350,000. The adjustment to the pool is as follows:

	Pool of qualifying expenditure		£
1 April 2009	Written down value brought forward		350,000
	Add: qualifying expenditure	20,000	
	Less: AIA (restricted)	(20,000)	
			—
			350,000
	WDA @ 20%		70,000
31 March 2010	Written down value carried forward		£280,000

For accounting periods commencing after 1 April 2009, it is possible to claim a temporary FYA of 40% on general plant and machinery (*CAA 2001, s 39*); (*FA 2009, s 24*). When this legislation was announced in Budget 2009, it was commented in BN 04 that 'business incurring expenditure in excess of the AIA cap that would normally be allocated to the main pool and qualify for a 20% WDA in the 12-month period beginning on 1 April 2009 will now be able to claim a 40% first year allowance instead'.

On this basis, in **Example 6.10**, Southco Ltd could make a 40% FYA claim on the balance of the expenditure.

Example 6.10

Southco Ltd carries on a manufacturing trade. During the 12-month accounting period to 31 March 2010 the company incurred £120,000 on new plant and machinery, which it uses in its manufacturing trade. The balance of its pool of general plant and machinery brought forward at 1 April 2009 amounts to £20,000. The company claims AIA and FYA.

The allowance is as follows:

Southco Ltd Capital Allowance claim for the year ended 31 March 2010:

	Pool of qualifying expenditure		£	*Total allowances claimed*
01.04.09	Written down value brought forward		20,000	
	20% writing down allowance		4,000	4,000
			16,000	
	Add: qualifying expenditure	120,000		
				50,000
	Less: AIA	(50,000)		
	Balance of expenditure	70,000	—	
	FYA @ 40%	28,000	42,000	28,000
31.03.10	Written down value carried forward		£58,000	
	Total allowances claimed			82,000

Common provisions

6.53   There are aspects of the legislation common to first year allowances and the AIA:

- the allowances are to be reduced to a just and reasonable amount, if the expenditure has been incurred for non-business purposes (*CAA 2001, s 205*);

- the allowances are to be reduced if a subsidy is received (*CAA 2001, s 210*);

- no allowance is given for disposals to connected persons, for transactions entered into for avoidance reasons, and in sale and leaseback transactions (*CAA 2001, s 217*);

- any additional VAT liability related to the original expenditure on which an allowance has been claimed is deemed to be incurred at the same time as the expenditure, and will also qualify for the allowance (*CAA 2001, s 236; FA 2008, Sch 24, para 6*).

Finance leasing accounting treatment

6.54 A finance lease is essentially a lending arrangement between two companies. The finance lessor company (the lender) retains ownership of the leased asset. The leased assets are not disclosed as fixed assets on the balance sheet but as a loan, which is normally the cost of the leased asset. The finance lessor's return is interest and loan repayment. Interest is recorded in the profit and loss account as income. Capital repayments reduce the amount of outstanding debt.

Although the finance lessee company (the borrower) does not own the asset it is recorded on the balance sheet as an asset under SSAP 21 (accounting for leases and hire purchase contracts) following the economic substance over form principle of FRS 5. Capital owed to the finance lessor is shown as a creditor. Interest payable is charged to the profit and loss account.

The finance lessee charges depreciation on the asset.

Finance leasing taxation treatment

6.55 Until 1 April 2006, the taxation legislation regarded the finance lessor as owner of the leased assets with entitlement to capital allowances. The lessor could only claim a 25% WDA. No FYA is available. Plant leased to companies not resident in the UK and whose activities are not charged exclusively to UK tax will only qualify for a 10% WDA during the designated period (*CAA 2001, s 105*). The designated period is ten years from the time that the plant and machinery is first brought into use. The equipment is placed in a separate pool.

FA 2006, Sch 8 introduced the concept of long funding leases, which applies with effect from 1 April 2006, or earlier if a written agreement was in place before 21 July 2005. A long funding lease is essentially a lease with a life of more than seven years. The effect being that the lessor company takes the finance element of the rentals arising under the lease as income. The lessee company deducts the finance element of the rentals payable over the life of the lease as an expense and will be entitled to capital allowances if it so chooses

(*FA 2006, s 81, Sch 8*). The Revenue's guidance is contained in its Business Leasing Manual.

Long funding leases

6.56   The lessor in a plant and machinery long funding lease arrangement is not entitled to capital allowances, but the lessee may be entitled to them (*CAA 2001, s 34A*). The lessee company must report the long-funding lease on its tax return (*CAA 2001, s 70H*).

In brief, a 'long funding lease' is a funding lease (see **6.58**) which meets the following conditions:

● 	it is not a short lease (see **6.57**);

● 	it is not an excluded lease of background plant or machinery for a building (see **6.61**);

● 	it is not excluded because it is plant or machinery of a low percentage value leased with land (see **6.62**) (*CAA 2001, s 70G*).

With effect for leases entered into on or after 13 December 2007, if the lessee of any plant and machinery is also the lessor of a long funding lease, both leases are treated as non-funding (*FA 2008, Sch 20, para 8*; *CAA 2001, s 70H(1A), (1B)*).

Short lease

6.57   A short lease is any lease with a term of five years or less. If the lease term is more than five years but less than seven years the lease is a short lease if the following three conditions A, B and C are met:

Condition A

The lease is one which, under generally accepted accounting practice, falls (or would fall) to be treated as a finance lease.

Condition B

The residual value of the plant or machinery which is implied in the terms of the lease, is not more than 5% of the market value of the plant or machinery at the commencement of the term of the lease, as estimated at the inception of the lease.

Condition C

Under the terms of the lease the total rentals falling due in the 12 months beginning on the day following the commencement of the lease are no greater than 10% or less than the total rentals falling due in the following 12 months and the total rentals falling due in the final year or in any successive 12-month period after the second 12-month period are not greater than 10% of the total rentals falling due in the second12-month period.

If plant and machinery is the subject of a lease and finance leaseback arrangement, it is not a short lease.

(CAA 2001, s 70I)

A funding lease

6.58　　A 'funding lease' is a plant or machinery lease (see *CAA 2001, s 70K*), which at its inception meets one or more of the following tests:

- the finance lease test—a lease which under GAAP falls to be a finance lease *(CAA 2001, s 70N)*;

- the lease payments test—the present value of the minimum lease payments is equal to 80 % or more of the fair value of the assets. The present value is calculated by using the interest rate implicit in the lease *(CAA 2001, s 70O)*; and

- the useful economic life test—the term of the lease is more than 65 % of the remaining useful economic life of the asset. The remaining useful economic life is the period beginning with the commencement of the term of the lease and ending when the asset is no longer used and no longer likely to be used by any person for any purpose as a fixed asset of the business *(CAA 2001, ss 70, 70P)*.

The minimum lease payments are the minimum lease payments over the entire term of the lease after deducting minimum amounts such as VAT and any residual amount at fair value reasonably expected to be recovered by the lessor at the end of the lease *(CAA 2001, s 70YE)*.

A non-funding lease

6.59　　A non-funding lease is outside of the scope of the new regime and may be treated as belonging to the hirer *(CAA 2001, s 70J(3))*. A lease is not a funding lease if prior to the commencement of the term of the lease the relevant asset has been leased under one or more other leases, the aggregate terms of which exceed 65% of the remaining useful economic life of the asset at the commencement term of the lease, provided none of the earlier leases was itself a funding lease *(CAA 2001, s 70J(4))*.

A lease is not a long funding lease of the lessor if prior to 1 April 2006 the asset had been leased out under one or more leases for an aggregate period of at least 10 years and the lessor was also the lessor of the asset on the last day before 1 April 2006 (*CAA 2001, s 70J(6)*).

Anti–avoidance

6.60   This anti-avoidance provision aims to allocate all a lessor's receipts to income. Any receipt not already included in income, which the provision terms as a 'capital payment' will be included in the lessor's accounts as lease income of the accounting period, in which the payment is made.

Where there is an unconditional obligation to make a 'capital payment', the lessor is treated as receiving lease income of the same amount in the accounting period, in which the obligation arises. A deduction may be claimed in the accounts, if it is expected that the amount will not actually be paid (*ICTA 1988, ss 785B and 785E; FA 2008, Sch 20, para 1*).

Anti-avoidance provisions designed to remove the advantages of sale and leaseback schemes are included in *FA 2009, Sch 32*.

Background plant and machinery

6.61   Background plant and machinery contributes to the functionality of the building. Plant and machinery leased with a building is excluded from the funding lease regime and is of the following type (*CAA 2001, s 70R*):

(a)   heating and air-conditioning installations;

(b)   ceilings which are part of an air-conditioning system;

(c)   hot water installations;

(d)   electrical installations that provide power to a building, such as high and low voltage switchgear, all sub-mains distribution systems and standby generators;

(e)   mechanisms, including automatic control systems, for opening and closing doors, windows and vents;

(f)   escalators and passenger lifts;

(g)   window cleaning installations;

(h)   fittings such as fitted cupboards, blinds, curtains and associated mechanical equipment;

(i)   demountable partitions;

(j)   protective installations such as lightning protection, sprinkler and other equipment for containing or fighting fires, fire alarm systems and fire escapes; and

(k)   building management systems.

The following types of plant or machinery are deemed to be background plant or machinery:

(a)   lighting installations including all fixed light fittings and emergency lighting systems;

(b)   telephone, audio-visual and data installations incidental to the occupation of the building;

(c)   computer networking facilities incidental to the occupation of the building;

(d)   sanitary appliances and other bathroom fittings including hand driers, counters, partitions, mirrors, shower and locker facilities;

(e)   kitchen and catering facilities for producing and storing food and drink for the occupants of the building;

(f)   fixed seating;

(g)   signs;

(h)   public address systems; and

(i)   intruder alarm systems and other security equipment including surveillance equipment.

The following descriptions of plant or machinery are deemed not to be background plant or machinery:

(a)   storing, moving or displaying goods to be sold in the course of a trade, whether wholesale or retail;

(b)   manufacturing goods or materials;

(c)   subjecting goods or materials to a process;

(d)   storing goods or materials—

    (i)   which are to be used in the manufacture of other goods or materials;

    (ii)   which are to be subjected, in the course of a trade, to a process;

    (iii)   which, having been manufactured or produced or subjected in the course of a trade to a process, have not yet been delivered to any purchaser; or

    (iv)   on their arrival in the United Kingdom from a place outside the United Kingdom (*SI 2007/303*).

Plant and machinery leased with land: low percentage value

6.62   An exclusion applies to low percentage value plant and machinery leased with land where:

* the plant and machinery is affixed to the building or otherwise installed on the land;

* the plant and machinery is not background plant and machinery for any building situated in or on the land; and

* the plant or machinery is leased with the land under a mixed lease, the sole purpose of which is to secure a tax advantage.

In these circumstances, the lease is not a long funding lease if the AMV does not exceed both 5% of the market value of the land (including fixtures and fittings) and 10% of the aggregate value of the background plant and machinery (*CAA 2001, s 70U*). The AMV is the aggregate of the relevant plant and machinery and the market value of all other plant and machinery leased with the land.

Change of company ownership

6.63   It follows, that through the benefit of capital allowances, a lessor company's profits chargeable to corporation tax will be lower in the earlier years of the leasing contract than in the later years. Where there is a change of ownership of a single company, group company (see **10.5**), consortium company (see **10.6**) or changes in a company's partnership share of an interest in a business the available loss relief is restricted, with effect from 5 December 2005.

For corporation tax purposes an accounting period ends and a new accounting period commences on the date of the change. On the date of the exchange an adjustment is calculated which is treated as income for the accounting period prior to the change and as an expense of the accounting period post the change. If the expense adjustment in the second period results in a trading loss which is not available for set off under *ICTA 1988, s 393A(1)(b)* against a prior accounting period (see **9.11**).

For these purposes a company is considered to be a lessor company or carrying on a leasing business if at least half the accounting value of its plant or machinery is relevant plant or machinery or that at least half of the company's income in the period of 12 months ending with the date of the change derives from qualifying leased plant or machinery (*FA 2006, Sch 10, para 6; FA 2009, Sch 31, para 2*). Relevant plant or machinery is the accounting value of the company's plant and machinery at the beginning of the relevant day plus the amounts of any plant and machinery transferred to it by its associates during that day (*FA 2006, Sch 10, para 7; FA 2009, Sch 31, para 3*). Long-funding leases and hire purchase are excluded (*FA 2006, Sch 10, para 7A; FA 2009, Sch 31, para 4*). Qualifying leased plant and machinery is plant and machinery bought wholly or partly for the purposes of the business, on which the company is entitled to plant and machinery capital allowances and which is leased at any time during the 12 months prior to the date of the change. Plant and machinery in let buildings owned by a property investment company does not fall into this category.

An associated company is defined according to *ICTA 1988, s 416(1)* (see **4.27**).

The adjustment that is to be made is calculated according to the formula:

$$PM - TWDV$$

PM = The amount of plant and machinery and the net investment in finance leases shown on the company's balance sheet at the start of the relevant day, together with that of its associates at the end of the relevant day.

TWDV = The total of the tax written down value of the single asset pools, the class pools and the main pool at the start of the relevant accounting period following the date of the change.

If the result is negative, it is assumed to be NIL.

(*FA 2006, Sch 10, paras 16–19*).

Example 6.11

Ludwig plc prepares accounts to 31 December each year. On 1 July 2009 the company is entirely taken over by Frank plc. At 30 June 2009 the balance sheet shows net investment in leased assets of £1,200 million. The same assets have a tax written down net book value of £640 million.

For corporation tax purposes, Ludwig plc:

(i) has two accounting periods, the six months to 30 June 2009 and the 6 months to 31 December 2009.

(ii) the required adjustment is £(1,200 – 640) million = £560 million.

(iii) If the expense adjustment in the period to 31 December 2009 results in a loss, Ludwig will not be able to utilise that loss in an *ICTA 1988, s 393A(1)(b)* claim.

These rules will continue to apply where there is a transfer of trade under *ICTA 1988, s 343 (FA 2007, Sch 6)*.

INDUSTRIAL BUILDINGS ALLOWANCES

Construction of an industrial building or structure

6.64 For many years a company was able to claim an industrial buildings allowance (IBA) if it had incurred expenditure on the construction of a building or structure. This allowance is being withdrawn over the period from 2008/09 until 2010/11.Until that time a transitional allowance may be claimed (see **6.74**). IBAs are completely withdrawn for expenditure incurred on or after 1 April 2011 (*FA 2008, s 84*). In order to claim the allowance, the company must actually incur the expenditure. The expenditure cannot be covered directly or indirectly by a third party. In order to qualify the building or structure must be:

- in use for the purposes of a qualifying trade;
- a qualifying hotel;
- a qualifying sports pavilion; or
- a commercial building in a qualifying enterprise zone,

and the expenditure must be qualifying (*CAA 2001, s 271*).

As a result of incurring the expenditure the company must have the relevant interest in the building (*CAA 2001, s 286*).

HMRC acknowledge that there is no definition of a building within the industrial buildings legislation, and will treat anything with four walls and a roof as a building, provided it is of a reasonably substantial size. Something that is too small or insubstantial will be a structure (HMRC Capital Allowances Manual CA 31050). A structure is artificially erected or constructed and is distinct from the earth surrounding it (HMRC Capital Allowances Manual CA 31110), and roads, car parks which have a hard concrete or asphalt surface, concrete surfacing, tunnels and culverts, walls, bridges, aqueducts, dams, hard tennis courts and fences would qualify as such.

Qualifying trade

6.65 A list of qualifying trades is given in Table A of *CAA 2001, s 274(1)* and consists of the following:

1	Manufacturing	A trade consisting of the manufacturing of goods or materials.
2	Processing	A trade consisting of subjecting goods or materials to a process. This includes subject to *s 276(3)* maintaining or repairing goods or materials.
3	Storage	A trade consisting of storing goods or materials:

      (a) which are to be used in the manufacture of other goods or materials,

      (b) which are to be subjected in the course of a trade to a process,

      (c) which having been manufactured or produced or subjected in the course of a trade to a process, have not yet been delivered to any purchaser, or

      (d) on their arrival in the UK from a place outside the UK.

4	Agricultural contracting	

      (a) Ploughing or cultivating land occupied by another person, or

      (b) carrying out any other agricultural operation on land occupied by another person, or

      (c) threshing the crops or vegetables of another person.

5	Working foreign plantations	A trade consisting of working land outside the UK used for:

      (a) growing and harvesting of crops and vegetables;

      (b) Husbandry, or

      (c) forestry.

6	Fishing	A trade consisting of catching or taking fish or shellfish.
7	Mineral extraction	A trade consisting of working a source of mineral deposits. Mineral deposits include any natural deposits capable of being lifted or extracted from the earth and for this purpose geothermal energy is to be treated as a natural deposit.

      'Source of mineral deposits' includes a mine, an oil well and a source of geothermal energy.

Manufacturing

6.66   Manufacturing includes the making of articles and the assembly of component parts made elsewhere (HMRC Capital Allowances Manual CA

32210). Cold storage premises that contained ice-making machinery and plant were held to be an industrial building (*Ellerker v Union Cold Storage Co Ltd; Thomas Borthwick & Sons Ltd v Compton* (1938) 22 TC 195).

Goods and materials

6.67 Goods and materials are understood to be raw goods and materials. In *Girobank plc v Clarke* (1997) 70 TC 387, [1998] STC 182, [1998] 1 WLR 942, [1998] 4 All ER 312 the bank's processing of cheques and credit card slips was not a qualifying trade. Cheques and credit card slips are not within the definition of goods and services.

Similar decisions were made in *Buckingham v Securitas Properties Ltd* (1979) 53 TC 292, [1980] STC 166, [1980] 1 WLR 380 regarding coins or notes used as currency, in *Bourne v Norwich Crematorium Ltd* (1967) 44 TC 164, [1967] 1 WLR 691, [1967] 2 All ER 576 regarding human remains and in *Carr v Sayer & Sayer* (1992) 65 TC 15, [1992] STC 396 with respect to dogs and cats.

Subject to a process

6.68 In *Kilmarnock Equitable Co-Operative Society Ltd v CIR* (1966) 42 TC 675, [1966] TR 185 a building in which coal was screened and packed qualified as an industrial building. In *Vibroplant Ltd v Holland* (1981) 54 TC 658, [1982] 1 All ER 792 IBA was claimed on a building used to repair individual plant hire items when not being hired to customers. The activity was not considered to be a process because the items were treated individually. Repairing goods or materials is now treated as a process unless the person who repairs the goods or materials uses them in a non-qualifying trade (*CAA 2001, s 276(3)*).

Bestway (Holdings) Ltd v Luff (1998) 70 TC 512, [1998] STC 357 claimed IBA on its cash and carry wholesale store. The claim was refused because the checking, unpacking and labelling of goods was not considered to be a process and the goods were not retained for sufficient time to qualify for storage.

Storage

6.69 The trade of storage particularly refers to storage of goods for manufacture or process or goods manufactured or processed but not yet delivered to customers and includes imports (*CAA 2001, s 274*).

A company examined, selected and graded used tyre casings, which it sold on for remoulding. It used a building for storage of the items that were only delivered to customers in small batches. The building qualified as an industrial building (*Crusabridge Investments Ltd v Casings International Ltd* (1979) 54 TC 246).

The storage of goods on their arrival in the UK refers to their immediate storage. In *Copol Clothing Ltd v Hindmarsh* (1983) 57 TC 575, [1984] STC 33, [1984] 1 WLR 411 an IBA claim on a Manchester warehouse was refused because the building was the goods' ultimate place of storage. HMRC consider that a building will qualify for an IBA for storage of goods when they first enter the country if the following conditions are satisfied:

- the goods have been imported;

- the goods are being stored for the first time since their arrival in the UK; and

- the goods are still in transit—that is they have not yet arrived at their final destination in the UK (HMRC Capital Allowances Manual CA 32224).

In *Maco Door & Window Hardware (UK) Ltd v Revenue and Customs Comrs* [2008] UKHL 54 the company, a UK subsidiary of an Austrian company, claimed industrial buildings allowance on a warehouse. The warehouse was used to house goods such as door locks and door handles, which were manufactured by the Austrian company and stored in the warehouse while awaiting sale to wholesalers and to manufacturers of doors and windows in the UK. The company contended that it carried on a trade of storage. The Court of Appeal held that the company's trade was that of import and sale of doors and windows hardware. Storage was part of that trade. The industrial buildings allowance claim was refused. The House of Lords upheld this decision, stating that storage was not part of the company's trade, not so much because it had been insignificant but because the storage of one's own goods could not amount to a trade.

Expenditure on which IBAs are available

6.70 IBAs are not given on the cost of land. Where repairs to an industrial building qualify as capital expenditure IBAs are given to that part as if it were a new construction at that time (*CAA 2001, s 272*). IBAs are given on the preparation of a site for building or for the installation of plant and machinery (if not allowed elsewhere).

Qualifying expenditure consists of the following:

- capital expenditure on the construction of a building;

- the purchase of an unused building without developer involvement;

- the purchase of an unused building from a developer;

- the purchase of a used building from a developer (*CAA 2001, s 292*).

IBAs are based on the cost of construction if the company erects the building (*CAA 2001, s 294*). HMRC regard the following expenditure as forming part of the cost of the building on which an IBA is available:

- expenditure on capital repairs (*CAA 2001, s 272(2), (3)*);

- demolition costs of the old building making way to erect a new building if these costs have not already been taken into account in calculating a balancing adjustment on the old building;

- professional fees relating to the design and construction of a building provided that the building is actually constructed (HMRC Capital Allowances Manual CA 31400).

Land preparation costs, including cutting, tunnelling or levelling land in readiness for the installation of plant and machinery, will qualify for an IBA if there are no other allowances available on that expenditure (*CAA 2001, s 273*).

HMRC do not consider that the following items of expenditure can be included within the cost of a building for IBA purposes:

- the cost of obtaining planning permission, except where included in the builder's quotation;

- capitalised interest;

- the cost of a public enquiry;

- the cost of land drainage and reclamation;

- landscaping;

- legal expenses;

- abortive expenditure.

These items do not qualify for IBA (HMRC Capital Allowances Manual CA 31400 and CA 31410).

If the company decides to sell the building without bringing it into use the new purchaser can claim IBAs on the lower of purchase price and construction cost (*CAA 2001, s 295*). If the company buys an unused building from a property developer it can claim IBAs on the purchase price (*CAA 2001, s 296*).

If the company buys a used building from a developer, ie one on which IBAs have already been claimed, the company claims IBAs as the second user (*CAA 2001, s 297*). IBAs are not available on the cost of land (*CAA 2001, s 272(1)*).

If the building is purchased with other assets the expenditure should be apportioned between the qualifying and non-qualifying assets on a just and reasonable basis (*CAA 2001, s 356*).

A dwelling house, a retail shop, or premises similar to a retail shop where retail trade or business (including repair work) is carried on, a showroom, a hotel or an office do not qualify for IBA (*CAA 2001, s 277(1)*). An office that forms part of the manufacturing process will qualify for IBA, such as a drawing office in the case of *CIR v Lambhill Ironworks Ltd* (1950) 31 TC 393. An 'industrial building' may have a non-industrial part such as an office. If the non-industrial part consists of 25% or less of the total cost of the building, allowances are given on the total cost of the building. If the non-industrial parts are more than 25% of the total cost, the allowances are only given on the industrial part. A drawing office in a factory qualifies as industrial usage. Staff welfare buildings in a qualifying trade will qualify for IBA (*CAA 2001, s 275*).

Hotels

6.71   A qualifying hotel has to be a permanent building, which is open during the year for at least four months during April to October. When the hotel is let during April to October:

• it must have ten or more letting bedrooms,

• the sleeping accommodation that it offers consists wholly or mainly of letting bedrooms, and

• the services provided for guests normally include the provision of breakfast and an evening meal, the making of beds and the cleaning of rooms (*CAA 2001, s 279(1)*).

Initial allowance

6.72   Initial allowances may no longer be claimed except on buildings in an enterprise zone where a 100% allowance is available. A list of enterprise zones can be found in HMRC Capital Allowances Manual CA 37600.

IBAs writing down allowance (WDA)

6.73   WDAs were, until the financial year beginning 1 April 2008, given at a rate of 4% per annum on a straight line basis on the assumption that the building had a tax life of 25 years (*CAA 2001, s 310*). The 4% allowance is now reduced by specified percentages during the transitional period from

1 April 2008 to 31 March 2011. Buildings in an enterprise zone continue to qualify for a straight line 25% WDA.

Transitional period

6.74 With the exception of qualifying enterprise zone expenditure, the writing down allowance claimed on an industrial building during the transitional period is reduced by the following formula:

If the whole of the accounting period falls within a financial year,

$$WDA \times P$$

WDA   writing down allowance subject to reduction

P   Specified percentage in relation to that year.

If the accounting periods spans financial years, the transitional allowance is calculated by apportioning the writing down allowance for each financial year in which the accounting period falls, and adding the amounts so calculated.

The apportioned writing down allowance for a financial year in which part of a transitional chargeable period falls is:

$$DCPY \times \frac{(WDA)}{DCP} \times P$$

DCPY   number of days in the accounting period which fall in that year

DCP   number of days in the accounting period

WDA   writing down allowance subject to reduction

P   Specified percentage in relation to that year

The specified percentage for the financial year is as follows:

Financial year beginning 1 April 2007 and earlier financial years	100%
Financial year beginning 1 April 2008	75%
Financial year beginning 1 April 2009	50%
Financial year beginning 1 April 2010	25%
Financial year beginning 1 April 2011 and later years	0%

(*FA 2008, s 85*)

Example 6.12

Sebastian Ltd's factory was built in December 1999 at a cost of £90,000. The company prepares accounts to 30 September each year. The annual writing down allowance available until 1 April 2008 was 4%. From 1 April 2008 the transitional annual available writing down allowance is calculated as follows:

£

Accounting Period ended 30 September 2008

Financial year beginning 1 April 2007

$$183 \times \frac{£3,600}{366} \times 100\%$$ 1,800

Financial year beginning 1 April 2008

$$183 \times \frac{£3,600}{366} \times 75\%$$ 1,350

Total allowances   £3,150

Accounting Period ended 30 September 2009

Financial year beginning 1 April 2008

$$183 \times \frac{£3,600}{366} \times 75\%$$ 1,350

Financial year beginning 1 April 2009

$$183 \times \frac{£3,600}{366} \times 50\%$$ 900

Total allowances   £2,250

Accounting Period ended 30 September 2010

Financial year beginning 1 April 2009

$$183 \times \frac{£3,600}{366} \times 50\%$$ 900

6.75 *Tangible fixed assets*

Financial year beginning 1 April 2010

$$183 \times \frac{£3,600}{366} \times 25\%$$
450

Total allowances <u>£1,350</u>

Accounting Period ended 30 September 2011

Financial year beginning 1 April 2010

$$183 \times \frac{£3,600}{366} \times 25\%$$
450

Financial year beginning 1 April 2011

$$183 \times \frac{£3,600}{366} \times 0\%$$
0

Total allowances <u>£450</u>

Qualifying enterprise zone expenditure: transitional provision

6.75 Where a 100% initial allowance on enterprise zone expenditure has not or has only partially been claimed, a straight-line writing down allowance on cost is available until 1 April 2011.

For an accounting period which begins before, and ends on or after, 1 April 2011, the company's entitlement to a writing down allowance is calculated according to the following formula:

$$\frac{DCPB \times WDA}{DCP}$$

DCPB   number of days in the accounting period before 1 April 2011, the relevant date

DCP   number of days in the accounting period

WDA   writing down allowance subject to reduction

(FA 2008, s 86)

Example 6.13

Investico Ltd bought a factory in an enterprise zone on 1 May 2008 for £100,000, which qualified for a writing down allowance. The annual available writing down allowances are calculated as follows:

	£
Accounting Period ended 30 September 2008	
WDA available in full	25,000
Accounting Period ended 30 September 2009	
WDA available in full	25,000
Accounting Period ended 30 September 2010	
WDA available in full	25,000
Accounting Period ended 30 September 2011	
$\dfrac{183}{366} \times £25.000$	12,500

Anti-avoidance

6.76   The buyer's writing down allowance is subject to reduction if:

- a purchase of a relevant interest is made from a connected party on or after 12 March 2008;

- both buyer and seller have different accounting periods;

- the purpose, or one of the main purposes, of the sale is for the buyer to obtain a tax advantage.

Parties are connected where one party has control of the other or both are under the same control (*CAA 2001, s 567*). Purchases made on or after 12 March 2008 in pursuance of a pre-commencement contract are not affected. A pre-commencement contract is an unconditional contract made up in writing before 12 March 2008 or if conditional, its conditions have been satisfied before 12 March 2008. In addition no terms remain to be agreed on or after 12 March 2008 and the contract is not varied in a significant way on or after that date (*FA 2008, s 87; CAA 2001, s 313A*).

Where restricted, the buyer's writing down allowance is calculated as follows:

$$\frac{DI \times WDA}{CP}$$

  where—

DI number of days in the accounting period for which the buyer is entitled to the relevant interest

CP number of days in the accounting period

WDA writing down allowance subject to reduction

Example 6.14

In pursuance of a tax advantage, Azron Ltd bought a building from Bulldozer Ltd on 12 March 2009. Both companies are owned and controlled by John Bulldog. The building qualifies a writing down allowance of £10,000. Azron Ltd prepares accounts to 31 March each year.

Azron Ltd's writing down allowance for the accounting period ended 31 March 2009 is calculated as follows:

$$20 \times \frac{£3,660}{366} = £200$$

With effect from 12 March 2008 onwards, where the whole or part of a trade is transferred from one company to another, the sole purpose of which is to obtain a balancing allowance, no balancing allowance is due (*FA 2008, s 89; CAA 2001, s 343ZA*). See **6.77**.

6.77 For the allowance to be given, the building must be in use as an industrial building at the end of the chargeable period (*CAA 2001, s 309*).

If the building is not in industrial use at the end of the year, no WDA is given to the company. However, a notional WDA reduces the tax written down value of the building, because in effect its 25-year life is expiring. If the chargeable period is more or less than one year, the allowance is adjusted proportionately. No adjustment is made if the building was acquired during the chargeable period.

Temporary disuse

6.78 A period of temporary disuse is ignored (*CAA 2001, s 285*). Temporary disuse infers that the building is to be used for an industrial purpose, but there has been a short break in activities and industrial use is to be resumed.

The building must have been in use as an industrial building immediately before the period of temporary disuse. The legislation states no time limit for the temporary disuse unless the building was a qualifying hotel. A qualifying hotel, which becomes temporarily disused, is treated as a qualifying hotel for two years after the end of the chargeable period in which the temporary disuse begins but for no longer.

HMRC will accept that a building is temporarily disused if it is capable of being used at all. It need not be capable of being used for a qualifying trade, but if it is not capable of further use for any purpose it is not temporarily disused. If a company breaks its manufacturing pattern and moves into another qualifying trade, this is clearly a period of temporary disuse.

If the building is left to deteriorate or left empty prior to development or demolition, this is not a period of temporary disuse and any IBA claims will be rejected.

A claim made in good faith for a period of disuse may be made only to find that the disuse becomes permanent. Earlier claims will remain although no further claims can be made once it is known that the building has no further use (HMRC Capital Allowances Manual CA 32800).

Example 6.15

Marmaduke Ltd prepares accounts to 31 March each year. The company incurs expenditure on 1 June 2005 of £100,000, which qualifies for IBAs. The building is used throughout as an industrial building except for the period 1 June 2007 to 31 May 2008. The available industrial buildings allowances (assuming the 4% WDA rate continues) are as follows:

		£	Allowances
Year ending 31 March 2006			
Expenditure		100,000	
	WDA (4%)	4,000	4,000
		96,000	

		£	Allowances
Year ending 31 March 2007	WDA (4%)	4,000	4,000
		92,000	
Year ending 31 March 2008	Notional WDA (4%)	4,000	4,000
		88,000	
Year ending 31 March 2009	WDA (4%) × 75%	4,000	3,000
		84,000	
Year ending 31 March 2010	WDA (4%) × 50%	4000	2,000
		80,000	

Disposal of an industrial building

Post-21 March 2007 regime

6.79 The available industrial buildings allowance has worked on the premise that a building has a 25-year tax life. Until 21 March 2007, if a building were sold before the 25-year life had expired a balancing event was deemed to occur and it was necessary to calculate a balancing adjustment on sale and to recalculate the industrial buildings allowance for the new purchaser. From 21 March 2007 balancing adjustments were withdrawn and instead the new purchaser takes over the balance of the expenditure known as the residue of qualifying expenditure (RQE).

Exceptions from the post-21 March 2007 regime

6.80 The pre-21 March 2007 regime is withdrawn except in respect of balancing events arising in the following two cases:

(i)   on qualifying enterprise zone expenditure or

(ii)   in pursuance of a relevant pre-commencement contract.

For details of qualifying enterprise zones, see HMRC Capital Allowances Manual CA 37600.

For this purpose a relevant pre-commencement contract is a written contract drawn up before 21 March 2007. The contract is unconditional or its conditions have been satisfied before 21 March 2007 and no terms remain to be agreed on or after that date. In addition, the contract is not varied in a significant way on or after 21 March 2007. The balancing event in order to qualify for the pre-21 March 2007 treatment must take place before 1 April 2011 (*FA 2007, s 36*).

Pre-21 March 2007 regime

6.81   These rules apply to all sales prior to 21 March 2007 and to the exceptions detailed in **6.59** above. If a building is sold before the expiry of its 25-year life and it has been used as an industrial building throughout its life, the lesser of the sale proceeds and the cost for IBA purposes is deducted from the tax written down value that is known for these purposes as the 'residue before sale' to give rise to a balancing event. If the proceeds are less than the residue before sale a balancing allowance arises, which is deductible from profits. If the sale proceeds are more than the residue before sale a balancing charge arises that is added to profits chargeable to corporation tax. The balancing charge is restricted to the amount of the allowances actually given.

If a building is sold before the expiry of the 25-year life that has not been used throughout as an industrial building and it is sold for less than cost then the balancing allowance is the difference between the adjusted net cost of the building and the allowances actually given.

The adjusted net cost is calculated by the formula:

$$(S - P) \times (I \div R)$$

where:

S = original expenditure

P = sale proceeds

I = the period of industrial use

R = the total period of use

(*CAA 2001, s 323*)

If the building is sold for more than cost the balancing charge amounts to the allowances actually given (*CAA 2001, s 319(5)*).

The purchaser of the building is able to claim IBAs on the residue of qualifying expenditure for the remainder of the building's 25-year life according to the following formula:

$$RQE \times (A \div B)$$

where:

RQE = the amount of the residue of qualifying expenditure after sale

A = length of chargeable period

B = length of the period from the date of sale to the end of the building's tax life

(*CAA 2001, s 311*)

Example 6.16

Pre-21 March 2007 regime, Herbert Ltd prepares accounts to 31 December each year. The company bought a new factory on 31 August 1997 for £100,000. On 1 January 2007, the company entered into a contract for the sale of the building to Maximillus Ltd. The contract was in writing and no changes were made until the eventual sale went through on 1 October 2007. Herbert Ltd and Maximillius Ltd have therefore entered into a pre-sale contract and the pre-21 March 2007 regime applies. The sale price is assumed to be (i) £90,000, (ii) £3,000, (iii) £120,000. Maximillius Ltd prepares accounts to 31 March each year.

Herbert Ltd

		(i)	(ii)	(iii)
		£	£	£
1 September 1997	Cost	100,000	100,000	100,000
Year ending 31 December 1997 to year ending 31 December 2006	WDA (4%) = £4,000 per annum for 10 years	(40,000)	(40,000)	(40,000)
	Residue before sale	60,000	60,000	60,000
1 October 2007	Proceeds	(90,000)	(3,000)	(120,000)
Year ending 31 December 2007	Balancing charge	(30,000)		(60,000)
	Balancing allowance		57,000	
	But restricted to allowances given			(40,000)

Maximillius Ltd

Maximillius Ltd obtains a transitional writing down allowance.

		(i)	(ii)	(iii)
		£	£	£
	Residue after sale (workings below)	90,000	3,000	100,000
Year ending 31 March 2008 (and transitional allowances available for a further three years)	WDA Residue × 1/15	6,000	200	6,667

At 31 August 2007 the building has a remaining life of 15 years.

Calculation of residue after sale

	(i)	(ii)	(iii)
	£	£	£
Residue before sale	60,000	60,000	60,000
+ balancing charge	30,000	0	40,000
− balancing allowance	0	(57,000)	0
Residue after sale	90,000	3,000	100,000

Example 6.17

Post-21 March 2007 regime

Herbert Ltd prepares accounts to 31 December each year. The company bought a new factory on 31 August 1997 for £100,000, which it sold to Maximillus Ltd on 1 October 2007. The sale price is assumed to be (i) £90,000, (ii) £3,000, (iii) £120,000. Maximillius Ltd prepares accounts to 31 March each year.

Herbert Ltd

		(i)	(ii)	(iii)
		£	£	£
1 September 1997	Cost	100,000	100,000	100,000
Year ending 31 December 1997 to year ending 31 December 2006	WDA (4%) = £4,000 per annum for 10 years	(40,000)	(40,000)	(40,000)
	Residue before sale	60,000	60,000	60,000

Neither a balancing charge nor a balancing allowance is calculated.

Maximillius Ltd

A full writing down allowance is available for the year ended 31 March 2008 and a transitional allowance for the next three years as follows:

		(i)	(ii)	(iii)
		£	£	£
	Residue after sale (understood to be the residue before sale)	60,000	60,000	60,000
Year ending 31 March 2008	WDA (4%)	4,000	4,000	4,000
Year ending 31 March 2009	WDA (4%) × 75%	3,000	3,000	3,000
Year ending 31 March 2010	WDA (4%) × 50%	2,000	2,000	2,000
Year ending 31 March 2011	WDA (4%) ×25%	1,000	1,000	1,000
Year ending 31 March 2012	WDA (4%) × 0%			

At 31 August 2007 the building has a remaining life of 15 years.

Fixtures qualifying for plant and machinery allowances

6.82   Although IBAs have been abolished, companies may still claim plant and machinery allowances on fixtures that were subject to a previous IBA. The maximum amount of claim is determined by the formula:

$$\frac{F \times R}{T}$$

F   Part of the consideration attributable to the fixture

T   Total consideration for that transfer

R   Residue of qualifying expenditure 'RQE' attributable to the relevant interest after sale on the assumption that all the RQE were sold

If the total consideration is less than the frozen RQE then the relief is restricted to the RQE (*CAA 2001, s 186; FA 2008, Sch 27, para 5*).

Example 6.18

Francis Ltd sold an industrial building on 1 January 2010, for £200,000. The residue of expenditure after sale amounted to £100,000, of which £20,000 was attributable to fixtures that qualified for plant and machinery allowances.

Francis Ltd may claim a plant and machinery allowance based on a calculated cost of:

$$20,000 \times \frac{100,000}{200,000} = £10,000$$

Successions

6.83   Where the whole of a trade is transferred to another company under *ICTA 1988, s 343* without a change of ownership, the successor takes over the predecessor's assets at tax written down value for capital allowance purposes.

Enterprise zones

6.84   A balancing charge may still arise in respect of qualifying enterprise zone expenditure on a building on which a qualifying enterprise zone allowance has been claimed if the building is disposed of within seven years after first being brought into use (*FA 2008, Sch 27, para 31*).

Example 6.19

Jojohnson Ltd bought a building in an enterprise zone which was first used on 1 December 2010 and on which it claimed an initial allowance for the accounting period ended 31 March 2011. The relevant interest in the building is sold on 1 October 2016. Any balancing event that would have given rise to a balancing charge (and only a balancing charge) will result in a balancing charge being made.

BUSINESS PREMISES RENOVATION ALLOWANCES

Introduction

6.85   A company that incurs qualifying expenditure (**6.86**) on the conversion of a qualifying building (**6.88**) to qualifying business premises (**6.90**) or incurs qualifying expenditure on the renovation of a qualifying building may be entitled to business premises renovation allowances if all conditions are satisfied (*CAA 2001, s 360A*). The company incurring the expenditure must have a relevant interest in the building. If that company acquires an interest after incurring the expenditure it will be treated as having the interest when the expenditure was incurred (*CAA 2001, s 360F*). The allowances are given as receipts or expenses of the trade or property income (*CAA 2001, ss 360Z–360Z1*).

Qualifying expenditure

6.86 Qualifying expenditure is capital expenditure on the conversion or renovation of the qualifying building into qualifying business premises. Repair work to a qualifying building or repairs incidental to the conversion or renovation work is also included. The expenditure must be incurred before 11 April 2012 being the fifth anniversary of the appointed day. The appointed day has now been set as 11 April 2007 (*Business Premises Renovation Allowances Regulations, SI 2007/945*).

Non-qualifying expenditure

6.87 Certain types of expenditure do not qualify for the business premises renovation allowance. This includes expenditure on:

● the acquisition of land or rights in or over land;

● the extension of a qualifying building (except to the extent required for the purpose of providing a means of getting to or from qualifying business premises);

● the development of land adjoining or adjacent to a qualifying building; or

● the provision of plant and machinery, unless it is or becomes a legally recognised fixture of the building within *CAA 2001, s 173(1)(a)*.

(*CAA 2001, s 360B(3)*)

Building repair expenditure not available for relief against the profits of a property business, or of a trade, profession or vocation, for tax purposes is treated as capital expenditure (*CAA 2001, s 360B(4)*).

A qualifying building

6.88 To be a qualifying building, the following conditions must be met at the date on which the conversion or renovation work begins. The building itself can be any building or structure, or part of a building or structure. The conditions are that the building:

● is situated in a designated disadvantaged area;

● was unused throughout the period of one year ending immediately before the date on which the conversion or renovation work began;

- had last been used:

  — for the purposes of a trade, profession or vocation; or

  — as an office or offices (whether or not for the purposes of a trade, profession or vocation);

- had not last been used as, or as part of, a dwelling; and

- in the case of part of a building or structure, on that date had not last been occupied; and

is used in common with any other part of the building or structure other than a part that was unused for a year before that date or which had last been used as a dwelling.

(*CAA 2001, s 360C*)

A disadvantaged area

6.89   A disadvantaged area is determined in accordance with Treasury regulations or in their absence in accordance with the designated disadvantaged areas for the purposes of the Stamp Duty disadvantaged areas relief (*FA 2003, Sch 6*), although this relief has now been withdrawn. See HMRC website Stamp Taxes section for the list of disadvantaged areas and the postcode search tool. If a building is partly situated in a disadvantaged area a just and reasonable apportionment of the expenditure will be made.

Qualifying business premises

6.90   Business premises can be any building or structure or part of a building or structure (*CAA 2001, s 360D(2)*), but must be a qualifying building (see **6.88**). The premises must be used or be available and suitable for letting for use for the purposes of a trade, profession or vocation, or as an office or offices. There is no requirement for any office to be used for the purposes of a trade, profession or vocation, therefore, a charitable organisation would qualify. Temporary periods of unsuitability are ignored if the building qualified in the immediate prior period (*CAA 2001, s 360D*). The premises must not be used, or be available for use as, or as part of, a 'dwelling'.

A dwelling

6.91   Premises that are in use or available for use as a dwelling will not qualify for business premises renovation allowance. There is no definition of 'dwelling' in *CAA 2001*.

A 'dwelling house' is defined in *CAA 2001, s 531* as having the same meaning as in the *Rent Act 1977*. HMRC confirm in Capital Allowances Manual CA 11520 that other references to a 'dwelling house' should be read in much the same way; namely for plant and machinery, industrial buildings and research and development. A dwelling house is defined as 'a building, or part of a building, which is a person's home. A person's second or holiday home is a dwelling house as is a flat that is used as a residence. A block of flats is not a dwelling house, although the individual flats within the block may be. University halls of residence, accommodation used for holiday letting, a hospital, a nursing home or a prison are not dwelling houses'. HMRC have since confirmed that a university hall of residence is a dwelling, as far as the individual student study bedrooms are concerned, but not for the common parts being the stairs, the corridors, the TV rooms and the kitchens etc. The view extends to other types of multi-occupancy accommodation such as those provided to key workers (HMRC Brief 66/2008).

It is for further consideration as to whether a 'dwelling' which is referred to for business premises renovation allowance purposes should not only include the separate unit of living accommodation but also any attached garden, yard, garage or other outbuildings, within the same occupancy.

Relevant interest

6.92 The relevant interest is the interest held by the company that incurred the qualifying expenditure or who incurs expenditure on conversion, if the person was entitled to more than one interest of which one was a reversionary interest, the reversionary interest becomes the relevant interest. If a leasehold and a reversionary interest are present, the leasehold interest merges with the freehold interest (*CAA 2001, ss 360E and 360F*).

Initial allowances

6.93 The company incurring the expenditure on qualifying business premises may claim an initial allowance of up to 100% of that expenditure in the accounting period in which it is incurred provided it continues to own the relevant interest at the time of the claim. Part of the allowance may be disclaimed (*CAA 2001, ss 360G and 360H*).

Writing down allowances

6.94 A company may claim a writing down allowance of 25% of the balance of unrelieved qualifying expenditure at the end of the chargeable period, if all the relevant conditions continue to apply, which are that:

- the company is entitled to the relevant interest in the qualifying building;

- the company has not granted a long lease (ie longer than 50 years) of the qualifying building out of the relevant interest in consideration of the payment of a capital sum; and

- the qualifying building constitutes qualifying business premises.

Part of the writing down allowance may be disclaimed (*CAA 2001, s 360I*). Any grant received is deducted from the qualifying expenditure for this purpose (*CAA 2001, s 360L*).

The writing down allowance is proportionately increased or reduced if the chargeable period is more or less than a year (*CAA 2001, s 360J*).

Balancing events

6.95 A balancing adjustment, ie a balancing charge or an allowance, is made on the company that incurred the expenditure when a balancing event takes place. There is no balancing adjustment if the balancing event occurs more than seven years after the time when the premises were first used, or suitable for letting for the purposes of a trade, profession or vocation or as an office or as offices (*CAA 2001, s 360M*).

A balancing event occurs in the following circumstances:

- the relevant interest in the qualifying building is sold; a long lease (ie a lease longer than 50 years) of the qualifying building is granted out of the relevant interest in consideration of the payment of a capital sum; if the relevant interest is a lease, the lease ends otherwise than on the person entitled to it acquiring the interest reversionary on it;

- the qualifying building is demolished or destroyed;

- the company is wound up;

- the qualifying building ceases to be qualifying business premises (without being demolished or destroyed).

(*CAA 2001, s 360N*)

The proceeds from a balancing event are as follows:

Balancing events and proceeds:

Balancing event	Proceeds from event
1 The sale of the relevant interest.	The net proceeds of the sale.
2 The grant of a long lease out of the relevant interest.	If the capital sum paid in consideration of the grant is less than the commercial premium, the commercial premium (ie an arm's length premium).
	In any other case, the capital sum paid in consideration of the grant.
3 The coming to an end of a lease, where a person entitled to the lease and a person entitled to any superior interest are connected persons.	The market value of the relevant interest in the qualifying building at the time of the event.
4 The death of the person who incurred the qualifying expenditure.	The residue of qualifying expenditure immediately before the death.
5 The demolition or destruction of the qualifying building.	The net amount received for the remains of the qualifying building, together with:
	(a) any insurance money received in respect of the demolition or destruction; and
	(b) any other compensation of any description so received, so far as it consists of capital sums.
6 The qualifying building ceases to be qualifying business premises.	The market value of the relevant interest in the qualifying building at the time of the event.

(*CAA 2001, s 360O*)

Balancing adjustment

6.96   A balancing allowance is the difference between proceeds and the asset's tax written down value (termed as the residue) before disposal. A balancing charge arises if the proceeds are more than the tax written down value. A balancing allowance arises if the opposite occurs.

A balancing charge cannot exceed the total amount of capital allowances granted to the company making the disposal (*CAA 2001, s 360P*).

Writing off qualifying expenditure

6.97 Initial allowances are written off the qualifying expenditure at the time when the qualifying business premises are first used, or suitable for letting for use. Writing down allowances are written off at the end of the chargeable period for which the allowance is made. A balancing event occurring at the end of the chargeable period will take into account all the allowances for the period (*CAA 2001, s 360R*).

Demolition costs

6.98 If the company, which is entitled to the allowances, also incurs the cost of demolition the net cost of the demolition (ie demolition costs less sale proceeds) is added to the residue of qualifying expenditure immediately before the demolition (*CAA 2001, s 360S*).

VAT

6.99 If an additional VAT liability accrues an additional allowance is given in the accrual chargeable period (*CAA 2001, s 360U*). An additional VAT rebate will not give rise to a balancing allowance but can give rise to a balancing charge (*CAA 2001, s 360X*). This occurs when the amount of the VAT rebate is more than the amount of the residue of qualifying expenditure or there is no residue (*CAA 2001, ss 360T–360Y*).

Termination of lease

6.100 Depending on the circumstances, the termination of a lease may be treated as a disposal or a continuation of the relevant interest.

The relevant interest continues in the following circumstances:

- If, with the consent of the lessor, the lessee of the qualifying building remains in possession of the qualifying building after the termination without a new lease being granted to him, the relevant interest continues as long as the lessee remains in possession.

- If, on the termination, a new lease is granted to a lessee as a result of the exercise of an option available to him under the terms of the first lease, the second lease is treated as a continuation of the first.

- If on the termination:
  - — another lease is granted to a different lessee; and
  - — in connection with the transaction that lessee pays a sum to the person who was the lessee under the first lease,

  the two leases are to be treated as if they were the same lease, which had been assigned by the lessee under the first lease to the lessee under the second lease in consideration of the payment.

The relevant interest ceases in the following circumstance:

- If on the termination the lessor pays a sum to the lessee in respect of business premises comprised in the lease, the lease is treated as if it had come to an end by surrender in consideration of the payment.

(*CAA 2001, s 360Z3*)

FLAT CONVERSION ALLOWANCES

Relevant interest in a flat

6.101   Capital allowances are available in respect of expenditure incurred after 10 May 2001 on the conversion of parts of business premises into flats.

In order to qualify the person must not only have incurred the expenditure, but also have the relevant interest in the flat. The flat must:

- be a separate set of premises (whether or not on the same floor);
- form part of a building; and
- be divided horizontally from another part of the building.

(*CAA 2001,s 393A*)

The relevant interest is the interest the person had when the expenditure was incurred. If the person holds a reversionary interest the original interest will merge with the conversion (*CAA 2001, s 393F*).

Expenditure qualifying for flat conversion allowances

6.102   The expenditure qualifying for flat conversion allowances is capital expenditure incurred on, or in connection with:

- the conversion of part of a qualifying building into a qualifying flat;

- the renovation of a flat in a qualifying building if the flat is, or will be, a qualifying flat; or

- repairs to a qualifying building, to the extent that the repairs are incidental to expenditure on the conversion or the renovation.

In addition, the expenditure must be made on a flat or part of a building that was unused or only used for storage through the year ending immediately before the date on which the conversion or renovation work began.

Expenditure not qualifying for flat conversion allowances

6.103 The following types of expenditure do not qualify for the flat conversion allowance:

- the acquisition of land or rights in or over land;

- the extension of a qualifying building (except to the extent required for the purpose of providing a means of getting to or from a qualifying flat);

- the development of land adjoining or adjacent to a qualifying building; or

- the provision of furnishings or chattels.

Whether or not repair expenditure constitutes a capital or a revenue item is determined in accordance with the property income rules (*CAA 2001, s 393B*).

A qualifying building

6.104 In order to qualify for the flat conversion allowances the flat must form part of a qualifying building, ie a building which meets the following requirements:

- all or most of the ground floor of the building must be authorised for business use;

- it must appear that, when the building was constructed, the storeys above the ground floor were for use primarily as one or more dwelling;

- the building must not have more than four storeys above the ground floor; and

- the construction of the building must have been completed before 1 January 1980 (building extensions on or after 1 January 1980 will meet the conditions provided the extension was completed on or before 31 December 2000).

(*CAA 2001, s 393C*)

A qualifying flat

6.105   The flat itself must be a 'qualifying flat' and hence meet the following requirements:

- the flat must be in a qualifying building;
- the flat must be suitable for letting as a dwelling;
- the flat must be held for the purpose of short-term letting (ie a lease no longer than five years);
- it must be possible to gain access to the flat without using the part of the ground floor of the building that is authorised for business use in accordance with the Town and County planning requirements;
- the flat must not have more than four rooms (kitchens and bathrooms are ignored together with any closet, cloakroom or hallway not exceeding 5 square metres in area;
- the flat must not be a high-value flat;
- the flat must not be (or have been) created or renovated as part of a scheme involving the creation or renovation of one or more high-value flats; and
- the flat must not be let to a person connected with the person who incurred the expenditure on its conversion or renovation.

Periods of temporary unsuitability for letting are ignored provided they are immediately preceded by a qualifying period (*CAA 2001, ss 393C, 393D*).

High-value flats

6.106   A flat is considered to be a high-value flat if the flat would command an anticipated notional set market rent on the date the expenditure was incurred based on the following assumptions:

- the conversion or renovation has been completed;
- the flat is let furnished;
- the lease does not require the tenant to pay a premium or make any other payments to the landlord or a person connected with the landlord;
- the tenant is not connected with the person incurring the expenditure on the conversion or renovation of the flat; and
- the flat is let on a shorthold tenancy (applies to England or Wales or Scotland).

The following notional rents have been set:

Notional rent limits

Number of rooms in flat	Flats in Greater London Price per week £	Flats elsewhere Price per week £
1 or 2	£350	£150
3	£425	£225
4	£480	£300

(*CAA 2001, s 393E*)

Initial allowances

6.107   If all conditions apply an initial allowance of 100% of the qualifying expenditure is available to the person who incurred the expenditure. The allowance may be disclaimed in whole or in part. If the flat is sold before the first let the initial allowance will not be available and if already claimed will be withdrawn (*CAA 2001, s 393I*). The allowances are granted in the chargeable period in which the flat is first suitable for letting as a dwelling (*CAA 2001, s 393R*).

Writing down allowances

6.108   A company that has incurred qualifying expenditure during the chargeable period and owns the flat at the end of the chargeable period is entitled to a writing down allowance for that chargeable period. The company must have a relevant interest in the flat and not have granted a long lease (a lease with a duration of more than 50 years) out of the flat. The flat must remain a qualifying flat (*CAA 2001, s 393J*). The allowance is 25% on a reducing balance basis of the qualifying expenditure and is increased or decreased proportionately if the chargeable period is more than or less than one year. The allowance may be disclaimed in whole or in part.

Balancing events

6.109   A balancing event occurs on the following occasions:

- the relevant interest in the flat is sold;

- a long lease of the flat is granted out of the relevant interest in consideration of the payment of a capital sum;

- if the relevant interest is a lease, the lease ends otherwise than on the person entitled to it acquiring the interest reversionary on it;
- the person who incurred the qualifying expenditure dies;
- the flat is demolished or destroyed;
- the flat ceases to be a qualifying flat (without being demolished or destroyed).

(CAA 2001, s 393N)

Balancing adjustment

6.110 A balancing adjustment occurs when a balancing event takes place, being the difference between the disposal proceeds and the tax written down value of the flat. A balancing allowance occurs if the disposal proceeds are less than the tax written down value and a balancing charge occurs in the opposite situation. There is no balancing adjustment if the balancing event occurs more than seven years after the time when the flat was first suitable for letting as a dwelling. If more than one balancing event occurs, a balancing adjustment is made only on the first of them *(CAA 2001, s 393O)*.

The proceeds from the balancing event are deemed to amount to the following:

Balancing events and proceeds

Balancing event	Proceeds from event
1. The sale of the relevant interest.	The net proceeds of the sale.
2. The grant of a long lease out of the relevant interest.	If the capital sum paid in consideration of the grant is less than the commercial premium (amount paid at arm's length rate), the commercial premium. In any other case, the capital sum paid in consideration of the grant
3. The coming to an end of a lease, where a person entitled to the lease and a person entitled to any superior interest are connected persons	The market value of the relevant interest in the flat at the time of the event.
4. The death of the person who incurred the qualifying expenditure.	The residue of qualifying expenditure immediately before the death.

Balancing event	Proceeds from event
5. The demolition or destruction of the flat.	The net amount received for the remains of the flat, together with: (a) any insurance money received in respect of the demolition or destruction; and (b) any other compensation of any description so received, so far as it consists of capital sums

Demolition costs are added to the residue of expenditure immediately before demolition (*CAA 2001, s 393S*). The allowance is given as a Schedule A expense or as a trading expense depending on the business activities of the lessor.

Chapter 7

Intangible assets

SCOPE PRE AND POST 1 APRIL 2002

7.1 The intangible assets regime was introduced by *FA 2002, s 84, Schs 29* and *30*, with effect from 1 April 2002, to provide companies with tax relief on their intangible assets and their intellectual property. These rules and their subsequent amendments have now been collated and redrafted, and are included in *Corporation Tax Act 2009 (CTA 2009), ss 711–931*, as part of the government's tax law rewrite project. The intention in drafting *CTA 2009* was not to change the existing legislation, but to make it clearer. The new corporation tax provisions apply to accounting periods beginning on or after 1 April 2009. The references, where applicable, in this chapter are to *CTA 2009*. For the previous legislation, please see *Corporation Tax 2008/09* (Tottel Publishing).

Existing assets

7.2 The pre 1 April 2002 rules have been in existence for many years and continue to apply to assets in existence on that date *(CTA 2009, s 882(1))*. The legislation terms these assets as 'existing assets' *(CTA 2009, s 881)*.

Chargeable intangible assets

7.3 The intangible asset regime rules apply to assets which are:

- intangible assets created by the company after 1 April 2002; or

- intangible assets that the company acquired after 1 April 2002, from a third party who was unrelated to the company at the time of the acquisition *(CTA 2009, s 882(1))*.

The legislation terms these assets as 'chargeable intangible assets', being assets on whose realisation any gain would be a chargeable realisation gain on the company *(CTA 2009, s 741(1))*. A chargeable realisation gain in relation to an asset means a gain on the realisation of that asset that gives rise to a credit to be accounted for under the intangible asset rules *(CTA 2009, s 741(2))*.

The intangible asset regime rules also apply to post 1 April 2002 chargeable intangible assets acquired from related third parties in the following circumstances:

- the asset at the time of sale was a chargeable intangible asset of the vendor company;

- if the asset is acquired from an intermediary who acquired the asset post 1 April 2002 from a third person, at the time of acquisition, the third person was neither a related party of the intermediary, nor of the company; or

- the asset was created after 1 April 2002 either by the person from whom it was acquired or by any other person (*CTA 2009, s 882(3), (4) and (5)*).

Transitional period

7.4   Therefore, the intangible asset regime does not apply to existing assets; namely those held by the company on 1 April 2002 or those acquired from a related party who held them on 1 April 2002. If an asset was internally generated, eg goodwill, and the business was in existence prior to 1 April 2002, the asset is treated as an existing asset prior to 1 April 2002. That being the case, the goodwill arising on incorporation of a sole trader or partnership business will remain as an existing asset and remain subject to capital gains on disposal if it was in existence prior to 1 April 2002. HMRC Corporate Intangibles Research and Development Manual CIRD 10145 gives a useful key to manual references applying to pre 1 April 2002 assets (grand-fathered assets). Goodwill is regarded as being created prior to 1 April 2002 if the business was carried on at any time by the company or by a related party, and on or after 1 April 2002 in any other case (*CTA 2009, s 884*).

Example 7.1

Ted commenced trading as a sole trader on 1 January 1987. Over recent years his business has expanded and he incorporates the business on 1 January 2010. He transfers the tangible fixed assets for £50,000 and the goodwill professionally valued at £20,000 to Ted Ltd, his newly formed company. Although Ted transfers the goodwill to the company after 1 April 2002, it was in existence prior to 1 April 2002 and is not within the intangible assets regime.

This example is continued in **7.10**, Example 7.3.

Example 7.2

Bill commenced trading as a sole trader on 1 January 2003. His business has expanded and he incorporates the business on 1 January 2010. He transfers the tangible fixed assets for £100,000 and the goodwill professionally valued at £40,000 to Bill Ltd his newly formed company. Bill's goodwill was not in existence prior to 1 April 2002 and is therefore within the intangible assets regime.

This example is continued in **7.10**, Example 7.3.

MEANING OF AN INTANGIBLE ASSET

7.5   The legislation gives intangible assets their accountancy meaning and includes an internally generated intangible asset. The inclusion of 'an internally generated intangible asset' is made by *FA 2009, s 70* with effect from 22 April 2009 to clarify a misunderstanding amongst taxpayers. The legislation always intended that internally generated assets were to be included within the meaning of intangible assets, but some companies were unsure. The amendment affects accounting periods beginning on or after 22 April 2009. An accounting period that covers 22 April 2009 is treated as two notional accounting periods, either side of that date.

The amendments are treated as always having had effect and are to apply for the purposes of calculating the future tax consequences of past transactions (*CTA 2009, s 712; FA 2009, s70(2)*).

Accountancy definition

7.6   FRS 10 (goodwill and intangible assets) defines intangible assets as:

'Non-financial fixed assets that do not have a physical substance but are identifiable and are controlled by the entity through custody or legal rights'.

Companies Act 2006, s 396 and the *Large and Medium-sized Companies and Groups (Accounts and Reports) Regulations 2008, SI 2008/410*, include intangible fixed assets under the following sub-headings:

- development costs;

- concessions, patents, licences, trade marks and similar rights and assets; and

- goodwill.

The assets may only be included in the balance sheet if they were acquired for valuable consideration or, with the exception of goodwill were created by the company itself.

For example, a company may include intangible assets under the following headings within intangible assets:

- patents, trade marks and other product rights;

- brand names;

- goodwill;

- publishing copyrights, rights and titles;

- newspaper titles;

- programmes, film rights and scores;

- databases;

- know-how agreements;

- development costs;

- betting office licences;

- trade value of retail outlets;

- exhibition rights and other similar intangible assets.

For taxation purposes intellectual property includes UK and overseas patents, trademarks, registered designs, copyright or design rights, plant breeders' rights, together with rights under *s 7* of the *Plant Varieties Act 1997* and the overseas equivalent. Assets owned outright and by licence are included, as are assets that are not protected by a legal right but which have an industrial, commercial or other economic value. Options or rights to acquire or dispose of an intangible asset are also included (*CTA 2009, s 713(2)*).

The intangible assets regime applies to goodwill, and the accounting meaning is adopted (*CTA 2009, s 715*), which defines goodwill as:

> 'The difference between the cost of an acquired entity and the aggregate of the fair values of that entity's identifiable assets and liabilities. Positive goodwill arises when the acquisition cost exceeds the aggregate fair values of the identifiable assets and liabilities. Negative goodwill arises when the aggregate fair values of the identifiable assets and liabilities of the entity exceed the acquisition cost'.

However, for accounting periods beginning on or after 22 April 2009, 'goodwill' for the purposes of the taxation of intangible assets régime includes internally generated goodwill and hence all goodwill is included, not just purchased goodwill. If an accounting period transverses 22 April 2009, it is divided for this purpose on a time basis between the period pre and post 22 April 2009. Goodwill is treated as created in the course of carrying on the business in question (*CTA 2009, s 715; FA 2009, s 70(3)*). If a company or a related party held an asset before 1 April 2002 (but not on or after) that did not qualify for capital allowances, it will also be excluded from the intangible assets regime (*FA 2009, s 70(6); CTA 2009, s 885*).

If a company has not drawn up accounts on this basis, it will be treated as having done so for the purposes of corporation tax. Therefore, HMRC will adjust accounts if they do not comply with GAAP and, in particular, FRS 10 (goodwill and intangible assets) (*CTA 2009, s 717(1)*).

For further discussion of the constituent parts of goodwill, see HMRC Capital Gains Manual CG 68050 to CG 68000 and *Balloon Promotions Ltd v HMRC* (2006) SpC 524.

Excluded assets

7.7   Assets entirely excluded from the intangible assets regime comprise rights over land or tangible moveable property, oil licences, financial assets, assets representing production expenditure on films, shares in a company, trust and partnership rights and powers and assets neither held for a business nor a commercial purpose (*CTA 2009, ss 803–809*).

The FRS 13 definition of financial assets (derivatives and other financial instruments: disclosure) is adopted, namely:

'cash, a contractual right to receive cash or another financial asset from another entity, a contractual right to exchange financial instruments with another entity under conditions that are potentially favourable or an equity instrument of another entity.'

Tax legislation adopts the same meaning (*CTA 2009, s 806(2)*).

Assets excluded in certain situations

7.8   Apart from royalties, all assets owned by a life assurance business and a mutual trade association are excluded from the definition of intangibles. Expenditure on films, sound recording and computer software expenditure (when accounted for with the hardware) is also excluded apart from expenditure on royalties (*CTA 2009, ss 810–813*). If the computer software is bought separately, the company may elect for the software to be removed from the intangible assets regime (*CTA 2009, s 813*).

The valuation of the intangible assets if need be is made on a just and reasonable basis.

Royalties and licences granted over existing assets from related parties are themselves treated as existing assets (*CTA 2009, s 896*).

Research and development expenditure

7.9   Research and development expenditure has its own taxation regime (see **Chapter 8**). The proceeds from the sale of research and development are included within the intangible assets regime (*CTA 2009, s 814(4)*).

CORPORATION TAX TREATMENT

Debits and credits

7.10   With effect from 1 April 2002, gains and losses relating to intangible assets bought or made for continuous use in a business are taxed generally as revenue items (*CTA 2009, s 747*).

Expenditure within the legislation is known as 'debits' and income as 'credits'.

The treatment of the debits and credits in calculating the taxable profits will depend on whether the assets are held for the purposes of a trade, a property business or if the company is non-trading.

Debits and credits in respect of assets held for the purposes of a trade are treated as receipts and expenses of the trade in calculating the profits of the trade for tax purposes.. Likewise, debits and credits held for a property business are treated as receipts and expenses of that property business. A property business includes an ordinary property business, furnished holiday lettings or an overseas property business.

Expenditure and the reversal of an earlier gain are deductible from profits as it is written off in the accounts. Depreciation is allowed on an accounting basis or on a revenue fixed rate basis (*CTA 2009, s 726(1)*).

HMRC will look to consistency with UK group accounting policies to determine whether the individual company's accounting treatment may be adopted for taxation purposes (*CTA 2009, s 718(2)*).

Example 7.3

Example continued from Examples 7.1 and 7.2.

Assuming the same facts as Examples 7.1 and 7.2, Bill Ltd but not Ted Ltd will be able to write off the cost of the goodwill on incorporation in its books. Assuming Bill decides a 10% deprecation rate, the annual write off is £4,000 (10% × £40,000).

This example is continued in Example 7.5.

Annual payments and patent royalties

7.11   Irrespective of when the intangible assets were acquired, the related annual payments and patent royalties are no longer deducted from total income as a charge on income. Instead they are deducted as a 'debit' on an accruals basis (*CTA 2009, s 728(5)*).

If the royalty is payable to or for the benefit of a related party and the payment is not made within 12 months after the end of the accounting period it cannot be allowed as a deduction for that period (*CTA 2009, s 851*). See **7.28** regarding related parties.

Depreciation

7.12   The company may select its own depreciation policy or it may adopt the legislation policy. If using the legislation policy, it must make a written irrevocable election to HMRC no later than two years after the end of the accounting period in which the asset is created or acquired. The asset is then depreciated at 4% per annum on a straight-line basis apportioned for accounting periods less than 12 months (*CTA 2009, ss 730* and *731*).

Non-trading debits and credits

7.13   Non-trading debits and credits are netted off against each other. A net gain is chargeable to corporation tax. A net loss is relieved in the following way:

- By claim within two years of the end of the accounting period to which the loss relates to set the loss against the company's total profits for that accounting period.

- By claim within two years of the end of the accounting period to which the loss relates to surrender by group relief under *ICTA 1988, s 403.*

- Any unutilised loss is carried forward to the next accounting period as if it were a non-trading debit of that period (*CTA 2009, s 753*).

PRESCRIBED DEBIT AND CREDIT ADJUSTMENTS

7.14   There are certain prescribed pro rata debit and credit adjustments. These are summarised in the following paragraphs.

Impairment review

7.15   The acquisition of an asset may be part of FRS 7 (fair values *in acquisition accounting*) impairment review because the acquisition cost is more than fair value. This could happen if a subsidiary was acquired in stages and deferred values are obtained. The accounting loss pro rata the tax and accounting cost is an allowable deduction from profits. The following formula is used to calculate the deductible debit in the year of acquisition:

$$L \times (E \div CE)$$

where:

L   =   the amount of the loss recognised for accounting purposes
E   =   the amount of expenditure on the asset that is recognised for tax purposes
CE =   the amount capitalised in respect of expenditure on the asset

In subsequent periods of account the following adjustment is made:

$$L \times (WDV \div AV)$$

where:

L   =   the amount of the loss recognised for accounting purposes
WDV   =   the tax written down value of the asset immediately before the amortisation charge is made or, as the case may be, the impairment loss is recognised for accounting purposes
AV   =   the value of the asset recognised for accounting purposes immediately before the amortisation charge or, as the case may be, the impairment review (*CTA 2009, s 729*)

Reversal of a previous accounting gain

7.16 If an accounting loss is recognised where the tax value and the accounting value of the asset differ, the amount of the loss is adjusted in accordance with the following formula:

$$RL \times (PC \div RG)$$

where:

RL = the amount of the loss recognised for accounting purposes
RG = the amount of the gain that is (in whole or in part) reversed
PC = the amount of the credit previously brought into account for tax purposes in respect of the gain (*CTA 2009, s 732*).

This could occur on a change in an accounting policy during an accounting period.

Income taxable

7.17 Receipts, revaluations, negative goodwill credits and reversals of any previous debits are all taxable as income on an accounting basis as they accrue (*CTA 2009, s 721*). Apart from assets for which an election has been made for the 4% fixed rate depreciation, accounting adjustments brought about by a revaluation of intangible assets or the restoration of past losses are adjusted by the following formula:

$$I \times (WDV \div AV)$$

where:

I = the amount of the increase in the accounting value of the asset
WDV = the tax written down value of the asset immediately before the revaluation
AV = the value of the asset by reference to which the revaluation is carried out (*CTA 2009, s 723*).

Any gain recognised in calculating negative goodwill is apportioned to the intangible assets on a just and reasonable basis and included in income accordingly (*CTA 2009, s 725*). Accounting gain reversals of previous losses recognised in the company's accounts is adjusted as follows:

$$RG \times (D \div RL)$$

where:

RG = the amount of the gain recognised for accounting purposes

RL = the amount of the loss that is (in whole or in part) reversed

D   = the amount of the tax debit previously brought into account in respect of the loss (*CTA 2009, s 725*).

Realisation of intangible fixed assets

7.18   Amounts arising from asset sale (proceeds less incidental costs of realisation) or balance sheet writing off are compared to the asset's tax written down value and the resultant net debit or credit is included in calculating profits chargeable to corporation tax. Abortive expenditure costs are allowed as a deduction (*CTA 2009, s 740*). In the case of a part realisation, the tax written down value is apportioned by the following formula:

$$\frac{(AVB - AVA)}{AVB}$$

where:

AVA = the accounting value immediately before the realisation compared with that immediately after the realisation.

AVB = the accounting value immediately before the realisation (*CTA 2009, s 737*).

Cost is substituted for tax written down value (WDV) – see **7.15** – if the asset has not been depreciated. Where there is no balance sheet valuation for the asset, possibly because it was created by the company, the full sale proceeds are brought into the profit and loss account as income.

Where the asset has been written down on an accounting basis, the tax written down value is calculated as follows:

$$\text{Tax cost} - \text{Debits} + \text{Credits}$$

where:

Tax cost = the cost of the asset recognised for tax purposes

Debits   = the total amount of the debits, ie depreciation previously brought into account for tax purposes

Credits   = the total amount of any credits, ie revaluation amounts, previously brought into account for tax purposes (*CTA 2009, s 742*).

The comparable adjustment for assets that have been written down on the fixed basis (see **7.12**) is as follows:

215

Tax cost − Debits

where:

Tax cost = the cost of the asset recognised for tax purposes

Debits = the total amount of the depreciation debits previously brought into account for tax purposes on the fixed rate basis (*CTA 2009, s 743*).

Part realisation of an asset

7.19   If there has been a partial sale of an intangible asset, the tax written down value of the asset immediately after the part realisation is calculated as follows:

$$\text{WDVB} \times (\text{AVA} \div \text{AVB})$$

where:

WDVB = the tax written down value of the asset immediately before the part realisation

AVA = the accounting value of the asset immediately after the part realisation

AVB = the accounting value immediately before the part realisation (*CTA 2009, s 744*).

An asset may cease to be a chargeable asset during its lifetime, in which case there is a deemed disposal for the company (*CTA 2009, s 859*).

SALE OF AN INTANGIBLE ASSET

Sale proceeds

7.20   Sale proceeds arising from a sale of intangible assets are credited to the profit and loss account. Disposal costs are allowed as a deductible debit. Relief is also given for abortive costs of sale (*CTA 2009, s 740*).

Roll-over and reinvestment relief

7.21   When a company sells an intangible asset it may, provided all conditions are met, be able to claim reinvestment relief. The effect being that it will avoid the credit (sale proceeds less incidental costs of sale) to its profits.

The conditions imposed are first that the asset disposed of must have been within the intangible assets regime throughout its ownership. Where the asset was within the intangible assets regime at the time of sale and for a substantial period of the ownership (but not the whole), it will be treated as a separate asset for the time that it so qualified. Sales proceeds are apportioned on a just and reasonable basis. Secondly, the sale proceeds must be greater than the original cost of the original asset or adjusted cost where there has been a part realisation.

The new assets acquired must be immediately chargeable intangible assets for the company as soon as they are acquired (as recognised for accounting purposes). The expenditure must be capitalised. The time limits for incurring the expenditure are 12 months before the sale of the old asset and three years thereafter (*CTA 2009, s 756*).

Any claims to HMRC must be in writing, must specify the old assets, identify the expenditure on new assets, and must state the amount of the relief claimed (*CTA 2009, s 757*). A company may make a provisional claim for relief if it has sold an intangible asset and intends to replace it with new intangible assets. The provisional claim continues until the earlier of its being withdrawn, replaced by a new claim or the expiry of four years after the end of the accounting period in which the realisation took place. Adjustments are then accordingly made to the corporation tax returns or are assessed regardless of time limits (*CTA 2009, s 761*).

The effect of the claim is to reduce the realisation proceeds and the tax cost of the new asset by the same amount.

The amount is calculated as follows:

- If the new expenditure on other assets is equal to or greater than the proceeds of realisation of the old asset, the amount available for relief is the amount by which the proceeds of realisation exceed the tax cost of the old asset.

- If the amount of the new expenditure on other assets is less than the proceeds of realisation of the old asset, the amount available for relief is the amount (if any) by which the new expenditure on other assets exceeds the tax cost of the old asset.

- If the new expenditure does not exceed the tax cost of the old asset no relief is given (*CTA 2009, s 758*).

Example 7.4

P Ltd makes up accounts to 31 December each year. The following accounting transactions take place:

7.22   *Intangible assets*

Year ended		Sale proceeds £000	Cost £000	Profit and loss account £000		Net book value £000
31 December 2009	Bought copyright with an estimated life of five years		50	10 debit	Annual depreciation	40
31 December 2010	Sold	70		30 credit	Profit on sale	Nil
	Bought copyright with an estimated life of five years		75	15 debit	Annual depreciation	60

For corporation tax purposes the company wishes to claim reinvestment relief on the first disposal. In order to do this it must first analyse the gain arising.

Year ended	Total gain £000	Arising from depreciation £000	Gain available for reinvestment relief £000	Actual new chargeable intangible asset purchased £000	Tax cost of new asset purchased £000
31 December 2010	30	10	20	75	55

The corporation tax deductions on these transactions are as follows:

Year ended 31 December		Purchase and sale transactions £000	Reinvestment relief £000	Opening tax value £000	Adjustment to profits for corporation tax £000	Closing tax value £000
2009	Bought			50	10 Debit	40
2010	Sold	70	20		10 Credit	Nil
	Bought	75	20	55	11 Debit	44

7.22   On a part realisation, the adjusted cost is calculated as follows:

$$\frac{(AVB - AVA)}{AVB}$$

where:

AVA = the accounting value immediately after the part realisation

AVB = the accounting value immediately before the part realisation (*CTA 2009, s 759*).

A company may wish to sell and reacquire the same asset. In which case this is treated as an independent disposal on which reinvestment relief is available. Deemed realisations are not recognised for reinvestment relief.

GROUPS

Meaning of a group

7.23   Group for intangible assets purposes adopts the capital gains tax definition: see **20.14**.

A group member must be an effective 51% subsidiary of the principal company, but the principal company cannot be a 75% subsidiary of another group and a company cannot be a member of more than one group.

Four criteria are applied to determine to which group a company belongs in the following order: voting rights, profits available for distribution, assets on a winding-up and percentage of directly and indirectly owned ordinary shares (*CTA 2009, s 768*).

The group remains intact until the principal company becomes a member of another group, in which case other companies join the group. The four criteria above must be applied to determine the group members.

Intra-group asset transfers

7.24   Intra-group transfers of assets have no tax effect except for tax-exempt friendly societies and dual resident investing companies. The transferee company adopts the asset as if it were its own.

Reinvestment relief is also available to group members but not in respect of intra-group asset transfers. Neither is it available to a dual resident investing company. Both companies involved are required to claim (*CTA 2009, s 777*).

Purchase by a company of the controlling interest in a non-group company that subsequently becomes a member of the group is treated for reinvestment purposes as a purchase of the underlying assets on which relief is available. Expenditure incurred by a company on its new purchase is treated as the lesser of the tax written down value of the underlying assets immediately before acquisition and the consideration paid for the controlling interest. If the relief applies the tax value of the underlying intangible assets is reduced by the amount of the relief (*CTA 2009, ss 778 and 779*).

Leaving a group

7.25 When a company leaves a group, having acquired a chargeable intangible asset by intra-group transfer within the past six years, there is a de-grouping charge on the transferee based on market value at the date of transfer. A debit or credit adjustment is made in the accounting period in which the company leaves the group (*CTA 2009, s 780*).

There is no de-grouping charge where two companies who have made intra-group transfers of assets within the time limits leave the group at the same time. There is no de-grouping charge if the entire group becomes a member of another group. If the transferee ceases to qualify as a member of the new group within six years of transfer, it is treated as having sold and reacquired the asset at the time of transfer. Any adjustment is included in the corporation tax computation for the period in which the company leaves the group. Group de-grouping charges can, by joint election between transferor and transferee company, be passed to the transferor company to form part of its income. It will be treated as a non-trading gain. The transferor company must be resident in the UK or be deemed to be carrying on a trade in the UK through a branch or agency. (The company must not be a friendly society or a dual resident holding company.) Unpaid tax may be recovered from any group members or controlling directors of non-UK resident companies carrying on a trade in the UK, if not paid by the relevant company. Inter company roll-over and de-grouping charge payments are left out of account for corporation tax purposes provided they do not exceed the amount of relief (*CTA 2009, s 799*). There is no de-grouping charge on a demerger carried out for bona fide commercial reasons.

Reconstructions

7.26 In general, reconstructions avoid a tax charge. In order to ensure this effect a clearance procedure is available (*CTA 2009, s 832*).

In a scheme of reconstruction where the whole or part of a business is transferred for shares or loan stock by a company, provided the company received no part of the consideration there is no tax charge. Although the consideration must be in shares apportionment is possible. The reconstruction must be made for bona fide commercial reasons and must not be part of a scheme of avoidance. (The company must not be friendly society or a dual resident holding company) (*CTA 2009, s 818*).

There is no tax charge on transfers of UK trades and companies resident in EU states follow the same lines provided the consideration is in securities issued by the transferor to the transferee. The intangible asset is transferred to the transferee company complete with its tax history (*CTA 2009, s 820*).

Where intangible assets are transferred from a UK company's overseas branch to a non-UK resident company the gain may be deferred, the trade must be transferred in exchange for securities. If the securities are later sold a taxable credit must be brought into account by the transferor equal to the deferred gain. Also, if at any time within six years after the transfer the transferee disposes of the relevant assets, taxable credit must be brought into account by the transferor equal to the deferred gain (*CTA 2009, s 829*). Relief for any foreign tax is available if there is no deferral of the gain (*CTA 2009, Sch 1, para 258*).

Where an existing intangible asset (see **7.2**) is transferred under a reconstruction to which *TCGA 1992, s 139 or s 140A* applies, the asset remains an existing asset in the hands of the transferee (*CTA 2009, s 818*).

Related parties

7.27 Transfers of intangible assets between related parties take place at market value (*CTA 2009, s 846*) subject to the transfer pricing provisions.

Example 7.5

Continued from Example 7.3.

Continuing with the same facts as Example 7.2 and Example 7.3, Bill had his goodwill upon incorporation professionally valued so there is no question of its value being adjusted.

However, if Bill had opted for a *TCGA 1992, s 165* hold-over claim (see *Capital Gains Tax 2008/09* (Tottel Publishing)) the amount held over will be deductible from the deemed market value of the goodwill for the purposes of calculating the annual write off (*CTA 2009, s 849(1)*).

Thus, supposing Bill's hold-over relief amounted to £10,000, the annual write off will be £3,000 (10% × (40,000–10,000)).

7.28 Part realisation roll-over relief is not available to a related party. Royalty payments to a related party not paid within 12 months of the accounting period in which they are accrued and not brought in as a credit by the recipient company are not allowed as a deduction for the payee.

A related party relationship exists where:

7.28 *Intangible assets*

Case 1

A company has control or a major interest in another company

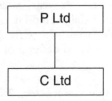

Case 2

Companies are under the control of the same person.

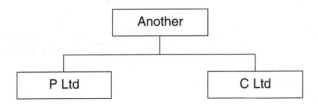

Case 3

C Ltd is a close company of which P is a participator or an associate of a participator (*ICTA 1988, s 417*; close company definitions apply: see **4.9**, **4.12**).

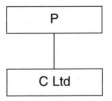

Case 4

P Ltd and C Ltd are companies in the same group.

Control means that a person is able to secure that the company's affairs are conducted in accordance with their wishes either by shareholdings, voting power or by powers conferred by the Articles of Association. A major interest exists if two persons have control of a company and each of them has at least 40% of the total shareholding (*CTA 2009, s 837(1), (2)*). Rights and powers owned singly and jointly are taken into account namely: rights and powers that he is entitled to acquire at a future date or will, at a future date, become entitled to acquire and others rights and powers that can be exercised on his behalf, under his direction or for his benefit. Rights and powers of a person connected with him are also taken into account, but not persons connected to a connected person (*CTA 2009, s 838*). Loan security arrangements are not taken into account. Rights and powers of a person as a member of a partnership are only taken into account if the person has a major interest (40%) in the partnership (*CTA 2009, s 840*).

Connected persons

7.29   Connected persons include spouses and civil partners, relatives and relatives of their spouses. Relatives are siblings, grandparents and grandchildren. (Great-grandparents and great-grandchildren etc are also included.) The trustee of a settlement is connected with the settlor, a person connected with the settlor and any company connected with the settlement. The company must be a close company (or only not a close company because it is non-UK resident) of which the trustees are participators (*CTA 2009, s 843*). (A company is a body corporate or unincorporated association (*ICTA 1988, s 832*) see **1.2**).

Grants

7.30   Regional development grants and certain Northern Ireland grants are not taxable credits for the purposes of computing corporation tax. All other grants received are taxable credits (*CTA 2009, ss 852 and 853*).

Finance lessors

7.31   Finance lessors are within the intangible assets regime for assets leased under finance leases to other companies. However, neither fixed rate depreciation nor reinvestment relief is available (*CTA 2009, s 855 and the Corporation Tax (Finance Leasing of Intangible Assets) Regulations 2002, SI 2002/1967*).

INTERNATIONAL ASPECTS

Company ceasing to be UK resident

7.32   There is a deemed disposal of a chargeable intangible asset at market value when a company ceases to be UK resident (*CTA 2009, s 859*). A UK holding company and a 75% subsidiary may jointly elect for the gain to be postponed on assets used for the purposes of the trade of the branch or agency where market value exceeds cost. The gain being the excess market value over cost is chargeable as a non-trading taxable credit on the UK holding company if the now non-resident subsidiary company disposes of the asset within six years of becoming non-resident. The gain is also chargeable on the holding company if it ceases to be UK resident or the non-resident company is no longer a subsidiary.

Controlled foreign companies

7.33   Gains relating to controlled foreign companies are brought into the assumed profits computation (see **13.23–13.63**) for *ICTA 1988, s 747* for apportionment purposes as taxable credits (*CTA 2009, s 870*).

Chapter 8

Research and development

INTRODUCTION

8.1　Relief is available for capital research and development (R&D) through the capital allowance rules, and for revenue R&D through the tax relief for expenditure on in-house and contracted-out research and development rules (*CTA 2009, ss 1039–1084*). Similar relief is available for expenditure on vaccine research (*CTA 2009, ss 1085–1142*).

CAPITAL EXPENDITURE

Capital allowances

8.2　Capital allowances on research and development allowances may be claimed by any size of company but only if the company carries on a trade. If the company does not already carry on a trade it must set up and commence a trade connected with the R&D after incurring the expenditure (*CAA 2001, s 439(1)*). The company need not carry on the research itself; a third party may carry on the research on the company's behalf. The R&D must be related to the trade that is being carried on, known as 'the relevant trade'. R&D capital allowances are treated as an expense of the trade, and any charge as a receipt of the trade (*CAA 2001, s 450*). Capital R&D expenditure qualifies for 100% first year allowance for capital allowance purposes. R&D is also available on oil and gas exploration. Thus the company is able to write off the full cost in the accounting period in which it is incurred (*CAA 2001, s 437*).

Meaning of research and development

8.3　For the purposes of claiming 100% capital allowances on R&D, the definition of R&D follows the accounting definition given in UK GAAP SSAP 13 (accounting for research and development) or IAS 38 (intangible assets) as appropriate (*ICTA 1988, s 837A*).

8.4 *Research and development*

The SSAP 13 definition

- Pure (or basic) research: experimental or theoretical work undertaken primarily to acquire new scientific or technical knowledge for its own sake rather than directed towards any specific aim or application.

- Applied research: original or critical investigation undertaken in order to gain new scientific or technical knowledge and directed towards a specific practical aim or objective.

- Development: use of scientific or technical knowledge in order to produce new or substantially improved materials, devices, products or services, to install new processes or systems prior to the commencement of commercial production or commercial applications, or to improving substantially those already produced or installed.

The IAS 38 definition

- Research is original and planned investigation undertaken with the prospect of gaining new scientific or technical knowledge and understanding.

- Development is the application of research findings or other knowledge to a plan or design for the production of new or substantially improved materials, devices, products, processes, systems or services before the start of commercial production or use.

8.4   Allowances are given for pure and applied research in order to gain new or scientific knowledge. Oil and gas exploration is included. The trade related R&D may be of a sort that may lead to or facilitate an extension of the company's trade. It may also be of a medical nature, which has a special relation to the welfare of workers employed in that trade (*CAA 2001, s 439(5)*). If the research is carried on by a third party on the company's behalf, the company must retain responsibility for the research and the expenditure must be undertaken directly.

Example 8.1

S Ltd had a part share in a petroleum exploration licence. It arranged for G Ltd to provide the funds and the equipment to conduct operations. In return S Ltd gave G Ltd the rights to the ownership of all the petroleum won and saved to which it was entitled. G Ltd claimed that the expenditure incurred under that agreement qualified as R&D capital expenditure because it was incurred on scientific research directly undertaken on its behalf.

G Ltd is not entitled to the R&D capital allowance because the research was not directly undertaken by or on behalf of G Ltd. The facts are those of *Gaspet Ltd v Ellis* (1987) 60 TC 91, [1987] STC 362, [1987] 1 WLR 769.

8.5   Medical research undertaken for the benefit of the community as a whole may qualify for R&D allowance if it may lead to or facilitate an extension of the trade. For example, medical research undertaken by a drug company for the purpose of its trade may qualify because it is related to its trade of manufacturing drugs (HMRC Capital Allowances Manual CA 60400). With effect from 1 April 2006 for large companies, and 1 August 2008 for small companies, R&D expenditure has been expanded to include payments made to clinical trial volunteers for taking part in such tests (*CTA 2009, Sch 2, para 124*).

Qualifying expenditure

8.6   Relief may be claimed on providing facilities to carry out the research (*CAA 2001, s 438*). Land does not qualify for relief, nor does the cost of a dwelling that is more than 25% of the cost of the building (*CAA 2001, s 438(4)*). Expenditure on the acquisition of rights in research and development or rights arising out of research and development does not qualify for R&D (*CAA 2001, s 438(2)*).

Example 8.2

Novotech plc is engaged in a qualifying research project and incurs the following expenditure:

- A building for £2.5m excluding the cost of the land. The cost of the building is apportioned between research laboratories £2m and living accommodation £500,000.

- A car for each researcher who is required to travel about the country carrying out research activities.

- The patent rights to a patented invention that Novotech considers may be of assistance with the current project.

The building, including the living accommodation, will qualify for R&D. This is because the living accommodation is less than 25% of the cost of the whole building. The motor cars qualify as expenditure on research and development. The cost of acquiring the patent rights does not qualify for R&D because it is expenditure incurred in acquiring rights arising out of R&D.

Allowances

8.7   A 100% capital allowance may be claimed on the expenditure during the accounting period in which the expenditure is incurred. A reduced claim may be made (*CAA 2001, s 441(3)*) but there is no facility to claim further allowances (such as writing down allowances) in subsequent accounting periods.

If ownership of the asset changes hands or if it destroyed, a disposal value must be included within the company's corporation tax computation. On sale it will be the net proceeds of sale or market value in other cases. If the asset is demolished or destroyed any insurance or compensation monies received are taken as the disposal value. In the accounting period of disposal a balancing charge will be included being the smaller of the difference between the disposal value and the balance of unclaimed expenditure and the R&D allowance claimed (*CAA 2001, s 442*). There is no facility in the legislation for claiming a balancing allowance.

The balancing charge and R&D allowance are treated accordingly as receipts and expenses of the trade (*CAA 2001, s 450*).

Example 8.3

In the year of acquisition of a £2.5m research building, Novotech plc makes a claim for £1m R&D. Some years later it sells the building for £5m. The balancing charge is the smaller of:

- the difference between the disposal value and the balance of unclaimed expenditure:

$$£5m - £(2.5m - 1m) = £3.5m$$

and

- the R&D allowance claimed:

$$£1m$$

The balancing charge is £1m, the R&D claim made.

8.8 If the company ceases to use the asset for the R&D purpose this is not a disposal for R&D purposes. The R&D allowance is eventually recouped when the asset is sold. On a change of use the asset may qualify for plant and machinery allowances or industrial buildings allowance (see **Chapter 6**). The R&D allowance is not clawed back at this stage. It is only clawed back on the eventual sale of the asset.

Disposal value

8.9 If an R&D asset on which an R&D allowance has been claimed is demolished and the demolition costs exceed the disposal value, (which in many cases may be nil), the excess demolition costs may qualify for R&D allowance. They will only qualify if the asset has not begun to be used for any purpose other than research and development (*CAA 2001, s 445*). The excess is not to be treated as expenditure on any property that replaces the demolished asset.

Any additional VAT liability incurred on the R&D asset qualifies for R&D allowances, provided that the company which incurred the original expenditure on the asset still owns it and the asset has not been demolished or destroyed. Any additional VAT rebate is treated as a disposal value, provided that the company that incurred the original expenditure on the asset still owns it and the asset has not been demolished or destroyed. If there is no unclaimed R&D allowance, the VAT rebate is treated as a balancing charge. If there is unclaimed R&D allowance and the additional VAT rebate is less than the unclaimed R&D allowance, the additional VAT rebate is deducted from the unclaimed R&D allowance, and the result treated as the unclaimed R&D allowance for future disposal events. If the additional VAT rebate is more than the unclaimed R&D allowance, the difference is treated as a balancing charge (*CAA 2001, ss 448, 449*). (See also HMRC Capital Allowances Manual CA 60750.)

REVENUE EXPENDITURE

Revenue deductions

8.10   The tax relief for expenditure on research and development provisions may be claimed by all companies. The rules applying to SMEs are contained in *CTA 2009, ss 1043–1073*, and the rules applying to large companies are contained in *CTA 2009, ss 1074–1079*. The relief only applies to companies and, for this purpose, the company definition given in *ICTA 1988, s 832(1)* applies, being 'any body corporate or unincorporated association but does not include a partnership, a local authority or a local authority association'. The company must also be within the charge to corporation tax (HMRC Corporate Intangibles Research and Development Manual CIRD 81200).

Companies qualify for an enhanced deduction if expenditure incurred is more than £10,000 in an accounting period. The enhanced deduction is included within the adjusted trading profits. Companies claim the enhanced relief by completing boxes 99 to 102 as appropriate. The following paragraphs provide a summary of the detailed rules.

Meaning of research and development expenditure

8.11   The same GAAP definitions are used as in **8.3**. In addition, the research must be within the DTI guidelines. HMRC recommend that the DTI guideline tests be applied before the SSAP 13 and IAS 38 tests. Essentially, a project will qualify as an R&D project if it is carried on in a field of science or technology and is undertaken with an aim to extend knowledge to which the relief applies (HMRC Corporate Intangibles Research and Development Manual CIRD 81300). The DTI guidelines are reproduced in HMRC Corporate Intangibles Research and Development Manual CIRD 81900. Paragraph 19 of the DTI guidelines defines the meaning of a project:

> 'A project consists of a number of activities conducted to a method or plans in order to achieve an advance in science or technology. It is important to get the boundaries of the project correct. It should encompass all the activities that collectively serve to resolve the scientific or technological uncertainty associated with achieving the advance, so it could include a number of different sub-projects. A project may itself be part of a larger commercial project, but that does not make the parts of the commercial project that do not address scientific or technological uncertainty into R&D.'

Therefore, in practice, every research activity should be broken down into its separate parts to ascertain whether or not it will qualify as R&D.

Relevant research and development

8.12 Relief can only be claimed on relevant R&D. Relevant R&D is defined in *CTA 2009, s 1042(1), (2)* to mean that it is R&D related to a trade carried on by the company, or from which it is intended that a trade to be carried on by the company will be derived.

The R&D expenditure may relate to a trade already carried on by the company, or the expenditure may lead to or facilitate an extension of that trade and, if medical research, it has a special relation to the welfare of workers employed in that trade (*CTA 2009, s 1042(1), (2)*). Relief is given for vaccine research to both SMEs and large companies regardless of trading activities (*CTA 2009, s 1042(3)*).

Qualifying R&D expenditure

8.13 Qualifying R&D expenditure for both the small and the large company schemes is similar but not identical. It can be summarised as follows:

The expenditure:

- must not be capital;
- is attributable to relevant R&D directly undertaken by the company or on its behalf;

- is incurred on staffing costs for directors or employees or on software or consumable items or on qualifying expenditure on externally provided workers or is qualifying expenditure on subcontracted R&D, and from 1 April 2006 on clinical trials;

- is not incurred by the company in carrying on contracted-out activities;

- is not subsidised (SME scheme only);

- any intellectual property created as a result of the R&D will be vested in total or in part in the company (SME scheme only); and

- if the expenditure is incurred in carrying on activities contracted out to the company, they are contracted out by:

  — a large company; or

  — a person otherwise than in the course of a trade, profession or vocation the profits of which are chargeable to tax as profits of a trade.

(*CTA 2009, ss 1052* and *1077*)

Staffing costs

8.14   Staffing costs for directors or employees include salary, benefits, secondary Class I contributions, UK staff pension fund and, from 1 August 2008, compulsory contributions under the social security legislation of an EEA State other than the UK or Switzerland (*CTA 2009, s 1123*).

Staffing costs attributable to the R&D include salaries and wages for all employees actively engaged in the research, together with employer's NIC and employer's pension fund contributions relevant to them. Benefits are not included in staff costs. Costs for employees only partly engaged in research are apportioned appropriately (*CTA 2009, s 1124*)). (Employees in this context includes directors.) Secretarial and administrative costs are excluded.

Software or consumable items

8.15   Expenditure on computer software and consumable or transformable items is relevant R&D expenditure. Consumable or transformable materials. include water, fuel and power (*CTA 2009, s 1125*).

Relevant payments to the subjects of a clinical trial

8.16   Relevant payments to the subjects of clinical trials are payments made to individuals for the purposes of participating in an investigation in human subjects undertaken in connection with the development of a health care treatment or procedure (*CTA 2009, s 1140*).

Intellectual property

8.17   Intellectual property includes:

- any industrial information or technique likely to assist in:

    — the manufacture or processing of goods or materials; or

    — the working of a mine, oil well or other source of mineral deposits or the winning of access thereto; or

    — the carrying out of any agricultural, forestry or fishing operations;

- any patent, trademark, registered design, copyright, design right or plant breeder's right or overseas equivalent (*CTA 2009, s 1139*).

The intellectual property, if vested, should be vested at the time when the intellectual property is created.

Externally provided workers

8.18   Externally provided workers are individuals engaged on the project who are not employed by the company but are under the company's supervision. The external workers' services must be supplied to the company through a staff provider (*CTA 2009, s 1128*). Self-employed consultants are not externally provided workers, although their costs may form part of subcontracted R&D (HMRC Corporate Intangibles Research and Development Manual CIRD 84100).

Where the staff provider and the company are not connected, 65% of the staff provision payment cost is treated as qualifying expenditure on externally provided workers (*CTA 2009, s 1131*).

If external workers are provided by a connected person, and the whole of the fee is included in the relevant provider's GAAP accounts for a period ending not more than 12 months after the end of the accounting period in which the company claiming the R&D allowance makes the payment, then the company may claim R&D tax credit on the lower of:

- the qualifying payment for staff that it makes to the staff provider, and

- the amount that the staff provider includes as relevant expenditure in its accounts (*CTA 2009, s 1129(1)–(7)*).

If the staff provided and the company are not connected, they may jointly elect in writing, within two years of the end of the accounting period in which the contract arrangement is entered into, for the connected persons treatment to apply. This election must apply to all staff under the same arrangement (*CTA 2009, s 1130*).

Subsidised expenditure

8.19   Subsidised expenditure is any expenditure for which a grant or assistance is directly or indirectly received (*CTA 2009, s 1138*).

Qualifying expenditure on contracted out R&D incurred by an SME

8.20   An SME's payments to its sub-contractors is qualifying expenditure if it meets all the following four conditions:

- the expenditure is attributable to relevant R&D undertaken on behalf of the company;

- that any intellectual property created as a result of the R&D to which the expenditure is attributable is, or will be, vested in the company (whether alone or with other persons;

- the expenditure is not incurred by the company in carrying on activities which are contracted out to the company by any person;

- that the expenditure is not subsidised.

(*CTA 2009, s 1053*)

Qualifying expenditure on contracted out R&D incurred by a large company

8.21   A large company's expenditure on contracted out R&D is qualifying expenditure if all of the following four conditions are met:

- the expenditure is incurred in making payments to:
    - a qualifying body,
    - an individual, or
    - a firm, each member of which is an individual in respect of research and development contracted out by the company to the body, individual or firm;

- the R&D is undertaken by the body, individual or firm itself;

233

- the expenditure is attributable to relevant R&D in relation to the company; and

- if the contracted out R&D is itself contracted out to the company, it is contracted out by a large company, or by any person carrying on activities that do not amount to a trade.

(*CTA 2009, s 1078*)

DEFINITION OF AN SME

8.22 An SME is defined in accordance with the European recommendation as detailed in *CTA 2009, ss 1119(1), (2), 1120(2)–(7)*, as amended by *Sch 2, para 118(1)–(3)*. The criteria for enlarging an SME were introduced with effect from 1 August 2008 (*SI 2008/1878*).

Definition of a Micro, Small and Medium-sized company – from 1 August 2008.

	Medium	*Small*	*Micro*
If the company has fewer than	500 employees	50 employees	10 employees
And **either** an annual turnover not exceeding	€100m	€10m	€2m
or A balance sheet total not exceeding	€86m	€10m	€2m

8.23

Definition of a Micro, Small and Medium-sized company – prior to 1 August 2008.

	Medium	*Small*	*Micro*
If the company has fewer than	250 employees	50 employees	10 employees
And **either** an annual turnover not exceeding	€50m	€10m	€2m
Or A balance sheet total not exceeding	€43m	€10m	€2m

(2003/361/EC 6 May 2003)

BASIS OF DEFINITION OF AN SME

8.24 The staff head count is based on the number of full-time person years attributable to people who have worked within or for the concern during the year in question. Part-time, seasonal and temporary workers are included on a pro-rata basis.

'Employees' includes actual employees, persons seconded to the enterprise, owner-managers and partners (other than sleeping partners). Apprentices or students engaged in vocational training with an apprenticeship or vocational training contract, or any periods of maternity or parental leave are excluded.

Turnover is taken per the accounts (net of VAT). The balance sheet total is the gross amount of assets shown in the accounts. Results are converted from sterling to euros to ascertain whether the tests are met.

The EC defines the enterprise as either autonomous, linked or partner. Autonomous means that there are no partner or linked enterprises. A linked enterprise is an enterprise whereby one company is able to exercise control directly or indirectly over the other. A partner enterprise exists where the enterprises are not linked but where one enterprise is able to exercise control either directly or indirectly over the affairs of the other. If a company has partner or linked enterprise relationships the results are aggregated. (See Flow Chart HMRC Corporate Intangibles Research and Development Manual CIRD 92850).

The conditions are relaxed for public investment corporations, and venture capital companies, 'business angels', provided the total investment of those business angels in the same enterprise is less than €1.25m, universities or non-profit research centres, institutional investors, including regional development funds and autonomous local authorities with an annual budget of less than €10m and fewer than 5,000 inhabitants.

Over time, as the company's trade and business activities develop, and it increases its staff and its financial performance, it may find that its status changes from SME to large company. In which case. a transition period allows the SME status to be retained until the limits have been exceeded for two consecutive accounting periods. Similarly, if a large company decreases in size or demerges from a larger group of entities, it will not attain SME status until the head count and the financial limits have been met for two consecutive accounting periods.

The situation where an SME is taken over by a larger enterprise is different. It was HMRC practice to accept that, if a company changed its status from SME to large company during an accounting period, it would be considered to be an SME for the remainder of that period. Being taken over by a large enterprise can involve being taken over by a single large company or a collection of smaller entities which, when taken together, are regarded as large. With effect from 1 December 2008, HMRC have changed their interpretation as regards loss of SME status due to merger, takeover or linking. Where such an event occurs during an accounting period, the company will lose its SME status for the whole of the accounting period concerned (HMRC Brief 55/2008, 17 November 2008).

SMALL OR MEDIUM-SIZED COMPANY

Tax relief for expenditure on research and development

8.25 A small or medium-sized company (SME) will qualify for an enhanced deduction from trading profits of 175% of its qualifying R&D expenditure if this expenditure amounts to £10,000 or more during a 12-month accounting period. For expenditure incurred prior to 1 August 2008, the rate was 150% (*CTA 2009, Sch 2, para 112(1), (2)*; *SI 2008/1933*).The amount is reduced proportionately if the accounting period is less than 12 months (*CTA 2009, s 1064*). (The £10,000 limit was introduced for accounting periods ending on or after 27 September 2003. Previously the limit was £25,000.) Qualifying expenditure is expenditure that would be allowable as a deduction in computing the taxable profits of a trade carried on by the company, or would have been allowable if the trade were being carried on at the time that the expenditure was incurred.

Relief

8.26 The company can obtain 175% relief if it is carrying on an R&D trade during that accounting period. An adjustment is included in the profits computation under the heading 'Deductible expenditure not included in the accounts' (*CTA 2009, s 1044(1), (4)–(8)*).

If the company has not yet started the trade, it may elect to treat 175% of the expenditure as a trading loss of the accounting period in which the expenditure was incurred. The relief for pre-trading expenditure (*CTA 2009, s 61*) is ignored. The election must be made in writing, within two years of the accounting period to which the loss relates, to a Revenue and Customs officer (*CTA 2009, s 1045*). However, this deemed trading loss may not be set off against profits of a preceding accounting period (where *ICTA 1988, s 393A(1)(b)* applies) where the company is also entitled to a deemed trading loss for that earlier period (*CTA 2009, s 1048*).

Alternatively, the company may surrender the loss for a cash payment of 14% of the loss for the chargeable period (*CTA 2009, ss 1054, 1058)*). For expenditure incurred prior to 1 August 2008 (*SI 2008/1933*), the rate was 16%. The cash payment cannot exceed the total of the company's PAYE and NIC liabilities for the period. Employee child tax credits, working tax credit, statutory sick pay and statutory maternity pay are ignored in these calculations (*CTA 2009, s 1059*). The relief claimed is included in box 89 of the company tax return. Trading losses carried forward are restricted accordingly. The time limit for making the claim is two years from the end of the relevant accounting period.

The relief is only available to SMEs. If the SME is owned by a consortium, no R&D relief may be surrendered to any group company that is not an SME (*CTA 2009, s 1049*).

RELIEF FOR SMEs: SUBSIDISED AND CAPPED EXPENDITURE ON R&D

Additional deduction in calculating profits of trade

8.27   An SME with R&D expenditure above the £10,000 threshold that incurs subsidised qualifying expenditure on in-house direct R&D (see **8.28**), or subsidised qualifying expenditure on contracted out R&D (see **8.29**) (*CTA 2009, s 1070*), and which has capped R&D expenditure (see **8.30**) can claim an additional 30% of this expenditure as a deduction from its trading profits (*CTA 2009, s 1068*).

Subsidised qualifying expenditure on in-house direct R&D

8.28   An SME's subsidised qualifying expenditure on in-house direct R&D is expenditure that meets all the following conditions:

- the expenditure is subsidised (see **8.19**);
- the expenditure is:
    - incurred on staffing costs (see **8.14**),
    - incurred on software or consumable items (see **8.15**),
    - qualifying expenditure on externally provided workers (see **8.18**), or incurred on relevant payments to the subjects of a clinical trial (see **8.16**);
- the expenditure is attributable to relevant R&D;
- the R&D is undertaken by the company itself;
- any intellectual property created as a result of the R&D to which the expenditure is attributable is, or will be, vested in the company (whether alone or with other persons) (see **8.17**); and

- the expenditure is not incurred by the company in carrying on activities which are contracted out to the company by any person.

(*CTA 2009, s 1071*)

Subsidised qualifying expenditure on contracted out R&D

8.29   An SME's subsidised qualifying expenditure on contracted out R&D is expenditure that meets all the following conditions:

- the expenditure is subsidised (see **8.19**);
- the sub-contractor is:
  - a qualifying body,
  - an individual, or
  - a firm each member of which is an individual;
- the body, individual or firm concerned undertakes the contracted out R&D itself;
- any intellectual property created as a result of the R&D to which the expenditure is attributable is, or will be, vested in the company (whether alone or with other persons); and
- the expenditure is not incurred by the company in carrying on activities which are contracted out to the company by any person.

(*CTA 2009, s 1072*)

Capped R&D expenditure

8.30   Capped R&D expenditure is any expenditure on which the company is not entitled to relief because of a cap on R&D aid (see **8.34**) which is not qualifying R&D sub-contracted expenditure, and which would have qualified as large company expenditure had the company been a large company throughout the accounting period in question (*CTA 2009, 1073*).

R&D SUB-CONTRACTED TO AN SME

Additional deduction in calculating profits of trade

8.31   An SME with R&D expenditure above the £10,000 threshold that incurs expenditure that relates to sub-contracted in-house or external R&D, contracted out to it by a large company, or any person that is not carrying on a trade, can claim an additional 30% of this expenditure as a deduction from its trading profits (*CTA 2009, ss 1063, 1065*).

Expenditure on sub-contracted R&D undertaken in-house

8.32 Three conditions are to be met in order for expenditure to qualify as sub-contracted R&D undertaken in-house:

- the R&D is undertaken by the SME itself;
- the expenditure is:
  - incurred on staffing costs (see **8.14**),
  - incurred on software or consumable items (see **8.15**),
  - qualifying expenditure on externally provided workers (see **8.18**), or
  - incurred on relevant payments to the subjects of a clinical trial (see **8.16**); and
- the expenditure is attributable to relevant R&D in relation to the company (see **8.12**).

(*CTA 2009, s 1066*)

Expenditure on sub-contracted R&D not undertaken in-house

8.33 Three conditions are to be met in order for expenditure to qualify as sub-contracted R&D not undertaken in-house:

- the expenditure is incurred in making payments to:
  - a qualifying body,
  - an individual, or
  - a firm, each member of which is an individual,

  in respect of research and development contracted out by the company to the body, individual or firm;
- the R&D is undertaken by the body, individual or firm itself; and
- the expenditure is attributable to relevant R&D in relation to the company (see **8.12**).

(*CTA 2009, s 1067*)

Cap on R&D aid

8.34   The maximum R&D relief or R&D tax credit that an SME may claim is restricted to €7.5m (£6m approximately) R&D aid (*CTA 2009, s 1113*). R&D aid is calculated according to the following formula:

$$A = (TC + R + (P \times CT)) - (N \times CT)$$

A   Total R&D aid,

TC   Total tax credits paid to the claimant in respect of expenditure attributable to that project and claims made, but not paid or applied unless refused by HMRC

R   Actual reduction in tax liability in respect of expenditure attributable to that project for all accounting periods concerned and for all companies concerned if a group or consortia exists and group relief has been claimed

P   Potential relief, being the aggregate of all relief other than a tax credit, for which the claimant has made a claim or election, unless refused by HMRC

CT   The main rate of corporation tax at the time when the total R&D aid is calculated

N   Notional relief that the company could have claimed if it were a large company throughout the accounting period

These rules come into effect from 1 August 2008 (SI 2008/1928). There is no restriction on expenditure incurred prior to this date (*CTA 2009, s 1114*).

Example 8.4

The Wonderco Ltd was an SME that made up accounts to 31 March each year. It incurred expenditure that qualified for R&D. The company wishes to know the amount of R&D relief available for the year ended 31 March 2012.

The company has received the following R&D relief:

Year ended 31 March 2009	R&D reduction in tax liability	£4m
Year ended 31 March 2010	R&D Tax credit	£1m
Year ended 31 March 2011	R&D reduction in tax liability	£3m

The main rate of corporation tax for the year ended 31 March 2012 is assumed to be 25%. If the company were to have been a large company it could have qualified for relief of £4m for the years ended 31 March 2009 and 2011. There were no claims outstanding.

The company's total R&D aid is calculated as follows:

$$Aid = £(1 + 7 + (0 \times CT)) - (4 \times 25) \text{ m}$$

$$= £7m$$

There is no R&D relief for the year ended 31 March 2012.

LARGE COMPANY

Tax relief for expenditure on research and development

8.35   A large company will qualify for an enhanced deduction from trading profits of 130% of its qualifying R&D expenditure if this expenditure amounts to £10,000 or more during a 12-month accounting period. For expenditure incurred prior to 1 April 2008, the rate was 125%.

The amount is reduced proportionately if the accounting period is less than 12 months (*CTA 2009, s 1075*). (The £10,000 limit was introduced for accounting periods beginning on or after 9 April 2003. Previously, the limit was £25,000.) Qualifying expenditure is expenditure that would be allowable as a deduction in computing the taxable profits of a trade carried on by the company, or it would have been allowable if the trade were being carried on at the time that the expenditure was incurred. Pre-trading expenditure is not treated as incurred on the first day of trading (*CTA 2009, s 61*) but when it is actually incurred.

Qualifying R&D expenditure

8.36   Large company R&D not only includes direct research and development expenditure (as discussed in **8.10** onwards) but also subcontracted R&D and contributions to independent R&D (*CTA 2009, s 1076*).

Subcontracted research and development

8.37   Subcontracted R&D may qualify for relief if it is subcontracted to an individual, or a partnership made up of individuals. It may also qualify for relief if it is subcontracted to a qualifying body. A qualifying body is a charity, a higher education institution, a scientific research organisation or a health service body.

The research carried out must be relevant revenue research directly undertaken on the company's behalf. In addition if the work is subcontracted out to the company it must be subcontracted by a large company or by a person otherwise than in the course of that person's trade (*CTA 2009, s 1078*).

Contributions to independent research and development

8.38 Contributions to independent R&D qualify for relief if the expenditure known as 'the funded R&D' is incurred in making payments to an individual, or a partnership made up of individuals or a qualifying body (as defined in **8.37**). The company must not be connected with an individual or any individual in the partnership when the payment is made. In addition the funded R&D must not be contracted out to the qualifying body, the individual or the partnership concerned by another person (*CTA 2009, s 1079*).

Location

8.39 There is no statutory provision restricting the location of the R&D work carried out. In fact, the ECJ has ruled that *art 49* of the EC Treaty precluded legislation of a Member State, which restricted the benefit of a tax credit for research to research carried out in that member state (*Laboratoire Fournier SA v Direction des Verifications Nationales et Internationales* Case C-39/04 [2006] STC 538, [2005] ECR I-2057).

Time limits for enhanced deduction

8.40 The time limit for claiming an enhanced deduction (see **8.25** and **8.35**) is two years from the end of the accounting period (*FA 1998, Sch 18, para 10*).

The transitional rules that expired on 31 Match 2008, allowed claims made up to six years after the end of the relevant accounting period. If such a claim were made the normal two-year time limit remains for all other corporation tax claims, such as loss relief (see **9.11**) or group relief (see **10.5**).

GOING CONCERN SME

8.41 Research and development relief being the additional deduction in calculating the profits of the trade and the deemed trading loss, see **8.26**, may only be claimed if the company is a going concern.

A company is a going concern for this purpose if its latest published accounts were prepared on a going concern basis, and nothing in those accounts indicates that they were only prepared on that basis because of an expectation that the company would receive R&D relief or R&D tax credits. 'Publication' is interpreted in accordance with the *Companies Act* in that the accounts are circulated in a way that invites members of the public or a class of members of the public to read them (*CA 2006, s 436(2)*; *CTA 2009, s 1106*).

If a company ceases to be a going concern after having made the claim, the claim becomes invalid (*CTA 2009, s 1057*).

TAX RELIEF FOR EXPENDITURE ON VACCINE RESEARCH

8.42 Similar rules also allow for companies to deduct an additional 40% of R&D expenditure on vaccines and medicines, from taxable profits, or to claim a 16% tax credit if the company is an SME and has a surrenderable loss (*CTA 2009, ss 1089, 1091* and *1107*). No relief may be claimed by SMEs that are not a going concern (*CTA 2009, s 1094*). Large companies submitting a claim must include a declaration that the availability of the relief has increased the amount, scope or speed of the company's R&D or the company's expenditure on R&D (*CTA 2009, s 1088*).

SPECIALIST HMRC UNITS FOR R&D TAX CREDIT CLAIMS

8.43 The Large Business Service and the seven specialist research and development (R&D) tax credit units deal with the R&D and vaccine research relief claims. These units should be approached if there are any queries.

The DTI has published a brochure of case studies setting out the experiences of 14 companies that have claimed the relief ' Applying for R&D Tax Credits: Case Studies of Companies' Experiences (URN 06/1930)'. The brochure is available from the DTI publications orderline via email from publications@dti.gsi.gov.uk or by calling 0845 015 0010, and for downloading from the R&D pages of the DIUS website www. dius.gov.uk.

Companies and agents should send corporation tax returns with R&D tax credit claims to the specialist unit dealing with the postcode for the location of the main R&D activity of the company, apart from companies dealt with by the Large Business Service and companies dealt with by the specialist pharmaceutical units in Manchester.

8.43 *Research and development*

Contact details for the new units are as below:

Cambridge R&D Unit,
Eastbrook,
Shaftsbury Road,
Cambridge CB2 2DJ.
Tel 01223 442534

Croydon R&D Unit,
Southern House.
Wellesley Grove,
Croydon,
Surrey CR9 1WW.
Tel 020 8633 4307

Leicester R&D Unit,
Saxon House,
1 Causeway Lane,
Leicester LE1 4AA.
Tel 0116 2535400

Maidstone R&D Unit,
Medvale House,
Mote Road,
Maidstone,
Kent M15 6AE.
Tel 01622 760403

Manchester R&D Unit,
6th floor Albert Bridge House,
1 Bridge Street,
Manchester M60 9AF.
Tel 0161 288 6118

Solent R&D and Pharma Unit
1 Northern Road,
Cosham,
Portsmouth PO6 3XB.
Tel 02392 22381

Cardiff R&D Unit (Wales, Scotland and Northern Ireland),
14 East Phase 2,
Ty Glas,
Llanishen,
Cardiff CF14 5FP.
Tel 029 2032 7003

Companies whose main R&D activities are located in one of the following postcodes should send their corporation tax returns containing R&D tax credit or relief claims to the appropriate office listed below.

Postcode	Office	Postcode	Office	Postcode	Office
AB	Cardiff	HD	Manchester	RG	Southampton
AL	Cambridge	HG	Manchester	RH	Maidstone
B	Leicester	HP	Croydon	RM	Maidstone
BA	Cardiff	HR	Cardiff	S	Leicester
BB	Manchester	HS	Cardiff	SA	Cardiff
BD	Manchester	HU	Leicester	SE	Maidstone
BH	Southampton	HX	Manchester	SG	Cambridge
BL	Manchester	IG	Cambridge	SK	Manchester
BN	Maidstone	IP	Cambridge	SL	Croydon
BR	Croydon	IV	Cardiff	SM	Croydon
BS	Cardiff	KA	Cardiff	SN	Southampton
BT	Cardiff	KT	Croydon	SO	Southampton
CA	Manchester	KW	Cardiff	SP	Southampton
CB	Cambridge	KY	Cardiff	SR	Manchester
CF	Cardiff	L	Manchester	SS	Maidstone
CH	Manchester	LA	Manchester	ST	Leicester
CM	Maidstone	LD	Cardiff	SW	Croydon
CO	Maidstone	LE	Leicester	SY	Cardiff
CR	Croydon	LL	Cardiff	TA	Cardiff
CT	Maidstone	LN	Cambridge	TD	Cardiff
CV	Leicester	LS	Manchester	TF	Leicester
CW	Manchester	LU	Cambridge	TN	Maidstone
DA	Maidstone	M	Manchester	TQ	Cardiff
DD	Cardiff	ME	Maidstone	TR	Cardiff
DE	Leicester	MK	Cambridge	TS	Manchester
DG	Cardiff	ML	Cardiff	TW	Croydon
DH	Manchester	N	Cambridge	UB	Croydon
DL	Manchester	NE	Manchester	W	Croydon
DN	Leicester	NG	Leicester	WA	Manchester
DT	Southampton	NN	Cambridge	WC	Cardiff
DY	Leicester	NP	Cardiff	WD	Cambridge
E	Maidstone	NR	Cambridge	WF	Manchester
EC	Maidstone	NW	Croydon	WN	Manchester
EH	Cardiff	OL	Manchester	WR	Cardiff
EN	Cambridge	OX	Southampton	WS	Leicester

Postcode	Office	Postcode	Office	Postcode	Office
EX	Cardiff	PA	Cardiff	WV	Leicester
FK	Cardiff	PE	Cambridge	YO	Leicester
FY	Manchester	PH	Cardiff	ZE	Cardiff
G	Cardiff	PL	Cardiff		
GL	Cardiff	PO	Southampton		
GU	Southampton	PR	Manchester		
HA	Cambridge				

RELIEF FOR EXPENDITURE ON REMEDIATION OF CONTAMINATED LAND

Introduction

8.44 Providing all conditions apply, a company may be able to obtain relief for expenditure incurred on the remediation of contaminated land. Relief has been extended to derelict land with effect from 1 April 2009. Capital expenditure and 150% of the revenue expenditure is relievable against the profits of a UK property business or against the profits of a trade (see **8.45**). Alternatively, if the company has a loss from a UK property business or trade, it can claim a repayable tax credit. Legislation is contained in *CTA 2009, ss 1143–1158*. There is no entitlement to relief for artificial arrangements (*CTA 2009, s 1169*).

Deduction for capital expenditure

8.45 In order to qualify for a deduction for capital expenditure, the company must have acquired a major interest in land situated in the UK for the purposes of its trade or UK property business that it carries on. At the time of the acquisition, all or part of the land must be either in a contaminated or a derelict state or both, and the company incurs qualifying land remediation expenditure. If the land is in a derelict state, in order to qualify it must be in a derelict state throughout the period beginning with the earlier of 1 April 1998 and the date the company, or a person connected with the company, acquired the major interest in that land (*CTA 2009, s 1147; FA 2009, Sch 7, para 9*).

The company may elect by notice in writing, to a Revenue and Customs officer, for this expenditure to be allowed as a deduction against PCTCT. The election must state the accounting period in which the relief is to be claimed and should be given within the normal time limit, ie within two years after the end of the accounting period concerned (*CTA 2009, s 1148*). Expenditure is incurred if it is recognised in the accounts drawn up under GAAP.

Expenditure incurred before trading commences is treated as being incurred on the first day of trading (*CTA 2009, s 1147(7)*).

A major interest in land can be either freehold or leasehold in land situated in Great Britain and Northern Ireland (*CTA 2009 s 1178A, FA 2009, Sch 7, para 22*). HMRC have commented that land includes the buildings on the land, and that an enforceable option to purchase land, and an enforceable agreement or contract for a lease, fall within this definition (HMRC Corporate Intangibles Research and Development Manual CIRD 60130).

Additional deduction for qualifying land remediation expenditure

8.46   In order to qualify for the enhanced relief, the company must have acquired a major interest in land situated in the UK for the purposes of its trade or UK property business. The company must carry on a trade of UK property business during the accounting period in which it makes the acquisition. At the time of the acquisition, all or part of the land must be either in a contaminated or in a derelict state or both. If the land is in a derelict state, it must have been in a derelict state throughout the period beginning with the earlier of 1 April 1998 and the date the company, or a person connected with the company, acquired the major interest in that land. The enhanced relief is available on expenditure that the company incurs in respect of that land that qualifies as a deduction in calculating the profits of the business or the trade for corporation tax purposes (*CTA 2009, s 1149; FA 2009, Sch 7, para 10*).

The land remediation relief is given in the accounting period in which the expenditure qualifies as a deduction from profits. The claim should be included on form CT600 at box 104.

Denial of relief

8.47   A company has no entitlement to relief for capital expenditure (see **8.45**) or revenue expenditure (see **8.44**) if the land is in a contaminated state or derelict state, wholly or partly as a result of a deed or omission brought about by the company or a person with a relevant connection to the company (*CTA 2009, s 1150*). A person has a relevant connection with the company if the person was connected with the company: at the time of the deed or omission; at the time of the land acquisition; or when the remediation work is undertaken. A relevant interest in land includes an interest (or an option) in a right over, or licence to occupy, the land, or the person has disposed of any estate or interest in the land for a value that reflects on the value of the remediation, contamination or dereliction (*CTA 2009, s 1179*).

Qualifying land remediation expenditure

8.48   In order to qualify, there are various conditions applying to the expenditure incurred:

- either all or part of the land must be in a contaminated or a derelict state;

- the expenditure must be incurred on relevant land remediation directly undertaken by the company or on its behalf;

- the expenditure must be incurred on relevant contaminated land remediation undertaken by the company or derelict land remediation so undertaken (see **8.51** and **8.52**);

- the expenditure must be incurred:

  — on employee costs, or

  — on materials,

  or is qualifying expenditure on relevant land remediation contracted out by the company to an unconnected person, or qualifying expenditure on connected sub-contracted land remediation;

- the expenditure would not have been incurred had the land not been in a contaminated or derelict state;

- the expenditure is not subsidised; and

- the expenditure is not incurred on landfill tax.

(*CTA 2009, s 1144; FA 2009, Sch 7, para 4*)

CONTAMINATED AND DERELICT STATE

Contaminated state

8.49   Land can only be in a contaminated state if relevant harm is being caused by something in, on or under the land, or there is a serious possibility that relevant harm will be caused. Relevant harm is defined as:

- death of living organisms or significant injury or damage to living organisms;

- significant pollution of controlled waters;

- a significant adverse impact on the ecosystem, or structural or other significant damage to buildings or other structures or interference with buildings or other structures that significantly compromises their use.

Land can only be in a contaminated state by reason of industrial activity but it cannot be in a contaminated state by reason of any living organisms or decaying matter deriving from living organisms, air or water living in or under it or any other such cause (*CTA 2009, s 1145; FA 2009, Sch 7, para 5*).

A nuclear site is not land in a contaminated state or in a derelict state (*CTA 2009, s 1145B*).

Derelict state

8.50   Land **is in** a derelict state **only if it** is not in productive use, and cannot be put into productive use without the removal of buildings or other structures (*CTA 2009, s 1145A*).

Relevant contaminated land remediation

8.51   The activities that a company carries out together with any relevant preparatory activities will be relevant remediation if the following two conditions are met:

- the activities comprise the doing of any works, the carrying out of any operations or the taking of any steps in relation to:

    (a)   the land in question,

    (b)   any controlled waters affected by that land, or

    (c)   any land adjoining or adjacent to that land;

- that the purpose of the activities is:

    –   to prevent or minimise, or remedy or mitigate the effects of, any relevant harm by virtue of which the land is in a contaminated state; or

    –   any other activity introduced by the Treasury.

A relevant preparatory activity must be connected to the company's remedial activities and involves an assessment of the conditions of: the land in question, any controlled waters affected by that land, or any land adjoining or adjacent to that land.

Controlled waters can only be affected by land in a contaminated state if something in, on or under the land causes the land to be in such a condition that significant pollution of those waters is being caused, or there is a serious possibility that significant pollution of those waters will be caused (*CTA 2009, s 1146*).

Relevant derelict land remediation

8.52   The activities that a company carries out, together with any relevant preparatory activities, will be relevant remediation if the following two conditions are met:

- the activities comprise the doing of any works, the carrying out of any operations or the taking of any steps in relation to the land in question; and

- the purpose of the activity is specified by Treasury Order.

A relevant preparatory activity must be connected to the company's remedial activities and involves an assessment of the conditions of: the land in question, any controlled waters affected by that land, or any land adjoining or adjacent to that land (*CTA 2009, s 1146A*).

Employee costs

8.53   Only the employee costs of directors or employees directly and actively engaged in the relevant land remediation can be attributed to the relevant land remediation. Administration and support services are not included. Employee costs consist of all salaries and benefits to the company's directors or employees, employer's Class 1 NI contributions and company pension fund contributions.

Employee costs of those not working full-time on the land remediation are calculated pro-rata except for two circumstances. If a director or employee spends less than 20% of his total working time on land remediation work, none of the employee costs relating to him are treated as attributable to relevant land remediation. If a director or employee spends more than 80% of his total working time on land remediation work, the whole of the employee costs relating to him are treated as attributable to relevant land remediation (*CTA 2009, ss 1170, 1171*).

Expenditure on materials

8.54   Expenditure on materials is attributable to relevant land remediation if the materials are employed directly in that relevant land remediation (*CTA 2009, s 1172*).

Expenditure incurred because of contamination

8.55   If expenditure incurred on the land is increased only because the land is in a contaminated state, that increased amount is relevant land remediation expenditure (*CTA 2009, s 1173*).

Subsidised expenditure

8.56   Company land remediation expenditure is treated as subsidised if a grant or subsidy is obtained or it is met by another person. Any receipt not allocated to a particular payment will be allocated on a just and reasonable basis (*CTA 2009, s 1177(1), (2)*).

Treatment of expenditure where company and subcontractor are connected persons

8.57   The company may incur subcontracted expenditure on land remediation. If the company and the subcontractor are connected persons, the amounts brought into account in accordance with normal accounting practice up to the subcontractor's relevant expenditure is treated as relevant expenditure (*CTA 2009, s 1175*). Connection is determined under *ICTA 1988, s 839* (see **4.25**).

A person has a relevant connection to a company, where the company's land is in a contaminated state wholly or partly as a result of anything done, or not done, at any time by that person, if:

- the person was connected to the company at that time;

- the person was connected to the company at the time when the land was acquired; or

- the person was connected to the company at any time when the land remediation is, or was, undertaken by the company.

(*CTA 2009, s 1316(1)*)

Treatment of subcontractor payment in other cases

8.58   Where the company is not connected to the subcontractor, the whole of the amount of the subcontractor payment is treated as qualifying expenditure on subcontracted land remediation (*CTA 2009, s 1176*).

Entitlement to land remediation tax credit

8.59   If the company incurs a UK property business or a trading loss in the same business or trade for which the contaminated land was acquired it may claim a land remediation tax credit if it has a 'qualifying land remediation loss' in an accounting period.

The 'qualifying land remediation loss' is the lower of:

- 150% of the related qualifying land remediation expenditure; and

- the unrelieved UK property loss or trading loss *(CTA 2009, s 1152)*.

The 'unrelieved' UK property loss or trading loss is the loss for the accounting period as reduced by the amount of any UK property loss *(ICTA 1988, s 392A)* or trading loss *(ICTA 1988, s 393A(1)(a))* claim that could be made in that accounting period and any other relief claimed by the company in respect of the loss for that accounting period. This will include losses relieved against profits of an earlier accounting period *(ICTA 1988, s 393A(1)(b))* and losses surrendered to group or consortium members *(ICTA 1988, s 403(1))*.

UK property losses *(ICTA 1988, s 392A(2))* and trading losses *(ICTA 1988, s 393(1))* brought forward from an earlier accounting period, and any trading losses carried back from a later accounting period *(ICTA 1988, s 393A(1)(b))*, are ignored for this purpose.

The corresponding loss carried forward is reduced accordingly *(CTA 2009, s 1153)*.

Example 8.5

Arthur plc incurs land remediation expenditure of £80,000 in the accounting period ended 30 September 2009. The expenditure is deductible against trading profits and the company claims land remediation relief.

The company's results for the year are as follows:

	£
Trading loss	(140,000)
Loan relationship	40,000

The company makes a claim to surrender the full amount of its qualifying land remediation loss in exchange for a payment of land remediation tax credit. It makes no other loss relief or group relief claims for the period.

The 'qualifying land remediation loss' is the lower of:

	£
150% of the qualifying land remediation expenditure (£80,000 × 150%) and	120,000
The company's unrelieved trading loss for the accounting period (£140,000 less £40,000)	100,000
Qualifying land remediation loss	100,000
The tax credit payable (£100,000 × 16%)	16,000
Trading loss available to carry forward to future accounting periods (£140,000 less £40,000)	100,000

Amount of land remediation tax credit

8.60   The company's entitlement to land remediation tax credit is 16% of the qualifying land remediation loss for the period (*CTA 2009, s 1154*). This is not income for taxation purposes (*CTA 2009, s 1156*). The credit is claimed on the form CT600 at box 144.

Payment in respect of land remediation tax credit

8.61   HMRC may use the credit to settle any outstanding corporation tax liability (*CTA 2009, s 1155(2)*).

The credit may be applied in discharging any liability of the company's to pay corporation tax, and to the extent that it is so applied the HMRC's obligation under *sub-s (1)* is discharged. If a return is under enquiry, the tax credit will not be repaid until the enquiry is complete, although a Revenue officer has discretionary powers to pay a provisional amount.

HMRC are not required to pay a tax credit for an accounting period if the company has outstanding PAYE and NIC liabilities for the same accounting period (*CTA 2009, s 1155*).

Certain qualifying land remediation expenditure excluded for purposes of capital gains

8.62   Qualifying land remediation expenditure that has been used in a tax credit claim is excluded expenditure for capital gains tax purposes (*CTA 2009,* *s 1157(1), (2)).* Capital expenditure on qualifying land remediation allowed as a deduction in computing the profits (losses) of a trade or UK property business, is not an allowable deduction for capital gains purposes (*TCGA 1992, s 39*).

Penalties

8.63   The company is liable to a penalty if it makes an incorrect claim for a land remediation tax credit or discovers that a claim is incorrect but fails to inform HMRC. See Chapter 18 Penalties for inaccuracies and errors.

Chapter 9

Single company trading losses

TRADE PROFITS AND LOSSES

Computation

9.1   The vagaries of business life will mean that a company can make a loss on its trading ventures just as easily as it can make a profit. A 'trade loss' as it is termed in the legislation is computed in exactly the same way as a trading income, which is the profit of the trade (*ICTA 1988, ss 393(7), (8), 393A(9)(a)*). When a company incurs a trading loss it must prepare its corporation tax computation in the normal way to send to HMRC together with form CT600 and the statutory accounts. If a trading loss is incurred during the accounting period the chargeable profits are recorded as 'nil'. This is achieved by leaving box 3 (trading and professional profits) of the company tax return CT600 blank. The legislation allows the company to claim relief for the loss against its other income (**9.11–9.17**) or to carry forward the loss against future profits of the same trade (**9.2–9.10**). A company that incurs expenditure on or after 1 April 2008 on the new technologies may surrender its loss and claim a repayable tax credit. For details, see **9.29–9.43**.

CARRY FORWARD OF TRADING LOSS AGAINST FUTURE TRADING PROFITS

Loss claim

9.2   Unless a trading loss is utilised in other ways it will automatically be carried forward to set against profits of the same trade in the next and subsequent accounting periods. The loss can only be used if there are available profits and once used it cannot be used again. There is no facility to disclaim the whole or even part of the loss, which must be matched consecutively year on year to available profits until depleted (*ICTA 1988, s 393(1)*). Companies that are in financial difficulties may enter into an agreement with the Treasury or another government department or agency. Part of the terms of the agreement may be the forfeiture of their right to tax loss. If such an arrangement is in place, loss relief will not automatically be given (*FA 2009, s 25*). If a market gardening or farming business makes a loss for five consecutive years, the next year's loss can only be carried forward against future profits of the same trade (*ICTA 1988, s 397*).

The loss relief is only available if the trade continues to be carried on, when the loss is to be relieved (*ICTA 1988, ss 393(1), 393A(1)*). What is more, the trade has to be the same trade. Commercial dictum dictates that business shifts from unprofitable to profitable sources. As business life moves swiftly it is often difficult to determine whether a new activity is in fact an extension of the existing trade or a new trade. The former situation will permit the loss relief but the latter will deny it. Case law has determined the following.

Case law

9.3   Gordon & Blair Ltd traded as brewers. The company's activities consisted of brewing and selling beer to third parties. After a period of time Gordon & Blair Ltd stopped brewing beer and engaged another company to brew to its specification. Gordon & Blair Ltd continued to sell the beer. It was held that the brewing trade had ceased and a new trade of beer selling had commenced. The effect being that the brewing trade's losses could not be set against the beer sales profits (*Gordon & Blair Ltd v CIR* (1962) 40 TC 358).

Bolands Ltd, an Irish company, traded in Ireland as millers and bakers. The company owned two mills and it used about half of the flour it produced in its own bakeries. The company hit dire times. The company made losses and closed the mills. A year later it reopened one of the mills mainly to supply the bakeries. It was held that a single trade was carried on throughout. Therefore it was able to utilise its trading losses (*Bolands Ltd v Davis* (1925) 1 ITC 91, (1925) 4 ATC 532).

In contrast, J G Ingram & Sons Ltd manufactured and sold surgical goods. At that time the company used rubber in its manufacturing process. The company suffered large losses. A receiver was appointed, the plant sold and the factory closed. The company continued to sell surgical goods under its own brand that were made by an associated company. A year later a change of ownership took place and the company recommenced manufacturing but used plastic rather than rubber in its production process. The sale of surgical goods continued. The company claimed that it carried on the continuing trade of the sale of surgical goods. The courts disagreed and deemed that a new trade commenced with the production of plastic surgical goods (*JG Ingram & Sons Ltd v Callaghan* (1968) 45 TC 151).

More recently in *Kawthar Consulting Ltd v HMRC*, the *JG Ingram* argument was used. Kawthar Ltd's trade was the provision of computers and monitors.

Unfortunately the company's client went into liquidation and Kawthar Ltd suffered large losses. Two to three years later, the company won a lucrative contract for the supply of compliance software. The company regarded itself as an IT company and set the earlier trading losses against the current profits under *ICTA 1988, s 393(1)*. The Special Commissioners decided that the company's trade of dealing in computers had ceased and a new trade of providing IT consultancy services had begun. The result being that Kawthar Ltd was unable to utilise its brought forward trading losses against its current profits (*Kawthar Consulting Ltd v HMRC* [2005] SWTI 1237, [2005] STC (SCD) 524).

Corporation tax self-assessment

9.4   As *s 393(1)* loss relief is automatic, the legislation requires no formal claim. (A formal claim was required for accounting periods ended before 1 October 1993.)

In order to satisfy the corporation tax self-assessment filing requirement the company, when completing form CT600, is required to state the amount of the loss to be relieved in box 4 of the return. Only the amount to actually be set against profits should be entered on the return. A separate loss calculation should be supplied with the company tax return to explain how the loss has been utilised. In particular, if more than one trade is being carried on, the computation should clearly show how the trading losses are utilised against each particular trade's income. As soon as the trade ceases it will no longer be possible to carry forward the loss.

The company in its corporation tax self-assessment submission must distinguish between an existing trade and a new or different trade when claiming loss relief.

This is where the practical difficulty lies.

From the earlier case law examples, it seems that, if a company changes its activities during the course of its existence, it must be able to demonstrate that these activities are sufficiently uninterrupted and interrelated to constitute a continuing trade.

Losses and HMRC enquiries

9.5   The fact that a company incurs a loss during the year rather than a profit has no effect on HMRC's powers of enquiry. They remain the same (see **Chapter 2**). A brought forward trading loss shown on a corporation tax computation cannot be enquired into under *FA 1998, Sch 18, para 25* if the

257

time limit of two years after the end of the accounting period in which the loss was incurred has expired. If HMRC wished to enquire into earlier losses, they would have to open a discovery enquiry under *FA 1998, Sch 18, para 43*. A discovery enquiry can only be opened if HMRC suspect fraud or negligence on the part of the company, its representative or anyone who was in partnership with the company at the relevant time. Alternatively, an enquiry may be opened into the use of a trading loss where there is a reconstruction (*ICTA 1988, s 343(3)*) or a change of ownership (*ICTA 1988, s 768*). *Section 343* permits losses to be transferred from one company to another company with substantially the same ownership, this is discussed in **15.24–15.25**. *Section 768* prevents loss utilisation where there is a change of ownership. (See **9.19**). HMRC have also stated that they will enquire into the use of a trading loss carried forward in a later accounting period where there is a dispute about whether a trade has continued or whether it has ceased and a new trade commenced (HMRC Company Taxation Manual CTM 04150).

Within the charge to corporation tax

9.6   In order to be granted loss relief, not only must the company be carrying on the same trade, but it must also be within the charge to corporation tax (*ICTA 1988, ss 393(10), 393A(9)(c)*). These clauses are most likely to affect companies who become resident in the UK after having been resident abroad.

When a company becomes UK resident it falls within the charge to corporation tax, if it has a source of income. If the company carries on the same trade when it becomes UK resident as it carried on before it became UK resident its loss relief capacity is restricted. The now resident, UK resident company will not be given relief for its trading losses incurred whilst non-UK resident against profits earned when it becomes UK resident. On the other hand a non-UK resident company that is carrying on a trade in the UK through a permanent establishment is within the charge to corporation tax (*CTA 2009, ss 5(2), 19(1)*). A permanent establishment may consist of a branch or agency. Therefore the branch or agency will obtain relief for any UK losses it incurs against the UK income that it earns. If the accounts and records are kept in a foreign currency, the loss should be converted to sterling using the same exchange rate as used for the conversion of profits entered in box 3.

CORPORATION TAX COMPUTATION

9.7   The following example details the presentation of a corporation tax computation in circumstances where there are trading losses brought forward to set against future trading income from the same traded under *ICTA 1988, s 393(1)*.

Example 9.1

The Abracadabra Trading Company Ltd has the following results for the year ended 31 March 2010.

	£000
Trade profits	200
Property income	1,600
Loan relationship	400
Chargeable gains	300
Gift aid payment	300
Loss brought forward under *ICTA 1988, s 393(1)*	5,000

The company calculates its profits chargeable to corporation tax and its trading loss carried forward as follows:

Corporation tax computation for the year ended 31 March 2010

	£000
Trade profits	200
Less: Loss brought forward under *ICTA 1988, s 393(1)*	(200)
	0
Property income	1,600
Loan relationship	400
Chargeable gains	300
Total profits	2,300
Less: Non-trade charge on income	(300)
Profits Chargeable to Corporation Tax	2,000

Loss utilisation

	£000
Loss brought forward	5,000
Used against trading income of the year	(200)
Loss carried forward *ICTA 1988, s 393(1)*	4,800

Charges on income

9.8   *ICTA 1988, ss 393(9), 393A(8)* allow excess trade charges to be added to a trading loss carried forward. With the introduction of the intangible assets regime on 1 April 2002, very few items will qualify from this time as 'trade charges'. From 25 July 2002 the definition of charges is restricted to:

- annuities or other annual payments,

- qualifying donations to charity,

- amounts allowed as charges on income, namely gifts of shares etc to charity.

Any amount that is deductible in computing profits cannot be allowed as a charge on income (*ICTA 1988, s 338A(2)*).

If trade charges were to be added to a loss claim the following format would be adopted.

Example 9.2

A company has a trading loss brought forward for its accounting period ended 30 June 2009 of £5,000. In that year it has excess trade charges of £10,000. The company has no other income. The trading loss carried forward to the accounting period ended 30 June 2010 is therefore £15,000.

Relief for trading losses against interest and dividends

9.9   *ICTA 1988, s 393(8)* allows the inclusion of interest and dividends as trading income that would be included as trading income but for the fact that tax has been deducted at source. Dividends from UK companies are excluded. In practice this section will only be applied where investment forms part of the trade. The treatment was refused in *Bank Line Ltd v CIR* (1974) 49 TC 307, [1974] STC 342 and *Nuclear Electric plc v Bradley* (1996) 68 TC 670, [1996] STC 405 (HMRC Company Taxation Manual CTM 04250 and HMRC Business Income Manual BIM 40805).

Companies entering into partnership

9.10   The business may determine that the company forms links with other companies in order to further its trading activities. Groups are discussed in **Chapter 10**. A company may be engaged in a certain trading activity and whilst carrying on this trade enters into partnership with another company or individual. Of concern to the company is whether and how it may utilise its trading losses. HMRC have confirmed that the company can relieve trading losses it incurred before it entered into partnership against profits earned whilst in partnership, provided the same trade is carried on. It can also relieve losses under *ICTA 1988, s 393(1)* against its share of the partnership trading income (HMRC Company Taxation Manual CTM 04200).

Set the loss against other profits in the same accounting period and then accounting periods falling within the previous 12 months

9.11   Rather than carry forward the trading loss to set against future trading profits, the company may, by claim, offset the loss against its other profits.

Example 9.3

A Ltd's results for the year ending 31 March 2010 show:

	£		£
Trading loss	(10,000)	Chargeable gains	7,200
Property income	3,000	Trade charges	(2,000)
Loan relationship	4,000	Non-trade charges	(1,000)

The loss may be relieved as follows.

	£
Property income	3,000
Loan relationship	4,000
Chargeable gains	7,200
	14,200
Deduct trading loss	(10,000)
	4,200
Deduct trade charges	(2,000)
Non-trade charges	(1,000)
Profits chargeable to CT	1,200
CT payable at 21%	252

9.12   The profits that are eligible are the total profits for the same accounting period as the loss followed by the total profits of the previous 12-month chargeable period, provided the trade was being carried on in that chargeable period. The relief must be taken in that order and the relief for the same chargeable period must be taken in full up to the amount of the chargeable profits. It is not possible to make a partial claim. Only after this relief is taken can the balance of the loss be set against the total profits of the accounting period ended within the previous 12 months.

Example 9.4

A company made a trading loss of £35,000 in the accounting period 1 January 2010 to 31 December 2010. Other corporation tax profits of the period amounted to £20,000. The company continues to trade. The corporation tax profits of earlier accounting periods were as follows.

	£
1 July 2009 to 31 December 2009	10,000
1 July 2008 to 30 June 2009	20,000

The trade in which the loss was incurred was carried on throughout the whole of the period from 1 July 2008 to 31 December 2010. The company claims relief under *ICTA 1988, s 393A(1)(b)* to extend the relief to the 'preceding period', the 12-month period which ends on 31 December 2009.

Relief is given as follows:

Against profits of the accounting period	£
1 January 2010 to 31 December 2010	20,000
1 July 2009 to 31 December 2009	10,000
1 July 2008 to 30 June 2009	5,000
Total amount of profits relieved	35,000

Example 9.5

The facts are the same as the previous example, except that the trading loss for the period from 1 January 2010 to 31 December 2010 was £45,000.

Relief is given as follows:

Against profits of the accounting period	£
1 January 2010 to 31 December 2010	20,000
1 July 2009 to 31 December 2009	10,000
1 July 2008 to 30 June 2009	10,000
Total amount of profits relieved	40,000

The set-off for the accounting period ended 30 June 2009 is limited to the proportion ($183/366 \times £20,000 = £10,000$) of the profits of the period that fall into the 12 months ending on 31 December 2009. The unused balance of the loss for accounting period ending 31 December 2010 (£5,000) is available for carry forward under *ICTA 1988, s 393(1)* (HMRC Company Taxation Manual CTM 04540 adapted).

Profits for the accounting period ended 30 June 2009 have been apportioned on a time basis. There is always the possibility to apportion the profits on an actual basis if this gives a more accurate result. For this see the discussion on *Marshall Hus & Partners Ltd v Bolton* (1980) 55 TC 539, [1981] STC 18 in **2.7**.

9.13   It is not compulsory to take *s 393A(1)* relief. The relief can be ignored and the loss can be carried forward in an automatic *s 393(1)* set-off. If *s 393A(1)* is claimed current year relief must always be taken before prior year relief.

Where there are losses arising in consecutive accounting periods and relief is claimed under *ICTA 1988, s 393A(1)* for each accounting period the order of set-off is:

(i)   loss of the first accounting period against total profits of the same accounting period;

(ii)   loss of the first accounting period against the preceding 12 months' profits;

(iii)   loss of the second accounting period against total profits of the same accounting period;

(iv)   loss of the second accounting period against profits of the preceding 12 months, which in effect amounts to the 'first accounting period'.

This can often result in insufficient profits against which to make a carry back election for the second accounting period.

Example 9.6

A company commenced trading on 1 January 2009 and prepares six monthly accounts for its first two years of trading. It makes trading losses of £25,000 in its six-month accounting period ended 30 June 2010, and £40,000 in its six-month accounting period ended 31 December 2010. The corporation tax profits of the preceding periods were as follows.

9.13 *Single company trading losses*

	£
Accounting period 6 months to 31 December 2009	20,000
Accounting period 6 months to 30 June 2009	10,000

Relief for the £25,000 loss for the period ended 30 June 2010 is given before relief for the £40,000 loss for the year ended 31 December 2010. Relief is given as follows:

Loss for the period to 30 June 2009

	Profit £	Loss £	Net £
Against profits of the accounting period:			
● 6 months to 31 December 2009	20,000	20,000	—
● 6 months to 30 June 2009	10,000	5,000	5,000
Total	30,000	25,000	5,000

Loss for the period to 31 December 2010

The profits against which the loss can now be set against are reduced as follows after the 30 June 2009 loss relief.

	Profit £	Loss £	Net £
Against profits of the accounting period:			
● 6 months to 31 December 2010	—	40,000	(40,000)
● 6 months to 30 June 2010	—	25,000	(25,000)
Total	—	65,000	(65,000)

This loss cannot be carried back. This is because all of the profits for accounting periods in the 12 months immediately preceding the accounting period ended 31 December 2010 (that is the 12 months to 30 June 2010) have already been covered by loss relief from the earlier period. The company would have preferred to claim relief for the period ended 31 December 2010 first. If it had been able to do this, relief for the period ended 31 December 2010 would have been given against the profits of the period ended 31 December 2009. The loss for the period ended 30 June 2010 could then have gone against the whole of the £10,000 profits for the period ended 30 June 2009. But the legislation does not allow this.

(HMRC Company Taxation Manual CTM 04550 adapted).

9.14 The loss can only be set against the total profits of the accounting period ended in the previous 12 months if and only if the trade in question was carried on at some time in that accounting period on a commercial basis. It is not necessary for the trade to have been carried on for the whole of the preceding 12-month period. If the trade was carried on at some time during the previous 12 months the loss will still be relievable against total profits of that period (HMRC Company Taxation Manual CTM 04510).

Again the facts of each case must be reviewed carefully to ascertain whether or not a trade is being carried on, on a commercial basis. The loss up to the full amount of the total profits must be utilised or if less the full amount of the loss. The balance of any unused loss is available to carry forward under *ICTA 1988, s 393(1)*.

A claim must be made within two years of the end of the accounting period in which the loss is incurred. The claim can be made by completing box 122 of the company tax return and by giving full details of the loss and the trade to which it refers (*ICTA 1988, s 393A*).

Set the loss against other profits in the same accounting period and then accounting periods falling within the previous 36 months

Temporary extension of loss carry back

9.15 The trading loss carry back rules have been temporarily extended from 12 months to three years, for accounting periods ending in the period 24 November 2008 to 23 November 2010 (*FA 2009, Sch 6, para 3(1)*). The rule that permits a company to set off its trading loss incurred in one year against its total income of the previous year is unchanged, but any remaining loss, up to a maximum of £50,000, can now be set against the two prior years, with relief being given for the latter year before the earlier year. There is a £50,000 limit for accounting periods ending in the 12-month period from 24 November 2008 to 23 November 2009, and another £50,000 limit for accounting periods ending in the 12-month period from 24 November 2009 to 23 November 2010 (*FA 2009, Sch 6, para 3(3)*).

Example 9.7

Multiloss Ltd's has the following results for the past four years ended 31 October:

9.15 Single company trading losses

Year ended 31 October	2010	2009	2008	2007
Trading income		—	100,000	80,000
Trading loss	120,000	177,000		
Property income	3,000	3,000	3,000	3,000
Loan relationship	4,000	4,000	4,000	4,000
Chargeable gains	1,000	7,000	6,000	4,000

The company seeks to maximise its loss relief under *ICTA 1988, s 393A*. The losses may be relieved as follows:

Year ended 31 October	2010 £	2009 £	2008 £	2007 £
Trading income		—	100,000	80,000
Trading loss				
Property income	3,000	3,000	3,000	3,000
Loan relationship	4,000	4,000	4,000	4,000
Chargeable gains	1,000	7,000	6,000	4,000
Total Income	8,000	14,000	113,000	91,000
Loss set off against				
Current profits	(8,000)	(14,000)		
Year 1 carry back		—	113,000	
Year 2 carry back			—	50,000
PCTCT	—	—	—	41,000
Trading loss c/f				

The loss utilisation summary is as below:

Year ended 31 October	Total Loss (2009) £	Total Loss (2010) £
Trading income		
Trading loss	(177,000)	(120,000)
Loss set off against		
Current profits	14,000	8,000
Year 1 carry back	113,000	
Year 2 carry back	50,000	
Trading loss c/f	—	(112,000)

The 2009 trading loss carry back to 2008 is unrestricted, but the carry back to 2007 is restricted to £50,000. The 2010 trading loss cannot be carried back at all, because the 2009 and 2008 profits available for loss relief have been fully relieved by the 2009 trading loss.

Charges on income

9.16   Charges on income are now in the main restricted to donations and gifts to charities (*ICTA 1988, s 338A*) (see **9.8**). As such payments are not related to a company's trading activity they are termed as 'non-trade charges' (*ICTA 1988, s 393A(1)(b)*); loss carry back is given before non-trade charges for the year. Excess non-trade charges can only be relieved against current year profits.

Example 9.8

Wizard Ltd prepares accounts to 30 June each year. The company has recently changed its accounting date from 31 December.

Wizard Ltd's results both actual and forecast are as follows:

	Year ended 31 December 2008 £000	*Six months ended 30 June 2009 £000*	*Year ended 30 June 2010 £000*	*Year ended 30 June 2011 £000*
Trade profit/(loss)	35	20	(120)	90
Property income	5	3	6	4
Chargeable gain	10	0	8	0
Gift aid payments	(3)	(2)	0	0

ICTA 1988, s 393A(1)(a) claim for the year ended 30 June 2010:

	Year ended 30 June 2010 £000
Property income	6
Chargeable gain	8
	14
Less: loss claim	(14)
Profits chargeable to corporation tax	0

9.16   *Single company trading losses*

ICTA 1988, s 393A(1)(b) for the previous 12 months:

	Year ended *31 December 2008* *£000*	*Six months ended* *30 June 2009* *£000*
Trade profit	35	20
Property income	5	3
Chargeable gain	10	0
	50	23
Less: loss claim	(25)	(23)
	25	0
Non-trade charges	(3)	0
Profits chargeable to corporation tax	(3)	0

The non-trade charges are lost for the six months ended 30 June 2009 as set-off is after loss relief.

ICTA 1988, s 393(1) loss carried forward against future trading profits:

	Year ended *30 June 2011* *£000*
Trade profit/(loss)	90
Less: loss claim	(58)
	32
Property income	4
Chargeable gain	0
Profits chargeable to corporation tax	36

Loss utilisation:

	£000
Trading loss for the year ended 30 June 2010	120
Less: *ICTA 1988, s 393A(1)(a)* claim for the current year	(14)
	106

Less: *ICTA 1988, s 393A(1)(b)* claim for the previous 12 months:

	£000
● Six months to 30 June 2009	(23)
● Six months to 31 December 2008	(25)
Loss carried forward (*ICTA 1988, s 393(1)*)	58
12 months to 30 June 2011	(58)
Total	0

Example 9.9—Losses carried forward and back with trade charges

B Ltd has carried on the same trade for many years. The results for the years ended 30 September 2008, 2009 and 2010 are shown below:

Year ended 30 September	*2008* £000	*2009* £000	*2010* £000
Trade profit/(loss)	(20)	20	(17)
Loan relationship	5	3	5
Chargeable gains	5.6	4.7	4
Trade charges	(3)	(9)	(5)
Non-trade charges	—	(1)	—

The losses may be relieved as follows:

Year ended 30 September	*2008* £000	*2009* £000	*2010* £000
Trade profits		20	
Deduct loss brought forward		(12.4)	
		7.6	
Loan relationship	5	3	5
Chargeable gains	5.6	4.7	4
	10.6	15.3	9
Trading losses of same period	(10.6)		(9)
Deduct trade charges		(9)	
		6.3	
Deduct trading loss carried back		(6.3)	
from year ended 30 September 2009			
Profits chargeable to CT	—	—	—
Non-trade charges unrelieved		1	

9.17 *Single company trading losses*

Loss memorandum:

Year ended 30 September	2008 £000	2009 £000	2010 £000
Trading loss	20		17
Trade charges	3	9	5
Non-trade charges		1	
	23	10	22
Losses used in current year	(10.6)		(9)
Charges used in current year		(9)	
Carried back to year ended 30 September 2008			(6.3)
Losses/charges carried forward	12.4	—	6.7
Non-trade charges unrelieved		1	

RELIEF FOR A TRADING LOSS AGAINST TOTAL PROFITS OF THE PRECEDING ACCOUNTING PERIODS WHEN A COMPANY CEASES TO TRADE

Cessation of trade

9.17   When a company ceases trading it is most likely to cease at or during its normal accounting period rather than on the last day of the accounting period. The legislation recognises this and allows the loss of the last 12 months of trading to be utilised in a carry back claim. The loss will most likely include the loss of the last trading period of less than 12 months and a proportionate part of a loss that falls into the preceding accounting period. In addition the loss carry back period of *ICTA 1988, s 393A(1)* is extended from a 12-month period to a three-year-period by *ICTA 1988 s 393A(2A)*, provided the trade was being carried on at that time. Losses are set off against profits of the preceding accounting period before earlier accounting periods.

For cessations of a trade on or after 21 May 2009, terminal loss relief is not available if the company ceased to carry on a trade, and a person or concern, any of whose members are not chargeable to corporation tax, began to carry it on. Nor is the relief given if the main purpose of the cessation was to bring about a tax advantage (*FA 2009, s 62*)) .

Example 9.10

Hardwood ceased trading on 30 June 2010. It had the following results:

Accounting period ended	Months	Trade profit £	Trade loss £
30 June 2010	6		30,000
31 December 2009	12		40,000
31 December 2008	12		3,000
31 December 2007	12	20,000	
31 December 2006	12	50,000	
31 December 2005	12	2,000	

ICTA 1988, s 393A(2A) and *(2B)* claims are made as follows:

	£
Loss arising in the accounting period falling wholly in the 12-month period prior to cessation—6 months to 30 June 2010	30,000
Proportion of the loss arising in the accounting period falling partly in the 12-month period prior to cessation—6 months to 31 December 2009: (183/365) × 40,000	20,000
Total	50,000

The £20,000 loss for the period to 31 December 2009 is utilised before the £30,000 loss for the later period to 30 June 2010.

The losses are relieved as follows:

Accounting period ended	Months	Trade profit £	Loss utilised £	Profit assessed £	ICTA 1988, s 393(2A), (2B) £	ICTA 1988, s 393A(1) £
30 June 2010	6				(30,000)	
31 December 2009	12				(20,000)	(20,000)
31 December 2008	12					(3,000)
31 December 2007	12	20,000	(3,000) (17,000)	Nil	17,000	3,000
31 December 2006	12	50,000	(3,000) (30,000)	17,000	3,000 30,000	
31 December 2005	12	2,000		2,000		
Total		72,000	(53,000)	19,000	Nil	(20,000)

It is not possible to utilise the £20,000 loss remaining for the year ended 31 December 2009, as there are no profits in the year ended 31 December 2008 against which it can be set.

LOSS RELIEF RESTRICTION

Changes in situation

9.18   Loss relief carry forward and carry back is denied where:

- in a three-year period there is both a change in the ownership of a company and a major change in the nature or conduct of the trade, or

- at any time after the scale of the company's activity becomes negligible and before any significant revival of the trade takes place there is a change in ownership of the company (*ICTA 1988, ss 768, 768A*).

Change of ownership of a company

9.19   A change of ownership of the company arises if a single person or a group of persons acquire more than half the ordinary share capital of the company. Holdings of 5% or less are ignored unless the acquisition is in respect of an existing holding (*ICTA 1988, s 769*). Any two points in a three-year period may be compared. Connected persons holdings are included. The *ICTA 1988, s 839* definition is used (see **4.25**), but unsolicited gifts of shares and legacies are not included. If the company is a 75% subsidiary, changes in ownership are ignored if it remains a 75% subsidiary of the same ultimate parent but a change in ownership of a holding company will extend to the subsidiary (*ICTA 1988, s 769*).

Major change in the conduct or nature of trade

9.20   What constitutes a major change in the nature or conduct of the trade is largely a question of fact, but *ICTA 1988, s 768(4)* includes the following:

- a major change in the type of property dealt in, or services or facilities provided, in the trade; or

- a major change in customers, outlets or markets of the trade.

The effect of the change is to restrict the loss relief both before and after the change, with the activity before and the activity after the change being treated as two separate accounting periods. Balancing adjustments will be calculated for capital allowance purposes.

Examples of HMRC's view of what would and would not constitute a major change in the conduct or nature of trade are given in SP 10/91.

These are:

Examples where a major change would be regarded as occurring:

(i) A company operating a dealership in cars switches to operating a dealership in tractors (a major change in the type of property dealt in).

(ii) A company owning a public house switches to operating a discotheque in the same, but converted, premises (a major change in the services or facilities provided).

(iii) A company fattening pigs for their owners switches to buying pigs for fattening and resale (a major change in the nature of the trade, being a change from providing a service to being a primary producer).

Examples where a change would not in itself be regarded as a major change:

(i) A company manufacturing kitchen fitments in three obsolescent factories moves production to one new factory (increasing efficiency).

(ii) A company manufacturing kitchen utensils replaces enamel by plastic, or a company manufacturing time pieces replaces mechanical by electrical components (keeping pace with developing technology).

(iii) A company operating a dealership in one make of car switches to operating a dealership in another make of car satisfying the same market (not a major change in the type of property dealt in).

(iv) A company manufacturing both filament and fluorescent lamps (of which filament lamps form the greater part of the output) concentrates solely on filament lamps (a rationalisation of product range without a major change in the type of property dealt in).

Government investment written off

9.21 It has been part of the government's policy to invest in certain companies. Where the government writes off the debt, the company's losses that are carried forward are reduced accordingly. The losses affected are:

- *ICTA 1998, s 393(1)*—loss carried forward against future trading profits from the same trade;

- *CTA 2009, ss 1219(3), 1221(1)*—excess management expenses or charges on income;

- *CAA 2001, s 260(1), (2)*—special leasing allowances; and

- *TCGA 1992, s 8*—capital losses.

Where a claim is made to set the loss against current profits under *ICTA 1988, s 393A* (trading loss set against profits of the same or earlier accounting period), *CAA 2001, s 260(3)* (special leasing allowance to be set against current profits) or *ICTA 1988, s 402* (group relief), it will not be disturbed (*ICTA 1988, s 400*).

SELF-ASSESSMENT

Loss claims and elections

9.22   If a company makes a loss claim it must quantify the amount of the loss at the time (*FA 1998, Sch 18, para 54*). Normally, this is included on the corporation tax computation and on the company tax return CT600 boxes 122–138. There is a general time limit of six years from the end of the accounting period to which the claim relates (*FA 1998, Sch 18, para 55*). This is overridden if the legislation gives a shorter time limit. In particular a loss claim under *ICTA 1988, s 393A(1)* must be made within two years of the end of the accounting period in which the loss arises. Normally, the loss is claimed on the company tax return CT600 and corporation tax computation for the year of the loss and this fulfils the claim requirement. If for any reason CT600 is delayed a separate quantified loss claim should be submitted to HMRC. Any errors in a claim or election can be corrected within the claim time limits (*FA 1998, Sch 18, para 56*).

The legislation differentiates between:

- claims affecting a single accounting period (*FA 1998, Sch 18, para 57*);

- claims or elections involving more than one accounting period (*FA 1998, Sch 18, para 58*); and

- all other claims and elections (*FA 1998, Sch 18, para 59*).

Claims affecting a single accounting period

9.23   As stated above, claims are usually included within the company tax return. If the company does not include the claim with the company tax return but submits it at another date, although still within the company tax return filing date period, the claim will be treated as an amendment to the return (*FA 1998, Sch 18, para 15*). The amendment should be made formally by letter; and more importantly the relief sought must be given a brief description and the amount of the claim must be quantified (HMRC Company Taxation Manual CTM 90625). If the 12-month period after the year end amendment period has expired, a claim can be made under *TMA 1970, Sch 1A*.

Claims or elections involving more than one accounting period

9.24   In this scenario a company makes a claim for an accounting period, which effects more than one accounting period. This will occur where a company claims to carry back a trading loss under *ICTA 1988, s 393A(1)* against its profits of the previous 12 months. The claim is made for the accounting period but it affects the previous accounting period. If the claim is made within the amendment period for the first accounting period, which contains the profits against which the losses are to be set, it will be treated as an amendment to the return. If the amendment period is past it is treated as an amendment under *TMA 1970, Sch 1A*. Depending on the circumstances the corporation tax repayment will either reduce the current year liability or be repaid direct to the company.

All other claims and elections

9.25   The corporation tax self-assessment enquiry period only runs to 12 months after the end of the filing date of the return. Some claims and elections may be submitted after this. This would mean that HMRC would be unable to enquire into the claim or election. Hence, such elections fall under *TMA 1970, Sch 1A*. HMRC have similar powers of enquiry but they are extended to one year and the quarter day after the claim is filed (*TMA 1970, Sch 1A, para 5*). HMRC can amend obvious errors within 12 months of the claim being made (*TMA 1970, Sch 1A, para 3(a)*), and the company may amend the claim at any time within 12 months of the claim, provided that it is not under enquiry.

HMRC AMENDMENTS TO TAX RETURNS AND CLAIMS AND ELECTIONS

9.26   HMRC acknowledge that they have the following powers to amend returns:

- Amendment of a company tax return under *FA 1998, Sch 18, para 34(2)(a)*.

- Discovery assessment made under *FA 1998, Sch 18, para 41*.

- An assessment to recover excess group relief under *FA 1998, Sch 18, para 76* (HMRC Company Taxation Manual CTM 90650)

In turn, the company may make, revoke or vary certain claims (*FA 1998, Sch 18, para 61*) outside the normal time limit. The extended time limit is one year from the end of the accounting period in which the HMRC adjustment was made (*FA 1998, Sch 18, para 62(1)*).

Certain liabilities can be reduced by the claim. These are:

- the increased liability resulting from the amendment or assessment;

- any other tax liability for the accounting period to which the amendment or assessment relates; or

- any other tax liability for any subsequent accounting period, which ends not later than one year from the end of the relevant accounting period (*FA 1998, Sch 18, para 62(3)*).

However, the claim cannot reduce the eventual liability by more than the additional assessment (*FA 1998, Sch 18, para 64*).

Where the claim affects another person's tax liability, the company must obtain the other person's consent (*FA 1998, Sch 18, para 62(3)*).

In situations of fraud and neglect a company can make additional claims but only those that can be given effect in HMRC's assessment. The claims must be made before the assessment is raised (*FA 1998, Sch 18, para 65(1), (2)*; HMRC Company Taxation Manual CTM 90665).

Assessments under appeal

9.27   If an HMRC amendment to a company tax return or an HMRC assessment is under appeal, claims cannot be made through the *FA 1998, Sch 18, para 54* etc claims procedures. Any claims that the company wishes to make must be made through an application to the First-tier Tribunal presiding over the appeal for a determination of the amount that is to be repaid, pending the final determination of the liability. The application is heard in the same way as an appeal (see **2.23–2.32**) (*TMA 1970, s 59DA(4), (5)*) (HMRC Company Taxation Manual CTM 92110).

REPAYMENTS

Repayment interest

9.28   A loss carry back under *ICTA 1988, s 393A* (or a non-trading deficit under *CTA 2009, s 459(1), (2)*) may bring about a corporation tax repayment for an earlier period. Repayment interest runs from the due date for the accounting period for which the loss is incurred (*ICTA 1988, s 826(7A), (7C)*).

The repayment interest will be calculated from the normal due date for the accounting period in which the loss or deficit is incurred (see **3.18**).

Example 9.11

Lettice Ltd made a trading loss in the accounting period ended 31 March 2010 of £100,000. It has no other income in the year and elects to carry the loss back against its total profits for the year ended 31 March 2009 of £90,000. Corporation tax of £17,100 was paid on 1 January 2010, the due date. The repayment interest is calculated from 1 January 2010.

If the loss is carried back further than 12 months, repayment interest is calculated with reference to the period for which the loss was incurred.

ENTITLEMENT TO FIRST-YEAR TAX CREDITS

9.29   If a company incurs relevant first year expenditure (**9.31**) on or after 1 April 2008, it may claim a first-year tax credit for an accounting period in which it has a surrenderable loss (**9.30**), unless it is an excluded company (**9.32**) for that accounting period.

Surrenderable loss

9.30   A company has a surrenderable loss for an accounting period if in that period:

- a first-year allowance is made to the company in respect of relevant first-year expenditure (see **9.31**) incurred for the purposes of a qualifying activity the profits of which are chargeable to corporation tax; and

- the company incurs a loss in carrying on that qualifying activity.

The amount of the surrenderable loss is equal to the lower of:

- the unrelieved loss; and

- the first-year allowance made in respect of the relevant first-year expenditure in the chargeable period in question.

Any first year tax credit claimed reduces the amount of the loss carried forward (*FA 2008, Sch 25, para 19*).

Relevant first-year expenditure

9.31   Relevant first-year expenditure is any expenditure which is incurred in the period commencing on 1 April 2008 and ending on 31 March 2013 and is either expenditure on:

- energy-saving plant or machinery (*CAA 2001, s 45A*) (see **6.23**); or

- environmentally beneficial plant or machinery (*CAA 2001, s 45H*) (see **6.21**).

Additional expenditure attributable to a VAT liability may be included (*CAA 2001, s 236*). Expenditure incurred before a qualifying period commenced cannot be included (*FA 2008, Sch 25, para 3*).

Excluded company

9.32   A company is an excluded company if it is disregarded for corporation tax purposes, being a co-operative housing association (*ICTA 1988, s 488*) or a self-build society (*ICTA 1988, s 489*). The company is also excluded if it is a charity (*ICTA 1988, s 505*) (see **5.70**) or a scientific research association (*ICTA 1988, s 508*; *FA 2008, Sch 25, para 1(4)*).

Amount of first-year tax credit

9.33   If a company has a surrenderable loss for the accounting period, it is entitled to claim a first-year tax credit of an amount equal to the lower of:

- 19% of the amount of the surrenderable loss for the accounting period; and

- the upper limit (*FA 2008, Sch 25, para 2(1)*).

The upper limit is the greater of:

- the total amount of the company's PAYE and NICs liabilities for payment periods ending in the accounting period; and

- £250,000 (*FA 2008, Sch 25, para 2(2)*).

A company may claim the whole or part of the amount that it is entitled to claim.

Total amount of company's PAYE and NICs liabilities

9.34   The total amount of the company's PAYE and NICs liabilities for payment periods ending in the accounting period is:

- PAYE due to HMRC for the period, disregarding child tax credit and working tax credit deductions; and

- Class 1 national insurance contributions due to HMRC for that period, disregarding statutory sick pay, statutory maternity pay, child tax credit or working tax credit deductions.

A payment period is a period which ends on the fifth day of a month and for which the company is liable to account for income tax and national insurance contributions to HMRC (*FA 2008, Sch 25, para 17*).

UNRELIEVED LOSS

Trade or a furnished holiday lettings business

9.35   For a qualifying activity that is a trade or a furnished holiday lettings business, the unrelieved loss is calculated as follows:

Trading loss for the period

less

any relief:

- available under *ICTA 1988, s 393A(1)(a)*, against profits of same accounting period (see **9.11**);

- obtained under *ICTA 1988, s 393A(1)(b)* or *393B(3)*, against profits of previous accounting period (see **9.11**);

- available under *ICTA 1988, s 403(1)*, group relief (see **10.8**);

- surrendered under a tax credit provision, of:

    - *CTA 2009, s 1043* (research and development), (see **8.26**);

    - *CTA 2009, ss 1143–1158* (remediation of contaminated land), (see **8.44**);

    - *CTA 2009, ss 1085–1142* (expenditure on vaccine research), (see **8.42**); and

    - *FA 2006, Sch 5(d)* (film tax credits); and

- set off against the loss under *ICTA 1988, s 400*, government investment write off (see **9.21**) (*FA 2008, Sch 25, para 11(2)*).

279

9.35 *Single company trading losses*

No account is to be taken of any loss:

- brought forward from an earlier accounting period under *ICTA 1988, s 393(1)* (see **9.2**);

- carried back from a later accounting period under *ICTA 1988, s 393A(1)(b)* or *s 393B(3)* (see **9.11**); or

- incurred on a leasing contract (*ICTA 1988, s 395*).

(*FA 2008, Sch 25, para 11(3)*)

Example 9.12

On 1 June 2008, Radius Ltd invests in a solar powered energy system that qualifies for a first year allowance of £100,000. The company has traded at a loss, but its prospects have now improved. Radius Ltd is not a member of a group. It has PAYE and NIC liabilities for the year of £18,000. It surrenders its loss for the year ended 31 March 2010 and claims a tax credit. Its results are as follows.

Year ended 31 March 2010:

	£
Trade loss	(500,000)
Property income	80,000
Loan relationship	5,000
First Year Allowance	100,000

There is no income for the year ended 31 March 2009.

The surrenderable loss for the year ended 31 March 2010 is calculated as follows:

	£	£
Loss for the year		500,000
Less relief against profits of the same accounting period		
Property income	80,000	
Loan relationship	5,000	85,000
Maximum surrenderable Loss		415,000
Restricted to first year allowance	100,000	

	£	£
The tax credit is restricted to the lower of:		
19% of the first year allowance and		
the upper limit which is the greater of		
(i) the total of the PAYE and NIC liabilities for the year – £18,000		
(ii) £250,000		
The company claims a tax credit of	19,000	
Loss restriction		100,000
Loss carried forward		315,000

Lettings business other than a furnished holiday lettings business

9.36   For a qualifying activity that is a lettings business other than a furnished holiday lettings business, the unrelieved loss is calculated as follows:

Loss from lettings for the period

less any relief:

* available under *ICTA 1988, s 392A(1)*, property income losses (see **12.33**);

* available under *ICTA 1988, s 403(1)*, group relief (see **10.8**);

* surrendered under a tax credit provision, of *CTA 2009, ss 1143–1158* (remediation of contaminated or derelict land) (see **8.44**);

* set off against the loss under *ICTA 1988, s 400*, government investment write-off (see **9.21**).

(*FA 2008, Sch 25, para 12(2)*)

No account is to be taken of any loss brought forward from an earlier accounting period under *ICTA 1988, s 392A(2)*, property income losses (see **12.33**).

(*FA 2008, Sch 25, para 12(3)*)

Overseas property business or a furnished holiday lettings business

9.37   For a qualifying activity that is an overseas property business trade or a furnished holiday lettings business, the unrelieved loss is calculated as follows:

Loss from lettings for the period

less any relief:

- set off against the loss under *ICTA 1988, s 400* government investment write-off (see **9.21**).

(*FA 2008, Sch 25, para 13(2)*)

No account is to be taken of any loss brought forward from an earlier accounting period under *ICTA 1988, s 392B(1)*, losses from an overseas property business.

Management of investments

9.38 For a qualifying activity that is the management of investments, the unrelieved loss is calculated as follows:

Excess management expenses for the period

less any relief:

- available under *ICTA 1988, s 403(1)*, group relief (see **10.8**).

- set off against the loss under *ICTA 1988, s 400*, government write-off (see **9.21**).

(*FA 2008, Sch 25, para 15(2)*)

No account is to be taken of any loss brought forward from an earlier accounting period under *CTA 2009, s 1223(2), (3)*, management expenses (see **12.15**) (*FA 2008, Sch 25, para 15(3)*).

Payment in respect of first-year tax credit

9.39 A first-year tax credit may either be repaid to the company, or together with any repayment interest (see **3.18**) be used to discharge any of the company's corporation tax liabilities (*FA 2008, Sch 25, para 18(1)–(3)*). If the return is under enquiry, HMRC are under no obligation to make a repayment until the enquiry is complete. However, they may make a repayment of an amount that they consider to be appropriate (*FA 2008, Sch 25, para 18(4)–(5)*). HMRC are precluded from making a repayment if any PAYE or Class 1 NIC is outstanding (*FA 2008, Sch 25, para 17(6)*). A payment in respect of a first-year tax credit is not chargeable to corporation tax (*FA 2008, Sch 25, para 23*).

CLAWBACK OF FIRST-YEAR TAX CREDIT

Circumstances in which first-year tax credit clawed back

9.40   If a company disposes of an item on which a first-year tax credit is paid before the end of the clawback period, the loss is restored and the first-year tax credit is treated as if it never should have been paid (*FA 2008, Sch 25, para 24*). The clawback period begins when the relevant first-year expenditure on the item is incurred, and ends four years after the end of the accounting period for which the tax credit was paid (*FA 2008, Sch 25, para 25(10)*).

A company disposes of an item of tax-relieved plant or machinery if the circumstances for a disposal of plant and machinery are met (see **6.31**) or the business is in new ownership. The disposal value of the item is the actual amount received, but this is replaced by market value if the disposal is made to a connected person for less than its market value, or the business is in new ownership (*FA 2008, Sch 25, para 25*). Broadly, this is one where there has been a transfer of a business and, for the purposes of making allowances and charges under the *Capital Allowances Act 2001*, anything done to or by the transferor is treated as having been done to or by the transferee.

Amount of restored loss

9.41   The amount of the restored loss is determined by the formula:

$$(LS - OERPM) - (OE - DV) - ARL$$

If the result is less than nil, the amount of the restored loss is nil.

LS   Amount of the loss surrendered in the accounting period for which the first-year tax credit was paid.

OERPM   Amount (or the aggregate of the amounts) of the original expenditure on the retained tax-relieved plant and machinery after the item is disposed of.

OE   Aggregate of the amount of the original expenditure on the item disposed of, and the amounts of the original expenditure on any items of tax-relieved plant and machinery, which the company has previously disposed of.

DV   Aggregate of the disposal value of the item disposed of, and the disposal values of any items of tax-relieved plant and machinery which the company has previously disposed of.

ARL   Amount of the restored loss (or the aggregate of the amounts of prior restored losses)

(*FA 2008, Sch 25, para 26*)

Example 9.13

For the accounting period ended 31 December 2009, Nonsuch Ltd incurred expenditure of £60,000 on plant that qualified as relevant first year expenditure. It surrendered a loss of £60,000 and obtained a tax credit. During the accounting period ended 31 December 2011 it sells part of the plant for £15,000. The original cost of the plant unsold was £10,000. There have been no other disposals or tax credit claims.

Nonsuch Ltd's restored loss is calculated as follows:

$$(LS - OERPM) - (OE - DV) - ARL$$
$$£(60,000 - 10,000) - (50,000 - 15,000) - 0 = £15,000$$

Clawback of first-year tax credits

9.42   If after submitting the corporation tax return the company becomes aware that the first- year tax credit has been included incorrectly in the tax return and the return is now incorrect; it must notify HMRC and give details of the amendment required. The notice must be given within three months beginning with the day on which the company became aware that a claw back was required (see **9.40**) (*FA 2008, Sch 25, para 27*).

Tax credit claim

9.43   The tax credit claim must be included in the corporation tax return.

The following details must be given:

- the plant or machinery on which the claim is made;
- the relevant first-year expenditure incurred; and
- the date on which that expenditure was incurred (*FA 1998, s 83ZA(1), (2)*).

The company must also provide a certificate for energy-saving plant and machinery (*CAA 2001, s 45B*) and environmentally beneficial plant and machinery (*CAA 2001, s 45I*).

A claim is ignored if arrangements are entered into wholly or mainly for a disqualifying purpose whose main object is to obtain a first-year tax credit to which the company would not otherwise be entitled, or of a greater amount than that to which it would otherwise be entitled (*FA 2008, Sch 25, para 28*).

The company will be liable to a penalty if it fraudulently or negligently makes a claim for a first-year tax credit which is incorrect, or discovers that a claim for a first-year tax credit made by it (neither fraudulently nor negligently) is incorrect, and does not remedy the error without unreasonable delay.

The maximum penalty is the excess first-year tax credit claimed for the accounting period, which is the difference between the company's tax credit entitlement and the amount of the first year tax credit claimed for the period (*FA 1998, s 83ZA(4)–(5); FA 2008, Sch 25, para 29*).

Chapter 10

Groups

BUSINESS STRUCTURE

10.1   As a business grows, its affairs develop and the company may consider whether a simple single company structure remains appropriate for its activities or whether it should consider other forms of organisation.

From a taxation perspective the single company offers many advantages. The absence of associated companies means that the small companies rate is not unduly dissipated (see **3.5**). Capital gains and losses can be set against one another without the *TCGA 1992, s 179* restrictions (see **20.32**). Possibly more importantly all the company's activities fall within one company. The merged activities may form one trade, whereas if the trades are split amongst group members they become separate trades in themselves. Retaining activities in one company also avoids the practicalities of preparing group relief claims and company tax returns for each separate entity.

However, taxation does not rule a commercial world and separate business structures may be required. The company may consider buying or forming another company (see **15.1**). Ownership of another company's shares by a company may bring about a group situation. The rapid changes in projects and deals may mean that a business structure is only required for a short amount of time and an acquisition or a new formation may not be the best structure for a deal. Before entering into a group arrangement the company may well be advised to consider a partnership or a joint venture, which it may find simpler to operate.

Corporate partners' share of profits and losses are assessed to corporation tax on the basis of a separate trade being carried on by each partner (*CTA 2009, s 1259*). The company's share of the partnership losses are available to the company to set against its other income for the same or previous year, if the partnership and its trade existed at that time, or to carry forward against its share of future partnership trading income. The partnership can prepare accounts in any format they wish, although they must be in accordance with GAAP. If a corporate partner exercises a dominant influence, the parent and subsidiary provisions of *CA 2006, s 1162* and FRS 2 (accounting for subsidiary undertakings) must be considered. Most notably each corporate partner will have joint and several liability. With this in mind, the business partners may decide upon a limited liability partnership (LLP) as introduced by the *Limited Liability Partnership Act 2000* with effect from 6 April 2001.

A joint venture between the business partners may be a simpler structure. No special legal form is required and the business activities are included within the accounts of the venturer thus easing the loss utilisation.

Companies committed to growth may form or acquire new companies and create a group structure. Specific taxation provisions and compliance issues affect groups of companies.

ACCOUNTING AND TAXATION REQUIREMENTS

Accounting

10.2   For company law, a group consists of parent and subsidiary undertakings (*CA 2006, s 474*. For these purposes an undertaking can be a body corporate, a partnership or an unincorporated association carrying on a business with a view to profit (*CA 2006, s 1161*). Groups of companies must prepare consolidated accounts unless they are exempted by the small group exemptions (*CA 2006, s 399*). Each company within the group must prepare its own individual company accounts (*CA 2006, s 394*).

Taxation

10.3   For corporation tax purposes each company within a group must submit its corporation tax computation, its company tax return and statutory accounts to HMRC (see **2.2**). Group accounts may be submitted as supporting information. Corporation tax is calculated in respect of each individual company's profits. Hence, there is no requirement to prepare a group company tax return. The group situation is brought into account when calculating the individual company's liability and when granting reliefs. Companies must prepare the supplementary form CT600C where group relief and eligible unused foreign tax is claimed or surrendered.

RELIEFS AVAILABLE TO GROUPS

10.4   The taxation legislation recognises that a group is one large trading or business entity made up of several components. Although each group company makes its own self-assessment return in its own name and is responsible for its own corporation tax liability, the taxation legislation permits a certain amount of loss sharing amongst group members. Groups have the opportunity to transfer losses to other group members to be relieved against that group member's profits and to transfer assets within the group without a charge to chargeable gain arising and to surrender eligible unused foreign tax (see **Chapter 13**). There are different definitions of a group applying to revenue losses, capital losses and consortium situations. These definitions are particular to the taxation legislation and will not always concur with the *Companies Act*.

GROUP RELIEF

Definition of a group

10.5 Various conditions must be satisfied before losses can be transferred in this way between group members. The first condition is that a group actually exists.

A group exists if one company is a 75% subsidiary of the other company and both companies are 75% subsidiaries of a third company. Shares held by share dealing companies as stock in trade are ignored (*ICTA 1988, s 413(3), (5)*). A 75% subsidiary is a company whose ordinary share capital is owned directly or indirectly by another company. 'Own' in this context means possessing the beneficial ownership (*ICTA 1988, s 838*).

Example 10.1

A Ltd owns 100% of the ordinary share capital of B Ltd.

B Ltd owns 80% of the ordinary share capital of C Ltd.

A Ltd, B Ltd and C Ltd are a group.

A Ltd owns 100% of B Ltd and effectively 80% of C Ltd (100 × 80).

Example 10.2

A Ltd owns 75% of the ordinary share capital of B Ltd.

B Ltd owns 80% of the ordinary share capital of C Ltd.

A Ltd and B Ltd are a group as A Ltd owns 75% of B Ltd.

A Ltd and C Ltd are not a group because A Ltd only effectively owns 60% of C Ltd (75 × 80).

B Ltd and C Ltd are a separate group.

Definition of a consortium

10.6   A company is owned by a consortium if 75% or more of the ordinary share capital of the company is beneficially owned by companies of which none owns less than 5%. The consortium member's share is measured by the lowest of the members' percentage interests in shares, profits or assets. Where these have varied over the year the weighted average is taken (SP/C 6). A 90% trading company subsidiary of a company which is itself a 75% owned consortium company is also included (*ICTA 1988, s 413(7)*). With effect from 1 April 2000 overseas companies are included within the count of group companies (*FA 2000, Sch 27, para 4*). The UK branch of a non-resident subsidiary may also claim or surrender group relief.

Example 10.3

P Ltd has an issued share capital of 1,000 ordinary shares, which are within the following beneficial ownership:

Q Ltd	200
R Ltd	100
S Ltd	100
T Ltd	100
U Ltd	100
V Ltd	100
X Ltd	50
Total	750

The remaining shares are held by individual shareholders.

P Ltd is owned by a consortium because 75% of the ordinary share capital is beneficially owned by companies of which none owns less than 5%.

Example 10.4

Z Ltd has an issued share capital of 1000 ordinary shares, which are within the following beneficial ownership:

Q Ltd	200
R Ltd	100
S Ltd	100
T Ltd	100
U Ltd	100
V Ltd	50
X Ltd	50
Total	700

The remaining shares are held by individual shareholders.

Z Ltd is not owned by a consortium because 75% of the ordinary share capital is not beneficially owned by companies of which none owns less than 5%.

Shares that are not treated as ordinary shares

10.7   A company may wish to finance its subsidiaries by issuing fixed rate preference shares to its external investors, thus guaranteeing them a fixed return and, at the same time, not jeopardising its own members' entitlement to group relief.

Until 1 January 2008, only preference shares that met the following conditions were not treated as ordinary shares:

- issued for new consideration, in whole or in part;

- carry no conversion rights except to shares in the company or its parent; and

- carry no right to a dividend except a fixed return at a commercial rate on the consideration given for the issue of the shares.

In the real world, external investors would lay claim to their dividend and, more often than not, their holding would not amount to that of fixed rate preference shares.

For accounting periods commencing after 1 January 2008, in addition to these requirements the company must not be able to reduce the dividend rate or be excused from payment, except in special circumstances that include its own financial difficulties or its necessity to comply with the law of a regulatory body relevant to its circumstances (*ICTA 1988, Sch 18, para 1* as amended by *FA 2009, Sch 9*), thus ensuring that the external investors receive their fixed return. The company can elect for these additional requirements not to apply either to shares issued or to agreements entered into for their issue before 18 December 2008.

Group relief

10.8   Group relief is the surrender of and claim of group and consortium members' trading losses (*ICTA 1988, s 402*).

Surrenderable losses are those incurred for the current year and include:

- trading losses,

- excess capital allowances,

- non-trading loan relationship deficits,

- charges on income,

- property income losses,

- management expenses, and

- a non-trading loss on intangible fixed assets (*ICTA 1988, s 403*).

Trading losses, excess capital allowances and non-trading loan relationship deficits may be set off against the claimant company's profits even though the surrendering company has other profits for the same accounting period against which they can be set.

Excess charges on income, property income losses, excess management expenses and a non-trading loss on an intangible fixed asset are only available for surrender if in total they exceed the surrendering company's gross profits for that period. If a surrender is made, the order of set-off is deemed to be:

(i)   charges on income,

(ii)   property income losses,

(iii)   management expenses, and

(iv)   a non-trading loss on an intangible fixed asset (*ICTA 1988, s 403*).

The surrendering company's gross profits are its profits for that period before deducting any trading losses, excess capital allowances, non-trade loan relationships deficits, charges, property income losses or management expenses, without any deduction for losses etc from other accounting periods (*ICTA 1988, s 403ZE*).

10.8 Groups

All losses arising from carrying on a trade are available for group relief. Losses from trades not carried out on a commercial basis and farming and market gardening losses within the *ICTA 1988, s 397* restriction may not be group relieved; there is a profit requirement every five years in order to be able to set these losses against the company's other income (*ICTA 1988, s 403ZA*). Excess capital allowances are allowances that are required to be set in the first instance against a specified class of income, eg special leasing (*ICTA 1988, s 403ZB*). A non-trading loan relationship deficit is discussed in **11.23**. Charges are the actual charges paid by the company during the period. A property income loss must be a commercial loss and must not include any loss brought forward from a previous period. Management expenses means the annual amount deductible by the company for the accounting period, but does not include amounts brought forward from earlier periods. See **7.13** for a non-trading loss on an intangible fixed asset (*ICTA 1988, s 403ZD*).

A claimant company must use its own trading losses brought forward before it makes a group relief claim (*ICTA 1988, s 393(1)*).

Example 10.5

Omega Ltd owns 75% of the shares and voting rights of Epsilon Ltd and Zeta Ltd. All companies prepare accounts to 31 March each year. There are no losses brought forward from previous accounting periods. The results for the year ended 31 March 2010 are as follows:

	Omega Ltd £	Epsilon Ltd £	Zeta Ltd £
Trade profits	400,000	90,000	−380,000
Property income	30,000	14,000	23,000
Loan relationship	6,000	1,000	2,000
Chargeable gain	40,000	—	10,000
Gift aid payment	1,000	—	—

Zeta Ltd is not expected to make a trading profit in the near future. Both Omega Ltd and Epsilon Ltd's future trading results are uncertain.

		Small companies rate
Upper limit	(1,500,000/3)	500,000
Lower limit	(300,000/3)	100,000

The position for each company prior to group relief is as follows:

	Omega Ltd £	Epsilon Ltd £	Zeta Ltd £
Trade profits	400,000	90,000	−380,000
Trade profits	400,000	90,000	—
Property income	30,000	14,000	23,000
Loan relationship	6,000	1,000	2,000
Chargeable gain	40,000	—	10,000
Gift aid payment	(1,000)	—	—
PCTCT	475,000	105,000	35,000
Marginal rate	29.75%	29.75%	21%

Omega Ltd should receive the maximum relief, in order to bring profits down to the lower limits for the small companies rate.

	Omega Ltd £	Epsilon Ltd £	Zeta Ltd £
PCTCT	475,000	105,000	35,000
Less: s 402 relief	375,000	5,000	
PCTCT	100,000	100,000	35,000
Corporation tax at 21%	21,000	21,000	7,350

Utilisation of loss

		£
Loss		380,000
(i)	Omega Ltd	375,000
(ii)	Epsilon Ltd	5,000
(iii)	Zeta Ltd	0
		380,000

Zeta Ltd will have trading losses in the next accounting period, which it can carry back against this year's profits. Both Omega Ltd and Epsilon Ltd's future profits are uncertain.

Example 10.6

A Ltd (a group member) has the following results.

	Year ending 31 December 2008 £	Year ending 31 December 2009 £
Trade (loss)brought forward	(500)	—
Trade profit (loss)	1,000	(1,000)
Loan relationship	500	500

For the accounting period ended 31 December 2008:

●   The loss brought forward must be relieved in priority to group relief. The maximum amount of group relief claimable will be £1,000.

●   If relief for this period is claimed for so much of the trading loss of the following period as cannot be relieved in that period, ie £500, such relief would be displaced by a group relief claim, and would then be available for carrying forward.

For the accounting period ending 31 December 2009:

No group relief is obtainable, whether or not the trading loss is carried back.

GROUP RELIEF RESTRICTIONS FOR THE CLAIMANT COMPANY

10.9   A company cannot claim group relief in excess of its own profits for the year less its own current and prior year losses.

The amount which a company can claim as group relief must not exceed its total profits as reduced by the following current and past losses:

●   any relief whatsoever for a loss from a previous period;

●   any trading loss brought forward from a previous accounting period under *ICTA 1988, s 393*;

●   any trading loss of the same accounting period under *ICTA 1988, s 393A* (irrespective of whether or not the company uses the loss);

●   any relief for UK property income losses of the same accounting period under *ICTA 1988, s 392A(1)*;

●   charges on income (*ICTA 1988, s 338*);

- any relief available to the company (whether claimed or not) for an excess of capital allowances under *CAA 2001, s 260(3)(a)* in the same accounting period; and

- any relief for non-trading loan relationship deficits under *CTA 2009, s 461* of the same accounting period.

There is no restriction on the amount of the loss claimed for losses from a later period.

(*ICTA 1988, s 407*)

AVAILABILITY OF GROUP RELIEF

UK losses

10.10   The next issue, assuming that losses as detailed in **10.8** have been incurred, is whether group relief is available.

A group relief loss claim for the items within the ambit of UK corporation tax may be made where:

- the surrendering company and the claimant company are both members of the same group,

- the surrendering company is resident in the UK or is not so resident but carries on a trade there through a permanent establishment, and

- the claimant company is resident in the UK or is not so resident but carries on a trade there through a permanent establishment (*ICTA 1988, s 402(2); FA 2006, Sch 1, para 1*).

UK group members and UK branches may, inter alia, claim and surrender losses, so may UK resident consortia.

Overseas losses

10.11   Following the decision in *Marks & Spencer v David Halsey* C-446/03 [2006] STC 237 with effect for accounting periods beginning on or after 1 April 2006, a 'qualifying overseas loss' may be surrendered for group relief (*ICTA 1988, s 403A, Sch 18A*).

For this to occur, the surrendering company must be chargeable to tax under the laws of any European Economic Area (EEA) territory and it must be:

- a 75% subsidiary of a UK resident claimant company, or

- both the surrendering company and the claimant company are 75% subsidiaries of a third company that is UK resident.

The company will be chargeable to tax in an EEA territory if it is resident in the territory or if it carries on a trade in any EEA territory through a permanent establishment (*ICTA 1988, s 402(2A), (2B)*; *FA 2006, Sch 1, para 1*).

The following countries are members of the EEA:

Austria	Finland	Italy	Norway	Sweden
Belgium	France	Latvia	Poland	UK
Bulgaria	Germany	Liechtenstein	Portugal	
Cyprus	Greece	Lithuania	Romania	
Czech Republic	Hungary	Luxembourg	Slovakia	
Denmark	Iceland	Malta	Slovenia	
Estonia	Ireland	Netherlands	Spain	

Comments in the *Marks & Spencer* case pointed to the fact that the UK was unfairly discriminating against overseas subsidiaries.

Marks & Spencer ECJ ruling

As Community law now stands, *Arts 43* and *48* of the EC Treaty do not preclude provisions of a member state, which generally prevent a resident parent company from deducting from its taxable profits losses incurred in another member state by a subsidiary established in that member state although they allow it to deduct losses incurred by a resident subsidiary. However, it is contrary to *Arts 43* and *48* to prevent the resident parent company from doing so where the non-resident subsidiary has exhausted the possibilities available in its state of residence of having the losses taken into account for the accounting period concerned by the claim for relief and also for previous accounting periods and where there are no possibilities for those losses to be taken into account in its state of residence for future periods either by the subsidiary itself or by a third party, in particular where the subsidiary has been sold to that third party.

Marks and Spencer plc v Revenue and Customs Commissioners TC5

At the First-tier Tribunal hearing held on 2 April 2009, the court re-examined the case in the light of the ECJ's ruling. The court reviewed whether the overseas companies had exhausted the possibilities of utilising the available loss against the profits for the year of the loss and previous periods, and whether there was 'no possibility' of the subsidiary or a third party using the loss in the future, bearing in mind the recognised possibilities given the objective facts of the company's situation at the relevant time. The trading losses in question arose from failed ventures in France, Belgium and Germany. The court rejected the losses used in the group relief claims that the company made whilst it was still trading, because such losses failed the 'no possibility' tests. These losses could have been claimed if the company had continued to trade or if it had started a new line of business. The court accepted, in principle, the group relief claims made by the Belgian and German subsidiaries made at the time they were in liquidation. The law in Belgium and Germany prohibits companies from carrying on a new activity, once liquidation has commenced. The losses arising in the liquidation period could be set against the income arising during that period, and the remainder would meet the 'no possibility' test.

Relief in respect of overseas losses of non-resident companies

10.12   An overseas loss of a non-resident company is available for surrender by way of group relief by a non-resident company if the 75% relationship is met.

The loss must meet the following conditions in relation to the EEA territory:

(a)   The equivalence condition: The loss must be of a kind that would be available for relief by a UK company.

(b)   The EEA tax loss condition:

For EEA resident companies:

- the loss is calculated under the laws of the EEA territory, and

- the loss is not attributed to a UK permanent establishment of the company.

For non-EEA resident companies:

- the company carries on a trade through a permanent establishment in the EEA territory,

- the loss is calculated under the laws of the EEA territory, and

- the activities are not exempt under a double tax treaty, as these would be ignored.

(c)   The qualifying loss condition:

- The loss cannot be given qualifying relief for any period ('the current period') or any past or future period, and

- the loss has not been given any other qualifying relief under the law of any territory outside the United Kingdom (other than the EEA territory concerned).

(d)   The precedence condition: The loss cannot be relieved in any other grouping (*ICTA 1988, s 403F; FA 2006, Sch 1, para 4(1)*).

The relevant accounting period concerned is the accounting period the company would have if it were UK resident (*ICTA 1988, Sch 18, para 1A; FA 2006, Sch 1, para 6(4)*). The loss will not qualify for relief if it arose from artificial arrangements (*ICTA 1988, s 403G; FA 2006, Sch 1, para 4(2)*). The qualifying loss condition must be satisfied at or up to the time when the company makes the group relief claim (*Marks and Spencer plc v Halsey (Inspector of Taxes)* (CA) 2007).

Application of UK rules to non-resident company

10.13   The corporation tax computation must be recalculated using the applicable UK tax rules. The calculated loss cannot exceed the non-resident company actual loss and if the result is a profit, no relief is available (*ICTA 1988, Sch 18A, para 11; FA 2006, Sch 1, para 7*).

On preparing the computation it is necessary to assume that the company is UK resident and that its trade is carried on wholly or partly in the UK. Rental income and income from land is calculated on the assumption that the land is based in the UK and on property income principles. The accounting period on which the computation is based is assumed to begin at the beginning of the loss period. If plant and machinery is purchased it is assumed that capital allowances are available (*ICTA 1988, Sch 18A, para 15; FA 2006, Sch 1, para 7*).

Arrangement for transfer of a company to another group or consortium

10.14   If a company has made arrangements that could result in it leaving the group, it will not be able to partake in the group relief claims by surrender of claim with other group companies (*ICTA 1988, s 410*). Its ineligibility for group relief will only last for the period in which the arrangements exist (*Shepherd v Law Land plc* (1990) 63 TC 692, [1990] STC 795).

Also all rights over shares are deemed to have been exercised at the earliest possible date. If rights differ over the ownership period the lowest common denominator is applied to the holdings to ascertain whether group relief is available (*ICTA 1988, Sch 18, para 5*).

Group relief claim

10.15 A group relief claim can be made for a corresponding accounting period. Often group member accounting periods are not co-terminous and the available profits and losses must be apportioned. The amount that may be surrendered is the smaller of:

- the unused part of the surrenderable amount for the overlapping period, and

- the unrelieved part of the claimant company's total profits for the overlapping period.

The overlapping period is the period common to both companies (*ICTA 1988, s 403A*).

Example 10.7

Mu Ltd owns 90% of the ordinary share capital of Nu Ltd.

Mu Ltd has prepared annual accounts to 30 June 2010.

Profits for the year amount to £48,000.

Nu Ltd has prepared annual accounts to 31 December 2010.

The trading loss for the year amounts to £56,000.

Although Mu Ltd and Nu Ltd are a group for group relief purposes, they can only claim and surrender losses pro rata to their common accounting periods.

Nu Ltd's maximum loss surrender

(1 January 2010 to 30 June 2010) ÷ (1 January 2010 to 31 December 2010) = 6/12

£56,000 × 6/12 = £28,000

The remaining £28,000 loss is available for relief against Nu Ltd's other income for the year.

Mu Ltd's maximum profits against which loss may be surrendered

(1 January 2010 to 30 June 2010) ÷ (1 January 2010 to 31 December 2010) = 6/12

£48,000 × 6/12 = £24,000

Only £24,000 of Nu Ltd's £56,000 trading loss can be group relieved against Mu Ltd's profits. The remaining £32,000 is available for relief against Nu Ltd's other income.

Consortium relief claim

10.16   Not only does the overlapping period restriction apply to consortium companies but also the claim is restricted to the members' interests in the consortium. The members' interest in the overlapping period for this purpose is the lower of the percentage of:

- ordinary share capital,
- profits available for distribution, and
- assets on a winding up.

If the percentages fluctuate over the period, the average is taken (*ICTA 1988, s 403C*).

Example 10.8

Delta Ltd is a consortium company, which is owned 60% by Alpha Ltd, 20% by Beta Ltd and 20% by Gamma Ltd. All companies prepare accounts to 31 December each year. In the accounting period ended 31 December 2009, Delta's trading loss amounts to £75,000. The maximum loss claim is as follows:

		£
Total loss		75,000
Alpha Ltd	60%	45,000
Beta Ltd	20%	15,000
Gamma Ltd	20%	15,000
		75,000

Loss relief will be given provided each company has sufficient profits.

In the accounting period ended 31 December 2010, Delta Ltd makes a profit of £80,000. Alpha Ltd makes a loss of £120,000, Beta Ltd makes a loss of £30,000 and Gamma Ltd makes a profit of £60,000.

The maximum surrenderable losses are calculated as follows:

		£	£
Delta Ltd	Profit		80,000
	Losses surrendered:		
Alpha Ltd	Loss made	(120,000)	
	Maximum surrender is 60% of £80,000	48,000	(48,000)
	Not available for surrender	(72,000)	
Beta Ltd	Loss made	(30,000)	
	Maximum surrender is 20% of £80,000	16,000	(16,000)
	Not available for surrender	(14,000)	
Gamma Ltd	Not applicable		
	PCTCT		16,000

Example 10.9

A Ltd owns 100% of the share capital of B Ltd.

B Ltd owns 40% of the share capital of D Ltd.

C Ltd owns 60% of the share capital of D Ltd.

D Ltd owns 100% of the share capital of E Ltd.

D Ltd owns 100% of the share capital of F Ltd.

This can be shown as follows.

```
          A
        100%
          B           C
         40%         60%
          D
        100%        100%
          E           F
```

10.16 *Groups*

There are two groups:

- A and B, and
- D, E and F.

D is owned by a consortium of B and C. All companies have the same accounting periods. None of the companies has any losses brought forward.

The companies have the following results for the year ended 31 July 2009:

A Ltd	£100,000	profit
B Ltd	(£30,000)	loss
C Ltd	Nil	
D Ltd	(£20,000)	loss
E Ltd	£10,000	profit
F Ltd	(£3,000)	loss

E Ltd claims group relief (in priority to consortium relief) as follows:

	£	£
Profit		10,000
Deduct:		
Group relief: loss surrendered by F Ltd	3,000	
Group relief: loss surrendered by D Ltd	7,000	
		(10,000)
		—

A Ltd can claim group relief first and then consortium relief as follows:

	£	£
Profit		100,000
Deduct:		
Group relief: loss surrendered by B Ltd	30,000	
Consortium relief: loss surrendered by D Ltd	5,200	
(£20,000 – £7,000) × 40%		
		(35,200)
		64,800

Group relief claimant company

10.17   The claimant company sets the relief against its total profits for the year to reduce its overall corporation tax liability. The claimant company is not required to pay the surrendering company for utilisation of the loss. There is no tax effect if a payment is made (up to the amount of the loss) (*ICTA 1988, s 402(6)*). If a payment is not made this may be viewed as a depreciatory transaction (*TCGA 1992, s 176*). HMRC have stated that they will not seek an adjustment (IR letter, 3 February 1981).

Company tax return

10.18   Details of the group relief claim are included on Company Tax Return Form—Supplementary Pages Group and Consortium CT600C. Both the claimant and the surrendering company must each complete their respective CT600C forms, which formalise the claim. The claimant company includes the amount of group relief and consortium relief claimed in box 36 of the main Company Tax Return CT600. The claim must be made within the normal self-assessment time limits, ie two years after the end of the chargeable period for which the claim is made. A claim made out of time can be refused (*Farmer v Bankers Trust International Ltd* (1990) 64 TC 1, [1990] STC 564).

Alternatively, 'an authorised group company', normally the holding company, may request HMRC in writing to grant it the power to furnish group relief claims and surrender notices on behalf of the other group and consortium companies. The application should include:

* the name and the tax office reference of the authorised company,

* the names and the tax office references of the authorising companies,

* details relating to the authorised company and each of the authorising companies that are sufficient to demonstrate that the company concerned is a member of the group of companies or, as the case may be, a consortium company, and

* a statement by the authorised company and the authorising companies that they agree to be covered by the arrangements and to be bound by claims, surrenders and withdrawals made under the arrangements.

The application must be accompanied by:

* a specimen copy of group relief claim and surrender statement that the authorised company proposes to use for the purpose of making and withdrawing surrenders and claims on behalf of itself and the authorising companies; or

303

- in the case of a company that is a consortium company, an agreement, signed by each member of the consortium and the consortium company, consenting to the authorised company acting on their behalf in relation to the arrangements.

The application must be signed on behalf of each of the companies concerned by an officer of the company, normally the company secretary and be sent to the tax office dealing with the tax affairs of the authorised company (*FA 1998, Sch 18, para 77*; *SI 1999/2975*).

Repayments of corporation tax

10.19   Groups of companies with an *ICTA 1988, s 402* group relationship are able to jointly elect for repayment due to one company to be surrendered to another company in payment of its corporation tax liability. The facility is aimed at reducing the group's exposure to interest on overdue tax. The companies involved must have the same accounting period and must be members of the same group throughout the accounting period (*FA 1989, s 102*). Any inter-company tax payment up to the amount of the tax is ignored. There is no prescribed format for the election. A letter to HMRC will suffice with details of the company and tax district reference numbers. Each company should appoint an authorised person to sign the form on its behalf.

The joint notice is not given in the return form CT600, but must be made separately. The surrendering company should use the 'repayment' section of the return form to claim its refund and show how much is to be surrendered by completing boxes 145 to 148 accordingly. A copy of the joint notice should be enclosed with the return. (See HMRC Company Taxation Manual CTM 92440 for further details.)

Refunds of quarterly instalments

10.20   The intra-group arrangement is also available for quarterly instalments (see **3.10**) (intra-group surrender: legislation *SI 1998/3175, reg 9*, as amended by *SI 1999/1929, reg 3*). A refund of tax that is paid under the instalment arrangements can be surrendered to fellow group members at the date of payment. Again the aim is to reduce the group's exposure to interest by netting off the debit and credit interest to eliminate the differential interest that it would otherwise suffer arising from underpaid and overpaid instalment tax.

The amended version only applies when a tax refund is due to be made to the surrendering company. The refund may be due under either *reg 6* or *TMA 1970, s 59D(2)*. HMRC explain the effects as follows, with the result that:

- payments made during the quarterly instalment payment period may retrospectively be allocated between group members to mitigate the interest position of the group, beyond that limited circumstance,

- *reg 9* only applies in relation to CT paid on account of the surrendering company's own liability,

- a group is unable to make a global payment in the name of a dormant company or one that will have no CT liability, and then reallocate it between group members retrospectively.

Under *reg 9* the surrendering company must give notice to HMRC, at the time when the joint surrender notice is given, specifying the payment(s) out of which the refund is to be treated as made (*FA 1989, s 102* or *reg 9(5C)*). The surrendering company then has 30 days in which to bring its specification into line with the amount of the repayment due. If it fails to do so within that time, the repayment can be made as if no notice of surrender had been given (*FA 1989, s 102* and *reg 9(5D), (5E)*) (HMRC Company Taxation Manual CTM 92740).

Example 10.10

Red Ltd and Blue Ltd are within the same group and they both qualify under the special rules of *FA 1989, s 102*.

Both companies have 31 December year ends and each company makes the following quarterly payments:

	Red Ltd £	Blue Ltd £
14 July 2010	500,000	500,000
14 October 2010	500,000	500,000
14 January 2010	250,000	500,000
14 April 2011	150,000	500,000
Total paid	1,400,000	2,000,000

The actual corporation tax liability for the year is as follows:

	Red Ltd £	Blue Ltd £
Corporation tax liability year ending 31 March 2010	10,000	3,500,000

305

10.21 *Groups*

Red Ltd makes a repayment claim for £1,390,000 under *reg 6* because it is now known that no instalment tax was due.

Blue Ltd should have paid quarterly instalments of £875,000.

So Blue Ltd's cumulative underpayment of instalments is:

	Instalments due £	Instalments paid £	Shortfall £
14 July 2010	875,000	500,000	375,000
14 October 2010	875,000	500,000	375,000
14 January 2011	875.000	500,000	375,000
14 April 2011	875,000	500,000	375,000
	3,500,000	2,000,000	1,500,000

Red Ltd makes a repayment claim for the overpaid instalments.

Red Ltd and Blue Ltd give joint notice of surrender, so that the instalment tax paid by Red Ltd is treated as paid by Blue Ltd with Red Ltd's payment dates.

Red Ltd is treated as if the overpaid tax had been repaid to it on those dates.

The claim results in Red Ltd not making any quarterly payments. Its corporation tax of £10,000 is now due by 1 January 2011. Blue Ltd has to make a further instalment payment as soon as possible of £100,000, which is calculated as follows:

	£
Corporation tax due year ending 31 March 2010	3,500,000
Quarterly instalments paid by Blue Ltd	(2,000,000)
Quarterly instalments paid by Red Ltd	(1,400,000)
Net amount due	100,000

10.21 *SI 1998/3175, reg 10* empowers HMRC, at any time after the filing date, to require a company to furnish such information as may reasonably be required about:

- the computation of any instalment payment,

- the reasons it omitted to make quarterly instalment payments, and

- a *reg 6* repayment claim.

The time allowed for providing the information must not be less than 30 days and must be shown on the notice.

Regulation 11 empowers HMRC to require the company to produce 'books, documents and other records in its possession or power' for the purposes of *reg 10*. HMRC accept photocopies, as long as the originals are available for inspection. These powers are not part of the enquiry procedures.

Group income

10.22 A UK company is not required to deduct tax at source from intra-group interest and royalty payments where the other company is UK resident or if not UK resident operates from a permanent establishment (*FA 2001, s 85*; *FA 2002, s 96*).

DEBT CAP

Introduction

10.23 *Finance Act 2009, Sch 15* introduced legislation, which is to take effect for accounting periods beginning on or after 1 January 2010, to cap the tax deduction for finance expenses payable by the UK members of a worldwide group of companies. The amount of the deduction is restricted to the consolidated gross finance expense of that group. Finance expenses and finance income are payments of interest and interest-like amounts. In brief, the restriction is calculated by comparing the UK group members' cost of borrowing with the cost of borrowing of the worldwide group. The result is allocated to one or more of the UK group companies, leading to a disallowance of part or all of their finance expenses. If the other UK members of the group have net finance income, this can be reduced in computing their corporation tax profits instead.

Meaning of a worldwide group

10.24 A worldwide group is any large group that contains one or more relevant group companies (*FA 2009, Sch 15, para 78*). A group has the same meaning as used for international accounting standards. If a group has more than one ultimate parent, each of those ultimate parents, together with its subsidiaries, is to be treated as a separate group. An entity that is a parent of the ultimate parent of a group is not to be treated as a member of the group (*FA 2009, Sch 15, para 79*). A group is large if it has no micro, small and medium-sized enterprises as members according to the Annex to Commission Recommendation 2003/361/EC of 6 May 2003 (see **8.22**). However, the rights of the liquidator or administrator are to be left out of account if the group member is in liquidation or administration (*FA 2009, Sch 15, para 85*).

A UK group company is UK resident and is a member of the worldwide group If non–resident, it must be carrying on a trade in the UK through a permanent establishment. In addition, the company must be either the ultimate parent of the worldwide group, or a relevant subsidiary of the ultimate parent of the worldwide group.

A relevant subsidiary of the ultimate parent of the worldwide group is a company:

- which is a 75% subsidiary of the ultimate parent;

- whose ultimate parent is beneficially entitled to at least 75% of any profits available for distribution to equity holders of the company; or

- whose ultimate parent would be beneficially entitled to at least 75% of any assets of the company available for distribution to its equity holders on a winding-up.

Arrangements to secure that a company is not treated as a member of a group are ignored (*FA 2009, Sch 15, para 86*). Foreign currency accounts are to be converted to sterling at the average rate of exchange for the period calculated from daily spot rates (FA *2009, Sch 15, para 91*).

Application of the debt cap rules

10.25 The rules apply to a worldwide group where, for any period of account, its UK net debt exceeds 75% of its worldwide gross debt of the group. (Percentages for future accounting periods are subject to Treasury override.) The rules do not apply to a qualifying financial services group (*FA 2009, Sch 15, para 2*). A qualifying financial services group is essentially a group that is engaged in financial services activities, including insurance (*FA 2009, Sch 15, para 7*).

Meaning of net debt and the relevant amount

10.26 UK net debt is the total of the UK net debt amounts of each group member during the accounting period. The net debt amount of each group member is the average of the net debt at the beginning and at the end of the accounting period. Averaged amounts of less than £3 million are treated as nil; £3 million is known as 'the relevant amount'. The net debt of a company that is dormant both at the beginning and at the end and throughout the accounting period is also treated as nil (a dormant company is defined according to *CA 2006, s 1169*. The beginning of the accounting period is the first day of the period of account of the worldwide group or, the date the company joined the group if later. The end of the accounting period is the last day of the period of account of the worldwide group or, the day the company ceased to be a group company, if earlier (*FA 2009, Sch 15, para 3*).

Calculation of a company's net debt

10.27 A company's net debt at any date is the difference between the total of its relevant liabilities and the total of its relevant assets, as disclosed in accordance with GAAP on the company's balance sheet at that date. The result can be negative.

Relevant liabilities are:

- all borrowings (whether by way of overdraft or other short-term or long-term borrowing);

- liabilities in respect of finance leases; or

- any other amounts as specified by regulation.

Relevant assets are:

- cash and cash equivalents;

- amounts loaned (by overdraft or short- or long-term loan);

- net investments or net cash investments in finance leases;

- national or foreign government securities; or

- any other amounts specified by regulation.

(*FA 2009, Sch 15, para 4*).

Calculation of a worldwide group's gross debt

10.28 To find the worldwide gross debt of the worldwide group, the average of the sum of the relevant liabilities of the group as at the day before the first day of the period, and the sum of the relevant liabilities of the group as at the last day of the period, is taken (*FA 2009, Sch 15, para 5*).

DISALLOWANCE OF DEDUCTIONS

Total disallowed amount

10.29 Worldwide groups may suffer a disallowed finance expense. This is known as the total disallowed amount, being the difference between the tested

309

expense amount (see **10.48**) and the available amount (see **10.50**) (*FA 2009, Sch 15, para 15*).

Appointment of authorised company for relevant period of account

10.30 The debt cap rules apply to all group companies, which are required to report jointly as one reporting body. The group can appoint one group company to assume this role, providing all group companies give their written agreement thereto. For the agreement to be valid, it must be signed by either a director, a company secretary or other authorised person (*FA 2009, Sch 15, paras 17, 18*). Companies to which the exemption of financing income rules apply (see **10.34**) may also appoint their own reporting body, and similar rules apply (*FA 2009, Sch 15, para 29*).

Statement of allocated disallowances: submission and financing expense amount

10.31 Within 12 months of the end of the accounting period concerned, HMRC must receive a statement of allocated disallowances for that period from the reporting body. HMRC will accept revised statements within 36 months of the end of the accounting period concerned. Revised statements must show how they differ from the previous statement (*FA 2009, Sch 15, paras 19,20*). All statements submitted must be signed by all companies concerned, or by the one reporting company, if so appointed (*FA 2009, Sch 15, para 21*). The statement of allocated disallowances must show:

- the tested expense amount;
- the available amount; and
- the total disallowed amount.

The statement must list the companies to which the disallowance applies, and give the relevant details for each disallowed amount. An amount is essentially a financing expense amount if it meets the conditions of A, B or C below, and these details, together with the accounting period in which the amount (apart from these rules) would normally be accounted, are the relevant details that must be supplied to HMRC (*FA 2009, Sch 15, para 21*). Conditions A, B or C require that the amount (apart from these rules) would respectively be accounted for as:

- a debit under a loan relationship (Condition A);
- financing cost implicit in payments made under finance leases (Condition B);

- financing cost payable on debt factoring or similar transactions (Condition C).

The debit arising under Condition A can be accounted for as trading or as a non-trading loan relationship (see **Chapter 11**), but it must not be an excluded debit by reason of it being:

- an impairment loss;

- an exchange loss; or

- a related transaction.

(*FA 2009, Sch 15, para 54*)

Debit or other amounts that do not entirely fall into the accounting period of the worldwide group are reduced pro-rata.

Statement of allocated disallowances: effect

10.32 Any financing expense that is included in the statement of disallowances is disallowed as a deduction when computing the corporation tax. If the statement is submitted after the company tax return, the company is treated as having amended its tax return (*FA 2009, Sch 15, para 23*).

Failure of reporting body to submit statement of allocated disallowances

10.33 If a reporting body fails to submit a statement of allocated disallowances or fails to submit a statement that complies with the requirements (see **10.30**), each company with a net financing deduction for the accounting period concerned must reduce the amounts that it brings into account in relevant accounting periods in respect of financing expense amounts.

This reduction is calculated by the formula

$$\frac{NFD \times TDA}{TEA}$$

where:

- NFD is the net financing deduction of the company for the relevant period of account, being the sum of the company's financing expense amounts for the period less the sum of the company's financing income amounts for the period (see **10.31** and **10.36**);

311

- TEA is the tested expense amount for the relevant period of account, being the sum of the net financing deductions for each relevant group company (*FA 2009, Sch 15, para 70 (1)*); and

- TDA is the total disallowed amount (see **10.29**).

Regulations will be issued that will determine how the particular financing expense amounts are to be reduced (*FA 2009, Sch 15, para 25*).

EXEMPTION OF FINANCING INCOME

Introduction

10.34 If a worldwide group suffers a disallowed finance expense, known as the total disallowed amount, (the difference between the tested expense amount (**10.48**) and the available amount (**10.50**)) certain conditions will apply (*FA 2009, Sch 15, para 27*).

Appointment of authorised company for relevant period of account

10.35 The debt cap rules apply to all group companies, which are required to report jointly as one reporting body. A UK group can appoint one group company to assume this role, providing all group companies give their written agreement thereto. For the agreement to be valid, it must be signed by either a director, a company secretary or other authorised person (*FA 2009, Sch 15, para 29*).

Statement of allocated exemptions and financing income amount

10.36 Within 12 months of the end of the accounting period concerned, HMRC must receive a statement of allocated exemptions for that period from the reporting body. HMRC will accept revised statements within 36 months of the end of the accounting period concerned. Revised statements must show how they differ from the previous statement (*FA 2009, Sch 15, paras 31,32*). All statements submitted must be signed by all companies concerned, or by the one reporting company, if so appointed (*FA 2009, Sch 15, para 33*). The statement of allocated exemptions must show:

- the tested expense amount;

- the available amount; and

- the total disallowed amount.

312

The statement must list the companies to which the exemption applies, and give the relevant details for each exempted amount. An amount is essentially a financing income amount if it meets the conditions of A, B or C below, and these details, together with the accounting period in which the amount (apart from these rules) would normally be accounted, are the relevant details that must be supplied to HMRC (*FA 2009, Sch 15, para 33(5)*).

Conditions A, B or C require that the amount (apart from these rules) would respectively be accounted for as:

● a credit under a loan relationship (Condition A);

● financing income implicit in amounts received under finance leases (Condition B);

● financing income receivable on debt factoring or similar transactions (Condition C).

The credit arising under Condition A can be accounted for as trading or as a non-trading loan relationship (see **Chapter 11**), but it must not be an excluded credit by reason of it being:

● the reversal of an impairment loss;

● an exchange gain; or

● a profit from a related transaction.

(*FA 2009, Sch 15, para 55*)

Credit or other amounts that do not entirely fall into the accounting period of the worldwide group are reduced pro-rata.

Statement of allocated exemptions: effect

10.37   Any financing income that is included in the statement of exemptions is non-taxable. If the statement is submitted after the company tax return, the company is treated as having amended its tax return (*FA 2009, Sch 15, para 35*).

Failure of reporting body to submit statement of allocated exemptions

10.38   If a reporting body fails to submit a statement of allocated exemptions or fails to submit a statement that complies with the requirements (see **10.36**), the net income of each company is reduced to nil.

10.39 *Groups*

If the total of the unrestricted reductions exceeds the lower of the total disallowed amount and the tested income amount, referred to as 'the excess', each unrestricted reduction is reduced by an amount as calculated by the formula

$$\frac{UR \times X}{TUR}$$

Where:

- UR is the unrestricted reduction in question,

- TUR is the total of the unrestricted reductions, and

- X is the 'excess' referred to above.

Regulations will be issued that will determine how the particular financing income amounts are to be reduced (*FA 2009, Sch 15, para 38*).

Intra-group financing income where payer denied deduction

10.39   Financing income received after introduction of this legislation is not chargeable to corporation tax if the payer and the recipient are both members of the same worldwide group, subject to satisfying the following conditions:

- *Condition A*

  at the time the payment is received, the payer is a relevant associate of the recipient (see **10.40**).

- *Condition B*

  at the time the payment is received the payer is: tax-resident in an EEA territory (see **10.41**); and

  the payer is liable to a tax of that territory that is chargeable by reference to profits, income or gains arising to the payer.

- *Condition C*

  qualifying EEA tax relief for the payment is not available to the payer in the period in which the payment is made ('the current period') or any previous period (see **10.41**); and qualifying EEA tax relief for the payment is not available to the payer in any period after the current period (see **10.42**).

An EEA territory is a territory outside the United Kingdom that is within the European Economic Area (see **10.11** for a list of countries that are within the EEA). A payer is tax-resident in a territory if it is liable, under the law of that territory, to tax by reason of domicile, residence or place of management.

(*FA 2009, Sch 15, para 40*)

Meaning of 'relevant associate'

10.40   The payer is a relevant associate of the recipient if the payer is:

- a parent of the recipient,

- a 75% subsidiary of the recipient, or

- a 75% subsidiary of a parent of the recipient.

(*FA 2009, Sch 15, para 41*)

Qualifying EEA tax relief for payment in the current period or a previous period

10.41   Qualifying EEA tax relief for a payment is not available to the payer in the current period or a previous period if conditions A and B are met in relation to the payment.

Condition A

- no deduction calculated by reference to the payment can be taken into account in calculating any profits, income or gains that:

    (a)   arise to the payer in the current period or any previous period, and

    (b)   are chargeable to any tax of the United Kingdom or an EEA territory

    for the current period or any previous period.

Condition B

- no relief determined by reference to the payment can be given in the current period or any previous period for the purposes of any tax of the United Kingdom or an EEA territory by:

    (a)   the payment of a credit,

    (b)   the elimination or reduction of a tax liability, or

    (c)   any other means of any kind.

This is on the proviso that all steps have been taken to secure the reliefs, and no double taxation provisions have been disregarded (*FA 2009, Sch 15, paras 42, 43*).

Qualifying EEA tax relief for payment in future period

10.42 Qualifying EEA tax relief for a payment is not available to the payer in a period after the current period if two conditions are met in relation to the payment:

- no deduction calculated by reference to the payment can be taken into account in calculating any profits, income or gains that:

  (a)   might arise to the payer in any period after the current period, and

  (b)   would, if they did so arise, be chargeable to any tax of the United Kingdom or an EEA territory for any period after the current period;

- no relief determined by reference to the payment can be given in any period after the current period for the purposes of any tax of the United Kingdom or an EEA territory by:

  (a)   the payment of a credit,

  (b)   the elimination or reduction of a tax liability, or

  (c)   any other means of any kind.

This is on the proviso that no double taxation provisions have been disregarded (*FA 2009, Sch 15, para 44*).

Financing income amounts of a company

10.43 Financing income is any amount that meets one of the following conditions, which require that the amount (apart from these rules) would respectively be accounted for as:

- a credit under a loan relationship (Condition A);

- financing income implicit in amounts received under finance leases (Condition B); or

- financing income receivable on debt factoring or similar transactions (Condition C).

The credit arising under Condition A can be accounted for as trading or as a non-trading loan relationship (see **Chapter 11**), but it must not be an excluded credit by reason of it being:

- the reversal of an impairment loss;

- an exchange gain; or

- a profit from a related transaction.

(*FA 2009, Sch 15, para 46*)

GROUP TREASURY COMPANIES

10.44 A treasury company can elect, within three years after the end of the relevant accounting period, whether or not it requires the debt cap rules to apply.

A treasury company must be a member of the worldwide group and undertake treasury activities. Treasury activities consist of:

- managing surplus deposits of money or overdrafts,

- making or receiving deposits of money,

- lending money,

- subscribing for or holding shares in another company which is a UK group company and a group treasury company,

- investing in debt securities, and

- hedging assets, liabilities, income or expenses.

In addition, at least 90% of the relevant income of the company for the relevant period must be group treasury revenue, ie revenue arising from the treasury activities it undertakes for the group. Dividends or other distributions are not group treasury revenue unless received from a UK group treasury company. Alternatively, if the company carries out treasury activities with another company, at least 90% of the aggregate relevant income of those companies for the relevant period must be group treasury revenue (*FA 2009, Sch 15, para 57*).

INTRA-GROUP SHORT-TERM FINANCE: FINANCING EXPENSE

10.45 A paying company can elect for its intra-group short-term financing expense not to be treated as a financing expense amount. An election can only be made if the payer and the recipient are both members of the same worldwide group. The election must be made within 36 months of the end of the accounting period of the worldwide group to which the relevant amount relates. The election is irrevocable. If this election is made the respective income of the recipient company is not treated as a financing income amount (*FA 2009, Sch 15, paras 61,62*). A short-term relationship is essentially a money debt that cannot or does not last for longer than 12 months (*FA 2009, Sch 15, para 62*).

STRANDED DEFICITS IN NON-TRADING LOAN RELATIONSHIPS: FINANCING EXPENSE AND FINANCING INCOME

10.46   A company may elect for its finance expense to be treated as non-deductible. The election can only be made if both parties are members of the worldwide group. The payer must be resident in the United Kingdom or, if non-resident, be carrying on a trade in the United Kingdom through a permanent establishment. The payer must then carry forward the amount of the non-trading deficit from the finance arrangement and set it off against non-trading profits of an accounting period that falls wholly or partly within the period of account of the worldwide group. The amount of non-trading deficit carried forward and set off is equal to, or greater than, the relevant amount.

Both companies may only make an election under this paragraph jointly within 36 months of the end of the accounting period of the worldwide group to which the relevant amount relates. In these circumstances, no financing income is deemed to arise on the payer *(FA 2009, Sch 15, paras 63, 64)*.

STRANDED MANAGEMENT EXPENSES IN NON-TRADING LOAN RELATIONSHIPS: FINANCING EXPENSE AND FINANCE INCOME

10.47   An investment company may elect for its finance expense to be treated as non-deductible. The election can only be made if both parties are members of the worldwide group. The recipient must be an investment company resident in the United Kingdom or, if non-resident, be carrying on a trade in the United Kingdom through a permanent establishment. The recipient is allowed a management expense deduction (see **12.6**) in respect of the accounting period that falls wholly or partly within the period of account of the worldwide group. The amount of the deduction must be equal to, or greater than, the relevant amount. In addition, the recipient's calculation of total profits for the relevant period for the purposes of corporation tax results in a loss if the recipient's credit is not included in that calculation.

Both companies may only make an election under this paragraph jointly within 36 months of the end of the accounting period of the worldwide group to which the relevant amount relates. In these circumstances, no financing income is deemed to arise on the recipient *(FA 2009, Sch 15, paras 65, 66)*.

THE TESTED EXPENSE AMOUNT

10.48   The tested expense amount for a period of account of the worldwide group is the sum of the net financing deductions of each relevant group company.

The net financing deduction is:

- the sum of the company's financing expense amounts for the period (see **10.31**),

    less

- the sum of the company's financing income amounts for the period (see **10.36**).

Negative results and results less than £500,000 are treated as nil.

Transactions that took place before this legislation came into force are ignored (*FA 2009, Sch 15, para 70*).

THE TESTED INCOME AMOUNT

10.49   The tested income amount for the period of account of the worldwide group is the sum of the net financing incomes of each UK group company.

The net financing income is

- the sum of the company's financing income amounts for the period (see **10.36**),

    less

- the sum of the company's financing expense amounts for the period (see **10.31**).

Negative results and results less than £500,000 are ignored. Transactions that took place before this legislation came into force are ignored (*FA 2009, Sch 15, para 71*).

THE AVAILABLE AMOUNT

10.50   The available amount for a period of account of the worldwide group is the sum of the amounts disclosed in the financial statements of the group for that period in respect of:

- interest payable on amounts borrowed;

319

10.50 *Groups*

- amortisation of discounts relating to amounts borrowed;

- amortisation of premiums relating to amounts borrowed;

- amortisation of ancillary costs relating to amounts borrowed;

- the financing cost implicit in payments made under finance leases;

- the financing cost relating to debt factoring, or

- amounts of such other description as may be specified in regulations made by the HMRC Commissioners.

Dividends payable in respect of redeemable preference shares that are recognised as a liability in the financial statements of the group for the period are ignored (*FA 2009, Sch 15, para 73*). Special rules apply to companies with income from oil extraction, shipping and ring fenced tax exempt business (*FA 2009, Sch 15, paras 74, 75*).

Chapter 11

Corporate finance

COMPANY FINANCE

Equity v loan finance

11.1   Companies raise finance by borrowing, issuing shares and exploiting their assets. A debt has a legal right to repayment whereas shares have no such rights. Various controls are exercised on a company's activities through the *Financial Services and Markets Act 2000*, the *Companies Act 2006* and the Stock Exchange.

For taxation purposes the basic premise is that equity finance, which relates to the issue of shares, will have no direct effect on the company's corporation tax liability. UK distributions received are not taxable on a company. On eventual disposal the profit on sale to the vendor will be assessable as a capital gain.

Loan finance does have an effect on the company's corporation tax liability. Lenders are rewarded by an interest payment. Lenders look to some form of asset security or guarantee regarding the loan repayment. Interest payments are deductible against a company's corporation tax liability and interest receipts are taxable.

The loan relationship provisions

11.2   The loan relationship rules governing corporate debt, principally aimed at aligning the taxation treatment of loan finance with the accounting treatment, were introduced by *Finance Act 1996, ss 80–105* and *Schs 8–15*. With the ever-increasing sophistication of the financial markets, the original rules were amended by subsequent *Finance Acts*; notably *FA 2002* (generally for accounting periods beginning on or after 1 October 2002), *FA 2004, F (No 2) A 2005* (generally for accounting periods beginning on or after 1 January 2005) and *FA 2006* for accounting periods ended on or after 22 March 2006. *Finance Act 2002* brought exchange gains and losses on loan relationships denominated in a foreign currency into the calculation of the overall profit or loss on the loan relationship. In general the *FA 1996* loan relationships legislation also applies to exchange gains and losses.

The original rules and their subsequent amendments have now been collated and redrafted and they are included in *Corporation Tax Act 2009 (CTA 2009), ss 292–710*, as part of the government's tax law rewrite project. The intention in drafting *CTA 2009* was not to change the existing legislation, but to make it clearer. The new corporation tax provisions apply to accounting periods beginning on or after 1 April 2009. The references, where applicable, in this chapter are to *CTA 2009*. For the previous legislation, please see *Corporation Tax 2008/09* (Tottel Publishing).

Ambit of the loan relationship provisions

11.3   The loan relationship rules treat capital and revenue receipts in a like manner and show no distinction between realised and unrealised amounts (*CTA 2009, s 293(3)*).

Profits and deficits are calculated according to the basis adopted in the accounts, and are termed 'credits' and 'debits' (*CTA 2009, ss 296, 307*).

Profits and losses from related transactions are also included within the meaning of a loan relationship (*CTA 2009, s 293(1), (2)*). A related transaction is any disposal or acquisition, in whole or in part, of rights or liabilities under the relationship. A disposal or acquisition includes the transfer or discharge by an outright sale, gift, exchange, surrender, redemption or release of any rights or liabilities under the loan relationship (*CTA 2009, s 304*). Rights and liabilities under a loan relationship refer to the arrangements as a result of which that relationship subsists. Rights and liabilities attached to any security that is issued in relation to the money debt are also included (*CTA 2009, s 305*). A debtor (borrower) may choose to settle an interest liability to a creditor (lender) by an issue of funding bonds. If so, the market value of the bonds at their issue date is treated as being the amount of interest paid. The later redemption of these bonds will not be treated as interest paid. Funding bonds can include any bonds, stocks, shares, securities or certificates of indebtedness (*CTA 2009, s 413*).

The loan relationship rules apply to both trading and non-trading companies, unincorporated associations subject to corporation tax, UK branches of overseas companies and controlled foreign companies. The rules apply to companies that are members of a partnership but not to individuals. Non-resident companies come within the loan relationship rules if they trade in the UK through a branch or agency, and the loan relationship is held for trading purposes by that branch or agency

Trading credits and debits

11.4   Trading credits and debits are included respectively as receipts and expenses of the trade, which are to be brought into account in calculating a company's profits for that period (*CTA 2009, s 297(2), (3)*) in the computation of trading income. Non-trading debits and credits are included within non-trading income.

Non-trading debits and credits

11.5   Non-trading debits and credits are netted off against each other. An excess of credits over debits results in a non-trading profit. An excess of debits over credits results in a non-trading deficit (*CTA 2009, s 301*).

Creditor and debtor loan relationship

11.6   The first issue that a company will want to address is whether the debt arrangement that it has entered into constitutes a loan relationship. In most situations this will be the case. A loan relationship exists where:

- the company stands in the position of a creditor or debtor as respects any money debt (whether by reference to a security or otherwise); and

- that debt is one arising from a transaction for the lending of money;

and references to a loan relationship and to a company's being a party to a loan relationship shall be construed accordingly (*CTA 2009, s 302(1)*).

For a company to be within the loan relationship provisions it must have a money debt. A normal trade debt is not a loan relationship. The loan relationship is termed accordingly.

A creditor relationship is a loan relationship where the company stands in the position of a creditor as respects the debt in question, ie the lender (*CTA 2009, s 302(5)*). A debtor relationship is a loan relationship where the company stands in the position of a debtor as respects the debt in question, ie the borrower (*CTA 2009, s 302(5)*).

MONEY DEBT

Legislative definitions

11.7   A money debt is a debt which falls to be settled by:

- the payment of money;

- the transfer of a right to settlement under a debt which is itself a money debt; or

- the issue or transfer of any share in a company.

A money debt is also any debt that has at any time fallen to be so settled or could at the option of the debtor or the creditor be so settled. If the debt can be settled in any other way this is ignored in deciding whether there is a money debt. If an instrument has been created that represents the rights under the debt then this will be within the loan relationship rules (*CTA 2009, s 303(3)*). A share is not within the loan relationship rules unless it is subject to outstanding third party obligations and is an interest-like investment (see **11.10**) (*CTA 2009, s 524*).

The following types of debt are included within loan relationships: overdrafts, mortgages, advances, gilts, bank loans and deposits, building society shares and deposits, debentures, certificates of deposit, company securities and eurobonds, government stock, discounts, premiums, bills of exchange and promissory notes. For corporation tax a qualifying corporate bond is a loan relationship. A qualifying corporate bond is a security which at all times has represented a normal commercial loan and which is only redeemable in sterling (*TCGA 1992, s 117*). A convertible loan note is not a qualifying corporate bond (*Weston v Garnett* [2005] EWCA Civ 742, [2005] STC 1134). A loan note or security that contains a currency conversion option on issue is not a qualifying corporate bond, even if the option were to lapse in the meantime (*Harding v Revenue and Customs Comrs* [2008] EWHC 99 (Ch)).

Certain relationships are treated as loan relationships: relevant non-lending arrangements; OEICs; unit trusts and offshore funds; building societies; industrial and provident societies; alternative finance arrangements; shares with guaranteed returns; returns from partnerships; manufactured interest; repos and investment life insurance contracts. These are all specialised situations and beyond the coverage of this book.

A debt arising from share rights granted in a company does not bring about a money debt (*CTA 2009, s 303*). A share in a company is any share that gives entitlement to a distribution (*CTA 2009, s 476(1)*).

Money debts included within the loan relationship rules

11.8   A money debt is not necessarily a loan relationship. Certain money debts are brought within the loan relationship rules as relevant non-lending relationships (*CTA 2009, ss 478–486*). A relevant non-lending relationship is a loan relationship that does not arise from the lending of money (*CTA 2009*, *s 479(1)*), but is a kind of debt on which interest is payable to or by the company, or an exchange gain or loss arises to the company, or there is an impairment loss resulting from an unpaid business debt. Such items will include interest on late payment for goods and services, interest on judgment debts, late payment interest on completion and late payment of tax. Only the interest and exchange gains and losses are treated as loan relationships and included as debits or credits. Interest imputed under transfer pricing (see **14.20–14.21**) is also included within loan relationships (*CTA 2009, ss 483, 484*). Whether the interest is trading or non-trading depends on whether it is receivable or payable for the purposes of the trade. Interest receivable from or payable to HMRC is always non-trading (*CTA 2009, s 482(1)*).

Interest in excess of a reasonable commercial return, which is treated as a distribution by virtue of *ICTA 1988, s 209(2)(d)* (see **16.7**), is not a loan relationship (*CTA 2009, s 465(1)*). *Section 465(1)* ensures that interest that is characterised as a distribution under *ICTA 1988, s 209(2)(d)* or *(e)* cannot be a debit or credit.

Discounts on money debts are also loan relationships (*CTA 2009, s 480(1)*), but discounts that are treated as distributions under *ICTA 1988, s 209(2)(e)* are not. Shares are treated as loan relationships in the following circumstances (see **11.9**).

Shares treated as loan relationships

11.9   Shares treated as loan relationships include:

- **Shares subject to outstanding third-party obligations**. The investing company holds a share in another company, the investee company that is subject to third party obligations and is an interest like investment. In other words another person must meet the calls on the shares and that its fair value increase represents a return at commercial rate of interest with no deviations (*CTA 2009, s 525*). In that case the investing company must treat the share as a creditor loan relationship. The distributions received are neither treated as a dividend nor a repayment of capital. The investing company must bring the debits and credits into account on an accounting fair value basis (*CTA 2009, s 524*).

- **Non-qualifying shares**. A non-qualifying share is a share held by an investing company in another company, the investee company, which is neither a holding in a unit trust, an OEIC nor an offshore fund. In addition, the share is not a dealer share (*CTA 2009, s 130*) but it satisfied one of three conditions:

    1   Its fair value increase represents a return at a commercial rate of interest with no deviations.

> 2   The share is redeemable such that its return equates with a return on invested money, eg redeemable preference shares.
>
> 3   The share and one or more derivative contracts are together designed to produce a return based on a commercial rate of interest.

In that case, the investing company must treat the share as a creditor loan relationship. The distributions received are neither treated as a dividend nor a repayment of capital. The investing company must bring the debits and credits into account on an accounting fair value basis.

Where condition 1 above applies, no debits or transactions are to be brought into account which prevent the value of the share increasing at a rate of return representing a commercial rate of interest.

If condition 3 applies, debits and credits are to be brought into account in respect of any associated transaction as if it were a derivative contract (*CTA 2009, s 526*).

Non-loan relationships

11.10   From the above it may be difficult to judge what arrangement can be considered not to be a loan relationship. However, the following are accepted as not being loan relationships: trade debts arising from the purchase of goods and services; finance leases; HP agreements; court settlement; loan guarantees; and contingencies, as they do not derive from the lending of money (*CTA 2009, s 302(1)*).

Accounting treatment

Amounts brought into account

11.11   The amounts that a company must bring into account as credits and debits are those that are recognised in determining the company's profit or loss for the accounting period in question in accordance with GAAP (*CTA 2009, s 307(2)*).

The amounts that the company must bring into account as regards its loan relationships are:

- all profits and losses from its loan relationships and related transactions, but excluding interest and expenses;

- all interest under those relationships; and

- all expenses incurred under or for the purposes of those relationships and transactions.

Expenses are only treated as incurred if they are incurred directly in:

- bringing the loan relationship into existence;

- entering or giving effect to any of the related transactions;

- making payments under any of those relationships or as a result of any of those transactions; or

- taking steps to ensure the receipt of payments under any of those relationships or in accordance with any of those transactions (*CTA 2009, s 307*).

Pre-loan relationship expenditure

11.12   Pre-loan relationship expenses and abortive expenses are deductible if they would be so deductible had the loan relationship been entered into at that time (*CTA 2009, s 329*). However, to be deductible as a trading debit, the company must elect within two years of the end of the accounting period in which the expenditure is incurred for the debit to be treated as a debit in connection with a trading loan relationship. This is on the proviso that the company begins to carry on the trade within seven years of the end of the accounting period from when the expenditure was incurred and the expenditure is of a type that would be deductible from that trading income, had the trade been carried on at that time (*CTA 2009, s 330*).

GAAP and accounting bases

11.13   If a company has not drawn up GAAP compliance accounts or no accounts at all, its results are re-calculated on an annual cumulative basis in accordance with GAAP and used for loan relationship purposes (*CTA 2009, s 309*). Where amounts are matched for accounts purposes, this is derecognised for loan relationships (*CTA 2009, ss 311, 312*).

Any basis of accounting may be adopted for bringing debits and credits into account, provided it complies with GAAP, including any amortised cost basis or a fair value basis, but particular accounting bases are required in the following circumstances:

Amortised cost basis:

- connected companies relationships (*CTA 2009, s 349(2)*);

327

- discounts arising from a money debt under a relevant non-lending relationship (*CTA 2009, s 482(2)*).

Fair value accounting:

- determination of credits and debits where amounts are not fully recognised for accounting purposes (*CTA 2009, s 312(5), (6)*);

- company partners using fair value accounting (*CTA 2009, s 382(2)*);

- index-linked gilt-edged securities (*CTA 2009, s 399(2)*);

- connected parties deriving benefit from creditor relationships (*CTA 2009, s 453(2)*);

- reset bonds etc (*CTA 2009, s 454(4)*);

- holdings in OEICs, unit trusts and offshore funds (*CTA 2009, s 490(3)*); and

- application of shares as rights under a creditor relationship by virtue of *s 523* (*CTA 2009, s 534(1)*).

Meaning of amortised cost and fair value accounting

11.14   The amortised cost basis of accounting is where an asset or liability representing the loan relationship is shown in the company's accounts at cost adjusted for cumulative amortisation and any impairment, repayment or release. The fair value basis of accounting is where assets and liabilities are shown in the company's balance sheet at their fair value (*CTA 2009. s 313(4), (5)*). Where there is a change in accounting basis from amortised cost to fair value, the Treasury may make regulations that debits and credits continue to be dealt with on an amortised cost basis (*CTA 2009, s 314*). A change in accounting policy from UK GAAP to IFRS, or vice versa, between two accounting periods may bring about a change in the carrying value of an asset or a liability between the earlier and the later period. If so, an adjusting debit or credit as appropriate is to be brought into the later accounting period (*CTA 2009, ss 315, 316*). This will also apply if there is a change in value following the cessation of a loan relationship (*CTA 2009, s 318*). The carrying value of an asset or liability includes accruals, payments in advance and impairment losses, together with provisions for bad or doubtful debts (*CTA 2009, s 317*). This impairment loss is a debit resulting from the uncollectability of a financial asset (*CTA 2009, s 476(1)*). The Treasury may by regulations make provision for cases where there is a change of accounting policy in drawing up a company's accounts from one period of account to the next which affects the amounts to be brought into account for accounting purposes in respect of the company's loan relationships (*CTA 2009, s 319*).

Debits or credits that are capital for GAAP remain as revenue if they refer to a loan relationship (*CTA 2009, s 320*). Where a debit or credit is recognised in shareholders' funds on the company's balance sheet or in equity, it is included in the profit and loss account for loan relationship purposes (*CTA 2009, s 321*).

Debits with no complementary credits

11.15 For accounting purposes, debits and credits complement each other but, if a debt is released, no complementary credit has to be recognised in the accounts if the release is part of a statutory insolvency arrangement or the debtor company meets one of the insolvency conditions and the debtor relationship is not a connected companies relationship. Neither does a complementary credit have to be recognised if the release is in consideration of shares forming part of the ordinary share capital of the debtor company, or in consideration of any entitlement to such shares. A company meets the insolvency conditions if it is in insolvent liquidation, in administration or in insolvent administrative receivership, or if an appointment of a provisional liquidator is in force. The insolvency conditions may be present either in the UK or abroad (*CTA 2009, s 322*).

If an asset is revalued, no debit is to be brought into account, with the exception of an impairment loss, or a debit resulting from a release by the company of any liability under the relationship. Credits, which correspond to the disallowed debits, are also not brought into account. This treatment does not apply if the company adopts fair value accounting (*CTA 2009, ss 324, 325*). Where a government debt is written off under *ICTA 1988, s 400(7)* and *(8)* (see **9.21**) by the release of a liability to pay an amount under a debtor relationship, no credit is required to be brought into account (*CTA 2009, s 326*). There is no relief for a loss incurred when the loan relationship was not subject to UK taxation (*CTA 2009, s 327*).

Connected companies

11.16 A company has a connected companies relationship if, as debtor, it has a connection with the creditor, or if, as creditor, it has a connection with the debtor, in respect of the relationship in question. A company can stand in the position of a debtor or creditor by indirectly standing in that position through a series of loan relationship or relevant money debts (*CTA 2009, s 348*).

CORPORATION TAX TREATMENT

Trading and non-trading loan relationships

11.17 It is necessary to distinguish between a trading and a non-trading loan relationship. Essentially, if a company owes funds or is due funds for the purposes of its trade, it is within a trading loan relationship (*CTA 2009, s 297(1)*). For lenders the test is tighter and they will only be within a trading loan relationship if it entered into the loan 'in the course of activities forming an integral part of its trade' (*CTA 2009, s 298(1)*). In practice only companies within the financial sector such as insurance companies, banks and finance trades which lend funds as an integral part of their trade will meet this requirement.

Group finance companies may be an exception.

Money lending was not deemed to be the integral part of the trade of an electrical energy producer and supplier. It was not the normal activity of an energy producer or supplier. Hence, interest earned on money set aside by to meet future liabilities was deemed to relate to a non-trading loan relationship (*Nuclear Electric plc v Bradley* (1996) 68 TC 670).

TRADING LOAN RELATIONSHIPS

Trading income

11.18 The appropriate accounting method will result in all credits and debits arising from profits, gains and losses, both capital and revenue, interest, charges and expenses, together with exchange gains and losses relating to the company's loan relationships, being brought into the corporation tax computation. Credits and debits resulting from a trading loan relationship are included as receipts or expenses of the trade (*CTA 2009, s 296*). The loan relationship legislation overrides the 'wholly and exclusively' provision (*CTA 2009, s 54*), the capital expenditure exclusion (*CTA 2009, s 53*) and patent royalties exclusion (*CTA 2009, s 59*) regarding trading income (see **5.13**) (*CTA 2009, s 297(4)*). Accounting matching procedures that result in the derecognition of matched income are ignored for corporation tax purposes (*CTA 2009, s 352*). Any subsequent profits or losses arising are assessable or relievable accordingly under the trading income rules. This is not the case for non-trading loan relationships, which have special computational rules (see **11.22, 11.23**).

Example 11.1

Aurora Ltd is a small trading company that requires additional finance for the purposes of its trade. The bank grants an additional £1m 6% fixed interest loan facility on 1 January 2009. The company is charged legal fees and other professional costs in relation to obtaining the loan of £5,000. The company applies the FRSSE. Accounts are prepared to 31 December each year.

The loan is a trading loan relationship as it has been taken out for trading purposes. As the company apples the FRSSE, the finance costs of borrowings are allocated to the accounting periods over the term of the borrowings at a constant rate on the carrying amount. The amounts charged will form the allowable debits and no adjustment to profits is required when preparing the corporation tax computation. The expenses will be allowable by reason of *CTA 2009, s 307(4)*: see **11.23**.

Example 11.2

Q plc acquires shares in a new subsidiary for £10m. It pays the vendor company £8m in cash, and issues loan notes for the remaining £2m. Subsequently, Q plc finds out facts about the financial position of its new subsidiary that had not come to light in the due diligence process. Discussions with the vendor company follow, as a result of which it is agreed that the purchase price should be reduced by £1m. Accordingly, £1m of the loan notes issued by Q plc is cancelled. It accounts for the transaction as:

| Cr | Cost of investment | £1 million |
| Dr | Creditors (loan notes) | £1 million |

For tax purposes, the loan notes are loan relationships since, although there has been no lending of money, an instrument has been issued representing security for the creditor's rights under the £2m money debt. The cancellation of £1m of the notes does not, however, give rise to a tax charge under the loan relationships rules. Although a credit appears in the company's books, there is no amount that has been recognised in determining the company's profit or loss for the period. Nothing therefore falls within *CTA 2009, s 307(2)* (HMRC Corporate Finance Manual CFM 5203a).

331

UNALLOWABLE PURPOSE

Non-business or non-commercial

11.19   Relief is denied for debits arising from an unallowable purpose.

An unallowable purpose is any non-business or non- business or commercial or any purpose that consists of securing a tax advantage (*CTA 2009, s 442(1)*).

Example 11.3

The CASH Bank plc grants the Village Tennis Club a loan to finance the construction of a new club house.

For corporation tax purposes the allowable and non-allowable interest expense is apportioned pro rata to the club's taxable income from non-members and non-taxable income from members.

Example 11.4

Chekov is the UK branch of Zagrev, a non-UK resident Russian holding company. The company uses British banks to fund its global activities. A £12m loan is raised from the CASH Bank plc to fund Zagrev's activities in Guatemala. Chekov has no involvement in these activities but agrees to pay the interest.

The interest charged is deemed to be 'an unallowable purpose' for Chekov, and hence is disallowable (*CTA 2009, s 442(2)*) (HMRC Corporate Finance Manual CFM 6214).

A tax avoidance purpose

11.20   A tax avoidance purpose is any purpose that consists in securing a tax advantage either for the company or for any other person (*CTA 2009, s 442(5)*). A tax avoidance purpose becomes an unallowable purpose when it is the main purpose or one of the main reasons that the company became a party to the relationship or entered into a related transaction. The usage of funds to secure or finance a tax avoidance scheme will amount to an unallowable purpose (*CTA 2009, s 443*).

Whether a tax avoidance purpose is the main, or one of the main, purposes is a question of fact, which depends on all the circumstances of the particular case.

Example 11.5

A company borrows £50m from a finance company at arm's length. The company becomes insolvent and disposes of all its assets. This leaves it with an outstanding debt of £40m. The company is not liquidated and interest continues to accrue on the debt. The finance company either omits to accrue the interest receivable or it accrues the interest and then writes it off as a bad debt. The company accrues the interest and makes a deficit on which group relief claims are made. The company has no activity which is within the charge to corporation tax *(CTA 2009, s 442(2))*. The purpose of the loan relationship is therefore specifically excluded from being a business or commercial purpose and it is an unallowable purpose. In addition, although the loan relationship was originally bona fide, its continued existence is not commercial. The relating debits to the loan relationship are disallowed.

The only purpose of the loan relationship in the current accounting period is to generate group relief thereby securing a tax advantage for another group company *(CTA 2009, s 442(5))* (HMRC Corporate Finance Manual CFM 6215a).

Write off of loans for an unallowable purpose

11.21   Write off of loans for an unallowable purpose will also not qualify for relief. For example, an interest-free loan made by a company, whose business consists of manufacturing kitchen tables, which had lent the money to a yacht club supported by one of the directors of the company for the purpose of providing financial support to the yacht club. If the company borrowed to make the loan to the yacht club, the interest will also be disallowed.

If the purpose of the loan included a commercial or other business purpose such as advertising, then this would be taken into account in arriving at the amount attributable to the unallowable purpose on a just and reasonable basis *(CTA 2009, s 441(1), (2))* (HMRC Corporate Finance Manual CFM 6224).

NON-TRADING LOAN RELATIONSHIPS

11.22   A company is party to a non-trading loan relationship if it is party to the relationship not for the purposes of the trade. For many companies, their only non-trading income will be bank interest received from an investment of surplus funds. A property business or an overseas property business is not a trade for these purposes.

Non-trading loan relationship debits and credits are aggregated to result in a non-trading profit or deficit. A non-trading profit is chargeable to corporation tax.

Example 11.6

On 1 January 2010, Aurora Ltd bought £20,000 nominal gilt-edged stock at £95 per £100 nominal stock. The investment was not for the purposes of trade. The securities are redeemable on 31 December 2014 at par. Interest at 3% is payable annually on 31 December.

As the investment has no relationship to the trade, this amounts to a non-trading loan relationship, and the interest and the discount are chargeable to corporation tax as profits from a non-trading loan relationship.

Again, the accounting treatment will be adopted and the assessable amounts are as follows:

Year ended	31 December 2010 £	31 December 2011 £	31 December 2012 £	31 December 2013 £	31 December 2014 £
Interest received	600	600	600	600	600
Discount	100	100	100	100	100
Non-trading loan relationship profit	700	700	700	700	700

RELIEF FOR NON-TRADING DEFICITS

Manner of non-trading deficit relief

11.23   The basic rule is for the deficit to be carried forward and set off against non-trading profits of the company for accounting periods after the deficit period (*CTA 2009, s 457(1)*).

Relief is given as follows for all or part of the deficit:

(a)   by claim in a group relief claim (*ICTA 1988, s 403*); or

(b)   by claim:

334

(i)   set against other profits of the company for the deficit period, in whole or in part *(CTA 2009, s 459(1)(a))*; or

(ii)   carried back and set against the chargeable non-trading loan relationship profits of the previous 12 months, in whole or in part *(CTA 2009, s 459(1)(b))*; or

(c)   any remaining amount will be carried forward and set against non-trading profits in succeeding accounting periods *(CTA 2009, s 457(3))*.

A claim under *ICTA 1988, s 403* can be made at any time up to the first anniversary of the filing date of the return *(FA 1998, Sch 18, para 74)*. A claim under *CTA 2009, s 459(1)* must be made within two years after the deficit period ends *(CTA 2009, s 460(1))*.

Example 11.7—Single company—No deficits in previous years

Aurora Ltd's results in years to come are shown below. Aurora Ltd has a non-trading deficit for the year ended 31 December 2012 of £10,000. There are no group companies.

Year ended	31 December 2009	31 December 2010	31 December 2011	31 December 2012	31 December 2013
	£	£	£	£	£
Trade profits	10,000	20,000	30,000	700	900
Non-trading loan relationship profits	1,000	1,000	5,000		300
PCTCT	11,000	21,000	35,000	700	1,200

Relief is obtained as follows:

	£	£
Total loss		10,000
Set against other profits of the company for the deficit period	700	
Carried back and set against the chargeable non-trading loan relationship profits of the previous 12 months	5,000	
Carried forward and set against non-trading profits in succeeding accounting periods *(CTA 2009, s 459(1))*	300	
Loss utilised		6,000
Balance available to carry forward		4,000

Example 11.8—Group company—No deficit in previous years

Horatio Ltd has the following results for the years ended 30 June 2008, 2009 and 2010.

Year ended	30 June 2008	30 June 2009	30 June 2010
	£	£	£
Trade profits	5,000	15,000	40,000
Non-trading loan relationship profit	10,000	10,000	
Non-trading loan relationship deficit			(5,000)

Horatio Ltd has the option of utilising the £5,000 deficit in:

(i)   a group relief claim (*ICTA 1988, s 403*), or

(ii)   against total profits for the year ending 30 June 2010 (*CTA 2009, s 459(1)(a)*), or

(iii)   against non-trading loan relationship profits for the year ending 30 June 2009 (*CTA 2009, s 459(1)(b)*), or

(iv)   carry forward against non-trading profits in succeeding periods (*CTA 2009, s 457(3)*).

Example 11.9—Single company partial loss claim for current year

Nelson Ltd has the following results for the year ended 31 March 2010 and makes a partial claim to set its non-trading deficit against profits of the same period.

	£
Trade profits	78,000
Profits of a property business	40,000
Non-trading deficit	152,000

Nelson Ltd's partial loss claim is as follows:

	Trade profits	Profits of a property business	Total	Non-trading loan relationship deficit utilisation memorandum
	£	£	£	£
Income	78,000	40,000	118,000	(152,000)
Partial deficit claim (*CTA 2009, s 459(1)(a)*)	(78,000)	(10,000)	(88,000)	88,000
PCTCT	0	30,000	30,000	
Corporation tax @ 28%			8,400	
Deficit available:				64,000
(i) to carry back under *CTA 2009, s 459(1)(b)*, or (ii) to carry forward (*CTA 2009, s 457(3)*)				

Current year order of non-trading deficit relief set-off

11.24   If the deficit is set against profits of the period the order of set-off is as follows:

(i)   after relief for trading losses carried forward,

but before relief for:

(ii)   losses of a property business set against profits for the same period (*ICTA 1988, s 392A(1)*),

(iii)   trading losses set against profits for the same period, or carried back from a later period (*ICTA 1988, s 393A(1)*),

(iv)   a non-trading deficit carried back from a later period (*CTA 2009, s 459(1)(b)*).

(*CTA 2009, s 461(5), (6)*)

Carry back previous year order of non-trading deficit relief set-off

11.25   If the deficit is carried back to the previous 12-month accounting period, the order of set-off is as follows:

after any amounts claimed that relate to:

(i)   deficits of the claim period to be set off against total profits (*CTA 2009, s 459(1)(a)*),

(ii)   losses or deficits from any period before the deficit period—or treated as coming from an earlier period,

(iii)   charges for trade purposes under *ICTA 1988, s 338* (normally before 24 July 2002), or

(iv)   trading losses set against profits of the same or preceding year under *ICTA 1988, s 393A.*

If the company is a company with investment business, the following are given prior relief:

●   capital allowances,

●   management expenses under *CTA 2009, s 1219,*

●   business charges under *ICTA 1988, s 338*, made wholly and exclusively for the purposes of the trade (*CTA 2009, s 463(5)*).

Example 11.10—Group company with deficit in previous year

If Horatio Ltd's results for the years ended 30 June 2008, 2009 and 2010 (see Example 11.8) had been as follows:

Year ended	30 June 2008	30 June 2009	30 June 2010
	£	£	£
Trade profits	—	15,000	40,000
Non-trading loan relationship profit		10,000	
Non-trading loan relationship deficit	(8,000)		(5,000)

Horatio Ltd can still use the £5,000 deficit for the year ended 30 June 2010 in a group relief claim or against other profits but can only relieve £2,000 of the deficit in 2009 as the brought forward deficit has priority.

Example 11.11—Single company with deficit in previous years

Kiora Ltd is a single company, prepares accounts to 31 March each year and has the following actual and forecast results:

Year ended	31 March 2009 £000	31 March 2010 £000	31 March 2011 £000
Trade loss brought forward	(90)		
Trade profits	400	200	500
Profits of a property business	50	50	20
Chargeable gain	100	100	2
Non-trading loan relationship			
Interest accrued (credits)	(10)	(8)	(20)
Interest accrued (debits)		400	400
Net deficit		392	380

The non-trading loan relationship deficit can be relieved as follows:

Year ended	31 March 2009 £000	31 March 2010 £000	31 March 2011 £000
Trade profits	400	200	500
Loss: *ICTA 1988, s 393(1)* brought forward	(90)		
Trade profits (post loss relief)	310	200	500

Year ended	31 March 2009 £000	31 March 2010 £000	31 March 2011 £000
Trade profits	310	200	500
Profits of a property business	50	50	20
Chargeable gain	100	100	2
Total non-trading profits	160	150	22
Total profits	470	350	522

Year ended	*31 March* *2009* £000	*31 March* *2010* £000	*31 March* *2011* £000
Set-off against current profits of whatever description (*CTA 2009, s 459(1)(a)*)		(350)	(380)
Set-off against non-trading loan relationship profits of the previous 12 months (*CTA 2009, s 459(1)(b)*)	(10)		
Carry forward to set against future non-trading profits (*CTA 2009, s 457(3)*)			(22)
Total relief	(10)	(350)	(402)
PCTCT	460	0	120
Non-trading deficit memorandum			
Net deficit		392	380
Current year relief		(350)	(380)
Prior year relief		(10)	
Future year relief		(22)	
Balance carried forward		10	0

Carry forward of non-trading deficit relief

11.26   If no other claim is made, the deficit will be carried forward by default under *CTA 2009, s 457*. The deficit may be set against the company's non-trading profits for the following years, which will include chargeable gains, and property and loan relationship income.

Disclaimer of carry forward non-trading deficit relief

11.27   Within two years of the end of the accounting period in which the brought-forward non-trading deficit would otherwise be utilised the company may claim that a specified amount of this deficit is not to be set against the non-trading profits of the following period. Any unused relief is carried forward to the following period and set against the non-trading profits of that period or disclaimed accordingly (*CTA 2009, s 458*).

Example 11.12—Single company partial claim for deficit brought forward

Josephine Ltd only carries on an overseas property business. A double tax agreement is in place. The profits for the year ended 30 September 2010 amounted to £90,000. The overseas tax paid was £16,800. Many years ago, Josephine Ltd incurred a non-trading loan relationship deficit. The balance brought forward under *CTA 2009, s 457* at 30 September 2009 is £100,000.

Josephine Ltd claims under *CTA 2009, s 458* that only part of the deficit be set against the current year's income, with the following result:

	Year ending 30 June 2009
	£
Overseas property business	90,000
Non-trading loan relationship part deficit	(30,000)
PCTCT	60,000
Corporation tax @ 28%	16,800
Overseas tax paid	16,800

The balance of deficit available to carry forward is £70,000.

Pre-loan relationship expenditure and pre-trading expenditure

11.28   Pre-loan relationship expenses and abortive expenses are classed as non-trading debits, and are deductible if they would be so deductible had the loan relationship been entered into at that time (*CTA 2009, s 329*).

If a company intends to trade, not only are its pre-loan relationship expenses and abortive expenses classed as a non-trading debit, but also any interest that the company incurs before it commences to trade (*CTA 2009, s 330*). If it would be allowed as a trading debit had trading commenced, the company may elect, within two years of the end of the accounting period in which the debit arose under the provisions of *CTA 2009, s 330(1)(b)*, that it is not to be brought in as a non-trading debit. Instead, it is to be treated as a trading debit for the accounting period in which the company commences to trade. The company must actually commence trading within seven years of the period in which the expenditure is incurred.

A trading company may wish to make this election because non-trading deficits carried forward can only be set against future non-trading income, which may not accrue to the company.

TRADING AND NON-TRADING LOAN RELATIONSHIPS

Costs of obtaining loan finance

11.29 HMRC consider that the following expenses directly incurred in the following activities are an allowable debit for both trading and non-trading loan relationships under *CTA 2009, s 307(4)*:

	Expense	*Examples*
CTA 2009, s 307(4)		
(a)	Bringing a loan relationship into existence	Arrangement fees with banks. Fee or commission for a loan guarantee. BIS fees for investing surplus cash in liquidation.
(b)	Entering into, or giving effect to, a related transaction	Broker's fees on purchase or sale of existing securities. Legal fees on the transfer of a security
(c)	Making a payment under a loan relationship or related transaction	Cost of making interest payments. Early redemption penalties.
(d)	Pursuing payments due under a loan relationship or related transaction	Solicitor's fees incurred in pursuing a debt defaulter.
CTA 2009, s 329	Attempting to bring a loan relationship into existence	This covers abortive expenditure. As long as the expense would have been allowable had the company raised the loan, it is still allowable even if the loan never exists.

Key person insurance premiums, other insurance policies or general investment advice, are not considered to be directly incurred (HMRC Corporate Finance Manual CFM 5210).

Costs of finance included in the accounts as required by GAAP

11.30 Under GAAP, when accounting for the incidental costs of purchase of shares in a subsidiary the costs of the loan finance to buy the shares are normally spread over more than one accounting period. Where this takes place relief will be granted in each respective accounting period. However, where the shares are held as a fixed asset and it is within GAAP to capitalise the costs, relief will be given by adjusting the corporation tax computation (*CTA 2009, s 320*) (HMRC Corporate Finance Manual CFM 5230b).

Interest and loan expenses on fixed capital assets, which have been capitalised according to GAAP, should be relieved against profits chargeable to tax by adjusting the corporation tax computation. This treatment is mandatory. Where capitalised interest on loans of this type is not included in the tax computation, the company must amend its self-assessment. HMRC will keep a record of the relief given, to check that the company makes an adjustment when amortisation of the asset is taken to profit and loss account, or when the asset is sold, and the interest then appears in the profit and loss account (*CTA 2009, s 321*) (HMRC Corporate Finance Manual CFM 5230). This treatment does not apply where interest is charged to work-in-progress. This is because interest has been charged in the profit and loss account albeit there has been a rise in the value of work-in-progress (HMRC Corporate Finance Manual CFM 5230a).

CONNECTED COMPANIES RELATIONSHIP

Meaning of connection

11.31 A company has a connected companies relationship if, as the debtor company in the relationship, it has a connection with the creditor company, or if, as the creditor company, it has a connection with the debtor company. A company can be in the connected companies relationship through a direct connection with the respective creditor or debtor company or indirectly through a series of loan relationships or relevant money debts. If there is a connected companies loan relationship at any time during an accounting period, it is treated as being in place for the whole of that accounting period (*CTA 2009, s 348*).

There is a connection between two companies if one controls the other, or both are under the same control (*CTA 2009, s 466(2)*).

Unless specifically applied, his definition does not disapply the definition given in *CTA 2009, s 1316*, which refers back to the definition in *ICTA 1988*, *s 839*, where connection to another company is defined as follows:

'A company is connected with another company–

(a)   if the same person has control of both, or a person has control of one and persons connected with him, or he and persons connected with him, have control of the other, or

(b)   if a group of two or more persons has control of each company, and the groups either consist of the same persons or could be regarded as consisting of the same persons by treating (in one or more cases) a member of either group as replaced by a person with whom he is connected.' *(ICTA 1988, s 839(5))*

Although an individual or a partnership cannot be a party to a loan relationship, in a loan relationship series he or she may be considered to stand indirectly in the position of debtor or creditor and so bring about a loan relationship *(CTA 2009, s 467)* (HMRC Corporate Finance Manual CFM 5416).

Meaning of control

11.32   'Control' in relation to a company means the power of a person to secure that the affairs of the company are conducted in accordance with the person's wishes:

(a)   by means of the holding of shares or the possession of voting power in or in relation to the company or any other company; or

(b)   as a result of any powers conferred by the articles of association or other document regulating the company or any other company *(CTA 2009, s 472(2))*.

Shares held as trading stock are not included *(CTA 2009, s 472(3))* and, in general, creditor relationships that result from activities forming an integral part of the trade carried on by that company during the accounting period are exempted.

This definition does not disapply the definition given in *CTA 2009, s 1316*, which refers back to the definition in *ICTA 1988, s 840*, on which *CTA 2009, s 471* seems to be based.

A partnership's property, rights or powers are apportioned between the partners in their profit-sharing ratios *(CTA 2009, s 467(4))*.

Example 11.13

Mr Link controls Right Ltd and Left Ltd. If Right Ltd lent money directly to Left Ltd, there would be a connection under *CTA 2009, s 466(2)*, because both companies are under the control of the same person.

Example 11.14

Right Ltd lends money to Ms Wong, who then lends it to Mr Wight who in turn lends it to Left Ltd. Right Ltd and Left Ltd are connected, because Mr Link controls them, but neither company is connected with Ms Wong, or Mr Wight. As a result of *CTA 2009, s 348(5))*, Left Ltd stands indirectly in the position of debtor in relation to Right Ltd's loan relationship in this series of loans. Note that there are no consequences for Ms Wong.

Example 11.15

Norman Ltd controls Saxon Ltd. If Norman Ltd lent money directly to Saxon Ltd there would be a connected companies relationship under *CTA 2009, s 466(2)* because one company is controlled by the other.

Angle Ltd is not connected to either Norman Ltd or Saxon Ltd. Norman Ltd lends £50,000 to Angle Ltd. There is no connection between Norman Ltd and Angle Ltd, so *CTA 2009, s 348* does not apply to the loan relationship.

Angle Ltd then lends £50,000 to Saxon Ltd on identical terms. There is no connection between Angle Ltd and Saxon Ltd, so *CTA 2009, s 466* does not apply to the loan relationship.

However, in relation to Norman's loan relationship, Saxon Ltd stands indirectly in the position of debtor through a series of loan relationships. Therefore, there is a connected companies relationship between Norman Ltd and Saxon Ltd by virtue of *CTA 2009, s 348(5)*.

CONSEQUENCES OF CONNECTION

Amortised cost basis of accounting

11.33   Where a loan relationship debtor and creditor are connected, certain rules are applied to the accounting treatment.

Regardless of the accounting method used in the company's accounts, the debits and credits brought into account must be determined according to the amortised cost basis of accounting (*CTA 2009, s 349(2)*).

The amortised cost of a financial asset or a financial liability is the amount at which the asset or liability is measured at initial recognition (usually its cost) less any repayments of principal, less any reduction for impairment or uncollectibility, and in addition or less the cumulative amortisation of the difference between that initial amount and the maturity.

HMRC comment that the amortised cost basis of accounting is broadly equivalent to the authorised accruals basis that applied in periods of account beginning before 1 January 2005. If a company does not adopt IAS 39 or FRS 26—for example, where a small company continues to use the FRSSE—and the company previously accounted for loan relationships on an authorised accruals basis, the *FA 2004* changes to the loan relationships legislation should not bring about any change in the basis on which its debt assets and liabilities are taxed (HMRC Corporate Finance Manual CFM 5151 and CFM 16025).

The amortisation is calculated using the effective interest rate. The effective interest rate is the internal rate of return (IRR), ie the rate at which the net present value of the instrument is nil.

Example 11.16

A £200,000 bond will pay £210,000 on maturity in a year's time.

The IRR is $£200,000 \times (1 + r)^1 = £210,000$

$$r = [(210,000 - 200,000) \div 200,000]$$
$$= 0.05$$
$$= 5\%$$

The future value of £200,000 @ 5% = $£200,000 \times (1 + 0.05)^1 = £210,000$

The present value of £210,000 = $£210,000 \times \{1 \div (1 + 0.5)^1\} = £200,000$

The present value of £200,000 less the initial investment of £200,000 equals the net present value, which is nil.

Therefore, the effective rate of return is 5%.

More complex calculations may be made by using the financial IRR (internal rate of return) function in Microsoft Excel (HMRC Corporate Finance Manual CFM 16025a).

Companies beginning and ceasing to be connected

11.34 Where there is a change in accounting basis brought about by companies becoming connected during the year, such that fair value basis is used before the connection and an amortised cost basis after the connection, the resulting differences in the valuation of an asset or a cost of a liability between the two periods are to be brought into account as a debit or a credit, as appropriate (*CTA 2009, s 350*). A similar rule in reverse operates for companies ceasing to be connected during the accounting period (*CTA 2009, s 351*).

If the creditor company is connected to the debtor in exempt circumstances, ie in the course of its financial trade, it is not required to apply the amortised cost basis of accounting or to follow the other provisions that apply to connected persons. The debtor company must apply the connected persons rules (*CTA 2009, s 469*).

Example 11.17

The CASH Bank plc issues listed security bonds worth £10m, which it places with its security trader subsidiary company Rowbowthams plc. Rowbothams plc is to place the bonds with unconnected investors.

The market is slow and Rowbothams plc holds the bonds for three months whilst it finds buyers. The bonds are part of its trading stock. It applies GAAP when preparing its accounts. The parties are connected under *CTA 2009, s 466(2)*. Without the *CTA 2009, s 469* exemption, Rowbothams plc would have to account for the bonds using the amortised cost basis of accounting. However, this is an ordinary commercial arrangement, with Rowbothams plc buying and selling the bonds as part of its trade. By applying *CTA 2009, s 469*, Rowbothams plc can continue to account for the debt as trading stock. The CASH Bank plc is not exempted by *s 469* and will therefore use the amortised cost basis when accounting for the securities (HMRC Corporate Finance Manual CFM 5421c).

Unpaid interest

11.35   There is no debit for accrued unpaid interest for the debtor relationship company, unless the creditor relationship company has a corresponding credit. If the accrued unpaid interest is not paid within 12 months of the end of the accounting period, relief will only be given when that interest is eventually paid (*CTA 2009, s 373*). With respect to accrual periods beginning on or after 1 April 2009, this rule only applies where the creditor company to the loan relationship is a company resident for tax purposes in a non-qualifying territory at any time in the actual accrual period, or effectively managed in a non-taxing non-qualifying territory. A non-qualifying territory is any territory with which the UK does not have a double tax agreement with a suitable non-discrimination clause (*FA 2009, Sch 20; CTA 2009, s 374*).

Discounted securities

11.36   Where the parties have a connection, relief on securities issued at a discount is deferred until redemption rather than being allowed as a debit over the life of the loan (*CTA 2009, s 407*).

Creditor relationships and benefit derived by connected persons

11.37   Benefit directly or indirectly received by a company that is connected with a company that has a third-party creditor loan relationship as a result of the loan relationship is treated as a credit, using fair value accounting of the creditor company if the actual return that the creditor company receives is below a commercial rate of interest (*CTA 2009, s 453*).

Bad debt relief and impairment losses generally

11.38   The loan relationship rules, in general, grant relief for bad debts. Impairment losses are accounted for using the IAS 39 or FRS 26 principles. The exception is a change in the rules relating to the acquisition of impaired debt (see **11.39**). The standards prescribe rules for identifying and measuring impairment losses at the year end. If the company correctly applies the relevant standard, to arrive at a debit for impairment losses (or a credit for reversal of impairment losses), the debit will be allowable (or the credit taxable) in accordance with the normal computational provisions of *CTA 2009, s 308*.

Connected parties and bad debt relief and impairment losses

11.39　Special rules apply to bad debt relief and impairment losses for connected parties. The general rule is that bad debt or impairment loss relief is denied if the companies to the loan relationship are connected (*CTA 2009, s 354*).

Impairment loss relief is not denied if the connection only arises because the debt is exchanged for equity, provided that the companies were not connected when the creditor company acquired possession of or entitlement to the shares (*CTA 2009, s 356(1)–(3)*). Neither is it denied if the creditor company goes into insolvent liquidation (*CTA 2009, s 357*).

The corresponding creditor company is not required to include a credit for the loss or bad debt relief reversal (*CTA 2009, s 360*), whether or not the companies are still connected when the reversal takes place.

If any rights or liabilities (known as related transactions) are acquired at a non-arm's length price, they are accounted for as though they were a transaction between independent persons (*CTA 2009, s 444*).

Release of trade debts between connected companies

11.40　The creditor company in a connected companies loan relationship has been at a disadvantage where it releases or waives a trade debt or a property business debt in favour of its connected debtor company. The debtor company is charged to tax on the release of a trade debt under *CTA 2009, s 94*, but the creditor company is denied tax relief under the loan relationship rules.

With effect from 22 April 2009, debts between connected companies that arise from a trade or a property business that are waived are taxed under the loan relationship provisions, the result being that there is no charge on the debtor on the release and no tax relief for the creditor on the cancellation (*FA 2009, s 42; CTA 2009, s 479*).

GROUPS AND CONSORTIA

11.41　Group companies are connected under the loan relationship rules. Loan relationship intra-group transfers are tax neutral (*CTA 2009, s 336*).

Consortium companies may not be connected under *CTA 2009, s 466(2)*, but consortium members are in a position to obtain not only consortium relief but also bad debt or impairment relief. Therefore, there are restrictions on the available amount of bad debt relief where there has been a claim to group relief. The group impairment losses and subsequent credits are first netted off against each other to result in the net consortium debit for the year,

The effect of the restriction is to reduce the net consortium debit by the amount of the group relief claimed (*CTA 2009, s 365*).

Example 11.18

Winston Ltd is a consortium company with £1,000 issued ordinary shares.

Its ownership is as follows:

	No of shares
A Ltd	400
B Ltd	400
C Ltd	200

All companies prepare accounts to 31 December.

Winston Ltd incurs a loss of £40,000 for the year ended 31 December 2010, which is used in a group relief claim by the consortium members.

On 1 January 2010, A Ltd made a £50,000 loan to Winston Ltd. At 31 December 2010, it seems unlikely that Winston Ltd will be able to repay A Ltd's loan. A Ltd writes off £25,000 as bad. *CTA 2009, s 365* will restrict A Ltd's impairment loss by the amount of the group relief claim, ie £16,000. Therefore, only £9,000 (25,000 – 16,000) may be claimed. The group relief claim remains intact, and the £16,000 restricted amount is carried forward, to be considered for future group and impairment loss claims.

The position for the year ended 31 December 2010 may be summarised as follows:

Impairment loss	Group relief	Impairment loss granted	Group relief allowed relief	Impairment loss carry forward
£	£	£	£	£
25,000	16,000	9,000	16,000	16,000

(HMRC Corporate Finance Manual CFM 5560a)

LOAN RELATIONSHIPS, DERIVATIVES AND FOREIGN EXCHANGE GAINS AND LOSSES (FOREX)

11.42 Exchange gains and losses are within the loan relationship regime. Therefore, 'credits' and 'debits' are brought into the corporation tax computation following the accepted accounting principles. All relevant capital and revenue profits, gains and losses must be included, together with charges and expenses for the year (*CTA 2009, s 329(1), (2)*).

A company may match its foreign currency non-monetary assets with its foreign currency borrowings to provide a commercial hedge. The tax treatment of such arrangements and other financial structures is covered in *CTA 2009, ss 501–710*. These are specialised transactions and are not within the coverage of this book.

COMPANY TAX RETURN

11.43 Companies provide details of their non-trade deficits on loan relationships in boxes 20 and 28 of the company tax return. All other details are supplied by means of the corporation tax computation and the accounts.

Chapter 12

Investment business

INTRODUCTION

12.1   A company's income from its investment business is chargeable to corporation tax. There are special rules to relieve expenditure as 'management expenses'.

INVESTMENT INCOME

12.2   A company's investment income will typically include profits of a property business and income from non-trading loan relationships, with a deduction for management expenses.

Example 12.1

XYZ Ltd draws up accounts to 31 March each year. Results for the year ended 31 March 2010 show the following:

	£000
Rents receivable	197
Interest receivable accrued (gross)	5
Chargeable gains	48
Management expenses	
● attributable to property	25
● attributable to management	40
Capital allowances	
● attributable to property	5
● attributable to management	1
Charitable charges on income	10

The company has unrelieved management expenses brought forward from previous accounting periods of £42,000.

XYZ Ltd corporation tax computations for the year ending 31 March 2010

	£000	£000
Profits of a property business		197
Less		
Capital allowances	5	
Management expenses	25	
		30
		167
Loan relationship		5
Chargeable gains		48
		220
Less:		
Management expenses unrelieved brought forward for year		
Unrelieved brought forward	42	
For year	40	
Capital allowances	1	
		83
		137
Less charges		10
PCTCT		127

MANAGEMENT EXPENSES

Definitions

12.3   The definition of a company with investment business is a company whose business consists wholly or partly of making investments (*CTA 2009, s 1218*). An investment company is any company whose business consists wholly or mainly in the making of investments and the principal part of whose income is derived therefrom. There are exemptions for savings banks (*ICTA 1988, s 130* amended by *CTA 2009 Sch 1 para 94*). Expenditure of a revenue nature is allowed as a deduction for management expenses in calculating total profits, if it relates to the company's business of making investments. The investments must not be held for an unallowable purpose, and there is no deduction for capital expenditure. In general, if expenditure can be charged against the company's other income, it cannot be included in management expenses, but there are exceptions (see **12.7**). Any apportionment of expenditure is to be done on a just and reasonable basis (*CTA 2009, s 1219*).

Unallowable purpose

12.4 Investments are held for an unallowable purpose during an accounting period if they are held for a purpose that is not a business or other commercial purpose of the company. This means that such investments are effectively held directly or indirectly as a result of, or in connection with, any arrangements that are designed to secure a tax advantage (*CTA 2009, s 1220*).

Expenses in connection with investments held for a non-business or non-commercial purpose, or in connection with activities not within the charge to corporation tax, are not chargeable as management expenses. Such activities will include:

- investments held by a company for social or recreational purposes;

- provision of services and facilities by a members' club to its members;

- UK branch expenses of a non-resident company in respect of activities not connected with the UK branch; and

- mutual trading activities).

However, a company that merely receives dividends from UK companies within *ICTA 1988, s 208* will still be classed as an investment company or a company with investment business, as will any company whose capital gains are covered by the substantial shareholding exemption or collective investment scheme gains exempt under *TCGA 1992, s 100(1)* (HMRC Company Taxation Manual CTM 08225).

Capital expenditure

12.5 Capital expenditure is specifically excluded as a deduction for management expenses purposes (*CTA 2009, ss 1219(3)*). HMRC's view is that expenditure incurred on appraising the purchase or sale of an investment up to the decision point is revenue, and expenditure following the decision to acquire or dispose of an investment is capital (HMRC Company Taxation Manual CTM 08260). Success fees that are only payable when the deal goes through must, by their very nature, be capital and therefore excluded from management expenses. It is necessary to examine the facts of each case and to apply *the same criteria to abortive expenditure*. The costs associated with purchase and sale are not regarded as management expenses. Brokerage and stamp duties were not allowed as management expenses (*Capital and National Trust Ltd v Golder* (1949) 31 TC 265, [1949] 2 All ER 956 and *Sun Life Assurance Society v Davidson* (1957) 37 TC 330).

Cost of asset valuations for accounts purposes (*SI 2008/409* and *SI 2008/410*) are considered to be management expenses, but valuations related to the acquisition and disposal of assets are not (HMRC Company Taxation Manual CTM 08420).

Capital expenditure on assets used for the purpose of management qualifies for capital allowances. The capital allowances are a management expense. Balancing charges are income of the investment business (see **12.6**) (*CAA 2001, ss 18, 253*).

Management expenses deduction

12.6   A deduction for management expenses for an accounting period is allowed against the total profits of the accounting period. Management expenses include all those expenses that are not otherwise deductible in computing profits, but do not include capital expenditure (*CTA 2009, s 1233(1), (2)*). Capital allowances may be claimed on capital expenditure (see **12.5**).

The description is specific and unlike the *CTA 2009, s 54* 'wholly and exclusively' trading company criteria. Expenses of management cannot just amount to general administration costs.

Running costs in connection with managing the company's investment business, including reasonable directors' remuneration, staff salaries and pension contributions are chargeable as management expenses (*LG Berry Investments Ltd v Attwooll* (1964) 41 TC 547). The same timing rules for remuneration payments apply as for trade profits (see **5.21**) (*CTA 2009, s 1249*). Company secretarial costs such as maintaining the share register, printing annual accounts and holding an AGM are regarded as expenses of management. Entertaining expenditure and expenditure involving crime is specifically prohibited (*CTA 2009, ss 1298, 1304*). No relief is given if the expenses are incurred for an unallowable purpose. An unallowable purpose occurs when the company holds investments neither for a business nor a commercial purpose or the company is not within the charge to corporation tax (see **12.7** below).

Management expenses are deductible from investment income of both UK resident companies and non-resident companies with a permanent establishment in the UK from where the income is derived (*CTA 2009, s 1222*).

Management expenses are the amounts shown in the accounts prepared under GAAP. If the accounts are not prepared under GAAP or are not prepared at all, the management expenses are calculated as if GAAP had applied (*CTA 2009, ss 1225, 1226* and *1227*). Credits for management expenses first reduce the management expenses for the year and are then brought into charge as other income. In practice, company expenditure may relate to a number of activities, in which case it should be allocated between them on a just and reasonable basis.

Amounts treated as expenses of management

12.7   Certain items of expenditure are treated as management expenses (*CTA 2009, s 1221*). These include:

- share incentive plans (*CTA 2009, s 1013*);

- costs of setting up an SAYE option scheme or an CSOP scheme (*CTA 2009, s 999*);

- costs of setting up an employee share ownership trust (*CTA 2009, s 1000*);

- employee share acquisitions: relief if shares acquired by employee or other person (*CTA 2009, s 1013*);

- employee share acquisitions: relief if employee or other person acquires option to obtain shares (*CTA 2009, s 1021*);

- manufactured dividends and interest (*ICTA 1988, Sch 23A, para 4(1A)*); and

- employers' contributions to pension schemes (*FA 1994, s 196*).

The following amounts are treated as management expenses only so far as they cannot be deducted from the company's other profits:

- excess capital allowances; see **6.7** (*CTA 2009, s 1233*);

- payment to employees for restrictive undertakings that are treated as employee earnings (*CTA 2009, s 1234*);

- employees seconded to charities and educational establishments where services are made available (*CTA 2009, s 1235*);

- payroll deduction schemes where the employer acts as an agent for an approved scheme (*CTA 2009, s 1236*);

- counselling and other outplacement services of an employee in connection with the cessation of employment (*CTA 2009, s 1237*);

- employee retraining courses upon cessation of employment (*CTA 2009, s 1238*);

- employee redundancy payments and approved contractual payments where the employee is engaged wholly or partly (for other services) in the investment business (*CTA 2009, ss 1239, 1240* and *1241*);

- contributions to local enterprise organisations or urban regeneration companies (*CTA 2009, s 1244*);

- payments to Export Credits Guarantee Department (*CTA 2009, s 1245*); and

- levies under FISMA 2000 (*CTA 2009, s 1246*).

Any complementary repayments from a local enterprise organisation or in respect of FISMA 2000 are taxable accordingly (*CTA 2009, ss 1253, 1254*).

Deductions restricted

12.8   The following expenses are not allowed as management expenses (*CTA 2009, s 1247*):

- employee benefit contributions (*CTA 2009, s 1290*);

- business entertainment and gifts (*CTA 2009, s 1298*);

- social security contributions (*CTA 2009, s 1302*);

- penalties, interest and VAT surcharges (*CTA 2009, s 1303*);

- crime-related payments (*CTA 2009, s 1304*);

- no other relief for employers in connection with contributions (*FA 2004, s 200*);

- restriction of deduction for non-contributory provision (*FA 2004, s 246*);

- employers' contributions: power to restrict relief (*FA 2004, s 196A*);

- expenses in connection with arrangements for securing a tax advantage (*CTA 2009, s 1248*);

- unpaid remuneration, as far as not paid within nine months of the end of the account period for which due (*CTA 2009, ss 1249, 1250*); and

- car or motor cycle hire; see **5.15** (*CTA 2009, s 1251*).

Credits that reverse debits

12.9   Credits for management expenses first reduce the management expenses for the year and any excess management expenses brought forward from a previous year; the remainder is then brought into charge as taxable income (*CTA 2009, ss 1229, 1230*).

Income from a source not charged to tax

12.10   A company's management expenses are reduced by any untaxed income that it may have in connection with its investment business.

Group companies

12.11   Group companies often recharge expenses to other group members such as administration charges. Provided the allocation is done on a reasonable basis, this will result in each group member deducting its share of administration costs from its relevant trade or activity; see **5.47** (HMRC Business Income Manual BIM 42140).

Management activities

12.12   Management expenses cannot be claimed unless the company is chargeable to corporation tax. This would, for example, exclude a mutual trading company, as its profits are not chargeable to corporation tax (see **5.76**). In order for a company to be chargeable to corporation tax it must have an activity, otherwise it would be totally dormant. On the assumption that the company had no other business, activities that would bring a company with investment business within the charge to corporation tax would be the holding of shares in another non-dormant company (*CTA 2009, s 9(2)*) or the disposal of an asset resulting in a chargeable gain or allowable loss (*TCGA 1992, s 8(3)*). The management expenses claim for the year is made by completing box 24. A claim for management expenses carried forward is included in box 136, with the maximum available for group relief surrender in box 137.

Insurance premiums

12.13   Premiums paid on assets used in the management of the company are considered to be management expenses but not premiums paid on the insurance of the investments. This is because the view is taken that the expenses incurred must relate to management and not to general administration (HMRC Company Taxation Manual CTM 08320). Depending on the circumstances such premiums may be classed as capital expenditure.

Self-assessment

12.14   The corporation tax computation for a company with investment business would normally show income and gains from the investment activity in full, rather than adjusted profits.

Management expenses set-off

12.15 Management expenses are deducted from the company's profits chargeable to corporation tax before charges and before loss relief claimed under *ICTA 1988, s 393A (CTA 2009, s 1219(1))*. Excess management expenses are carried forward to be used in the subsequent accounting period as management expenses of that period (*CTA 2009, s 1223*). A company may group relieve management expenses for the chargeable period against group income.

A company may only surrender management expenses that exceed the gross profits for the accounting period (*ICTA 1988, ss 402, 403(1)*). The order of set-off being charges on income, property business losses and management expenses or a non-trading loss on intangible fixed assets in that order (see **10.8**).

Example 12.2

Kappa Ltd owns 90% of the ordinary share capital of Lamda Ltd. Kappa Ltd is the group investment holding company.

Both companies prepare accounts to 31 December each year.

Results for the year ended 31 December 2009 are as follows:

	Kappa Ltd	*Lamda Ltd*
	£000	£000
Trade profits		50
Profits of a property business	10	20
Loan relationship	40	30
Charges		2

Kappa Ltd's corporation tax liability after management expenses and management expenses for group relief are as follows:

	£000
Management expenses	
(*CTA 2009, s 1219(1)*) for the year	100
(*CTA 2009, s 1223(3)*) brought forward	5
	105

	£000
Excess management expenses for group relief	
Management expenses	
(*CTA 2009, s 1219(1)*) for the year	100
Less:	
Profits of a property business	(10)
Loan relationship	(40)
Excess management expenses for group relief	50
Group relief	(50)
	0
Excess management expenses brought forward and carry forward	5

Lamda Ltd corporation tax computation after group relief is as follows:

	£000
Trade profits	50
Profits of a property business	20
Loan relationship	30
	100
Less Charges	(2)
Total profits	98
Group relief (management expenses)	(50)
PCTCT	48

Companies ceasing to trade

12.16   Practical considerations may arise when a company ceased to trade. The holding of a static bank account when trading ceased classifies a company as 'dormant' (*Jowett v O'Neill & Brennan Construction Ltd* (1998) 70 TC 566). In such circumstances, it would be necessary for the company to show that it intends to continue with an investment activity if it wishes to claim management expenses for that period. The same criteria will apply to a company that is in liquidation. It will be necessary to show that it is 'making investments'.

Pensions paid to former employees by a company that ceases to trade, and becomes an investment company or a company with investment business, are not expenses of management if the former employees were not at any time employees of the company after it ceased to trade. This is because the pension payments relate to the former trade and not to the investment activity (HMRC Company Taxation Manual CTM 08350).

Restriction on management expenses

12.17 Management expenses are restricted where there is a change of ownership and after the change there is a significant increase in the company's capital. Alternatively, within a period of six years beginning three years before the change, there is a major change in the nature or conduct of the business, or the change in ownership occurs after the scale of activities has become small or negligible and before any considerable revival of the business (*ICTA 1988, s 768B*).

A change of ownership occurs where:

(i)   a single person acquires more than half the ordinary share capital of the company or

(ii) two or more persons each acquire a holding of 5% or more of the ordinary share capital of the company, and those holdings together amount to more than half the ordinary share capital of the company or

(iii) two or more persons each acquire a holding of the ordinary share capital of a company, and those holdings together amount to more than half the ordinary share capital of the company. Holdings of less than 5% are disregarded unless it is in addition to an existing holding and the two holdings together amount to 5% or more of the ordinary share capital (*ICTA 1988, s 769*).

The 5% threshold means there is no need to examine small shareholdings, particularly those of public companies.

Note, it is possible for more than half of a company's shares to change hands and yet not trigger a change of ownership if the shares are purchased by a number of unconnected persons, each of whom acquires a holding of less than 5%.

A major change in the nature or conduct of the business includes a major change in the nature of the investments held, even if that change was the result of a gradual process which began before the period of six years within which the change has to take place (*ICTA 1988, s 768B(3)*).

INVESTMENT IN PROPERTY

12.18 If a company invests in property, it will show the property as a fixed asset on the balance sheet and will record letting income as property income. Property disposals will attract a capital gain. Letting income will be assessable under the profits of a property business rules contained in *CTA 2009, ss 202–291*.

A company could be a property dealer or developer in which case the property cost is shown in trading stock on the balance sheet. The company earns its income from the sale of properties and its profits are assessed as trade profits (see **Chapter 5**).

Transactions between property dealing companies and their non-dealing associates are brought into charge on the associate as trade profits, if they so elect, or other income under *CTA 2009, s 979* (*ICTA 1988, s 774*).

PROFITS OF A PROPERTY BUSINESS

Income from UK land and buildings

12.19 Companies are charged to corporation tax on income arising from the letting of land and property situated in the UK and abroad. The income generated from land situated in the UK is treated as a single property business (*CTA 2009, s 205*), and the income generated from land situated overseas is treated as the company's overseas property business (*CTA 2009, s 206*).

Generating income from land is defined as exploiting an estate, interest or right in or over land as a source of rents or other receipts. Rents include not only the periodical payments referred to in a lease, but also any payments that a tenant makes for work carried out in maintaining or repairing the leased premises, which the lease does not require him to carry out.

Other receipts include:

- payments for a licence to occupy, use or exercise a right over land;

- rent charges, ground annuals, feu duties and other annual payments in respect of land; and

- income from furnished lettings, including furnished holiday lettings; and income from caravans or houseboats where their use is confined to one location in the UK (*CTA 2009, s 207*).

Profits of a property business are included in box 11 of form CT600.

Certain activities carried out on land are treated as a trade: farming or market gardening in the UK; certain commercial occupation of UK land and mining and quarrying (*CTA 2009, s 208*) (see **5.58–5.62**). Income from other activities may be treated as income of a trade: tied premises, caravan sites where a trade is carried on, surplus business accommodation, and payments for wayleaves (*CTA 2009, s 213*).

Computation of profit

12.20   The profits of a property business are calculated in the same way as the profits of a trade (see **Chapter 5**). The trade profits provisions found in *CTA 2009, ss 61* and *68–92*, that allow a deduction against income, also apply to property income. The following trade profits receipts provisions also apply to property income: *CTA 2009, ss 93, 94, 101–104, 108, 131, 133* and *172–175*. Matters relating to loan relationships and derivative contracts are excluded (*CTA 2009, s 210*).

Capital allowances are available on plant used in the letting business, eg a motor vehicle used in connection with site visits, and are deductible as an expense from the profits of a property business. Credits and debits in respect of an intangible fixed asset, held by a company for the purposes of a property business carried on by it, are treated as receipts and expenses of the business (*CTA 2009, s 212*). The general calculation rules that restrict deductions (see **5.12**) also apply. Overall, a relevant permissive rule has priority over a relevant prohibitive rule (*CTA 2009, s 214*).

LEASE PREMIUMS

Landlord tax receipts

12.21   Where the landlord company grants a lease that has an effective duration of 50 years or less (a 'short' lease (*CTA 2009, s 216*)), any amounts that the landlord company receives that are:

(a)   paid as a premium (*CTA 2009, s 218(4)*);

(b)   paid instead of rent (*CTA 2009, s 219(4)*);

(c)   payable as consideration for the surrender of the lease (*CTA 2009, s 220(4)*);

(d)   payable as consideration for the variation or waiver of the terms of the lease (*CTA 2009, s 221(4)*); or

(e)   arising under an assignment for profit of lease granted at undervalue (*CTA 2009, s 222(4)*);

are treated partly as a disposal for capital gains and partly as property income.

The income portion known as the 'taxed receipt' is treated as rental income in the year in which the lease is granted. The income portion is calculated according to the following formula:

$$P \times \frac{(50 - Y)}{50}$$

where:

- P, for (a)–(d) above, is the amount in question; for (e), P is the lesser of the profit on the assignment and the amount by which the undervalue exceeds the total of the profits (if any) made on previous assignments of the lease.

- Y is the number of complete periods of 12 months (other than the first) comprised in the effective duration of the lease, for (a), (c) and (e), or the period for which the sum is payable for (b), or the period for which the variation or waiver has effect for (d).

A premium is deemed to arise if the terms of the lease impose an obligation on the tenant to carry out work on the premises. The amount of the premium is the amount by which the value of the landlord's estate or interest immediately after the commencement of the lease exceeds what its value would have been at that time, if the terms of the lease did not impose the obligation on the tenant.

An obligation to carry out excepted work is ignored. Excepted work is work the cost of which would be deductible as an expense in calculating the profits of the landlord's property business had the landlord and not the tenant been obliged to carry it out (*CTA 2009, s 218*).

The effective lease term is the length of time that the lease is expected to last for that tenancy, given the current state of affairs and conditions. This may not be the length of time that is stated in the agreement (*CTA 2009, s 243*).

A Revenue officer is required to certify the accuracy of any statement made by the company in respect of any assignment for profit, as at (e) above (*CTA 2009, s 237*).

If the taxed receipts from (a)–(d) are payable over a period of time, the corporation tax due can be paid by instalments to HMRC over the same amount of time, or eight years if less (*CTA 2009, s 236*).

Additional deduction

12.22 The tenant company may decide to sublet part of the property within its own property business. If so, the amount that it receives from its tenants will become a 'taxed receipt' and will be taxable in the same way, but it will be able to take relief for premiums that it has paid to the head landlord. Relief is given by the following formula:

$$\frac{A \times LRP}{TRP}$$

where:

- A is the unreduced amount of the taxed receipt,

- LRP is the receipt period of the receipt under calculation, and

- TRP is the receipt period of the taxed receipt.

The receipt period varies according to the amounts paid, as detailed in **12.21**:

(a) the effective duration of the lease;

(b) the period in relation to which the sum payable instead of rent is payable;

(c) the effective duration of the lease;

(d) the period for which the variation or waiver has effect; and

(e) the effective duration of the lease remaining at the date of the assignment.

(*CTA 2009, s 228*)

If the lease does not extend to the whole premises the formula can be adjusted on a just and reasonable basis (*CTA 2009, s 229*).

Example 12.3

Horatio Ltd and Eustace Ltd are property companies. Horatio Ltd granted a 30-year lease to Eustace Ltd on 1 January 2010 with a £50,000 premium and £60,000 annual rent. Horatio Ltd prepares accounts to 31 December each year. Horatio Ltd's property business receipts for the year ended 31 December 2010 are as follows:

Profits of the property business	£
Income portion of the premium receivable	

$$£50,000 \times \frac{50-29}{50} \text{ years} \qquad\qquad 21,000$$

Plus:	
rent for the year ended 31 December 2010	60,000
Profits of the property business	81,000

On 1 January 2013, Eustace Ltd grants a 21-year lease to Ferrero Ltd with a £40,000 premium and £35,000 annual rent. EustaceLtd prepares accounts to 31 December each year. Eustace Ltd's property business receipts for the year ended 31 December 2013 are as follows:

Profits of the property business	£
Income portion of premium receivable	

$$£40,000 \times \frac{50-20}{50} \text{ years} \qquad\qquad 24,000$$

Less:	
reduction for taxed receipt paid to Horatio Ltd	

$$£21,000 \times \frac{21}{30} \qquad\qquad (14,700)$$

	9,300
Plus:	
rent for the year ended 31 December 2013	35,000
Profits of a property business	44,300

Tenant

12.23   Where the company is the tenant and pays a lease premium, the income portion is an allowable deduction from property income, spread over the life of the lease (*CTA 2009, ss 62, 231–234*). Where this applies, the additional calculation is taken into account (*CTA 2009, s 233*) and, if the lease does not extend to the whole premises, the formula is adjusted on a just and reasonable basis (*CTA 2009, s 234*). A daily amount is calculated according to the following formula:

$$\frac{A}{TRP}$$

where:

- A is the taxable receipt given by the formula, and

- TRP is the number of days in the receipt period of the taxed receipt (*CTA 2009, s 233(6)*).

If applicable, the additional calculation is also taken into account and the daily reduction is calculated by the following formula:

$$\frac{AR}{RRP}$$

where:

- AR is the reduction, and

- RRP is the number of days in the receipt period of the lease period receipt (*CTA 2009, s 233(6)*).

If the lease does not extend to the whole premises the formula is adjusted on a just and reasonable basis (*CTA 2009, s 234*).

Example 12.4

Eustace Ltd and Ferrero Ltd will be able to claim not only a deduction for rent paid from their property income but also for part of the premium paid.

Profits of a property business	£
Eustace Ltd	
Daily deduction for premium payable:	
$\dfrac{£21,000}{365 \times 30}$	1.92
Annual deduction for premium payable:	
£1.92 × 365	700
Ferrero Ltd	
Daily deduction for premium payable:	
$\dfrac{£24,000}{365 \times 21}$	3.13

Daily amount of the additional deduction:	£
$\dfrac{£14,700}{365 \times 21}$	1.92
Net daily deduction	1.21
Annual deduction for premium paid:	
£1.21 × 365	442

Reverse premiums

12.24   Where a landlord pays a sum to induce a tenant (or a person connected with the tenant) to take a lease (a reverse premium) then (unless it reduces expenditure qualifying for capital allowances) it is generally treated as a receipt of the profits of a property business of the tenant corresponding with the treatment of the rental payments (*CA 2009, s 250*). Other benefits, such as the grant of a rent-free period, are not taxable under these rules. If the landlord is a property development company, the payment will be a deduction against trade profits. If the landlord is a property investment company, the payment will be treated as a capital payment that enhances the value of the underlying asset. The premium will not be deductible from rental income (see HMRC Business Income Manual BIM 41060).

Sales with right to reconveyance and sale and leaseback

12.25   A proportion of the sales proceeds derived from a sale under terms for reconveyance to the seller and a proportion of the sales proceeds derived from a sale under terms for the granting of a lease to the seller are included in the profits of a property business.

The amount to be included is determined by the formula:

$$E \times \frac{50 - Y}{50}$$

where:

- E is the amount by which the sales price exceeds the reconveyance price or the value of the leaseback (premium plus reversion).

- Y is the number of complete periods of 12 months (other than the first) comprised in the period beginning with the sale and ending with the earliest date on which the terms of the sale the lease would be satisfied (*CTA 2009, ss 224, 225*).

The seller is required to pay the corporation tax due on the calculated income amount, even though the reconveyance or sale and leaseback transaction may not have taken place, in which case the seller can claim repayment of the excess corporation tax paid, being the difference between the tax actually paid and the tax that would have been payable had the calculation been made at the date of reconveyance or the grant of the lease to the seller (*CTA 2009, ss 238, 239*).

Corporation tax deduction for expenditure on energy-saving items

12.26   Companies which operate a residential property letting business, either in the UK or overseas, can deduct the cost of acquiring and installing certain energy-saving items in the residential properties which they let, from the rental business profits assessable to corporation tax (*CTA 2009, s 251(2)*).

There is a maximum amount of allowable expenditure of £1,500 for each property (or 'dwelling house'). Any contributions received from persons not entitled to a deduction reduce the amount of the deduction. A property for this purpose means a separate dwelling ie a separate unit; therefore, the £1,500 limit will be applied to each flat in a block of separate apartments rather than the entire building. The deduction is only available for expenditure incurred before 1 April 2015. See **6.91** for a discussion on 'dwelling' and 'dwelling house'.

The qualifying expenditure in question is capital expenditure, which does not qualify for capital allowances or the annual investment allowance, but is incurred 'wholly and exclusively' for the purposes of the letting business and is of an energy saving nature. The qualifying expenditure is expenditure on hot water system insulation, draught proofing, cavity wall insulation, solid wall insulation, floor insulation and loft insulation.

If a landlord incurs qualifying expenditure that benefits more than one property then this should be apportioned amongst the relevant properties on a just and reasonable basis (*CTA 2009, s 251(4)*). No deduction for the cost of the energy-saving item is permitted if it is installed in the property during the course of construction. The landlord must have a legal title to the property. If the energy-saving item is installed whilst the landlord is in the course of acquiring a legal title or changing that legal title, no deduction is permitted. No deduction is permitted in respect of property used in a commercial letting of furnished holiday accommodation (see **5.57**). The expenditure only qualifies as pre-trading expenditure under *CTA 2009, s 61* if it is incurred no more than six months before the residential letting business commenced. In addition, the acquisition and the installation expenditure must have been incurred solely for the purposes of the dwelling-house (*CTA 2009, s 252*).

In practice, more than one party can have a legal interest in the property, and any apportionment of the relief or the expenditure should be made on a just and reasonable basis. The company has the right of appeal should there be a dispute (*CTA 2009, s 251*; *SI 2008/1520*; *SI 2008/1521*).

Deductions accepted in practice

12.27 The *Corporation Tax Act 2009* allows deductions from the profits of a property business on the same basis as deductions from trade profits. Property businesses tend to have recurring expenditure on property repairs, legal fees, and recurring expenditure on furnished lettings. Prior to the introduction of *CTA 2009*, the following treatment was given and there is no reason to suggest that this, in principle, should not continue in the future.

Repair expenditure

12.28 Property repair expenditure is an allowable deduction. If the repair takes the asset beyond its condition prior to the repair, this will be deemed a capital expense and hence disallowable. Repair expenditure of the subsidiary parts of an asset is classed as revenue expenditure (HMRC Property Income Manual PIM 2020).

Legal fees

12.29 Legal fees of a revenue nature, wholly and exclusively in connection with the rental business, are deductible.

The expenses incurred in connection with the first letting or subletting of a property for more than one year are capital expenditure and therefore not allowable. The expenses may include legal expenses, lease preparation costs, agent's and surveyor's fees, and commission. If the lease is for less than one year, the expenses are deductible.

Legal and professional costs incurred in respect of the renewal of a lease for less than 50 years are allowable. Legal costs in relation to the payment of a premium on the renewal of a lease are not deductible.

Legal expenses in connection with letting arrangements that closely follow the terms of previous arrangements are considered to be a revenue expense and will not be disallowable, except for the legal or other costs that relate to the payment of a premium on the renewal of a lease.

Legal costs in connection with a change of use of the premises in between lets will be treated as a capital expense and hence disallowable.

HMRC have identified the following legal and professional costs as allowable:

- costs of obtaining a valuation for insurance purposes,
- the normal accountancy expenses incurred in preparing rental business,
- subscriptions to associations representing the interests of landlords,
- the cost of arbitration to determine the rent of a holding, and
- the cost of evicting an unsatisfactory tenant in order to relet the property.

The following costs are disallowable:

- legal costs incurred in acquiring, or adding to, a property,
- costs in connection with negotiations under the *Town and Country Planning Acts*,
- fees pursuing debts of a capital nature, for example, the proceeds due on the sale of the property.

Normal accountancy costs are deductible, including, by concession, agreeing the taxation liabilities. However, legal costs in connection with acquisition of a property or costs in connection with negotiations under the *Town and Country Planning Acts* are not deductible. Legal fees on drawing up a new lease are allowable if the lease is for less than one year. If more than one year, it is not allowable because the expense is capital (HMRC Property Income Manual PIM 2205).

Furnished lettings

12.30 A furnished letting provides a tenant with the use of premises and furniture. Capital allowances are not available for plant let for use in a dwelling house (*CAA 2001, s 35*). *CTA 2009, s 248* allows a deduction for the use of furniture. In practice, relief is normally given by allowing 10% of rental income (net of the landlord's outlay on council tax and water rates, if any) as a wear and tear deduction. Alternatively, relief can be claimed on a renewals basis for capital items replaced in a let property. Interest is excluded from profits of a property business computation and dealt with as a non-trading 'debit' under the loan relationship rules.

Treatment as trade profits

12.31 Moderate rental income from the temporary letting of part of the trader's business premises may be treated as trade profits. This treatment only

371

applies to the letting of accommodation and not to the letting of land.The letting income from properties held as trading stock is a profit of a property business rental income. Expenses must be apportioned on a reasonable basis. Property development is a trade. Any property held awaiting sale would be included in trading stock. If that property were to be let for a short time, the costs of letting would be deducted from the letting receipts and the net profit would be part of the rental business income assessable as profits of a property business. If there is an excess of expenditure over income, that excess is deducted from the property dealing or development trade (HMRC Property Income Manual PIM 4300).

Rents and premiums received from tied premises are trade profits and not profits of a property business income. The same applies to the taxable amount of any premium received. Any expenditure on the tied premises will be deducted in the computation of the trading profits and should similarly be excluded from the rental business (*CTA 2009, s 42(1)–(3)*). If other services are provided that go beyond those normally provided by a landlord, they might constitute a separate trade and not a rental business. Services normally provided by a landlord are:

- the cleaning of stairs and passages in multi-unit premises,

- the provision of hot water and heating,

- supervision involving rent collection and arranging new tenancies, and

- arranging for repairs to the property.

The facts of each case must be examined on their merits to see if a separate trade is being carried out (HMRC Property Income Manual PIM 4300).

Travelling expenses to and between properties, when incurred wholly and exclusively for the rental business, are deductible (HMRC Property Income Manual PIM 2210).

Appeals against proposed determinations

12.32   HMRC may require the company to provide information in respect of its leases and arrangements. A Revenue and Customs officer may prepare a provisional determination of income. If the company disagrees with the amount it has 30 days to lodge an objection notice. The amount is then determined by a tribunal, in much the same way as an appeal. See **Chapter 2** for the appeals process. If the company raises no objection, the determination becomes final (*CTA 2009, ss 240 and 242*).

PROPERTY BUSINESS LOSSES

12.33 A company's property business losses are set against its total profits for the same accounting period. The business must be carried on on a commercial basis. If there are insufficient profits against which to set the loss, it is carried forward to the next accounting period and treated as a loss of that period to be set against total profits. Excess losses are carried forward in this way until the property business ceases. When the property business ceases, the remaining loss will be carried forward and treated as management expenses under *CTA 2009, s 1219(1)* (*ICTA 1988, s 392A(3)*).

Where there is a change of company ownership, as described in **12.17**, the losses arising before the change of ownership cannot be carried forward to be set against profits arising after the change of ownership. If the change of ownership occurs during an accounting period, losses pre and post the change are apportioned according to the length of the accounting bases or, if this produces an unjust result, on a just and reasonable basis (*ICTA 1988, s 768D*).

Property business losses are included in CT600 boxes 127 and 128.

INVESTMENT IN OTHER LIMITED COMPANIES

12.34 An investment in another limited company will bring about share ownership for the company. The subsequent disposal of the shares will bring about a capital gain. Income will take the form of dividend receipts. UK dividends have in effect already borne corporation tax and with effect from 1 July 2009 foreign dividends are generally exempt (see **1.1** and **13.46–13.50**). There are important reliefs for share disposals:

- losses on shares in unquoted trading companies,

- substantial shareholding exemption, and

- corporate venturing scheme relief.

Capital losses

12.35 An investment company may claim relief against income for capital losses arising on the disposal of shares in unquoted qualifying trading companies, which had been subscribed for by the investment company. The loss incurred, which is calculated under normal CGT rules, may be set-off against income (before management expenses and charges) of the same and (if not wholly relieved) preceding accounting periods (*ICTA 1988, s 573*). A loss claim may also be made where an asset has proven to be of negligible value

(*TCGA 1992, s 24*). A computation must be prepared by taking the negligible value of the asset as its sale proceeds.

Loss relief for allowable capital losses is available to an investment company (irrespective of whether it is a close investment-holding company), which has subscribed for shares in a qualifying trading company (*ICTA 1988, s 573*). The relief must be claimed, in writing, within two years after the end of the accounting period in which the loss was incurred.

The investment company obtains relief for its capital loss by set-off against its income chargeable to corporation tax. The loss relief is set against income of the accounting period in which the loss is incurred and income of previous accounting periods ending within the 12 months immediately preceding the accounting period in which the loss was incurred. Where an accounting period falls partly within and partly outside the 12-month period, only a proportion of its income can be relieved.

The loss relief against income is given before deduction of charges on income and expenses of management. Where loss relief is given under these provisions, the loss is ignored for the purpose of corporation tax on chargeable gains.

The main conditions to be satisfied in order to qualify for this relief against income are as follows:

- The company subscribing for shares and incurring the capital loss must, generally, have been an investment company for the whole of the previous six years.

- The shares subscribed for must be share capital of a qualifying trading company as defined in *ICTA 1988, s 576(4)*.

- The investment company must not control the trading company, the two companies must not be under common control, and the two companies cannot be members of the same group.

For this purpose the distinction between an investment company and a trading company is maintained. An investment company has the same meaning as *ICTA 1988, s 130* (see **12.3**) but does not include the holding company of a trading group. A trading company is defined as a company whose business consists wholly or mainly of the carrying on of a trade or trades (*ICTA 1988, s 576*).

Substantial shareholdings exemption

The relief

12.36   Provided all relevant conditions are met, the gain on the disposal of shares or an interest in shares held by a company in another company will not be a chargeable gain. However, if a loss were to arise on the disposal of the shares, this loss will not be an allowable loss and hence not available for set-off against other gains. The company has the benefit of no tax payable on the gain but all loss relief is 'lost'.

The exemption does not apply where disposal is deemed to be a no gain/no loss transfer for capital gains under *TCGA 1992, s 171* (see **20.16**).

Substantial shareholding

12.37   Essentially the investing company must hold at least 10% of the investee company's share capital and be entitled to at least 10% of the profits and assets available for distribution to equity holders by the investee company. The investing company must have held the shares for a continuous period of at least 12 months ending not more than one year before the disposal (*TCGA 1992, Sch 7AC*).

Group member holdings can be aggregated in order to calculate whether the 10% holding criteria is met (*TCGA 1992, Sch 7AC, para 26*). The capital gains tax group definition is used (see **20.14**) using a 51% relationship rather than a 75% relationship.

Even if shares are vested in a liquidator the company continues to be treated as the beneficial owner of the assets (*TCGA 1992, Sch 7AC, para 16*). The shares must have been held for at least 12 months ending not more than one year before disposal. If some of the shares have been sold during the 12-month period the remainder of the holding will continue to qualify, provided that all other conditions are met (*TCGA 1992, Sch 7AC, para 7*). The period of ownership also looks back through the no gain/no loss transfers and share reorganisations so that this time of ownership is also brought into consideration (*TCGA 1992, Sch 7AC, paras 10, 14*). However, for deemed sales and reacquisitions, the time of ownership commences with the reacquisition of the holding (*TCGA 1992, Sch 7AC, para 11*). Repurchase agreement arrangements treat the time of ownership as that commencing with the original owner (*TCGA 1992, Sch 7AC, para 12*). Similarly, stock lending arrangements have no effect on the original ownership time span (*TCGA 1992, Sch 7AC, para 13*). A demerger that has a reorganisation treatment (*TCGA 1992, s 192*) is also looked through when calculating the period of ownership

(*TCGA 1992, Sch 7AC, para 15*). In addition, if the 10% shareholding exemption applies as described above, the exemption will also be extended to an option or conversion right connected with the shares (*TCGA 1992, Sch 7AC, para 2*).

Conditions affecting the investing company

12.38   The investing company must have been a sole trading company or a member of a trading group throughout the 12-month period and immediately after the disposal (*TCGA 1992, Sch 7AC, para 18*). The relief also applies in a group situation where the company holding the shares does not qualify, but assuming an intra-group transfer under *TCGA 1992, s 171* another company would qualify. Where there is a deferral of the completion date on disposal the investing company must qualify at the time of completion (*TCGA 1992, Sch 7AC, para 18*).

Conditions affecting the investee company

12.39   The investee company must have been a trading company or the holding company or a trading group during the 12-month period and also be a trading company immediately after the disposal of the shares (*TCGA 1992, Sch 7AC, para 19*). The responsibility for determining whether a company, in which shares (or interests in shares or assets related to shares) are held and since disposed of, was a qualifying company, lays with the investor company concerned. However, in cases of uncertainty it is possible to request HMRC's opinion through the non-statutory business clearance service (HMRC Capital Gains Manual CG 53120). As for the investor, where there is a contract for sale with delayed completion the investee company must qualify at the time of sale (*TCGA 1992, Sch 7AC, para 19*).

Trading activities

12.40   A 'trading company' is defined as a company which is either 'a company existing wholly for the purpose of carrying on one or more trades' or a company that would fall within that definition 'apart from any purposes capable of having no substantial effect on the extent of the company's activities'.

In this context 'wholly' means solely, ie the company had no purpose other than to trade. Wholly for a trading purpose is considered according to the requirements of the company's trade. The generation of investment income does not necessarily mean that a company is not trading. For example, the company may set aside funds short-term for the expansion of the business or a cyclical business may hold large funds from time to time that it needs to settle its trading debts. A company's purpose is understood to mean its actual or its intended activities; this will mean examining the directors' intentions.

Trading activities for these purposes will include activities carried on by a company:

- in the course of, or for the purposes of, a trade it is carrying on;
- for the purposes of a trade it is preparing to carry on;
- with a view to it acquiring or starting to carry on a trade;
- with a view to it acquiring a significant interest in the share capital of a trading company, or the holding company of a trading group or subgroup (subject to the restrictions outlined below).

The company's view to acquire or start a trade or its view to acquire a shareholding must materialise as soon as is reasonably practical in the circumstances. 'Significant' for these purposes only refers to ordinary share capital and the company to be acquired must not already be a member of the same group (*TCGA 1992, Sch 7AC, para 20*).

Holding funds for a longer term may prove to be insubstantial.

Any non-trading activities should be insubstantial. This is normally understood to be 20% of all the activities or less (HMRC Capital Gains Manual CG 53116). Included in the criteria applied are the proportion of turnover, assets and management time derived from or employed in the non-trading activity. HMRC have stated that these are not pass/fail tests and are not the only indicator of whether a company is a trading company. In general, HMRC attach less importance to the assets measure than to turnover or management time. HMRC will examine the situation over a period of time.

A holding company of a trading group is 'a company whose business (disregarding any trade carried on by it) consists wholly or mainly of the holding of shares in one or more companies which are its 51% subsidiaries'. HMRC interpret 'wholly or mainly', in this context, as more than half of whatever measure is reasonable in the circumstances of the case. Intra-group activities are disregarded for the purpose of the financial tests.

Trading activities also include a qualifying interest in a joint venture company (*TCGA 1992, Sch 7AC, para 20*).

Example 12.5

Atlantic Ltd is a trading company, with two wholly-owned subsidiary companies, India Ltd and China Ltd.

On 1 July 2008, Atlantic Ltd acquired 25% of the ordinary share capital of Pacific Ltd.

On 1 September 2008, Pacific Ltd is taken over by Adriatic Ltd.

Atlantic Ltd received an exchange of shares under the no gain/no loss treatment (*TCGA 1992, s 135* applied *TCGA 1992, s 127*). As a result, Atlantic Ltd now owns 20% of Adriatic Ltd.

On 1 March 2008, Atlantic Ltd transfers its holding in Adriatic Ltd on a no gain/no loss basis so that *TCGA 1992, s 171* applies to its 100% subsidiary India Ltd.

On 1 July 2009, India Ltd sells the holding to a third party.

The holding was bought on 1 July 2008 and sold on 1 July 2009. It is necessary to look back through the period of ownership to ascertain whether the substantial shareholdings exemption applies (*TCGA 1992, Sch 7AC, para 10*). The holding throughout has remained within the group. India Ltd is treated as owning the shares for 12 months prior to disposal, and so the substantial shareholding exemption applies.

Corporate venturing scheme

12.41   The corporate venturing scheme rules are contained in *FA 2000, Sch 15* The rules offer companies relief for investment in qualifying shares in other companies during the period from 1 April 2000 until 1 April 2010. The companies involved can be of any size, but more usually between a larger company and a smaller one in the same line of business; thus providing the smaller company with another form of finance.

The larger company may invest in the smaller company. The connection provides an alternative or supplementary source of finance for the investee firm and a useful business outlet for the investor company. The investor company may take an interest in the investee by offering its skills and financial advice but must not have a major interest in the company.

Tax reliefs

12.42   There are three types of relief available:

- **Investment relief**. Relief against corporation tax of up 20% of the amount subscribed for the full-risk ordinary shares held for three years.

- **Deferral relief**. Any gain on the sale of shares can be rolled into the cost of new shares acquired under the scheme.

- **Loss relief**. Any loss on the sale of the shares can be relieved against income or chargeable gains.

The investing company

12.43   The investing company's interest in the investee company must not be more than 30% and it must not be in a position to control the company (*FA 2000, Sch 15, paras 5–8*). Connected company interests are taken into account together with directors' and the directors' relatives' interests. A relative is taken to mean a spouse, civil partner, parent and grandparent, child and grandchild etc. No reciprocal arrangements must exist regarding the investment (*FA 2000, Sch 15, para 6*). The investing company must be a trading company or the holding company of a trading group and financial activities are precluded. If the investment does not qualify for some reason the relief will be withdrawn.

The issuing company

12.44   The issuing company must be an unquoted trading company or the holding company of a trading group, when the shares are issued (AIM and PLUS market shares are unquoted for this purpose). The company can be preparing to carry on a trade. It must not have made any arrangements to become a quoted company.

The company must have gross assets of no more than £7m immediately before, and £8m immediately after the issue (if the issuing company is the parent company of a group, this test is applied to the group as a whole). For shares issued before 6 April 2006, the limits are £15m before and £16m after.

With effect from 6 April 2007 if the issuing company is a single company, there must be less than 50 full-time or equivalent employees when the shares are issued (*FA 2000, Sch 15, para 22A*). The equivalent number of full-time employees is found by taking the actual number of full-time employees and adding to this the fractional apportionment for each additional employee (*FA 2007, Sch 16*).

Throughout the qualification period the issuing company must not be a member of a group of companies, unless it is the parent company of the group, and must not be under the control of another company. With effect from 6 April 2007, if the issuing company is a parent company, there must be less than 50 full-time or equivalent employees (as calculated above) for that company and for each of its qualifying subsidiaries when the shares are issued (*FA 2000, Sch 15, para 22A*) (*FA 2007, Sch 16*).

At least 20% of the issuing company's ordinary share capital must be held by individuals other than directors or employees (or their relatives) of an investing company, or any company connected with it (*FA 2000, Sch 15, para 18*).

The investment

12.45   The investment must be in cash and the shares must be fully paid-up at the time they are issued. There can be no arrangement in force to protect investors from normal commercial investment risk.

The investing company must use 100% of the funds it receives from issuing the shares for the purposes of a qualifying trade, or for research and development intended to lead to or benefit a qualifying trade. For share issues prior to 22 April 2009, at least 80% had to be used on share issue, with the remaining 20% in the following 12 months. The funds must be used no later than the end of the period of two years starting with the issue of the shares, or the two years following the commencement of the trade if later. The period was 12 months for share issues prior to 22 April 2009 (*FA 2000, Sch 15, para 36*). With effect from 6 April 2007, the total investment in the company's relevant investments is restricted to £2 million. The company's relevant investments include investments made in any company that is, or has at any time during the year in question been, a subsidiary of the issuing company, regardless of whether it was a subsidiary at the time when the investment was made. Relevant investments are investments included on a *FA 2000, Sch 15, para 42* compliance statement, which confirms that the scheme conditions are met (*FA 2007, Sch 16*).

Trading activities

12.46   In order to qualify for the relief, the company must be carrying on a qualifying trade during the qualification period. The qualification period commences with the issue of the shares and ends immediately before the third anniversary of the issue date. If the money raised wholly or mainly for the purposes of the trade had not been used for that trade by the issuing company or its qualifying 90% subsidiary, the qualification period ends on the third anniversary of the trading date.

A qualifying 90% subsidiary of the issuing company is any company in which the issuing company owns not less than 90% of the issued share capital, not less than 90% of the voting power, has entitlement to not less than 90% of the assets in a winding-up and has entitlement to not less than 90% of the profits on a distribution. In addition no other person has control according to the meaning in *ICTA 1988, s 840* (see **14.4**) and no arrangements are in existence so that any of the aforementioned conditions would cease to be effective (*FA 2000, Sch 15, para 23A*).

Qualifying trade

12.47   A qualifying trade is a trade carried out wholly or mainly in the UK, on a commercial basis with a view to the realisation of profits, and which does not consist wholly or substantially in carrying out excluded activities (*FA 2000, Sch 15, para 25*).

The following activities are excluded from a 'qualifying trade':

- dealing in land, commodities or futures or in shares, securities or other financial instruments;

- dealing in goods otherwise than in the course of an ordinary trade of wholesale or retail distribution;

- banking, insurance, money lending, debt factoring, hire purchase financing or other financial activities;

- leasing (including letting ships on charter or other assets on hire) or receiving royalties or other licence fees;

- providing legal or accountancy services;

- property development;

- farming or market gardening;

- holding, managing or occupying woodlands, any other forestry activities or timber production;

- operating or managing hotels or comparable establishments or managing property used as a hotel or comparable establishment; and

- operating or managing nursing homes or residential care homes, or managing property used as a nursing home or residential care home. (*FA 2000, Sch 15, para 26*).

The carrying out of research and development activities is treated as a qualifying trade if it is expected that a connected qualifying trade will be derived therefrom. This is a qualifying trade carried on by the company itself or, if the company is a member of a group, the issuing company or any of its 90% subsidiaries.

Obtaining clearance

12.48   The investee company can obtain clearance before the shares are issued (*FA 2000, Sch 15, para 89*). If the issue goes ahead, the issuing company should complete form CVS 1 confirming it has met all the necessary conditions with which it must comply. The company must submit the form to HMRC and, if satisfied, HMRC will authorise the issuing company to provide the investing company with a compliance certificate to enable it to claim investment relief (and, where applicable, deferral relief). The compliance certificate can only be issued after the issuing company has been carrying on the trade (or, where appropriate, research and development) for which the funds were raised for at least four months.

Obtaining relief

12.49   The investing company claims investment relief against its corporation tax liability by completing the corporate venturing scheme CT600G supplementary pages and including the relief claimed in box 71 of the main return. Loss relief is included in CT600 box 22.

The necessary conditions must be complied with for three years or else the relief is withdrawn. The relief is only available during the accounting period for which the investment is made. The relief is given against corporation tax after marginal relief but before any double taxation relief.

Example 12.6

If, during an accounting period, an investing company subscribes £30,000 for 3,000 shares in company A and £90,000 for 6,000 shares in company B, then the maximum investment relief available is £24,000 (20% of £30,000 + £90,000).

If the investing company's corporation tax liability for the accounting period is £18,000 before taking account of any investment relief, then only three-quarters of the available investment relief can be used.

So, the amount attributable to the shares in A is:

$$£30,000 \times \frac{£18,000}{£120,000} = £4,500$$

The amount attributable to the shares in B is:

$$£90,000 \times \frac{£18,000}{£120,000} = £13,500$$

It would also be possible for the investing company to claim investment relief only in respect of the shares in company B, so all the investment relief would be attributable to those shares. But, this would prevent shares in company A from qualifying for CVS loss relief and deferral relief, because there would be no investment relief attributable to the shares in company A immediately before any future disposal.

12.50   If value, other than insignificant value, is received from the investee company, relief is withdrawn accordingly, being 20% of the value received. Receiving value could amount to acquiring an asset at undervalue, money lending etc. The provision of goods and services at market rates during the course of trade is not understood to be receipt of value (*FA 2000, Sch 15, para 47*).

An insignificant amount is £1,000 or if more, the amount is insignificant in relation to the amount subscribed for the shares (*FA 2000, Sch 15, para 47(7)*) (HMRC Venture Capital Manual VCM 50630).

Deferral relief

12.51   The reinvesting company may claim deferral relief on its disposal of qualifying shares, if investment relief was attributable to the shares immediately before the disposal and, if the investing company holds the shares continuously from the time they were issued until the disposal. The new company in which the investee company invests must comply with the investment relief conditions. The gain must be reinvested in the other qualifying company at any time beginning four years before the deferred gain arose.

The gain is deferred until the shares in the other company are disposed of, or an event occurs (such as, a receipt of value or certain share reorganisations), which causes any of the investment relief attributable to the shares to be withdrawn.

The investing company claims deferral relief on the corporate venturing scheme supplementary pages. It may do so after it has received the second investment's compliance certificate. The amount of the deferral must be shown on the claim.

If the investment relief is withdrawn for any reason, this does not affect the deferral relief.

Relief for losses

12.52   A loss on disposal can be set against a chargeable gain, or carried forward to set against future chargeable gains, in the normal way. Alternatively, the investing company may claim that the loss be set against its income for the accounting period in which the disposal was made, with any excess carried back to periods ending in the 12 months before that period.

The loss must have arisen from an arm's-length disposal and not arise from a scheme or arrangement. The company must have held the shares continuously since issue. The amount of the loss is reduced by the amount of any investment relief retained (*FA 2000, Sch 15, paras 67–71*).

Example 12.7

An investing company subscribes £100,000 for 100,000 shares (obtaining investment relief of £20,000).

It retains the shares for four years before disposing of them all for £55,000.

The allowable loss is calculated as follows:

Disposal proceeds £55,000 – £80,000 (consideration given for shares less investment relief given and not withdrawn).

So the allowable loss is £25,000.

Any unutilised loss cannot be carried forward as a trading loss but may be carried forward as a capital loss.

Other reliefs

12.53   The investing company will hold the shares in the investee company as an investment. Corporate venture scheme holdings will not qualify for group relief, but if all necessary conditions apply, they may qualify for consortium relief (see **10.16**). For further information see HMRC Guidance, The Corporate Venturing Scheme: www.hmrc.gov.uk/guidance/cvs.

Further developments

12.54 In April 2009, the European Commission gave the scheme its formal State Aid approval. In order to secure the approval, the rules regarding the location of the qualifying trade are to be relaxed (see **12.47**) and a restriction is to be introduced to exclude companies in difficulty from the scheme. Legislation will be introduced in *Finance Bill 2010* (Treasury Press Release, 29 April 2009).

INVESTMENT IN COMPANY OR GOVERNMENT LOAN STOCK

12.55 Loan stock investments are within the loan relationships regime (see **Chapter 11**).

COMMUNITY INVESTMENT TAX RELIEF

Eligibility for tax relief

12.56 Companies that make investments in an accredited community development finance institution (CDFI) may obtain community investment tax relief (*FA 2002, Sch 16, para 1*). The investor company itself cannot be a CDFI (*FA 2002, Sch 16, para 16*). There must be no tax avoidance purposes (*FA 2002, Sch 16, para 18*). The investment may take the form of a secured or unsecured loan subscription to a securities or share issue but not in the form of an overdraft (*FA 2002, Sch 16, para 2*).

The relief is given over a five-year period, which commences on the day that the investment is made (*FA 2002, Sch 16, para 3*).

The relief

12.57 The company must claim on box 72 of form CT600 for its corporation tax liability to be reduced by the smaller of 5% of the invested amount and the amount which reduces the investor's corporation tax liability to zero. The claim can be made for the accounting period in which the investment is made and in each of the following four accounting periods (*FA*

2002, Sch 16, para 20). The company must have received a tax relief certificate relating to the investment from the CDFI.

Accreditation

12.58 The company must apply for accreditation as a community development finance institution to provide finance, or business advice for SMEs in disadvantaged communities (*SI 2003/96* and *SI 2008/383*). SMEs in disadvantaged communities include both SMEs located in disadvantaged areas, and SMEs owned or operated by, or designed to serve, members of disadvantaged groups (*FA 2002, Sch 16, para 4*).

No claim can be made unless the company is an accredited CDFI (*FA 2002, Sch 16, para 24*). If the investor company itself becomes a CDFI no claim is possible (*FA 2002, Sch 16, para 25*). When granted a period of accreditation will last for three years (*FA 2002, Sch 16, para 7*).

Conditions to be satisfied in relation to loans

12.59 There are conditions related to loans. First the CDFI either receives the full amount of the loan on the investment date or the draw down period must commence no later than 18 months after the investment date. Secondly, the loan must not carry any present or future rights for conversion to shares or securities redeemable within the five-year period beginning with the day the investment is made. Thirdly, the loan must not be repayable during the first two years; no more than 25% of the loan outstanding at the end of the first two years can be repaid in the third year; no more than 50% of the loan capital can be repaid before the end of the fourth year and no more than 75% of the loan capital can be repaid before the end of the loan period. Other normal commercial conditions may be imposed (*FA 2002, Sch 16, para 9*).

Conditions to be satisfied in relation to securities

12.60 Any securities issued must be subscribed for wholly in cash and be fully paid for on the investment date. The securities must not carry any present or future right to be redeemed within the five-year period, or any present or future right to be converted into or exchanged for a loan which is, or securities, shares or other rights which are, redeemable within that period (*FA 2002, Sch 16, para 10*).

Conditions to be satisfied in relation to shares

12.61 Shares must be subscribed for wholly in cash, and be fully paid up on the investment date. In addition, akin to the rule for securities above, the shares must not be redeemable *per se* or be redeemable in exchange for a loan for other securities within that five year period. Shares are not fully paid up on the investment date, if there is any undertaking to pay cash to the CDFI at a future date in connection with the acquisition of the shares.

(*FA 2002, Sch 16, para 11*).

Tax relief certificates

12.62 Tax relief certificates may be issued by the CDFI in respect of retail investments made in the CDFI in that period with an aggregate value exceeding £10m, and in any other case, in respect of investments made in the CDFI in that period with an aggregate value exceeding £20m (*FA 2002, Sch 16, para 12*). The investment consists of the amount of the loan or the investment in shares. There is a £3,000 penalty for any tax relief certificates issued fraudulently or negligently.

There can be no risk exclusion other than normal commercial risks (*FA 2002, Sch 16, para 13*). At any time during the five-year period the investor or a connected party must not control the CDFI. When considering control, all future rights and powers are attributed to the investor and the investor must be the sole beneficial owner of the investment or loan repayment entitlement when it is made (*FA 2002, Sch 16, para 14*).

Investment

12.63 As regards securities or shares, the invested amount for a tax year or accounting period is the amount subscribed by the investor for the securities or shares. The shares must have been held by the investor throughout the accounting period (*FA 2002, Sch 16, para 23*).

The amount of a loan investment is determined according to its average capital balance. The average capital is the mean of the daily balances of capital outstanding during the period. The investment is as follows:

- for the tax year or accounting period in which the investment date falls, the average capital balance for the first year of the five-year period;

- for the tax year or accounting period in which the first anniversary of the investment date falls, the average capital balance for the second year of the five-year period;

- for any subsequent tax year or accounting period:

  — the average capital balance for the period of one year beginning with the anniversary of the investment date falling in the tax year or accounting period concerned; or

  — if less, the average capital balance for the period of six months beginning 18 months after the investment date.(*FA 2002, Sch 16, para 21*).

The loan must be outstanding at the end of the accounting period concerned (*FA 2002, Sch 16, para 22*).

Where more than one investment is made the relief is attributed pro-rata (*FA 2002, Sch 16, para 26*).

Withdrawal of relief

12.64   If the relief is withdrawn or reduced for any reason, an income assessment will be made on the company for the accounting period for which the relief was obtained (*FA 2002, Sch 16, para 27*). An assessment may be made at any time not more than six years after the end of the accounting period for which the relief was obtained, but if a loss of tax is brought about deliberately by the company or a related person, the period is extended to 20 years (*FA 2008, Sch 39, para 48*).

In the case of a loan the relief is withdrawn if the investor disposes of the loan within the five-year period other than through the dissolving or winding up the CDFI or the CDFI loses its accreditation. A full or partial loan repayment is not treated as a disposal (*FA 2002, Sch 16, para 28*).

In the case of share or securities the relief is withdrawn if the investor disposes of the whole or any part of the investment within the five-year period other than through the dissolving or winding up the CDFI, or the CDFI loses its accreditation, or the repayment, redemption or repurchase of securities or shares included in the investment (*FA 2002, Sch 16, para 29*).

In addition, the disposal must be at arm's length or for full consideration.

Repayments of loan capital

12.65   The relief is withdrawn if loan capital is repaid and the average capital balance of the loan for the period of six months beginning 18 months after the investment date is less than the prescribed percentage being 75% for the third year, 50% for the fourth year and 25% for the final year. The relief is not withdrawn if the amount does not exceed £1,000.

The average capital is the mean of the daily balances of capital outstanding during the period disregarding any non-standard repayment.

A repayment is non-standard if it is made at the choice or discretion of the CDFI and not as a direct or indirect consequence of a contractual obligation (*FA 2002, Sch 16, para 30*). The same situation applies if value is received in repayment of a loan (*FA 2002, Sch 16, para 31*).

Excessive returns to an investor

12.66 Relief is withdrawn or pro rata partially withdrawn, if the investor receives excess value from the company during the first three years of the period of six years beginning one year before the investment date (the period of restriction). Amounts of less than £1,000 are ignored.

Relief is also withdrawn if the aggregate amount of value received by the investor before the beginning of the fifth year of the period of restriction (as mentioned above) is more than 25% of the invested capital or 50% before the final year and 75% during the final year. Amounts of less than £1,000 are ignored (*FA 2002, Sch 16, para 32*).

Value received

12.67 An investor received value from a CDFI at any time when the CDFI:

(a) repays, redeems or repurchases any securities or shares included in the investment;

(b) releases or waives any liability of the investor to the CDFI or discharges, or undertakes to discharge, any liability of the investor to a third person:

   (i) A CDFI shall be treated as having released or waived a liability if the liability is not discharged within 12 months of the time when it ought to have been discharged.

(c) makes a loan or advance to the investor, which has not been repaid in full before the investment is made:

   (i) A loan is treated as made by the CDFI to the investor if there is a debt incurred by the investor to the CDFI (other than an ordinary trade debt) or a debt due from the investor to a third person which has been assigned to the CDFI.

(d) provides a benefit or facility for:

    (i) the investor or any associates of the investor; or

    (ii) if the investor is a company, directors or employees of the investor or any of their associates.

(e) disposes of an asset to the investor for no consideration or for a consideration which is or the value of which is less than the market value of the asset;

(f) acquires an asset from the investor for a consideration which is or the value of which is more than the market value of the asset; or

(g) makes a payment to the investor other than the following:

    (i) any payment by any person for any goods, services or facilities provided by the investor (in the course of his trade or otherwise) which is reasonable in relation to the market value of those goods, services or facilities;

    (ii) the payment by any person of any interest, which represents no more than a reasonable commercial return on money, lent to that person;

    (iii) the payment by any company of any dividend or other distribution which does not exceed a normal return on any investment in shares in or securities of that company;

    (iv) any payment for the acquisition of an asset, which does not exceed its market value;

    (v) the payment by any person, as rent for any property occupied by the person, of an amount not exceeding a reasonable and commercial rent for the property; and

    (vi) a payment in discharge of a trade debt for goods or services supplied in the ordinary course of a trade or business with credit terms of not more than six months and not longer than that normally given to customers of the person carrying on the trade or business (*FA 2002, Sch 16, para 35*).

Reconstructions

12.68 If there is a restructuring by the CDFI the new investment is treated as made and not when the original investment was made (*FA 2002, Sch 16, para 40*). A share exchange is treated as a disposal of shares and the relief may be lost (*FA 2002, Sch 16, para 41*).

If the relief is to be withdrawn, the investor company must inform HMRC within the period of 12 months beginning with the end of the accounting period in which the event occurred (*FA 2002, Sch 16, para 42*). An investor must notify HMRC of value received by any person no later than 60 days beginning when the investor comes to know of that event, if this is later than the period of 12 months beginning with the end of the accounting period.

Chapter 13

Foreign matters

INTRODUCTION

13.1 Companies may be resident in the UK with overseas income, or vice versa. Alternatively, they may invest abroad, in which case they will be able to receive tax relief on their income, or their investment may fall within the controlled foreign companies regime.

COMPANY RESIDENCE

13.2 A company is resident in the UK if it is incorporated in the UK (*CTA 2009, s 14*).

If a company is not incorporated in the UK if will be resident in the UK if it is centrally managed and controlled in the UK. The case of *De Beers Consolidated Mines Ltd v Howe* (1906) 5 TC 198, [1906] AC 455 involved a company that was registered in South Africa where it worked diamond mines. The company's head office and shareholders' general meetings were held in South Africa, but the directors' meetings took place in both South Africa and the UK. The majority of directors lived in the UK. The company claimed that it was not resident in the UK. It was held that the company was resident in the UK because the majority of the directors who had the overall control were situated in London.

The place where the management and control is exercised from then on has been interpreted as the place where the effective management decisions are taken and not necessarily where it was constitutionally managed. In *Wood v Holden (Inspector of Taxes)* [2006] EWCA Civ 26, [2006] 2 BCLC 210 although a company's board meetings took place in London, the authority given by those board meetings was usurped by the overseas parent and the company was held to be non-UK resident. Thus it is necessary for the courts to apply two tests; first the *situs* of the management and control of its own constitutional organs and secondly where that control is usurped. These tests were applied in the later case of *News Datacom Ltd v Atkinson (Insp of Taxes); News Data Security Products Ltd v Atkinson (Insp of Taxes)* [2006] STC

(SCD) 731 where there was no usurpation and the company was deemed to be non-UK resident on its facts (*CTA 2009, s 15*).

Double tax treaty

13.3   If a double tax treaty is in place between the UK and the overseas territory it should be consulted in order to verify the company's deemed place of residence.

A company may be 'treaty non-resident'; in other words, solely resident in the other country. A discussion is given in HMRC International Manual INTM 120070.

If residence is or could be awarded to the treaty partner, the company becomes treaty non-resident. A treaty non-resident company is not resident for UK tax purposes (*CTA 2009, s 18*).

A double tax treaty ensures that companies that carry on business in more than one country are only taxed once on their income. A reciprocal provision to the effect that the profits of a non-resident company, which carries on a trade, profession or business that is controlled or managed outside the UK are only subject to UK tax if those profits are attributable to a permanent establishment in the UK is often included. In relation to income arising on or after 12 March 2008, the inclusion of such a clause does not prevent the company's other income from being chargeable to UK tax (*FA 2008, s 59; ICTA 1988, s 815ZA*).

UK RESIDENT COMPANY WITH OVERSEAS INCOME

13.4   A company resident in the UK is chargeable to corporation tax on all its profits wherever the income arises and wherever the assets on which the gain on whose disposal the gain was calculated were situated and whether or not received or transmitted to the UK. Trading income of a UK trade earned abroad is included within the trade profits computation.

NON-UK RESIDENT COMPANY CARRYING ON A TRADE IN THE UK

Circumstances in which chargeable to UK corporation tax

13.5   A non-resident company is chargeable to corporation tax if, and only if, it carries on a trade in the UK through a permanent establishment, in which case the following becomes chargeable:

- any trading income arising directly or indirectly through or from the permanent establishment;

- any income from property or rights used by, or held by or for, the permanent establishment;

- chargeable gains accruing on the disposal of assets situated in the UK used for the purposes of the trade of the use of the permanent establishment (*CTA 2009, ss 5, 19; TCGA 1992, s 10*).

Meaning of 'permanent establishment'

13.6   Non-resident companies are assessed to UK corporation tax (subject to treaty override: see **13.3**), if they have a permanent establishment in the UK. A permanent establishment can be a branch or agency, or other establishment. *FA 2003, s 148* states that a company has a permanent establishment in a territory if, and only if, it has a fixed place of business there through which the business of the company is wholly or partly carried on, or an agent acting on behalf of the company has and habitually exercises there authority to do business on behalf of the company.

A fixed place of business

13.7   A fixed place of business can be a place of management, a branch, an office, a factory, a workshop, an installation or structure for the exploration of natural resources, a mine, an oil or gas well, a quarry or any other place of extraction of natural resources or a building site or construction or installation project (*FA 2003, s 148(1), (2)*).

Circumstances in which there is no permanent establishment

13.8   A company is not regarded as having a permanent establishment if it carries on business there through an independent agent acting in the ordinary course of the agency business. A company is regarded as having a permanent establishment if it maintains a fixed place of business for the purpose of carrying on activities that have not yet commenced. Neither will the company be regarded as having a permanent establishment if an agent carries on preparatory or auxiliary activities in relation to the business of the company as a whole.

The legislation provides examples of preparatory or auxiliary activities, of a company as a whole, which will not be considered sufficient business activities to constitute the existence of a permanent establishment. The list is not exhaustive but includes:

- the use of facilities for the purpose of storage, display or delivery of goods or merchandise belonging to the company;

- the maintenance of a stock of goods or merchandise belonging to the company for the purpose of storage, display or delivery;

- the maintenance of a stock of goods or merchandise belonging to the company for the purpose of processing by another person (*FA 2003, s 148(4), (5)*).

NON-RESIDENT COMPANY BECOMING LIABLE TO UK CORPORATION TAX

Assessment, collection and recovery of corporation tax

13.9   When an overseas company commences trading in the UK it should notify HMRC that it is within the charge to corporation tax. This will be the commencement of an accounting period (*CTA 2009, s 41*). When it becomes chargeable to UK corporation tax, it is chargeable to corporation tax, subject to any exceptions provided for by the *Corporation Tax Acts*, on all profits, wherever arising, that are attributable to its permanent establishment in the UK on the same principles as UK resident companies (*CTA 2009, s 21*).

Only where the UK has a tax treaty with the permanent establishment's home country and there is a conflict between the treaty and the UK corporation tax domestic law the effect of the treaty will be to modify or prevent the application of UK corporation tax principles. *ICTA 1988, s 788(3)* specifies that relevant treaty provisions take precedence over domestic legislation.

CTA 2009, s 21(1) adopts the wording of Article 7(2) of the OECD model tax convention and states that the permanent establishment's taxable profits are the profits that it would have made if it were a distinct and separate enterprise, engaged in the same or similar activities under the same or similar conditions, dealing wholly independently with the rest of the non-resident company of which it is a part. In accordance with the separate enterprise principle, transactions between the UK permanent establishment and other parts of the non-resident company are treated as being dealt with at arm's length (*CTA 2009, s 22*).

When calculating the profits, it is assumed that the permanent establishment has the same credit rating as the non-resident company of which it is a part and has such equity capital and loan capital as it could reasonably be expected to have in regard to its circumstance (*CTA 2009, s 21(2)*).

A deduction is given for expenses, wherever they are incurred, if they are incurred for the purposes of the permanent establishment and if they would be deductible if incurred by a company resident in the UK. These include executive and general administrative expenses. (*CTA 2009, s 29(1)*). The non-resident company may supply its permanent establishment with goods and services. If the supplies are at arm's length and within the non-resident company's normal business, they are treated as a trading or business transaction; and, if not, they are treated as an expense (*CTA 2009, s 23*).

A non-resident company pays corporation tax at the full rate. No claim can be made for the small companies rate (*ICTA 1988, s 13(1)*).

Responsibility for UK corporation tax

13.10 The UK representative of the overseas company is responsible for the permanent establishment's corporation tax affairs (*FA 2003, s 150*). The company in turn is bound by the acts or omissions of the UK representative. However, a non-resident company is not bound by mistakes in information provided by its UK representative in pursuance of an obligation imposed on the representative by this section, unless the mistake is the result of an act or omission of the company itself, or to which the company consented or in which it connived. Therefore, the UK representative of a non-resident company can only be prosecuted for a criminal offence if it committed the offence itself, or consented to or connived in its commission (*FA 2003, s 150*).

NON-UK RESIDENT COMPANY NOT CARRYING ON A TRADE IN THE UK BUT WITH OTHER UK INCOME

Liability to income tax

13.11 A non-resident company not carrying on a trade in the UK through a branch or agency is chargeable to income tax at the basic rate on any other UK income. Therefore a UK property investment business operated by a non-resident company will be subject to income tax at the basic rate on its profits. The profits are computed according to income tax rules (see *Income Tax 2009/10* (Bloomsbury Professional)).

Where tax is deducted at source from such income the tax payable is limited to the tax deducted at source. This includes savings and dividend income (*FA 2003, s 151*).

FOREIGN TAX

13.12   If, after 22 April 2009, foreign tax is repaid to a person connected with the company, any credit that the company is to receive is reduced by that amount. A connected person is defined according to *ICTA 1988, s 839*; see **4.25** (*FA 2009, s 59; ICTA 1988, s 804G*).

INTERNATIONAL MOVEMENT OF CAPITAL

Reporting rules prior to 1 July 2009

13.13   For transactions carried out prior to 1 July 2009, it was unlawful, without Treasury consent, for a UK resident company to cause or permit a non-UK resident company over which it had control to create or issue any shares or debentures. It was also unlawful, without Treasury consent, for a resident company to dispose of any shares or debentures in a non-resident company that it controlled (*ICTA 1988, s 765*). These were criminal offences. A £10,000 fine could have been levied, and those involved could have been sentenced to two years' imprisonment (*ICTA 1988, s 766*). These rules have now been abolished (*FA 2009, Sch 17, para 1*).

Reporting rules from 1 July 2009 onwards

13.14   As from 1 July 2009, an issue of shares in excess of £100m by a foreign subsidiary must be reported to HMRC, within six months of occurring. Other similar types of transaction must also be reported unless they are excluded transactions. Transitional rules allow an extended reporting deadline until 1 April 2010 for transactions entered into before 1 October 2009 (*FA 2009, Sch 17, para 14*).

The reporting body is responsible for making the report. A reporting body is a UK corporate parent that meets one of the following conditions:

Condition A

● it is not controlled by a foreign parent;

Condition B

● it is the only relevant UK parent or body corporate that is controlled by the foreign parent; or

Condition C

● the foreign parent controls the UK parent and other UK parents, but it has not nominated a single reporting body, or the foreign parent controls the UK parent and other UK parents and it is the nominated group reporting body (*FA 2009, Sch 17, para 5*).

Control of company means a person's ability, or a group of persons, to guarantee that the company's affairs are carried out in accordance with his or their wishes. This can be achieved through shareholdings or voting power or through powers conferred by the articles of association or other document (*FA 2009, Sch 17, para 12*).

Two or more UK corporate parents can select one of their number to be the reporting body ((*FA 2009, Sch 17, para 6*).

A UK corporate parent is essentially a totally independent UK resident company that controls one or more non-resident companies, and is not itself controlled by another UK resident company or companies (*FA 2009, Sch 17, para 7*).

The purpose of the report is to enable HMRC to establish whether any person gains a direct or indirect tax advantage from the transaction (*FA 2009, Sch 17, para 4*). If a company fails to comply, it is chargeable to a special returns penalty under *TMA 1970, s 98* (see **2.3**).

Reportable events and transactions

13.15   An event or transaction is reportable to HMRC if:

- it exceeds £100 million,

- it applies to the foreign subsidiary holdings (see **13.16**), and

- it is not an excluded transaction (see **13.17**).

(*FA 2009, Sch 17, para 8(1)*).

Conditions applying to foreign subsidiaries

13.16   The conditions that apply to foreign subsidiary holdings referred to in **13.15** are:

- an issue of shares or debentures by a foreign subsidiary;

- a transfer of shares or debentures of a foreign subsidiary in which the reporting body has an interest;

- the reporting body is a party to a transfer of shares or debentures of a foreign subsidiary in which the transferor has an interest;

- it results in a foreign subsidiary becoming, or ceasing to be, a controlling partner in a partnership, or

- it is of a description specified in regulations made by the Commissioners.

A foreign subsidiary is a controlling partner if it controls the partnership alone or with other subsidiaries (*FA 2009, Sch 17, para 8(3)*).

Excluded transactions

13.17   A transaction is excluded from the reporting rules if:

- it is carried out in the ordinary course of a trade;
- all the parties to the transaction are resident in the same territory at the time that the transaction is carried out;
- it is a security payment given to the bankers of a foreign subsidiary in the ordinary course of banking business;
- it is a security payment given to an insurance company by a foreign subsidiary in the ordinary course of banking business; or
- it is of a description specified in regulations made by HMRC.

(*FA 2009, Sch 17, para 9*).

UK COMPANY BECOMING NON-UK RESIDENT

HMRC notification and outstanding liabilities

13.18   When a company ceases to be chargeable to corporation tax, for example, by becoming non-UK resident it must comply with *FA 1988, s 130* requirements. It must notify HMRC of the date that it intends to become non-resident, provide a statement of all amounts owing and provide details of the arrangements it will make for payment. HMRC will require a payment guarantor to be provided and the arrangements must be approved by HMRC or otherwise they are void. (Treasury consent is not required for companies ceasing to be UK resident from 15 March 1988 onwards.) If a company becomes non-resident without HMRC approval, it and its directors together with controlling company directors may be liable to a penalty based on its outstanding liabilities (*FA 1988, s 131*). Outstanding amounts of tax may be recovered from the company directors or directors of other companies in the group (*FA 1988, s 132*).

The company's UK departure will be the cessation of an accounting period (*CTA 2009, s 41*). Therefore, balancing adjustments must be calculated for capital allowance purposes.

Deemed disposal of chargeable assets

13.19   Also the company will be deemed to have disposed of all its chargeable assets at market value thus creating a chargeable gain under *TCGA 1992, s 185*. A charge under *TCGA 1992, s 185* will also arise where a company becomes treaty non-resident. Roll-over relief is not available. If the chargeable assets are assets used in a trade that the company carries on, say through a branch or agency in the UK, there is no chargeable gain and therefore roll-over relief would be available. Following *Hughes de Lasteyrie du Saillant v Ministère de l'Économie, des Finances et de l'Industrie* Case C-902/02, the European Commission has invited member states to improve the coordination of their national exit tax rules on accrued capital gains (EC 19 December 2006). No changes have been made to the UK legislation as yet.

Postponement of exit charge

13.20   Postponement of the exit charge may occur if:

- the assets are situated outside the UK and are used in or for the purposes of a trade carried on outside the UK ('foreign assets'),

- the company is a 75% subsidiary (by ordinary shares) of a UK resident company (the 'principal company'), and

- both companies make an election within two years of the company becoming non-resident.

The postponed gain becomes a chargeable gain of the principal company, in whole or in part, if:

- the asset is disposed of within six years of the company becoming non-resident; and

- the company ceases to be a 75% subsidiary:

  — by disposal of ordinary shares;

  — for any other reason; or

  — by the principal company ceasing to be UK resident.

HMRC do not consider that the issue of new shares by the principal company to a third party will bring the gain into charge (*TCGA 1992, s 187*).

The capital gains charge under *TCGA 1992, s 185* also applies to companies who become treaty non-resident.

DUAL RESIDENT COMPANY

Restrictions

13.21   The transfer of the central management and control of a non-UK resident company to the UK will result in the company being UK resident. In practical terms the foreign jurisdiction may determine that the company remains resident abroad because of incorporation or because of trading activities. Hence, the company becomes a dual resident company. In such situations the relevant double tax treaty, if any, should be examined.

A dual resident investment company (ie a non-trading company) cannot claim or surrender group relief for the chargeable period (*ICTA 1988, s 404*). Neither can it make intra-group asset transfers on a no gain/no loss basis (*TCGA 1992, s 171*). Group roll-over relief is unavailable (*TCGA 1992, s 175(2)*).

The carry forward of trading losses on a succession to a trade without a change of ownership is also prohibited, together with the transfer of assets at written-down value for capital allowance purposes (*ICTA 1988, s 343(2)*).

Double tax relief

13.22   The double tax treaty between the UK and the country concerned may exempt the income in question from corporation tax. It should be examined in every case. (Double tax agreements can be viewed in HMRC Double Taxation Relief Manual DT 2140 onwards).

Credit relief for overseas corporate taxes paid is available against UK corporation tax payable. A claim should be made according to the terms of the double taxation agreement (*ICTA 1988, s 793A*).

Where there is no entitlement to relief under a double taxation agreement, unilateral relief (*ICTA 1988, ss 790, 793*) together with relief for withholding tax may be claimed. The general rule is that income is calculated according to UK principles (*George Wimpey International Ltd v Rolfe* [1989] STC 609) and the credit cannot exceed the calculated UK corporation tax.

CONTROLLED FOREIGN COMPANIES

Meaning

13.23   A company resident outside the UK, that is controlled by UK residents and which pays less than three quarters of the tax in its country of residence, which it would have paid on its income had it been resident in the UK is known as a controlled foreign company 'CFC' (*ICTA 1988, s 747(1)*). This being the case, the CFC's income may be apportioned to the UK resident owners.

The CFC legislation is contained in *ICTA 1988, ss 747–756, Schs 24–26*. Its aim is to prohibit UK resident companies artificially diverting their profits to controlled companies in low tax territories, by apportioning the diverted profits to UK residents with a relevant interest in the non-resident company and taxing them accordingly.

Developments in controlled foreign companies legislation

13.24 The controlled foreign companies legislation was brought to the European Courts with the case of *Cadbury Schweppes plc and Another v Inland Revenue Commissioners* (Case-196/04). The company concerned was an international group with a UK parent company. The group included two subsidiaries in Ireland who were established at the International Financial Services Centre in Ireland whose business was the financing of subsidiaries in the group. The two Irish subsidiaries were subject to a 10% rate of corporation tax and HMRC assessed the profits under the CFC legislation. Cadbury Schweppes plc appealed on the grounds that the legislation was contrary to *Arts 43* and *48* of the EC Treaty. *Article 43* prevents restrictions on the freedom of establishment of nationals of Member States in another Member State. *Article 48* provides that companies shall be treated in the same way as individuals.

The court ruled that *Arts 43* and *48* precluded the inclusion of the profits of a controlled foreign company, which had been subject to a lower rate of tax, in the tax base of a resident company, unless the inclusion related only to wholly artificial arrangements intended to escape the national tax normally payable. The inclusion was not to be applied where despite the existence of tax motives the controlled company was actually established in the host Member State and carried on economic activities there.

The ECJ decided that the rules were compatible with European Law provided they were not applied to companies carrying on genuine economic activities in other EU member states. However, as a result several changes were made to the UK's CFC legislation (*FA 2007, s 48, Sch 15*). In particular the 'exempt activities test' was extended (**13.33**), the public quotation condition (**13.37**) was removed and a formal claim procedure was introduced to enable a CFC company to be able to demonstrate that it is carrying on economic activities in the country concerned (**13.44–13.45**). These changes have effect for accounting periods beginning on or after 6 December 2006. If an accounting period straddles 6 December 2006, for CFC purposes there are deemed to be two accounting periods: the first to 5 December 2006 and the second to the end of the accounting period in question.

Residence

13.25 For these purposes the company is resident in the country where its place of management is situated. A company may be resident in two countries. In order to decide the country of residence it is taken to be the country which has the greatest amount of assets at the accounting year end. The assets are valued at market value (*ICTA 1988, s 749*).

A company may make an irrevocable election for a CFC to be treated as resident in a certain territory. The election must be made within 12 months of the end of the first accounting period to which it is to apply (*ICTA 1988, s 749A*).

If HMRC deem a country of residence, they must give notice to all persons with an interest in the CFC. A person has an interest in a company if he can secure that the assets or income can be applied directly or indirectly for his benefit or if either alone or with others he has control of the company.

A UK company that becomes treaty non-resident after 1 April 2002 (see **13.2**) remains UK resident for controlled foreign company purposes (*ICTA 1988, s 747*). (This does not apply to companies that migrated before 1 April 2002.)

Self-assessment requirements

13.26 Under self-assessment companies are required to make their own assessment of any liability. Form CT600B is used. The information that is required is:

- a calculation of the profits chargeable to tax on a UK corporation tax basis (exclusive of capital gains);

- an apportionment of the profits among those with an interest in the company; and

- corporation tax self-assessment where 25% or more of the profits are allocated.

Associates are included when considering the 25% threshold but are not included in the calculation of corporation tax due.

For accounting periods commencing before 16 March 2005, the self-assessment the accounts are prepared in accordance with the accountancy rules of the country concerned. If no accounts are required they are drawn up along *Companies Act* principles (*ICTA 1988, s 747A*). Profits computed in a foreign currency are converted to sterling at the rate for the last day of the accounting period (*ICTA 1988, s 748(4), (5)*). For accounting periods commencing on or after 16 March 2005, the accounts are drawn up in accordance with GAAP (*FA 2005, Sch 4, para 24*).

Apportionment

13.27   Apportionment can be made to persons who have a relevant interest in the CFC (*ICTA 1988, s 752*). The following persons who have an interest in the company:

- members of the company who are entitled to acquire voting rights and to participate in distributions,

- loan creditors entitled to a premium on redemption,

- persons who are able to secure that income or assets are applied directly or indirectly for their benefit,

- those who alone or with others control the company (*ICTA 1988, s 749B*).

A relevant interest, in general, can be direct or indirect (*ICTA 1988, s 752A*).

Calculation of the profits chargeable

13.28   Each year the company should calculate its chargeable profit irrespective of HMRC direction or whether an apportionment is required (*ICTA 1988, Sch 24, para 1*).

Assumptions made for the calculation of the profits chargeable

13.29   The profits chargeable to corporation tax are calculated in the normal way with the following added criteria:

- The company is assumed to be UK resident from the beginning of the first accounting period for which a direction is given. The company then continues to be notionally UK resident for subsequent accounting periods until it ceases to be controlled by UK residents (*ICTA 1988, Sch 24, para 2*).

- The company is assumed to be an open company (ie not a close company) (*ICTA 1988, Sch 24, para 3*).

- The company assumed to make full use of any claims or reliefs against corporation tax (*ICTA 1988, Sch 24, para 4*).

- Group relief is denied. If the company is a member of a group and relief has already been given, it is added back to the chargeable profits (*ICTA 1988, Sch 24, para 5*).

- If a CFC transfers a trade to a UK company the *ICTA 1988, s 343* succession treatment for losses carried forward from the CFC predecessor company to the UK successor company will apply (see **15.12–15.22**). The same does not apply to a transfer of trade from another company to a CFC company (*ICTA 1988, Sch 24, para 8*).

- Losses incurred within six years before the first year in which a direction or apportionment is made on a non-UK resident CFC may be treated as incurred within the first year. A claim must be made within 20 months of the CFC's first accounting period (*ICTA 1988, Sch 24, para 9*).

- Notional capital allowances are given in calculating the tax due (*ICTA 1988, Sch 24, para 10*).

- Unremittable income is ignored in the calculation until it is remitted to the UK (*ICTA 1988, Sch 24, para 12*).

Chargeable profits for an accounting period include income which accrues during that accounting period to the trustees of a settlement in relation to which the company is a settlor or a beneficiary. Any distributions made by the company to the trustees are excluded from that income. Income from any settlement can only be included once. Where there is more than one settlor or beneficiary in relation to the settlement, the income is to be apportioned between the company and the other settlors or beneficiaries, on a just and reasonable basis (*ICTA 1988, Sch 25, para 2A; FA 2008, s 64(2)*).

Control

13.30 A person has control of a company if he or she has the power to secure that the affairs of the company are conducted in accordance with his or her wishes. This is brought about by the ownership of the greater part of the share capital or voting rights or by powers granted by any document regulating the affairs of the company.

There are additional rules for determining whether two or more persons taken together control acompany. A UK resident and a non-UK resident may control a company together if the UK person has interests, rights and powers representing at least 40% of the holdings, rights and powers by which the company is controlled and the non-UK person has interests, rights and powers representing at least 40% but not more than 55% of such holdings, rights and powers. Attribution of connected persons' rights and powers applies (*ICTA 1988, s 755D*).

With effect from 12 March 2008, a person also controls a company if he or she possesses, or is entitled to acquire, such rights as would:

- if the whole of the income of the company were distributed, entitle the person to receive the greater part of the amount so distributed;

- if the whole of the company's share capital were disposed of, entitle the person to receive the greater part of the proceeds of the disposal; or

- in the event of the winding-up of the company or in any other circumstances, entitle the person to receive the greater part of the assets of the company which would then be available for distribution.

(*FA 2008, s 64(3); ICTA 1988, s 755D*)

Exclusion from profit apportionment

13.31   A series of exemptions exclude companies that can be reasonably assumed not to exist so as to artificially divert profits from the UK from the scope of the CFC rules.

No apportionment of profits is required for an accounting period in which:

- the CFC pursues an acceptable distribution policy (for accounting periods beginning before 1 July 2009), or

- the CFC is engaged in exempt activities throughout the period (only for local holding companies, except for accounting periods beginning before 1 July 2011), or

- the CFC has a public quotation, or

- the chargeable profits are £50,000 or less, or

- the CFC is situated in one of the exempt territories (*ICTA 1988, s 748*).

For accounting periods ending before 6 December 2006, the public quotation condition was still in force. This was abolished for subsequent accounting periods (*FA 2007, Sch 15, para 8*).

With effect from accounting periods beginning on or after 1 July 2009, the acceptable distribution policy exemption has been repealed, and the special rules applying to holding companies, apart from those applicable to local holding companies, have been removed from the exempt activities exemption.

Acceptable distribution policy

13.32   The acceptable distribution policy exemption relieved overseas companies, which paid most of their profits back to shareholders in the UK, from the CFC rules. This rule has now been repealed and takes effect for accounting periods commencing on or after 1 July 2009 (*FA 2009, Sch 16, para 1*). Where an accounting period straddles 1 July 2009, it is treated as split, on a just and reasonable basis, between the relevant periods (*FA 2009, Sch 16, para 7*). Dividends paid after that date, in respect of accounting periods before that date, are not affected (*FA 2009, Sch 16, para 8*).

An acceptable distribution policy was in place if the company paid a dividend equal to or greater than 90% of its net chargeable profits within 18 months of the end of its accounting period to UK resident persons (*ICTA 1988, Sch 25, paras 1–4A*).

For income accruing after 12 March 2008, the company had to satisfy a further condition. The distributed profits must have included:

- any income accruing during the relevant accounting period to the trustees of a settlement in relation to which the company was a settlor or a beneficiary; and

- any other income which accrued during that period to a partnership of which the company was a partner, apportioned between the company and the other partners on a just and reasonable basis.

A partnership could have been any entity established under the law of another territory of a similar character to a partnership, with the respective owners being treated as partners (*FA 2008, s 64(4); ICTA 1988, Sch 25, paras 4A–4D*).

Exempt activities test

13.33   The exempt activities test is met if the company satisfies the following requirements throughout the accounting period:

- it has a 'business establishment' in its territory of residence (see **13.44**);

- its business affairs are 'effectively managed' in its territory of residence; and

- its main business at no time consists of certain defined activities; namely investment business, import and exports and trading with connected or associated persons (*ICTA 1988, Sch 25, paras 5–12A*).

The affairs of the business will not be considered to be effectively managed unless there are sufficient individuals working for the company in the territory who have the competence and authority to undertake all or substantially all the company's business. Individuals are regarded as working for a company in the other territory if they are employed by the CFC or their working activities are controlled in another way by the CFC (*FA 2007, Sch 15, para 8*).

A company may be exempt from the charge if the holding company carries out an exempt activity. A holding company's gross income accruing after 12 March 2008 includes any income to which it is entitled and any income accruing to a trustee of a trust of which it is a settlor or beneficiary (*FA 2008, s 64(5); ICTA 1988, Sch 25, para 6*).

13.34   The special rules applying to holding companies, apart from those applicable to local holding companies, have been removed from the exempt activities exemption, with effect from 1 July 2011.

Subject to transitional rules, the exemption from the CFC rules under the holding company exemption will continue to apply for accounting periods beginning before1 July 2011, after which time it is to be repealed (*FA 2009, Sch 16, para 12*).

A controlled foreign company, that was an exempt holding company in respect of the last accounting period to end before 1 July 2009, is known as a qualifying holding company.

Where the accounting period of a controlled foreign company straddles 1 July 2009, it is treated as split on a time basis (*FA 2009, Sch 16, para 14*). Where the accounting period of a qualifying holding company straddles 1 July 2011, it is treated as split on a time basis (*FA 2009, Sch 16, para 15*). The qualifying holding company's accounting period in this instance is any accounting period that begins on or after 1 July 2009 and ends on or before 1 July 2011 (*FA 2009, Sch 16, para 16*).

Transitional rules

13.35   The transitional exempt activities test rules will not apply to a qualifying holding company during the period 1 July 2009 until 1 July 2011, unless the following conditions A and B are met:

Condition A

- At all material times the company was a member of a group with the same ultimate corporate parent. Material times are periods beginning 9 December 2008, and all times during the accounting period in question. The ultimate corporate parent is a company that is neither a direct nor an indirect subsidiary of another company. Government and crown bodies are excluded, and international accounting standards are used for the meaning of group and subsidiary (*FA 2009, Sch 16, para 18*).

Condition B

- For the accounting period in question, the company's non-qualifying gross income (X) does not exceed its non-qualifying gross income (Y), calculated according to the number of reference periods in relation to the company before 1 December 2008, during which the company was an exempt holding company.

    Where:

    - there are three reference periods, Y is equivalent to the greatest of the amounts of the company's non-qualifying gross income in each of those periods;

    - there are two reference periods, Y is equivalent to the greater of the amounts of the company's non-qualifying gross income in each of those periods;

    - there is one reference period, Y is equivalent to the amount of the company's non-qualifying gross income in that period, or

    - there is no reference period, Y is equivalent to the amount of the company's non-qualifying gross income in the period of 12 months ending with 9 December 2008 (*FA 2009, Sch 16, para 17(7)*).

Non qualifying gross income is income which does not assist a CFC to satisfy the existing non-local and superior holding company rules of *ICTA 1988, Sch 25, para 6(3), (4)* or *(4A)*, being the full amount of any income to which a CFC is entitled during an accounting period before any expenses are deducted.

Exemption is available under the existing holding company rules where at least 90% of a holding company's gross income during the accounting period comes from companies that it controls and which, if not themselves holding companies, are engaged in exempt activities. The income that can qualify as part of the 90% for each of the different types of holding company is summarised as follows:

Local holding company

Income from companies it controls which are:

- resident in the territory in which the holding company is resident, and

- are not themselves holding companies or superior holding companies but are engaged in exempt activities or is an exempt trading company.

Holding company

Income from companies it controls which are:

- local holding companies, or

- are not themselves holding companies or superior holding companies, but are engaged in exempt activities or are an exempt trading company.

Superior holding company

- represents qualifying exempt activity income of its subsidiaries, and

- is derived directly from companies which it controls and which are not superior holding companies but are engaged in exempt activities or are an exempt trading company.

Apportionment

13.36   If the number of days in the transitional period varies, then the following formula is applied:

$$Y \times \frac{DX}{DY}$$

where:

- DX is the number of days in the period by reference to which amount X is determined, and

- DY is the number of days in the period by reference to which amount Y is determined.

See **13.35** above for X and Y (*FA 2009, Sch 16, para 17(8)*).

Public quotation condition

13.37   The public quotation condition which existed for accounting periods ended before 6 December 2006 (see **13.31**) was met if the public held at least 35% of the company's voting rights and the shares were dealt with on a recognised stock exchange. The condition was not met if at any time the principal members owned more than 85% of the voting power. A principal member is a member holding 5% or more of the voting power (*ICTA 1988, Sch 25, paras 13–15*).

De minimis exclusion

13.38   The de minimis test excludes a company's chargeable profits of £50,000 or less in a 12-month accounting period from the apportionment requirements *(SI 1998/3081, reg 5)*.

Debt cap reductions

13.39   For accounting periods ended on or after 1 January 2010, upon application to HMRC amounts brought into account in connection with the debt cap can reduce an apportionment. HMRC will grant the application if the amount does not exceed the relevant amount *(ICTA 1988, s 751AA; FA 2009, Sch 16, para 23)*.

Motive test

13.40   Transactions that result in a minimal reduction in UK tax and for which the main purpose was not to achieve a reduction in tax by diversifying profits away from the UK will satisfy the motive test and will not be included in the apportionment calculation *(ICTA 1988, Sch 25, paras 16–19)*.

Territorial exclusion from exemption

13.41   No apportionment is required if the company is situated in one of the excluded countries. See *Pt I* or *II* of the *Excluded Countries Regulations 1998, SI 1998/3081, regs 4, 5*.

Creditable tax and reliefs

13.42   A company can claim set-off of:

- trading losses,

- charges on income,

- non-trading deficits on loan relationships,

- management expenses,

- certain capital allowances, and

- group relief *(ICTA 1988, Sch 26, para 1)*.

Tax suffered but unrelieved in any other way may be offset in the capital gains computation if the shares are later sold *(ICTA 1988, Sch 26, para 1(5))*.

Dividends from controlled foreign companies

13.43   Dividends paid by CFCs to UK companies are assessable to corporation tax. If the dividend is paid out of apportioned profits the apportioned tax paid is treated as underlying tax in respect of the dividend received (*ICTA 1988, Sch 26, para 4*).

Genuine economic activities

13.44   For CFC purposes a genuine economic activity is considered to be carried on if the following three conditions are satisfied throughout the accounting period concerned:

- the controlled foreign company must have a business establishment in the EEA territory;

- there are individuals who are employed by and work for the controlled foreign company in that territory; and

- UK resident company has a relevant interest in the controlled foreign company.

HMRC will remove those profits representing the net economic value attributable to the persons and work undertaken by that EEA business establishment. Net economic value does no include any value which derives directly or indirectly from the reduction or elimination of any liability of any person to any tax or duty imposed under the law of any territory.

A 'business establishment' means premises which are to be occupied with a reasonable degree of permanence and from which the company's business is wholly or mainly carried on (*ICTA 1988, Sch 25, para 7*).

Formal claim procedure

13.45   A company that carries on a genuine activity in another EEA state may make a formal claim to HMRC for some or all of its profits to be exempted from the controlled foreign companies legislation. The claim can be made for an accounting period in which an apportionment would be due.

The application must be made at any time before the normal self-assessment filing date (see **2.10**) and may be amended or withdrawn at any time before it is agreed by HMRC. If HMRC have agreed the application and the company has delivered its tax return, the company has 30 days beginning with the day on which the application is granted to amend that application. If refused, the company has the right of appeal (*ICTA 1988, s 751A* inserted by *FA 2007, Sch 15, para 5*).

HMRC have indicated that the information to be included in applications under *s 751A* is as follows:

1. Name of controlled foreign company (CFC).

2. United Kingdom company's interest in the CFC's share and loan capital (by virtue of *s 749B*).

3. Tax district and reference number of United Kingdom interest holders where known.

4. Territory of residence of the CFC and details of branches including those in the United Kingdom.

5. Place, and for new companies, date of incorporation of the CFC.

6. Confirmation that no other exemption is available to the CFC under the legislation at *s 748*.

7. The other EEA state(s) where the CFC has a business establishment and individuals working for the CFC in the state(s).

8. A copy of the most recent accounts of the CFC (or where these have not yet been drawn up, management accounts or financial projections).

9. Actual or expected equity at the beginning and end of the CFC's accounting period.

10. Details of all investments held by the CFC and actual or projected income from these during the accounting period for which the application is made.

11. Details of all direct or indirect transactions between group affiliates and in particular between the United Kingdom and the CFC. This will include interest on loans (direct or indirect), royalties, payments for services, purchase or sale of goods etc.

12. Full details (including address) of the CFC's business establishment(s), the number of hours, days etc. occupied on the company's business, the size of premises, whether premises are shared, in particular with group affiliates, the amount of rent paid by the CFC etc.

13. Full details of staff working for the CFC in business establishment(s) in EEA states, including details of duties, experience, position of authority and salary.

14. Details of any outsourced business activity.

15. Full details of the business activity undertaken by the CFC. Where there is more than one business activity, details of where each activity is

carried out and which individuals in each territory as detailed above at 13 are involved in carrying out each business activity.

16. Details of sources of funding for the CFC's activities, in particular sources of equity and intra-group borrowing.

17. A computation of the CFC's chargeable profits and creditable tax for the relevant accounting period.

18. The computation of how the specified amount was arrived at and the reasons why it is considered that this amount is a part of the CFC's chargeable profits that represents the net economic value created directly by the work of individuals working for the CFC in another EEA state where the CFC has a business establishment. Include details of the work directly carried out by individuals and how the net economic value to relevant interest holders or other members of the group was arrived at.

19. Provide a computation of the amount by which the creditable tax of the CFC for the relevant accounting period should be reduced and an explanation of why you consider this to be the correct amount on a just and reasonable basis.

Applications, or potential applications under the new rules, should be sent to:

CFC Team,
International CT,
HMRC03C/01,
100 Parliament Street,
London SW1A 2BQ.
For Attn: Mary Sharp, Team Leader
Telephone 020 7147 2656

Note: In considering applications, HMRC may request further information and documentation in relation to the application, though it is thought that the above information should be sufficient in most cases (HMRC Draft Guidance 6 December 2006—*Changes to Controlled Foreign Companies Rules*).

FOREIGN DIVIDENDS

Finance Act 2009 changes

13.46 *Finance Act 2009, Sch 14* has changed the taxation of foreign dividend and distribution receipts. Prior to the *FA 2009* changes, foreign dividends and other distributions received were chargeable to corporation tax, with a credit given for any foreign tax withheld from a dividend. For shareholdings of 10% or more, relief was also given for the underlying foreign tax, being tax charged on the profits out of which the dividend was paid. For full commentary, please refer to *Corporation Tax 2008/09* (Tottel Publishing).

FA 2009 now treats foreign and UK distributions in the same way.

Distributions are generally exempt unless anti-avoidance provisions apply. These changes come into effect for dividend payments on or after 1 July 2009. Where foreign dividends are not exempt, or if the company elects for them not to be exempt, relief for underlying tax may be available.

DISTRIBUTIONS RECEIVED

General provision

13.47   There is a general rule that a company is chargeable to corporation tax on all the distributions that it receives unless the distribution is exempt. The exemption rules depend on whether the recipient company is small or large (*CTA 2009, s 931A*).

Small company

13.48   A company is small if, in that accounting period, it meets the micro or small enterprise criteria, as defined in the Annex to Commission Recommendation 2003/361/EC of 6 May 2003 (see **8.22**). A company is not small if, at any time during the accounting period, it is an open-ended investment company, an authorised unit trust scheme, an insurance company, or a friendly society (*CTA 2009, s 931S*).

SMALL COMPANY EXEMPTION RULES

Exemption

13.49   The dividend received by a small company is exempt if:

- the payer is UK resident or resident of a qualifying territory at the time that the distribution is received; dual residence with a non-qualifying territory is not permitted;

- the distribution does not result from an interest payment in excess of a normal commercial rate of return (see **16.7**);

- in the case of a dividend paid by a non-UK resident, no deduction is available for that dividend under the laws of that foreign jurisdiction; and

- the distribution is not made as part of a scheme that is designed to gain a tax advantage (*CTA 2009, s 931B*).

Qualifying territory

13.50 In general, a qualifying territory is a territory that has a double taxation agreement with the UK, and this agreement contains a non-discrimination provision which broadly ensures that foreign concerns are taxed no less fairly than national concerns. However, this rule is subject to HM Treasury override. A company that is liable to tax under the laws of a territory by reason of its domicile, residence or place of management is resident in that territory. A company is not resident in that territory just because it has income arising or capital situated there (*CTA 2009, s 931C*).

Large company exemption rules

13.51 The dividend received by a large company is exempt if:

- the dividend is of a statutory exempt class (see **13.52** below);
- the distribution does not result from an interest payment in excess of a normal commercial rate of return (see **16.7**); and
- in the case of a dividend paid by a non-UK resident, no deduction is available for that dividend under the laws of that foreign jurisdiction (*CTA 2009, s 931D*).

Statutory exempt dividends

13.52 Classes of dividends that are statutory exempt are:

- distributions paid to a parent company that controls the company making the distribution. Control is defined by reference to the controlled foreign company (CFC) control rules (see **13.30**) (*CTA 2009, s 931E*);
- distributions paid in respect of non-redeemable ordinary shares (*CTA 2009, s 931F*); for the meaning of ordinary shares, see **13.53** below;
- distributions in respect of portfolio holdings, if the recipient holds less than 10% of the holding by reference to share capital, income rights and capital distribution rights on a winding up. The evaluation is made for each class of share held, and shares are not treated as of the same class if the amounts paid up on them (otherwise than by way of premium) are different (*CTA 2009, s 931G*);

- dividends derived from transactions that are not designed to reduce tax (transactions entered into before 1 July 2008 are excluded) (*CTA 2009, s 931H*); or

- dividends in respect of shares not accounted for as liabilities and the loan relationship rules of *CTA 2009, s 521*, because the investing company does not own the share for an unallowable purpose, being the gaining of a tax advantage (transactions entered into before 1 July 2008 are excluded) (*CTA 2009, s 931I*).

Meaning of ordinary and redeemable shares

13.53 Ordinary shares are understood to carry neither present nor future preferential dividends rights nor rights to assets on the company's winding up. Redeemable shares are those that, as a result of their terms of issue or any collateral arrangements, either require redemption or entitle the holder to require redemption, or entitle the issuing company to redeem them (*CTA 2009, s 931U*).

ANTI-AVOIDANCE

General anti-avoidance rules

13.54 Anti-avoidance rules have been introduced to ensure that the exemption rules are not abused. In general, a dividend is not exempt if it artificially falls into an exempt class because it forms part of a scheme or tax advantage scheme. A scheme is defined as any scheme, arrangement or understanding of any kind whatever, whether or not legally enforceable, that involves a single transaction or two or more transactions. A tax advantage scheme is a scheme the main purpose, or one of the main purposes, of which is to obtain a tax advantage, other than a negligible tax advantage (*CTA 2009, s 931V*). A tax advantage is the payment of less UK tax because of a foreign tax credit gain because of artificial arrangements (*ICTA 1988, s 804ZA, Sch 28AB*).

Particular exemption anti-avoidance rules

13.55 As regards the statutory exemption dividends listed in **13.52** above, dividends paid to a parent company under are not exempt if they artificially fall into an exempt class because they form part of a scheme or arrangement and are paid in respect of pre-control profits, ie profits that arose before the company was part of the group. If a dividend is partially paid out of pre-control profits, it is treated as two separate dividends (*CTA 2009, s 931J*).

Distributions paid in respect of non-redeemable ordinary shares are not exempt where the rights obtained under an avoidance scheme are equivalent to the rights of either a preferential shareholder or a holder of a redeemable preference share (*CTA 2009, s 931K*). Distributions paid in respect of portfolio holdings are not exempt if the holding has been manipulated to a smaller holding (*CTA 2009, s 931L*).

Further anti-avoidance rules

13.56   There are further anti-avoidance rules for:

- schemes that yield a return economically equivalent to interest (*CTA 2009, s 931M*);

- situations where a deduction is given in respect of the distribution (*CTA 2009, s 931N*);

- situations where a person connected to the recipient makes a payment or gives up income in return for a distribution (*CTA 2009, s 931O*);

- schemes involving payments not on arm's-length terms, which prevent the supply of goods and services on terms for a reduced payment that is then compensated for by the payment of a dividend (*CTA 2009, s 931P*); or

- schemes that divert trade income whereby a dividend is received by another company in respect of the trading income reduction (*CTA 2009, s 931Q*).

Election that distribution should not be exempt

13.57   A company can elect, within two years of the end of the accounting period in which the distribution is paid, for it to be non-exempt (*CTA 2009, s 931R*). In practice, a company may wish that its taxed dividend be taken into account for the purposes of the CFC acceptable distribution policy (ADP) exemption, in which case it may elect under those provisions for the dividend payment, in whole or in part, to be non-exempt. Also, the company may wish to elect that the dividend be non-exempt if it considers that this could lead to an increased rate of withholding tax or relief for underlying tax.

OVERSEAS DIVIDENDS

Underlying tax

13.58   If the dividend received is not exempt, the company can claim relief for underlying tax. Also, the dividend must have been a bona fide dividend and not designed to reduce tax (*ICTA 1988, s 799*). Underlying tax is the tax on profits out of which the dividend is paid, whereas withholding tax is tax deducted at source from the dividend payment.

Example 13.1

England Ltd, a UK resident company, receives a dividend of £9,000 net of 10% withholding tax, from Overseas Ltd, a foreign company in respect of the accounting period ended 31 March 2010.

Extracts from Overseas Ltd's profit and loss account (converted to sterling) show the following:

	£
Profit before tax	450,000
Provision for corporation tax	90,000
Distributable profits	360,000

Corporation tax paid £140,000.

Computation of underlying tax

	£
Distributable profits	360,000
Foreign tax paid	140,000
	500,000

The effective rate of underlying tax is 28%.

The UK corporation tax is satisfied by the overseas underlying tax and there is no additional corporation tax to pay.

Profits for calculating underlying tax

13.59   The distributable profits for these purposes are the profits shown in the company's accounts drawn up in accordance with the law of the company's home state. No provision is permitted for reserves, impairment losses or contingencies other than as required by the company's home state law. The home state is the country or territory of incorporation or formation (*ICTA*

1988, s 799(5)–(7)). The company must take all reasonable steps to reduce the amount of foreign tax paid (*ICTA 1988, s 795A*).

If a company pays tax in another country on the aggregated profits of itself and other companies as if they were a single entity, for the purposes of calculating credit relief the relevant profits of these companies are regarded as a single aggregate figure in respect of a single company, and the foreign tax paid by the responsible company as if it were paid by that single company. For the purposes of calculating the underlying tax, only the profits of companies that are resident as a matter of fact in the country concerned may be included in the calculations of relevant profits and foreign tax for the deemed single entity (*ICTA 1988, s 803A*). Therefore, dividend resolutions for such a group of companies, specifying the profits from which the dividends are paid, are inappropriate. HMRC will accept dividend resolutions from, or board resolutions of, the paying company specifying the accounting period from which the dividend is paid (HMRC International Manual INTM 164130).

Credit relief: 'mixer cap'

Limit

13.60   The credit relief given is limited to the lower of the overseas tax paid and the UK corporation tax. The following formula is used:

$$(D + U) \times M\%$$

where

D = the dividend,

U = the amount of underlying tax paid overseas, and

M = the UK corporation tax rate when the dividend was paid (*ICTA 1988, s 799(1A)*).

The formula looks back through the paying company to the source of the dividends.

Example 13.2

England Ltd receives two dividends from Overseas Ltd of £9,000 each arising in its accounting period ended 31 March 2010. The dividends are paid out of the foreign company's profits for the years ended 31 December 2009 and 31 December 2010, with respective underlying rates of tax of 28% and 50%. Each net dividend plus withholding tax amounts to £10,000.

Dividend income:

	£	£
Dividend 1: £10,000 + £2,800 underlying tax	12,800	
Dividend 2: £10,000 + £5,000 underlying tax	15,000	
	27,800	
UK corporation tax: £27,800 at 28%		7,784
Less credit		
Dividend 1	2,800	
Dividend 2 (restricted to £15,000 at 28%)	4,200	
		7,000
Corporation tax payable		784

If a company's accounting period straddles 1 April 2008, its rate of corporation tax will be based on the number of days falling into the financial years 2007 and 2008, with the respective rates of 30% and 28% being adjusted accordingly. Dividend income is also apportioned on the same time basis. Credit relief is given at the rate when the dividend was paid or, if there was more than one dividend, at the average rate for the year. Companies are not therefore disadvantaged by a reduction in the main rate of corporation tax from 30% to 28%. The rules have effect for dividends paid on or after 1 April 2008 (*ICTA 1988, s 799(1A); FA 2009, s 57*).

FOREIGN CURRENCY ACCOUNTING

General rules

13.61　In general, foreign profits and losses arising in an accounting period must be converted into sterling at the average exchange rate for that accounting period. If there is only one transaction, an appropriate spot rate should be used for that transaction. If there are a few transactions, a rate derived on a just and reasonable basis from appropriate spot rates for those transactions should be used (*FA 2009, Sch 18, paras 5 and 6; FA 1993, ss 92D and E*).

Special rules apply in circumstances where losses are carried back or forwards and where adjustments are made to the amounts of those losses carried back or forwards. These rules depend on the company's operating currency in each of the two accounting periods. The operating currency is the currency employed in preparing accounts under GAAP. A company's functional currency is the currency that it uses to record its daily transactions.

The commencement date for these rules to apply is 29 December 2007, but the company can elect for 21 July 2009, being the date that *Finance Act 2009* was passed, to be its commencement date, in which case the transitional rules (see **13.66** and **13.67**) do not apply. The election must be made within 30 days from the commencement of the first accounting period beginning on or after 21 July 2009 and is irrecoverable.

Special rules for losses carried back

13.62 Where a loss is carried back under *ICTA 1988, s 393A(1)(b)* (see **9.11–9.15**), or a non trading loan relationship deficit is carried back under *CTA 2009, s 459(1)(b)* (see **11.25**), the following rules apply:

- If the same operating currency is used for the earlier and the later accounting period, the general rule applies (see **13.61**).

- If sterling is the operating currency for the earlier accounting period, but a foreign currency is used for the latter period, the spot rate of exchange for the last day of the earlier accounting period must be used to convert the loss into sterling.

- If different operating currencies are used for the earlier and the later accounting period, neither of which is sterling, the loss must first be translated into the earlier operating currency using the spot rate of exchange for the last day of the earlier accounting period. The loss is then converted into sterling at the same rate as is used for the earlier profits against which the loss is to be set. The earlier profits are translated according to the general rule; see **13.61** (*FA 2009, Sch 18, para 5; FA 1993, s 92DA*).

Adjustment of sterling losses carried back amounts

13.63 Subject to the three conditions below being met, if there is an adjustment to the sterling loss that is carried back, the loss must first be translated into the earlier operating currency by applying the spot rate of exchange for the last day of the earlier accounting period. The loss is then converted into sterling at the same rate as is used for the earlier profits against which the loss is to be set. The earlier profits are translated according to the general rule (see **13.61**).

The three conditions that must be met are:

- the company is UK resident and prepares accounts in accordance with GAAP for a period of account in sterling, or in a foreign currency but identifies sterling as its functional currency;

- the loss computed under GAAP is a carried back amount; and

- the operating currency of the earlier accounting period is not sterling (*FA 2009, Sch 18, para 5*; *FA 1993, s 92DC*).

Special rules for losses carried forward

13.64   Where a loss is carried forward under *ICTA 1988, s 392A(2)* or *(3)* for a UK property business (see **9.36**), or under *s 392B(1)(b)* for a foreign property business (see **9.37**), or under *s 393(1)* from a trade (see **9.2**), or under *s 396(1)* losses from miscellaneous transactions, or a non-trading loan relationship deficit is carried forward under *CTA 2009, s 457(3)* (see **11.26**), or a non-trading loss on an intangible fixed asset is carried forward under *CTA 2009, s 753(3)*, or management expenses are carried forward under *CTA 2009, s 1223*, the following rules apply:

- If the same operating currency is used for the earlier and the later accounting period, the general rule applies (see **13.61**).

- If sterling is the operating currency for the later accounting period, but another currency is used for the earlier period, the spot rate of exchange for the first day of the later accounting period must be used to convert the loss into sterling.

- If different operating currencies are used for the earlier and for the later accounting period, neither of which is sterling, the loss must first be translated into the earlier operating currency by applying the spot rate of exchange for the first day of the earlier accounting period. The loss is then converted into sterling at the same rate as is used for the later profits against which the loss is to be set. The later profits are translated according to the general rule; see **13.61** (*FA 2009, Sch 18, para 5*; *FA 1993, s 92DB*).

Adjustment of sterling losses carried forward amounts

13.65   Subject to the three conditions below being met, if there is an adjustment to the sterling loss that is carried forward, the loss must first be translated into the later operating currency by applying the spot rate of exchange for the first day of the later accounting period. The loss is then converted into sterling at the same rate as is used for the later profits against which the loss is to be set. The later profits are translated according to the general rule (see **13.61**).

The three conditions that must be met are:

- the company is UK resident and prepares accounts in accordance with GAAP for a period of account in sterling, or in a foreign currency but identifies sterling as its functional currency;

- the loss computed under GAAP is a carried forward amount; and

- the operating currency of the earlier accounting period is not sterling (*FA 2009, Sch 18, para 5; FA 1993, s 92DD*).

Transitional rules for losses carried back

13.66   The general rule (see **13.61**) is used to convert a loss to sterling that is to be carried back to an accounting period which contains the commencement date (*FA 2009, Sch 18, para 8*). A sterling loss carried back to a pre-commencement period cannot be adjusted (*FA 2009, Sch 18, para 10*).

Transitional rules for losses carried forward

13.67   If a loss that is to be carried forward arises in an accounting period beginning before the commencement date, that loss is converted to sterling by applying the following steps:

Step 1

- translate the loss into its sterling equivalent by reference to the appropriate exchange rate;

Step 2

- translate the sterling equivalent as calculated in *Step 1* to the original currency by reference to the spot rate of exchange for the first day of the first accounting period of the company beginning on or after the commencement date;

Step 3

- translate the loss as translated in *Step 2* into its sterling equivalent in accordance with the applicable conversion rule as detailed in **13.68** below.

(*FA 2009, Sch 18, para 9*)

Conversion rules

13.68

- If the same operating currency is used for the earlier and the later accounting period, the general rule applies (see **13.61**).

- If sterling is the operating currency for the later accounting period, but another currency is used for the earlier period, the spot rate of exchange for the first day of the later accounting period must be used to convert the loss into sterling.

- If different operating currencies are used for the earlier and for the later accounting period, neither of which is sterling, the loss must first be translated into the later operating currency by applying the spot rate of exchange for the first day of the later accounting period. The loss is then converted into sterling at the same rate as is used for the later profits against which the loss is to be set. The later profits are translated according to the general rule; see **13.61** (*FA 2009, Sch 18, para 9*).

- If an adjustment to the sterling loss carried forward is required, the rules detailed in **13.65** apply (*FA 2009, Sch 18, para 11*).

Chapter 14

Transfer pricing

INTRODUCTION

14.1　The transfer pricing modus operandi dictates that transactions between connected parties should be treated for tax purposes as if the same transactions had taken place between unconnected parties. The 'arm's-length principle' should apply. Modern business these days is transacted globally with many business partners and associates. Groups are able to pick the country or regime that best suits their business in order to minimise their corporation tax liabilities. To prevent any unfairness taxation legislation requires that the 'arm's-length principle' be applied to all relevant transactions. The UK transfer pricing rules are included in *ICTA 1988, s 770A, Sch 28AA*. It is more than likely that other countries will have their own comparable domestic legislation. For countries that have a double taxation treaty it is included in the OECD Model Tax Convention on Income and on Capital (OECD Model Treaty), Art 9.

For periods beginning 1 April 2004 inter-company UK trading is brought within the ambit of transfer pricing.

THE UK TRANSFER PRICING RULES

14.2　The rules apply for accounting periods ending on or after 1 July 1999. The transfer pricing rules cover:

- the purchase and sale of goods,
- the provision of management and other services,
- rents and hire charges,
- transfers of intangible property, such as trademarks, patents and know-how,
- sharing of expertise, business contacts, supply systems, etc,
- provision of finance, and other financial arrangements, and
- interest.

The legislation aims to mitigate the loss of tax arising from non-arm's-length pricing; irrespective of a tax motive.

Application of transfer pricing

14.3   Transfer pricing rules apply for accounting periods ending on or after 1 July 1999 if there is a provision by means of a transaction or a series of transactions between any two companies under common control where:

- one of the affected persons was directly or indirectly participating in the management, control or capital of the other, or

- the same person or persons was or were directly or indirectly participating in the management, control or capital of each of the affected persons.

The controlling person may be an individual.

The provision made is different to an arm's-length provision that would be made between independent parties and gives one of the two affected parties a UK taxation benefit (*ICTA 1988, Sch 28AA, para 1*). An adjustment must be made to the taxable profits of the person or persons enjoying the tax advantage.

These rules also apply to securities issued by one company to another for accounting periods beginning after 31 March 2004 (*ICTA 1988, Sch 28AA, paras 1A, 1B*).

Control

14.4   Control is defined by *ICTA 1988, s 840* as the power to secure that the company's affairs are conducted in accordance with a person's wishes. The powers so recognised are voting power, power given by the Articles of Association and the actual ability of a person to direct the affairs of the company in the absence of the visible signs of such rights.

Indirect participation examines the following issues.

A person participates indirectly in another entity if:

- he would be participating directly had certain rights and powers been attributed to him, or

- he is one of the major participants in the other entity.

The rights and powers that can be attributed are those:

- which the potential participant is entitled to acquire at a future date,
- exercisable by other persons on behalf of the potential participant or under his direction or for his benefit and
- of connected persons.

A person is a major participant in a company or partnership if the participant and another person together have a 40% interest therein thus creating a joint venture (*ICTA 1988, Sch 28AA, para 4(7)*).

Transfer pricing only applies to transactions between at least one of the joint venture parties and the joint venture itself and not between the two joint venturers unless they are under common control.

Corporation tax self-assessment

14.5   Transfer pricing is within the self-assessment regime. It closely follows the OECD Model Treaty, Art 9. From 1 April 2004, transactions between UK entities are included within the transfer pricing rules (previously, only transactions between foreign entities and UK entities were included). Also from 1 April 2004 small and medium-sized enterprises and dormant companies are excluded from the legislation.

Companies are required to include the adjustment to profits within their own self-assessment.

The transaction

14.6   The basic pricing rule follows the OECD Model Tax Convention (*ICTA 1988, Sch 28AA, para 2*). The meaning of transactions is extremely wide and includes binding and unbinding arrangements, understandings and mutual practices. A series of transactions is considered to be a sequence in any order that is in connection with a single arrangement (*ICTA 1988, Sch 28AA, para 3*). In comparing the actual provision with the arm's-length provision it is necessary to look at all of the terms and conditions of the transactions in question and to adjust them to arm's-length terms if necessary.

A third party can be involved in a series of transactions. Interest payments to third parties under finance arrangements guaranteed by related companies.

A potential advantage arises from a non-arm's-length price, if, as a result, taxable profits are reduced, or losses together with expenses of management or group relief are increased. The transfer pricing adjustment may only increase profits or reduce losses (*ICTA 1988, Sch 28AA, para 5*).

SMALL AND MEDIUM-SIZED ENTERPRISES

Exemption

14.7   In this context SMEs are defined according to the European Commission Recommendation 2003/361/EC. They are exempt from the basic transfer pricing except in the following circumstances:

- where the company irrevocably elects to disapply the provision in relation to a chargeable period or

- where the company enters into transactions with a company resident in a territory with which the UK does not have a tax treaty containing a suitable non-discrimination clause (*ICTA 1988, Sch 28AA, para 5B*).

- Alternatively, HMRC may issue the company with a transfer pricing notice for that chargeable period (*ICTA 1988, Sch 28AA, para 5C(1)*).

If an SME carries on activities with overseas associates it must indicate on the front of the return if it qualifies for an SME exemption. This will not be possible if the company transacts business in a country with which the UK does not have a tax treaty with a suitable non discrimination clause. See **14.12**.

Definition

14.8   The SME definition follows that given by the European Commission Recommendation (2003/361/EC). The definition and the User Guide can be viewed on http://ec.europa.eu.int/comm/enterprise/enterprise_policy/sme_definition/index_en.htm

The definition not only applies to companies but to any entity engaged in an economic activity, irrespective of its legal form and includes entities subject to income tax as well as corporation tax.

An entity qualifies as either small or medium if it meets the staff headcount ceiling for that class and either one or both of the following financial limits.

	Maximum number of staff	And less than one of the following limits:	
		Annual turnover	Balance sheet total
Small enterprise	50	£10 million	£10 million
Medium enterprise	250	£50 million	£43 million

This test is made and determined solely by reference to the period for which a return is being made.

Staff includes employees, persons seconded to work for a business, owner managers and partners; proportioned accordingly to the amount of time that they work.

Turnover and balance sheet totals are net of VAT and otherwise have their ordinary meaning for accounting purposes. Balance sheet total means total gross assets without any deduction for liabilities.

Conversion to sterling should be made at the average exchange rate for the period of account whose profit is being computed or the exchange rate on the date the account was drawn up if this produces a fairer result.

As with any of the thresholds, companies close to the limit should not rely on changes to the exchange rate but should plan in advance to meet the requirements (if any) which changing designation requires.

If the entity is a member or a group or has an associated entity the limits are applied to the whole group. For this purpose the company is said to have linked or partnership enterprises (HMRC International Manual INTM 432112).

Linked enterprises

14.9   A linked enterprise is an enterprise which has the right either directly or indirectly to control the affairs of another enterprise. Control can be by shareholding, voting rights or contractual rights.

In order to ascertain which is the dominant linked company the following is taken into consideration:

- majority of the shareholders or members' voting rights in another enterprise;

- the right to appoint or remove a majority of the members of the administrative, management or supervisory body of another enterprise;

- the right to exercise a dominant influence over another enterprise pursuant to a contract entered into with that enterprise or to a provision in its memorandum or articles of association.

The data for all linked companies and partnership companies must be aggregated to ascertain whether the SME limits have been exceeded.

Partnership enterprises

14.10   A partnership enterprise is one that holds 25% or more of the capital or voting rights of another company but is not a linked company. Where linked enterprises jointly hold rights these must be aggregated to see if the 25% threshold has been passed.

Excluded holdings

14.11   Holdings and investments by the following are ignored for the purposes of aggregation: public investment corporations, venture capital companies, individuals or groups of individuals with a regular venture capital investment activity who invest equity capital in unquoted businesses ('business angels'), provided the total investment of those business angels in the same enterprise is less than €1,250,000; universities or non-profit research centres; institutional investors, including regional development funds; autonomous local authorities with an annual budget of less than €10m and fewer than 5,000 inhabitants.

The rights of a person in office as a liquidator or administrator are not to be taken into account when considering partnership or linked enterprises (HMRC International Manual INTM 432112). Dormant companies are excluded (*ICTA 1988, Sch 28AA, para 5A*) but there is the possibility that the party to the transaction may remain within transfer pricing (HMRC International Manual INTM 432114).

Appropriate non-discrimination clause

14.12   With effect from 1 April 2004, small and medium-sized companies may be exempted from the transfer pricing rules. The exemption does not apply where a business has transactions with or provisions that include a related business in a territory with which the UK does not have a double tax treaty with an appropriate non-discrimination article. Such transactions remain subject to the transfer pricing rules.

An appropriate non-discrimination article is one that ensures that the nationals of a contracting state may not be less favourably treated in the other contracting state than nationals of that latter state in the same circumstances (in particular with respect to residence).

HMRC regard the following double taxation treaties as containing an appropriate non-discrimination article as at 1 April 2004 (except where stated otherwise):

Argentina	Luxembourg
Australia	Macedonia
Austria	Malaysia
Azerbaijan	Malta
Bangladesh	Mauritius
Barbados	Mexico
Belarus	Mongolia
Belgium	Morocco
Bolivia	Myanmar
Bosnia-Herzegovina	Namibia
Botswana	Netherlands
Bulgaria	New Zealand
Canada	Nigeria
Chile (wef 21/12/2004)	Norway
China	Oman
Croatia	Pakistan
Cyprus	Papua New Guinea
Czech Republic	Philippines
Denmark	Poland
Egypt	Portugal
Estonia	Reunion
Falkland Islands	Romania
Fiji	Russian Federation
Finland	Serbia and Montenegro
France	Singapore
Gambia	Slovak Republic
Georgia	Slovenia
Germany	South Africa
Ghana	Spain
Greece	Sri Lanka
Guyana	Sudan
Hungary	Swaziland
Iceland	Sweden
India	Switzerland
Indonesia	Taiwan
Ireland	Tajikistan
Israel	Thailand

Italy	Trinidad & Tobago
Ivory Coast	Tunisia
Jamaica	Turkey
Japan	Turkmenistan
Jordan	Uganda
Kazakhstan	Ukraine
Kenya	USA
Korea	Uzbekistan
Kuwait	Venezuela
Latvia	Vietnam
Lesotho	Zambia
Lithuania	Zimbabwe

The Treasury has the power to make regulations adding to the list of territories that qualify even if the double taxation treaty in question does not contain an appropriate non-discrimination article, or to exclude territories even if the treaty in question does contain such an article (HMRC International Manual INTM 432112).

Election to remain subject to transfer pricing rules

14.13   There may be occasions where a business wishes to apply transfer pricing rules even though it would qualify for exemption. A business can elect that the exemption will not apply. An election can be made for a specified chargeable period and will cover all transactions or provisions made in that period. It will be irrevocable.

A pre-existing dormant company

14.14   A dormant company that was dormant for an accounting period ending on 31 March 2004, or for the whole of the three months prior to 1 April 2004, is exempt from transfer pricing for accounting periods commencing on or after 1 April 2004 as long as it remains dormant. If it engages in any business activity it will lose its exemption (*ICTA 1988, Sch 28AA, para 5A*).

Compensating relief

14.15   Where transactions take place between two UK taxpayers and a transfer pricing adjustment is made to the corporation tax return of one taxpayer, the other party may claim compensating relief in its corporation tax return in order to prevent profits being taxed twice (*ICTA 1988, Sch 28AA, para 6*). The claimant company is required to indicate on the front of CT600 if a compensating adjustment has been claimed.

This may bring about other adjustments if the effects are worked through, for example, to the double tax credit if double taxation is involved (*ICTA 1988, Sch 28AA, para 7*).

Balancing payments

14.16   If the claimant company makes a payment to the tax advantage company up to the amount of the compensating relief this is without any tax effect (*ICTA 1988, Sch 28AA, para 7A*).

Transfer pricing does not apply to FOREX or to financial instrument legislation.

Other provisions deal with transactions not at arm's length in these cases (*CTA 2009, s 694*), but transfer pricing rules apply to sales of oil and gas produced by a company in which the buyer and linked companies have an interest of 20% or more (*ICTA 1988, Sch 28AA, para 9*).

Appeal hearings

14.17   Appeal hearings are heard by the First-tier Tribunal (*ICTA 1988, Sch 28AA, para 12*).

Capital allowances and chargeable gains

14.18   The transfer pricing rules do not apply to capital allowances (including balancing charges), chargeable gains or allowable capital losses (*ICTA 1988, Sch 28AA, para 13*).

Matching loans and derivatives

14.19   A corporate group structure may assist with the external borrowing facilities for the individual group members. Further advantage may be taken of the group structure by one group member taking out a foreign currency loan to match a non-monetary asset acquired by another group member. The loan may then be further lent to the asset acquiring company interest-free. In addition, the company may enter into a forward exchange contract to cover the forward exchange risk. From 1 April 2004 no transfer pricing adjustment is required for foreign exchange gains and losses on 'matching' loans (*CTA*

2009, s 694(8)). However, from 22 March 2006 artificial losses created by contrived arrangements were disallowed (*Loan Relationships and Derivative Contracts (Disregard and Bringing into Account of Profits and Losses) Regulations 2006, SI 2006/843, reg 5* and *Loan Relationships and Derivative Contracts (Disregard and Bringing into Account of Profits and Losses) (Amendment) Regulations 2006, SI 2006/936, reg 5*).

Interest-free loans

14.20   Under the transfer pricing regulations an interest-free loan between related parties will attract a tax charge on the lender (*ICTA 1988, Sch 28AA, para 1*) and a compensating adjustment for the ultimate borrower (*ICTA 1988, Sch 28AA, para 6*). The borrowing capacity of a UK company is assessed in isolation without regard to the borrowing capacity of the whole group. This also applies where a guarantee is made by a fellow group company. Any adjustment will be met by a compensating adjustment (HMRC International Manual INTM 561000).The foreign exchange element of these adjustments is ignored for transfer pricing purposes (*CTA 2009, s 694(2)*).

Where asset backed matching loans are involved, the company with the debtor loan relationship would normally follow SSAP 20 and take the foreign exchange gains and losses on both the asset and the matching loan to reserves. The company with the creditor loan relationship will record foreign exchange gains and losses on the loan to the group company and the loan from a third party (external to the group) in its loans in its profit and loss account.

Foreign exchange gains and losses of the debtor loan relationship company are excluded from taxable income for corporation tax purposes, where they can be matched against gains and losses from an asset (*CTA 2009, s 328(3)*). *Loan Relationships and Derivative Contracts (Disregard and Bringing into Account of Profits and Losses) Regulations 2004, SI 2004/3256, reg 3*, from 1 January 2005 to 22 March 2006, will apply to disregard such exchange differences. Where an arm's length adjustment is required, only the arm's-length element will become chargeable. If the company would not have been able to borrow at all in an arm's-length situation no amount of the foreign exchange gain or loss will be taxable.

Foreign exchange gains and losses of the creditor loan relationship are brought to account immediately through the profit and loss account (*CTA 2009, s 328)*).

Loans on which interest is charged

14.21   If interest is charged on an intra-group loan the tax treatment for the company with the debtor loan relationship is exactly the same. This is because the effect of the matching rules is to disregard the foreign exchange gain or loss arising.

The company with a non-arm's-length creditor loan relationship that receives a less than arm's-length amount of interest is in the same position as if no interest had been charged on the loan.

If the amount of interest receivable on the loan is more than an arm's-length amount the non-arm's-length amount of the foreign exchange gain or loss is disregarded. If a group company acts as guarantor it can make a compensating adjustment claim (*ICTA 1988, Sch 28AA, para 6D*).

Otherwise the result is that the creditor does not have a symmetrical position as far as its foreign exchange gains and losses on its lending and borrowing are concerned.

Currency contracts

14.22   In general the foreign exchange gains and losses on 'matching' currency contracts are also disregarded for transfer pricing purposes (*CTA 2009, s 447*).

However, transfer pricing rules will apply to premium receipts and to non-arm's-length interest payments. Arrangements to assign, terminate or vary a currency contract may also fall within the transfer pricing conditions. *FA 2002, Sch 26, para 27* applies to tax the amount of the gain that would have been taxed had an arm's-length rate applied.

SELF-ASSESSMENT

14.23   There are no supplementary pages to a tax return, which relate to transfer pricing; businesses make computational adjustments in their returns in cases where transactions as recorded in their accounts are not at arm's length. A business (as in **14.13**) wishing to make an election to remain subject to transfer pricing rules should do so as part of its computation of taxable income in its return.

Companies are required to make tax returns in accordance with the arm's-length principle. If a company submits a fraudulent or negligent return (see **Chapter 2**) a tax-related penalty may be charged (*ICTA 1988, Sch 18, para 20*). The maximum penalty is the tax lost. A Revenue officer authorised by HMRC has the power to determine a penalty at any amount he considers appropriate (*TMA 1970, s 100(1)*).

Such a penalty can ensue if a company fails to comply with the transfer pricing requirements. This is the case if the company had been negligent.

Negligence must be judged on its own facts and merits, with the guiding principle being that a company will not have been negligent if it has done what 'a reasonable person would do'. Where a company can show that it has made an honest and reasonable attempt to comply with the legislation, there will be no penalty even if there is an adjustment. Indeed, the onus will be on HMRC in this area, as it is more generally, to show that there has been fraudulent or negligent conduct by the taxpayer before any penalty can be charged.

There is, therefore, an obligation on taxpayers to do what a reasonable person would to ensure that their returns are made in accordance with the arm's-length principle. This would involve, but not be limited to:

- using their commercial knowledge and judgment to make arrangements and set prices, which conform to the arm's-length standard (or to make computational adjustments in their returns where they do not);

- being able to show (for example, by means of good quality documentation) that they made an honest and reasonable attempt to comply with the arm's-length standard and with the legislation; and

- seeking professional help where they know they need it.

Taxpayers should document what they do to the extent necessary to enable them to sustain the arm's-length nature of their arrangements and prices in any discussions with HMRC. The documentation will include the following:

- the relevant commercial or financial relations falling within the scope of the new legislation;

- the nature and terms (including prices) of relevant transactions (including transactions which form a series, and any relevant offsetting transactions). Transactions which are clearly in one family (eg regular purchases made by a distributor throughout a return period of the same or similar products for resale) may be aggregated, provided any significant changes during the period in the nature or terms of the transactions are recorded;

- the method or methods by which the nature and terms of relevant transactions were arrived at, including any study of comparables and any functional analysis undertaken;

- how that method has resulted in arm's-length terms etc or, where it has not, what computational adjustment is required and how it has been calculated. This will usually include an analysis of market data or other information on third party comparables;

- the terms of relevant commercial arrangements with both third party and affiliated customers. These will include commercial agreements (eg service or distribution contracts, loan agreements), and any budgets, forecasts or other papers containing information relied on in arriving at arm's-length terms etc or in calculating any adjustment made in order to satisfy the requirements of the new transfer pricing legislation.

In order to be adequate the documentation must show that the company had good grounds for believing their arrangements and prices were in accordance with the arm's-length principle.

HMRC have provided the following examples for illustration purposes.

Example 14.1

A company, whose business is to provide services to other group members, charges out its services at cost plus 5%. 5% accords with a policy in place throughout the group, and is documented in correspondence involving members of the main Board, the Finance Directorate, and the Tax Department; and in a group agreement. It is established in discussion with HMRC that the arm's-length range for the services in question is 10%–15%. The company cannot show from its records that it even considered whether its own 5% rate complied with the arm's-length principle. HMRC would view any tax lost as a result of the undercharge as having been lost through negligence, and would wish to consider a penalty.

Example 14.2

As Example 14.1, except that in the correspondence it is asserted several times that the group's policy is to comply with the arm's-length standard, and that 5% is an arm's-length price. However, the company is unable to bring forward any convincing evidence in support of its assertions, while HMRC are able to show that an arm's-length price would be in the 10%–15% range. HMRC would wish to consider a penalty.

Example 14.3

As Example 14.1, except that the company charges out at cost plus 8%, and can show that at the time the rate was set it had run a check of available

438

industry data, and had found what it considered to be a comparable uncontrolled price supporting the 8% rate. In discussion with HMRC, the company agrees that the comparable it used was flawed, and that the weight of evidence points towards a price in the 10%–15% range. HMRC accept that the company had made an honest and reasonable attempt to comply with the arm's-length principle. There is an adjustment but no penalty.

Example 14.4

A company, whose business is to provide services to other group members, charges at cost plus 5%. As in Example 14.1, 5% accords with a policy in place throughout the group, and is documented in correspondence and a group agreement. The company includes an adjustment in its computation, bringing the effective rate of charge-out up to 8%. It did so after searching available industry data for possible comparable uncontrolled prices, this search being made at the time the tax computation was being prepared. As with Example 14.3, the company sees this information as supporting its opinion that 8% accorded with the arm's-length principle, but it later agrees that the price should have fallen in the 10%–15% range. Once again, HMRC accept that the company had made an honest and reasonable attempt to comply with the arm's-length principle, and there is an adjustment but no penalty.

14.24   When considering the abatement in relation to the size and gravity of the failure, HMRC will take into account the absolute size of the adjustment; the size of the adjustment relative to the turnover and profitability of the business against which the adjustment is being made; and where this is possible, the size of the adjustment in relation to the volume and value of the related party transactions giving rise to the adjustment (Tax Bulletins, Issue 37 (October 1998) and Issue 38 (December 1998)).

Record keeping

14.25   The record keeping in **14.23** above was suggested in 1998. Under self-assessment, the requirement is for companies to keep records to support its transfer pricing policy, its arm's-length justification policy and the adjustments made to the corporation tax return. The records kept will vary to each country and to each particular company's circumstances. General guidance is given in Chapter V of the OECD Transfer Pricing Guidelines.

The self-assessment penalties will ensue upon the company if the company were unable to supply supporting records. As a transitional measure, businesses were relieved from penalty exposure for failure to provide 'arm's-length evidence for the two years ended 31 March 2006.

As regards evidence to support an arm's-length policy, HMRC have now suggested the following:

- Associated businesses should be identified and the form of association.

- Description of business activity in which transactions took place.

- Details of contractual relationship and understanding between the parties involved.

- Description and justification for method used to establish the arm's-length result.

- Evidence need not be provided where companies do not fall within the UK transfer pricing rules.

- Useful to provide supporting information regarding the company's general strategy.

- English translations of documentation should also be given.

The European Commission has adopted a proposal for a Code of Conduct to standardise the documentation that multinationals must provide to tax authorities on their pricing of cross-border intra-group transactions. The documentation would consist of two main parts namely a 'blueprint' master file of the transfer pricing system together with business information and standardised documents for intra-group transactions.

It is expected that Member States would implement the Code by legislating for it in national law or through administrative guidelines. Until then companies must comply with the national documentation requirement IP/05/1403 and MEMO/05/414.

Enquiries

14.26 An enquiry would follow normal HMRC enquiry procedures. Details are to be found in HMRC International Manual INTM 434020 onwards. In particular, HMRC would seek evidence to support the arm's-length policy. Additional guidance as to the conduct of the enquiry is given in HMRC Guidance Notes 10 July 2008 – Guidance for the conduct of transfer pricing enquiries. Here, HMRC explain that cases are normally to be settled within 18 months and possibly 36 months for more complex cases. Although aimed at transfer pricing, similar procedures will be adopted in determining the attribution of a profit to a permanent establishment. All enquiries will commence with a risk assessment, which is based on the quantum risk, the behaviour risk and the transaction risk of the matters that are being enquired into. Following the risk assessment, HMRC may decide to investigate further and develop a business case, whereupon a thorough enquiry into the nature of the transactions, their treatment and the supporting information will take place. HMRC will specify the transactions that are subject to the enquiry.

Example 14.5

A UK company is engaged to provide research and development (R&D) activities on behalf of its overseas affiliate. The group employs a cost-plus pricing method under which the overseas affiliate pays the UK company a sum consisting of the UK company's costs plus a mark-up of 10%. This is characterised in the UK company's transfer pricing documentation as a 'contract research arrangement'.

HMRC's criteria and the areas for enquiry are as follows:

Criterion	*Area of enquiry*
1. The transactions subject to the enquiry.	The provision of research and development facilities by the UK company to the overseas affiliate.
2. The aspect(s) of the transaction and its pricing to be tested	HMRC will test whether cost-plus is an appropriate method to set the pricing between the UK company and its overseas affiliate.
3. The criteria by which the transaction is to be tested	HMRC will consider whether the actual functions carried out by the UK company are consistent with their respective characterisations as low-risk research provider and research contractor.
4. What HMRC need to understand in order to achieve this.	How decisions are made concerning the identification and prioritisation of research projects, who makes these decisions and where the people making them are located.
	The process for reviewing and assessing R&D projects. Who is involved in this and where are they located.
	The ownership of any value, including the intellectual property, arising from the R&D.
	Whether the UK company uses the intellectual property it created in its wider range.

Thin capitalisation

14.27   Where a UK group member company borrows more from an internal or external lender than it would do if it were not part of a group, it is said to be thinly capitalised. Interest payments are deductible from taxable profits but dividend payments are not so deductible. Companies who structure their investments in subsidiaries by means of inordinate large loans may also fall within the thin capitalisation rules.

The result is that the admissible interest deduction from assessable profits is restricted to an arm's-length amount. All parts of the borrowing arrangement will be examined to ascertain if thin capitalisation is involved including guarantees and the like. See **10.23–10.50** regarding the introduction of the Debt cap rules.

Thin capitalisation falls within the transfer pricing regime (*ICTA 1988, Sch 28AA*). Until 1 April 2004 it was dealt with by treating the amount as a dividend (*ICTA 1988, s 209(2)(da)*). *ICTA 1988, s 209(2)(da)* only applied where there was a 75% overseas relationship (together with effective 51% subsidiaries) between borrower and lender, whereas transfer pricing applies to all UK and overseas relationships with no 75% demarcation.

Payments of interest abroad

14.28   Subject to any existing double taxation agreement, payments of annual interest to an overseas lender are made net of withholding tax. The rate of withholding tax is linked to the basic rate of income tax (HMRC International Manual INTM 542010) (*ICTA 1988, s 349(2)*). Assessments can be raised to recover any outstanding withholding tax together with any accrued interest (*ICTA 1988, Sch 16; TMA 1970, s 87*).

Advance pricing agreement (APA)

14.29   A company with more complex affairs can enter into an APA with HMRC (*FA 1999, s 85*). APAs are written agreements between a taxpayer and HMRC, which determine a method for resolving intricate transfer pricing issues in advance of a return being made. If the terms of the arrangement are complied with, the company can be assured that HMRC will accept those transfer issues covered by the agreement.

The matters that can be covered include the determination of:

- the arm's-length provision for the purposes of *ICTA 1988, Sch 28AA, s 770A*;

- the profits attributable to a branch or agency through which a trade is carried on in the UK; and

- the amount of any income arising outside the UK and attributable to the overseas branch of a UK company.

HMRC recommend bilateral agreements rather than unilateral agreements. The APA will be operative for a specified number of years from the date of entry into force as set out in the agreement. The term is normally for a minimum of three, and a maximum of five, years. The formal submission of an APA request should normally be made no later than six months before the start of the first chargeable period to be covered by the APA. The APA process will typically comprise four stages: expression of interest, formal submission of application for clarification, evaluation, and agreement. In essence, when agreed if prices are set in accordance with the APA they will satisfy the transfer pricing regulations. SP 3/99 gives further details.

Advance thin capitalisation agreements (ATCA)

14.30   The UK thin capitalisation rules are aimed at insuring that investors do not finance their UK sub-groups with large sums of debt that give rise to excessive interest deductions, but maintain an arm's-length standard by reference to the amount and the terms of their debt (see **14.27**).

Transactions with countries with a double taxation treaty may be agreed in advance with HMRC in accordance with the treaty (HMRC International Manual INTM 574000). For transactions with countries with which there is no double tax treaty, the company may enter into an advance thin capitalisation agreement (ATCA) under the APA legislation (*FA 1999, s 85*). (HMRC Statement of Practice 04/07). See also Advance Thin Capitalisation Agreements – frequently asked questions. HMRC Brief 1/2009.

Chapter 15

Reconstructions and amalgamations

BUYING AND SELLING A COMPANY

Buying a company

15.1   Purchase of another company's share capital requires careful consideration. Depending upon the percentage acquired, the new acquisition will be a subsidiary or an investment for the acquiree. All taxation aspects of the transaction must be considered, not only corporation tax but also VAT and stamp duty land tax (for VAT, see *VAT 2009/10* (Bloomsbury Professional)).

Asset purchase

15.2   Alternatively the company may wish to consider an asset purchase. In this case the acquired company is absorbed into the existing company rather than being maintained as a separate corporate unit. Apart from the normal funding and synergy issues the acquiring company will need to consider a variety of issues affecting the taxation impact of the transaction.

The purchased tangible and intangible assets will be included within the company's fixed assets as shown on the balance sheet. In particular, the excess of the purchase price of the assets acquired over the price paid: namely the goodwill will also be shown on the balance sheet. This in turn will form an intangible asset for which an annual tax-deductible write down is available (see **7.10**).

The company will also be able to utilise the newly acquired asset in a roll-over relief claim for fixed assets (see **20.6**) and intangible assets (see **7.21**). The assets are also established at a high base cost for capital gains tax purposes, because the gain to date is assessed on the predecessor company.

The acquisition of stock will be a deduction from trading profits. Importantly the purchaser avoids taking over any of the vendor's liabilities.

For capital allowances purposes the assets in question are disposed of by the vendor; balancing charges and allowances arising and acquired by the successor. If the companies are connected within the definition given by *ICTA 1988, s 839* then *ICTA 1988, s 343* may apply as described later in this chapter. If *s 343* does not apply both companies may elect for the assets to be transferred at tax written-down value. If this occurs during an accounting period the allowances are proportioned pro-rata (*CAA 2001, ss 266, 569*).

The purchaser and the vendor may wish to make use of the provisions of *CAA 2001, s 198*, which allows the parties to jointly elect that sale proceeds relating to a building inclusive of fixtures be allocated as agreed by the parties. The value must not be more than cost (*CAA 2001, s 198*).

Acquisition finance costs

15.3   Regardless of a share or asset purchase, the company will invariably require the use of borrowed funds to finance the acquisition. Any interest or finance costs charged in acquiring a company are non-trading debits within the loan relationship regime. They are not costs in connection with the trade (see **11.29** for relief for costs of obtaining loan finance).

Selling a company

15.4   The 'reversed' considerations to acquiring a company must be considered when selling a company. If the assets are to be sold a chargeable gain may arise within the company. The company may be cash-rich, which then presents a problem for cash extraction. If the company is owned by individual investors they will need to consider their own capital gains position if the company is to be wound up or sold (see *Capital Gains Tax 2009/10* (Bloomsbury Professional)). In practical terms the sale may be negotiated to make use of the *s 343* relief as described in **15.12** onwards.

If shares are to be sold and another company owns the company it may be able to make use of the substantial shareholdings exemption, see **12.36–12. 40**. If a company cannot make use of the substantial shareholdings exemption in order to reduce the chargeable gain on sale the investor company may wish to consider the payment of a pre-sale dividend by the investee company. This in effect reduces the sale price but results in tax-free funds being received by the investor company; hence the company's sale price must be renegotiated accordingly. Under the *Companies Act* a pre-sale dividend is permitted financial assistance for the company's purchase of its own shares (*CA 2006, s 681(2)(a)*). In this respect it is necessary to consider the capital gains anti-avoidance provisions (see **20.24–20.31** re value shifting).

COMPANY RECONSTRUCTIONS AND AMALGAMATIONS

Introduction

15.5   The development of a limited company's trading activity may mean that it has to change its structure. Shares in a corporate structure can be bought or sold or created or cancelled. Shares may be owned by individuals or large corporations alike. A change in a company's capital structure may be a necessity to enable it to carry on its future activities. Such changes will have taxation consequences. This may involve the formation of a new company and the transfer of the predecessor's assets to the new company. The result being that the ownership of the business remains in the same hands, but is earned through a different corporate structure. The shareholders receive a share for share exchange.

Companies Act

15.6   The *Companies Act* permits reconstructions and amalgamations subject to certain conditions. The requirements are detailed in *Companies Act 2006, ss 895–941* and *Insolvency Act 1986, s 110*.

The court will sanction an arrangement with the members (or creditors) of the company provided this is voted on with 75% agreeing to the scheme at the company meeting (*CA 2006, ss 899, 907* and *922*). *Insolvency Act 1986, s 110* permits a liquidator to transfer the company's business or property to another company. The liquidator will receive shares for the distribution. Any dissenting member may require the liquidator to purchase his shares.

CAPITAL GAINS TAX

Reorganisation of share capital

15.7   In effect the action that the company takes is to transfer the company's assets to another company in exchange for shares. A reorganisation of share capital whereby the shareholder receives new shares in exactly the same proportion as the old shares is tax neutral. No charge to CGT arises. The new shares are deemed to have been acquired at exactly the same time as the old shares (*TCGA 1992, ss 126–131*). If the original shares or the new holding consist of or include qualifying corporate bonds, *TCGA 1992, s 116(5)* disapplies *TCGA 1992, ss 127–130*.

Any cash received is treated either as a capital distribution or as a part disposal (*TCGA 1992, ss 122, 128*). Consideration given for the new holding is treated as being given for the original holding but is indexed from the time that it is given rather than from the time that the original shareholding was acquired.

Company reconstructions

15.8   The no gain/no loss treatment contained in *TCGA 1992, ss 127–131*, will also apply to a company reconstruction in the following situation. The situation is such that a company issues shares or debentures to a person in exchange for shares or debentures that person owns in another company and:

- as a result of the exchange, the successor company holds or will hold more than 25% of the ordinary share capital of the original company, or

- the successor company issues shares or debentures as a result of a general offer made conditional upon the successor company acquiring control over the original company to the members of the successor company or any class of them, or

- the successor company holds or will hold as a result of the exchange the greater part of the voting power of the original company (*TCGA 1992, s 135*).

Further rules apply if the shares in the successor company are cancelled. The shareholders will benefit from the no gain/no loss treatment provided the following conditions are satisfied. Conditions one and two must be met, together with either condition three or condition four.

Condition 1. The successor must only issue ordinary shares to the original company's ordinary shareholders (*TCGA 1992, Sch 5AA, para 2*) and not to any other party.

Condition 2. The original ordinary shareholders in the same class all obtain the same proportional entitlement to ordinary shares in the new company. There is no requirement that all the shareholders of the old company become shareholders in the new company but the shares must be issued to the same persons (*TCGA 1992, Sch 5AA, para 3*).

Condition 3. There must be continuity of the business. The whole of the business must be carried on by one successor company or by two or more successor companies of which the original company may be one (*TGCA 1992, Sch 5AA, para 4*).

Condition 4. The scheme is carried out in pursuance of a compromise arrangement under *CA 1985, s 425* or foreign equivalent and no part of the business is transferred to any other person (*TCGA 1992, Sch 5AA, para 5*).

Bona fide commercial arrangements

15.9   The conditions only apply if the scheme is made for bona fide commercial arrangements where the main purpose is not the avoidance of capital gains tax. This restriction does not apply to holders of less than 5% of the shares. If the conditions are not met or there is found to be an anti-avoidance purpose, HMRC can collect the tax from any of the shareholders concerned (*TCGA 1992, s 137*). A tax avoidance purpose was found in *Snell v HMRC Comrs* SpC 532, [2006] STC (SCD) 296. On advice received from an adviser, a taxpayer became non-resident to avoid a capital gains tax liability. The Special Commissioners decided that as the taxpayer had full knowledge and understanding of the proposed course of action it arose from a tax avoidance purpose.

The company may apply for a clearance to HMRC that the proposed reconstruction or reorganisation is for bona fide commercial purposes. The full facts of the transaction should be given to HMRC, who have 30 days to reply. If HMRC do not issue a clearance notice to the company, the company may refer its case to the Tribunal (*TCGA 1992, s 138*). See **18.42** for further details regarding clearance procedures.

Reconstruction involving transfer of business

15.10   Where the whole or part of a business is transferred to another company for no consideration apart from taking over the liabilities, the asset transfer apart from the trading stock is deemed to take place for such consideration that provides neither gain nor loss (*TCGA 1992, s 139*). More often than not the consideration in such circumstances is a share exchange for the shareholders concerned.

Again for this section to apply the transfer must be made for bona fide commercial purposes. Similar provisions relate to intangible assets (*CTA 2009, s 818*). A clearance procedure is also available (*CTA 2009, ss 832, 833(1)*). Where an existing intangible asset (see **7.2**) is transferred under a reconstruction to which *TCGA 1992 s 139* or *s 140A* applies, the asset remains as an existing asset in the hands of the transferee (*CTA 2009, s 892*).

This situation whereby some or all of a company's assets or liabilities are transferred from one company to a successor company is commonly known as 'a hive down'. The successor company is often newly formed. Such a transaction is used to facilitate a company sale; so that only the chosen activities and assets and liabilities are taken over. The transaction may also facilitate a division in a group's activities.

Company reconstruction example

Example 15.1

A scheme of reconstruction can be used to break up an existing business into separate undertakings. This can involve the liquidation of the original company. See **Chapter 19** for liquidations.

Facts

The issued share capital of Union Ltd is of one class of share and is held as follows:

Shareholders	£1 Ordinary Shares
	£
Jack	50,000
Jill	50,000
	£100,000

The company has two businesses; it rents holiday homes in the UK and arranges tours of Great Britain, mainly for overseas visitors.

Original structure

It is proposed to separate the two businesses. There are four possible solutions that will satisfy the conditions of *TCGA 1992, Sch 5AA* (see **15.8**). Solutions 1 and 2 both involve the liquidation of Union Ltd.

Reconstruction Solution 1

Union Ltd enters into a scheme under *Insolvency Act 1986, s 110*. The original shares in Union Ltd are organised into A shares and B shares. The holdings are now as follows:

Shareholders	Total	£1 A Ordinary Shares	£1 B Ordinary Shares
	£	£	£
Jack	50,000	25,000	25,000
Jill	50,000	25,000	25,000
	100,000	50,000	50,000

The assets and liabilities of the holiday home rental business are allocated to the A shares. The assets and liabilities of the tours of Great Britain business are allocated to the B shares.

Union Ltd is placed in liquidation. The liquidator transfers the holiday home rental business to a new company, Country Homes Ltd (a successor company). Country Homes Ltd issues ordinary shares to the holders of the A shares in proportion to their respective holdings. The tours of Great Britain business is transferred to a new company Roving Ltd (a successor company) which issues ordinary shares to the holders of the B shares in proportion to their respective holdings.

Structure post Reconstruction 1

Example 15.2

Reconstruction Solution 2

The same facts apply as in *Reconstruction Solution 1* except that the new A shares are issued to Jack and the new B shares are issued to Jill. The new shareholdings are as follows:

Shareholders	Total	£1 A Ordinary Shares	£1 B Ordinary Shares
	£	£	£
Jack	50,000	50,000	—
Jill	50,000	—	50,000
	100,000	50,000	50,000

The assets and liabilities of the holiday home rental business are allocated to the A shares. The assets and liabilities of the tours of Great Britain business are allocated to the B shares.

Union Ltd is placed in liquidation. The liquidator transfers the holiday home rental business to a new company, Country Homes Ltd (a successor company). Country Homes Ltd issues ordinary shares to the holders of the A shares in proportion to their respective holdings. The tours of Great Britain business is transferred to a new company Roving Ltd (a successor company) which issues ordinary shares to the holders of the B shares in proportion to their respective holdings.

Structure post Reconstruction 2

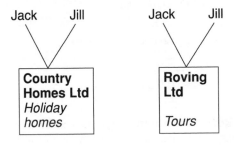

Example 15.3

Reconstruction Solution 3

The same facts apply as in Reconstruction Solution 2 except that it is not necessary to liquidate Union Ltd.

Instead, Union Ltd declares a dividend on the B shares, which it pays by transferring the assets and liabilities of the touring business to Roving Ltd. Roving Ltd then issues Jill with ordinary shares. The B shares in Union Ltd are now worthless. Jack now owns all the shares in Union Ltd which holds the holiday home business.

Structure post Reconstruction 3

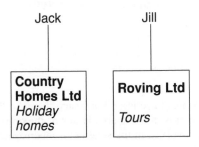

Example 15.4

Reconstruction Solution 4

Solution 4 takes place under the demerger rules. See **16.14** Example 16.3 (ii). There is no requirement to liquidate Union Ltd. The original shareholdings in Union Ltd are:

Shareholders	£1 Ordinary Shares
	£
Jack	50,000
Jill	50,000
	100,000

A new company Roving Ltd is formed with Jack and Jill each owning 50% of the issued ordinary share capital. The tours of Great Britain business is transferred to Roving Ltd. The holiday home letting business continues to be operated by Union Ltd

Structure post Reconstruction 4

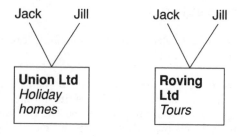

In all four solutions, the conditions of *TCGA 1992, Sch 5AA* (see **15.8**) are met:

Reconstruction—Conditions satisfied

Condition 1

The successor companies have issued ordinary shares to the holders of ordinary shares in the share classes of the original company, which are involved in the scheme of reconstruction and to no other person.

TCGA 1992, Sch 5AA, para 2

Condition 2

The original ordinary shareholders in the same class all obtain the same proportional entitlement to ordinary shares in the new company.	*TCGA 1992, Sch 5AA, para 3*

Condition 3

If the activities of the successor companies are taken together they carry on the whole of the business of the original company.	*TCGA 1992, Sch 5AA, para 4*

The result is that the disposal of Jack and Jill's holdings in Union Ltd in solutions 1 & 2, and the disposal of Jill's holding in solution 3, and the acquisition of the respective new holdings, is a no gain/no loss transaction (*TCGA 1992, s 136*). In solution 4, there is no disposal of the original holding.

The liquidator's transfer of the two businesses to Holiday Homes Ltd and Roving Ltd in solutions 1 and 2 is a no gain/no loss disposal (*TCGA 1992, s 139*).

In practice, these steps would not be taken in isolation of other factors; in particular the stamp duty costs and company procedural matters must be considered. In addition, if the trades have accumulated loss the utilisation of these losses will be hampered if there is cessation of the relevant trades concerned.

Solutions 1 and 2 will involve a cessation of Union Ltd's trade. Solution 1 offers the protection of *ICTA 1988, s 343* (see **15.11** and **15.12**) but not solution 1, because the same ownership structure pre and post reconstruction is not retained.

Solutions 3 and 4 involve the cessation of the touring trade. *Section 343* protection will be given to Roving Ltd in solution 4 but not in solution 3 because the same ownership structure pre and post reconstruction is not retained. Union Ltd's holiday home trade continues.

Groups

15.11   If the reconstruction involves a group relationship (see **20.14** for a definition of a group), company assets can be transferred between group members without a charge to capital gains arising (*TCGA 1992, s 171*). However, if the company subsequently leaves the group a capital gains tax charge will crystallise. The capital gain is based on the market value of the asset at the date of transfer. The gain is deemed to arise at the end of the accounting period in which the company leaves the group (*TCGA 1992, s 179*).

This provision does not apply to inter-group asset transfers between associated companies who cease to be group members at the same time (*TCGA 1992, s 179(2)*). The companies must have been associated at the time that the asset transfer was made (*Johnston Publishing (North) Ltd v Revenue and Customs Comrs* [2007] All ER (D) 240 (Mar)). The companies must remain associated after they leave the group. For this purpose 'associated companies' are defined as companies that would themselves form a group (*TCGA 1992, s 179(10)*).

TRADING LOSSES

Company reconstruction without a change of ownership

15.12   The utilisation of trading losses is restricted where a trade ceases and where there is a change of ownership of the company (*ICTA 1988, ss 768, 768A*), as discussed in **9.17–9.19**. Where there is a company reconstruction without a change of ownership and a continuing trade, the losses incurred by the previous company will be available to set against profits earned by the new company provided the same ownership and charging conditions apply pre and post transfer (*ICTA 1988, s 343*). Loss relief is given automatically without claim. It is necessary for the same trade to continue.

There is also a restriction on management expenses and property business losses. See **12.17** and **12.33** (*ICTA 1988, s 768C and s 768D*).

Ownership

15.13   Ownership of the trade is the beneficial ownership obtained by ownership of the share capital. The ownership condition is met if, at any time within two years after the transfer of trade, the beneficial ownership was held by the same person or persons as at any time within the 12 months prior to the transfer of trade (*ICTA 1988, s 343(1)(a)*). No minimum period of ownership is required but, in practice, HMRC may query short periods of ownership.

In *Barkers of Malton Ltd v Revenue and Customs Commissioners* SpC 689 it was held that trading should continue for some time and there should be evidence of trading. *ICTA 1988, s 343* prescribes no length of time for which the new trade should be carried on, but HMRC would expect to see profits and losses being realised for tax purposes.

Charge to corporation tax

15.14   The charging condition is met if the trade has been carried on by companies within the charge to corporation tax within the prescribed period of ownership (*ICTA 1988, s 343(1)(b)*). The situation not only applies to UK resident companies but also to non-resident companies chargeable to corporation tax in respect of a trade carried on by a UK branch or agent. The relief applies to a 'trade' and will also apply if part of a trade is transferred (*ICTA 1988, s 343(8)*).

Relief

15.15 Normally, when a company ceases to trade, its corporation tax liability is computed as though this was a discontinuance (*CTA 2009, s 41*). This is not the case under *s 343*.

Essentially the trade is not treated as discontinued and a new one commenced. Capital allowances continue uninterrupted with balancing charges falling on the successor company (*ICTA 1988, s 343(2)*). The loss carried forward by the successor is reduced by any excess of liabilities taken over (*ICTA 1988, s 343(4)*).

It should be noted that the relief only applies to trade losses: property business losses, the remaining trade losses, management expenses, and non-trading loan relationship deficits etc are not included.

Beneficial ownership

15.16 Ownership of the ordinary share capital for these purposes is the beneficial ownership. Ordinary share capital is defined in *ICTA 1988, s 832* and means all the issued share capital of the company, by whatever name it is called, other than capital whose holders have only a right to a dividend at a fixed rate, but have no other right to share in the profits.

A beneficial owner is not necessarily the person in whose name the ordinary shares are registered. A person who holds shares as a nominee is not a beneficial owner (*ICTA 1988, s 344(3)(a)*). Beneficial ownership is established by looking through to the ultimate owners.

15.17 The ownership of a trade is established whenever the *s 343* and *s 344* trade ownership tests are met. Ownership can fall to the holders of the ordinary share capital of the company carrying it on under *ICTA 1988, s 344(2)(a)*, or to the parent of the company carrying on the trade under *ICTA 1988, s 344(2)(b)*. Ultimately, the holders of the ordinary share capital of the parent under *ICTA 1988, s 344(2)(b)* may be the beneficial owners of the company. Finally, as will apply in most owner-manager controlled companies, the person or persons who by voting power, or by powers given in the Articles of Association or other document regulating the company, can direct or control the affairs of a company, which directly or indirectly owns the ordinary share capital of the company carrying on the trade (*ICTA 1988, s 344(2)*). HMRC will look to the person who can control the company 'by other means', which seems to imply that they may accept an arrangement not formalised by a written document (HMRC Company Taxation Manual CTM 06020).

A 75% parent and subsidiary ownership relationship is required for *ICTA 1988, s 344(2)(b)* above, under *ICTA 1988, s 344(3)(b)*. Relatives are treated as a single person and include spouses, civil partners (with effect from 5 December 2005), siblings, children and grandchildren etc, and parents and grandparents etc.

Example 15.5

Matthew, Mark and Luke each own 33.33% outright of the ordinary share capital of the publishing company W Ltd. H Ltd takes over the publishing trade from W Ltd. Matthew, Mark, Luke and John each own 25% of H Ltd.

Common ownership of the trade is achieved because the same group of persons owns not less than 75% of both companies.

Example 15.6

Sleekstyles Ltd manufactured hairdressing products but is now dormant. On 1 January 2009, Sleekstyles Ltd's trade was taken over by Crazystyles Ltd. The percentage ownership of the ordinary shares of both companies is as follows:

	Sleekstyles Ltd	*Crazystyles Ltd*
	%	%
William	60	40
Nathan	20	40
Roger	10	8
Susan	5	7
Clementine	3	3
Nadia	2	2
Total	100	100

William and Nathan formalised their relationship by entering into civil partnership on 5 December 2006. Roger and Susan became engaged to be married on 1 January 2008. Clementine and Nadia are senior employees. William and Nathan's shares are aggregated. Common ownership of the trade is achieved because the same group of persons owns not less than 75% of both companies.

15.18   For the relief to be given, beneficial ownership of the shares must be in place.

In *Wood Preservation Ltd v Prior* (1969) 45 TC 112, [1969] 1 All ER 364, the carry forward of loss relief was denied because Wood Preservation Ltd's trade was transferred after its parent company lost beneficial ownership of Wood's shares. HMRC explain that beneficial ownership passes from vendor to purchaser where an unconditional sale document is signed. If the contract is subject to a condition the beneficial ownership does not pass until the condition is satisfied. Equally, a legal owner of shares can lose the beneficial ownership if that person entered into an unconditional contract to sell the shares in advance of signing a contract. An oral agreement can be an unconditional contract (HMRC Company Taxation Manual CTM 06030). Therefore, a potential vendor should be particularly vigilant with respect to the point in time at which beneficial ownership is transferred.

Transfer of trade

15.19   HMRC have identified the following four practical situations where either a trade or part of a trade is transferred between companies. Firstly, a succession to an entire trade, arising under *ICTA 1988, s 343(1)*, where a company ceases to carry on a trade and another company begins to carry it on. Secondly, a transfer of the activities of a trade under *ICTA 1988, s 343(8)*, where a company ceases to carry on a trade and another begins to carry on the activities of that trade as part of its trade. Thirdly, a transfer of the activities of part of a trade, where a company ceases to carry on part of a trade and another company begins to carry on the activities of that part as its trade, again under *ICTA 1988, s 343(8)*. Finally, also under *ICTA 1988, s 343(8)*, where a company ceases to carry on part of a trade and another company begins to carry on the activities of that part as part of its trade (HMRC Company Taxation Manual CTM 06060).

Succession

15.20   In practical terms sufficient of the predecessor's trading activities must be transferred to the new company. For example, if, as in the case of

Example 15.6, Sleekstyles Ltd transferred its factory, its manufacturing operations and its employees to Crazystyles Ltd without its book debts or its sales distribution unit, this may be a sufficient trading activity transfer to qualify as a succession. In *Malayam Plantations Ltd v Clark* (1935) 19 TC 314 the acquisition of a rubber plantation and its employees without the book debts or the selling organisation was considered to be a 'succession'. The fact that one company actually succeeds to the trade of another company within the same ownership will bring about the relief as in *Wadsworth Morton Ltd v Jenkinson* (1966) 43 TC 479, [1967] 1 WLR 79, [1966] 3 All ER 702.

Activities of a trade

15.21   The relief is also given if the predecessor's trade is added to the successor's trade in an identifiable form. For example, two shoe-manufacturing companies supplied shoes wholesale to their parent company for retail sale. The parent company wound up the subsidiaries. It took over the factories and the staff, and manufactured the shoes itself. The parent company was denied use of the subsidiaries' losses because although the manufacturing activities continued the wholesale activities failed to continue. The trade was not carried on in the same identifiable form as before the transfer (*Laycock v Freeman Hardy and Willis Ltd* (1938) 22 TC 288, [1939] 2 KB 1, [1938] 4 All ER 609). In *Rolls Royce Motors Ltd v Bamford* (1976) 51 TC 319, [1976] STC 152, it was held that the successor trade was different to that of the predecessor and *s 343* loss relief was denied.

A jeans and casual clothing company made trading losses. A company with which it was associated marketed its merchandise. The marketing company bought the manufacturing company and carried on its trade. The trading losses were available for relief after transfer because the trade continued, although the profits were not earned separately (*Falmer Jeans Ltd v Rodin* (1990) 63 TC 55, [1990] STC 270).

The identifiable form test was also met in *Briton Ferry Steel Co Ltd v Barry* (1939) 23 TC 414, [1940] 1 KB 463, [1939] 4 All ER 541.

Activities of part of a trade

15.22   There is no definition of part of a trade within the legislation. HMRC regard part of a trade as being a free-standing apparatus and making profits or losses in its own right. A part of a trade does not have to amount to anything as distinctive as a branch or a division (HMRC Company Taxation Manual CTM 06060).

LATER EVENTS

15.23 When a trade is transferred between two companies but the full ownership test is never met, although within two years there is a transfer to a company that does meet the ownership test, then *s 343* still applies and it is still possible to transfer losses to the third company (*ICTA 1988, s 343(7)*).

PRACTICAL EFFECTS OF SECTION 343 RELIEF

Trading losses carried forward

15.24 If all conditions apply, the successor is able to utilise the remaining predecessor's loss in an *ICTA 1988, s 393(1)* claim against future income from the same trade (*ICTA 1988, s 343(4)*). The remaining loss is the loss that the predecessor has not utilised less the relevant liabilities restriction. The relevant liabilities restriction is the difference between the retained relevant liabilities, the retained relevant assets and the consideration (*ICTA 1988, s 343(4)*).

The relevant liabilities are taken at their actual value immediately before the predecessor ceased to trade. Relevant liabilities exclude share capital, share premium, reserves or relevant loan stock and any liabilities transferred to the successor. Inter-group debts are included in relevant liabilities (*ICTA 1988, s 344(6)*). Relevant loan stock can be secured or unsecured but not that arising from a person carrying on the trade of money lending (*ICTA 1988, s 344(11), (12)*).

Relevant assets are the assets that the company owned immediately before it ceased to trade (*ICTA 1988, s 344(5)(a)*) and are valued at market value (*ICTA 1988, s 344(7)*).

The consideration is the amount given by the predecessor to the successor of the trade. Liabilities assumed by the successor are not included within the consideration (*ICTA 1988, s 344(5)(b)*). However, if a liability is transferred to the successor and the creditor agrees to accept less than the full amount due in settlement of the outstanding debt, the shortfall is treated as a liability for the purposes of the restriction.

If losses exceed the net relevant liabilities there is no restriction. Any losses disallowed are not available to the predecessor company (*ICTA 1988, s 343(4)*). Where part of a trade is transferred, a just apportionment of receipts, expenses, assets or liabilities is to be made for this purpose (*ICTA 1988, s 343(9))*. The restriction only applies to trading losses and not to capital allowances and balancing charges.

The release of a trading debt will be a taxable receipt of the trade (*CTA 2009, s 94*).

Example 15.7

Alfonso Ltd took over the trade and assets of Bertino Ltd on 1 January 2010. *Section 343* relief applies. Bertino Ltd's unutilised trading losses amount to £150,000. Neither cash nor trade creditors are included in the sale. The balance sheet at 31 December 2009 directly before transfer is shown below. The business is assumed to be sold by Alfonso Ltd to Bertino Ltd for:

(i)   £10,000, and

(ii)   £100,000.

Bertino Ltd: Balance sheet at 31 December 2009

	£000	£000
Fixed assets		
Plant and machinery		60
Current assets		
Stock	20	
Debtors	10	
Cash	5	
	35	
Current liabilities		
Trade creditors	30	
		5
		65
Shareholders' funds		
Share capital		50
Profit and loss account		15
		65

The restriction is calculated as follows:

(i)   Sale proceeds: £10,000

	£000
Trade creditors	30
Less cash	(5)
	25
Less sale consideration	(10)
Loss relief restriction	15

The losses that are available for relief are £150,000 – 15,000 = £135,000

(ii)   Sale proceeds: £100,000

	£000
Trade creditors	30
Less cash	(5)
	25
Less sale consideration	(100)
Loss relief restriction	(75)

As the sale consideration exceeds the value of the liabilities and assets not taken over there is no loss restriction.

If only £50,000 of the plant were taken over, the restriction would be calculated as follows:

Sale proceeds	£10,000	£100,000
	£000	£000
Trade creditors	30	30
Less plant retained	(10)	(10)
Less cash	(5)	(5)
	15	15
Less sale consideration	(10)	(100)
Loss relief restriction	5	(75)

If the company is sold for £10,000, the losses that are available for relief are:

$$£150,000 - £10,000 = £140,000$$

If the company is sold for £100,000, there is no loss restriction as the sale consideration continues to exceed the value of the liabilities and assets not taken over.

Capital allowances

15.25 For capital allowances purposes where a company is sold to a successor such that the original company's trade ceases (*CTA 2009, s 41(2)*), the assets are deemed to be sold to the new company at market value. Therefore, balancing charges and allowances will ensue for the predecessor (*CAA 2001, s 559*).

If the conditions of *s 343* apply the assets are transferred from predecessor to successor at tax written-down value. If the transfer is made during the accounting period the writing-down allowances are reduced proportionately. When the assets are eventually sold any balancing charge or allowances will fall upon the party carrying on the trade at the time, ie the successor as if he had always owned the assets (*ICTA 1988, s 343(2)*).

European mergers and reconstructions

15.26 Reconstructions and mergers that involve a company resident in another Member State are in general tax neutral (*CTA 2009, ss 817–833*).

Chapter 16

Distributions

INTRODUCTION

16.1 A dividend is a shareholder's expected reward for an investment in a limited company. Under company law, a company may declare and distribute a dividend out of its realised profits. The dividend is then payable to the shareholders pro rata to their shareholdings (*CA 2006, Pt 23*).

For corporation tax purposes, the distribution rules apply whenever cash or assets are passed to the members of the company. For taxation purposes, a dividend is a distribution of profits falling within *ICTA 1988, s 209(2)(a)*. If the payment relates to the member's services to the company it is not a distribution but a payment for services performed for the company. The payment will be chargeable upon the member as employment income under the rules of *ITEPA 2003* and any payments so made should be relievable by the company for corporation tax purposes.

However, a distribution can take a variety of forms and includes capital (other than a repayment of capital) or assets. For a company shareholder a distribution constitutes franked investment income (if non group) and dividend income for an individual assessable under *ITTOIA 2005, s 384* (see *Income Tax 2009/10* (Bloomsbury Professional)).

MEANING

16.2 Distribution for corporation tax purposes does not have the same meaning as the company law meaning of distribution of share capital in a winding up. The former deals with allocating profits and the latter with apportioning a company's assets (*ICTA 1988, s 209(1)*).

PAYMENTS CLASSED AS A DISTRIBUTION

16.3 Particular payments are classed as distributions. These include not only dividends but also bonus securities or redeemable shares, transfers of assets and of liabilities between a company and its members, payments of interest or other distributions to the extent that they exceed a commercial rate, payments of interest or other distributions on certain securities, a bonus issue on or following a repayment of share capital and any other distributions out of assets of the company in respect of shares in the company.

Dividend

16.4   In general a dividend paid by a company including a capital dividend is a distribution (*ICTA 1988, s 209(2)(a)*). Exceptions are stock dividends and dividends paid by building societies and industrial provident societies. If a company transfers an asset to a member, the amount of the distribution is the market value of the asset less the market value of any new consideration given by the member (*ICTA 1988, s 209(4)–(6)*).

A distribution of shares by a close company to its members when they are worth more is not a distribution but can be a transfer of value between members (*IHTA 1984, s 94*). A dividend waiver may constitute a settlement if there is an element of bounty in the arrangement (*ITTOIA 2005, ss 619–648*).

Distribution of assets

16.5   If a distribution of a company's asset is made to members at an undervalue, the difference between that and the market value of the asset is treated as a distribution (*ICTA 1988, s 209(4)*). If the person to whom the asset is passed is also a director then it is a matter of fact whether he or she receives the asset as shareholder or as employee. If received as an employee the amount will be assessed as employment income. There is no distribution if the payer and the recipient are both UK companies and one is a subsidiary of the other or both are subsidiaries of a third company (*ICTA 1988, s 209(5)*). Again there is no distribution between two independent companies, neither of which is a 51% subsidiary of a non-resident company where the companies are not under common control. The *ICTA 1988, s 416* definition of control is used here (*ICTA 1988, s 209(6)*). If an asset is transferred from one company to another, any material difference between the market value and the consideration given should be treated as a distribution within *ICTA 1988, s 209(4)* or *ICTA 1988, s 209(2)(b)* as appropriate unless *ICTA 1988, s 209(5)* or *ICTA 1988, s 209(6)* applies.

Unless the payments are intra company for *ICTA 1988, s 209(5), (6)* purposes other payments or asset transfers may be classed as distributions (*ICTA 1988, s 209(2)(b)*).

A repayment of share capital is not a distribution.

Bonus issue subsequent to a repayment

16.6 A bonus issue subsequent to a repayment of share capital (other than fully paid preference shares) is deemed to be a distribution of the nominal value of the shares so issued and is added to the purchase price of the shares (*ICTA 1988, s 210*). This does not apply to a bonus issue of non-redeemable share capital by a non-close listed company, which takes place more than ten years after the repayment of capital (*ICTA 1988, s 211*).

The distribution is calculated as follows:

the nominal amount of the bonus issue up to the amount of the capital repaid,

minus

the new consideration received,

minus

any amounts in respect of the same repayment of capital, already treated as distributions under *ICTA 1988, s 210(1)* (HMRC Company Taxation Manual CTM 15420).

Example 16.1

A Ltd repays £200,000 of its share capital.

It then issues:

- 100,000 fully paid £1 ordinary shares at 30p per share, and later
- 500,000 fully paid £1 preference shares for no new consideration.

The issue of ordinary shares results in a distribution of:

$$100,000 \times (£1 - £0.30) = £70,000$$

The second (bonus) issue is of shares with par value of £500,000 (500,000 × £1).

This distribution is restricted to a maximum of the repayment of share capital less the earlier distribution. The amount of this distribution is, therefore:

$$£200,000 - £70,000 = £130,000$$

465

Interest and other situations

16.7   Interest payments in excess of a normal commercial rate of return may be treated as a dividend (*ICTA 1988, s 209(2)(d), (e)*). HMRC have confirmed that there is no requirement to deduct income tax at source, under *ITA 2007, s 874*, from interest payments treated as a distribution (HMRC Brief 47/2008).

Distributions in a winding up are not income distributions and are subject to capital gains tax. A distribution has an extended meaning for close companies (*ICTA 1988, s 418*) (see **4.13**).

There is a general anti-avoidance provision where two companies enter into reciprocal arrangements. Each company makes payments to the other company's members. In this instance the payments are classed as distributions (*ICTA 1988, s 254(8)*).

NON-QUALIFYING DISTRIBUTION

16.8   Non-qualifying distributions are bonus issues of redeemable shares or securities. They can be issued directly or issued from bonus redeemable shares or securities received from another company (*ICTA 1988, s 209(2)(c)*).

The amount of the non-qualifying distribution for the purposes of *ICTA 1988, s 209(2)(c)* for redeemable share capital is the excess of the nominal amount of the share capital together with any premium payable on redemption, in a winding up or in any other circumstances over any new consideration received.

Individual shareholders receive a 10% credit and may be charged at the 32.5% upper rate. The company must notify HMRC on form CT2 within 14 days after the end of the quarter in which the non-qualifying distribution is made (*ICTA 1988, s 234(5)*).

SMALL COMPANY DIVIDEND PAYMENTS

16.9   Small private company owner managers generally take their reward from their companies in the form of dividends and/or remuneration. Remuneration is deductible for corporation tax purposes. Dividend payments are not tax deductible.

Under *Companies Act 2006, s 19*, statutory model articles (SMA) apply from 1 October 2009; see *SI 2008/3229* (*arts 30–36* concern dividends and other distributions).

Dividends may be declared by the company in general meeting but no dividend shall exceed the amount recommended by the directors (*SMA, art 30*). Interim dividends may be paid by directors from time to time (*SMA, art 30*).

The timing of the dividend payment may have a marked impact on the directors' personal taxation situation. A dividend is not paid until the shareholder receives the funds direct or the dividend amount is unreservedly put at his or her disposal, for example by a credit to a loan account from which the shareholder has the power to draw.

Final dividends are normally due and payable on the date of the resolution unless a future date is set for payment. Interim dividends are not an enforceable debt and can be varied or rescinded prior to payment. Interim dividends are due when paid or when the funds are placed at the disposal of the director/shareholders as part of their current accounts with the company. HMRC state that 'payment is not made until such a right to draw on the dividend exists (presumably) when the appropriate entries are made in the company's books. If, as may happen with a small company, such entries are not made until the annual audit, and this takes place after the end of the accounting period in which the directors resolved that an interim dividend be paid, then the "due and payable" date is in the later rather than the earlier accounting period' (HMRC Company Taxation Manual CTM 20095).

For taxation purposes an 'illegal dividend' will be treated in the same way as a legal dividend. However, there is the possibility that if the directors were to pay an interim dividend during an accounting period and it is not possible to demonstrate that the interim dividend payment was paid out of available profits (or alternatively as a repayment of loans due from the company) that HMRC could attack that nature of the payment classing it as remuneration and assess the company for PAYE and NIC. If a shareholder knew or was in a position to know that a dividend was illegal at the time of payment it is refundable to the company. See **4.18**. Companies must therefore be meticulous in their statutory record keeping as regards interim dividend payments.

A final dividend can only be waived before payment. An interim dividend must be waived before entitlement to payment because payment and entitlement take place at the same time. If waiver takes place afterwards it is not an effective waiver but merely a transfer of income.

With effect for accounting periods commencing on or after 1 January 2005 a company may not recognise a dividend in its accounts unless it is a liability at the balance sheet date (FRS21 and IAS10). See also ICAEW Technical Release Tech 57/05.

SURPLUS ACT

16.10   Post 6 April 1999 there is no liability to corporation tax if a company makes a distribution payment. Prior to 6 April 1999 if a company made a dividend payment it had to account for advance corporation tax (ACT). ACT was calculated as 1/4 of the dividend paid. The ACT paid was, as its name describes, an advance payment of corporation tax. The advance payment could be set against the mainstream liability up to a 20% limit. Any surplus was carried forward for relief in the next year. The problem for companies post 6 April 1999 is to obtain relief for its pre-6 April 1999 surplus ACT against its post-6 April 1999 mainstream corporation tax. It can only do this if it takes account of its 'shadow' or notional ACT.

The company is required to follow this procedure:

1   Calculate the ACT that it would have paid on its distributions.

2   Calculate the maximum ACT set-off.

3   Calculate the remaining offset capacity after the notional ACT has been used.

This can be used to set off the surplus ACT.

Example 16.2

Lotus Ltd's profits chargeable to corporation tax for the year ended 31 March 2010 amount to £300,000. The company paid a dividend of £35,000 during the year. Surplus ACT brought forward at 1 April 2009 amounts to £90,000. The position is as follows:

	£
Maximum ACT set-off £300,000 × 20%	60,000
Less shadow ACT £35,000 × 20/80	8,750
Surplus ACT set-off	51,250
Surplus ACT brought forward	90,000
Less set-off for accounting period ended 31 March 2010	51,250
Surplus ACT carried forward	38,750
The final corporation tax liability is:	
Corporation tax	63,000
Less surplus ACT set-off	51,250
Final tax liability	11,750

16.11 If a company wishes to make large payments to shareholders it may choose to do so in the form of share capital rather than as a distribution. However, from 6 April 1999 non-qualifying distributions are included with qualifying distributions for the purposes of calculating shadow ACT (*FA 1998, s 32*; *Corporation Tax (Treatment of Unrelieved Surplus Advance Corporation Tax) Regulations 1999, SI 1999/358*).

EXEMPTIONS FROM THE DISTRIBUTION RULES

16.12 Certain transactions are relieved or exempted from the overall distribution rules. These include:

- Demergers by *ICTA 1988, s 213* and *TCGA 1992, s 192*.

- Purchase by a company of its own shares (*ICTA 1988, s 219*).

- Distributions in a winding up by ESC C16.

DEMERGERS

16.13 It may be seen as beneficial for a subsidiary company to leave a group. For this to happen the ownership of the subsidiary's shares passes out of the control of the ultimate holding company to another company or group. This transfer of capital will not be treated as a distribution provided certain conditions apply. Both the distributing and the subsidiary company, whose share are transferred, must be trading companies or holding companies of a trading group at the time of the distribution (*ICTA 1988, s 213*). Both companies must be resident in the UK at the time of the distribution.

16.14 *ICTA 1988, s 213* facilitates three types of transaction where subject to additional conditions such a transaction is treated as an exempt distribution. SP 13/80 provides additional interpretation and guidance. Exempt distributions may consist of:

(i) A distribution by a company of its shares in one or more 75% subsidiaries.

(ii) A transfer of a company's trade to one or more companies in consideration for the issue of shares in the transferor company.

(iii) A distribution of shares in a 75% subsidiary or subsidiaries to one or more companies which issue their shares to the members of the distributing company.

Example 16.3—(i) A distribution by a company of its shares in one or more 75% subsidiaries (*ICTA 1988, s 213(3)(a)*)

This results in a direct demerger.

In this situation B Ltd, a group company, leaves the group, but its ultimate ownership remains with A and B.

Before the demerger:

- A and B owned A Ltd, and
- A Ltd owned B Ltd and C Ltd.

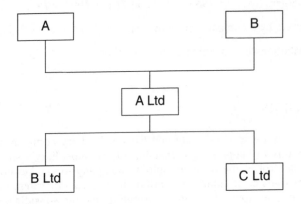

After the demerger:

- A and B own A Ltd and B Ltd, and
- A Ltd owns C Ltd.

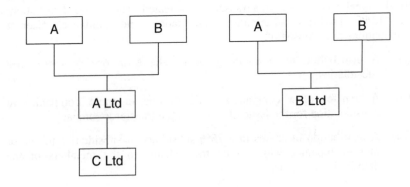

In particular, in this situation, the B Ltd shares that are distributed by A Ltd to A and B, must be non-redeemable and must be the whole or substantially the whole of the ordinary shares and voting rights that A Ltd holds in B Ltd (*ICTA 1988, s 213(6)(a)*). 'Whole' is interpreted as around 90% or more (SP 13/80).

Example 16.4—(ii) A distribution of a company's trade or shares in one or more 75% subsidiary companies in consideration for the issue of shares in the transferor company (*ICTA 1988, s 213(3)(b)*)

This is known as an indirect demerger.

A & B Ltd carries on a trade or trades and the desired effect is for another company to carry on some of its activities. A new company, B Ltd, is formed to which part of the trade is transferred. A & B Ltd remains in active existence.

Before the demerger:

- A and B owned A & B Ltd, which is involved in trade A and trade B.

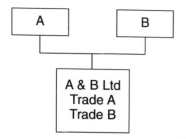

After the demerger:

- A and B own A & B Ltd, which is involved in trade A, and
- A and B own B Ltd, which is involved in trade B.

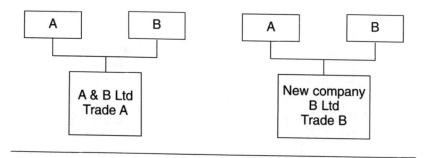

Example 16.5—(iii) A distribution of shares in a 75% subsidiary or subsidiaries to one or more companies, which issue their shares to the members of the distributing company

B Ltd, a subsidiary company, leaves the group to be within the ownership of a newly formed company but remains within A and B's ultimate ownership.

Before the demerger:

●   A and B owned A Ltd, and

●   A Ltd owned B Ltd and C Ltd.

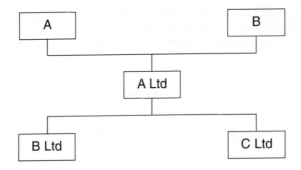

After the demerger:

●   A and B own A Ltd and the new company D Ltd,

●   A Ltd owns B Ltd, and

●   D Ltd owns C Ltd.

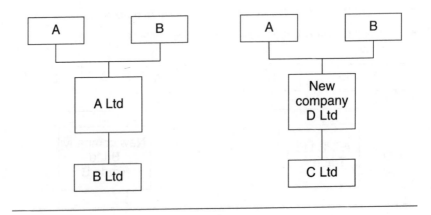

16.15   In the cases above, the transferor, ie A & B Ltd in Example 16.4 and A Ltd in Example 16.5, must not retain any material interest in the transferred trade (*ICTA 1988, s 213(8)(a)*). HMRC give a wide meaning. If the transferor company retained control of the trade or assets or had a material influence on the profit destination, this would amount to retaining an interest in the trade. Otherwise, a minor interest would amount to around 10% (SP 13/80).

If shares in a subsidiary are transferred those shares must constitute the whole or substantially the whole of the distributing company's holding of the ordinary share capital of the subsidiary and must confer the whole or substantially the whole of the distributing company's voting rights in the subsidiary (*ICTA 1988, s 213(8)(b)*).

The only or main activity of the transferee company or each transferee company after the distribution must be the carrying on of the trade or the holding of the shares transferred to it (*ICTA 1988, s 213(8)(c)*).

The shares issued by the transferee company or each transferee company must not be redeemable, must constitute the whole or substantially the whole of its issued ordinary share capital and must confer the whole or substantially the whole of the voting rights in that company (*ICTA 1988, s 213(8)(d)*).

After (but not 'for ever after' SP13/80) the distribution the distributing company must be either a trading company or the holding company of a trading group unless the transfer relates to two or more subsidiaries and the transferor is dissolved and has no other assets available for distribution or it is itself a 75% subsidiary (*ICTA 1988, s 213(6)(b), (8)(d)*). ESC C11 permits the company to retain funds to meet the costs of liquidation and to repay a negligible amount of share capital remaining. Negligible is interpreted as meaning £5,000 or less.

There are certain conditions if the distributing company is itself a 75% subsidiary of another company. The group to which the distributing company belongs must be a trading group (*ICTA 1988, s 213(12)(a)*). The distribution by the subsidiary must be followed by one or more of the Example 16.3 or Example 16.4 distributions (*ICTA 1988, s 213(12)*).

Shareholders effectively enter into a share for share exchange. The trade or business remains with the companies.

Reliefs

16.16   The share transfer is an exempt distribution and is not taxable on the individual shareholders (*ICTA 1988, s 213*).

The direct demerger is not treated as a capital distribution under *TCGA 1992, s 122* but instead is treated as a paper for paper reconstruction under *TCGA 1992, ss 126–130*. Thus the capital gains base cost is apportioned to the shares in the transferee company and in the distributing company in proportion to their values at the time of the distribution. There is no charge if the company leaves the group provided the company has not made a chargeable payment within five years of making the exempt distribution. A chargeable payment is a payment that is neither for money's worth nor for commercial purposes but will possibly be part of a tax avoidance scheme (*ICTA 1988, s 214; TCGA 1992, s 192*). In the case of an indirect demerger, capital gains relief is obtained in practice under *TCGA 1992, s 136* because the demerger is often a reconstruction (see HMRC Capital Gains Manual CG 52720/1 and CG 33920A for HMRC's comments).

General conditions

16.17 All companies involved in the transactions must be UK resident at the time of the distribution (*ICTA 1988, s 213(4)*). The distributing company and any company whose shares are distributed must be a trading company or a member of a trading group (*ICTA 1988, s 213(5)*). The distribution must be made wholly or mainly for the benefit of some or all of the trading activities formerly carried on by a single company or group and after the distribution carried on by two or more companies or groups (*ICTA 1988, s 213(10)*). The distribution must not form part of a scheme or arrangement for:

- the avoidance of tax;
- the making of a chargeable payment;
- the transfer of control of a relevant company to persons other than members of the distributing company;
- the cessation of a trade or its sale after the distribution (*ICTA 1988, s 213(11)*).

Clearance procedure

16.18 A clearance procedure is available under *ICTA 1988, s 215* for the distributing company and also for any person considering making a chargeable payment within five years of an exempt distribution. A chargeable payment is any payment not made for money's worth. This will be treated as a company distribution if made during the five-year period of an exempt distribution. Individuals receiving a chargeable payment will be charged to income tax in full. Companies receiving a chargeable payment will be charged to corporation tax on the full amount of the receipt (*ICTA 1988, s 214(1A), (1B)*). A return of exempt distributions must be provided to HMRC within 30 days of making the distribution (*ICTA 1988, s 216*). See **18.48** for further details regarding clearance procedures.

PURCHASE OF OWN SHARES

Effects of the legislation

16.19 The Companies Act permits a company to purchase and redeem their own share capital. In absence of any relieving legislation a distribution will arise under *ICTA 1988, s 209(2)(b)* on the difference between the subscribed capital and the purchase or redemption proceeds.

Relief is given under *ICTA 1988, s 219* for payments made by an unquoted trading company or the unquoted holding company of a trading group on the purchase or redemption of their own shares. A quoted company is 'a company whose shares are listed in the official list of the Stock Exchange' (*ICTA 1988, s 229(1)*). Shares dealt in by the unlisted securities market or the alternative investment market are unquoted for these purposes (HMRC Corporation Tax Manual CTM 17507).

Payments on purchase and redemption to quoted companies remain within the distribution legislation. The excess of the payment above the refund of share capital is treated as a distribution. If certain conditions are complied with there is no distribution treatment. Instead the disposal receives the capital gains treatment in the hands of the vendor shareholder.

Conditions—purpose

16.20 The purpose of the transaction must be to benefit the company's trade or any of its 75% subsidiary's trade. It must not form part of a scheme or arrangement to enable a shareholder to participate in company profits without receiving a dividend, or any other form of tax avoidance (*ICTA 1988, s 219(1)(a)*). HMRC will review the circumstances of each case. The case of *Allum v Marsh* SpC 446; [2005] STC (SCD) 191 was subject to such a review. The facts are as follows: Mr and Mrs A owned 99% and their son 1% of the ordinary shares in A Ltd an unquoted trading company. Mr and Mrs A and their son were all directors. The company owned a property from which the business was carried out and there was a large loan due to the directors. The company approved a contract for the sale of the property and when the sale had been completed it voted to purchase Mr and Mrs A's shares in A Ltd. Mr and Mrs A resigned as company directors. A new company secretary was appointed and the board voted to make voluntary payments to Mr and Mrs A in appreciation for their services to the company. Their shareholdings were duly purchased by the company. The next year the company's activities became small and negligible and the company could not find suitable premises from which to carry out its activities. Mr and Mrs A were assessed to a distribution on the basis that the exemption under *ICTA 1988, s 219(1)(a)* did not apply because the purchase of the shares was not made wholly or mainly for benefiting the company's trade. The voluntary payments were assessed as emoluments. Therefore it is necessary to demonstrate that the purchase takes place for the benefit of the trade.

Alternatively, the whole of the payment (apart from any sum applied in paying capital gains tax charged on the redemption, repayment or purchase) may be applied by the recipient in discharging a liability of his for inheritance tax charged on a death and is so applied within the period of two years after the death (*ICTA 1988, s 219*).

Conditions—shareholder residence

16.21 The vendor shareholder must be resident and ordinarily resident in the UK in the year of assessment in which the purchase is made. If the shares are held through a nominee, the nominee must also be so resident and ordinarily resident (*ICTA 1988, s 220(1)*).

The shares must have been owned by the vendor throughout the period of five years ending with the date of the purchase (*ICTA 1988, s 220(5)*). For an individual a spouse's period of ownership is also taken into consideration (*ICTA 1988, s 220(6)*).

Shareholder's interest in the company

16.22 Immediately after purchase the shareholder's interest or the combined interests with associates must be substantially reduced (*ICTA 1988, s 221(1), (2)*). By this it is meant first that the total nominal value of the shares owned by him immediately after the purchase, expressed as a fraction of the issued share capital of the company at that time, does not exceed 75% of the corresponding fraction immediately before the purchase (*ICTA 1988, s 221(4)*). Second, if the share of profits available for distribution immediately after purchase exceeds 75% of the corresponding fraction immediately before the purchase, the shareholding will not be treated as substantially reduced (*ICTA 1988, s 221(5)*).

In a group situation other group members' and associates' interests are also taken into account (*ICTA 1988, s 222(4)*). Group for these purposes is a 51% relationship (*ICTA 1988, s 222(7)*).

After the purchase the ex-shareholders must not be connected with the company making the purchase or with any company that is a member of the same group as that company (*ICTA 1988, s 223(1)*).

Clearance procedure

16.23   An advance clearance procedure is available under *ICTA 1988, s 225*. The full procedure is set out in SP 2/82. 60 days after making the payments the company must make a return to HMRC giving details of the payment and the circumstances (*ICTA 1988, s 226*).

Associated persons

16.24   Associated persons include spouses who are living together and children under the age of 18 together with their respective associates. With effect from 5 December 2005, civil partners are also associated persons. Two or more companies are connected if they are both under the same control. Trustees are connected with the settlor, the beneficiaries and the respective associates.

A personal representative is associated with the beneficiaries. A person connected with a company is an associate of the company and of any company controlled by it, and the company and any company controlled by it are his associates. Trustees are associated with the settlor or an associate of his or the beneficiaries if any one of the beneficiaries has an interest of more than 5%. Personal representatives are associated with beneficiaries if the beneficiary has an interest of more than 5% in the estate.

Also, if one person is accustomed to act on the directions of another in relation to the affairs of a company, then in relation to that company the two persons are associates of one another. Exempt approved pension schemes and employee trusts are not included in these arrangements (*ICTA 1988, s 227(8)*).

Connected persons

16.25   A person is connected with a company if he directly or indirectly possesses or is entitled to acquire more than 30% of the issued ordinary share capital, 30% of the combined loan capital and issued share capital, 30% of the voting power or 30% of the assets available for distribution on a winding up.

An interest in loan capital, acquired during the normal course of a money lending business, is disregarded, if the person takes no part in the management or conduct of the company.

DISTRIBUTIONS IN A WINDING UP BY ESC C16

Striking off a defunct company

16.26   If the registrar of companies believes that a company is not carrying on a business he may strike it off. The procedure involves the registrar writing to the company. If a reply is not received within a month a second letter is sent within 14 days, this time by registered post. If no reply is received within one month, the registrar may publish a notice in the London Gazette and will send a notice to the company stating that within three months from the date of the notice the company will be struck off the registrar and dissolved (*CA 2006, s 1001* – now applicable from 1 October 2009).

Request for striking off by a private company

16.27   A private company may voluntarily request that the registrar strike it off. In practice the company completes a Companies House form DS01, which it sends to the registrar of companies, together with a fee. The form must be signed by all or a majority of the directors. The directors must confirm that in the previous three months it has not carried on any business, or changed its name, disposed of any of its assets or engaged in any other activities apart from making the application, settling its affairs or meeting a statutory requirement. The company must, of course, not be involved in any other insolvency proceedings (*CA 2006, s 1003* – now applicable from 1 October 2009). The registrar then publishes a notice in the London Gazette. Within seven days of sending the form to the Registrar, all members, creditors, Crown departments, employees and any directors who have not signed the form should be sent full information as to the company assets and liabilities and should have a copy of the letter that was sent to the Registrar of Companies. Creditors should be invited to petition for the winding up of the company as an alternative. In most cases, creditors would not wish to take up this option, as to do so would involve them in material court costs which they could not substantially recover. If no objections are received, three months after the date of the notice, a further notice will be placed in the London Gazette and the company will be removed (See form BVC 17 on the Bona Vacantia website www.bonavacantia.gov.uk).

ESC C16

16.28   As a *CA 2006, s 1000* or *s 1003* method of striking off is not a formal winding up, HMRC regard any distribution of assets as an income distribution within *s 209*. By concession, HMRC will treat the distribution as a capital distribution, provided certain criteria are complied with; namely that the shareholders accept personal liability for the company's unpaid taxation liabilities. HMRC will require written signed statements from the company and its shareholders.

The company must provide assurances that it:

- does not intend to trade or carry on business in future;

- intends to collect its debts, pay off its creditors and distribute any balance of its assets to its shareholders (or has already done so); and

- intends to seek or accept striking off and dissolution.

The company and its shareholders agree that:

- they will supply such information as is necessary to determine and will pay any corporation tax liability on income or capital gains; and

- the shareholders will pay any capital gains tax liability (or corporation tax in the case of a corporate shareholder) in respect of any amount distributed to them in cash or otherwise as if the distributions had been made during a winding up (ESC C16).

This method of winding up is widely used by small private companies. Assuming all other conditions apply, the capital gains tax treatment enables the shareholders to take advantage of business asset taper relief. As the capital gains tax treatment is only a concession, HMRC could refuse to apply it if they perceived a tax avoidance motive.

HMRC are currently reviewing their list of statutory concessions. Consultation on ESC C16 closed on 1 May 2009. Subject to the result of the review, it is anticipated that ESC C16 will be enacted or withdrawn.

Treatment of assets and liabilities

16.29 Before a company is dissolved, the members should ensure that its assets are transferred out of its ownership. If this is not done, any assets owned at the date of dissolution will pass to the Crown and become *bona vacantia*. Assets held in trust by the company for another do not pass to the Crown (*CA 2006, s 1012* – now applicable from 1 October 2009).

The company should request well in advance and whilst the company is still in existence for any corporation tax repayments to be made to the shareholders or directors. Otherwise with a closed bank account the company will not be able to receive the repayment and with a company no longer in existence it will not be possible to give alternative payment instructions to HMRC with the result that the corporation tax repayment will also be *bona vacantia*.

The company's liabilities are extinguished on dissolution unless the debt is secured on the company's property by a mortgage or charge. The creditor's remedy for unsecured debts is to restore the company to the Register, and then bring legal proceedings against the restored company. The time limit for which a company can be restored to the Register is six years in the case of *CA 2006, s 1000* – now applicable from 1 October 2009 or *s 1003* now applicable from 1 October 2009 strike off (*CA 2006, ss 1024* and *1029*).

Bona vacantia

16.30   *Bona vacantia* or 'vacant goods' is ownerless property, which passes to the Crown. The collection of the assets of dissolved companies in England and Wales is dealt with by the Treasury Solicitor as nominee for the Crown. The Treasury Solicitor has published guidelines in respect of companies registered under the *Companies Acts 1929* to *1985* at: www.bonavacantia.gov.uk.

Unauthorised distribution

16.31   If there is an unauthorised return of the share capital to the members, the company has a right to recover that money from its members. That right of recovery from the members is a 'right' for the purposes of *CA 2006, s 1012* – now applicable from 1 October 2009, which would pass to the Crown as *bona vacantia* when the company is dissolved. If there was an unauthorised distribution of share capital to the members prior to dissolution, therefore, the Crown would be entitled to recover that distribution from the members. The only legal way to avoid this 'right' passing to the Crown as *bona vacantia* is to put the company into formal liquidation prior to dissolution, or to legally reduce the amount of the share capital legally prior to the company dissolution (Form BVC 17 www.bonavacantia.gov.uk).

Permitted distributions

16.32   It has been recognised that it would be unreasonable for the Treasury Solicitor to expect that a company is put into formal liquidation when that would be uneconomic, especially bearing in mind that HMRC ESC C16 permits a distribution for tax purposes without the company having to incur the costs of a formal liquidation. It has, therefore, been agreed with HM Treasury that if:

- a company has been struck off under either *CA 2006, s 1000* or *1003* – now applicable from 1 October 2009; and

- the shareholders have taken advantage of ESC C16; and

- the amount of the distribution is less than £4,000,

as a concession the Treasury Solicitor will waive the Crown's right to any funds, which were distributed to the former members prior to dissolution. (£4,000 is considered to be the average cost of putting a company into liquidation.) (Form BVC 17 www.bonavacantia.gov.uk).

Example 16.6

Beat Ltd is a private company, which has made trading losses for the past few years.

The directors plan to sell the company's assets, settle the company debts, distribute the balance and apply for the company to be struck off. HMRC have agreed to the application of ESC C16.

The shareholders funds are:

	£
Issued Ordinary Shares	1,000
Share Premium	50
Retained Profits	250
	1,300

The company distributes £1,300 to the former members. The Treasury Solicitor will not attempt to recover any of that distribution from the members.

Example 16.7

Deadbeat Ltd is a private company, which has made trading losses for the past few years.

The directors plan to sell the company's assets, settle the company debts, distribute the balance and apply for the company to be struck off under *CA 2006, s 1003* – now applicable from 1 October 2009. HMRC have agreed to the application of ESC C16. The shareholders funds are:

	£
Issued Ordinary Shares	2,000
Share Premium	50
Retained Profits	3,250
	5,300

16.32 *Distributions*

If the company distributes £5,300 to the former members, the Treasury Solicitor will attempt to recover the distribution from the members. In order to avoid this, the company could:

- pay an unauthorised distribution of less than £4,000. £1,300 of assets will be sacrificed but the overall cost may be less than a formal liquidation;

- abandon a *s 1003* striking off application – now applicable from 1 October 2009, approach and appoint a liquidator under a formal winding-up; and

- consider a redemption or purchase of own shares out of capital (*CA 2006, s 709* – now applicable from 1 October 2009).

Chapter 17

Accounting and taxation

GENERALLY ACCEPTED ACCOUNTING STANDARDS

17.1   For accounting periods beginning from 1 January 2005, either UK GAAP or international accounting standards (IAS) as set out in EC Regulation 1606/2002 may be used (*FA 2004, s 50*). UK GAAP will be applied in cases of inter-group transactions where one group member to the transaction obtains a tax advantage by the use of UK GAAP whilst the other group member to the transaction uses IAS (*FA 2004, s 51*).

Those companies whose securities are traded on an EU regulated market are required to prepare their consolidated accounts in accordance with IAS for accounting periods ended on or after 1 January 2005.

A change in accounting practice following UK accounting principles from 1 January 2005, a change from UK GAAP to IAS, may bring about a prior period adjustment. Positive adjustments are taxed as receipts and negative adjustments are allowed as expenses. For accounting periods beginning on or after 1 January 2005, these prior period adjustments are treated as arising on the first day of the first period of account for which the new basis is adopted. For accounting periods beginning before 1 January 2005, the prior period adjustment was treated as taking place on the last day of the first period of account for which the new basis was adopted (*CTA 2009, s 181*).

Companies qualifying as small under the *Companies Act* definition (see **1.13–1.14**) may opt to apply the financial reporting standard for smaller entities (FRSSE). The FRSSE replaces all other accounting standards and Urgent Issue Task Force (UITF) abstracts. An IFRS for small and medium-sized companies has also been published.

ACCOUNTING POLICIES

17.2   A company's accounts prepared in accordance with GAAP form the basis for the company's corporation tax computation (see **1.8–1.10**). This rule applies to trading profits, a letting business, an overseas property business, loan relationships, derivatives, intangible property, management expenses and leases.

Taxation law has no authority to impose compliance with the *Companies Act* or to impose any requirements as to audit disclosure upon the company (*CTA 2009, s 46(2)*). Accounts prepared according to GAAP and in accordance with the *Companies Act* form the basis of the corporation tax computation. The profits are then normally adjusted further because the laws of taxation take precedence over accounting principles (see **Chapter 5**).

As regards the accounts basis, HMRC employ revenue accountants with wide auditing and accounting experience to whom they refer all their accountancy queries (see Tax Bulletin, Issue 58, April 2002). If HMRC open an enquiry into a company's corporation tax return, the Revenue accountants may also enquire into the accounting policies which the company has adopted (see 'TAXline', February 2003 and Working Together, Issue 13, June 2003).

17.3   A synopsis of the current UK and international standards is given on the accompanying pages, together with notes on the interaction of accounting and taxation principles where appropriate. The UK accounting standards are published by the Accounting Standards Board (ASB) and are based on overriding principles rather than detailed prescription.

17.4   UITF assists the ASB where unsatisfactory or conflicting interpretations have developed (or seem likely to develop) about a requirement of an accounting standard or the *Companies Act*. The UITF seeks to arrive at a consensus on the accounting treatment within the ASB framework that should be adopted. UITF consensuses are published in the form of UITF Abstracts. Compliance with UITF Abstracts is necessary (other than in exceptional circumstances) in accounts that claim to give a true and fair view. International accounting standards are published by the International Accounting Standards Board. Overall there is a general convergence between UK GAAP and IAS.

UK GAAP

17.5

	Financial Reporting Standards	Commentary
FRS 30	Heritage assets	
FRSSE (2008)	Financial reporting standard for smaller entities (replaces FRSSE (2007)) (IFRS for SMEs)	**17.8**
FRSSE (2007)	Financial reporting standard for smaller entities (replaces FRSSE (2005))	**17.8**

	Financial Reporting Standards	Commentary
FRS 29	(IFRS 7) Financial instruments: disclosures	
FRS 28	Corresponding amounts	
FRSSE (2005)	Financial reporting standard for smaller entities (replaces FRSSE (2002))	**17.8**
FRS 27	Life assurance	
FRS 26	(IAS 39) Financial instruments: measurement	**17.9**
FRS 25	(IAS 32) Financial instruments: disclosure and presentation	
FRS 24	(IAS 29) Financial reporting in hyperinflationary economies	
FRS 23	(IAS 21) The effects of changes in foreign exchange rates	**17.10**
FRS 22	(IAS 33) Earnings per share	
FRS 21	(IAS 10) Events after the balance sheet date	**17.11**
FRS 20	(IFRS 2) Share-based payment	
FRSSE (2002)	Financial reporting standard for smaller entities	
FRS 19	Deferred tax	**17.30**
FRS 18	Accounting policies	**17.12**
FRS 17	Retirement benefits	**17.21**
FRS 16	Current tax	**17.28**
FRS 15	Tangible fixed assets	**17.13, 17.14**
FRS 14	Earnings per share (FRS 22)	
FRS 13	Derivatives and other financial instruments: disclosures	
FRS 12	Provisions, contingent liabilities and contingent assets	**17.15, 17.16**
FRS 11	Impairment of fixed assets and goodwill	
FRS 10	Goodwill and intangible assets	**17.17**
FRS 9	Associates and joint ventures	
FRS 8	Related party disclosures	
FRS 7	Fair values in acquisition accounting	
FRS 6	Acquisitions and mergers	
FRS 5	Reporting the substance of transactions	**17.18**
FRS 4	Capital instruments	
FRS 3	Reporting financial performance	**17.19, 17.20**

	Financial Reporting Standards	Commentary
FRS 2	Accounting for subsidiary undertakings	
FRS 1	Cash flow statements	
	Statements of Standard Accounting Practice	
SSAP 25	Segmental reporting	
SSAP 24	Accounting for pension costs	**17.21**
SSAP 21	Accounting for lease and hire purchase contracts	**17.22**
SSAP 20	Foreign currency translation (FRS 23)	
SSAP 19	Accounting for investment properties	**17.23**
SSAP 17	*Accounting for post balance sheet events* (FRS 21)	**17.11**
SSAP 13	Accounting for research and development	**17.17**
SSAP 9	Stocks and long-term contracts	**17.24**
SSAP 4	Accounting for government grants	**17.25**
SSAP 5	Accounting for value added tax	

Notes
Bracketed references show the equivalent IFRS or IAS.
Superseded standards are italicised. Replacement standard is shown in brackets.

INTERNATIONAL GAAP

17.6

	International Financial Reporting Standards	Commentary
IFRS 1	First-time adoption of international financial reporting standards	**17.26**
IFRS 2	Share-based payments	
IFRS 3	Business combinations	
IFRS 4	Insurance contracts	
IFRS 5	Non-current assets held for sale and discontinued operations	
IFRS 6	Exploration for and evaluation of mineral assets	
IFRS 7	Financial instruments disclosures	
IFRS 8	Operating segments	
IFRS for SMEs	IFRS for small and medium-sized entities	**17.8**
	International Accounting Standards	
IAS 1	Presentation of financial statements	**17.19**

	International Financial Reporting Standards	*Commentary*
IAS 2	Inventories	**17.24**
IAS 7	Cash flow statements	
IAS 8	Accounting policies, changes in accounting estimates and errors	**17.20**
IAS 10	Events after the balance sheet date	**17.11**
IAS 11	Construction contracts	**17.24**
IAS 12	Income taxes	**17.29, 17.39**
IAS 14	Segment reporting	
IAS 16	Property, plant and equipment	**17.13**
IAS 17	Leases	**17.22**
IAS 18	Revenue	
IAS 19	Employee benefits	**17.21**
IAS 20	Accounting for government grants and disclosure of government assistance	**17.25**
IAS 21	The effects of changes in foreign exchange rates	**17.10**
IAS 23	Borrowing costs	**17.14**
IAS 24	Related party disclosure	
IAS 26	Accounting and reporting by retirement benefit plans	
IAS 27	Consolidated and separate financial statements	
IAS 28	Investments in associates	
IAS 29	Financial reporting in hyperinflationary economies	
IAS 31	Interests in joint ventures	
IAS 32	Financial instruments: presentation	
IAS 33	Earnings per share	
IAS 34	Interim financial reporting	
IAS 36	Impairment of assets	**17.17**
IAS 37	Provisions, contingent liabilities and contingent assets	**17.15**
IAS 38	Intangible assets	**17.17**
IAS 39	Financial instruments: recognition and measurement	**17.9**
IAS 40	Investment property	**17.23**
IAS 41	Agriculture	

INTERACTION OF ACCOUNTING AND TAXATION PRINCIPLES

17.7 Accounting standards deal with accounting treatments. Certain aspects of the accounting treatment may have a direct impact for taxation purposes.

FRSSE

17.8 The FRSSE consolidates and modifies the relevant accounting requirements and disclosures from the other accounting standards and UITF Abstracts for smaller entities and was originally introduced in November 1997. Companies who qualify as 'small' under the *Companies Act* may apply the standard (see **1.13–1.14**). In April 2008 the FRSSE (2008) was introduced to reflect changes in the *Companies Act* and other legislation and accounting standards. A company complying with the FRSSE complies with GAAP.

On 9 July 2009, the International Accounting Standards Board (IASB) published the first International Financial Reporting Standard for small and medium-sized entities (IFRS for SMEs), which provides a common set of accounting standards that is much simpler than the full IFRS. The UK Accounting Standards Board will consult on its implementation in the UK.

FRS 26 Financial instruments: measurement and IAS 39 Financial instruments: recognition and measurement

17.9 IAS 39 and FRS 26 require assets and liabilities to be measured at fair value (see **11.13**). Fair value is the amount for which an asset could be exchanged between knowledgeable, willing parties in an arm's-length transaction. An impairment loss of a financial asset should be recognised only when it is incurred. An impairment loss is the amount by which the carrying amount of an asset exceeds its recoverable amount. The Standard provides additional guidance about how to evaluate impairment that is inherent in a group of loans, receivables or held-to-maturity investments that cannot be identified with any individual financial asset in the group. The guidelines state that if an asset is found to be individually impaired it should not be included in a group of assets that are collectively assessed for impairment. A collective assessment of impairment should be based on credit risk, the debtors' ability to pay together with contractual cash flows and historical loss experience. Historical loss rates should be adjusted to reflect current economic conditions. The impairment review procedures should ensure that the loss is not recognised on the initial recognition of an asset (IAS 39 Introduction).

FRS 23 The effects of changes in foreign exchange rates and IAS 21 Currency accounting

17.10 Under IAS 21 and FRS 23, income and expenditure of foreign operations (including branches) are translated at actual or average rates (not at closing or average rates).

FA 1993, s 92D requires that foreign currency be converted at the average exchange rate for the current accounting period of the appropriate spot rate of exchange for the transaction in question.

For accounting periods beginning on or after 1 January 2005, accounts for taxation purposes must be prepared in sterling (*FA 1993, s 92*). If a UK resident company prepares accounts in a currency other than sterling, for corporation tax purposes the accounts must be computed for GAAP in sterling (*FA 1993, s 92A*). If a UK resident company prepares accounts in a currency other than sterling, but then uses another non-sterling currency as its functional currency, that functional currency is used for preparing accounts according to GAAP. The resulting profits or loss are then converted to sterling (*FA 1993, s 92B*). Similar rules apply if a UK resident company prepares accounts in a currency other than sterling and neither *s 92A* nor *s 92B* applies, or if a non-resident company prepares its accounts in a non-sterling currency. The accounts currency is used for preparing accounts according to GAAP. The resulting profits or loss are then converted to sterling (*FA 1993, s 92C*). See (**13.61–13.68**).

FRS 21 (IAS 10) Events after the balance sheet date and SSAP 17 Accounting for post balance sheet events

17.11 FRS 21 specifies the accounting treatment to be adopted (including the disclosures to be provided) by entities for events occurring between the balance sheet date and the date when the financial statements are authorised for issue. It replaces SSAP 17 Accounting for post balance sheet events.

FRS 21 sets out the recognition and measurement requirements for two types of event after the balance sheet date:

- **Adjusting events**. Those events that provide evidence of conditions that existed at the balance sheet date for which the entity shall adjust the amounts recognised in its financial statements or recognise items that were not previously recognised (adjusting events). For example, the settlement of a court case that confirms the entity had a present obligation at the balance sheet date.

- **Non-adjusting events**. Those events that are indicative of conditions that arose after the balance sheet date for which the entity does not adjust the amounts recognised in its financial statements. For example, a decline in market value of investments between the balance sheet date and the date when the financial statements are authorised for issue.

Dividends declared after the balance sheet date should no longer be reported as liabilities. The FRS removes the requirement to report dividends proposed after the balance sheet date in the profit and loss account and instead requires disclosures in the notes to the financial statements.

The FRS sets out other disclosure requirements. These include:

- the disclosure of the date when the financial statements were authorised for issue;

- the disclosure of information received about conditions that existed at the balance sheet date; and

- if non-adjusting events after the balance sheet date are material and non-disclosure could influence the economic decisions of users, the entity should disclose the nature of the event and an estimate of its financial effect, or a statement that such an estimate cannot be made.

The FRS also requires that an entity shall not prepare its financial statements on a going concern basis if management determines after the balance sheet date that it intends to liquidate the entity or to cease trading or that it has no realistic alternative but to do so (see Chapter 19).

When SSAP 17 (Accounting for post balance sheet events) applied, HMRC found that companies paid insufficient or no attention to adjusting post balance sheet events as regards stock obsolescence provisions, impairment provisions (where the debts are recovered in full) and provisions for claims against an entity that were settled for less in the post balance sheet period (Working Together, Issue 11, June 2003).

FRS 18 Accounting policies

17.12   HMRC have commented that, in some cases, work completed before the year end has been invoiced after the year end but not correctly accounted for (FRS 18, para 26; Working Together, Issue 11, June 2003).

FRS 15 Tangible fixed assets and IAS 16 Property, plant and equipment

17.13   For taxation purposes the distinction between capital and revenue expenditure is maintained. Revenue deductions will follow the timing of recognition in the accounts. FRS 15 provides principles for measurement, valuation and depreciation of fixed assets that are not recognised for taxation purposes (HMRC Business Income Manual BIM 31060).

FRS 15 permits renewals accounting (FRS 15, para 97) on infrastructure assets only in specified circumstances; that is, where the infrastructure is treated as a single system, is maintained by continuing replacement of parts according to a projected asset management plan (AMP) calculated by a qualified and independent person. The system or network has to be in a mature or steady state. Under renewals accounting, the estimated level of expenditure required to maintain the operating capacity (over the AMP period) is treated as depreciation and is charged to the profit and loss account. Actual maintenance expenditure is capitalised. There is no direct link between the actual expenditure in any one year and the amount charged to the profit and loss account. Renewals accounting provides a mechanism to smooth the profile of maintenance expenditure (HMRC Business Income Manual BIM 31065).

FRS 15 renewals accounting is not specifically permitted under IAS 16. If a company adopts IAS 16 there may be a change of accounting policy adjustment (*CTA 2009, s 181*; HMRC International Accounting Standards—the UK Tax Implications, July 2006).

FRS 15 Tangible fixed assets and IAS 23 Borrowing costs

17.14   IAS 23 and FRS 15 permit the capitalisation of borrowing costs. UK tax law departs from FRS 15 by allowing relief for capitalised borrowing costs as if they were a profit and loss account item but only where they relate to a fixed asset or project (*CTA 2009, s 320*). The same approach will continue where IAS 23 is followed (HMRC International Accounting Standards—the UK Tax Implications, July 2006).

FRS 12 Provisions, contingent liabilities and contingent assets and IAS 37 Provisions, contingent liabilities and contingent assets

17.15   There is no significant difference between IAS 37 and FRS 12, which is followed for tax purposes (subject to adjustment where the expenditure is capital for tax purposes or otherwise disallowable).

Under FRS 12 provisions must satisfy the definition of liabilities: 'obligations of an entity to transfer economic benefits as a result of past transactions or events'. Mere anticipation of future expenditure, however probable and no matter how detailed the estimates, is not enough, in the absence of an obligation at the balance sheet date. Provisions are defined by FRS 12 as 'liabilities of uncertain timing or amount' (HMRC Business Income Manual BIM 46515).

Under FRS 12 a provision should be recognised when:

- an entity has a present obligation (legal or constructive) as a result of a past event;

- it is probable that a transfer of economic benefits will be required to settle the obligation; and

- a reliable estimate can be made of the amount of the obligation.

If these conditions are not met, no provision should be recognised.

FRS 12 does not apply to trade creditors, accruals, adjustments to the carrying value of assets, insurance company provisions arising from contracts with policy holders, provisions that are specifically addressed by other accounting standards, such as losses on long-term contracts (SSAP 9), provisions relating to leases (SSAP 21) other than operating leases that have become onerous and pension costs (SSAP 24).

Trade creditors are understood to be liabilities to pay for formally invoiced received goods or services. Accruals are understood to be liabilities to pay for received goods or services, not yet formally invoiced.

HMRC have commented that because of the changes brought about by FRS 12 (effective for accounting periods ending on or after 23 March 1999), the following provisions are no longer allowable for tax purposes:

- provisions for 'future operating losses' that is, losses that will or may arise from obligations entered into subsequent to the balance sheet date;

- restructuring provisions until the business has a 'detailed formal plan' for restructuring and has created a 'valid expectation' in those affected that it will carry it out;

- provisions where the only event that might require them is an unpublished decision of the directors;

- provisions for future expenditure required by legislation where the business could avoid the obligation by changing its method of operation, for example, by stopping doing whatever is affected by the legislation;

- provisions for future repairs of plant and machinery owned by the business (HMRC Business Income Manual BIM 46535).

HMRC have commented that the following provisions will be allowable:

- in the period of sale for the cost of work under a warranty which a trader gives on the sale of merchandise (or under consumer protection legislation);

- for commission refundable by an insurance intermediary on the lapse of a policy where the commission is recognised as income at the inception of the policy;

- by builders for rectification work, including retentions up to the level that these have been recognised as income within accounts (HMRC Business Income Manual BIM 46545).

FRS 12 Provisions, contingent liabilities and contingent assets

17.16 If HMRC wish to challenge a provision, they will firstly ascertain whether it accords with GAAP and then possibly look into the accuracy of the provision. Under FRS 12 a provision should only be recognised if a company has a present obligation as a result of a past event, it is probable that a transfer of economic benefits will be required to settle the obligation, and a reliable estimate can be made of the amount. HMRC comment that, when enquiring into company accounting matters, they have found problems with refurbishment expenditure, onerous contracts and the debtor's ability to pay when applying this standard.

Major refurbishment expenditure should only be provided for if it is in excess of normal repairs and maintenance expenditure. For example, if the lining of a furnace needs to be replaced every five years and at the balance sheet date has been in use for three years, there is no present obligation to make a provision. Similarly, no annual provision is required in the accounts of an airline that is required to overhaul its aircraft once in every three years, the cost being expended when incurred (FRS 12, para 19 and example 11).

In contrast, provisions should be made for onerous contracts, but only those that are truly onerous. When providing for onerous leases, for example, the expected rental income or surrender or sale of the lease should be taken into account (FRS 12, para 73). If the facts show that there is no real likelihood of having to pay, for example where the creditor company has already been wound up and the liquidator has decided not to pursue the debt, then practically speaking, no provision is required (FRS 12, para 23). Finally, provisions have been made to 'smooth profits' rather than to comply with FRS 12, para 14 (Working Together, Issue 13, June 2003).

With effect from 2 January 2007, producers of electrical and electronic equipment are responsible for financing waste management costs. These costs will include the costs of collection, treatment, reuse, recovery and environmentally sound disposal (*SI 2005/3289*). UITF Abstract 45 (IFIRC Interpretation 6) Liabilities arising from Participating in a Specific Market—Waste Electrical and Electronic Equipment implements FRS 12 and IAS 17 principles in providing for these costs.

FRS 10 Goodwill and intangibles; SSAP 13 Accounting for research and development; IAS 38 Intangible assets and IAS 36 Impairment

17.17   IAS 38 does not permit goodwill amortisation. Under IFRS 1 a company has the option of keeping goodwill at the amortised cost at the date of the opening comparative balance sheet in a company's first IAS accounts, and only impairing from that basis figure. *CTA 2009, ss 871, 873* ensure that any write up on the transition from UK GAAP to IAS will be a taxable credit for the intangible fixed assets regime, and *CTA 2009, s 872* ensures that any such credit is limited to the net amount of relief already given. Any impairment from written up cost will be deductible.

IAS 38 requires the capitalisation of development expenditure in R&D. *FA 2004, s 53* nevertheless permits a revenue deduction.

IAS 38 requires website costs, when capitalised, to be treated as an intangible asset.

Where website costs have been the subject of capital allowance claims, but are reclassified as intangible fixed assets under IAS 38, *CTA 2009, s 804* disapplies the intangibles rules so that capital allowances may continue. If intangible asset costs have been written off to the profit and loss account and are then brought into the balance sheet under IAS 38 as an asset, there will be an intangibles credit and possibly an adjustment under *CTA 2009, s 181*. Rules for the transition from UK GAAP to IAS are within *CTA 2009, ss 871–879*. See **6.15**.

FRS 5 Reporting the substance of transactions

17.18   In general, the reporting of revenue in accounts is followed for tax purposes. There is no general standard for revenue recognition in UK GAAP, but the recently added Application Note G to FRS 5 goes some way to dealing with certain aspects of IAS 18. In March 2005 the UITF of the ASB issued UITF Abstract 40 (Revenue recognition and service contracts) to provide further guidance on Note G. *FA 2005, Sch 15* permits a spreading adjustment (see *Corporation Tax 2008/09* Tottel Publishing).

FRS 3 Reporting financial performance and IAS 1 Presentation of financial statements

17.19 UK tax law uses the balance on a profit and loss account as the starting point for the basis of corporation tax computation. Amounts are recognised when they are included in the profit and loss account or in the statement of recognised gains and losses or the IAS equivalent statement of changes in equity or other statement used for calculating the company's profit (*CTA 2009, s 308*; HMRC International Accounting Standards—the UK Tax Implications, July 2006).

FRS 3 Reporting financial performance and IAS 8 Accounting policies, changes in accounting estimates and errors

17.20 Prior period accounting adjustments are brought into the trade profits computation, in the year of change (*CTA 2009, s 181*). A change in valuation from a realisation basis to a market to market basis (possibly occurring in a financial trade) may be spread over six years (*CTA 2009, ss 185, 186*). Where amounts have been allowed as a deduction on an old basis, they will not be allowed again on a new basis (*CTA 2009, s 183*).

CTA 2009, s 180 does not apply to fundamental errors. In such cases, prior periods must be restated. This is effected by an amendment to the corporation tax return (see **2.10**).

SSAP 24 Accounting for pension costs; FRS 17 Retirement benefits and IAS 19 Employee benefits

17.21 The accounts figures for contributions to and changes in value of pension schemes are irrelevant for tax purposes. Relief is given on a paid (and sometimes deferred basis). For pension scheme contributions, see **5.25–5.27**. See **5.23**, **5.41–5.42** for non-pension employee benefits (HMRC International Accounting Standards—the UK Tax Implications, July 2006).

SSAP 21 Accounting for lease and hire purchase contracts and IAS 17 Leases

17.22 UK tax law is not entirely consistent with SSAP 21 (see **6.36–6.37**). IAS 17 is drawn up along similar lines to SSAP 21.

SSAP 19 Accounting for investment properties and IAS 40 Investment property

17.23 The accounts treatment of investment properties is generally irrelevant for tax, as the capital gains rules apply. There may be cases where a property developer uses land for investment purposes before sale, and in such cases IAS 40 may apply. If the company adopts the fair value basis, an adjustment may arise falling within *CTA 2009, s 180*.

Where a company elects to treat an interest in a property held, which it holds as a lessee under an operating lease, as an investment property it is required to account for it as a finance lease. Where this happens the tax rules applying to finance leases will apply (HMRC International Accounting Standards—the UK Tax Implications, July 2006).

SSAP 9 Stocks and long-term contracts; IAS 2 Inventories and IAS 11 Construction contracts

17.24 According to GAAP, stocks should be valued at the lower of cost and net realisable value (SSAP 9). Net realisable value is used where there is no reasonable expectation of sufficient future revenue to cover cost incurred, for example, as a result of deterioration, obsolescence or 'change in demand'. Ideally, stocks should be considered item by item, but this may be impractical and groups of items may be considered. Provisions may be made on a justifiable basis and in consideration of age, past and future movements and estimated scrap values, to reduce valuation from cost to net realisable value. Long-term contracts are valued on a pro-rata completion stage basis.

IAS 2 adopts the same basic principle that inventories should be measured at the lower of cost and net realisable value. Net realisable value is the estimated selling price in the ordinary course of business, less the estimated costs of completion and the estimated costs necessary to make the sale.

Companies Act 2006, s 396 (SIs 2008/409 and *2008/410)* permits the addition of incidental costs of acquisition to the stock cost. The company may include production costs and interest on funds borrowed to finance the asset's production in the stock valuation. Interest should be separately disclosed in a note to the accounts.

SSAP 9 is followed for tax purposes. If a trade ceases, the stock is valued at market value. If the stock is transferred to an unconnected party for the purposes of their trade, stock is valued at the consideration given. If stock is sold to a connected party, it is valued at an arm's-length value (*CTA 2009, s 166*). If stock is taken for a participator's own use, it is valued at selling price

(*CTA 2009, s 157*; *Sharkey v Wernher* (1955) 36 TC 275, [1956] AC 58, [1955] 3 All ER 493). HMRC have in the past commented that they have found problems with aspects of SSAP 9.

In particular, they have found that where companies have made stock provisions they have not been supported by the facts of the case. Long-term contracts are not always identified and accounted for as such (SSAP 9, para 22). Companies have sometimes valued stock and work in progress at net realisable value on the theoretical basis that it would have to be sold as an emergency sale in its current condition, rather than being sold in the normal course of business (SSAP 9, Appendix 1, paras 19, 20; Working Together, Issue 11, June 2003).

HMRC comment that they see no difference between SSAP 9, IAS 2 and IAS 11, except that they do not recognise the IAS 2 LIFO (last in first out) stock valuation method (HMRC International Accounting Standards—the UK Tax Implications, July 2006).

SSAP 4 Accounting for government grants and IAS 20 Government grants

17.25 For both taxation and accounting purposes, grants are treated as income (HMRC International Accounting Standards—the UK Tax Implications, July 2006).

IFRS 1 First time adoption of international financial reporting standards

17.26 Differences between the previous GAAP and the current IFRS treatment are recognised in the opening comparative balance sheet thus enabling any adjustments to be made under *CTA 2009, s 180*.

ACCOUNTING FOR TAX

17.27 Tax is represented in the accounts in both the profit and loss account and the balance sheet. The two types of tax to be shown are current year tax and deferred tax.

FRS 16 Current tax

17.28 Current tax is the estimated tax charge payable based on the taxable profits for the company for the year. Current tax is measured using the tax rates and laws applicable at the balance sheet date.

17.28 *Accounting and taxation*

Dividends received from UK companies are reported as the net amount received. Dividends received from other countries are reported gross only to the extent that they have suffered a withholding tax. Interest received or receivable is shown gross of withholding tax.

Current tax for the period must be recognised in the profit and loss account except to the extent that it relates to gains or losses that have been recognised directly in the statement of total recognised gains and losses. Such tax should also be recognised in the statement of total recognised gains and losses (STRGL).

The profits per the accounts are usually different from the profits chargeable to corporation tax. This is because the nature of the accounts is to attain a profit that incorporates all the expenses and income that have been charged and received as true business expenses and income and incurred during the accounting period, irrelevant of whether payment has actually been made or not. Taxable profits on the other hand have disallowable expenses and income, which must be added back or removed from the profit. In instances where there are timing differences between the accounting profits and the taxable profits an adjustment is made for deferred tax (see **17.31**).

For accounts purposes, the current year's tax provision is disclosed as a current liability, together with a disclosure note. The format of the note is as follows:

Illustration of profit and loss account disclosure

	£000	£000
UK Corporation tax		
Current tax on income for the period	a	
Adjustments in respect of prior periods	b	
	C	
Double taxation relief	(d)	
		E
Foreign tax		
Current tax on income for the period	f	
Adjustments in respect of prior periods	g	
		H
Tax on profit in ordinary activities		I

If an item of tax relates to an item in the statement of total recognised gains and losses, where the tax is also recognised there, then it should not be recognised in the profit and loss account per FRS 16. This includes gains on disposals of fixed assets previously revalued and differences on foreign currencies. The format for the STRGL as per FRS 3 is set out below:

Statement of total recognised gains and losses for the year

	£000
Profit for the financial year (per the profit and loss account)	X
Items taken directly to reserves:	
Unrealised surplus on revaluation of fixed assets	X
Surplus/deficit on revaluation of investment principles	X
Foreign currency exchange differences	X
Total recognised gains and losses for the year	X
Prior period adjustments	(x)
Total gains and losses recognised since last annual report	X

IAS 12 Income taxes

17.29   IAS 12 is drawn up along similar lines with the following notable differences. IAS 12 requires current tax to be shown separately on the face of the balance sheet. FRS 16 has no such requirement. IAS 12 also requires items to be charged to equity if they relate to equity. FRS 16 does not have this requirement. IAS 12 also requires disclosure of the tax expense relating to discontinued operations. FRS 16 does not require this. IAS 12 has no requirement as to the presentation of outgoing or incoming dividends.

FRS 19 Deferred tax

FRS 19's objective

17.30   Deferred tax is sometimes considered more of an accounting issue as opposed to a tax issue. This is largely due to the nature of deferred tax and what it intends to cover. Income and expenditure are often recognised in the accounts at different times to when they are necessarily taxable or relievable. FRS 19 prescribes timing different accounts adjustments to enable the accounts to show a true and fair view.

The overall objective of FRS 19 is to require 'full provision to be made for deferred tax assets and liabilities arising from timing differences between the recognition of gains and losses in the financial statements and their recognition in a tax computation' (FRS 19 Summary).

Deferred tax should be recognised as a liability or asset if the transactions or events that give the entity an obligation to pay more tax in future or a right to pay less tax in future have occurred by the balance sheet date.

Deferred tax should be recognised on most types of timing difference, including those attributable to:

- accelerated capital allowances;
- accruals for pension costs and other post retirement benefits that will be deductible for tax purposes only when paid;
- elimination of unrealised intra-group profits on consolidation;
- unrelieved tax losses;
- other sources of short-term timing differences.

FRS 19 prohibits the recognition of deferred tax on timing differences arising when:

- a fixed asset is revalued without there being any commitment to sell the asset;
- the gain on sale of an asset is rolled over into replacement assets;
- the remittance of a subsidiary, associate or joint venture's earnings would cause tax to be payable, but no commitment has been made to the remittance of the earnings.

As an exception to the general requirement not to recognise deferred tax on revaluation gains and losses, the FRS requires deferred tax to be recognised when assets are continuously revalued to fair value, with changes in fair value being recognised in the profit and loss account.

There is also the requirement that deferred tax assets are to be recognised to the extent that they are regarded as more likely than not that they will be recovered.

Calculation of deferred tax

Fixed assets

17.31 FRS 19 deals with the depreciation, disposal and revaluation aspects of fixed assets.

The depreciation charge within the accounts is likely to differ to the capital allowances granted for tax purposes. The difference is usually removed when the asset is sold, however, whilst the asset is still owned by the company, the difference in depreciation of the asset can result in timing differences and thus the asset will have a differing value to that of the accounts and as recognised in the accounts. Thus, an adjustment will be made to reflect the timing differences within the accounts. When the asset is sold, an adjustment will be made in the tax computation reversing the excess capital allowances previously given.

The timing differences for accelerated capital allowances for an asset bought in 2006 for £5,000 with a depreciation charge of 25% straight line and sold at the end of 2008 can be shown thus:

Year	2007	2008	2009
	£	£	£
Depreciation charge	1,250	1,250	1,250
Capital allowances	2,000	750	563
Timing differences	750	(750)	(687)

The cumulative timing difference at 31 December 2009 is £(687). The cumulative timing difference at 31 December 2008 is nil, being £750 at 31 December 2007 and £(750) at 31 December 2007.

Deferred tax should not be recognised on timing differences arising where fixed assets are revalued or sold unless by the balance sheet date the reporting entity has entered into a binding agreement to sell the revalued asset and has recognised the gains and losses expected to arise on sale. There is an exception to this rule, however, in that if the asset is to be replaced and roll-over relief is obtained or expected to be obtained then no deferred tax should be recognised. Even if the gain from the sale of the asset is to be rolled over for use in replacement assets, as long as no roll-over relief is obtained or expected to be obtained then an adjustment for deferred tax should be made.

Pension costs

17.32 Another element of deferred tax where an adjustment may need to be made is with pension liabilities. The FRS describes the use of deferred tax here as when the liabilities are 'accrued in the financial statements but are allowed for tax purposes only when paid or contributed at a later date'. Pension costs are only allowable in a tax computation for the period in which they are paid. Thus, where they have not been paid in the accounts, but are shown in the profit and loss account in the accounts, then an adjustment for the deferred tax will be made as it relates to a timing difference between expenses in an accounting period and in a tax period.

Tax losses

17.33 Timing differences may occur with unrelieved tax losses leading to a tax reduction or refund. If, however, they are used against future profits a deferred tax asset may arise as per FRS 19 a timing difference can arise if a tax loss is not relieved against past or present taxable profits but can be carried forward to reduce future taxable profits.

Unremitted earnings of subsidiaries, associates and joint ventures

17.34 As regards the unremitted earnings of subsidiaries, associates and joint ventures FRS 19 states that tax that could be payable (taking account of any double taxation relief) on any future remittance of the past earnings of a subsidiary, associate or joint venture should be provided for in certain circumstances. These are only to the extent that, at the balance sheet date, dividends have been accrued as receivable or a binding agreement to distribute the past earnings in the future has been entered into by the subsidiary, associate or joint venture. This again refers to timing differences between the accounting and tax periods, as all earnings by the parent or related company are either accrued or past profits.

Full provision liability method

17.35 FRS 19 adopts the full provision liability method as opposed to the partial provision deferral method. Full provision rationale records the tax effect of all gains and losses in the accounts in full. Partial provision provides for tax liabilities that are expected to arise.

The deferral method provides for deferred tax at the rate of taxation in use when the differences occur. No adjustment is made if the rates subsequently change. If the timing differences reverse, the tax is calculated again at the rate in force when the differences first arose. The liability method provides for deferred tax at the rate that is expected to apply when the timing differences reverse. This method is considered to more accurately reflect the amount of tax that is expected to be paid.

Discounting

17.36 FRS 19 permits but does not require a company to discount its deferred tax assets and liabilities to reflect the time value of money. The discount period being the number of years between the balance sheet dates and the date on which it is estimated that the underlying timing differences will reverse (FRS 19, para 47). The discount rates prescribed are the post-tax yields to maturity that could be obtained at the balance sheet date on government bonds with maturity dates and in currencies similar to those of the deferred tax assets or liabilities (FRS 19, para 52).

Recognition of deferred tax assets

17.37   Deferred tax assets should be recognised to the extent that they are regarded as recoverable. This judgment should be made from all available evidence (FRS 19, para 23). Deferred tax should only be recognised if it is likely that the company has sufficient taxable profit to cover any future reversal of the underlying timing differences. In making this assessment the company should also consider its tax planning opportunities.

Accounts presentation

17.38   FRS 19 requires that deferred tax be recognised in the profit and loss account for the period, except to the extent that it is attributable to a gain or loss that is or has been recognised directly in the statement of total recognised gains and losses.

Within the profit and loss account the charge for the period should be included under the heading *Tax on profit or loss on ordinary activities*. The deferred tax balance will be shown separately in the balance sheet within either *Provisions for liabilities and charges* if the balance is a net deferred tax liability or within *Debtors* should the balance be a net deferred tax asset.

The deferred tax debit and credit balance should only be offset within the debtor and creditors if they relate to taxes levied by the same tax authority and arise in the same taxable entry or in a group of taxable entries where the tax losses of one entity can reduce the taxable profits of another meaning that the liabilities have to match in time period and transaction and so be offset without confusion in the accounts.

The accounts must also show within the balance sheet the total deferred tax balance showing the amount recognised for each significant type of timing difference separately showing the impact of discounting on, and the discounted amount of, the deferred tax balance and the movement between the opening and closing net deferred tax balance analysing separately:

- the amount charged or credited in the profit and loss account for the period;
- the amount charged or credited directly in the statement of total recognised gains and losses for the period; and

- movements arising from the acquisition or disposal of businesses.

The deferred tax will also need to be shown in a disclosure note showing the different elements as per the example below.

Example 17.1

Taxation on profit on ordinary activities

(a) Analysis of charge in the period

	£000	£000
Current tax		
UK corporation tax on profits of the period	40	
Adjustments in respect of previous periods	10	
Total current tax		50
Deferred tax		
Origination and reversal of timing differences	27	
Adjustments in respect of previous periods		
Total deferred tax		27
Total tax charge		77

(b) Factors affecting the tax charge for the period

The difference between the tax charge based on applying the UK corporation tax rates to the reported profit before taxation to the actual current tax charge is reconciled below.

	£000
Profit on ordinary activities before taxation	536
Profit on ordinary activities before taxation multiplied by the standard rate of corporation tax in the UK of 28%	150
Effects of:	
Expenses not deductible for tax purposes	30
Capital allowances (more than) less than depreciation	(60)
Utilisation of tax losses	(80)
Current tax charge for the period	40

(c) Factors that may affect future tax charges

Based on current capital investment plans, the company expects to be able to continue to claim capital allowances in excess of depreciation in future years but at a slightly lower level than in the current year. The company has tax losses that have not been recognised due to the uncertainty over their availability. If they become available they will reduce the future tax charge.

Provisions for deferred tax

(a) Deferred tax liability/(asset) provided in the accounts comprises:

	£000
Accelerated capital allowances	140
Tax losses	(60)
Other short-term timing differences	(1)
	(79)

(b) Deferred tax liability/(asset) not provided in the accounts comprises:

	£000
Chargeable gains subject to roll-over relief	70
Tax losses	(20)
Other short-term timing differences	(1)
	49

The potential deferred tax asset has not been recognised in the accounts because it is unlikely that the losses will be utilised in the foreseeable future.

(c) Analysis of movement in the period

	£000
Deferred tax asset at 1 April 2009	(106)
Deferred tax charge in the profit and loss account	27
Deferred tax asset at 31 March 2010	(79)

Deferred tax has been calculated at 28% being the prevailing rate of UK corporation tax rate at 31 March 2010.

As can be seen, FRS 19 provides in-depth analysis to assist account users in comprehending the effects of the overall tax charge. There are significant differences between FRS 19 and IAS 12 that are summarised below.

IAS 12 Income tax

17.39   IAS 12 (Income tax) deals with deferred taxation. It is drawn up on similar lines except that provisions are required in the following circumstances:

- on a revaluation of a non-monetary asset whether or not it is intended that the asset will be sold and whether or not roll-over relief could be claimed;

- on a sale of assets where the gain has been or might be rolled over into replacement assets;

- where adjustments recognise assets and liabilities at their fair values on the acquisition of a business;

- on the unremitted earnings of subsidiaries, associates and joint ventures;

- on exchange differences on consolidation of non-monetary assets;

- on unrealised intra-group profits eliminated on consolidation, provision is required on the temporary difference rather than on the timing difference of the profit that has been taxed but not recognised in the consolidated financial statements.

Chapter 18

Compliance assurance

INTRODUCTION

18.1   HMRC have been granted new powers in order to monitor the accuracy of the submission of company tax returns (**18.2–18.15**). The penalty provisions for: the failure to submit a company tax return (**18.16–18.20**),for inaccuracies (**18.21–18.30**) and for the company's failure to make itself known to HMRC (**18.31–18.36**) have been updated. The senior accounting officer has been made responsible for the accuracy of certain large company returns (**18.37–18.43**). Anti-avoidance clauses are included within all new legislation, and companies are required to disclose any tax mitigation scheme to HMRC when submitting their company tax return (**18.44–18.49**).

HMRC POWERS TO OBTAIN INFORMATION AND DOCUMENTS

18.2   With effect from 1 April 2009 (*SI 2009/404*), HMRC have powers to:

- request supplementary information from the taxpayer and from third parties;

- inspect records; and

- visit premises and inspect records, assets and premises.

Supplementary information

18.3   The request for *supplementary* information to either the company or a third party must be made in writing (*FA 2008, Sch 36, paras 1* and *2*). A notice to a third party can only be given with the approval of the company or the First-tier Tribunal, and an application to the tribunal for approval of a taxpayer or third party notice is heard without the taxpayer being present (*FA 2008, Sch 36, para 3*). A third party request must name the person to whom it relates, unless this has been disapplied by the First-tier Tribunal. A copy of a third party notice must be given to the taxpayer unless the First-tier Tribunal disapplies this requirement (*FA 2008, Sch 36, para 4*). If there are reasonable grounds for believing that a company has not complied with the *Taxes Acts*, HMRC may request a notice approval from the First-tier Tribunal, even though the identity of the company is unknown to them (*FA 2008, Sch 36, para 5*). A decision of the tribunal regarding the approval of a giving of a notice is final (*FA 2008, Sch 36, para 6(4)*; *FA 2009, Sch 47, para 4*). HMRC's notice may request the production of an original or copy document. The notice must be complied with in full (*FA 2008, Sch 36, para 8*).

Inspect records

18.4   The Commissioners may authorise a person to access and inspect the operation of any computer and associated apparatus used in connection with a relevant required document at any reasonable time (*FA 2008, s 114(3)*).

Any person who obstructs the exercise of this power, or does not provide assistance within a reasonable time, is liable to a penalty of £300 (*FA 2008, s 114(6)*).

Powers to inspect businesses

18.5   Subject to at least 24 hours' notice being given, an HMRC officer may inspect the business premises and the business assets or the business documents that are on the premises at any time, if the inspection is required for checking the company's tax position (*FA 2008, Sch 36, para 10*). Business assets consist of any assets that a Revenue officer believes are owned, leased or used in connection with carrying on the business. Only business documents that are trading stock or plant, as defined in *CAA 2001* (see **6.10** et seq), and statutory documents may be inspected. Business premises consist of any premises that an officer believes are used for the purposes of carrying on a business and include any building or structure, and land or any means of transport. If the First-tier Tribunal has approved the inspection, the company has no right of appeal (*FA 2008, Sch 36, para 13(3)*; *FA 2009, Sch 47, para 8*).

Other powers

18.6   Revenue officers have powers to copy documents and to remove and retain a document for a reasonable time if it appears necessary to do so (*FA 2008, Sch 36, para 15*). HMRC are liable to pay the owner reasonable compensation should they cause any damage to the document (*FA 2008, Sch 36, para 16*). In addition, HMRC have powers to mark documents and assets that have been inspected (*FA 2008, Sch 36, para 17*).

Restriction on powers

18.7   An information notice only requires a person to produce a document if it is in his possession or power (*FA 2008, Sch 36, para 18*). An information notice may not require a person to produce a document if the whole of the document originates more than six years before the date of the notice, unless the notice is given by, or with the agreement of, an authorised officer (*FA 2008, Sch 36, para 20*).

If a company has made a tax return under *FA 1998, Sch 18, para 3*, a notice may not be given for checking the company's corporation tax position. A notice may be given if an enquiry has commenced under *FA 1998, Sch 18, para 21* but has not yet been completed, or if the Revenue and Customs officer has reason to suspect that there has been an under-assessment or excessive relief granted (*FA 2008, Sch 36, para 21*). Documents protected by legal privilege need not be supplied (*FA 2008, Sch 36, para 23*). Similarly, an auditor cannot be required to provide copies of his working papers (*FA 2008, Sch 36, para 24*), and a tax adviser cannot be required to supply copies of his client correspondence or working papers (*FA 2008, Sch 36, para 25*). The tax adviser's legal privilege does not extend to explanatory material supplied to the client in relation to a document already supplied to HMRC or name and address details of a person to whom an information notice relates or of any person who acts or has acted on his or her behalf (*FA 2008, Sch 36, para 27*).

Right of appeal

18.8   A company has a right of appeal to the First-tier Tribunal against an information notice (*FA 2008, Sch 36, para 29*). There is no right of appeal if the document formed part of the statutory records or the First-tier Tribunal approved the information notice. Statutory records are documents that the company is required to keep under the *Taxes Acts* and CGT legislation. Records that do not relate to the business or need to be kept for VAT purposes become statutory records once the chargeable period to which they relate has ended, and they need only be kept for the relevant statutory retention period (*FA 2008, Sch 36, para 62*).

Any person given a third party notice may also appeal to the First-tier Tribunal on the grounds that it would be unduly onerous to comply. There is no right of appeal if the notice relates to i the company's statutory records or that of its parent or subsidiary (*FA 2008, Sch 36, para 35(3)*), or if the First-tier Tribunal approved the giving of the notice (*FA 2008, Sch 36, para 30*). A company has a right of appeal if given a notice, where the identity of the person is unknown, on the grounds that it would be unduly onerous to comply with the notice or the requirement (*FA 2008, Sch 36, para 31*).

Appeal procedure

18.9   Notice of appeal must be given in writing, within 30 days of the date when the information notice was given, and to the Revenue and Customs officer who gave the notice. The appeal must state the grounds. The First-tier Tribunal's decision is final, and on receipt of the appeal it will either confirm, vary or set aside the information notice or a requirement in the information notice. Confirmations and variations must be complied with within the time limits set by the Tribunal and, if not set, within any reasonable time limit specified in writing by a Revenue and Customs officer following the Tribunal's decision (*FA 2008, Sch 36, para 32*).

Third party information notices given to any person to check the tax position of the parent undertaking and any subsidiary need only state this and the name of the parent, and not every subsidiary, which need only be sent to the parent (*FA 2008, Sch 36, para 35*). No consent is required from either the subsidiary or the First-tier Tribunal, and no copy need be given to the subsidiary. The information notice restrictions in *FA 2008, Sch 36, para 21* (see **18.7**), in relation to the CTSA return and enquiry framework, apply as if the notice was a taxpayer notice given to a subsidiary. If a notice is given to the parent to check the tax position of a subsidiary whose identity is not known to the officer, the approval of the First-tier Tribunal is not required. The parent company cannot appeal against a requirement to produce documents which are part of the statutory records.

The definition of parent and subsidiary follows that of the *Companies Act 2006.*

An undertaking is a parent undertaking in relation to another undertaking if:

- it holds a majority of the voting rights of the other undertaking; or

- it is a member of the undertaking and has the right to appoint or remove a majority of its board of directors; or

- it has the right to exercise a dominant influence over the undertaking:

    — by virtue of provisions contained in the undertaking's articles; or

    — by virtue of a control contract; or

- it is a member of the undertaking and controls alone, pursuant to an agreement, with other shareholders or members, a majority of the voting in the undertaking.

(*CA 2006, s 1162*)

Change of ownership of companies

18.10   A change of ownership of a company is determined under *ICTA 1988, s 769* (see **9.19**). In such circumstances, there are no restrictions on the giving of an information notice only during the course of an enquiry or where a Revenue and Customs officer has reason to suspect that there has been an under-assessment or excessive relief granted; see **18.7** (*FA 2008, Sch 36, para 36*).

Penalties

18.11   A penalty of £300 is invoked, and followed by a daily penalty not exceeding £60 per day, for:

- failure to comply with an information notice;

- deliberate obstruction of a Revenue officer in the course of an inspection;

- concealment or destruction of documents following and information notice; or

- an informal information notice.

(*FA 2008, Sch 36, paras 39* and *40*)

If a company supplies inaccurate information or produces a document that contains an inaccuracy when complying with an information notice, and the inaccuracy is careless or deliberately caused by the person failing to take reasonable care, HMRC may charge a fixed rate penalty of £3,000. Similarly, where a company discovers the inaccuracy some time later, but fails to take reasonable steps to inform HMRC, a penalty of £3,000 may be charged. If the information or document contains more than one inaccuracy, a penalty is payable for each inaccuracy (*FA 2008, Sch 36, para 40A; FA 2009, Sch 47, para 15*).

DESTRUCTION OF DOCUMENTS

18.12   A company must not conceal, destroy or dispose of a document which is the subject of an information notice addressed to that company. If the document has already been produced to the Revenue and Customs officer, the prohibition no longer applies unless the officer notified the person that the document must continue to be available for inspection. Copies of documents produced to a Revenue and Customs officer under *FA 2008, Sch 36, para 8(1)* may be destroyed six months thereafter, unless the officer previously notified the person that the document must continue to be available for inspection (*FA 2008, Sch 36, para 42*).

511

A company must not conceal, destroy or dispose of a document if an officer has informed the person within the previous six months that that document is likely to be the subject of an information notice (*FA 2008, Sch 36, para 43*).

Reasonable excuse

18.13 No penalty arises if there was a reasonable excuse for the failure or obstruction. Reasonable excuse is not defined, but it does not include an insufficiency of funds, unless this is outside the company's control, or reliance on the work of others, unless reasonable care to avoid failure or obstruction is taken (*FA 2008, Sch 36, para 45*). A company liable for a penalty will be assessed within 12 months of the relevant date, being:

- the end of the period in which an appeal against the information notice could have been given;

- the date on which the appeal is determined or withdrawn, if an appeal is given; or

- in any other case, the date on which the person became liable to the penalty.

(*FA 2008, Sch 36, para 46*)

Right of appeal

18.14 A company has a right of appeal to the First-tier Tribunal against a penalty notice and the amount of the penalty (*FA 2008, Sch 36, para 47*). The notice of appeal must be made in writing and must state the grounds. It must be made within 30 days of the day on which the notice was issued.

If a Revenue and Customs officer believes that a significant amount of tax is at stake through the company's failure to comply with a penalty notice, the officer may apply to the Upper Tribunal for an additional penalty within 12 months of the relevant date (*FA 2008, Sch 36, para 50*). The penalty is due for payment within 30 days of its notification (*FA 2008, Sch 36, para 51*).

Offence

18.15 Any person found guilty of an offence is liable on summary conviction to a fine not exceeding the statutory maximum. On conviction or indictment, he may be liable to imprisonment for a term not exceeding two years or a fine or both (*FA 2008, Sch 36, para 55*).

A person is guilty of an offence if he is found to be concealing, destroying or otherwise disposing of documents required for an information notice which has been approved by a First-tier Tribunal. This is not the case if the person concerned acted after the document or copy has been produced to an officer, unless an officer notified that the document should continue to be available. Nor is there an offence if the person acted six months after a copy document was produced to an officer, unless an officer previously requested the original document (*FA 2008, Sch 36, para 53*).

A person is also guilty of an offence if the person concealed, destroyed or otherwise disposed of a document after an officer has informed the person in writing that that document is likely to be the subject of an information notice and the officer intended to seek the First-tier Tribunal's approval. There is no offence if the person acts at least six months after the person was informed or a notice was given (*FA 2008, Sch 36, para 54*).

FAILURE TO DELIVER A COMPANY TAX RETURN ON TIME

Penalty rules post Finance Act 2009, Sch 55

18.16   *Finance Act 2009, Sch 55* introduced new penalty regulations for the failure to deliver a company tax return under *FA 1998, Sch 18, para 3* on time. The date of introduction is to be notified by Treasury Order. The amount of each penalty depends on the length of time the return is outstanding after the penalty date. The penalty date is the day after the filing date, being the date on which the penalty is first payable. The penalties are not interdependent. There are unlimited fixed-rate penalties, but the total of the tax-related penalties may not exceed 100% of the tax at issue (*FA 2009, Sch 55, paras 1(3) and 17(3)*). The company has a right of appeal ((*FA 2009, Sch 55, para 20*) and no penalty can be charged if the company has a reasonable excuse for its failure.

Penalties invoked

18.17   Penalties raised if the company fails to meet the company tax return filing deadline are as follows:

Company tax return outstanding for 3 months or less

- a £100 penalty;

Company tax return outstanding for more than 3 months

- HMRC may issue a notice to charge a penalty of £10 per day from the penalty date for a period of 90 days or until the company tax return is filed;

18.18 *Compliance assurance*

Company tax return outstanding for more than 6 months

- HMRC may charge a penalty amounting to the greater of £300 and 5% of the corporation tax at issue;

Company tax return outstanding for more than 12 months after the penalty date

- the penalty is dependent on whether the failure amounts to the withholding of information which would enable or assist HMRC to assess the company's liability to tax.

Withholding information failure

18.18   The penalty is dependent upon whether HMRC consider that the:

Withholding of information is deliberate and concealed

- the penalty is the greater of 100% of any liability to tax which would have been shown in the return in question and £300;

Withholding of information is deliberate but not concealed

- the penalty is the greater of 70% of any liability to tax which would have been shown in the return in question and £300;

In any other case

- the penalty is the greater of 5% of any liability to tax which would have been shown in the return in question and £300 (*FA 2009, Sch 55, paras 1–6*).

Reductions for unprompted and prompted disclosure

18.19   There are reductions in the penalties charged for unprompted and prompted disclosure brought about by: informing HMRC; assisting HMRC in quantifying any tax unpaid; and allowing HMRC access to records for the purpose of checking how much tax is so unpaid.

The maximum reduced penalty that may be applied is as follows but, if the withholding of information is deliberate, irrespective of whether it was concealed, the penalty cannot fall below £300:

Penalty	Maximum reduced penalty for an unprompted disclosure	Maximum reduced penalty for a prompted disclosure
30%	0%	15%
70%	20%	35%
100%	30%	50%

(*FA 2009, Sch 55, para 15*).

An unprompted disclosure can be made at any time when the person making it has no reason to believe that HMRC have discovered or are about to discover the inaccuracy or under-assessment. In all other cases, the disclosure is prompted. The quality of the disclosure depends on its timing, nature and extent.

HMRC have the discretion to reduce a penalty if they consider that special circumstances apply. The special circumstances do not include the company's inability to pay, or the fact that a potential loss of revenue from one taxpayer is balanced by a potential over-payment by another.

An insufficiency of funds is not a reasonable excuse, unless it is attributable to events outside the company's control. Where the company relies on another person to do anything, that is not a reasonable excuse unless the company took reasonable care to avoid the failure. Where the company had a reasonable excuse for the failure, but the excuse has ceased, the company is treated as having continued to have the excuse if the failure is remedied without unreasonable delay after the excuse ceased (*FA 2009, Sch 55, para 23*).

HMRC also have the discretion not to bring proceedings in relation to a penalty, and to agree a compromise during any proceedings that should take place (*FA 2009, Sch 55, para 16*).

This penalty is reduced by any other penalty or surcharge applied to the same tax liability (*FA 2009, Sch 55, para 17(1)*).

Penalty assessment

18.20   In order to charge the penalty, HMRC must raise an assessment, notify the company, and state in the notice the period in respect of which the penalty is assessed. The company must pay the penalty within 30 days beginning with the day on which notification of the penalty was issued (*FA 2009, Sch 55, para 18*). The time limit for assessing the penalty is the last day of the period of two years beginning with the filing date. If there is an appeal, the time limit is the last day of the period of 12 months beginning with either the end of the appeal period for the assessment of the liability to tax which would have been shown in the return or, if there is no such assessment, the date on which that liability is ascertained or it is ascertained that the liability is nil (*FA 2009, Sch 55, para 19*).

PENALTIES FOR INACCURACIES

New penalty regime effective after 1 April 2009

18.21 *Finance Act 2007 (FA 2007, s 97, Sch 24* as amended by *FA 2008, Sch 40*) introduced a new penalty regime which comes into effect for returns or other documents for tax periods commencing on or after 1 April 2008 that are due to be filed on or after 1 April 2009 (HMRC Brief 19/2008, 2 April 2008; *SI 2008/568*). These rules apply not only to corporation tax but also to income tax, capital gains tax, construction industry deduction and VAT. See Revenue and Customs Brief 29/08 for HMRC learning package. HMRC have also introduced a new manual on this topic – Compliance Handbook Manual.

As regards corporation tax, HMRC will raise a penalty if the company or another person has either carelessly or deliberately supplied a document from the type listed below, containing an inaccuracy that leads to a tax understatement, or a false or inflated allowable loss, or a false or inflated claim to repayment of tax, or a payment of a corporation tax credit. Separate penalties are charged for each inaccuracy contained in the document (*FA 2007, Sch 24, paras 1, 1A*).

The types of documents on which a penalty is payable are as follows:

- Company Tax Return (CT600 and/or supplementary pages) as required by *FA 1998, Sch 18, para 3*;

- any return, statement or declaration in connection with a claim for an allowance, deduction or relief;

- accounts in connection with ascertaining liability to tax; or

- any document which is likely to be relied upon by HMRC to determine, without further inquiry, a question about:

  — the company's tax liability;

  — the company's corporation tax payments or in connection with corporation tax;

  — any other payment made by the company including penalties; or

  — repayments or any other kind of payment or credit to the company.

Special returns subject to special penalties under *TMA 1970, s 98* are excluded: see **2.3** (*FA 2007, Sch 24, para 12*). Where the company or its officer (see **18.22**) has been convicted of an offence, there is no liability to any further penalty (*FA 2007, Sch 24, para 21*).

Provided that the company takes reasonable care to avoid an inaccuracy in the supply of a document to HMRC, the company is not liable to a penalty in respect of any actions or omissions of its corporation tax agent (*FA 2007, Sch 24, para 18*).

The penalty rules imposed on companies that fail to notify HMRC that they are within the charge to corporation tax (see **2.3**) are contained in *FA 2008, Sch 41*. These rules mirror those of *FA 2007, Sch 24*; see **18.22**.

Circumstances in which a penalty is payable

18.22   If HMRC under-assess the company's corporation tax liability and the company has failed to take reasonable steps to notify HMRC within a 30-day period commencing with the date of the under-assessment, HMRC will raise a penalty. In deciding what is reasonable, HMRC will consider whether the company knew or should have known of the under-assessment and, if so, what steps would have been reasonable to notify HMRC. A loss of tax by an under-assessment includes a loss of tax by an under-determination on HMRC's part, and the same rules apply (*FA 2007, Sch 24, para 2*). See **2.22** for determination assessments.

There are three degrees of inaccuracy on the part of the company, each with increasing degrees of seriousness, on which a penalty may be charged: careless, deliberate but not concealed, and deliberate and concealed. There is only one penalty if the error is attributable to another person. The penalty is based on a percentage of the potential lost revenue. The relevant percentages are:

Degree of inaccuracy	Percenatage penalty based on potential lost revenue
Careless	30%
Deliberate but not concealed	70%
Deliberate and concealed	100%
Error attributable to another person	100%

A careless inaccuracy arises when the company fails to take reasonable care when supplying the document to HMRC. A deliberate but not concealed inaccuracy arises when the company wilfully supplies a document containing

517

incorrect information, but takes no steps to conceal the fact. A deliberate and concealed inaccuracy arises when the company wilfully supplies false evidence, but this time takes steps to conceal the fact.

Even if the company delivered a document containing an inaccuracy to HMRC with neither a careless nor a deliberate intent, but which later was discovered to contain an inaccuracy, the circumstance is treated as careless if the company has not taken reasonable steps to inform HMRC (*FA 2007, Sch 24, para 3*).

A penalty can be reduced if the company makes an unprompted error disclosure. A disclosure is unprompted if it is made at a time when the company has no reason to believe that HMRC has made or is about to discover the error. In calculating the reduction, HMRC will consider the quality of the information provided, the assistance given to HMRC in calculating the additional liabilities, and the access given to the company's books and records. Companies are expected to take reasonable care, in proportion to their circumstances, when maintaining their books and records. They should seek assistance when dealing with unfamiliar transactions. HMRC may suspend a penalty that is invoked for failing to take reasonable care. See HMRC Brief 19/2008 2 April 2008 'New Penalties for errors in returns and documents'.

Potential lost revenue: normal rule

18.23   If tax is under-assessed because a company omits to submit a return, the penalty is 30% of the potential lost revenue. The potential lost revenue is the additional tax due or payable as a result of correcting the inaccuracy in a document, including that attributable to a supply of false information or the withholding of information, or the assessment. The additional tax includes all tax due and any over-payments (*FA 2007, Sch 24, para 5*).

Group relief claims and repayments of tax on loans from a company under *ICTA 1988, s 419(4A)* are ignored for the purposes of calculating the potential lost revenue, but inaccurate claims can still attract a penalty (*FA 2007, Sch 24, para 5(4)*).

Potential lost revenue: multiple errors

18.24   In the case of multiple inaccuracies in a document, careless inaccuracies are treated as being corrected first, followed by a deliberate but not concealed inaccuracy, and followed by a deliberate and concealed inaccuracy. For the purposes of calculating potential lost revenue, an overstatement of tax by the company is brought into consideration when calculating the penalty. The set-off is first against understatements for which the taxpayer is not liable to a penalty, and then against careless understatements, then against deliberate but not concealed understatements, and then against deliberate and concealed understatements. No consideration is to be given to the increased tax revenue from another taxpayer as a result of the company's action (*FA 2007, Sch 24, para 6*).

Potential lost revenue: losses

18.25   If an inaccuracy results in a loss being incorrectly recorded, the penalty is calculated according to the utilisation of the loss.

A penalty based on the potential lost revenue is also applied if a loss arises or if no loss would have arisen apart from the inaccuracy, and that loss has been used to reduce the amount of tax payable. If a different loss is recorded to the actual true loss, the penalty is based on the potential lost revenue from the differential. The potential lost revenue is the amount of the additional tax due or payable as a result of correcting the inaccuracy or the assessment (*FA 2007, Sch 24, para 7(1)*). If the loss has been partially used to reduce the amount of tax payable and the balance remains unutilised, the penalty is the additional tax due or payable as a result of correcting the inaccuracy or the assessment for the loss used plus 10% of the part of the loss that has not been utilised (*FA 2007, Sch 24, para 7(2)*).

Group relief can be taken into account if the inaccuracy creates or increases an aggregate loss for the group (*FA 2007, Sch 24, para 7(4)*).

The potential lost revenue will be reduced to nil if the company's circumstances are such that neither it nor any other company would be able to utilise the loss (*FA 2007, Sch 24, para 7(5)*).

Potential lost revenue: delayed tax

18.26   Where tax is declared late because of an inaccuracy, but a penalty based on lost revenue does not apply, a penalty will still be calculated. This penalty is based on 5% of the delayed tax for each year of the delay. Part years are treated on a pro rata basis (*FA 2007, Sch 24, para 8*).

Reductions for disclosure

18.27   HMRC will give a penalty reduction for both prompted and unprompted disclosures. The reduction is based on the seriousness of the penalty and the quality of the disclosure.

For the purposes of these regulations, a company makes a disclosure to HMRC if that company:

- admits to HMRC that there is or may be an inaccuracy, a supply of false information or the withholding of information;

- takes active steps in giving HMRC reasonable help in quantifying the inaccuracy, supply of false information or the withholding of information, or the under-assessment; and

- allows HMRC access to records for the purpose of ensuring that the inaccuracy, supply of false information or the withholding of information, or under-assessment is fully corrected.

An unprompted disclosure can be made at any time when the person making it has no reason to believe that HMRC have discovered or are about to discover the inaccuracy or under-assessment. In all other cases, the disclosure is unprompted. The quality of the disclosure depends on its timing, nature and extent.

The maximum reduced penalty that may be applied is as follows:

Penalty	Maximum reduced penalty for an unprompted disclosure	Maximum reduced penalty for a prompted disclosure
30%	0%	15%
70%	20%	35%
100%	30%	50%

(*FA 2007, Sch 24, para 10*)

HMRC have the discretion to reduce a penalty if they consider that special circumstances apply. The special circumstances do not include the company's ability to pay, or the fact that a potential loss of revenue from one taxpayer is balanced by a potential over-payment by another. HMRC also have the discretion not to bring proceedings in relation to a penalty, and to agree a compromise during any proceedings that should take place (*FA 2007, Sch 24, para 11*).

This penalty is reduced by any other penalty or surcharge applied to the same tax liability (*FA 2007, Sch 24, para 12*).

Procedures

18.28 HMRC will assess the penalty and notify the company. The notice will specify the tax period for which the penalty is assessed. The assessment will be treated and enforced in the same way as a corporation tax assessment. It may also be combined with an actual corporation tax assessment (*FA 2007, Sch 24, para 13(1)* and *(2)*).

The penalty assessment for a tax understatement must be made within 12 months of the period beginning with the end of the appeal period for the decision correcting the inaccuracy or, if there is no penalty assessment, the date on which the inaccuracy is corrected. The penalty assessment for a false or inflated loss must be made within 12 months of the period beginning with the end of the appeal period for the assessment of tax, which corrected the understatement (*FA 2007, Sch 24, para 13(3)* and *(4)*). An appeal period is a period during which an appeal could be brought or during which an appeal has been brought but has not been determined or withdrawn. The penalty is due for payment within 30 days of notification (*FA 2007, Sch 24, para 13(1A)*).

Suspension

18.29   HMRC may suspend a penalty for a careless inaccuracy leading to a tax understatement. The period of suspension must not exceed two years. HMRC must issue a notice specifying the part of the penalty to be suspended and stating the suspension conditions with which the company must comply. HMRC may suspend all or part of a penalty if they think that compliance with a condition of suspension would help the company to avoid becoming liable to further penalties (*FA 2007, Sch 24, para 14*). The conditions of the suspension may specify the action to be taken and a period within which it must be taken. If, on the expiry of the extension period, HMRC are then satisfied that the conditions of the suspension have been complied with, the suspended penalty may be cancelled in whole or in part.

The company has the right of appeal to the First-tier Tribunal against the imposition, the amount, the denied suspension and the conditions of the penalty, in which case no penalty is due until the appeal is determined (*FA 2007, Sch 24, paras 15* and *16*). The tribunal may affirm or cancel the decision or recalculate the penalty (*FA 2007, Sch 24, para 17*).

Liability of company officers

18.30   In the case of a deliberate inaccuracy, which was attributable to an officer of the company, both the company and the officer are liable for the penalty (*FA 2007, Sch 24, para 19*). For this purpose an officer of the company includes a director, a shadow director (as defined in *CA 2006, s 251*), a manager and a secretary (*FA 2007, Sch 24, para 19(3)*). There is no liability if the person concerned had already been convicted of an offence by reason of the inaccuracy (*FA 2007, Sch 24, para 21*).

COMPANY FAILING TO MAKE ITSELF KNOWN TO HMRC

Penalty rules post Finance Act 2008, Sch 41

18.31 *Finance Act 2008, Sch 41* introduced a new penalty regime for companies that fail to notify HMRC that they are within the charge to corporation tax (see **2.3**). The rules apply to obligations arising on or after 1 April 2009. If HMRC omits to issue a company with a notice requiring a company tax return and the company fails to notify HMRC that it is chargeable to corporation tax, within 12 months of the end of the accounting period concerned it will incur a penalty based upon the behaviour of the company in these circumstances (*FA 1998, Sch 18, para 2*).

The amount of the penalty is based on the percentage of potential lost revenue arising. This is any corporation tax that remains unpaid 12 months after the end of the accounting period by reason of the failure (*FA 2008, Sch 41, para 7*).

There are three degrees of failure: deliberate and concealed; deliberate and not concealed; and any other case. The first most serious arises where the company intentionally refrains from making its activities known to HMRC and hides the fact that it should. The second most serious is where although the failure is intentional; there is no attempt to cover it up. The third failure encompasses all other situations (*FA 2008, Sch 41, para 5*).

Penalties invoked

18.32 The relevant percentages are:

Degree of inaccuracy	Percentage penalty based on potential lost revenue
Deliberate and concealed	100%
Deliberate but not concealed	70%
Any other case	30%

(*FA 2008, Sch 41, para 6*).

Penalty reduction

18.33 The penalty can be reduced if the company makes an unprompted disclosure. A disclosure is unprompted if it is made at a time when the company has no reason to believe that HMRC has made or is about to discover the failure. In calculating the reduction, HMRC will consider the quality of the information provided, the assistance given to HMRC in calculating the additional liabilities, and the access given to the company's books and records (*FA 2008, Sch 41, para 12*).

The maximum reduced penalty that may be applied is as follows:

Penalty	Maximum reduced penalty for an unprompted disclosure	Maximum reduced penalty for a prompted disclosure
100%	30%	50%
70%	20%	35%
30%		
	0%*	
	10%*	
30%	10%**	20%**

* Notification less than 12 months after corporation tax becoming unpaid
** Notification more than 12 months after corporation tax becoming unpaid

(*FA 2008, Sch 41, para 13*).

An unprompted disclosure can reduce a 30% penalty to nil, if HMRC are made aware of the failure within 12 months of the time that the corporation tax becomes unpaid by reason of the failure. In any other case the percentage cannot be below 10%. A prompted disclosure can reduce a 30% penalty to 10% if HMRC are made aware of the failure within 12 months of the time that the corporation tax becomes unpaid by reason of the failure. In any other case the percentage cannot be below 20%.

HMRC have the discretion to reduce a penalty if they consider that special circumstances apply. The special circumstances do not include the company's ability to pay or the fact that a potential loss of revenue from one taxpayer is balanced by a potential over-payment by another. HMRC also have the discretion not to bring proceedings in relation to a penalty and to agree a compromise during any proceedings that should take place (*FA 2008, Sch 41, para 13*). This penalty is reduced by any other penalty or surcharge applied to the same tax liability (*FA 2008, Sch 41, para 15*).

Assessment procedures

18.34 HMRC will assess the penalty and notify the company. The notice will specify the tax period for which the penalty is assessed. The assessment will be treated and enforced in the same way as a corporation tax assessment. It may also be combined with an actual corporation tax assessment (*FA 2008, Sch 41, para 16)*).

The penalty assessment for a tax understatement must be made within 12 months of the period beginning with the end of the appeal period for the assessment of tax unpaid by reason of the failure or where there is no such assessment, the date on which the amount of tax unpaid by reason of the relevant act or failure is ascertained.

An appeal period is a period during which an appeal could be brought or during which an appeal has been brought but has not been determined or withdrawn. The penalty is due for payment within 30 days of notification (*FA 2008, Sch 41, para 16*).

Right of appeal

18.35   The company has the right of appeal to the First-tier Tribunal against the imposition and the amount of the penalty, in which case no penalty is due until the appeal is determined (*FA 2008, Sch 41, para 17*). The appeal is treated for procedural purposes in the same way as a corporation tax appeal. The tribunal may affirm or cancel the decision or recalculate the penalty, in recalculating the amount the First-tier Tribunal can make the same percentage reductions as HMRC. See **2.10** (*FA 2008, Sch 41, paras 18* and *19*). A company with a non deliberate failure and a reasonable excuse may if the court so decides be excused of a penalty. A reasonable excuse does not include an insufficiency of funds unless this is outside the company's control or reliance on a third party unless the company took reasonable care to avoid the failure. If there was a reasonable excuse for the failure, which has now ceased it will be treated as continuing if the failure is remedied without unreasonable delay after the excuse has ceased.

Liability of company officers

18.36   In the case of a deliberate failure, which was attributable to an officer of the company, both the company and the officer may be liable for a portion of the penalty, which in total may not be more than 100% of the penalty (*FA 2008, Sch 41, para 22*). For this purpose an officer of the company includes a director, a shadow director (as defined in *CA 2006, s 251*), a manager, a secretary or any other person purporting to manage the company's affairs. There is no liability if the person concerned had already been convicted of an offence by reason of the inaccuracy (*FA 2008, Sch 41, para 22*).

DUTIES OF SENIOR ACCOUNTING OFFICERS OF A QUALIFYING COMPANY

Introduction

18.37 With effect for accounting periods beginning on or after 28 July 2009, the senior accounting officer of a qualifying company is mandated to ensure that the company's accounting systems are sufficiently robust in order to supply HMRC with accurate information. A qualifying company is a company whose relevant turnover is more than £200 million and whose relevant balance sheet total is more than £2 billion. The balance sheet total is the amount shown as assets as at the end of the previous financial year. If the company is a member of a group, the aggregate group member totals for assets and turnover are taken instead. (*FA 2009, Sch 46, para 15*). A group relationship is determined by a 51% holding in another company.

A senior accounting officer is a director or the company officer, ie the company secretary, who, in the company's reasonable opinion, has overall responsibility for the company's financial accounting arrangements. If the company is a member of a group, it is the group director or officer who, in the company's opinion, has overall responsibility for the company's financial arrangements (*FA 2009, Sch 46, para 16*). The name of the individual concerned must be given to HMRC before the accounts filing date. The fixed penalty for non-compliance is £5,000. HMRC published a guidance notice 'Duties of Senior Accounting Officers of Qualifying Companies' on 13 August 2009.

Main duty of the senior accounting officer

18.38 The senior accounting officer is charged to take reasonable steps to ensure that the company establishes and maintains appropriate tax accounting arrangements and, in particular:

- to monitor the company's accounting arrangements; and

- to identify any respects in which those arrangements are not appropriate tax accounting arrangements (*FA 2009, Sch 46, para 1*).

The fixed penalty, to which the senior accounting officer would be liable, for non-compliance is £5,000.

Appropriate tax accounting arrangements are defined as arrangements that enable the company's relevant liabilities to be calculated accurately in all material respects. Relevant liabilities are not only corporation tax and amounts assessable as corporation tax, but also other direct and indirect taxes and levies that may fall upon a company. Accounting arrangements includes arrangements for keeping accounting records (*FA 2009, Sch 46, para 14*).

Certificate to HMRC

18.39 The senior accounting officer must provide HMRC with a certificate to confirm that appropriate tax accounting arrangements were in place throughout the financial year and, if not, to give an explanation of the shortfall. This certificate must be supplied by the accounts filing date, or such later time as agreed by HMRC. The certificate can relate to more than one company (*FA 2009, Sch 46, para 2*). The fixed penalty, to which the senior accounting officer would be liable, for non-compliance is £5,000 (*FA 2009, Sch 46, para 5*).

Non-compliance

18.40 Non-compliance not only includes the failure to provide a certificate, but also the provision of a certificate that contains a careless or deliberate inaccuracy. A careless inaccuracy results from a failure by the senior accounting officer to take reasonable care. A careless inaccuracy also arises if the senior accounting officer supplied a certificate in good faith but, upon discovery of an inaccuracy some time later, failed to take reasonable steps to inform HMRC (*FA 2009, Sch 46, para 8*).

Assessment of penalties

18.41 A penalty must be assessed by HMRC within six months after the failure or inaccuracy first comes to the attention of a Revenue and Customs officer, or not more than six years after the end of the period for filing the accounts for the financial year. If there has been more than one senior accounting officer during the year, the penalty will fall on the last accounting officer (*FA 2009, Sch 46, para 6*).HMRC may cancel a penalty if they are satisfied at the time or on appeal that there is a reasonable excuse. If the conditions for a reasonable excuse cease, the failure must be remedied within a reasonable time for the excuse to remain accepted. Appeal is to the First-tier Tribunal or the Upper Tribunal under Tribunal Procedure Rules, see **2.23**.

The following are not accepted as a reasonable excuse:

- an insufficiency of funds, unless attributable to events outside the person's control; or

- reliance on a third party, unless the first person took reasonable care to avoid the failure (*FA 2009, Sch 46, para 8*).

Although a person can be a senior accounting officer of more than one company, that person will only be charged one penalty if two or more of the companies that he or she is attached to are in default in relation to notification of his or her name to HMRC or supplying HMRC with a certificate.

DISCLOSURE OF TAX AVOIDANCE SCHEMES

HMRC strategy

18.42 *FA 2004, ss 307–319* introduced procedures for the disclosure of tax avoidance schemes with effect from 18 March 2004. HMRC are determined to crack down on those who use the system to their advantage. Their strategy in this matter is as follows:

- To discourage taxpayers from using schemes. This includes a critical appraisal of all new legislation to reduce the potential for tax avoidance as well as publicising successes in closing down avoidance schemes.

- To identify as early as possible schemes that are being used.

- To challenge avoidance schemes by contesting returns and, where necessary, pursuing the matter through the courts.

- To produce legislative changes that will close down avoidance schemes where litigation is not appropriate or where the amount of tax at stake is particularly large.

On tax avoidance schemes, Dawn Primarolo has commented:

'HMRC has not prosecuted any accountancy firm for selling aggressive tax avoidance schemes; selling an avoidance scheme would not normally involve activity that amounts to a criminal offence.' (*House of Lords Hansard* col 1428 W 28 June 2005)

However, with the proposed introduction of extended criminal investigatory powers (see **18.2**), practitioners and taxpayers must remain ever vigilant.

When first introduced in 2004, the disclosure rules only applied to employment and financial products. This has resulted in a number of tax avoidance methods being legislated against in *FA 2006, s 76, Sch 6*.

From 1 August 2006 the disclosure rules were widened to include corporation tax together with income tax, capital gains tax and stamp duty land tax. The *Tax Avoidance Schemes (Prescribed Descriptions of Arrangements) Regulations 2006, SI 2006/1543* came into force on 1 August 2006 to replace the *Tax Avoidance Schemes (Prescribed Descriptions of Arrangements) Regulations 2004, SI 2004/1863* regarding notification to HMRC of any tax avoidance scheme (*FA 2004, ss 306–319*). The *Tax Avoidance Schemes (Information) Regulations 2004, SI 2004/1864* (as amended by *SI 2004/2613, SI 2005/1869,SI 2006/1544* and *SI 2009/611*) and the *Tax Avoidance Schemes (Promoters and Prescribed Circumstances) Regulations 2004, SI 2004/1865* (as amended by *SI 2004/2613*) are still currently in force.

NOTIFICATION

18.43 A notifiable arrangement is anything which obtains a tax advantage. Persons who are responsible for the design of such arrangements, or who make the arrangement notifiable for implementation by other persons, could be promoters.

A promoter is required to notify HMRC of the scheme within five days of it becoming available. Form AAG 1 (notification of scheme by promoter) is used for this purpose. The user may be required to notify HMRC if the promoter is based outside the UK, or an adviser has legal privilege or there is no promoter. Form AAG 2 (notification of scheme by user where the promoter is offshore) is available for use. HMRC will then issue the promoter with an eight-digit scheme reference number (SRN), which the promoter must pass to those clients to whom he provides services in connection with the scheme. A person who designs and implements a hallmarked scheme (own scheme) must disclose the scheme within 30 days of implementation. Form AAG 3 (notification of scheme by user in other circumstances) (eg where legal privilege applies or the scheme is devised for use 'in-house') is used for these purposes. Form AAG 5 (continuation sheets) are also available. (See HMRC Disclosure of Tax Avoidance Schemes, June 2006 for further guidance.) The company client must include the SRN details from HMRC on the corporation tax return for the accounting period in which the advantage is being obtained. A co-promoter is not required to disclose a scheme to HMRC if another promoter has disclosed the scheme, or a scheme substantially the same, to HMRC (*FA 2004, ss 308–313*). HMRC published disclosure guidance in October 2008, which took effect from 1 November 2008 'Disclosure of Tax Avoidance Schemes'.

DISCLOSABLE ARRANGEMENTS

Pre 1 August 2006

18.44 Prior to 1 August 2006, disclosure of anti-avoidance measures was determined according to a series of filters. These included the premium test, the confidentiality test and the off-market test. If the promoter charged a fee for his advice aligned to the tax savings advantage from the scheme, disclosure was required. If the promoter's advice was provided on a confidential basis, so that the promoter could obtain it to maintain the premium fee potential, disclosure was required. If the 'off-market' test involved the promoter charging a small fee for the arrangement but a much larger fee for the financial product that he sold as part of the tax avoidance arrangement, disclosure was required.

From 1 August 2006

18.45 From 1 August 2006, a scheme is disclosable if it meets any one of a series of hallmark tests. 'Disclosable' is defined by HMRC as 'the requirement to provide prescribed information to HMRC'. 'Hallmarks' is defined as the descriptions prescribed, for the purpose of *FA 2004, s 306(1)(a), (b),* and the *Tax Avoidance Schemes (Prescribed Descriptions of Arrangements) Regulations 2006.*

Hallmark tests

18.46 HMRC have devised a series of tests to determine whether a hallmarked scheme exists, which, when applied to corporation tax, are as follows:

Test	Question	Consequence for a positive answer Positive	Consequence for a negative answer Negative
1	Are there arrangements (including any scheme, transaction or series of transactions), or proposals for arrangements, that enable, or might be expected to enable, any person to obtain an advantage in relation to income tax, corporation tax or capital gains tax?	Yes: apply test 2	No: not a hallmarked scheme
2	Are those arrangements or proposals such that the main benefit, or one of the main benefits that might be expected to arise from them, is the obtaining of that advantage?	Yes: apply test 3	No: not a hallmarked scheme benefit, or one of the main benefits that might be expected to arise from them, is the obtaining of that advantage?

Test	Question	Consequence for a positive answer	Consequence for a negative answer
		Positive	Negative
3	Is there a promoter of the arrangements or are they devised for use 'in-house'?	Yes, a promoter: apply test 4. Yes, in-house: apply test 5	
4	Do any of the hallmarks for arrangements where there is a promoter apply?	Yes: a hallmarked scheme	No: not a hallmarked scheme
5	Is the tax advantage intended to be obtained by a business that is not a small or medium enterprise?	Yes: apply test 6	No: not a hallmarked scheme
6	Do any of the in-house hallmarks apply?	Yes: a hallmarked scheme	No: not a hallmarked scheme

Hallmarks

18.47 The hallmarks for arrangements where there is a promoter are as follows:

1 Confidentiality from other promoters.

2 Confidentiality from HMRC.

3 Premium fee.

4 Off-market terms.

5 Standardised tax products.

6 Loss schemes.

7 Leasing arrangements.

The hallmarks for in-house arrangements are:

2 Confidentiality from HMRC.

3 Premium fee.

7 Leasing arrangements.

The small business definition is the same as is used for research and development (see **8.22**).

The 'confidentiality', 'premium fee' and 'off-market terms' hallmarks follow through from the pre-1 August 2006 filters mentioned in **18.46**. The 'confidentiality from HMRC' hallmark has been added and applies to a promoter who would wish to keep matters confidential from HMRC, for example, to secure future fee income.

A 'standardised tax product' hallmark exists where there is a promoter of a mass-marketed product that needs little or no alteration to suit a client's situation. Enterprise investment schemes (EIS), venture capital trust schemes (VCTs) and corporate venturing schemes (CVS) arrangements are specifically excluded; as are approved employee share schemes and regulated pension schemes. The hallmark for a loss scheme is the existence of a promoter and is intended to capture various loss creation schemes used by wealthy individuals. The leasing arrangement applies to promoted and in-house arrangements. In-house arrangements do not apply if the party intended to benefit from the arrangement is an SME. The hallmark applies to certain high value sale and leaseback arrangements which involve a party outside the charge to corporation tax and a removal of risk from the lessor.

Clearances

18.48 There are special rules to avoid the duplication of information where the arrangement includes transactions for which a statutory clearance exists (*SI 2004/1864, reg 5*).

They apply for the purposes of:

- purchase of own shares by an unquoted company (*ICTA 1988, s 215*) (see **16.19–16.25**);

- company demergers (*ICTA 1988, s 225*) (see **16.13–16.18**);

- transfer of business (*CTA 2009, s 832*);

- transactions in securities (*ICTA 1988, s 707*);

- reconstruction of company or trade (TCGA 1992, *ss 138, 139, 140B* or *140D*) (see **15.7–15.10**).

Where statutory clearance is available then the promoter or user may apply for clearance at the same time as making the disclosure. If there is no clearance request the promoter must make the disclosure not later than five working days following the day on which reasonable intention to make a clearance application ceased, or the normal 'relevant date' if this is later.

Where a transaction occurs prior to the submission of a clearance application, the disclosure must be made within five working days of any transaction that is part of the scheme occurring.

HMRC have confirmed that clearance applications will be considered in the usual way, and clearance will not be refused merely on the grounds that some part of the proposed transaction involves a disclosable scheme.

Disclosures made in this way should be sent with the clearance application.

CORPORATION TAX SELF-ASSESSMENT

CT600 completion

18.49 Companies who use a tax avoidance scheme are required to put an 'X' in the box so named on the first page of CT600 and to complete the disclosure of tax avoidance schemes supplementary pages form CT600J. The scheme number is required in box J and the accounting periods that benefit in JA.

Penalties

18.50 Failure to notify incurs the following penalties:

Taxpayer failing to disclose a scheme	Initial penalty maximum	£5,000
	Daily penalty	£600 per day
Promoters failing to give registration number to client	Initial penalty maximum	£5,000
Taxpayer failing to disclose scheme registration numbers on returns	Initial penalty	£100
	Second failure penalty	£500
	Third and subsequent failure penalty	£1,000

Subject to right of appeal, the Tribunal will determine the initial penalties for both the promoters and the taxpayers.

Chapter 19

Liquidations

INSOLVENCY

Insolvent company

19.1   If a company becomes insolvent, the only option may be to 'wind up' or liquidate the company. A solvent company may also be put into liquidation.

If a company becomes insolvent, there are various courses or mixtures of courses of action that it can take. Firstly, the company can enter into a 'voluntary arrangement' with its creditors. Secondly, a secured creditor, with either a fixed or floating charge, such as the bank, may appoint a receiver who then assumes control of the company's business, who then becomes an administrative receiver. Thirdly, the court may make an administration order. An administrator will then take control of the company. An administrator has similar powers to a receiver. Finally, a compulsory liquidation may take place with the company being wound up by a court order under *Insolvency Act 1986, s 73* or a voluntary liquidation may take place following a resolution passed at a general meeting of the company.

Solvent company

19.2   A solvent company may be put into liquidation when there is no further use for the company, say in a group reconstruction or when the shareholders or directors of a family company want to extract their capital. When such a course is contemplated the company directors, or a majority of them, must make a statutory declaration of solvency to the Registrar of Companies to the effect that the company will be able to pay or provide for all of its debts (including interest) within 12 months. Within five weeks of that declaration the directors must pass a resolution to wind up the company. A members' voluntary winding-up starts on the day the resolution to wind up the company is passed.

ADMINISTRATION PROCEEDINGS

Administration order

19.3   An administration order is a court order placing a company that is, or is likely to become, insolvent under the control of an administrator following an application by the company, its directors or a creditor. The purpose of the order is to preserve the company's business, allow a reorganisation or ensure the most advantageous realisation of its assets whilst protecting it from action of its creditors.

Receivers and administrators

19.4   A receiver takes his appointment from a secured creditor. Sometimes this is through a court order on behalf of the creditor. The receiver is assigned to take control of the secured assets on behalf of the creditor and to sell them if need be to pay off the creditors. If the receiver succeeds in this work, the directors continue with their responsibilities. If the receiver is unable to discharge the secured debt it normally follows that the company is put into liquidation. Prior to 15 September 2003, a receiver normally assumed control of the company's business as an administrative receiver with statutory powers. An administrative receiver is an insolvency practitioner. Administrative receivership was abolished for floating charges created on and after 15 September 2003 with certain exceptions (such as financial market transactions and public private partnerships). Under the *Enterprise Act 2002*, lenders appoint administrators in situations that would previously have been dealt with by administrative receivership. From 15 September 2003, an administrative receiver in post must vacate office on the appointment of an administrator (HMRC Insolvency Manual INS 1203).

The administrator may be appointed by the court, the creditors or the directors to manage the affairs, business and property of company. Essentially, the administrator seeks to rescue the company and if possible seek better results for the creditors. Eventually he may realise property in order to make a distribution.

Effect of appointment

19.5   The appointment does not affect the corporate existence of the company. The directors and officers retain their respective positions and are not relieved of their duties and liabilities although the administrator has effective control of the company.

Corporation tax in administration

19.6   For companies entering administration on or after 15 September 2003, a new accounting period begins where the company enters into administration (*CTA 2009, s 10(2)–(5)*), and an accounting period ends where it ceases to be in administration (*CTA 2009, s 10(1)*). Within this time the accounting period may run to the next 12 months or to the original accounting date if so required. If the company is to be dissolved at the end of the administration period, the corporation tax will be charged on the company's profits for the final year based on current rates available at the time (*ICTA 1988, s 342A*). If the company receives any interest on overdue tax in the final accounting period, provided that it does not exceed £2,000, it will not be subject to corporation tax.

When a company enters into administration it does not cease to be the beneficial owner of its assets. Therefore the reconstruction procedure described in **15.5–15.10** will still apply.

Whether the company may claim group relief is a debatable point. As the administrator or receiver is effectively controlling the company, the company's shareholders cannot secure that the affairs of the company are conducted in accordance with their wishes (*ICTA 1988, s 840*). Therefore it could cease to be grouped with parent and subsidiaries for group relief (*ICTA 1988, s 410(1)(b)(ii)*). If the company arranges to dispose of a subsidiary it may lose entitlement to group relief (*ICTA 1988, s 410*).

Effect of cessation of trade

19.7   A company may continue to trade during its administration or liquidation period. However, such an event is unlikely. The date of cessation of trade marks the end of an accounting period (*CTA 2009, s 10(1)*).

A cessation of trade has various corporation tax implications. Trading stock, if sold to an unconnected UK trade, is valued at sales price. In other circumstances, such as a sale to a connected party or an overseas trader it is valued at market value. The company should provide for all known bad debts and impairment losses. If trading ceases and a debt proves to be irrecoverable it can only be relieved against post-cessation receipts. Similarly, all known expenses should be provided for.

The permanent cessation will give rise to a balancing charge or balancing allowance in the final period (*CAA 2001, s 65*). Disposal proceeds will be the sale price if sold to an unconnected third party or market value in any other case. The connected parties may elect in writing within two years of the end of the accounting period in which the trade ceased to substitute the higher of the sales price or the actual cost price. The purchaser will use the same stock valuation (*CTA 2009, s 167*). Trading losses in the final period accounting period can be utilised in a group relief claim (see **10.8**) or carried back in a terminal loss claim (see **9.17**).

When a company ceases to trade its unrelieved trading losses are not available to shelter other income received in the period. It may still offset its non-trading deficits against its non-trading credits.

Unrelieved trading losses may be set against post cessation receipt income (*CTA 2009, s 196*). In addition any balancing charge arising from the disposal of a building that is temporarily out of use may be relieved by the unutilised losses (*CAA 2001, s 354*).

LIQUIDATION PROCEEDINGS

Winding-up

19.8   The winding-up of a company may be 'voluntary' by company or creditor's resolution or be 'compulsory' by order of the court (*IA 1986, s 73*). Following the winding-up order or resolution a liquidator is appointed to 'wind up' the affairs of the company; namely to realise the assets and settle outstanding liabilities. The liquidator will then apply to have the company dissolved and removed from the Register at Companies House. The company will then cease to exist. In a member's voluntary winding-up the company is dissolved three months after the date on which the Registrar of Companies is advised that the winding-up is complete.

Liquidator

19.9   A liquidator can be appointed by the creditors, the members or the court, depending on the type of liquidation. The liquidator is assigned to realise all company assets within his control and to apply the proceeds in payment of the company's debts in order of priority. If any surplus funds remain, the liquidator will repay the members the amounts paid up on their shares. If any further surplus remains he will distribute the surplus amongst the members according to their entitlement.

Commencement

19.10   A voluntary winding-up commences on the date that the resolution is passed or the date that the company went into administration if the liquidation follows an administration (HMRC Insolvency Manual INS 1612). A compulsory winding-up commences on the date that the resolution is passed, or the date of the order, when the company has applied for an administration order, or the date of the petition in any other case (HMRC Insolvency Manual INS 1520). On hearing a petition the court will make an order for the winding-up of the company if all necessary conditions have been followed and the court is satisfied that the company is unable to pay its debts. (HMRC Insolvency Manual INS 1612).

Corporation tax

19.11   The date of the winding-up order marks the end of one accounting period and the beginning of the next. Thereafter the accounting periods run to the 12-month anniversary of the winding-up (*CTA 2009, s 12*). The profits during the winding-up remain chargeable to corporation tax on the company and not on the liquidator (*ICTA 1988, s 344(2)*). If the company receives any interest on overdue tax in the final accounting period, provided that it does not exceed £2,000 it will not be subject to corporation tax (*ICTA 1988, s 342(3A)*).

The liquidator will provide HMRC with a provisional date for completion of the winding-up. The corporation tax will be charged on the company's profits for the final year based on current rates available at the time (*ICTA 1988, s 342(2)(a)*).

If it transpires that the provisional date is incorrect an accounting period is deemed to end on that date and a new one commences (*ICTA 1988, s 342(6)*).

Effect of winding-up order

19.12   When a company has entered into liquidation it loses the beneficial interest in its assets (*Ayerst v C & K (Construction) Ltd* (1975) 50 TC 651, [1975] STC 345, [1976] AC 167, [1975] 2 All ER 537). Hence group relief both for groups and consortiums is no longer available (*ICTA 1988, s 410(1)(b)(ii)*) and reconstruction hive down utilising *ICTA 1988, s 343* (see Chapter 15) is also prohibited. The company remains a group member for capital gains purposes (*TCGA 1992, s 170(11)*); therefore the liquidator may transfer assets to group members with *TCGA 1992, s 171* continuing to apply (see **20.16**).

No distributions of profits may be made to shareholders in respect of their share capital (*ICTA 1988, s 209(1)*). The close company distribution rules of *ICTA 1988, s 418* continue to apply. However, distributions of assets may still be made (*ICTA 1988, s 209(4), (5), (6)*) (see **16.5**).

Loans to participators

19.13   Loans to participators may either be called in, in order to pay out the shareholders or alternatively they will be written off. The normal procedures will follow as described in **4.16–4.22**.

ESC C16

19.14   Where a company has ceased business it may ask the Registrar of Companies to strike it off under *CA 2006, s 1003: CA 1985, s 652A* or wait for the Registrar of Companies to strike off the company (see **16.26–16.28** and HMRC Company Taxation Manual CTM 36220).

Taxation liabilities of office holders

19.15   Although a receiver deals with all preferential claims, the corporation tax arising during receivership remains the responsibility of the company and will be dealt with by any subsequent liquidator either as an unsecured claim or to the extent that the income and gains arose after the commencement of winding-up as a liquidation expense.

When appointed a liquidator or an administrator becomes the proper officer of the company dealing with its corporation tax affairs (*TMA 1970, s 108(3)*).

Corporation tax arising prior to appointment is an unsecured claim; post appointment it is an administration or liquidation expense and strictly must be paid ahead of the liquidator's remuneration (*Re Mesco Properties Ltd* (1979) 54 TC 238, [1979] STC 788, [1980] 1 WLR 96, [1980] 1 All ER 117).

Subsidiary company in liquidation

19.16   The substantial shareholding exemption (*TCGA 1992, Sch 7AC*) prevents a capital gain and a capital loss accruing where more than 10% of the shares of a trading company are owned by another UK company (see **12.36–12.40**) if the shares are held throughout a 12-month period beginning not more than two years before the date of disposal. In other circumstances the holding company may be able to make a negligible asset claim under *TCGA 1992, s 24*.

During the liquidation period it is unlikely that the company will be carrying on a trade. Therefore the liquidator's costs will not be relievable. They may form part of the incidental costs of disposal of certain assets, but apart from that no relief will be given.

A close company in liquidation may be treated as a close investment holding company (CIC) (see **4.23–4.26**). Where a close company commences liquidation, *ICTA 1988, s 13A(4)* provides that it is not to be treated as a CIC in the accounting period immediately following the commencement of winding-up if it was not a CIC in the accounting period immediately before liquidation commenced. In any subsequent accounting period a close company in liquidation will be excluded from being a CIC only if it then meets the usual conditions of *ICTA 1988, s 13A(2)* (see **4.24**). HMRC have commented that it may happen that there is a very short gap between the end of a period in which the company was not a CIC and the commencement of winding-up, so that strictly the company will not have the benefit of *s 13A(4)*. This may cause difficulties in some cases and an undertaking has been given to review the position where a company has not been able to avoid a short gap and would suffer significantly if not given the protection of *s 13(4)* (HMRC Company Taxation Manual CTM 60780).

From a practical perspective, HMRC should be contacted to ascertain whether any enquiries are to be made. Any distributions to shareholders during the liquidation period are capital distributions and do not fall within *ICTA 1988, s 209(1)*.

Chapter 20

Capital gains

INTRODUCTION

Chargeable gains for companies

20.1   Companies are not liable to capital gains tax, but instead pay corporation tax on chargeable gains, at the same rate as trading profits and other income. Gains arising on the disposal of assets are chargeable to capital gains tax except where exemptions apply (*TCGA 1992, s 1*). From a company's perspective disposals that are most likely to fall within the capital gains net are disposals of land and property held on capital account and share holdings. The disposal of loan stock comes within the loan relationship rules (see **Chapter 11**) and the disposal of intangible assets comes within the intangible asset rules (see **Chapter 7**).

Capital gains are broadly computed in accordance with normal CGT principles (*see Capital Gains Tax 2009/10* (Bloomsbury Professional)), but there is no taper relief (before removal) or annual exemption. A company's chargeable gains are adjusted for post-March 1982 indexation allowances. The reform of CGT for individuals, trustees and personal representatives, which froze indexation relief at April 1998 and introduced taper relief provisions, did not extend to the capital gains of companies. Gains on the disposal of a company's chargeable assets are included in box 16 of the corporation tax self-assessment return.

There are a number of relieving provisions that are discussed as follows:

Roll-over relief	**20.6–20.13, 20.21**
Intra-group asset transfers	**20.14–20.17**
Losses on shares in unquoted trading companies	**12.25**
Substantial shareholdings exemption	**12.26–12.30**
Corporate venturing schemes	**12.31–12.43**
CGT on reconstructions	**15.7–15.10**

Special computational provisions apply to:

There are also many anti-avoidance provisions which are discussed as follows:

BASIC CAPITAL GAINS COMPUTATION

20.2   The gross sale proceeds less the allowable items of expenditure and indexation results in the chargeable gain. Allowable items include the purchase cost and the costs of acquisition and disposal (*TCGA 1992, s 38*). Indexation based on purchase and acquisition costs is still available to companies from the date of purchase or 31 March 1982 if later, until date of sale.

When preparing the capital gains computation the incidental costs of sale are deducted from sale proceeds and may include such items as valuation fees, auctioneers' or estate agency fees, costs of advertising or legal costs. These costs do not qualify for the indexation allowance. Allowable expenditure includes the original cost of the asset, any enhancement expenditure and the incidental costs of sale. All this expenditure qualifies for indexation allowance.

Enhancement expenditure

20.3   Enhancement expenditure is capital expenditure, which adds to, improves or enhances the value of the asset. Expenditure deductible on revenue account such as repairs, maintenance and insurance are excluded since such costs only maintain the value of an asset. Conversely, capital expenditure that has not qualified as a deduction on revenue account may qualify as a deduction for capital gains purposes, so long as it enhances the value of the underlying asset.

Indexation

20.4   Indexation allowance is calculated by multiplying the relevant allowable expenditure by the indexation factor. The indexation factor is computed by expressing the following fraction as a decimal (to three decimal places) (*TCGA 1992, s 54*).

$$(RD - RI) \div RI$$

Where RD is the retail prices index (RPI) for the month of disposal and RI is the RPI for the later of:

- March 1982; or

- the month in which the expenditure was incurred. (See Appendix 1 for Retail Price Indices)

If there should be a decrease in RPI between the base month and the month of disposal, the indexation allowance is nil. If expenditure is incurred on two or more dates, separate indexation calculations are required for each. No indexation is available if proceeds less costs results in a loss before indexation is calculated (*TCGA 1992, s 53(2A)*). Neither can indexation allowance be deducted so as to turn a gain before indexation into a loss. Instead, the gain is reduced to nil (*TCGA 1992, s 53(1)(b)*).

Capital losses

20.5   The company's chargeable gains for the accounting period are reduced by allowable losses of the same period, and any unrelieved allowable capital losses brought forward from previous accounting periods. Capital losses may only be set against capital gains of the current year or carried forward to set against future capital gains.

Unused capital losses are carried forward for offset against capital gains of subsequent accounting periods. There are no provisions allowing for the carry back of capital losses, the surrender of capital losses between group companies, or the offset of capital losses against trading or other income (except for losses of investment companies on shares in qualifying unquoted trading companies, or losses of trading companies on shares within the Corporate Venturing Scheme: see **12.41–12.55**).

Allowable capital losses including losses brought forward are recorded in box 17 of the company tax return.

Example 20.1

The West End Trading Co Ltd prepares accounts to 31 March each year. The company disposes of an office block on 3 December 2010 for £40m. The incidental costs of sale are £1m. The block was purchased in January 2003 for £15.5m. Costs of acquisition amounted to £0.5m. In January 2004 a new frontage at a cost of £2m was added to the building that was deemed to be capital expenditure. The chargeable gain to be included within the corporation tax computation for the year ended 31 March 2011 is calculated as follows:

		£000	£000
December 2010	Gross sale proceeds		40,000
	Less: Incidental costs of sale		1,000
	Net sale proceeds		39,000
	Less: Relevant allowable expenditure:		
January 2003	Acquisition cost	15,500	
January 2003	Incidental costs of acquisition	500	
January 2004	Enhancement expenditure	2,000	
			18,000
	Unindexed gain		21,000
	Less: Indexation allowance		
	Cost 16,000 × 0.233	3,728	
	Enhancement 2,000 × 0.202	404	
			4,132
	Chargeable gain		16,868

Workings: calculation of indexation factor

RPI	December 2010	*220.0
RPI	January 2003	178.40
RPI	January 2004	183.10

Factor		
Cost	(RPI December 2010—RPI January 2003) ÷ RPI January 2003	0.233
Enhancement	(RPI December 2010—RPI January 2004) ÷ RPI January 2004	0.202

* assumed

RELIEVING PROVISIONS

Roll-over relief

20.6   Assets sold in excess of cost may bring about a chargeable gain, assessable upon the company. If the assets are of a certain class and if new assets have been purchased to replace them the gain may qualify for roll-over relief under *TCGA 1992, s 152*. This will enable the gain to be deferred within the cost of the new asset.

The assets that can qualify for relief are listed under *TCGA 1992, s 155*.

The relevant classes of assets are as follows:

Class 1

Assets within heads A and B are given below.

Head A

(i)   Any building or part of a building and any permanent or semi-permanent structure in the nature of a building, occupied (as well as used) only for the purposes of the trade.

(ii)   Any land occupied (as well as used) only for the purposes of the trade. Head A has effect subject to *s 156*.

Head B

Fixed plant or machinery which does not form part of a building or of a permanent or semi-permanent structure in the nature of a building.

Class 2

Ships, aircraft and hovercraft ('hovercraft' having the same meaning as in the *Hovercraft Act 1968*).

Class 3

Satellites, space stations and spacecraft (including launch vehicles).

Class 4

Goodwill (but only prior to 1 April 2002).

Class 4

Goodwill no longer qualifies after 1 April 2002 as it is included within the intangible assets regime. See **Chapter 7** for intangible assets.

Conditions affecting the old assets and the new assets

20.7   The old assets must have been used solely for the purposes of the trade throughout the period of ownership. The consideration received must be used in acquiring new assets or an interest therein. Upon acquisition the new assets must also be used solely for the purposes of the trade. The new assets must not be acquired for the purposes of realising a gain, ie as an investment (*TCGA 1992, s 152(5)*).

The trading company can then claim that the consideration on the sale of the old assets is reduced up to the amount reinvested that produces neither a gain nor a loss on disposal. The acquisition cost of the new asset is reduced by the same amount. The relief is given after indexation.

The new assets must be acquired during the period commencing 12 months before and ending three years after the disposal of, or of the interest in, the old assets. A provisional claim may be made if the company enters into an unconditional contract for purchase.

Apportionment takes place if the old asset is not used throughout the period of ownership for the purposes of the trade or if only part of an asset is used for the purposes of a trade. Periods before 31 March 1982 are ignored in calculating the period of ownership.

Assets only partly replaced

20.8   If only part of the asset is replaced it follows that the gain on disposal of the old asset is limited to the amount of consideration reinvested with the balance of the gain being rolled over (*TCGA 1992, s 153*).

New assets which are depreciating assets

20.9   If the new assets are depreciating assets the chargeable gain is not deducted from the cost of the new asset but is held over and becomes chargeable at the earliest of the following events:

●   the new asset is disposed of;

●   the asset is no longer used for the purposes of the trade; or

●   10 years have elapsed since the acquisition of the new asset.

A depreciating asset is any asset that will become a wasting asset within 10 years of acquisition. A wasting asset is an asset with a predictable life of 50 years or less (*TCGA 1992, s 44*). Fixed plant and machinery installed in a building with a life of more than 60 years to run will not be a depreciating asset. A leasehold building with less than 60 years to run will be a depreciating asset (Tax Bulletin, Issue 7, May 1993).

Land and buildings and roll-over relief

20.10   Land and buildings are treated as separate assets for roll-over relief purposes. HMRC wish to see separate computations to support a claim together with an appropriate apportionment of costs (HMRC Capital Gains Manual CG 60990). No roll-over relief is available for land held or property dealt with in the course of trade by a property dealing or development company other than land and buildings that it used for the purposes of the trade. Lessors of tied premises are treated as occupying and using the premises for the purposes of their trade (*TCGA 1992, s 156(4)*).

New assets not purchased

20.11   By concession proceeds used from the disposal of old assets may be used to enhance the value of qualifying assets already held. The other assets must only have been used for the purposes of the company's trade and on completion of the work undertaken the assets are immediately taken back for use in the trade (ESC D22).

Similarly, by concession if proceeds from the sale of old assets are used to acquire a further interest in another asset that is already being used for the purposes of the trade that new interest is treated as a new asset if it is taken into use for the purposes of the trade (ESC D25).

New asset not brought immediately into trading use

20.12   If a new asset on acquisition is not taken immediately into use for the purposes of the trade, roll-over relief will still be available in the following circumstances:

- the owner proposes to incur capital expenditure for the purposes of enhancing its value;
- any work arising from such capital expenditure begins as soon as possible after acquisition and is completed within a reasonable time;
- on completion of the work the asset is taken into use for the purpose of the trade and for no other purpose; and
- the asset is neither let nor used for any non-trading purpose in the period between acquisition and taking into use for trade purposes (ESC D24).

Assets owned personally but used for the purposes of the trade of a personal company

20.13   If an individual exercises no less than 5% of the voting rights of a company, which uses an asset owned by that individual for the purposes of its trade, that individual will be entitled to roll-over relief if all other conditions apply (*TCGA 1992, s 157*).

INTRA-GROUP ASSET TRANSFER

Group structure

20.14 For chargeable gains purposes, a group consists of a company (known as the principal company) and all its 75% subsidiaries together with each subsidiary's 75% subsidiary company. Each subsidiary must be an effective 51% subsidiary of the principal company. A principal company must not be a 75% subsidiary of another company. The principal company can be UK or overseas resident and the inclusion of a non-resident subsidiary does not disturb the group relationship.

Example 20.2

A Ltd owns 75% of the ordinary share capital of B Ltd.

B Ltd owns 80% of the ordinary share capital of C Ltd.

A Ltd and B Ltd are a group, as A Ltd owns 75% of B Ltd.

A Ltd and C Ltd are a group because A Ltd effectively owns 60% of C Ltd (75 × 80).

20.15 A company can only be a member of one group. Where the conditions qualify so that a company would be a member of two or more groups the group that it is deemed to be a member of is determined establishing its links to the principal company and if the group conditions are not met the links should be established with the next group (*TCGA 1992, s 170*).

Example 20.3

A Ltd owns 75% of the ordinary share capital of B Ltd.

B Ltd owns 80% of the ordinary share capital of C Ltd.

C Ltd owns 75% of the ordinary share capital of D Ltd.

D Ltd owns 75% of the ordinary share capital of E Ltd.

A Ltd and B Ltd are a group.

A Ltd and C Ltd are a group.

A Ltd and D Ltd are not a group because A Ltd effectively owns 45% of D Ltd (75 × 80 × 75).

D Ltd and E Ltd are a group.

Relief

20.16 For chargeable gains purposes intra-group transfers of assets are always deemed to be made at a price that results in neither gain nor loss for the transferee company (*TCGA 1992, s 171*) (*Innocent v Whaddon Estates Ltd* (1981) 55 TC 476, [1982] STC 115).

The relief is automatically applied and given without claim, but does not apply where a transfer arises in the satisfaction of a debt, a disposal of redeemable shares on redemption, a disposal by or to an investment trust, Venture Capital Trust (VCT) or qualifying friendly society; or a disposal to a dual resident investing company. On a company reconstruction where *TCGA 1992, s 135* applies (see **15.8**), *s 135* takes preference so *s 171* does not apply.

Although a non-UK company can be a member of the group, it cannot take part in the asset transfer unless it trades in the UK through a permanent branch or agency. The asset must be in the UK and be used for the branch or agency trade.

When a company eventually disposes of the asset to a third party the company selling adopts the original base cost of the asset to the group plus indexation for the capital gains computation.

Election to treat a disposal as if made by another group member

20.17 In order to fully utilise the group's capital losses, a group company was able to treat a disposal of an asset outside the group as though it were made by another group member. This enabled the asset to be placed in the company that had the capital losses. Both companies had to make a joint election for the deemed transfer to apply, within two years of the end of the chargeable period in which the transfer took place (*TCGA 1992, s 171A*).

This rule has now been amended by *FA 2009*. The chargeable gain or the allowable loss can be transferred to another group member, instead of the asset which is to be disposed of. The companies must jointly elect for this treatment within two years of the end of the chargeable period in which the gain or the loss accrues (*FA 2009, s 31, Sch 12*). This change relieves the group of the formalities of transferring ownership of a capital asset from one group member to another. The rule does not apply when a company leaves a group (see **20.22**), but negligible value claims are not prohibited. The change has effect for chargeable gains or losses accruing on or after the day on which *FA 2009* is passed (i.e. 21 July 2009).

SPECIAL COMPUTATIONAL PROVISIONS

Transfers of assets to trading stock

20.18 Where one group member acquires a capital asset, from another member, that it appropriates to trading stock, the intra-group asset transfer will be at no gain/no loss, but as soon as the asset is transferred to stock a chargeable gain arises on the transferee. The transferee adopts the transferor's asset base cost and indexation. Alternatively, the transferee can elect under *TCGA 1992, s 161(3)* to treat the asset as acquired at market value less the capital gain arising. The gain will, therefore, be taken as part of the trading profit on the asset.

Example 20.4

O Ltd transfers a fixed asset to its holding company N Ltd. N Ltd appropriates the asset to its trading stock. The indexed cost of the asset was £12,500 to O Ltd and the market value on transfer is £20,000. N Ltd eventually sells the asset to a third party for £30,000.

Without a *TCGA 1992, s 161(3)* election the position is as follows:

N Ltd	£
Market value	20,000
Indexed cost	12,500
Capital gain	7,500
Sale proceeds	30,000
Deemed cost	20,000
Trading profit	10,000

20.19 *Capital gains*

With a *TCGA 1992, s 161(3)* election the position is as follows:

N Ltd	£
Sales proceeds	30,000
Indexed cost	12,500
Trading profit	17,500

20.19 There is the potential here to turn a capital loss into a trading loss. The loss will only be allowed if there is a true trading intention (*Coates v Arndale Properties Ltd* (1984) 59 TC 516, [1984] STC 637, [1984] 1 WLR 1328, [1985] 1 All ER 15).

Transfers of assets from trading stock

20.20 Where a group company transfers an asset that it holds as trading stock to another group company that holds it as an asset it is deemed to be transferred at market value in the transferor's books giving rise to a trading profit. When the transferee company sells the asset outside the group it adopts the market value of the asset when it was transferred from the transferor company as base cost on which is based indexation allowance, etc.

Example 20.5

N Ltd transfers a chargeable asset from its trading stock to its subsidiary company O Ltd. O Ltd will hold the asset as an investment. The cost of the asset was £10,000 and the market value on transfer is £30,000. O Ltd then sells the asset to a third party for £40,000. The indexation from the time of transfer is £500.

N Ltd	£	£
Market value		30,000
Cost		10,000
Trading profit		20,000
O Ltd		
Sale proceeds		40,000
Deemed cost	30,000	
Indexation	500	
		30,500
Capital gain		9,500

Replacement of business asset by members of a group

20.21 *TCGA 1992, s 152* roll-over relief is extended to group situations. For this purpose all group assets and trades are treated as one. The new assets must be purchased outside the group (*TCGA 1992, s 175*). See **20.6** et seq.

Companies leaving the group

20.22 If a company leaves a group within six years of an inter-group transfer a chargeable gain arises on retained assets acquired, on a no gain/no loss basis, from other group members within the previous six years (*TCGA 1992, s 179*). The chargeable gain is calculated on the basis that the company leaving the group sold and repurchased the asset at market value on the day that it was acquired from the other group member (*TCGA 1992, s 179(3)*) but the gain is charged in the accounting period in which the company leaves the group.

There is no de-grouping charge if two or more associated companies leave the group at the same time (*TCGA 1992, s 170(2)*). In *Johnston Publishing (North) Ltd v Revenue & Customs Commissioners* [2008] EWCA Civ 858 it was decided that not only must companies be associated at the time of leaving the group, but also the same group of companies must be associated at the time of the acquisition of the asset, for the exemption to apply. HMRC have since confirmed their approach and given the following example of when the *TCGA 1992, s 170(2)* exemption will apply.

Example 20.6

P is the principal company of a capital gains group. Q is one of its 100% subsidiaries.

Q has a 100% subsidiary, R, which in turn has two 100% subsidiaries, A and B.

A also has an 80% subsidiary, S.

A transfers an asset to B; *TCGA 1992, s 171* applies and no gain or loss arises.

Later, R is liquidated and its shareholdings passed to Q.

S is then transferred elsewhere in the group.

B then acquires a new 100% subsidiary, T.

HMRC consider that if P sells Q, along with its subsidiaries at that time, to a third party then there will be no degrouping charge in respect of the asset transferred from A to B. This is because Q, A and B formed a group of companies by themselves when the asset transfer took place (A and B were both 100% indirect subsidiaries of Q) and at the time when P left the main group (A and B were both 100% direct subsidiaries of Q).

TCGA 1992, s 170(2) defines a group by reference to a principal company and its 75% subsidiaries. *TCGA 1992, s 170(10)* provides that a group remains the same while the principal company remains the same. Applying these to the provision at *TCGA 1992, s 179(10)*, HMRC would expect the sub-group to remain defined by reference to the same company from the time of the asset transfer to the time the companies leave the group.

(HMRC Brief, 17 December 2008)

The company and the other group member from whom the asset was acquired may jointly elect that the capital gain on leaving the group be treated as that of the other company (*TCGA 1992, s 179A*). If qualifying, the asset will be available for roll-over relief (*TCGA 1992, s 179B*).

Example 20.7

In 1989, N Ltd acquired a freehold property for £280,000. In 2005, when the market value was £500,000 and the indexation to date was £20,000, N Ltd transferred the freehold property to P Ltd, a fellow group member. P Ltd leaves the group on 1 January 2009. Both companies prepare accounts to 30 June each year.

The *s 179* gain for the year ended 30 June 2009 is calculated as follows:

P Ltd	£
Market value	500,000
Indexed cost	300,000
Capital gain	200,000

If P Ltd purchases another qualifying asset, P Ltd will be able to make a roll-over relief claim under *TCGA 1992, s 152*.

If N Ltd and P Ltd could jointly elect for the gain to fall in N Ltd only, N Ltd will be able to make a roll-over relief claim, which must be against its acquisition of a qualifying asset.

20.23 HMRC have confirmed that a degrouping charge will not be imposed on assets transferred to the parent of a two-company group, which disposes of its single subsidiary (HMRC Capital Gains Tax Manual CG 45450).

ANTI-AVOIDANCE

Value shifting

20.24 The shareholders own a company through its share structure. A share or security is a chargeable asset for capital gains purposes (*TCGA 1992, s 21*). Transactions that affect the value of these shares could fall within the capital gains rules for value shifting found in *TCGA 1992, ss 29–34* or the depreciatory transaction rules found in *TCGA 1992, ss 176–181*.

General application

20.25 If a shareholder exercises his control over the company, so that value passes out of that person's or the shares of a connected party a disposal is deemed to have taken place at market value (*TCGA 1992, s 29(2)*). Similarly, a loss on disposal arising in this situation will not be an allowable loss (*TCGA 1992, s 29(3)*). Similar rules apply for intangible assets *TCGA 1992, s 33A*. The value shifting rules are applicable to all companies.

Free benefits

20.26 A disposal at market value is also deemed to take place where a scheme or arrangement materially reduces the value of an asset and gives rise to a tax-free benefit on the person making the disposal or on a connected party (*TCGA 1992, s 30(1)*). (These rules do not apply to disposals between husband and wife or between civil partners (*TCGA 1992, s 58(1)*), disposals by personal representatives to legatees (*TCGA 1992, s 62(4)*).

A benefit arises when a person becomes entitled to any money or money's worth, when the value of an asset increases or when a liability is reduced or cancelled (*TCGA 1992, s 30(3)*). It follows that, post an HMRC value shifting uplift, there is a complementary asset value uplift for future chargeable gains purposes.

These rules do not apply to group asset transfers groups (*TCGA 1992, s 171(1)*) (see **20.16**) and companies ceasing to be a member of a group (*TCGA 1992, ss 178 and 179*) (see **20.22**).

Again these rules do not apply if it is shown that avoidance of tax was not the main purpose or one of the main purposes of the scheme or arrangements in question (*TCGA 1992, s 30(2)*).

Distributions within a group followed by a disposal of shares

20.27   *TCGA 1992, s 31* is particularly drawn up to deal with situations where an intra-group dividend payment and an intra-group asset transfer is followed by the disposal of the subsidiary.

In normal circumstances before the sale of a subsidiary takes place, the payment of a dividend by the subsidiary to the holding company out of profits that have already suffered tax is not a depreciatory dividend for the purposes of *TCGA 1992, s 31*. It is recognised that such a transaction avoids a double taxation charge.

The legislation, however, applies where a company has profits that in some way it has engineered which have not been charged to tax. A revaluation of assets or the transfer of an asset on a no gain no loss basis under *TCGA 1992, s 171* may create such profits (*TCGA 1992, ss 31A, 32*).

Profits are chargeable in this circumstance if they satisfy the three conditions of *TCGA 1992, s 31*.

First, there must be a transaction that gives rise to distributable commercial profits, but which does not give rise to taxable profits. Such transactions are:

- an intra-group disposal at no gain/no loss under *TCGA 1992, s 171(1)*;

- an intra-group exchange of shares or debentures, or a reconstruction or amalgamation, which is treated as a reorganisation of share capital by *TCGA 1992, s 135(3)*; or

- a revaluation of an asset.

In practice, an asset revaluation will not give rise to distributable profits as a dividend may only be paid out of realised profits (*CA 2006, s 830*). However, this matter may require consideration when dealing with overseas groups (*TCGA 1992, s 31(6)*).

Secondly, there must be no real disposal of the asset other than a no gain/no loss disposal under *TCGA 1992, s 171(1)* and there has been no deemed disposal under *TCGA 1992, s 178* or *179* (*TCGA 1992, s 31(7)*).

Thirdly, immediately after the disposal the asset must be owned by a third party who remains outside the group (*TCGA 1992, s 31(8)*).

HMRC will investigate the following type of transactions:

Intra-group 'depreciatory' dividends:

- before the disposal the subsidiary paid a dividend out of reserves which were created by the intra-group transfer of an asset at a commercial (book) gain, and the transferred asset left the group at the same time as the shares in the subsidiary,

Intra-group asset transfers:

- before the disposal there was an intra-group transfer of an asset at a commercial (book) loss, (HMRC Capital Gains Manual CG 46803).

The *s 31* rules do not apply to trading assets (*TCGA 1992, s 31(9)*).

Asset holding company leaving the group

20.28 *TCGA 1992, s 31A* imposes subsequent conditions (applicable on or after 9 March 1999), which apply even though the third condition in **20.27** is not satisfied because the asset remains in the group. The asset may remain within the group if it is transferred to a non-UK company group member before disposal to a third party. If the UK transferee company ceases to be a member of the group within six years of transfer without a de-grouping charge arising, the value-shifting rules will apply to the transaction. This results in an increase in the gain being brought into charge at the time of the sale of the UK subsidiary company outside the group.

If that company no longer exists or has left the group, HMRC may by notice designate a company to be the chargeable company. This company will have been a group member immediately before the transferor company left the group (*TCGA 1992, s 31A(9)*).

Distributable profits are those profits, computed on a commercial basis, which a company may distribute in accordance with company law and any further restrictions in its own articles of association. A proper provision should be made for any tax payable (*TCGA 1992, s 31(4)*). Distributable profits are chargeable profits if they are within *s 31*. Distributable profits are first identified with non-chargeable profits for value shifting purposes and then with the chargeable profits (*TCGA 1992, s 31(10)*) (HMRC Company Taxation Manual CTM46851).

Example 20.8

Archer Ltd sold its 100% subsidiary Longfellow Ltd on 1 December 2009.

The substantial shareholdings relief is not available. Prior to sale Longfellow Ltd pays a dividend of £1,050,000 to Archer Ltd.

The details are as follows:

	£000
Value shifting non-chargeable profits	
– Distributable profits from normal operations	800
Value shifting chargeable profits	
– Distributable profits from intra-group transfer	900
Pre-sale distribution	1,050

Result

£1,050,000 is identified with the non-chargeable profits of £800,000. The £250,000 remainder is identified with the chargeable profits. An additional £250,000 is added to the consideration for the sale of Longfellow Ltd.

The legislation permits dividend tracing through tiers of companies (*TCGA 1992, s 31(3)*).

Disposals within a group followed by a disposal of shares

20.29   The value shifting provisions of *s 30* do not apply to disposals within *TCGA 1992, s 171(1)* unless particular conditions apply. These conditions are if the underlying asset is disposed of for less than its market value or less than cost unless the disposal was made for bona fide commercial reasons and does not form part of a scheme or arrangements of which the main purpose, or one of the main purposes, is avoidance of liability to corporation tax (*TCGA 1992, s 32(2)*). Cost incurred include all capital expenditure on acquiring and enhancing the value of the asset whilst in the company's ownership (*TCGA 1992, s 32(3)*).

The value shifting provisions do not apply on a disposal resulting from a capital distribution in the course of winding up the company, which has made the intra-group transfer of the underlying asset (*TCGA 1992, s 32(5)*).

Value shifting: reorganisation of share capital

20.30   If a parent company depreciates shares in a subsidiary, which is followed by a company reconstruction to which *TCGA 1992, ss 127, 135(3)* apply (see **15.8**) there is a chargeable gain or allowable loss in relation to the value-shifting portion (*TCGA 1992, s 34*).

Where a company ceases to be a member of a group and there is a deemed disposal of shares or securities at market value under *TCGA 1992, s 178* or *179*, the amount of the notional market value consideration for the deemed disposal may be increased under the value shifting provisions. The relevant increase is the amount of any adjustment, which could have been made under the value shifting provisions if the deemed disposal had been an actual disposal (*TCGA 1992, ss 178(7), 179(9)*).

Disposal of shares in another company

20.31   Where a company disposes of shares in, or securities of, another company, the value shifting rules cover a reduction in value, not only of the asset disposed of, but of any 'relevant asset', as defined by *TCGA 1992, s 30(2)*. An asset is a relevant asset if, at the time of the disposal to which *TCGA 1992, s 30* applies, it is owned by a company in the same group as the company making the disposal.

The extension to relevant assets only applies if the following conditions are satisfied.

During the period beginning when the relevant asset was depreciated and ending with the *s 30* disposal, the relevant asset has not been the subject of a disposal, other than a disposal at no gain/no loss under *TCGA 1992, s 171(1)*, or of a deemed disposal under the degrouping provisions in *TCGA 1992, ss 178* and *179*. For this purpose, *TCGA 1992, s 33(2)* disregards disposals of part of the asset. Assuming that all other circumstances had been the same, except that the relevant asset had not been depreciated, the value of the asset disposed of would have been materially greater.

LOSSES ATTRIBUTABLE TO DEPRECIATORY TRANSACTIONS

Depreciatory transactions within a group

20.32   If assets are transferred to group members at below market value this could fictitiously deflate the value of the company. If the shares were later sold, the market price would reflect the deflated price and hence a capital loss would arise. Such a loss will not be an allowable loss for CGT purposes (*TCGA 1992, s 176*).

The depreciatory transactions legislation in *TCGA 1992, ss 176* and *177* restrict the allowable loss on a disposal of shares or securities but do not convert a loss into a gain or increase the amount of a gain. A depreciatory transaction occurs when value is extracted from an asset. The aim of the legislation is to prevent artificial losses for both the shareholder and the company.

TCGA 1992, s 176 deals with depreciatory transactions involving groups of companies. *TCGA 1992, s 177* extends these rules to cover depreciatory distributions to a company with at least a 10% interest in the class of shares or securities to which the distribution relates. The provisions dealing with depreciatory distributions in respect of 10% holdings adopt the same general rules as apply to depreciatory transactions within groups.

For the legislation to apply, there must have been a disposal of shares or securities (referred to in the legislation as 'the ultimate disposal') and the value of the shares or securities has been materially reduced, by a depreciatory transaction (*TCGA 1992, s 176(1)*).

A depreciatory transaction' is a disposal of assets at other than market value by one group member to another. The adjustment is made on the basis that the allowable loss should not reflect any diminution in the value of the relevant company's assets, which was attributable to a depreciatory transaction. HMRC interpret 'materially reduced' as meaning that the value of the shares or securities is reduced other than by a negligible amount (HMRC Capital Gains Manual CG 46540).

Dividend stripping

20.33   This legislation is aimed at situations where a company might hold 10% or more of the same class securities of another company in a non-dealing non-group situation. A distribution is then made, the effect of which reduces the value of the other company dramatically. If the shares are then sold the distribution is not taken into account when calculating the chargeable gain on disposal (*TCGA 1992, s 177*).

Pre-entry losses and gains

20.34   A pre-entry asset is any asset owned by a company before it joined a group. The asset may have been transferred to other group members. An asset derived from a pre-entry asset is deemed to be part of the same asset, eg if the freehold reversion of a leasehold property is acquired (*TCGA 1992, Sch 7A, para 2(8)*).

For changes in ownership prior to 5 December 2005, restrictions were in place whereby, if a company joined a group, it was prevented from utilising its unrelieved losses arising prior to the time it joined the group against gains on the disposal of assets transferred (or deemed to be transferred) from another group member (*TCGA 1992, Sch 7AA*, repealed by *FA 2006, s 70(4)*).

Similarly, if a company joins a group and in the same accounting period realises a chargeable gain it is prevented from relieving the gain against the loss on sale of group assets transferred to the company during the same accounting period (*TCGA 1992, Sch 7AA*). See **20.35–20.43** for the situation with effect from 5 December 2005.

A realised pre-entry loss belonging to a company on joining a group can be set against a profit on disposal of any asset made before it joined the group or against the profit on disposal of any asset that the company owned when it joined the group and sells after joining. The losses can also be set against the gains on disposal of any assets that it acquired from outside the group and used for the purposes of the trade, which it has continued to carry on since it joined the group (*TCGA 1992, Sch 7A(1)*).

The pre-entry unrealised losses are apportioned accordingly to the time that the company joined the group (*TCGA 1992, Sch 7A(2)*).

It was confirmed in *Revenue and Customs Commissioners v Prizedome Ltd and another* [2009] EWCA Civ 177 that, where a company together with all the members of its original group joins a second group, the pre-entry losses that it incurred whilst a member of the first group are not available for offset whilst it is a member of a second group (*TCGA 1992, s 1(7)*). See also *Five Oaks Properties Ltd v Revenue and Customs Comrs* (2006) SpC 563.

CAPITAL LOSSES

Restrictions on allowable losses

20.35   A capital loss is a valuable tool for a company, as it can be carried forward indefinitely and set against future capital gains (see **20.5**). Improper utilisation of capital losses was targeted in *FA 2006* and *FA 2007*. With effect from 5 December 2005, a company's allowable losses exclude losses generated as part of a company tax avoidance scheme (*FA 2006, s 69; TCGA 1992, s 8(2)*). From 6 December 2006, these rules were extended to any person in situations where a taxpayer's capital loss will not be an allowable capital loss if it accrues in disqualifying circumstances. A loss accrues in disqualifying circumstances if it accrues directly or indirectly in consequence of or in connection with any arrangements of which the main purpose is to secure a tax advantage. The rationale is that capital loss relief should only be available in circumstances where there has been a true commercial disposal of an asset accompanied by a genuine commercial loss because of economic conditions existing at that time. Losses created by schemes that result in a tax loss greater than the actual loss or leave the economic ownership of the asset virtually intact are not allowed (*TCGA 1992, s 16A*).

Targeted anti-avoidance rules

20.36   With effect from 5 December 2005, three targeted anti-avoidance rules (TAARs) were introduced. The legislation is aimed at (1) the buying of capital losses and gains (*TCGA 1992, ss 184A* and *184B*), (2) the conversion of an income stream into a capital gain, or a capital gain matched by an income stream, thus covering the gain with an allowable loss (*TCGA 1992, s 184G*), and (3) the artificial generation of capital losses (*TCGA 1992, s 184H*).

Measures to counter bed and breakfast arrangements existed up to 5 December 2005 (*TCGA 1992, s 106*). This prevented companies selling and buying shareholdings within a short space of time in order to utilise a capital loss. The current anti-avoidance rule supersedes the bed and breakfast rule.

Restrictions on buying losses: tax avoidance schemes (TCGA 1992, s 184A)

20.37   The restriction of pre-entry loss rules within *TCGA 1992, Sch 7A* remains (see **20.34**) but *TCGA 1992, s 184A* has precedence (*TCGA 1992, s 184F(3)*). The pre-entry gains legislation of *TCGA 1992, Sch 7A* ceases to have effect (*TCGA 1992, s 184F(4)*). The *TCGA 1992, Sch 7A* rules are aimed at a group acquiring another company with latent losses. *TCGA 1992, s 184A* focuses on a company with latent losses changing its ownership. The rule only applies where there is an arrangement to avoid tax.

Situations where the restriction is applied

20.38   A group company is able to set its capital loss against the capital gain of another group company. However, this will be denied in the following circumstances:

- where there is a direct or indirect change of ownership of a company,

- where a loss accrues to the company or any other company on the disposal of an asset acquired prior to the change in ownership (a pre-change asset),

- where the main purpose of the change of ownership is to secure a tax advantage, and

- where the advantage involves the deduction of a qualifying loss from any chargeable gains, whether or not any other transactions or events are involved.

The resulting loss is not deductible from gains arising on assets belonging to the new owners.

Arrangements include any agreement, understanding, scheme, transaction or series of transactions whether or not they are legally enforceable. It is irrelevant as to whether the loss accrues before or after the change of ownership. It is irrelevant whether there are any chargeable gains at the time against which it can be utilised or whether the tax advantage accrues to the company to whom the loss has accrued or to any other company.

A qualifying change of ownership occurs at any time that:

- a company joins a group of companies,

- the company ceases to be a member of a group of companies,

- the company becomes subject to different control (*TCGA 1992, s 184C*).

A group is determined by *TCGA 1992, s 170* (see **20.14**) (*TCGA 1992, s 184C*).

Group off-set of losses is only available if both the companies in question were members of the same group immediately before the disposal and have remained members until immediately after the disposal (*FA 2006, s 70(12)*).

A tax advantage means relief or increased relief from corporation tax or repayment or increased repayment of corporation tax. It also means the avoidance or reduction of a charge to corporation tax or an assessment to corporation tax or the avoidance or a possible assessment to corporation tax (*TCGA 1992, s 184D*).

Example 20.9

Sam Arkwright and Bill Weatherspoon each own 50% of Solo Ltd, a single company with substantial capital losses. Solo Ltd owns Nevercourt, a property that it is in negotiations to sell. Solo Ltd issues ordinary shares that amount to

30% of the nominal value of the ordinary share capital to Alfonso Roderigo (an unconnected third party). Mr Roderigo's shares only have dividend rights. Sam Arkwright and Bill Weatherspoon then sell the original shares in Solo Ltd to the Multi Group plc. Although, in economic terms, Solo Ltd has joined the Multi Group plc, it has not joined the Multi Group plc's capital gains group, because Multi Group plc owns less that 75% of the issued share capital. Multi Group plc intends to transfer all of its assets that have not yet risen in value, but that it expects to rise in value, to Solo Ltd in the expectation that any resulting chargeable gains could be covered by the purchased losses. The issue of shares in Solo Ltd to Alfonso Roderigo is clearly intended to prevent Solo Ltd joining the Multi Group plc when the original shareholders sell their shares. This prevents *TCGA 1992, Sch 7A* (Pre-entry loss restriction) from applying.

Solo Ltd has neither left nor joined a chargeable gains group but it has become subject to a different control. There has, therefore, been a qualifying change of ownership as defined by *TCGA 1992, s 184C*. Solo Ltd has accrued losses on pre-change assets. The change of ownership has occurred in connection with arrangements, the main purpose of which is to secure a tax advantage for the Multi Group plc. *TCGA 1992, s 184A* applies and Solo Ltd's losses are qualifying losses and are not to be deducted from any gains arising to the company, except those accruing to Solo Ltd on a disposal of pre-change assets. If Nevercourt, the property owned by Solo Ltd at the time of the change of ownership, is then sold, giving rise to a chargeable gain, this gain can be covered by the losses.

Restrictions on buying gains: tax avoidance schemes (TCGA 1992, s 184B)

20.39   The same criteria apply to a change of company ownership and the realisation of a chargeable gain to be relieved by capital losses, which accrued prior to the change in ownership.

Disposal of pre-change assets

20.40   If a company has disposed of a pre-change asset but still retains an interest in the asset, that interest will remain as a pre-change asset.

The capital gain on the following disposals may be deferred:

- Reconstructions involving transfers of business (*TCGA 1992, s 139*).

- Postponement of charge on transfer of assets to non-resident companies (*TCGA 1992, s 140*).

- Transfer of a UK trade (*TCGA 1992, s 140A*).

- Merger leaving assets within UK tax charge (*TCGA 1992, s 140E*).

- Replacement of business assets (*TCGA 1992, ss 152, 153*).

- Postponement of charge on deemed disposal under *s 187* (*TCGA 1992, s 185*).

Any gain or loss accruing as a result of any subsequent event will be treated as accruing on a pre-change asset (*TCGA 1992, s 184E*).

Pre-change securities are pooled. Any disposal is matched first for these purposes; pre-change securities are pooled separately from post-change securities. A disposal of securities after the change is to be matched first against the post-change pool, then against the pre-change pool, and then in accordance with the usual share identification rules (*TCGA 1992, s 184F*).

Avoidance involving losses: schemes converting income to capital (TCGA 1992, s 184G)

20.41   This situation arises where a company receives a receipt directly or indirectly on the disposal of an asset in connection with any arrangements. A chargeable gain accrues to the company on the asset disposal but capital losses accrue on other assets before or after the first asset's disposal as part of the arrangements. The arrangements enable a capital receipt to be accounted for instead of an income receipt, which would indeed have happened had the arrangements not been in place. The main purpose of the arrangement is to obtain a capital loss deduction from the capital gain irrespective of any other purpose.

Avoidance involving losses: schemes securing a deduction (TCGA 1992, s 184H)

20.42   This situation arises where a chargeable gain accrues to a company directly or indirectly in consequence of or in connection with any arrangements and losses accrued on any disposal of any asset before or after the first asset's disposal as part of the arrangements. Also as part of the arrangements the company or a connected company incurs expenditure which is allowable as a deduction in computing total profits but is not allowable in computing its chargeable gains. The main purpose of the arrangement is to obtain a deduction for the expenditure in computing profits and a capital loss deduction from the relevant gain irrespective of any other purpose.

Arm's-length arrangements, arrangements in respect of land, unconnected party arrangements and certain sale and leaseback arrangements are excluded.

HMRC notice

20.43   If HMRC consider that the purpose of these arrangements is to secure a tax advantage, they may give the company a notice under *TCGA 1992, s 184G* or *184H*. If all conditions are satisfied, no loss accruing to the relevant company may be deducted from the relevant gain.

If a company submits its tax return within a 90-day period after the receipt of the notice, it may disregard the notice in preparing the return and, within the 90-day period, amend the return in order to comply with the notice.

If the company has already submitted its company tax return, HMRC can only give the company a notice in respect of these anti-avoidance schemes if a notice of enquiry has also been given to the company in respect of the return for the same period.

HMRC may give the company a notice after any enquiries into the return have been completed if two conditions are satisfied. First, that at the time the enquiries into the return were completed, HMRC could not have been reasonably expected, on the basis of information made available to them before or at that time or to an officer of theirs before that time, to have been aware that the circumstances necessitated the issue of a notice. The second condition is that the company or any other person was requested to produce or provide information during an enquiry into the return for that period and, if the request had been duly complied with, HMRC could have been reasonably expected to give a notice in relation to that period.

Chapter 21

The construction industry scheme

INTRODUCTION

21.1 Companies whose trade involves construction or building may find that they are required to comply with the construction industry scheme. Such businesses will include construction businesses, property developers, speculative builders and construction work gang leaders. *FA 2004* introduced the current construction industry scheme, which is effective from 5 April 2007. Legislation is contained in *FA 2004, ss 57–77, Schs 11, 12*; *CTA 2009, ss 1303(1), 1306(1)*. Secondary legislation is contained within *SI 2005/2045*. The Construction Industry Scheme applies not only to companies but also to individuals and partnerships.

FA 2004 scheme replaced the 6 April 1993 scheme. In brief, the new scheme replaces the CIS4 registration card and CIS6 tax certificates with a verification service. There is also a new employment status declaration. Monthly returns replace the old vouchers and a declaration of the employment status of those engaged is included with the monthly returns.

Sub-contractor companies are now required subject to conditions to register for gross or net payments. Sub-contractors registered under the old scheme are carried over to the new scheme. A contractor company engaging a sub-contractor must verify with HMRC whether to make payment gross or net.

Where a contractor company has a recent connection with the sub-contractor it need not carry out any verification procedures. HMRC will notify any change in the payment status of the sub-contractor to any contractor who has engaged that sub-contractor in the current or previous two years. Each month, the contractor will be required to make a return, including a nil return, of all payments made to sub-contractors in that month.

CONSTRUCTION CONTRACT

Meaning of a construction contract

21.2 A construction contract is a contract relating to construction operations carried out in the UK, which is not a contract of employment (*FA*

2004, s 57(2)). The UK for this purpose consists of England, Scotland, Wales and Northern Ireland and its territorial waters but not the Channel Islands nor the Isle of Man (HMRC Manual CISR 11090 and 12130). For a construction contract to exist there must be a contract and a sub-contractor. Certain payments under construction contracts are to be made under deduction of sums on account of tax *(FA 2004, s 57(1))*. Reverse premium payments (see **12.24**) are not payments under a construction contract *(SI 2005/2045, reg 20)*.

Sub-contractor

21.3   The status of a sub-contractor is determined by the construction contract. If an individual or a company by reason of the construction contract has a duty to the contractor to carry out the operations of the construction contract or to furnish his own labour or to furnish the labour of the employees or officers of the company or indeed to furnish the labour of others or is answerable to the contractor for the work of others that individual or that company is considered to be a sub-contractor for these purposes *(FA 2004, s 58)*.

Construction operations

21.4   Activities falling under one of more of the following headings are considered to be construction operations:

1   The construction, alteration, repair, extension, demolition or dismantling of buildings or structures (whether permanent or not), including offshore installations.

2   The construction, alteration, repair, extension or demolition of any works forming, or to form, part of the land, including (in particular) walls, roadworks, power-lines, electronic communications apparatus, aircraft runways, docks and harbours, railways, inland waterways, pipe-lines, reservoirs, water-mains, wells, sewers, industrial plant and installations for purposes of land drainage, coast protection or defence.

3   The installation in any building or structure of systems of heating, lighting, air-conditioning, ventilation, power supply, drainage, sanitation, water supply or fire protection.

4   The internal cleaning of buildings and structures, so far as carried out in the course of their construction, alteration, repair, extension or restoration.

5   The painting or decorating the internal or external surfaces of any building or structure.

6   Operations which form an integral part of, or are preparatory to, or are for rendering complete, such operations as are previously described in this subsection, including site clearance, earth-moving, excavation, tunnelling and boring, laying of foundations, erection of scaffolding, site restoration, landscaping and the provision of roadways and other access works.

(FA 2004, s 74(2))

The following activities are not construction operations:

1   The drilling for, or extraction of, oil or natural gas.

2   The extraction (whether by underground or surface working) of minerals and tunnelling or boring, or construction of underground works, for this purpose.

3   The manufacture of building or engineering components or equipment, materials, plant or machinery, or delivery of any of these things to site.

4   The manufacture of components for systems of heating, lighting, air-conditioning, ventilation, power supply, drainage, sanitation, water supply or fire protection, or delivery of any of these things to site.

5   The professional work of architects or surveyors, or of consultants in building, engineering, interior or exterior decoration or in the laying-out of landscape.

6   The making, installation and repair of artistic works, being sculptures, murals and other works, which are wholly artistic in nature.

7   Signwriting and erecting, installing and repairing signboards and advertisements.

8   The installation of seating, blinds and shutters.

9   The installation of security systems, including burglar alarms, closed circuit television and public address systems

(FA 2004, s 74(3))

HMRC offer a CIS helpline 0845 366 7899 for cases of doubt over a particular activity.

Contractors

21.5   A company carrying on a construction operation will be a contractor. Any business or public body, government department or agency or NHS trust will also be a contractor if the average annual expenditure on construction operations in the period of three years ending with the end of the last period of account before that time exceeds £1,000,000 *(FA 2004, s 59(1))*. The business will cease to be a contractor if the construction business annual expenditure is less £1,000,000 for three successive years. Any business will also be a contractor if it was not carrying on the business at the beginning of that period of three years but one-third of the total expenditure on construction operations for the part of that period during which business was carried on exceeds £1,000,000 (*FA 2004, s 59*). The amounts paid will only be treated as contract payments if the property is held for sale of letting or held as an investment property. Incidental use of the property is ignored (*SI 2005/2045, reg 22*). The property may be owned by the company, a fellow group member (see **10.5**) or another company in which the company in question has a 50% or more holding.

A contractor may elect to be treated as different contractors in relation to different groups of sub-contractors, with the result that for each group the contractor was a different contractor. The election must give information to identify the groups of sub-contractors, and contain a certificate that there are no other sub-contractors besides those identified.

The election must be made before the beginning of the tax year for which it is to have effect. If a contractor company acquires the whole or part of any business from another contractor the company may elect within 90 days of the acquisition to be treated as a different contractor in relation to the acquired sub-contractors and to add some or all of the acquired sub-contractors to existing groups of sub-contractors in respect of whom an election is already in force. The election continues in effect until it is revoked. For a revocation to be effective it must be given before the beginning of the tax year for which it is to apply (*SI 2005/2045, reg 3*).

Transfer of a trade

21.6   If the company transfers the whole or part of a trade to another company to which *ICTA 1988 s 343* applies, the transferee company is deemed to have incurred the expenditure actually incurred by the transferor. Where only part of the trade is transferred a just and reasonable apportionment of the expenditure will be made.

DEDUCTIONS ON ACCOUNT OF TAX FROM CONTRACT PAYMENTS TO SUB-CONTRACTORS

Contract payments

21.7   A contract payment is any payment made by the contractor under a construction contract to either the sub-contractor, a person nominated by the sub-contractor or the contractor, or a person nominated by a sub-contractor under another contract in connection with all or some of the construction operations. A payment is not a subcontract payment if it is treated as employment earnings of an employed person or an agency worker (*FA 2004, s 60*). A payment does not include the cost of materials, VAT or an amount in respect of the Construction Industry Training Board (CITB) levy, but depending on the terms of the contract may include payments for subsistence and/or travelling expenses (HMRC Manual CISR 11100).

Deductions on account of tax from contract payments

21.8   It is necessary to be able to distinguish between the direct cost of materials for the construction operation and all other costs. The contractor must deduct tax when making a contract payment to the sub-contractor, which does not relate to the direct material costs (*FA 2004, s 61*). The sum deducted and payable to HMRC is treated as satisfying the sub-contractor's tax liability either for income tax if an individual or corporation tax if a company (*FA 2004, s 62*).

There is no requirement to deduct tax from a contract payment if the contractor is an approved public body or any company carrying on a business which includes construction operations as highlighted in **21.5** (*FA 2004, s 59(1)(b)–(l)*) and the total payments (excluding the direct cost of materials) are lower than or likely to be lower than £1,000 (*SI 2005/2045, reg 18*). Similarly, there is no requirement to deduct tax if the company carrying on a business, which includes construction operations on land, owned by the company and the total payments (excluding the direct cost of materials) are lower than or likely to be lower than £1,000 (*SI 2005/2045, reg 19*).

Penalties introduced by *FA 2009, Sch 56* have been introduced for failure to pay tax on time, see **21.35**. These are to take effect from a date yet to be announced by Treasury Order.

Rate of tax on deductions from contract payments

21.9   The rate of tax applied to the payment to the sub-contractor depends on the sub-contractor's status. For registered and verified sub-contractors the rate is 20%. For unregistered or unverified sub-contractors the rate is 30%. The rate is nil for those sub-contractors that are registered for gross payment (HMRC Manual CISR 11100 and *SI 2007/46*).

Monthly payment

21.10   The return period is the tax month, ie the fifth day of each month. Payment is due within 17 days of the end of the month if the payment is made electronically and within 14 days if the payment is made by any other means (*SI 2005/2045, reg 7*). If HMRC have not received payment in full within 17 days they may issue a notice requiring a return to be completed (*SI 2005/2045, reg 10*). HMRC may also make an estimation based on past payment criteria (*SI 2005/2045, reg 11*).

If the contractor makes an error in good faith or after enquiry genuinely believed that the scheme did not apply any amounts not deducted by the contractor company can be recovered from the sub-contractor. Also, the contractor may ask HMRC to issue a direction that the contractor is not liable to any excess tax (*SI 2005/2045, reg 9*). If there is a dispute between the contractor and the sub-contractor HMRC may make a determination of the amount due. Both contractor and sub-contractor have the right of appeal (*SI 2005/2045, reg 13*). Interest is charged on unpaid tax for a fiscal year (year ended 5 April) from 19 April until date of payment (*SI 2005/2045, reg 14*). HMRC have the power to bring proceedings against the contractor for unpaid tax and unpaid interest (*SI 2005/2045, reg 16*). A return for 50 sub-contractors or less will attract a penalty of £100 for each month that it is outstanding. The monthly penalty is increased progressively by £100 for the addition of 50 sub-contractors or less. Therefore a return for 40 sub-contractors that is two months late will attract total penalties of £200, and a return for 90 contractors that is also two months late will attract total penalties of £400. See HMRC 4 October 2007, CIS – Penalty regimes.

Overpayments attract interest from the end of the tax year after the tax year in which the payment was made until date of repayment. If a payment was made more than 12 months after the end of the tax year then the repayment interest will run from the end of the tax year in which the payment was made until date of payment (*SI 2005/2045, reg 15*). Any tax overpaid during the year may be reclaimed from HMRC (*SI 2005/2045, reg 17*).

Default surcharge

21.11 If the company fails to pay the tax deducted by the due date it will fall liable to a default surcharge unless there is a reasonable excuse. Inability to pay is not a reasonable excuse (*SI 2005/2045, reg 46*). The company has the right of appeal (*SI 2005/2045, reg 47*).

The surcharge percentage is applied to the difference between the tax deducted from payments under the construction industry scheme and the amounts deducted under the following:

● *Statutory Maternity Pay (Compensation of Employers) and Miscellaneous Amendment Regulations 1994, regs 4–6,*

- *Statutory Paternity Pay and Statutory Adoption Pay (Administration) Regulations 2002, regs 3 and 5*, and

- if the company is a sub-contractor against relevant liabilities in the following order in that year:

  — Employee Class 1 NIC contributions

  — Employer Class 1 NIC contributions

  — PAYE

  — Student Loan deductions

  — Construction industry deductions from its sub-contractors.

The default percentage charged depends on the number of defaults and is calculated according to the following table:

Default number (within a surcharge period)	Specified percentage
1st	0%
2nd	0%
3rd	0.17%
4th	0.17%
5th	0.17%
6th	0.33%
7th	0.33%
8th	0.33%
9th	0.58%
10th	0.58%
11th	0.58%
12th	0.83%

A surcharge period begins on the day following the payment date and ends on the last day of the tax year for which there is no default for any specified payment. The surcharge is payable within 30 days after the issue of the surcharge notice (*SI 2005/2045, reg 48*). A contractor has the right of appeal against the notice within 30 days of the issue of the notice (*SI 2005/2045, reg 49*).

Penalties introduced by *FA 2009, Sch 56* have been introduced for failure to pay tax on time, see **21.35**. These are to take effect from a date yet to be announced by Treasury Order.

Quarterly payment

21.12   A contractor company may pay quarterly if it has reasonable grounds for believing that the average monthly amount will be less than £1,500 and the company chooses to pay quarterly.

The average monthly amount is based on the current year's tax month. The following formula is applied:

$$(P + N + L + S) - (SP + CD)$$

The formula uses the following amounts that would be payable in the circumstances:

P   =   PAYE due for the period less any PAYE repayments as calculated according to the *Income Tax (Pay As You Earn) Regulations 2003, SI 2003/2682, reg 68.*

N   =   Employees' class 1 primary contribution excluding and secondary contributions transferred from the employer to the employee under an *SSCBA 1992, Sch 1, para 3B(1)* election.

L   =   Student Loan repayments less tax credits under *Education (Student Loans) (Repayment) Regulations 2000, reg 39(1)* and *(3).*

S   =   Tax due by the contractor for the tax month (*SI 2005/2045, reg 7*).

SP =   statutory sick pay, statutory maternity pay, statutory paternity pay and statutory adoption pay under *SSCBA 1992.*

CD =   the amount which others would deduct from payments to the company, in its position as a sub-contractor.

(*SI 2005/2045, reg 8*)

REGISTRATION

Registration of sub-contractors

21.13   HMRC will register a sub-contractor company for gross payment on submission of the relevant information and documentation. In other circumstances the company will be registered for net payment. The company is required to comply with the business, turnover and compliance test conditions in order to be eligible for gross payments:

In turn, the Board may direct that the conditions shall apply to the company directors, the beneficial shareholders if the company is a close company or specified persons as if each were an applicant for gross payment registration (*FA 2004, s 64(5)*).

Information to be supplied to HMRC

A sub-contractor company must supply the following information to HMRC:

- the name, address, national insurance number and unique taxpayer reference of the directors of the company or, if the company is a close company, the persons who are the beneficial owners of shares in the company,
- utility bills,
- council tax bills,
- current passport,
- driving licence,
- company registration number and
- company's memorandum and articles of association.

(*SI 2005/2045, reg 25*)

Penalties introduced by *FA 2009, Sch 55* apply if the information is not submitted on time (see **21.30** and **21.32**). These rules are to take effect from a date yet to be announced by Treasury Order.

COMPANY CHANGE OF CONTROL

21.14   If there has been a change in the control of a company that is or that is applying for gross payment registration, HMRC may ask for information regarding the changes in control of the company (*FA 2004, s 65*).

The definition of control for this purpose is *ICTA 1988, s 840* (see **14.4**).

Where there is a change of control of a close company by reason of an issue or transfer of shares in the company to a person who was not a shareholder in the company immediately before the issue or transfer, the company must notify HMRC, within 30 days of the issue or of receiving information as to the transfer. The company must supply HMRC with details of the name and address of the person to whom the shares were issued or transferred (*SI 2005/2045, reg 53*).

CANCELLATION OF REGISTRATION FOR GROSS PAYMENT

Reasons for cancellation

21.15   HMRC may issue a determination stating the reasons to cancel a gross payment registration if at any time it appears to them that:

- if an application to register the person for gross payment were to be made at that time, the Board would refuse so to register him,

- If he has made an incorrect return or provided incorrect information (whether as a contractor or as a sub-contractor) under any provision of this Chapter or of regulations made under it, or

- he has failed to comply (whether as a contractor or as a sub-contractor) with any such provision.

The gross payment cancellation takes effect from the end of a prescribed period after the making of the determination.

On receipt of the determination the sub-contractor company must register for net payment. The sub-contractor company is debarred from re-applying for gross payment registration for a year from cancellation.

Fraudulent conduct

21.16 HMRC may issue a determination stating the reasons, to cancel a company's gross payment registration if at any time if they have reasonable grounds to suspect that the person:

- became registered for gross payment on the basis of information which was false;

- has fraudulently made an incorrect return or provided incorrect information (whether as a contractor or as a sub-contractor) under any provision of this Chapter or of regulations made under it; or

- has knowingly failed to comply (whether as a contractor or as a sub-contractor) with any such provision.

In such circumstances the cancellation takes immediate effect on the issue of the determination. On receipt of the determination, if HMRC thinks fit, the sub-contractor company may register for net payment. Again, the sub-contractor company is debarred from re-applying for gross payment registration for a year from cancellation (*FA 2004, s 66*).

Registration cancellation right of appeal

21.17 The company has the right of appeal to the General Commissioners (or to the Special Commissioners if so elected), against the determination. The appeal must give the full grounds and be made within 30 days after the refusal or cancellation. A refusal or cancellation under appeal does not take effect until the later of:

- the abandonment of the appeal,
- the Commissioners determination of the appeal or
- the determination of the appeal by the appropriate higher court.

(*FA 2004, s 67*)

Verification, returns etc and penalties

21.18 HMRC may make regulations requiring the contractor company to verify the status of the sub-contractor company (*FA 2004, s 69*).

A contractor must verify with HMRC the status of the sub-contractor to whom gross payments are to be made or that person's nominee.

The contractor company must provide details of

- the company name, unique taxpayer reference (UTR), accounts office reference and employer's reference, and
- in relation to the person to whom it is proposing to make the payment and, where that person has appointed a nominee, his nominee:
  - (i) if that person or nominee is an individual, his name, unique taxpayer reference (UTR) and national insurance number;
  - (ii) if that person or nominee is a partner in a firm, the name of the firm and that partner, the unique taxpayer reference (UTR) of the firm, and if the partner is an individual his unique taxpayer reference (UTR) or national insurance number or if the partner is a company the unique taxpayer reference (UTR) or the company registration number;
  - (iii) if that person or nominee is a company, the name of the company, unique taxpayer reference (UTR) and the company registration number.

Verification is not possible until a contract is in place.

Situations where verification is not required

21.19 Verification is not required if:

- the sub-contractor has been included in a sub-contract return in the current or previous two tax years;
- the payment is made within two years of 6 April 2007;

- if the person to whom he is proposing has been included in a return of the previous construction industry scheme within the current or previous two years;

- if the company or a company within the same group to whom it is proposed to make the payment has been included in a return of the previous construction industry scheme within the current or previous two years;

- the contractor has elected under *SI 2005/2045, reg 3* (see **21.5**);

- the contractor acquired the contract under which the payment is to be made in a transfer of a business as a going concern in one of the situations as described above.

(SI 2005/2045, reg 6)

Record-keeping

21.20   HMRC may make regulations requiring contractor companies that make payments under construction contracts to carry out the following:

- to make returns to HMRC,

- to keep records as prescribed relating to the payments, or

- to provide such information as may be prescribed the to persons to whom the payments are made *(FA 2004, s 70)*.

Records must be kept for three years *(SI 2005/2045, reg 51(10))*.

In particular the company making the return must state that none of the contracts to which the return relates is a contract of employment, that the regulations have been complied with, the returns contain in the necessary information and confirmation that the verification status requirements of the sub-contractor have been complied with *(SI 2005/2045, reg 6)*. The sub-contractor need not seek verification if the sub-contractor has been included in a monthly return in the current or previous two years of the same company or group company. (A group is defined according to *ICTA 1988, s 413(3)*; see **10.5** *(SI 2005/2045, reg 6)*.)

Inspection of records of contractors and sub-contractors

21.21   A contractor or sub-contractor must produce records for the previous three years to HMRC when required to do so *(SI 2005/2045, reg 51)*. HMRC may make copies, remove or make extracts from these records. HMRC will issue a receipt for all documents removed and provide copies on request free of charge to the contractor or sub-contractor from whom the documents were removed.

Penalties

21.22   A sub-contractor company may be liable to a £3,000 penalty if it knowingly or recklessly makes a false statement, or provides a false document (*FA 2004, s 72*). An interest payable in connection with the scheme is neither taxable nor deductible for corporation tax purposes (*CTA 2009, s 1303(1)*).

HMRC charge penalties for all CIS returns not received by the due date.

Monthly return

21.23   Contractor companies are required to make monthly returns, either online or manually, within 14 days of the end of each month to HMRC. The contractor company may appoint another company in the same group as the scheme representative (*SI 2005/2045, reg 5*).

The return must show:

- the contractor's name,

- the contractor's unique taxpayer reference (UTR) and Accounts' Office reference,

- the tax month to which the return relates, and

- in respect of each sub-contractor to whom, or to whose nominee, payments under construction contracts were made by the contractor during that month:

  (i)   the sub-contractor's name;

  (ii)   the sub-contractor's national insurance number (NINO) or company registration number (CRN), if known;

  (iii) the sub-contractor's UTR;

  (iv)   if the sub-contractor is registered for gross payment the total amount of payments which would be contract payment exceptions (see **21.7**) made by the contractor to the sub-contractor during the tax month;

  (v)   if the sub-contractor is registered for payment under deduction of tax, the total amount of the contract payments (see **21.7**) made by the contractor to the sub-contractor during the tax month, the total amount included in those payments which the contractor is satisfied represents the direct cost to any person other than the contractor of materials used or to be used in carrying out the construction contract to which the contract payment relates, and the amount of tax deducted; and

(vi) if the sub-contractor is not registered for gross payment or payment under deduction of tax, the total amount of the contract payments (see **21.7**) made by the contractor to the sub-contractor during the tax month, the total amount included in those payments which the contractor is satisfied represents the direct cost to any person other than the contractor of materials used or to be used in carrying out the construction contract to which the contract payment relates, and the amount of tax deducted together with the verification reference for higher rate deduction.

The return may be submitted electronically. Online filing can only be accepted via HMRC's free filing facility or Electronic Data Interchange (EDI). Alternatively third party agent filing is recognised.

The CIS300 and the CIS300(Man) are the only acceptable paper forms. Nil returns may be obtained from the CIS Helpline 0845 366 7899.

HMRC will not accept photocopies, PDFs, computer listings and paper substitute returns of any description. See HMRC Guidance Note 29 August 2007, The contractor monthly return – further guidance on its completion.

Penalties introduced by *FA 2009, Sch 55* apply if the return is not submitted on time (see **21.30** and **21.31**). These rules are to take effect from a date yet to be announced by Treasury Order.

Declaration

21.24 The company must declare that none of the contracts to which the return relates is a contract of employment. The company must indicate whether it has verified each sub-contractor status. The contractor must provide the sub-contractor with details of the payments not later than 14 days after the end of the tax month to which the payment relates. Details for a sub-contractor on a net payment basis will include: the contractor's name, the contractor's employer's reference, the tax month to which the payments relate or the date of the payment, the sub-contractor's name, the sub-contractor's unique taxpayer reference (UTR), the total amount of contract payments made by the contractor to the sub-contractor during the tax month, the total amount included in those payments which the contractor is satisfied represents the direct cost to any person other than the contractor of materials used or to be used in carrying out the construction contract to which the contract payment relates, and the total tax deducted. Amount deducted from the payments and the verification reference if the sub-contractor is not registered. If not payments are made, nil returns are still required (*SI 2005/2045, reg 6*).

If the company fails to submit a return, there is an automatic penalty of £100 per month for 50 sub-contractors. If the return is made over 12 months late, there is a penalty of up to the tax (*SI 2005/2045, reg 4; TMA 1970, s 98A*).

GROSS PAYMENT TESTS

21.25 If a company applies for gross payment registration it must satisfy the business test, the turnover test and the compliance test (*FA 2004, Sch 11, para 9*).

The business test

21.26 The company must satisfy HMRC that:

- it is carrying on a business in the UK, which

- consists of or includes the carrying out of construction operations or the furnishing or arranging for the furnishing of labour in carrying out construction operations, and is substantially carried on through a bank account.

The following evidence must be supplied to HMRC:

- the company's address;

- invoices, contracts or purchase orders for construction work carried out by the company;

- details of payments for construction work;

- the books and accounts of the company;

- details of the company bank account, including bank statements.

(*SI 2005/2045, reg 27*)

The turnover test

21.27 The company must either satisfy HMRC with evidence that it is likely to receive the minimum turnover in the year in which the application is made, or satisfy HMRC that the only persons with shares in the company are companies, which are limited by shares and themselves, are registered for gross payment.

The minimum turnover for the period is the smaller of:

- £30,000 × number or relevant persons for the company, or
- £200,000.

Company directors are relevant persons. Beneficial owners of shares in a close company are also relevant persons (*FA 2004, Sch 11, para 11*).

The company must be able to supply evidence of turnover and relevant payments together with documentary evidence to demonstrate that operations during the period amounted to construction operations (*SI 2005/2045, reg 29*). In the case of a new business, evidence of turnover and relevant persons during the qualifying period should be supplied. Evidence should also be supplied of construction contracts entered into by the company including payment schedules where the aggregate value of these contracts exceeds £200,000 and that payments of at least £30,000 have been made.

If a company's business does not consist mainly of construction operations HMRC will treat the turnover test as met, if not actually met, if the following conditions are met. These conditions are that in the year prior to making the application the total turnover of the business exceeded the relevant turnover threshold, and in the year following making the application the company is likely to receive relevant payments in relation to construction operations which are incidental to the company's main business (*SI 2005/2045, reg 31*).

The compliance test

21.28 Within 12 months of the registration application, the company must have complied with all HMRC requests concerning information and documentation (*FA 2004, Sch 11, paras 12* and *14*). HMRC will treat the following prescribed obligations as being satisfied by the following prescribed circumstances:

Prescribed obligations		Prescribed circumstances
Obligation to submit monthly contractor return within the required period.	1 2	Return is submitted not later than 28 days after the due date, and the company— (a) has not otherwise failed to comply with this obligation within the previous 12 months, or (b) has failed to comply with this obligation on not more than two occasions within the previous 12 months.

Prescribed obligations		Prescribed circumstances
Obligation to pay—	1	Payment is made not later than
(a) the tax deducted from	2	14 days after the due date, and
payments made		the company—
		(a) has not otherwise failed to comply with this obligation within the previous 12 months, or
Prescribed obligations		Prescribed circumstances
during that tax period, or		(b) has failed to comply with
(b) tax liable to be deducted under the PAYE Regulations.		this obligation on not more than two occasions within the previous 12 months.
Obligation to pay income tax.	1	Payment is made not later than
	2	28 days after the due date, and the applicant has not otherwise failed to comply with this obligation within the previous 12 months.
Obligation to submit an annual return under the PAYE regulations 73, 74 and 85 within the required period.		Return is submitted after the due date.
Obligation to pay corporation tax	1	Payment is made not later than
for which the applicant or	2	28 days after the due date, and
company is liable.		any shortfall in that payment has incurred an interest charge but no penalty.
Obligation to submit a self-assessment return within the required period.		Return is submitted after the due date.
Obligations and requests to supply information in support of the compliance test.		The failure to comply occurred before 6 April 2007 but complied with previous requirements.
Obligation to make a payment under the *Tax Acts* or *TMA 1970*		Late or non-payment of an amount under £100.

(*SI 2005/2045, reg 32*; *SI 2008/1282*)

HMRC will carry out a 'Scheduled Review', also known as an 'Ongoing TTQT' (Tax Treatment Qualification Test), to check whether companies holding gross payment status comply with their obligations. See HMRC Technical Note 29 October 2007 – Construction industry scheme – tax treatment qualification test.

APPLICATION OF SUMS DEDUCTED FROM CONTRACT PAYMENTS

21.29   The sums that a contractor company deducts from payments made to a sub-contractor may be applied as follows:

- employee Class 1 NIC contributions;

- employer Class 1 NIC contributions;

- PAYE;

- student loan deductions;

- refunds due to HMRC for statutory sick pay, statutory maternity pay, statutory paternity pay or statutory adoption pay; and

- construction industry deductions from its sub-contractors.

HMRC will not repay any tax deducted by a contractor from a sub-contractor's payment until after the end of the tax year in which the deduction was made and the contractor has delivered its annual PAYE return.

Any remaining amount will either be repaid to the contractor or used to off-set any outstanding corporation tax (*SI 2005/2045, reg 56*).

CIS PENALTIES

Returns outstanding for less than 12 months

21.30   If the CIS return is outstanding for more than two months after the penalty date, HMRC may charge a penalty of £200. The penalty date is the day after the filing date, being the date on which the penalty is first payable. If the CIS return is outstanding for more than six months after the penalty date, HMRC may charge a penalty amounting to the greater of £300 and 5% of any liability to make payments which would have been shown on the return. If the CIS return is outstanding for more than 12 months after the penalty date, the penalty liability is dependent upon the circumstances. These provisions will take effect from a date yet to be announced by Treasury Order.

Returns outstanding for more than 12 months

Contractor company

21.31   If, by failing to make the return (see **21.23**), the contractor company withholds information which would enable or assist HMRC to assess its liability to tax, the penalty depends on whether or not the withholding of information is deliberate and concealed.

If withholding of information is deliberate and concealed:

• the penalty is the greater of 100% of any liability to tax which would have been shown in the return in question and £3,000;

If the withholding of information is deliberate but not concealed:

• the penalty is the greater of 70% of any liability to tax which would have been shown in the return in question and £1,500;

In any other case:

• the penalty is the greater of 5% of any liability to make payments which would have been shown in the return and £300.

Returns outstanding for more than 12 months – withholding information where gross payment registration

21.32   If information relating to persons registered for gross payments (see **21.13**) remains outstanding for 12 months beginning with the penalty date, an additional penalty may be charged. If, by failing to make the return, the contractor company withholds information which relates to such persons, the penalty arising is dependent on whether the withholding of information is deliberate or concealed.

If the withholding of information is deliberate and concealed:

• the penalty is £3,000;

If the withholding of information is deliberate but not concealed:

• the penalty is £1,500;

If the company has just entered the CIS régime:

• the total of the fixed rate penalties is capped at £3,000.

(*FA 2009, Sch 55, paras 7–13*)

Reductions for unprompted and prompted disclosure

21.33 There are reductions in the penalties charged for unprompted and prompted disclosure brought about by either informing HMRC in advance, or giving HMRC reasonable help in quantifying any tax unpaid, and allowing HMRC full access to the company's records for checking the unpaid tax calculations.

The maximum reduced penalties follow the normal percentages. However, there are restrictions: a penalty for deliberately withholding and concealing information cannot fall below £3,000, and the amount cannot fall below £1,500 if the information is withheld deliberately but is not concealed.

Penalty	Maximum reduced penalty for an unprompted disclosure	Maximum reduced penalty for a prompted disclosure
30%	0%	15%
70%	20%	35%
100%	30%	50%

(*FA 2009, Sch 55, para 15*)

An unprompted disclosure can be made at any time when the person making it has no reason to believe that HMRC have discovered or are about to discover the inaccuracy or under-assessment. In all other cases, the disclosure is unprompted. The quality of the disclosure depends on its timing, nature and extent.

HMRC have the discretion to reduce a penalty if they consider that special circumstances apply. The special circumstances do not include the company's ability to pay, or the fact that a potential loss of revenue from one taxpayer is balanced by a potential over-payment by another. HMRC also have the discretion not to bring proceedings in relation to a penalty, and to agree a compromise during any proceedings that should take place (*FA 2009, Sch 55, para 16*).

This penalty is reduced by any other penalty or surcharge applied to the same tax liability (*FA 2009, Sch 55, para 17(1)*).

Assessing the penalty

21.34 In order to charge the penalty, HMRC must raise an assessment, notify the company, and state in the notice the period in respect of which the penalty is assessed. The company must pay the penalty within 30 days beginning with the day on which notification of the penalty was issued (*FA 2009, Sch 55, para 18*). The time limit for assessing the penalty is the last day of the period of two years beginning with the filing date. If there is an appeal, the time limit is the last day of the period of 12 months beginning with either the end of the appeal period for the assessment of the liability to tax which would have been shown in the return or, if there is no such assessment, the date on which that liability is ascertained or it is ascertained that the liability is nil (*FA 2009, Sch 55, para 19*).

An insufficiency of funds is not a reasonable excuse, unless it is attributable to events outside the company's control. Where the company relies on another person to do anything that is not a reasonable excuse, unless the company took reasonable care to avoid the failure. Where the company had a reasonable excuse for the failure, but the excuse has ceased, the company is treated as having continued to have the excuse if the failure is remedied without unreasonable delay after the excuse ceased (*FA 2009, Sch 55, para 23*).

Penalties for failure to pay tax

21.35   HMRC may charge a penalty on late payment of deductions on account of corporation tax from contract payments payable under *FA 2004, s 62* (see **21.8–21.11**). The penalty is based on the number of defaults made during the tax year, being the company's failure to pay tax on time in full. These provisions will take effect from a date yet to be announced by Treasury Order.

Number of failures to pay tax in full and on time	*Number of defaultsduring the tax year*	*Penalty*	*Amount on which penalty is based*
1	0	0%	Nil
2, 3 or 4	1, 2 or 3	1%	Total amount of defaults 1–3
5, 6 or 7	4, 5 or 6	2%	Total amount of defaults 1–6
8, 9 or 10	7, 8 or 9	3%	Total amount of defaults 1–9
11	10 or more	4%	Total amount of defaults in the period

The amount of a default is the amount which the company fails to pay, and a default is still counted for penalty purposes even if the default is remedied before the end of the tax year.

If any amount of the tax is unpaid after the end of the period of six months beginning with the penalty date, the company is liable to an additional penalty of 5% of that amount. If any amount of the tax is unpaid after the end of the period of 12 months beginning with the penalty date, the company is liable to an additional penalty of 5% of that amount (*FA 2009, Sch 56, paras 5,6*).

The penalty may be reduced for special circumstances, and there is an appeals procedure. See **Chapter 2** for details.

Chapter 22

The year end

CORPORATION TAX COMPUTATION

22.1 Shortly after the year end, the company will prepare its annual accounts, whereupon it will be able to prepare its corporation tax computation and self-assessment return. Sample returns have been reproduced in the following pages by kind permission of HMRC.

Corporation tax computation

22.2 The company will then bring all its income into charge under the various schedule headings to calculate its PCTCT (profits chargeable to corporation tax).

Corporation tax computation for the accounting period of ... months ended on ...

	£	£
Trade profits		
Property income		
Non-trading loan relationship profits		
Other income		
Chargeable gains		
Less:	Expenses of management	
	Charges on income	
Profits chargeable to corporation tax (PCTCT)		

Capital allowance computation

22.3   The company will also prepare its capital allowances claim. The following is an outline computation.

Capital allowances—plant and machinery computation for the ... months ended on ...

	Main pool 20% £	Special rate allowances 10% £	Expensive car £	Short-life asset 20% £	Allowance given £
Allowable qualifying expenditure b/f					
Additions not qualifying for FYA					
Annual investment allowance maximum £50,000					
Disposal proceeds					
Balancing allowance/ balancing charge					
WDA					
WDA					
Additions qualifying for FYA					
Less: FYA					
Allowable qualifying expenditure c/f					
Total allowances for year					

Capital gains

22.4   A company's chargeable gains incurred during an accounting period are assessed to corporation tax together with its other income for that accounting period. Capital gains legislation is often used as an incentive to provide tax breaks or as an anti-avoidance regulator. See **Chapter 20** for areas discussed.

PLANNING

22.5   A company's accounts and corporation tax computation are based on its transactions for a set period. Once that period has ended, the time has passed to make any changes to the transactions. Hence all planning should ideally take place before the year end.

The minimisation of corporation tax liabilities and the maximisation of reported profits is possibly each and every company's ultimate goal. Under corporation tax self-assessment the company should be aware that planning also looks to ensuring that the company's returns are accurate and timely to avoid interest and penalties and to minimise any adverse consequences arising from an enquiry. Companies should also be fully aware of HMRC procedures and their own appeal rights.

The following list is a summary of some of the new legislation of which the company should be aware, and of the areas that a company may wish to consider with respect to the year end. The list is by no means exhaustive:

- **Accounting dates**. If a company pays corporation tax by quarterly instalments it will pay its first instalment six months and 13 days after the beginning of the accounting period. If the trade is seasonal it might not have sufficient funds to pay the corporation tax. Consider changing the accounting date so that the high-earning period falls at the beginning of the year rather than the end. See **3.11**.

- **Activities**. Consider the type of activities that the organisation carries out and whether it would qualify for charitable or mutual status. See **5.76**.

- **Appeals**. New procedures were introduced with effect from 1 April 2009. A company can appeal an HMRC decision directly to the First-tier Tribunal or ask HMRC to carry out an internal review of the decision. See **2.23–2.32**.

- **Apportionment of profits**. If an accounting period is longer than 12 months, taxable profits are normally apportioned pro rata on a time basis. However, an actual basis may be used if this gives a more accurate result. See **2.7**.

- **Associated companies**. Associated companies eradicate the benefit of the small companies rate of corporation tax. Prepare a company structure in good time to ascertain whether the separate companies are actually necessary. See **4.27**. A participator's partners are only associated persons for small company rate purposes, if the relationship has come about through a tax planning arrangement. This rule is only effective from 1 April 2008, but HMRC have given their assurance that, unless the case is selected for full enquiry, the existence of associated companies is relevant only in cases where the amount of tax at risk is significant. See **4.29**.

- **Business renovation allowance**. Expenditure on the renovation of unused business premises in a disadvantaged area may qualify for the 100% business renovation allowance. Check the stamp duty section of HMRC website to carry out a postcode check. See **6.85–6.100**.

- **Business premises**. Expenditure on surplus business premises turned into residential accommodation may attract the 100% flat conversion allowance. See **6.101–6.110**.

- **Cars** qualify for capital allowances according to their CO_2 emissions. There are three bands: 0–109g/km, 110–159g/km, and 160g/km and above. The respective reliefs are a 100% FYA, a 20% WDA, and a 10% WDA. There are no expensive car pools for expenditure after 1 April 2009, but existing expensive car pools are retained and WDA granted according to the vehicle's emissions with a maximum of £3,000 per annum. See **6.24** and **6.40**.

- **CIS penalties**. New penalty regulations have been introduced for the late submission of contractor returns and information to support a sub-contractor's gross payment application. See **21.30–21.34**. New penalty provisions have also been introduced for late payment of monthly tax liabilities. See **21.35**.

- New rules regarding **claims for overpaid corporation tax** are to be introduced with effect from 1 April 2010, that replace the error and mistake claim rules. See **3.30**. Specific circumstances are given, and companies are recommended to ensure that they monitor their corporation tax calculations and payments carefully so that they are able to identify where a mistake has occurred should such a situation arise. See **3.30–3.31**.

- **Close investment holding company**. Where a company is making investments in land and property, and that property is used by a person connected with the company, the company may be classed as a close investment holding company (CIHC), liable to pay corporation tax at the full rate. See **4.23–4.26**.

- **Companies Act 2006**. The new provisions are being introduced over the period to 1 October 2009and may have an influence on a company's chosen status. See **1.3**. They may also have an influence on the directors' approach to the management of the company's corporation tax affairs. See **1.15**.

- **Companies in financial difficulties** can agree to vary the timing of their corporation tax payments through the HMRC Business Payment Support Service. This operates where companies are in genuine difficulty but, given time, will be able to pay their corporation tax. See

3.34. Companies that prefer to spread their corporation tax payments may agree a managed payment plan with HMRC. See **3.35**.

- **Company tax return**. New penalty provisions for the failure to deliver a company tax return are to be introduced. The penalty could amount to up to 100% of the tax at issue. See **18.16–18.20**.

- Assets eligible for capital allowances may be transferred between **connected parties** at tax written-down value. Both parties must submit an election to HMRC within two years from date of sale (*CAA 2001, s 569(1)*). See**6.4**.

- Both **contaminated land and land in a derelict state** qualify for the land remediation allowance, which gives full relief for capital expenditure and 150% of revenue expenditure against profits. If the company is engaged in building projects on a brown field site, full details of the work should be obtained in order to assess whether the necessary conditions are met. See **8.44–8.63**.

- **Controlled foreign companies**. Changes have been made to the apportionment calculation. With effect for accounting periods beginning on or after 1 July 2009, the acceptable distribution policy exemption has been repealed, and the special rules applying to holding companies, apart from those applicable to local holding companies, have been removed from the exempt activities exemption. For accounting periods ended on or after 1 January 2010, amounts brought into account in connection with the debt cap can reduce an apportionment. See **13.23–13.45**.

  Review interest in overseas companies. The CFC legislation will not apply if a CFC company carries on a genuine economic activity in the country concerned. A formal claim can be made to HMRC. See **13.45**.

- **Corporate venturing scheme**. The investee company must now use 100% of the funds it receives from the share issue for the purposes of a qualifying trade, or for research and development intended to lead to or benefit a qualifying trade. Qualifying trades are, in general, non-financial services or non-property related trades. See **12.45** and **12.46**.

- **Corporation Tax Act 2009** came into force on 1 April 2009. It has not 'changed' the law as such. Types of income are referred to by name rather than by Schedule reference. See **Chapter 5** for references to the calculation of trade profits.

- **Debt cap**. The finance expense tax deduction of the UK members of a worldwide group of companies is to be capped for accounting periods beginning on or after 1 January 2010. See **10.23–10.50**.

- **Dividends**. Interim dividends are due and payable on the day they are declared. For this reason, they may not be effective in clearing an overdue director's loan account. See **4.18**.

591

22.5 *The year end*

- **Dormant company**. Check to see if any of the associated companies are dormant throughout the accounting period. If so, they will not be included within the count of associated companies. See **4.30**.

- **Enquiries**. For single companies and small groups, there is an incentive to file the corporation tax return as soon as possible after the end of the accounting period because the enquiry window is 12 months after the return was delivered to HMRC. See **2.16**. On a non-statutory basis, HMRC will endeavour to follow this procedure for medium and large companies. Companies must notify HMRC when the last group return is filed. See **2.17**.

- **Enterprise Zone** expenditure qualifies for a 100% initial allowance and, if not fully claimed, any balance of expenditure qualifies for a writing down allowance (*FA 2008, s 86*), but a balancing charge may still arise on disposal. See **6.75** and **6.84**.

- **Environmentally beneficial plant and machinery and energy saving plant or machinery** qualify for a 100% FYA. Loss-making companies may claim a repayable tax credit. See **6.22** and **9.29**.

- **Equitable liability**. With effect from 1 April 2010, HMRC will withdraw their concessional practice to accept evidence after the statutory deadlines had expired in support of a claim against an excessive assessment. See **3.33**.

- **Failure** to pay corporation tax on time. A new penalty regime will shortly be introduced for corporation tax that is unpaid for three months or more. The penalties apply to quarterly instalments and the main liability. See **3.25–3.29**.

- **First year allowance**. Companies can claim a temporary 40% first year allowance for capital expenditure incurred on general plant and machinery during the 12 months commencing 1 April 2009. Expenditure on long life assets, integral features and motorcars is not included. See **6.20**.

- **Foreign currency accounting** rules have been introduced for converting transactions from foreign currencies into sterling, in particular where losses are carried backwards and forwards and where adjustments are made to the losses. The rules must be applied when preparing corporation tax computations for accounting periods ended after 29 December 2007, but the company can elect for 21 July 2009 to be the start date of the new rules. See **13.61–13.68**.

- **Foreign dividends** that a company receives after 1 July 2009 are, in the main, exempt from tax. Different exemption rules apply to small and large companies. If the dividends are not exempt, relief for underlying tax may be available. See **13.46–13.60**.

- The meaning of a **group** is determined by the measurement of the controlling interests, normally through ordinary share ownership. The rules for determining which shares qualify as fixed rate preference shares have been relaxed to enable group companies to obtain external finance and to enable group members to continue to qualify for group relief. See **10.7**.

- **Group asset transfers**. Group companies can now transfer a chargeable gain or an allowable loss accruing on a third party disposal to another group member, instead of the asset which is to be disposed of, in order to be able to utilise another group member's capital losses. The companies must jointly elect for this treatment within two years of the end of the chargeable period in which the gain or the loss accrues. The change relieves the group of the formalities of transferring ownership of a capital asset from one group member to another and can be used for a negligible value claim. See **20.17**.

- **Group payment arrangements**. Consider whether it would be administratively efficient for one company in a group to attend to the group's corporation tax payments. See **3.22**.

- New **HMRC powers** came into effect on 1 April 2009. HMRC have powers to request supplementary information from the company and third parties, to inspect records, and to visit premises. It is unlikely that a compliant company will fall foul of these new powers. However, in order to be prepared, a company is well-advised to ensure that the Revenue officer dealing with its affairs has all the necessary information in support of the corporation tax return, for example providing the Revenue officer with an analysis of repair expenditure or legal expenses. If a different interpretation of the law is taken from that viewed by HMRC, this should be clearly explained. It is also advisable for the company to retain all details in support of the preparation of the corporation tax computation on its files. See **18.2–18.15**.

- New penalties for **inaccuracies** in returns and other documents submitted to HMRC are effective from 1 April 2009. The penalty is dependent on how the inaccuracy arose. Companies are recommended to retain details on file of the source of information used to complete their company tax returns. See **18.21–18.30**.

- **Intangible assets** allow debits and credits to follow the accounting treatment. A company might wish to ensure that its depreciation policy is suitable. See **7.10**.

- **International movement of capital**. From 1 July 2009, companies must report share issues in excess of £100m by a foreign subsidiary, within six months of issue, to HMRC. Similar transactions must also be reported to HMRC, unless they are an excluded transaction. See **13.14–13.17**.

- A company's failure to make itself **known** to HMRC will be charged a penalty based on the potential lost revenue. See **18.31–18.36**.

- Corporate **Landlords** may claim an allowance of up to £1,500 per dwelling when installing energy-saving items in residential property. See **12.26**.

- **Large company**. Check if the company is large. If it is large, for one year it will not need to make quarterly payments of corporation tax unless it is large for the second year, subject to conditions. See **3.10–3.11**.

- **Loans to directors**. Outstanding loans to a director at the year end attract a charge under *ICTA 1988, s 419* if not repaid within nine months of the year end. Ensure there are no outstanding loans and that they are repaid promptly. See **4.14–4.22**.

- The trading **loss** carry back rules have been temporarily extended from 12 months to three years, for accounting periods ending in the period 24 November 2008 to 23 November 2010. Loss relief is restricted to £50,000 in each of the earlier two years. See **9.15–9.16**. A trade must continue for losses to be utilised. For a carry back, the trade must have been in existence at some time during the previous periods. For a carry forward, the loss continues to be available until the trade ceases. See **9.2**.

- Terminal **loss relief** upon the cessation of a trade is not available where the trade is disposed of to a purchaser who is not within the charge to corporation tax. See **9.17**.

- **Marginal rates of corporation tax**. The claim for marginal relief takes a company's franked investment income (FII) into account. With effect from 1 July 2009, the foreign dividends that a company receives are included within its FII. See **3.5**.

- **Online filing**. Consider whether it will be more expedient to file the company's corporation tax online for the year. See **2.12**. Online filing is being seen as compulsory from 31 March 2011 for accounting periods ending after 31 March 2010. It is envisaged that all corporation tax payments will be made electronically after 31 March 2011.

- **Pension contributions**. A small company may consider making additional pension contributions on behalf of its directors/shareholders. In applying the spreading rules, the company should be aware of the possible business purpose test restriction. See **5.24–5.27**.

- **Property business**. Both UK and overseas property businesses are treated as though they were trades for the purposes of allowing deductions, but only certain of the *CTA 2009* trade relief provisions apply; see **12.19–12.20**

- **Research and development**. An SME can claim an enhanced deduction of 175% of its R&D expenditure against its taxable profits or a repayable tax credit of 14%. See **8.20**. A large company can claim an enhanced deduction of 130% on its qualifying expenditure. See **Chapter 8**.

Claims must be made within the normal corporation tax timescale of two years after the end of the accounting period.

- **Residential property**. Capital allowances are not available on residential property. HMRC have confirmed that individual units in a multi-occupancy building are residential property, but the common parts are not, thus allowing claims to be submitted. See **6.91**.

- **Roll-over relief**. If a company is disposing of tangible assets or intangible assets, it is well advised to consider purchasing new assets either 12 months before, or within three years after, sale to claim roll-over relief to reduce the chargeable gain. See **20.6–20.13** and **7.20-7.22**.

- **Senior accounting officers** of very large companies are required to ensure that the company has appropriate systems for calculating the company's tax liabilities. He or she is also required to monitor these systems and supply a certificate to HMRC. These rules will not affect the vast majority of limited companies, but the rules should be reviewed carefully because group membership may mean that they apply. See **18.37–18.43**.

- **Short life assets**. The balance of expenditure may be written off in full if it is less than £1,000. See **6.33**.

- If a **subsidiary company** with surplus funds is in liquidation, it could invest in quoted shares in UK companies to avoid the 28% corporation tax rate on attaining a CIHC status. The dividends will not be taxable, so the 28% corporation tax rate cannot apply. See **4.23–4.24**.

- **Substantial shareholding exemption**. HMRC offer guidance on whether an investor and/or an investee company meet the conditions for the relief. See **12.39**.

- **Surrenderable losses** for group relief purposes may need to be set off against the company's other profits before surrender. The following is a brief summary. See **10.8** for full details.

	Required to be set off against claimant company's profits before used in a group relief claim
Trading losses	No
Excess capital allowances	No
Non-trading loan relationship debits	No
Charges on income	Yes
Property business losses	Yes
Management expenses	Yes
Non-trading loss on a loan relationship	Yes

22.5 *The year end*

- The company's **trading status** is important to retain loss and investment reliefs. Consideration should be given to the company's long-term plans. Restructuring may be seen as necessary to separate the investment and the trading activities. See **15.7–15.24** and **16.13–16.18**.

- **Transfer pricing** rules now apply to all companies entering into transactions with associates. Ensure that documentation is in place to support the inter company arrangement. See **Chapter 14**. If a company with which the company trades has a transfer pricing adjustment the company should ensure that it claims the compensating relief. See **14.15**.

- A loss on disposal of shares in an **unquoted trading company** may be set against income of an investment company. The claim must be made within two years from the end of the accounting period in which the loss occurred (*ICTA 1988, s 573(2)*). See **12.35**.

- **Winding-up**. With no formal liquidation procedure a private company may now have funds remaining of up to £4,000 without them being claimed as *bona vacantia*. See **16.32**.

Appendix 1

Retail price index

	Jan	Feb	Mar	Apr	May	Jun
1982	78.73	78.76	79.44	81.04	81.62	81.85
1983	82.61	82.97	83.12	84.28	84.64	84.84
1984	86.84	87.20	87.48	88.64	88.97	89.20
1985	91.20	91.94	92.80	94.78	95.21	95.41
1986	96.25	96.60	96.73	97.67	97.85	97.79
1987	100.00	100.40	100.60	101.80	101.90	101.90
1988	103.30	103.70	104.10	105.80	106.20	106.60
1989	111.00	111.80	112.30	114.30	115.00	115.40
1990	119.50	120.20	121.40	125.10	126.20	126.70
1991	130.20	130.90	131.40	133.10	133.50	134.10
1992	135.60	136.30	136.70	138.80	139.30	139.30
1993	137.90	138.80	139.30	140.60	141.10	141.00
1994	141.30	142.10	142.50	144.20	144.70	144.70
1995	146.00	146.90	147.50	149.00	149.60	149.80
1996	150.20	150.90	151.50	152.60	152.90	153.00
1997	154.40	155.00	155.40	156.30	156.90	157.50
1998	159.50	160.30	160.80	162.60	163.50	163.40
1999	163.40	163.70	164.10	165.20	165.60	165.60
2000	166.60	167.50	168.40	170.10	170.70	171.10
2001	171.10	172.00	172.20	173.10	174.20	174.40
2002	173.30	173.80	174.50	175.70	176.20	176.20
2003	178.40	179.30	179.90	181.20	181.50	181.30
2004	183.10	183.80	184.60	185.70	186.50	186.80
2005	188.90	189.60	190.50	191.60	192.00	192.20
2006	193.40	194.20	195.00	196.50	197.70	198.50
2007	201.60	203.10	204.40	205.40	206.20	207.30
2008	209.80	211.40	212.10	214.00	215.10	216.80
2009	210.10	211.40	211.30	211.50	212.80	213.40

Appendix 1

	Jul	Aug	Sep	Oct	Nov	Dec
1982	81.88	81.90	81.85	82.26	82.66	82.51
1983	85.30	85.68	86.06	86.36	86.67	86.89
1984	89.10	89.94	90.11	90.67	90.95	90.87
1985	95.23	95.49	95.44	95.59	95.92	96.05
1986	97.52	97.82	98.30	98.45	99.29	99.62
1987	101.80	102.10	102.40	102.90	103.40	103.30
1988	106.70	107.90	108.40	109.50	110.00	110.30
1989	115.50	115.80	116.60	117.50	118.50	118.80
1990	126.80	128.10	129.30	130.30	130.00	129.90
1991	133.80	134.10	134.60	135.10	135.60	135.70
1992	138.80	138.90	139.40	139.90	139.70	139.20
1993	140.70	141.30	141.90	141.80	141.60	141.90
1994	144.00	144.70	145.00	145.20	145.30	146.00
1995	149.10	149.90	150.60	149.80	149.80	150.70
1996	152.40	153.10	153.80	153.80	153.90	154.40
1997	157.50	158.50	159.30	159.50	159.60	160.00
1998	163.00	163.70	164.40	164.50	164.40	164.40
1999	165.10	165.50	166.20	166.50	166.70	167.30
2000	170.50	170.50	171.70	171.60	172.10	172.20
2001	173.30	174.00	174.60	174.30	173.60	173.40
2002	175.90	176.40	177.60	177.90	178.20	178.50
2003	181.30	181.60	182.50	182.60	182.70	183.50
2004	186.80	187.40	188.10	188.60	189.00	189.90
2005	192.20	192.60	193.10	193.30	193.60	194.10
2006	198.50	199.20	200.10	200.40	201.10	202.70
2007	206.10	207.30	208.00	208.90	209.70	210.90
2008	216.50	217.20	218.40	217.70	216.00	212.90

Appendix 2

Company tax return forms

HM Revenue & Customs

Company Tax Return form
CT600 (2008) Version 2

for accounting periods ending on or after 1 July 1999

Your company tax return

If we send the company a *Notice* to deliver a company tax return (form *CT603*) it has to comply by the filing date or we charge a penalty, even if there is no tax to pay. A return includes a company tax return form, any Supplementary Pages, accounts, computations and any relevant information.
Is this the right form for the company? Read the advice on pages 3 to 6 of the Company tax return guide (the *Guide*) before you start.
The forms in the CT600 series set out the information we need and provide a standard format for calculations. Use the *Guide* to help you complete the return form. It contains general information you may need and box by box advice
Please note that some boxes on form *CT600* are not in order, reflecting changes made since the form was first published in 2004.

Company information

Company name

Company registration number   Tax Reference as shown on the CT603   Type of Company

Registered office address

Postcode

About this return

This is the above company's return for the period
from (dd/mm/yyyy)   to (dd/mm/yyyy)

Put an 'X' in the appropriate box(es) below

A repayment is due for this return period

A repayment is due for an earlier period

Making more than one return for this company now

This return contains estimated figures

Company part of a group that is not small

Disclosure of tax avoidance schemes
Notice of disclosable avoidance schemes

Transfer pricing
Compensating adjustment claimed

Company qualifies for SME exemption

Accounts
I attach accounts and computations
• for the period to which this return relates

• for a different period

If you are not attaching accounts and computations, say why not

Supplementary Pages
If you are enclosing any Supplementary Pages put an 'X' in the appropriate box(es)

Loans to participators by close companies, form *CT600A*

Controlled foreign companies, form *CT600B*

Group and Consortium, form *CT600C*

Insurance, form *CT600D*

Charities and Community Amateur Sports Clubs (CASCs), form *CT600E*

Tonnage tax, form *CT600F*

Corporate Venturing Scheme, form *CT600G*

Cross-border royalties, form *CT600H*

Supplementary charge in respect of ring fence trade, form *CT600I*

Disclosure of tax avoidance schemes, form *CT600J*

Appendix 2: CT600 (2008) Version 2

Company tax calculation

Turnover

1 Total turnover from trade or profession   **1** £

2 Banks, building societies, insurance companies and other financial concerns. *Put an 'X' in this box if you do not have a recognised turnover and have not made an entry in box 1*   **2**

Income

3 Trading and professional profits   **3** £

4 Trading losses brought forward claimed against profits   **4** £

5 Net trading and professional profits   *box 3 minus box 4*   **5** £

6 Bank, building society or other interest, and profits and gains from non-trading loan relationships   **6** £

7 *Put an 'X' in box 7 if the figure in box 6 is net of carrying back a deficit from a later accounting period*   **7**

8 Annuities, annual payments and discounts not arising from loan relationships and from which income tax has not been deducted   **8** £

9 Overseas income within Sch D Case V   **9** £

10 Income from which income tax has been deducted   **10** £

11 Income from UK land and buildings   **11** £

12 Non-trading gains on intangible fixed assets   **12** £

13 Tonnage tax profits   **13** £

14 Annual profits and gains not falling under any other heading   **14** £

15 Income within Sch D Case VI   *total of boxes 12, 13 and 14*   **15** £

Chargeable gains

16 Gross chargeable gains   **16** £

17 Allowable losses including losses brought forward   **17** £

18 Net chargeable gains   *box 16 minus box 17*   **18** £

19 Losses brought forward against certain investment income   **19** £

20 Non-trade deficits on loan relationships (including interest), and derivative contracts (financial instruments) brought forward   **20** £

21 Profits before other deductions and reliefs   *net sum of boxes 5, 6, 8, 9, 10, 11,15, & 18 minus sum of boxes 19 and 20*   **21** £

Deductions and reliefs

22 CVS loss relief, and losses on unquoted shares under S573 ICTA 1988

22 £

23 *Put an 'X' in box 23 if the entry in box 22 includes CVS loss relief, complete and attach form CT600G*

23

24 Management expenses under S75 ICTA 1988

24 £

25 Interest distributions under S468L ICTA 1988

25 £

26 Schedule A losses for this or previous accounting period under S392A ICTA 1988

26 £

27 Capital allowances for the purposes of management of the business

27 £

28 Non-trade deficits for this accounting period from loan relationships and derivative contracts (financial instruments)

28 £

29 Non-trading losses on intangible fixed assets

29 £

30 Trading losses of this or a later accounting period under S393A ICTA 1988

30 £

31 *Put an 'X' in box 31 if amounts carried back from later accounting periods are included in box 30*

31

32 Non-trade capital allowances

32 £

33 Total of deductions and reliefs

total of boxes 22, 24 to 30 and 32

33 £

34 Profits before charges and group relief

box 21 minus box 33

34 £

35 Charges paid

35 £

36 Group relief

36 £

37 Profits chargeable to corporation tax

box 34 minus boxes 35 and 36

37 £

169 Ring fence profits included

169 £

Appendix 2: CT600 (2008) Version 2

Tax calculation

38 Franked investment income   **38** £

39 Number of associated companies in this period   **39**
    or
40 Associated companies in the first financial year   **40**

41 Associated companies in the second financial year   **41**

42 *Put an 'X' in box 42 if the company claims to be*   **42**
    charged at the starting rate or the small companies'
    rate on any part of its profits, or is claiming
    marginal rate relief

Enter how much profit has to be charged and at what rate of tax

Financial year *(yyyy)*	Amount of profit	Rate of tax	Tax	
43	**44** £	**45**	**46** £	p
	47 £	**48**	**49** £	p
	50 £	**51**	**52** £	p
53	**54** £	**55**	**56** £	p
	57 £	**58**	**59** £	p
	60 £	**61**	**62** £	p

total of boxes 46, 49, 52, 56, 59 and 62

63 Corporation tax   **63** £   p

64 Marginal rate relief   **64** £   p

65 Corporation tax net of marginal rate relief   **65** £   p

66 Underlying rate of corporation tax   **66** • %

67 Profits matched with non-corporate   **67** £
    distributions

68 Tax at non-corporate distributions rate   **68** £   p

69 Tax at underlying rate on remaining profits   **69** £   p

See note for box 70 in CT600 Guide

70 Corporation tax chargeable   **70** £   p

Reliefs and deductions in terms of tax

71 CVS investment relief   **71** £   p

72 Community investment relief   **72** £   p

73 Double taxation relief   **73** £   p

74 *Put an 'X' in box 74 if box 73*   **74**
    includes an Underlying Rate relief claim

75 *Put an 'X' in box 75 if box 73 includes*   **75**
    any amount carried back from a later period

76 Advance corporation tax   **76** £   p

total of boxes 71, 72, 73 and 76

77 Total reliefs and deductions in terms of tax   **77** £   p

CT600 (2008) Version 2

Calculation of tax outstanding or overpaid

box 70 minus box 77

78 Net corporation tax liability | **78** £ | p

79 Tax payable under S419 ICTA 1988 | **79** £ | p

80 Put an 'X' in box 80 if you completed box A11 in the Supplementary Pages CT600A | **80**

81 Tax payable under S747 ICTA 1988 | **81** £ | p

82 Tax payable under S501A ICTA 1988 | **82** £ | p

total of boxes 78, 79, 81 and 82

83 Tax chargeable | **83** £ | p

84 Income tax deducted from gross income included in profits | **84** £ | p

85 Income tax repayable to the company | **85** £ | p

box 83 minus box 84

86 Tax payable - this is your self-assessment of tax payable | **86** £ | p

Tax reconciliation

87 Research and Development tax credit, including any vaccines tax credit, or film tax credit | **87** £ | p

88 Land remediation or life assurance company tax credit | **88** £ | p

170 Capital allowances first-year tax credit | **170** £ | p

box 87 minus box 86

89 Research and Development tax credit payable, including any vaccines tax credit, or film tax credit payable | **89** £ | p

total of boxes 87 + 88 minus boxes 86 and 89

90 Land remediation or life assurance company tax credit payable | **90** £ | p

boxes 87, 88 and 170 minus boxes 86, 89 and 90

171 Capital allowances first-year tax credit payable | **171** £ | p

161 Ring fence corporation tax included | **161** £ | p

166 Tax under S501A ICTA 1988 included | **166** £ | p

91 Tax already paid (and not already repaid) | **91** £ | p

box 88 minus boxes 87, 88, 170 and 91

92 Tax outstanding | **92** £ | p

total sum of boxes 87, 88, 170 and 91 minus box 96

93 Tax overpaid | **93** £ | p

94 Tax refunds surrendered to the company under S102 FA 1989 | **94** £ | p

Indicators

Put an 'X' in the relevant box(es) if, in the period, the company

95 *should have made (whether it has or not) instalment payments under the Corporation Tax (Instalment Payments) Regulations 1998* | **95**

96 *is within a group payment arrangement for this period* | **96**

97 *has written down or sold intangible assets* | **97**

98 *has made cross-border royalty payments* | **98**

Appendix 2: CT600 (2008) Version 2

Information about enhanced expenditure

Research and Development (R&D) or films enhanced expenditure

167 *Put an 'X' in box 167 if the claim is for films expenditure* **167** [ ]

99 *Put an 'X' in box 99 if the claim is made by a small or medium-sized enterprise (SME), including a SME subcontractor to a large company* **99** [ ]

100 *Put an 'X' in box 100 if the claim is made by a large company* **100** [ ]

101 R&D or films enhanced expenditure **101** £ [ ]

102 R&D enhanced expenditure of a SME on work sub-contracted to it by a large company **102** £ [ ]

103 Vaccines research expenditure **103** £ [ ]

Land remediation enhanced expenditure

104 Enter amount equal to 150% of actual expenditure **104** £ [ ]

Information about capital allowances and balancing charges

Charges and allowances included in calculation of trading profits or losses

	Capital Allowances	Balancing Charges
172 Annual investment allowance	**172** £	
105-106 Machinery and plant - special rate pool	**105** £	**106** £
107-108 Machinery and plant - main pool	**107** £	**108** £
109-110 Cars	**109** £	**110** £
111-112 Industrial buildings and structures	**111** £	**112** £
162-163 Business premises renovation	**162** £	**163** £
113-114 Other charges and allowances	**113** £	**114** £

Charges and allowances not included in calculation of trading profits or losses

	Capital Allowances	Balancing Charges
173 Annual investment allowance	**173** £	
164-165 Business premises renovation	**164** £	**165** £
115-116 Other non-trading charges and allowances	**115** £	**116** £
117 *Put an 'X' in box 117 if box 115 entry includes flat conversion allowances*	**117** [ ]	

Qualifying expenditure

118 Machinery and plant on which first year allowance is claimed **118** £ [ ]

174 Designated environmentally friendly machinery and plant **174** £ [ ]

120 Machinery and plant on long-life assets and integral features **120** £ [ ]

121 Other machinery and plant **121** £ [ ]

Losses, deficits and excess amounts

		Arising	Maximum available for surrender as group relief
122-123	Trading losses Case I	122 £ *(calculated under S393 ICTA 1988)*	123 £ *(calculated under S393A ICTA 1988)*
124	Trading losses Case V	124 £ *(calculated under S393 ICTA 1988)*	
125-126	Non-trade deficits on loan relationships and derivative contracts	125 £ *(calculated under S82 FA 1996)*	126 £ *(calculated under S83 FA 1996)*
127-128	Schedule A losses	127 £ *(calculated under S392A ICTA 1988)*	128 £ *(calculated under S403 ICTA 1988)*
129	Overseas property business losses Case V	129 £ *(calculated under S392B ICTA 1988)*	
130	Losses Case VI	130 £ *(calculated under S396 ICTA 1988)*	
131	Capital losses	131 £ *(calculated under S16 TCGA 1992)*	
132-133	Non-trading losses on intangible fixed assets	132 £ *(calculated under S29 FA 2002)*	133 £ *(calculated under S403 ICTA 1988)*
		Excess	
134	Excess non-trade capital allowances		134 £ *(calculated under S403 ICTA 1988)*
135	Excess charges		135 £ *(calculated under S403 ICTA 1988)*
136-137	Excess management expenses	136 £ *(calculated under S75 ICTA 1988)*	137 £ *(calculated under S403 ICTA 1988)*
138	Excess interest distributions	138 £ *(calculated under S469L(7) ICTA 1988)*	

Overpayments and repayments

Small repayments

If you do not want us to make small repayments please either put an 'X' in box 139 or complete box 140 below. 'Repayments' here include tax, interest, and late-filing penalties or any combination of them.

Do not repay £20 or less **139** [ ] Do not repay sums of **140** £ [ ] or less. *Enter whole figure only*

Repayments for the period covered by this return

141	Repayment of corporation tax	141 £	p
142	Repayment of income tax	142 £	p
143	Payable Research and Development tax credit	143 £	p
168	Payable film tax credit	168 £	p
144	Payable land remediation or life assurance company tax credit	144 £	p
175	Payable capital allowances first-year tax credit	175 £	p

Surrender under S102 FA 1989 (including surrenders under Regulation 9 of the Instalments Regulations)
Repayments of advance corporation tax cannot be surrendered.

145 The following amount is to be surrendered under S102 FA 1989, and either **145** £ [ ] p

146 the joint Notice is attached **146** [ ]
or *(put an 'X' in either box 146 or box 147)*
147 will follow **147** [ ]

148 Please stop repayment of the following amount until I send you the Notice **148** £ [ ] p

Page 8

Bank details (for person to whom the repayment is to be made)

Repayment is made quickly and safely by direct credit to a bank or building society account. Please complete the following details:

Name of bank or building society

149

Branch sort code

150

Account number

151

Name of account

152

Building society reference

153

Payments to a person other than the company

Complete the authority below if you want the repayment to be made to a person other than the company.
I, as *(enter status - company secretary, treasurer, liquidator or authorised agent, etc.)*

154

of *(enter name of company)*

155

authorise *(enter name)*

156

(enter address)

157

Postcode

Nominee reference

158

to receive payment on the company's behalf.

Signature

159

Name *(in capitals)*

160

Declaration

Warning - Giving false information in the return, or concealing any part of the company's profits or tax payable, can lead to both the company and yourself being prosecuted.

Declaration
The information I have given in this company tax return is correct and complete to the best of my knowledge and belief.

Signature

Name *(in capitals)*

Date *(dd/mm/yyyy)*

Status

CT600 (2008) Version 2

606

Company - Short Tax Return form
CT600 (Short) (2008) Version 2
for accounting periods ending on or after 1 July 1999

Your company tax return

If we send the company a *Notice* to deliver a company tax return (form *CT603*) it has to comply by the filing date, or we charge a penalty, even if there is no tax to pay. A return includes a company tax return form, any Supplementary Pages, accounts, computations and any relevant information.

Is this the right form for the company? Read the advice on pages 3 to 6 of the Company tax return guide (the *Guide*) before you start.

The forms in the CT600 series set out the information we need and provide a standard format for calculations. Use the *Guide* to help you complete the return form. It contains general information you may need and box by box advice.

Company information

Company name

Company registration number

Tax Reference as shown on the CT603

Type of company

Registered office address

Postcode

About this return

This is the above company's return for the period

from (dd/mm/yyyy)   to (dd/mm/yyyy)

Put an 'X' in the appropriate box(es) below

A repayment is due for this return period

A repayment is due for an earlier period

Making more than one return for this company now

This return contains estimated figures

Company part of a group that is not small

Disclosure of tax avoidance schemes

Notice of disclosable avoidance schemes

Transfer pricing

Compensating adjustment claimed

Company qualifies for SME exemption

Accounts
I attach accounts and computations

• for the period to which this return relates

• for a different period

If you are not attaching accounts and computations, say why not

Supplementary Pages
If you are enclosing any Supplementary Pages put an 'X' in the appropriate box(es)

Loans to participators by close companies, form *CT600A*

Charities and Community Amateur Sports Clubs (CASCs), form *CT600E*

Disclosure of tax avoidance schemes, form *CT600J*

Page 2

Company tax calculation

Turnover

1   Total turnover from trade or profession   **1** £

Income

3   Trading and professional profits   **3** £

4   Trading losses brought forward claimed against profits   **4** £

5   Net trading and professional profits   *box 3 minus box 4*   **5** £

6   Bank, building society or other interest, and profits and gains from non-trading loan relationships   **6** £

11   Income from UK land and buildings   **11** £

14   Annual profits and gains not falling under any other heading   **14** £

Chargeable gains

16   Gross chargeable gains   **16** £

17   Allowable losses including losses brought forward   **17** £

18   Net chargeable gains   *box 16 minus box 17*   **18** £

21   **Profits before other deductions and reliefs**   *sum of boxes 5, 6, 11, 14 & 18*   **21** £

Deductions and Reliefs

24   Management expenses under S75 ICTA 1988   **24** £

30   Trading losses of this or a later accounting period under S393A ICTA 1988   **30** £

31   Put an 'X' in box 31 if amounts carried back from later accounting periods are included in box 30   **31**

32   Non-trade capital allowances   **32** £

35   Charges paid   **35** £

37   **Profits chargeable to corporation tax**   *box 21 minus boxes 24, 30, 32 and 35*   **37** £

Tax calculation

38   Franked investment income   **38** £

39   Number of associated companies in this period   **39**
    or

40   Associated companies in the first financial year   **40**

41   Associated companies in the second financial year   **41**

42   Put an 'X' in box 42 if the company claims to be charged at the starting rate or the small companies' rate on any part of its profits, or is claiming marginal rate relief   **42**

Enter how much profit has to be charged and at what rate of tax

Financial year *(yyyy)*	Amount of profit	Rate of tax	Tax	
43	**44** £	**45**	**46** £	p
53	**54** £	**55**	**56** £	p

63   Corporation tax   *total of boxes 46 and 56*   **63** £   p

64   Marginal rate relief   **64** £   p

65   Corporation tax net of marginal rate relief   **65** £   p

66   Underlying rate of corporation tax   **66** • %

67   Profits matched with non-corporate distributions   **67**

68   Tax at non-corporate distributions rate   **68** £   p

69   Tax at underlying rate on remaining profits   **69** £   p

70   **Corporation tax chargeable**   *See note for box 70 in CT600 Guide*   **70** £   p

CT600 (Short) (2008) Version 2

79 Tax payable under S419 ICTA 1988 — 79 £   p

80 Put an 'X' in box 80 if you completed box A11 in the Supplementary Pages CT600A — 80

84 Income tax deducted from gross income included in profits — 84 £   p

85 Income tax repayable to the company — 85 £   p

86 **Tax payable - this is your self-assessment of tax payable** — total of boxes 70 and 79 minus box 84 — 86 £   p

Tax reconciliation

91 Tax already paid (and not already repaid) — 91 £   p

92 Tax outstanding — box 86 minus box 91 — 92 £   p

93 Tax overpaid — box 91 minus box 86 — 93 £   p

Information about capital allowances and balancing charges

Charges and allowances included in calculation of trading profits or losses

		Capital allowances	Balancing charges
172	Annual investment allowance	172 £	
105 - 106	Machinery and plant - special rate pool	105 £	106 £
107 - 108	Machinery and plant - main pool	107 £	108 £
109 - 110	Cars	109 £	110 £
111 - 112	Industrial buildings and structures	111 £	112 £
113 - 114	Other charges and allowances	113 £	114 £

Charges and allowances not included in calculation of trading profits or losses

		Capital allowances	Balancing charges
173	Annual investment allowance	173 £	
115 - 116	Other non-trading charges and allowances	115 £	116 £
117	Put an 'X' in box 117 if box 115 includes flat conversion allowances	117	

Qualifying expenditure

118 Expenditure on machinery and plant on which first year allowance is claimed — 118 £

174 Designated environmentally friendly machinery and plant — 174 £

120 Machinery and plant on long-life assets and integral features — 120 £

121 Other machinery and plant — 121 £

Losses, deficits and excess amounts

122 Trading losses Case I	calculated under S393 ICTA 1988 — 122 £	124 Trading losses Case V	calculated under S393 ICTA 1988 — 124 £
125 Non-trade deficits on loan relationships and derivative contracts	calculated under S82 FA 1996 — 125 £	127 Schedule A losses	calculated under S392A ICTA 1988 — 127 £
129 Overseas property business losses Case V	calculated under S392B ICTA 1988 — 129 £	130 Losses Case VI	calculated under S396 ICTA 1988 — 130 £
131 Capital losses	calculated under S16 TCGA 1992 — 131 £	136 Excess management expenses	calculated under S75 ICTA 1988 — 136 £

Overpayments and repayments

Small repayments

If you do not want us to make small repayments please either put an 'X' in box 139 or complete box 140 below. 'Repayments' here include tax, interest, and late-filing penalties or any combination of them.

Do not repay £20 or less **139** ☐   Do not repay sums of **140** £ ☐   or less. *Enter whole figure only*

Bank details (for person to whom the repayment is to be made)

Repayment is made quickly and safely by direct credit to a bank or building society account. Please complete the following details:

Name of bank or building society   Branch sort code

149 ☐   **150** ☐☐☐☐☐☐

Account number   Name of account

151 ☐   **152** ☐

Building society reference

153 ☐

Payments to a person other than the company

Complete the authority below if you want the repayment to be made to a person other than the company.
I, as *(enter status - company secretary, treasurer, liquidator or authorised agent, etc.)*

154 ☐

of *(enter name of company)*

155 ☐

authorise *(enter name)*

156 ☐

(enter address)

157 ☐

                                            Postcode

Nominee reference

158 ☐

to receive payment on the company's behalf.

Signature

159 ☐

Name *(in capitals)*

160 ☐

Declaration

Warning - Giving false information in the return, or concealing any part of the company's profits or tax payable, can lead to both the company and yourself being prosecuted.

Declaration

The information I have given in this company tax return is correct and complete to the best of my knowledge and belief.

Signature

Name *(in capitals)*   Date *(dd/mm/yyyy)*

☐   ☐☐☐☐☐☐☐☐

Status

☐

CT600 (Short) (2008) Version 2

HM Revenue & Customs

Company Tax Return form - Supplementary Pages
Loans to participators by close companies
CT600A (2006) Version 2
for accounting periods ending on or after 1 July 1999

Company information

Company name

Tax reference as shown on the CT603

Period covered by these Supplementary Pages (*cannot exceed 12 months*)

from (dd/mm/yyyy)   to (dd/mm/yyyy)

You need to complete these Supplementary Pages if

the company is close and has made a loan (or loans) to an individual participator, or associate of a participator, in this period which has not been repaid within the period. Tax is due under S419 ICTA 1988.

Important points

- These Supplementary Pages, when completed, form part of the company's return.
- These Pages set out the information we need and provide a standard format.
- Complete the boxes with whole figures only, except where pence or decimals are indicated.
- The notes below will help you understand any terms that have a special meaning and notes on these Pages will help with the completion of this form.
- These Pages are covered by the Declaration you sign on back page of form *CT600*.
- The warning shown on form *CT600* about prosecution, and the advice about late and incorrect returns, and late payment of tax also apply to these Pages.

Notes

A '**close company**' is one which is under the control of five or fewer participators, or of any number of participators who are directors (S414 ICTA 1988).

A '**loan**' within S419 ICTA 1988 includes the situation where a participator incurs a debt to the close company (S419(2)(a) ICTA 1988), for example by overdrawing a current or loan account. There are two exceptions where S419 ICTA 1988 does not apply
- a debt incurred for the supply by the close company of goods or services in the ordinary course of its trade or business, unless the credit given exceeds six months, or is longer than that normally given to the company's customers (S420(1) ICTA 1988), and
- certain loans made to full-time working directors or employees who do not have a material interest in the close company (S420(2) ICTA 1988).

A '**participator**' is a person having a share or interest in the capital or income of the company and includes any loan creditor of the company (S417(1) ICTA 1988).

An '**associate**' of a participator includes any relative or partner of the participator and the trustees of any settlement of which the participator or their relative is, or was, a settlor (S417(3)(a) and (b) ICTA 1988).

Methods by which a loan can be 'repaid' include depositing money into the company's bank account, crediting the participator's current or loan account with a dividend, director's remuneration or bonus, or book entry.

The term '**release**' refers to a formal procedure that normally takes place under seal for a consideration, whereas '**write off**' is a wider term that does not necessarily require formal arrangements and could include acceptance by the company that the loan will not be recovered and has given up attempts to recover it.

Appendix 2: CT600A (2006) Version 2

1: Loans made during the return period

You must complete part 1 if the company is close and has made a loan to an individual participator, or associate of a participator, during the return period which has not been repaid within the return period.
Enter in the table below, details of any outstanding loans made to a participator or associate of a participator during the return period. If the participator or associate has a current or loan account with the company, enter details of each participator's or associate's account. The amount you enter in column 2 of the table is the total of all debit entries on the account, less any credit entries and less any credit balance brought forward from the previous return period. In arriving at this figure you must exclude any credit entries that represent repayment, release or write off of loans made in earlier return periods.

A1 *Put an 'X' in this box if loans made during the period have been released, or written off before the end of the period* | A1 |

A2 Information about loans made during the return period and outstanding at the end of the period

Name of participator or associate	Amount of loan
	£
	£
	£
	£
	£

Total loans within S419 ICTA 1988 made during the return period which have not been repaid, released or written off before the end of the period   Total | A2 | £

If a continuation sheet is used, please put an 'X' in box A2A   A2A

A3 Tax chargeable on loans -
     (Tax due before any relief for loans repaid, released, or written off after the end of the period) box A2 multiplied by 25%   A3 £ ___ p

2: Relief for amounts repaid, released or written off after the end of the period but *earlier than* nine months and one day after the end of the period - for loans made during the return period

Complete part 2 to obtain relief for loans included in box A2 that were repaid, released or written off if
- the return is for the period in which the loans were made and
- the loan was repaid, released or written off after the end of the period but **earlier than** nine months and one day after the end of the accounting period in which the loan was **made**.

Enter in the table details for each participator or associate. If there have been a number of repayments on an account, enter only the total repayments for that account and give the date of the last repayment. A separate entry must be made for each loan or part loan that has been released or written off.

Example

A company makes a loan during the accounting period ended 31 December 2004 and it is all repaid to the company on 30 June 2005. The company's tax return for the accounting period ended 31 December 2004 is sent to HM Revenue & Customs on 1 November 2005. Part 2 should be completed because the loan was repaid after the end of the accounting period but earlier than nine months and one day after it.

A4 & A5 Information about loans repaid, released or written off after the end of the period but *earlier than* nine months and one day after the end of the period

Name of participator or associate	Amount repaid	Amount released or written off	Date of repayment, release or write off
	£	£	
	£	£	
	£	£	
	£	£	
	£	£	
	£	£	
Totals A4	£	£	A5

If a continuation sheet is used, please put an 'X' in box A5A   A5A

A6 Total amount of loans made during the return period which have been repaid, released or written off after the end of the period but **earlier than** nine months and one day after the end of the period   total of boxes A4 and A5   A6 £

A7 Relief due for loans repaid, released or written off after the end of the period but **earlier than** nine months and one day after the end of the period   box A6 multiplied by 25%   A7 £ ___ p

CT600A (2006) Version 2

612

Most companies will not need to complete part 3 below

Only complete part 3:
- where the loan was made during the return period, and
- where repayment, release or write off was more than nine months after the end of the period in which the loan was made, and
- the return is submitted after the date on which relief is due (if the return is sent in very late, at least twenty-one months after the end of the return period).

If you are unsure whether or not to complete part 3, apply the following questions to each claim.

Put an 'X' in this box if the loan was made in the return period.
If it was not, then you cannot complete part 3; if it was then go on to the next box

                                                  dd/mm/yyyy

End date of accounting period in which the loan was repaid, released or written off   **a**

Enter the date 9 months after the end of that accounting period   **b**

Date you are sending in the company tax return for the period in which the loan was made   **c**

If the date at **c** is earlier than the date at **b** you cannot complete part 3, but can make a separate claim for the relief which is not due until the date in **b**.

If the date at **c** is later than the date at **b** you can complete part 3 below to obtain the relief now.

3: Relief for loans made during the return period repaid, released or written off *more than* nine months after the end of the period and *where relief is due now*

Complete part 3 only if loans made during the return period, that have not been included in part 2, have been repaid, released or written off and where relief is due now (see the notes above under 'Most companies will not need to complete part 3').

Example

A company makes a loan during the accounting period ended 31 December 2004 and it is all repaid on 30 November 2005. The company's return for the accounting period ended 31 December 2004 is sent to HM Revenue & Customs on 1 December 2005. Part 3 of this form **should not** be completed because, although the loan was repaid more than nine months after the end of the return period, the return is sent earlier than nine months after the end of the return period in which the loan was repaid.

Relief for the repayment cannot be given until the due date of the accounting period in which the repayment was made, in this case 1 October 2006 (Ss419(4A) and (4B) ICTA 1988). The company must make a separate claim for relief.

Example

Same as example above except that the return is not sent in until 3 December 2006. Relief for the repayment is due on or after 1 October 2006. In this case part 3 can be completed because the repayment was made more than nine months after the end of the accounting period in which the loan was made, and the relief is due at the time the return is sent in.

A8 & A9 Information about loans made during the return period which have been repaid, released or written off *more than* nine months after the end of the period *and relief is due now*

Name of participator or associate	Amount repaid	Amount released or written off	Date of repayment, release or write off
	£	£	
	£	£	
	£	£	
	£	£	
	£	£	
	£	£	
Totals **A8** £		£	**A9**

If a continuation sheet is used, please put an 'X' in box A9A   **A9A**

A10 Total amount of loans made during the return period which have been repaid, released, or written off *more than* nine months after the end of the period *and relief is due now*   total of boxes A8 and A9   **A10** £

A11 Relief due now for loans repaid, released or written off *more than* nine months after the end of the period. *Put an 'X' in box 80 on form CT600 if you have completed box A11*   box A10 multiplied by 25%   **A11** £   p

CT600A (2006) Version 2

Appendix 2: CT600A (2006) Version 2

Page 4

4: Other information

A12 Total of all loans outstanding at end of return period - including all loans outstanding at the end of the return period, whether they were made in this period or an earlier one.

5: What S419 ICTA 1988 tax is payable?

A13 Tax payable under S419 ICTA 1988
Copy the figure in box A13 to box 79 on form CT600

What to do when you have completed these Supplementary Pages

- Copy the figure from box A13 in part 5 to box 79 of the form *CT600*.
- Put an 'X' in box 80 of form *CT600* if you have completed box A11 in part 3 of these Pages.
- Follow the advice shown under 'What to do when you have completed the return' on page 23 of the *Guide.*

HM Revenue & Customs

Company Tax Return form - Supplementary Pages
Controlled foreign companies
CT600B (2006) Version 2
for accounting periods ending on or after 1 July 1999

Company information

Company name

Tax reference as shown on the CT603

Period covered by these Supplementary Pages (*cannot exceed 12 months*)
from (*dd/mm/yyyy*)   to (*dd/mm/yyyy*)

You need to complete these Supplementary Pages if

at any time in this period, the company, held a relevant interest of 25% or more in a foreign company which is **controlled** from the UK. No controlled foreign company (CFC) need be included on these pages where it satisfies the **Excluded Countries Regulations**.

A UK company may also include companies which may not be CFCs but which would satisfy one of the exemptions if they were. This applies to foreign companies which may not be subject to a lower level of tax, or may not be controlled from the UK. It also applies where the UK company's relevant interest in the foreign company may be less than 25%. The purpose of this is to save UK companies the cost of working out whether a foreign company is in principle a CFC in cases where it is clear that one of the exemptions would be passed if it were.

Important points

- These Supplementary Pages, when completed, form part of the company's return.
- These Pages set out the information we need and provide a standard format.
- Notes below will help with the completion of this form.
- These Pages are covered by the Declaration you sign on the back page of form *CT600*.
- The warning shown on form *CT600* about prosecution, and the advice about late and incorrect returns, and late payment of tax also apply to these Pages.

Notes

The following information is required on pages 2 and 3:

- **Name of the CFC** Enter the full name of the CFC.

- **Territory of residence** If a residence election is made this should be noted and if a company is conclusively presumed to be resident in a territory in which it is subject to a lower level of tax then this should be indicated by the entry 'S749(5) ICTA 1988'.

- **Exemption due** Companies exempt under the provisions may indicate one (or more) exemptions here. Only one exemption need be noted, and not including an exemption will not prejudice whether it applies. If an exemption applies there is no need to complete page 3 of the supplementary return in respect of the CFC.

- **Percentage measure for apportionment** This will usually be the percentage of ordinary share capital held directly or indirectly by the UK company (but not by associated or connected persons). In all other circumstances the appropriate percentage should be calculated on a just and reasonable basis.

- **Chargeable profits** These are the chargeable profits (after reliefs available under Sch 25 ICTA 1988) apportioned to the UK company.

- **Tax on chargeable profits** This is the amount of tax apportioned on the basis of the company's share of chargeable profits before reliefs are given under Sch 26 ICTA 1988 or relief is given for advance corporation tax.

- **Creditable tax** This broadly represents tax already paid on the chargeable profits and is deductible.

- **Reliefs in terms of tax** Any reliefs available under Sch 26 should be shown at the appropriate rate of corporation tax.

- **ACT as restricted** Unrelieved surplus ACT to the extent not restricted should be shown here.

- **S747 tax chargeable** This is the column J total which is the sum of the figures in column F less the sum of the figures in columns G to I. The net figure should be copied to box 81 of form *CT600*.

What to do when you have completed these Supplementary Pages

- Copy the figure from the Summary box J13 on these Pages to box 81 of form *CT600*.
- Follow the advice shown under 'What to do when you have completed the return' on page 23 of the *Guide*.

HMRC 08/06   CT600B (2006) Version 2

Appendix 2: CT600B (2006) Version 2

	A Name of CFC	B Territory of residence for S749 Purposes	C Exemption due (if any)
1			
2			
3			
4			
5			
6			
7			
8			
9			
10			
11			
12			

Put an 'X' in this box if a continuation sheet is used for page 2 ☐

CT600B (2006) Version 2

616

D Percentage of apportionable profits and creditable tax	E Chargeable profits	F Tax on charge-able profits	G Creditable Tax	H Reliefs in terms of tax	I ACT as restricted	J S747 tax chargeable	
%	£	£ p	£ p	£ p	£ p	£ p	1
%	£	£ p	£ p	£ p	£ p	£ p	2
%	£	£ p	£ p	£ p	£ p	£ p	3
%	£	£ p	£ p	£ p	£ p	£ p	4
%	£	£ p	£ p	£ p	£ p	£ p	5
%	£	£ p	£ p	£ p	£ p	£ p	6
%	£	£ p	£ p	£ p	£ p	£ p	7
%	£	£ p	£ p	£ p	£ p	£ p	8
%	£	£ p	£ p	£ p	£ p	£ p	9
%	£	£ p	£ p	£ p	£ p	£ p	10
%	£	£ p	£ p	£ p	£ p	£ p	11
%	£	£ p	£ p	£ p	£ p	£ p	12
		F	G	H	I	J	
Totals		£ p	£ p	£ p	£ p	£ p	13

Enter this amount in box 81 of form CT600

Put an 'X' in this box if a continuation sheet is used for page 3

CT600B (2006) Version 2

HM Revenue & Customs

Company Tax Return form - Supplementary Pages
Group and consortium
CT600C (2006) Version 2

for accounting periods ending on or after 1 July 1999

Company information

Company name

Tax reference as shown on the CT603

Period covered by these Supplementary Pages (*cannot exceed 12 months*)
from (*dd/mm/yyyy*)   to (*dd/mm/yyyy*)

You need to complete these Supplementary Pages if

- you are claiming or surrendering any amounts under the group and/or consortium relief provisions.
- you are claiming or surrendering eligible unrelieved foreign tax (for accounting periods ending on or after 31 March 2001).

Important points

- These Supplementary Pages, when completed, form part of the company's return.
- These Pages set out the information we need and provide a standard format.
- Complete the boxes with whole figures only, except where pence or decimals are indicated.
- There are notes on these Pages to help you when you complete this form.
- These Pages are covered by the Declaration you sign on back page of form *CT600*.
- The warning shown on form *CT600* about prosecution, and the advice about late and incorrect returns, and late payment of tax also apply to these Pages.

1: Claims to group relief

You need to complete this part if you are claiming group relief in your calculation of corporation tax payable. Attach a copy of each surrendering company's notice of consent to the claim. Include claims made under the consortium provisions and attach a copy of the notice of consent of each member of the consortium. If a simplified arrangement is in force, the claim may be authorised below.

Name of surrendering company	Accounting period [1] of surrendering company	Tax reference [2]	Amount claimed £

[1] Enter the start and end dates of any period that is different from that covered by this return

[2] Enter the HM Revenue & Customs office number and taxpayer reference. If you do not know these show whatever information you can that will help us to identify the company, such as the company registration number

enter in box 36 of form *CT600*

Total **C1** £

Put an 'X' in box C1A if a continuation sheet is used **C1A**

Put an 'X' in box C1B if a group relief claim involves losses of a trade carried on in the UK through a Permanent Establishment by a non-resident company **C1B**

Put an 'X' in box C1C if a group relief claim involves losses of a non-resident company other than those covered by box C1B **C1C**

A claim involves a non-resident if the claimant, the surrendering company, or any other company by reference to which their group relationship is established, is non-resident

Claim authorisation - *complete if simplified arrangements apply and copies of notices of consent are not supplied*

Signature

Name *(in capitals)*

Name of authorised company

Date *(dd/mm/yyyy)*

Any person authorised to sign on behalf of the company that is authorised to act for the companies within the arrangement should sign this authorisation.

CT600C (2006) Version 2

Page 2
2: Amounts surrendered as group relief

You need to complete this part if the company is surrendering any amount under the group (or consortium) provisions.
Unless a simplified arrangement is in force
- a notice of consent to each claim is needed
- this part is acceptable as a notice of consent, if the surrendering company details are entered and it is signed by an authorised person in the space below.
- send a copy of the notice of consent to the HM Revenue & Customs office dealing with the claimant company's return before or at the same time as the claimant company submits its return claiming the group relief
- the consent of all the other consortium members is needed for consortium relief.

Surrender as group relief

Trading losses	£
Excess non-trade capital allowances over income from which they are primarily deductible	£
Non-trading deficit on loan relationships	£
Non-trading losses on intangible fixed assets	£
Excess charges over profits	£
Excess of Schedule A losses over profits	£
Excess of management expenses over profits	£
Total	£

Details of surrender

Name of claimant company	Accounting period [1] of claimant company	Tax reference [2]	Amount surrendered £

		Total **C2**	£

[1] Enter the start and end dates of any period that is different from that covered by this return

[2] Enter the HM Revenue & Customs office number and taxpayer reference. If you do not know these show whatever information you can that will help us to identify the company, such as the company registration number

Put an 'X' in box C2A if a continuation sheet is used.　　**C2A**

Details of company surrendering relief
You must complete and sign this section if you are using this form as the notice of consent to surrender.

Company name

Tax reference	Accounting period Start date (dd/mm/yyyy)	End date (dd/mm/yyyy)

I certify that all the information I have given on these pages is correct and complete to the best of my knowledge and belief.

Signature *(needed if you are using this form as the notice of consent to surrender)*

Name *(in capitals)*	**Status**

Except where a liquidator or administrator has been appointed, any person who is authorised to do so may sign on behalf of the company. A photocopy of a signature is not acceptable.

CT600C (2006) Version 2

Appendix 2: CT600C (2006) Version 2

Eligible Unrelieved Foreign Tax (EUFT)

You need to complete this part if you are claiming EUFT in your calculation of corporation tax payable, or part 4 on page 4 if the company is surrendering any amount of EUFT under the Double Taxation Relief (Surrender of Relievable Tax within a Group) Regulations. These regulations apply to income arising on or after 31 March 2001.

You must attach a copy of each surrendering company's notice of consent to the claim.

Claims to EUFT do not apply to consortium companies and, unlike the claims to and surrenders as group relief covered by parts 1 and 2 of this form, there can be no simplified arrangement for EUFT.

3: Claims to EUFT

You need to complete this part if you are claiming EUFT in your calculation of corporation tax payable.

Remember to include any box C3 figure in your calculation of corporation tax payable on form CT600.

Details of claim

Name of surrendering company	Accounting period [1] of surrendering company	Tax reference [2]	Amount claimed £	p

[1] Enter the start and end dates of any period that is different from that covered by this return

[2] Enter the HM Revenue & Customs office number and taxpayer reference. If you do not know these show whatever information you can that will help us to identify the company, such as the company registration number

Put an 'X' in box C3A if a continuation sheet is used

Include in box 73 entry on form CT600

Total C3 £ _____ p

C3A [ ]

Appendix 2: CT600C (2006) Version 2

Page 4
4: Amounts of EUFT surrendered

You should complete this part if the company is surrendering any amount of EUFT under the Double Taxation Relief (Surrender of Relievable Tax Within a Group) Regulations.
- A notice of consent to each claim is needed.
- This part is acceptable as a notice of consent, if the surrendering company details are entered and it is signed by an authorised person in the space below.
- Send a copy of the notice of consent to the HM Revenue & Customs office dealing with the claimant company's return before or at the same time as the claimant company submits its return claiming the EUFT.

Details of surrender

Name of company claiming	Accounting period [1] of claimant company	Tax reference [2]	Amount surrendered £	p

Total **C1** £ _____ p

[1] Enter the start and end dates of any period that is different from that covered by this return

[2] Enter the HM Revenue & Customs office number and taxpayer reference. If you do not know these show whatever information you can that will help us to identify the company, such as the company registration number

Put an 'X' in box C4A if a continuation sheet is used **C4A** ▢

Details of company surrendering EUFT
You must complete and sign this section if you are using this form as the notice of consent to surrender.
Company name

Tax reference   **Accounting period**
                           Start date (dd/mm/yyyy)   **End date (dd/mm/yyyy)**

I certify that all the information I have given on these pages is correct and complete to the best of my knowledge and belief.

Signature *(needed if you are using this form as the notice of consent to surrender)*

Name *(in capitals)*   **Status**

Except where a liquidator or administrator has been appointed, any person who is authorised to do so may sign on behalf of the company. A photocopy of a signature is not acceptable.

What to do when you have completed these Supplementary Pages

- Copy any figure from box C1 in part 1 to box 36 of form *CT600*.
- Include any figure from box C3 in part 3 in box 73 of form *CT600*.
- Follow the advice shown under 'What to do when you have completed the return' on page 23 of the *Guide*.

CT600C (2006) Version 2

621

Appendix 2: CT600E (2006) Version 2

HM Revenue & Customs

Company Tax Return form - Supplementary Pages
Charities and Community Amateur Sports Clubs (CASCs)
CT600E (2006) Version 2

for accounting periods ending on or after 1 July 1999

Company information

Company name

Tax reference as shown on the CT603

Period covered by these Supplementary Pages (*cannot exceed 12 months*)
from (*dd/mm/yyyy*)   to (*dd/mm/yyyy*)

You need to complete these Supplementary Pages if

the charity/CASC claims exemption from tax on all or any part of its income and gains.

Important points

- These Supplementary Pages will form the charity's/CASC's claim to exemption from tax on the basis that its income and gains have been applied for charitable or qualifying purposes only.
- Please use the notes on page 2 to help you complete this form.
- Please enter whole figures or '0' where appropriate.
- How often you are asked to make a return will depend on the extent and nature of your activities.
- These Pages, when completed, form part of the company's return.
- These Pages set out the information we need and provide a standard format.
- These Pages are covered by the Declaration you sign on the back page of form *CT600*.
- The warning shown on form *CT600* about prosecution, and the advice about late and incorrect returns and late payment of tax, also apply to these Pages.

Claims to exemption

This section should be completed in all cases

Charity/CASC repayment reference

Charity Commission Registration number, or Scottish Charity number (if applicable)

Put an 'X' in the relevant box if during the period covered by these Supplementary Pages:

- the company was a charity/CASC and is claiming exemption from all tax on all or part of its income and gains.

- all income and gains are exempt from tax and have been, or will be, applied for charitable or qualifying purposes only.

  If the company was a charity/CASC but had no income or gains in the period, then put an 'X' in the first box 'claiming exemption from all tax' above.

or

- some of the income and gains may not be exempt or have not been applied for charitable or qualifying purposes only, and I have completed form *CT600*.
  See the note on Restrictions of relief for non-qualifying expenditure on page 2.

I claim exemption from tax

Signature   **Date** (*dd/mm/yyyy*)

Name (*in capitals*)

Status

Except where a liquidator or administrator has been appointed, any person who is authorised to do so may sign on behalf of the company. For CASCs the treasurer should sign. A photocopy of a signature is not acceptable.

HMRC 08/06   CT600E (2006) Version 2

622

Page 2

Notes

Repayments boxes E1/E1a, E2/E2b and E1a - E4d

Transitional relief only applies on qualifying distributions made on or after 6 April 1999 and before 6 April 2004. The time limit for claims is 2 years after the end of the charity's accounting period in which the distribution was made.

In boxes E1/E1a:

- Enter the amount of income tax and transitional relief claimed on forms *R68(2000)* or *R68(CASC)* for the period covered by these Pages.
- This should relate only to income arising in the period.
- Do not include amounts claimed for earlier periods.

In Box E2/E2b enter the total amount due for income received in the period on which a charity/CASC can claim.

CASCs should leave boxes E1a to E4d blank.

Trading income box E5

Enter details of the turnover of trades, the profits of which will be exempted by

a) S505(1)(e) ICTA 1988, S46 FA 2000 or ESC C4 (for charities), or

b) Schedule 18, Paragraph 4, FA 2002 (for CASCs).

If the charity/CASC has carried on a trade during the return period which falls outside the exemption, complete the *Company Tax Calculation* on form *CT600*. Do not include in the calculation sources of income which are otherwise exempt from tax. Also, complete the *About this return* section on page 1 and *Declaration* on the back page of form *CT600*.

Gifts boxes E11 and E12

Include in box E11 the value of any gifts of shares or securities received under S587B ICTA 1988.

Include in box E12 the value of any gifts of real property received under S587B/S587C ICTA 1988.

Other sources box E13

Enter details in box E13 of income received from sources other than those included in the boxes above where the income is exempt from tax in the hands of a charity/CASC. This will include Case VI income exempted by S505(1)(c)(iic) ICTA 1988.

Investments and loans within Sch 20 ICTA 1988 box E26 charities only

Qualifying investments and loans, for the purposes of S506 ICTA 1988, are specified in Parts I and II of Sch 20 ICTA 1988.

Charities can make claims to HM Revenue & Customs for any loan or other investment not specified in Sch 20 but made for the benefit of the charity and not for avoidance of tax, to be accepted as qualifying.

Put an 'X' in box E26 only if all investments and loans are qualifying investments and loans:

- automatically, because they are specified in Sch 20, or
- because the charity has either claimed (with this return or separately) that they are under Paragraphs 9 or 10 of Sch 20 ICTA 1988, or is prepared to do so on request.

For a claim for qualifying status to succeed, the loan or investment must be made for the benefit of the charity and not for the avoidance of tax (whether by the charity or any other person). Claims should be in writing and specify

- the nature of the item (loans, or shares for example)
- the amount
- the period
- whether the claim is under Paragraph 9 or 10.

It is helpful if a claim includes full details, for example the terms of a loan.

Investments and loans made outside Sch 20 ICTA 1988 box E27 charities only

If the charity has made any investments or loans which do not fall within Schedule 20 ICTA 1988, and no claim is being made with this return, enter the total of such loans or investments in box E27.

Restrictions of relief for non-qualifying expenditure

Relief under S505(1) ICTA 1988 and S256 TCGA 1992 may not be available to some charities.

The charity should attach a calculation of restriction of relief under S505(3) ICTA 1988 and send it with this return. If you need help with this calculation please telephone our helpline on **08453 020203** or email **charities@hmrc.gov.uk**

Where a CASC has incurred non-qualifying expenditure its exemptions from tax may need to be restricted. The CASC should include a calculation of the restriction of relief under Schedule 18, Paragraph 8 FA 2002 with this return. If you need help with this calculation please telephone our helpline on **08453 020203** or email **charities@hmrc.gov.uk**

Further guidance

Further guidance on the reliefs available to charities and CASCs is available on our website at **www.hmrc.gov.uk/charities**

Appendix 2: CT600E (2006) Version 2

Repayments

Enter details of repayments of Income Tax/payments of Transitional Relief for income arising during the period covered by these Supplementary Pages

		Income Tax	Transitional Relief *Charities only*
E1/E1a	Amount already claimed for period using form R68(2000) or R68(CASC)	**E1** £	**E1a** £
E2/E2b	Total repayment/payment due	**E2** £	**E2b** £
and either			
E3/E3c	Further repayment/payment due *Where E2/E2b is more than E1/E1a*	**E3** £	**E3c** £
or			
E4/E4d	Amounts overclaimed for period *Where E1/E1a is more than E2/E2b*	**E4** £	**E4d** £

If any of the amounts in boxes E3/E3c have been included in any repayment/payment claim on form R68(2000) or R68(CASC) put an 'X' in this box.

Information required

Enter details of any income received from the following sources, claimed as exempt from tax in the hands of the charity/CASC. Enter the figure included in the charity's/CASC's accounts for the period covered by this return
Do not include amounts which are not taxable. Non-exempt amounts should be entered on form CT600 in the appropriate boxes.

Type of income	Amount
E5 Enter total turnover from exempt trading activities	**E5** £
E6 Investment income - exclude any amounts included on form *CT600*	**E6** £
E7 UK land and buildings - exclude any amounts included on form *CT600*	**E7** £
E8 Deed of covenant - exclude any amounts included on form *CT600*	**E8** £
E9 Gift Aid or Millennium Gift Aid - exclude any amounts included on form *CT600*	**E9** £
E10 Other charities - exclude any amounts included on form *CT600*	**E10** £
E11 Gifts of shares or securities received	**E11** £
E12 Gifts of real property received	**E12** £
E13 Other sources	**E13** £

Enter details of expenditure as shown in the charity's/CASC's accounts for the period covered by these Supplementary Pages

Type of expenditure	Amount
E14 Trading costs in relation to exempt activities (in box E5)	**E14** £
E15 UK land and buildings in relation to exempt activities (in box E7)	**E15** £
E16 All general administration costs	**E16** £
E17 All grants and donations made within the UK	**E17** £
E18 All grants and donations made outside the UK	**E18** £
E19 Other expenditure not included above, or not used in calculating figures entered on the form *CT600*	**E19** £

continued on page 4

624

Page 4

continued from page 3

Charity/CASC Assets		Disposals in period (total consideration received)	Held at the end of the period (use accounts figures)
E20/E20a	Tangible fixed assets	E20 £	E20a £
E21/E21b	UK investments (excluding controlled companies)	E21 £	E21b £
E22/E22c	Shares in, and loans to, controlled companies	E22 £	E22c £
E23/E23d	Overseas investments	E23 £	E23d £
E24e	Loans and non-trade debtors		E24e £
E25f	Other current assets		E25f £
E26	Qualifying investments and loans. *Applies to charities only. See note on Page 2*		E26
E27	Value of any non-qualifying investments and loans. *Applies to charities only*		E27 £
E28	Number of subsidiary or associated companies the charity controls at the end of the period. *Exclude companies that were dormant throughout the period*		E28

What to do when you have completed these Supplementary Pages

Follow the advice shown under 'What to do when you have completed the return' on page 23 of the *Guide*.

CT600E (2006) Version 2

HM Revenue & Customs

**Company Tax Return form - Supplementary Pages
Corporate Venturing Scheme**
CT600G (2006) Version 2
for accounting periods ending on or after 1 July 1999

Company information

Company name

Tax reference as shown on the CT603

Period covered by these Supplementary Pages (*cannot exceed 12 months*)
from (*dd/mm/yyyy*)   to (*dd/mm/yyyy*)

You need to complete these Supplementary Pages if

for shares issued **on or after 1 April 2000 but before 1 April 2010** the company is claiming under the Corporate Venturing Scheme (CVS):

- investment relief on the amount subscribed for shares, **or**

- relief against income for losses on certain disposals of shares, whether effect is to be given to the claim in this period or an earlier period, **or**

- postponement of certain chargeable gains where the gains are reinvested in shares under the Corporate Venturing Scheme.

Important points

- These Supplementary Pages, when completed, form part of the company's return.

- They set out the information we need and provide a standard format.

- They are covered by the Declaration you sign on the back page of form *CT600*.

- The warning shown on form *CT600* about prosecution, and the advice about late and incorrect returns, and late payment of tax also apply to these Pages.

- **You are advised to read the relevant notes on page 4 of this form before you complete these Pages.**

What to do when you have completed these Supplementary Pages

- Copy the figure from box G1 to box 71 of the form *CT600*.

- Follow the advice shown under 'What to do when you have completed the return' on page 23 of the *Guide*.

Claims

A company making a claim in its company tax return must do so using these Supplementary Pages.

If a company makes a claim later, but within the time limit for amending its return, it should make the claim on an amended return, giving the same details as are required by forms *CT600* and *CT600G*. (For instance this could be the case if the form CVS 3 to support a deferral relief claim is not received until after the return has been delivered.) No specific form is provided for an amended return, but as long as it is signed by a person authorised to do so and includes a declaration that the information is correct and complete to the best of his or her knowledge and belief, it will be accepted as an amended return.

If the time for amending a return has passed, but the claim is still in time, the company should again give the same details as are required by forms *CT600* and *CT600G*. The claim should be signed by a person authorised to do so and include a declaration that the information is correct and complete to the best of his or her knowledge and belief.

Page 2   *Use this page together with page 3*

If there is not enough space in any section, please continue on a separate sheet and attach it to the form.

Investment Relief

For each issue of shares in respect of which investment relief is claimed, please enter the following details:
All this information, except the actual amount of investment relief claimed, is on the form CVS3 that the issuing company sent to the investing company.

1

Name of qualifying issuing company	Number of shares subscribed for

Relief for losses on disposals of shares

For each disposal in respect of which a claim is being made, please enter the following details:

2

Name of qualifying issuing company	Description of shares disposed of

Deferral relief

For claims to postpone chargeable gains or parts of gains, please enter the details below. Use a separate line for each gain or part of gain.

3

Name of qualifying issuing company whose shares have been disposed of, or in relation to which another chargeable event has occurred	Where the gain was previously postponed under the CVS, enter name of qualifying issuing company on which original gain arose	Date of disposal or of other chargeable event

CT600G (2006) Version 2

Appendix 2: CT600G (2006) Version 2

If there is not enough space in any section, please continue on a separate sheet and attach it to the form.

Nominal value of shares subscribed for £	Date of issue (given on form CVS 3)	Amount subscribed for the shares £	Amount of investment relief claimed net of any reduction for value received £	Small Company Enterprise Centre reference	1

Total investment relief claimed *Copy the figure in box G1 to box 71 of form CT600*	G1	£	

Number of shares disposed of	Date of issue of shares	Date of disposal of shares	Accounting period(s) of claim, and amount of loss relief claimed for (each) period			2
			From	To	£	

Amount of chargeable gain (or of part of chargeable gain) matched against unused qualifying expenditure on new qualifying shares £	Name of qualifying issuing company that issued the new qualifying shares	Date of issue of new qualifying shares	3

CT600G (2006) Version 2

628

Page 4

Notes

These notes do not provide a full explanation of the Corporate Venturing Scheme.
More guidance is available on our website at www.hmrc.gov.uk/guidance.htm

Investment relief

A company must not claim the relief on any investment unless it has received a compliance certificate on form CVS 3.
You may be asked to produce the certificate relating to that investment.

Investment relief takes the form of a reduction in the investing company's corporation tax liability for the accounting
period in which the shares were issued. Except as mentioned below, the amount of that reduction is 20% of the amount
of any subscriptions (excluding any associated costs) or, if that would exceed the corporation tax liability, such an
amount as will reduce that liability to nil. The amount subscribed will be shown on form CVS 3.

Where the investing company (or any person connected with it) has received value from the issuing company (or from
any person connected with that company) so that paragraph 47 of Sch 15 FA 2000 applies, the amount of relief is
reduced. The amount of the reduction is usually 20% of the amount of value received, but it will be less where
paragraph 51 or 52 of Sch 15 FA 2000 apply. Any amount of value received by the investing company from the issuing
company (or any connected person) that was known to the issuing company at the time the form CVS 3 was issued
should be shown on that form.

Loss relief

A claim to set an allowable loss on a share disposal against income may be made under the CVS only if

- investment relief was attributable to the shares disposed of at the time of the disposal, and
- the investment relief is not withdrawn in full as a result of the disposal, and
- the shares were held continuously from the date the shares were issued until disposal, and
- the disposal is
  - a disposal by way of a bargain at arm's length for full consideration, or
  - by way of a distribution in the course of dissolving or winding up the issuing company, or
  - a disposal within S24(1) TCGA 1992, or
  - a deemed disposal following a claim under S24(2) TCGA 1992, and
- the disposal does not occur in consequence of any company reconstruction or amalgamation for the purposes
  of tax avoidance.

CVS loss relief may be claimed against income of the accounting period in which the loss arises. Any loss not so relieved
may be claimed against income of accounting periods ending in the previous 12 months, subject to the apportionment
provision in paragraph 69(2) of Sch 15 FA 2000. To the extent that the loss is not set off against income it may be
deducted from chargeable gains in the usual way.

The amount of an allowable loss is calculated according to the rules in TCGA 1992, as modified by paragraph 94,
Sch 15 FA 2000.

Deferral relief

A claim may be made to postpone

- a chargeable gain accruing on a disposal of shares to which investment relief was attributable immediately before
  the disposal, provided that the shares were held continuously from the date they were issued until the disposal, or
- a chargeable gain previously postponed under the CVS in respect of an investment in shares which is revived
  because of a 'chargeable event' (that is a disposal or an event other than a disposal which causes any investment
  relief attributable to the shares to be reduced or withdrawn).

To be eligible for the relief the company must have subscribed - during the period starting one year before and ending
three years after the date on which the gain accrued - for shares to which investment relief is attributable. Before deferral
relief can be claimed a form CVS 3 must be held in respect of those shares. If those shares were issued before the gain
accrued, the company must have held the shares continuously from the date they were issued until the gain accrued
and investment relief must be attributable to them at the time the gain accrued.

However, deferral relief is not available where the gain to be deferred accrues on a disposal of shares and the shares
subscribed for are in the same company or in any member of its group. Similarly, deferral relief is not available where the
gain to be deferred has been revived because of a chargeable event and the shares subscribed for are in the company
whose shares were involved in that event, or in any member of its group.

Appendix 2: CT600H (2006) Version 2

 **HM Revenue & Customs**

Company Tax Return form - Supplementary Pages
Cross-border Royalties
CT600H (2006) Version 2
for accounting periods ending on or after 1 July 1999

Company information

Company name

Tax reference as shown on the CT603

Period covered by these Supplementary Pages (*cannot exceed 12 months*)
from (*dd/mm/yyyy*)   to (*dd/mm/yyyy*)

You need to complete these Supplementary Pages if

- the company is a UK company and made cross-border royalty payments after 1 October 2002, and reasonably believed that the recipient of the royalties would be entitled to treaty relief on any tax deducted. The company is entitled to make such payments without deduction of tax or at the rate specified by reference to the double taxation treaty appropriate to the country of residence of the payee. Further information about countries or territories that have double taxation agreements with the UK can be found on our website at **www.hmrc.gov.uk**

and/or

- the company is a UK company or UK permanent establishment of an EU company, and made royalty payments to an associated company in another Member State of the EU on or after 1 January 2004 (1 May 2004 for States joining the EU on that date) and reasonably believed that the beneficial owner of the royalties is exempt from UK income tax on those payments following the implementation of the Interest and Royalties Directive. Such payments should be made without deduction of tax.

In this context 'permanent establishment' is a fixed place of business situated in a Member State through which the business of a company of another Member State is wholly or partly carried on.

Important points

- These Supplementary Pages, when completed, form part of the company's return.
- These Pages set out the information we need and provide a standard format.
- Complete the boxes with whole figures only, except where pence or decimals are indicated.
- These Pages are covered by the Declaration you sign on the back page of form *CT600*.
- The warning shown on form *CT600* about prosecution, and the advice about late and incorrect returns, and late payment of tax also apply to these Pages.
- There are additional penalty provisions for failure to observe the law regarding royalty payments. Details are contained in S349E(1)(7) ICTA 1988, S98(4D) TMA 1970 and S98(4DA) TMA 1970 and there is provision for a Direction to be issued under S349E(1)(3) ICTA 1988 or S96(3) FA 2004, as appropriate.

What to do when you have completed these Supplementary Pages

- Complete box 98 of form *CT600* to show that you have made cross-border royalty payments under reasonable belief.
- Follow the advice shown under 'What to do when you have completed the return' on page 23 of the *Guide*.

HMRC 08/06

CT600H (2006) Version 2

Page 2

Details of payments made

	Name of recipient of the royalty	Full address of recipient of the royalty	Type of royalty payment made
1			
2			
3			
4			
5			
6			
7			
8			
9			
10			
11			
12			

Put an 'X' in this box if a continuation sheet is used.

CT600H (2006) Version 2

Appendix 2: CT600H (2006) Version 2

Gross amount of royalty paid £	Agreement under which relief claimed: (a) Interest and Royalties Directive *or* (b) country with double taxation agreement with UK	Rate of tax deducted from payment %	Amount of tax deducted from payment £ p	Additional notes	
	(a) _____ (b) _____				1
	(a) _____ (b) _____				2
	(a) _____ (b) _____				3
	(a) _____ (b) _____				4
	(a) _____ (b) _____				5
	(a) _____ (b) _____				6
	(a) _____ (b) _____				7
	(a) _____ (b) _____				8
	(a) _____ (b) _____				9
	(a) _____ (b) _____				10
	(a) _____ (b) _____				11
	(a) _____ (b) _____				12

CT600H (2006) Version 2

632

HM Revenue & Customs

**Company Tax Return form - Supplementary Pages
Disclosure of tax avoidance schemes**
CT600J (2006) Version 2

for notifiable arrangements on or after 18 March 2004

Company information

Company name

Tax reference as shown on the CT603

Period covered by these Supplementary Pages (*cannot exceed 12 months*)
from (*dd/mm/yyyy*)   to (*dd/mm/yyyy*)

You need to complete these Supplementary Pages if

you are a party to any notifiable arrangements under S308, 309, 310 Finance Act 2004 (FA 2004) and you have received a reference number.

Under S313(1) FA 2004 you are required to provide HM Revenue & Customs with
- any reference number notified to you in the accounting period covered by this return, **and**
- the time when you obtain or expect to obtain a tax advantage from the notifiable arrangements either in the accounting period covered by this return or in a period covered by a future return.

You should not use this form if
- you are an employer and the notifiable arrangements concerned are arrangements connected with employment. A scheme reference number for employment products should be notified separately using form AIU4.
- you are a party to any notifiable arrangements in the accounting period covered by this return that have not otherwise been notified to HM Revenue & Customs you should do so now by completing form AIU3.

Forms AIU3 and AIU4 are available on our website at **www.hmrc.gov.uk/aiu/index.htm** or from the Orderline by telephoning **0845 300 6555.**

Important points

- These Supplementary Pages, when completed, form part of the company's return.
- These Pages set out the information we need and provide a standard format.
- These Pages are covered by the Declaration you sign on back page of form *CT600*.
- The warning on form *CT600* about prosecution and the advice about late returns and late payment of tax also apply to these Pages. Other penalties that apply are shown overleaf.

Disclosable tax avoidance schemes

See notes overleaf before completing these boxes.

Scheme Reference Number	Accounting period in which the expected advantage arises (*dd/mm/yyyy*)
J1	J1A
J2	J2A
J3	J3A
J4	J4A
J5	J5A
J6	J6A
J7	J7A
J8	J8A
J9	J9A
J10	J10A

Appendix 2: CT600J (2006) Version 2

Page 2

Scheme Reference Number

Enter the reference number given to you by the promoter or by HM Revenue & Customs (as appropriate) for each notifiable proposal or notifiable arrangement if you

- have received the scheme reference number in the accounting period covered by this return, or
- expect to obtain a tax advantage in the accounting period covered by this return, or
- expect to obtain a tax advantage in an accounting period covered by a later return.

You should enter the reference number even if you have already entered the number on a return covering an earlier period, unless you no longer expect any tax advantage to arise from the notifiable arrangements either in this accounting period or in any later accounting period.

Accounting period in which the expected advantage arises

You should enter the last day of the accounting period in which you currently expect any tax advantage resulting from the notifiable arrangements to arise, using the format *dd/mm/yyyy*. If you expect the tax advantage to cover more than one accounting period, enter the earliest.

Penalties

If the company fails
- to provide any reference number given to it by the promoter or by HM Revenue & Customs for any notifiable proposal or arrangement, **or**
- to report the last day of the accounting period in which you first expect any tax advantage to arise, as required by S313(1) FA 2004,

the company may be liable to a penalty under S98C(3) Taxes Management Act 1970.

The amount of the penalty will vary as follows:
- £100 for each scheme to which the failure relates unless either of the bullets below applies -
  - £500 for each scheme where the company has previously failed to comply on one and only one occasion during the period of 36 months ending with the date of the current failure, whether or not the failure relates to the same scheme.
  - £1000 for each scheme where the company has previously failed to comply on two or more occasions during the period of 36 months ending with the date of the current failure, whether or not the failure relates to the same scheme.

Glossary

Tax advantage here means
- relief or increased relief from, or repayment or increased repayment of corporation tax, or the avoidance or reduction of a charge to that tax, or an assessment to that tax, or the avoidance of a possible assessment to that tax
- the deferral of any payment of tax or the advancement of any repayment of tax, or
- the avoidance of any obligation to deduct or account for any tax.

Arrangements connected with employment means any notifiable proposal or arrangements which are disclosable under S308, 309, or 310 FA 2004 by virtue of Part 1 of the Schedule to the Tax Avoidance Schemes (Prescribed Descriptions of Arrangements) Regulations 2004 (as amended). A copy of the Regulations giving the prescribed descriptions of arrangements can be seen at **www.hmrc.gov.uk/aiu/index.htm**

Notifiable proposal and **Notifiable arrangements** have the meanings given in S306 FA 2004.

Reference number in relation to the notifiable arrangements, has the meaning given by S311(3) FA 2004.

What to do when you have completed these Supplementary Pages

Follow the advice shown under 'What to do when you have completed the return' on page 23 of the *Guide*.

CT600J (2006) Version 2

634

Index

[All references are to paragraph numbers]

Capital gains – *contd*
indexation 20.4
intra-group asset transfer
  election to treat disposal as if
    made by another member
    20.17
  group structure 20.14–20.15
  relief 20.16
limited companies
  capital losses 12.35
  corporate venturing scheme 12.41–
    12.52
  group relief 12.53
  other reliefs 12.53
  shares in unquoted trading
    companies 12.35
  substantial shareholdings
    exemption 12.36–12.40
  taper relief 12.53
pre-entry losses and gains 20.34
reconstructions and amalgamations,
    and
  bona fide commercial
    arrangements 15.9
  groups 15.11
  reorganisation of share capital
    15.7
  share for share exchange 15.8
  transfer of business 15.10
reliefs
  intra-group asset transfer 20.14–
    20.17
  introduction 20.1
  roll-over relief 20.6–20.13
replacement of assets by members of
    group 20.21
roll-over relief
  assets only partly replaced 20.8
  assets owned personally but used
    in the trade 20.13
  conditions 20.7
  depreciating assets 20.9
  introduction 20.6
  land and buildings 20.10
  new assets as depreciating assets
    20.9
  new assets not brought
    immediately into trading use
    20.12
  new assets not purchased 20.11

Capital gains – *contd*
shares in unquoted trading companies
  12.35
substantial shareholdings exemption
  conditions 12.38–12.39
  generally 12.36
  substantial shareholding 12.37
  trading activities 12.40
tangible fixed assets, and
  conditions affecting assets 20.1
  new assets not brought
    immediately into trading use
    20.12
  new assets not purchased 20.11
  new, depreciating assets 20.9
  partly replaced assets 20.8
  personally-owned assets used in
    trade 20.13
  roll-over relief 20.6
taper relief 12.53
transfer of assets from trading stock
  20.20
transfer of assets to trading stock
  20.18–20.19
transfer pricing, and 14.18
value shifting
  asset holding company leaving
    group 20.28
  disposal of shares in another
    company 20.31
  disposals within group followed by
    share disposal 20.29
  distributions within group followed
    by share disposal 20.27
  free benefits 20.26
  general application 20.25
  introduction 20.24
  reorganisation of share capital
    20.30
year end, and 22.4
Capital losses
anti-avoidance, and
  avoidance involving 20.41–20.42
  disposal of pre-change assets
    20.40
  generally 20.36
  HMRC Notice 20.43
  restrictions on buying gains 20.39
  restrictions on buying losses
    20.37–20.38